Christianity for Seekers and Skeptics

"This explanation and defense of what C. S. Lewis called 'mere Christianity' is irenic, ecumenical, accurate, fair to all sides, reasonable, readable, clear, concrete, and comprehensive. It contains a lifetime of learning—theological, historical, biblical, philosophical, psychological, sociological, and personal. There are far more than one thousand pages' worth in this less than five hundred–page book."

—**Peter Kreeft**, professor of philosophy, Boston College

"Clinton McLemore presents an honest and open account of Christian faith for thoughtful readers. . . . An account of Christian faith such as this is needed in a time like ours where 'Christian' has become a contentless and often heresy-ridden political/cultural label. *Christianity for Seekers and Skeptics* is valuable reading for Christians as well as seekers and skeptics."

—**Warren S. Brown**, professor, Fuller Theological Seminary

"*Christianity for Seekers and Skeptics* is a difficult book to describe, but an easy one to love. McLemore's honesty, intellectual curiosity, and existential passion lead him to discuss a range of questions from a host of different fields, including philosophy, theology, science, biblical studies, psychology, and human history and culture generally. He offers engaging arguments for his views and presents them with a commendable spirit of intellectual humility. Many will be inspired to think in new ways about the most important questions that face human persons, as well as the resources Christian faith offers in answering those questions."

—**C. Stephen Evans**, emeritus professor of philosophy and humanities, Baylor University

"*Christianity for Seekers and Skeptics* is clearly written, concise, and full of rich content.... Those searching for greater meaning and purpose in their faith journey will find this work to be most stimulating and deeply satisfying. Dr. McLemore offers keen insights about the basics of a religious worldview and lifestyle. I find his writing to be clear, concise and consequential—a much-needed antidote to the superficiality so prevalent in contemporary society."

—**Richard E. Butman**, emeritus professor of psychology, Wheaton College

"Clinton McLemore's *Christianity for Seekers and Skeptics* is a one-stop shop for everything a person would want to know about the Christian faith—what it is, why it's believable, and how it affects our personal lives. McLemore's knowledge is encyclopedic, but he presents what he knows in an unpretentious and easily accessible way.... But beyond the audience identified in the book's title, this book also serves as a reference for believers to keep on the shelf, not only as a store of information to which they will often return, but as a resource to consult when knowing how to address the concerns of seekers and skeptics."

—**Dennis Okholm**, emeritus professor of theology, Azusa Pacific University

CHRISTIANITY *for* SEEKERS *and* SKEPTICS

Critical Thinking and Passionate Faith

CLINTON W. MCLEMORE

WIPF & STOCK · Eugene, Oregon

CHRISTIANITY FOR SEEKERS AND SKEPTICS
Critical Thinking and Passionate Faith

Copyright © 2024 Clinton W. McLemore. All rights reserved. Except for brief quotations in critical publications or reviews, no part of this book may be reproduced in any manner without prior written permission from the publisher. Write: Permissions, Wipf and Stock Publishers, 199 W. 8th Ave., Suite 3, Eugene, OR 97401.

Wipf & Stock
An Imprint of Wipf and Stock Publishers
199 W. 8th Ave., Suite 3
Eugene, OR 97401

www.wipfandstock.com

PAPERBACK ISBN: 979-8-3852-1915-5
HARDCOVER ISBN: 979-8-3852-1916-2
EBOOK ISBN: 979-8-3852-1917-9

VERSION NUMBER 11/14/24

Excerpt from Conor McPherson, *The Seafarers*, used by permission.

Excerpt from Paul Baloche, "Open the Eyes of My Heart," used by permission.

Scripture quotations marked (ESV) are from the English Standard Version, copyright © 2001 Crossway. Used by permission. Crossway reserves all rights for all of the content of the ESV Global Study Bible, including but not limited to all print, electronic, and audio rights.

Scripture quotations marked (KJV) are from the King James Bible, public domain.

Scripture quotations marked (GNT) are from the Good News Translation in Today's English Version Second Edition, Copyright © 1992 by American Bible Society. Used by Permission.

Scripture quotations marked (NIV) are taken from the Holy Bible, New International Version®, NIV®. Copyright © 1973, 1978, 1984, 2011 by Biblica, Inc.™ Used by permission of Zondervan. All rights reserved worldwide. www.zondervan.com The "NIV" and "New International Version" are trademarks registered in the United States Patent and Trademark Office by Biblica, Inc.™

Scripture quotations marked (NLT) are taken from the *Holy Bible*, New Living Translation, copyright ©1996, 2004, 2015 by Tyndale House Foundation. Used by permission of Tyndale House Publishers, Carol Stream, Illinois 60188. All rights reserved.

Scripture quotations marked (NRSV) are from New Revised Standard Version Bible, copyright © 1989 National Council of the Churches of Christ in the United States of America. Used by permission. All rights reserved worldwide.

Scripture verses marked (Phillips) are taken from The New Testament in Modern English by J. B. Phillips, copyright © J. B. Phillips, 1958, 1959, 1960, 1972. All rights reserved.

Scripture quotations marked (REB) are taken from the Revised English Bible, copyright © Cambridge University Press and Oxford University Press 1989. All rights reserved.

Other Books by Clinton W. McLemore

CLERGYMAN'S PSYCHOLOGICAL HANDBOOK: Clinical Information for Pastoral Counseling

THE SCANDAL OF PSYCHOTHERAPY: A Guide to Resolving the Tensions between Faith and Counseling

GOOD GUYS FINISH FIRST: Success Strategies from the Book of Proverbs for Business Men and Women

HONEST CHRISTIANITY: Personal Strategies for Spiritual Growth

STREET-SMART ETHICS: Succeeding in Business without Selling Your Soul

TOXIC RELATIONSHIPS AND HOW TO CHANGE THEM: Health and Holiness in Everyday Life

INSPIRING TRUST: Strategies for Effective Leadership

STAYING ONE: How to Avoid a Make-Believe Marriage (With Anna M. McLemore)

LEADER'S GUIDE for Workshops Based on STAYING ONE

WORKBOOK for Workshops Based on STAYING ONE

Website: www.obstaclestofaith.org

*To my beloved daughter Anna-Marie
whose loving heart and superb mind
fill me with joy and thanksgiving*

Contents

Acknowledgments | xi

Introduction | 1
Synopsis of Questions to Be Addressed | 11

Part I. FOUNDATIONS

1 Sense and Fire | 17
2 Faith, Knowledge, and the Logic of Belief | 24
3 Why Beliefs Matter | 41
4 Religion, Culture, and Values | 56
5 Philosophy, Theology, and Rigorous Thinking | 67
   Addendum: Modes of Philosophy and Theology | 80
6 The Deep Structure of Existence | 84
7 Spiritual Knowledge as Interpersonal | 95

Part II. COMING TO TERMS

8 Reports of God's Demise | 115
9 Appointment in Samarra | 127
10 Psychologically Defending Against Death | 135
11 Avoidance Through Distraction | 143

CONTENTS

Part III. PIVOTAL QUESTIONS

12 What Does Christianity Owe to Judaism? | 159
13 Can We Trust the New Testament? | 177
14 What Can We Conclude About Jesus? | 197
15 Are Science and Religion at War? | 218
16 Is Evil an Outdated Concept? | 240
    Addendum: A Brief Compendium of Evil | 257
17 How Have Philosophers Addressed Evil? | 261
18 What Has Christianity Contributed to Civilization? | 290
19 How Have Christians Contributed to the Modern World? | 310
20 What of Violence in the Name of Christ? | 322
21 Is There Life After Death? | 340

Part IV. TRANSFORMATION IN CHRIST

22 Important Christian Beliefs | 361
23 Awkward Realities | 383
24 Becoming a Christian | 392
25 Authentic Prayer | 399
26 Responding to God's Gifts | 411

Part V. CHRISTIANITY AND OTHER PEOPLE

27 Dynamic Relationships | 421
28 Helping Others | 431
29 Representing Christ | 439

Part VI. TAKING THE PLUNGE

30 All Things Made New | 447

Appendix I. The Apostles' Creed | 453
Appendix II. The Nicene-Constantinopolitan Creed | 454
About the Author | 457
Bibliography | 459
Index | 471

Acknowledgments

I HAVE BEEN BLESSED with many gifted friends who were gracious enough to spend considerable time and energy reading through all or parts of this book. They gave me scores of constructive suggestions. When I went my own way, it was usually in the service of trying to ensure that any Christian, regardless of church affiliation, would feel at home with the book and perhaps also be inclined to share it with others who may be seekers or skeptics.

Fourteen people carefully read the entire manuscript, including in many cases the footnotes, and made helpful and well-reasoned suggestions for how to improve it. The meticulous care with which they undertook this formidable task was impressive and touching. For their considerable help, I remain grateful and express deep appreciation. Their wise counsel turned this into a far better book than it otherwise would have been. Each is or has held one or more of the following positions: professor of theology, philosophy, psychology, or nuclear medicine; business executive, manager, or consultant; chief financial officer; television reporter and communications professional; front-line pastor; certified public accountant; or award-winning novelist. I list them below in alphabetical order.

Warren Brown, a lifelong friend and former faculty colleague, provided many insightful comments and recommendations. Rich Butman, who has been encouraging from the beginning, gave me many pages of useful feedback. William Edgar corrected several of my errors and encouraged me more strongly to emphasize certain theological themes. Peter Esser made suggestions for improvements and was consistently enthusiastic about the book. Steve Evans corrected my misunderstandings about certain philosophers, pointed out philosophical mistakes, and made many other helpful suggestions. Terry and Diana Fleskes each meticulously read the manuscript and made scores of constructive suggestions for improving it. Tom Gastil shared many thoughtful reflections, some on theology and others on softening passages that some might find off-putting. Warren Lamb made astute substantive suggestions and, in many places, provided sound advice on word choice and literary tone, which I nearly always followed. Ken McLemore closely read the draft and highlighted sections that needed more clarity, advice I also followed. Anna-Marie Michael used her impressive skill and knowledge of the written word to make a large number of recommendations for enhancing readability and eliminating irrelevancies. Duncan Merritt, with his well-honed awareness of theological nuances and subtleties, wisely encouraged me to take stronger stances and cite passages in the Bible more often where appropriate. Dennis Okholm, whom I greatly respect for how well his life matches his message, used his fine theological mind to offer many excellent suggestions. Mark Pocino, who combines high intellectual capacity with admirable humility, also made many recommendations for improving the book.

Peter Kreeft, whose steadfast commitment to the Christian faith and formidable intellect I much admire, read sections of the manuscript and was generously encouraging. Others, listed in alphabetical order, also read sections and made helpful suggestions: Dan Ballinger, Paul Cardenas, Diana Firestone, Gary Hessenauer, Mark Juergensen, Barbara Lamb, Cathy Marshall, Trevor Milliron, Dick Neu, Sherilee Pocino, Paul Sharkey, and Susan Whitcomb.

I also want to acknowledge and honor three clergypersons from my church, who routinely bless me through their messages, teachings, and authentic lives. They are Senior Pastor Jackson Clelland, Executive Pastor Daryl Ellis, and Associate Pastor Courtney Ellis, who has herself written many fine books.

For over forty years, Anna has been the epitome of a loving and supportive wife. Years ago, she and I were walking through a shopping mall early one morning when I told her that I needed to replace a significant amount of lost income by acquiring another corporate client. A sign on a mannequin in the window of a department store urged, *Reinvent Yourself!* When Anna saw it, she said, "You've done that before, so do it again. You said you wanted to write more. Here's your chance." The following

ACKNOWLEDGMENTS

year, I wrote two books. Not many wives would have made the choice she did. Writing pays considerably less than consulting. Referring to the contents of this book, she has often said, "You need to get this down on paper." As you can see, Anna, I finally have.

Introduction

I DID NOT GROW up in a religious home. My father was a Navy chief who had been on a ship in Pearl Harbor when the bombs came down in December of 1941. That was the end of all religion for him. As for my mother, who had experienced a rough childhood, religion to her was a racket, a way for unscrupulous scoundrels to fleece sheep. She did, however, think it fitting that we own a Bible, so she acquired one. I do not know if she ever opened it, but I did, and somewhere along the way I came to believe there is a God and to sense God's presence in my life.

As a college student, I grew tired of living without a purpose beyond getting into graduate school. Life seemed empty. One Friday afternoon, I asked a graduate student who served as faculty advisor to a small Christian organization to go with me to an empty classroom to pray. What I experienced in that room was life-changing. God shook me to my foundations. I remained the same person of course, but my view of existence changed radically.

The word *radical* comes from a Latin term meaning *having or relating to roots*. It suggests a return to origins, to basics.[1] My return involved surrendering to God, whom I came to recognize as the ultimate source of truth and goodness. It became clear that we inhabit God's universe, we are God's creations, and it is to God we are responsible. I also came to realize that God does not just love people in general, in a kind of vague and impersonal way. God loves me as an individual, and I believe also loves you.

---

1. *Chambers Dictionary of Etymology*, "Radical," 880.

INTRODUCTION

God has purposes, desires, and intentions for human beings and therefore has something like what we think of as consciousness. Becoming a Christian means undergoing a fundamental change that better aligns us with those purposes, desires, and intentions. It is a revision of basic assumptions about God, people, human nature, and the meaning of life. This revision results in the transformation of day-to-day experience. All things become new, and what may have been puzzling or confusing begins to make sense and come more sharply into focus.

People become Christians when, in response to God's Spirit operating on their minds and hearts, they come to terms with what they are, who God is, and how much God cares. To reveal that love, God gave us the gift of Jesus, who went to the cross to demonstrate God's nature and restore our broken relationship with our creator. That God loved humanity to such an extent that he allowed us to crucify Jesus is beyond astonishing.

Many people find all this implausible and believe that, in the face of evil, the existence of a loving God is so unlikely as to border on the impossible. Such a conclusion is not new. Although people living in prior centuries might not have labelled it the way contemporary philosophers do—the problem of evil—they could not get past evil as a stumbling block. This, however, is not the only stumbling block that stands in the way of people coming to faith, and in this book, I will address many of them.

As the twentieth century came to a close, Americans indicated that they had become more rather than less religious, and early in the twenty-first century religion was still on the rise.[2] With a colleague, Inglehart first analyzed data on religious trends from 1981 to 2007 in forty-nine countries, plus "a few subnational territories such as Northern Island." Researchers asked those surveyed to indicate how important God was in their lives, on a scale from one ("not at all important") to ten ("very important"). In thirty-three (67 percent) of the forty-nine countries and territories, people reported having become more religious as defined by their ratings, and during this period, the United States ranked among the world's more religious countries. Contrary to what experts had predicted, industrialization, scientific knowledge, and prosperity had not eroded religious belief, and those in the United States remained among the most religious people on the planet.

2. Inglehart, "Giving Up on God," 110–118.

INTRODUCTION

Since the end of the first decade of the present century, however, the importance of religion has declined. Inglehart continues, "But since 2007, things have changed with surprising speed." People in the United States have shown a decline in how important they believe God to be. In the period ending in 2007, the mean rating of Americans on the ten-point scale was 8.2. By 2017, it had dropped to 7.0. Many Americans seem to have abandoned their search for God and lost interest in religion, or at least the hope of finding a form of faith that to them makes sense. They have given up on God, who however has not given up on them.

Many people have also given up the quest for truth[3] and are likely to say, "Your truth is your truth, and my truth is my truth." For them, the subjective has displaced the objective, and opinions are taken to be trustworthy guides to truth. Freedom to believe what they want has devolved into the belief that truth depends on one's point of view. They seem to live according to the maxim popularized by French philosopher Michel Foucault,[4] "truth does not exist."

You and I may have different likes and dislikes. Perhaps you prefer the mountains over the seashore, while I prefer the seashore to the mountains. It would make little sense to debate which of us is right. When we make claims about the world beyond preferences, feelings, and attitudes, however, the game changes. We must now justify our claims and subject them to the principles of reason. The most important of these principles is the law of non-contradiction. Something cannot be A and not-A at the same time and in the same respect. If you claim Kenya to be in Africa and I insist it is in South America, one of us is mistaken, and it would be ridiculous to talk about your truth versus my truth.

Confusion about the difference between truth-claims relating to subjective preferences and those concerning the objective world has become epidemic. It is rooted in misunderstandings that have to do with fairness, equality, and tolerance. These ideals are admirable in some domains but out of place in others, such as deciding what is objectively true.

It can be difficult to determine what is true, especially when it comes to religion, which confronts us with many questions relating to beliefs, which may or may not mirror reality. Some claim there is no God. But perhaps there is. Yet, both cannot be true. God cannot both exist and not exist. Nor can a personal God exist for you but not for me.

3. Andersen, "How America Lost Its Mind," 76–91.

4. Theologian Bill Edgar pointed out that there is a lot more to Foucault than this one-liner.

INTRODUCTION

Religious affirmations will always, at root, remain beliefs, and the relationship between belief and knowledge is not as straightforward as it may appear. We accept some beliefs as knowledge. Kenya *is* in Africa. Which beliefs can be accepted as knowledge is open to debate. Claims of knowledge are sometimes right but often wrong, and what some take to be knowledge, others regard as mistaken opinion.[5] If there is a God, and if how we relate to that God is important, distinguishing between true and false beliefs, and therefore between true or false religion, is vitally important.

Not long ago, a history professor at the University of California wrote an article in which he describes how, given his occupation, he is naturally curious about theology, but that it is difficult to persuade students that the subject is worth their time and attention.[6] He reports how, in discussing assigned readings on the sixteenth-century theologian John Calvin, they erupt in protest. If all goes well, he writes, what follows are powerful conversations having to do with religion and secular life. They discuss whether the universe has a purpose and order, and if so, who or what is behind it. If it has no purpose, how can we live meaningful lives? What are the implications of believing or not believing in God? The author points out that theological questions, however alien they may seem within the ethos of secular culture, "shade into politics, history, social life."

Christianity for Seekers and Skeptics is neither about, nor intended to promote, Christianity as a set of narrow-minded, unreflective beliefs. Such beliefs provide a person with a ready-to-hand ideology for making sense of experience, but they also allow him or her to rely on the shaky explanatory comfort of unexamined assumptions. Rigidly minded Christianity is a kind of chauvinism, expressed through fealty to a set of ambiguously related and loosely connected beliefs by like-minded people, but not by much rigorous thinking. The collective faith of these believers, which may be quite genuine, is based on the beliefs and opinions of others, rather than on what they have reasoned out for themselves. They may have read the Apostle[7] Paul's exhortation to work out their own salvation with fear and trembling (Phil 2:12), which entails working cooperatively with God to become ever more like Christ. But they have often missed the import of Paul's message. Comforted by recycled clichés, they are like

---

5. See Frankfurt, *On Bullshit*.
6. Sheehan, *International New York Times*, September 12, 2016.
7. *Apostle* means messenger, one sent on a mission.

INTRODUCTION

medieval knights who, while they see only through small slits in their helmets, remain formidably defended. Wrestling with an invisible God through a dark night of the soul would, to them, make no sense.[8]

The French essayist Montaigne wrote centuries ago about the need to remain wary of accepting what others claim to be knowledge and not become lazy. Blind faith reminded him of someone who needing fire, goes to a neighbor's house to get some, where he sits down to warm himself but forgets to take any of it home.[9]

At the other end of the spectrum are many thoughtful people who would never step foot in a church. For some, this is because they have no expectation that, once inside, they would find credible answers to important questions. They may not know the words intellectuals use to frame such questions, but they still have them. What is the meaning of life? Is there any point to it all? Where can we find hope?

Such questions can prove troubling, which is the condition in which we find ourselves as human beings: haunted by hope.[10] There are religious questions to which no one has satisfactory answers, which as we will see reflect the interesting relationship between faith and knowledge. But there are also questions to which the answers seem relatively clear. And, there are others whose answers seem so certain to Christians that many would stake their lives on them.

I hope you find this book to be an honest and intellectually informed introduction to the Christian faith. It is intended for thoughtful people, whether they work in business, teach in a secondary school, study at or serve on the faculty or staff of a college, university, or other educational institution, work in the home, serve in the military, or devote their time to raising children. I have tried to avoid glossing over difficult questions, succumbing to arbitrary biases, or hiding behind five-syllable words.

Although fewer and fewer hotel rooms now contain Bibles, there are many stories of people who, having read passages from a Bible they found in a nightstand, became Christians. Whether someone must hear or read the exact words of the New Testament can be debated, but to become a Christian a person must understand and respond to its central message. Christians hold different opinions about the nature of the Bible, but they all agree it discloses the character of God. They also view the life and teachings of Jesus as God's self-disclosure. Beginning with the story of the

8. See Luscombe, *Medieval Thought*.
9. Montaigne, "Pedantry," 58.
10. See Digges, CSJ., *Haunted by Hope*.

Jews and their relationship with the Creator-God in the Old Testament, the Bible culminates in the life, death, and resurrection of Christ.

Two statements about the Bible are worth noting, one by John Calvin, a leader in the Protestant Reformation in the mid-1500s, and the other by Paul Johnson, a contemporary Roman Catholic intellectual. Calvin, who was a French lawyer living in Geneva, wrote, "For anyone to arrive at God the creator he [or she] needs Scripture as [the] Guide and Teacher."[11] Johnson, who is a British writer and scholar, suggests, "The only way to grasp [the teaching of Jesus] is to read all the Gospels repeatedly, until its essence permeates the mind."[12] One could always say in response to Johnson's comment, "But, of course! Read anything long enough and you'll end up believing it." Allowing these narratives to realign how you view God, yourself, and your relationship to God, could be nothing more than a way to narrow your perspective—unless there is a God who, as you read, is trying to broaden it

Every translation of the Bible reflects attempts to convey the essential meaning of material written two thousand years ago, in Greek, Hebrew, or Aramaic. Some translations are word-for-word, others thought-for-thought, and still others akin to paraphrases. All translations of the Bible necessarily involve interpreting, for a contemporary audience, what authors in antiquity were trying to communicate to their readers and listeners. Biblical scholars think of translations as ranging from literal to dynamic. A *literal* translator, attempting to translate the Bible for an Inuit people living in a remote area near the Arctic, might insist on retaining some form of the word lamb, even though no Inuit had any knowledge of sheep. A *dynamic* translator, by contrast, might substitute for lamb an Inuit term for baby seal. Millions of people, reading or hearing the words contained in any good translation of the Bible, literal or dynamic, continue to find it compelling.

If you are thinking about becoming a Christian, a good place to start would be to read the New Testament, perhaps beginning with its fourth book, the Gospel of John. Then, move on to the Epistle (letter) to Christians living in Ephesus, the ruins of which you can still visit near the western shore of Turkey. After reading the book of Ephesians, read the related Epistle to the Colossians, then the book of Romans. Next, read another of the Gospels, perhaps the shortest one, which is Mark's.

---

11. Parker, *Calvin*, 21.

12. Johnson, *Jesus: A Biography*, 82–83.

INTRODUCTION

Although there is little challenge to the claim that Paul wrote several letters in the New Testament, for example Romans, scholars are less certain about the authorship, for example, of Ephesians and Colossians. Regardless of who wrote down the words, there is little doubt that both epistles reflect the thought-forms of Paul, since they capture his understanding of who Jesus was and what he accomplished.

Even for an atheist, life may come down to something resembling a quest to figure out what gives it meaning and significance. We generally try to align with whatever we believe this to be, which partly determines how we spend our *life energy*.[13] It is ultimately what we serve. This could be the pursuit of money, pleasure, status, or power. Or, devotion to a family, a marriage, or a charity. It could be a cause, social movement, political party, or ideology. Human beings serve all sorts of things, some noble and others base. We vote with our feet, calendars, and bank accounts. On the Apostle Paul's view, we are all, knowingly or unknowingly, captive to whatever we seek and serve (see Rom 6:16–23). If we care about the big questions, the challenge becomes to develop insight into who or what we serve. Having done that, the next challenge is to determine if there is a God, what God's nature is, and whether what we serve helps us connect with that God.

It is worth noting that medieval theologians included sloth among their list of deadly sins. Theologian Dennis Okholm pointed out to me that sloth can be busyness as well as laziness. The word derives from two Latin words, *tristitia* (sadness) and *acedia* (apathy). It suggests neglect of duty. What have been called *deadly* sins were originally called *capital* sins, not because they are worse than the others but because indulging in them tends also to involve a person in other sins. Each is the 'capita" of a lot of "mischief and wrongdoing."[14]

The basic dilemmas of human existence have not changed. Questions raised by Plato several hundred years before Jesus remain relevant today. One example is a question Plato raised, is the pious (holy) loved by the gods because it is pious, or is it pious because it is loved by the gods?[15] Referring to the wealth of ideas scattered throughout Plato's writings, Alfred North Whitehead (1861–1947) went as far as to suggest that the European philosophical tradition reflects footnotes to Plato.[16] Whitehead

---

13. Dominguez and Robin, *Your Money or Life*, 59.
14. Sykes, "Lust," 67–76.
15. Plato, *Euthyphro*.
16. Whitehead, *Process and Reality*, 39.

was the mentor and later the collaborator of the equally eminent philosopher and mathematician Bertrand Russell (1872–1970). Some of the questions Plato raised were the same ones Jesus addressed as he climbed the hills of Palestine, which from the vantage point of geologic time, was but a moment ago. Many of the Egyptian pyramids were constructed thousands of years before Jesus, and ancient Middle Eastern civilizations were also making jewelry over five thousand years ago. Human artifacts have been around, in one form or another, for at least a hundred thousand years, which means that Jesus lived in comparatively recent times.

There are philosophic and religious questions to which neither I nor anyone else can supply satisfying answers. Mysteries that we cannot get our minds around permeate our existence, such as when time began or where space ends. Yet, I will argue that voting in God's favor makes as much sense, indeed more, than voting against God, a point made centuries ago by the seventeenth-century French mathematician and philosopher Blaise Pascal.[17] Christianity remains at least as reasonable as any other alternative on the market.

Three parables in the Gospel of Luke point to God's desire for us to return to God. A parable is a short illustrative narrative, often a story but sometimes a simile, metaphor, or analogy, revolving around human characters, that conveys a moral or spiritual lesson. The first concerns a person who, having lost one sheep (Luke 15:3–7), leaves the other ninety-nine, finds the lost one, and rejoices. Next comes the parable of the lost coin (Luke 15:8–10). A woman has ten valuable pieces of silver and loses one. She turns on a lamp, sweeps the house, and diligently searches until she finds it. Then, she invites her friends and neighbors to join her in rejoicing over its recovery. The third and most moving of the three describes a father who has two sons, one of whom asks for his inheritance (Luke 15:11–32). This son soon departs for a distant region, where through foolish extravagance and reckless living, he squanders everything the father gave him. Reduced to poverty, he returns home to the father who, seeing him a long way off, rejoices that his son is still alive, runs to meet him, then kisses and embraces him. He immediately instructs his servants to dress the son in the finest robe, put a ring on his finger and sandals on his feet, and slaughter the fatted calf for a celebration. The one who was lost is now found. Jesus tells these parables

---

17. See Kreeft, *Christianity for Modern Pagans*.

to communicate how God rejoices over anyone who finds God, accepts God's love, and loves God in return.

I pray that, if you are not a Christian, you will become one. And, if you are already a Christian, that what I have written will strengthen your faith and better equip you to respond to those inclined to challenge it. May the creator of the cosmos bless you in all that you do.

Synopsis of Questions to Be Addressed

MANY THOUGHTFUL PEOPLE WHO reflect on Christianity come up against one or more of the following questions. Philosophers refer to them collectively as the *problem of God.*

1. Was the universe created by a purposeful being? A creator with intentions is a lot different from an impersonal force, or from taking God to mean everything that exists, from the bricks in a wall to the sand on a beach.
2. Is there a cosmic intelligence behind the workings of the universe, and if so what is the character of this intelligence?
3. Might God, if God exists, take notice of us, or are we irrelevant, like earthworms crawling along the surface of an insignificant and dying planet?
4. Is the universe hurtling toward cataclysmic annihilation when God or impersonal nature turns off the sun and the lights go out forever?
5. Do we continue to exist after death, or is life permanently over at the end of our days on earth? Are we, or can we become, in some sense eternal, and if so in what sense?
6. If we live on after death, will we recognize ourselves and each other, or will we lose all sense of ourselves, and everyone else, as individuals?

SYNOPSIS OF QUESTIONS TO BE ADDRESSED

7. Are we self-determining? Do we have at least limited free will, or is all choice mere illusion? Are we completely predestined by God, nature, or both?

8. Which of our choices, if any, affect whether we continue to exist beyond the grave, and if so in what mode or form might we do so?

9. If a supreme being pays us notice, is this the scrutiny of a condemning judge, the compassion of a loving parent, or something else entirely?

10. Does God, if God exists, have an overarching plan and purpose, and if so, what is it, will it bring us joy, and how might we come to know it?

11. Might we be able to participate in and partner with God in furthering God's intentions?

12. How are we to make sense of the terrible things that happen in life, especially to innocent children, and how can we possibly square such events with the idea of a benevolent God?

13. Is it the case, as some have suggested, that God is too weak or uncaring to prevent tragedy?

14. Are some ways of living better than others, or are all approaches to life arbitrary and perhaps in the end meaningless?

15. Should we regard traditional morals as mere conventions, or perhaps as hoaxes perpetuated by the strong to prey more effectively on the weak?

16. What, if anything, is special about Christianity? Is it different in any important way from other religions, such as Animism, Buddhism, Confucianism, Hinduism, Islam, Jainism, Judaism, Shinto, Taoism, Zoroastrianism, or a hundred others? If so, does this mean other religions are completely wrong?

17. Does it make a difference what you believe, so long as you believe something?

18. Is there more to Christianity than an ethical code?

19. Is it important to join a church, or can you do just as well on your own, living as a solitary Christian?

20. What does it mean to become and live as a Christian?

SYNOPSIS OF QUESTIONS TO BE ADDRESSED

These or similar questions often arise in discussions about Christianity. Paleolithic paintings, created on the walls of caves over 40,000 years ago, suggest that some of these questions may have existed in rudimentary form since prehistoric times.

Part I. **FOUNDATIONS**

Chapter 1. Sense and Fire

MANY PEOPLE WOULD LIKE to explore Christianity but are put off by how Christians behave. It is not always easy for Christians to represent Christ well when they need sleep, someone endangers their family on the highway, or catastrophe intrudes into their lives. Even if you accept that Christians are imperfect, your spiritual quest may bring you face to face with a subtler difficulty. Specific groups of Christians tend to focus either on religious experience or conceptual precision, but not both. Some encourage emotion to the exclusion of reason, while others emphasize reason to the neglect of emotion.

A lot of people would be open to religious belief if it held up to critical scrutiny, they found it inspiring, and it warmed their hearts. They instinctively realize that there is more to faith than following rules and that meaningful religion involves an ongoing relationship with God. Many people would like nothing better than to connect with God, if only they believed a divine creator to exist and that a living relationship with this creator would meet their deepest needs.

Rigorous Thinking and Spiritual Passion

Christianity in the Western World tends to reflect either sense (reason) or fire (emotion). A congregation or pastor may be intellectually precise *or* fervently spiritual. This is less the case in Eastern Orthodox and Roman Catholic churches than in Protestant ones, but it remains a reasonable generalization even for them. In theory, sound thinking and deep spirituality are not mutually exclusive and they ought to enhance each other. In practice, however, many churches foster one to the relative neglect of the other. If you are in search of faith that is both intelligent and heartfelt, you may find yourself in a dilemma.

Opting for sense, you might try a church whose members care about ideas, culture, and clear thinking. They may, however, be without much spiritual passion. Such a congregation may foster a nice-to-have communal glow, but it may lack meaningful prayer or serious religious commitment. The members of such a congregation may be well-educated, up on current events, and concerned for the poor and the environment. But the idea of a moment-by-moment relationship with a God who is involved in human lives might seem oddly out of place. The price of admission to such a church may be quietly to check your passion at the door or at least to suppress it.

Choosing the path of fire, you might try a church whose members abound in pietistic fervor. But they may tend to be isolationist or doctrinaire. They may be relatively uninformed, perhaps distrustful of intellectuals, and so focused on religious experience that they remain unaware of and unconcerned about the world around them. Such members are likely to be wary of those who do not use the same words or phrases to identify the faithful, those who belong. The price of admission, this time, may be to check your intellect at the door.

This book is for readers who are looking for both fire and sense, for those who would like to connect with God without having to turn off their minds. Although I will do my best to make clear what a Christian is, and what I believe it means to be one, I do not believe that becoming a Christian means belonging to one group of believers as opposed to another, whether Anglican, Baptist, Coptic, Lutheran, Methodist, Orthodox, Pentecostal, Presbyterian, Roman Catholic, or any other. It may not make much difference to God whether someone is more comfortable with medieval chants or gospel choruses. But there is something that does make a difference, which is whether the person has a relationship, an ongoing conversation, with God through Christ. If you encounter God more authentically in one Christian church than another, that is far better than not encountering God at all. The important thing is that you meet God somewhere.

CHAPTER 1. SENSE AND FIRE

Defining Religion

Religion is notoriously difficult to define, and no one has come up with a definition on which everyone, including experts, agree. I will not attempt, therefore, to do what others have failed to do. But I want to introduce the best characterization of the nature of religion I have found, which is suggested by Geddes MacGregor. His characterization, which he does not offer as a rigorous definition, is complex because religion is nuanced and multifaceted. Here it is:

> Religion is characterized by (1) interest in, (2) concern for, (3) encounter with, (4) sense of absence from, (5) sacrificial love of, (6) commitment to, and (7) joy over, that which is judged to be more important than anything else in one's experience and which, so conceptualized, is taken to be a symbol of that which lies at the heart of all possible experience.[1]

Some may take exception to one or another aspect of what MacGregor suggests, but it will do for our purposes.

MacGregor's characterization is complicated, I realize, but it does suggest why religion may best be thought of in terms of *family resemblances*. The idea of defining something according to family resemblances was popularized by the philosopher Ludwig Wittgenstein a century ago. Some have suggested that he picked up the idea from Nietzsche, who as a philologist employed it in relation to language families. We may not like that we cannot precisely define religion, but we tend to recognize it when we see it, an idea made famous by United States Supreme Court Justice Potter Stewart, in 1964.

All religions reflect a set of assertions, however consistent or inconsistent, that at least roughly conform to MacGregor's characterization, which suggests the difference between faith and belief. Faith presupposes belief, but as we will see, belief does not guarantee faith. Although faith involves accepting a set of claims, mentally assenting to various affirmations, it also involves taking an existential risk grounded in trust, what Danish philosopher Søren Kierkegaard (1813–55) called a leap. If nothing else, the leap of faith involves investing, and therefore risking, one's time and energy. Given that life is a finite resource, this risk is not trivial.

From the beginning of the Renaissance in the fifteenth century to at least the late 1700s, humanism did not necessarily imply atheism, but

---

1. MacGregor, *Philosophical Issues*, 20.

that is what it means to many people today. This has been dubbed secular humanism, according to which "man is the measure of all things," a phrase coined by the Greek philosopher Protagoras. In response to this, the atheistic philosopher Bertrand Russell writes, "There is a widespread philosophic tendency towards the view which tells us that man is the measure of all things, that truth is man-made, that space and time and the world of universals are properties of the mind, and that, if there be anything not created by the mind, it is unknowable and of no account for us. This view . . . is untrue . . . and has the effect of robbing philosophic contemplation of all that gives it value."[2]

Overarching Contours of Christianity

It can be almost as difficult to define Christianity as to define religion because Christianity is the name for a bewildering variety of assertions and practices.[3] There are exemplary Christians all over the world who attend churches of which neither you nor I have ever heard, and in which we might be uneasy. A set of core beliefs, however, runs through many if not most of them. Although the boundary between Christian and quasi-Christian can be fuzzy, a religious body that strays from these beliefs runs the risk of no longer remaining Christian. There is no merit in so watering down the meaning of Christianity that it becomes unrecognizable when viewed in the light of what mainstream Christians have asserted for two thousand years.

I am going to understand Christianity to be consistent with the Apostles' (Appendix I) and the Nicene-Constantinopolitan (Appendix II) Creeds. These creeds are not exhaustive. They do, however, express *in whom* Christians have faith. Nor were they without controversy (see introductory comments to Appendix II). Although they do not contain everything Christians believe, they are centrally important defining documents. The Apostles' Creed was developed between the second and ninth centuries, with the earliest written version apparently dating to AD 215. It outlines basic Christian affirmations. The Nicene Creed was first drafted in AD 325 under Emperor Constantine, and the church ratified the final version over fifty years later, in AD 381. It primarily addresses challenges to Christianity that came to a head in the fourth century.

2. Russell, *The Problems of Philosophy*, 121.
3. Walls, "Christianity," 53–161.

CHAPTER 1. SENSE AND FIRE

To modern eyes, the language of these statements of faith may appear outdated, but the ideas expressed in them continue to shape and reflect belief throughout the Christian world. Limiting our definition of Christianity to what accords with these statements allows us a certain measure of conceptual precision. Yet, even with the addition of the Chalcedonian Creed framed in AD 451,[4] these creeds do not specifically address what some believe is a principal theme of the Gospels, what Jesus taught about the arrival of the kingdom of God on earth[5] This kingdom has a long way to go, but it has existed since Jesus inaugurated it two thousand years ago.

For the word *Christian* to apply to a person, Jesus must be integral to that person's life. Some people seem to go to church week after week without much awareness of God as a living presence in their lives or of Christ as their ultimate authority. Exactly what it means for Jesus to be one's ultimate authority, what the Bible calls *Lord*, may not be obvious, so we will return to this subject. Nor is the meaning of the term *Christ* self-evident, which is not a last name but a title. It is the Greek word for Anointed One, in Hebrew *Messiah*, which carries with it the ideas of king, savior, liberator, deliverer, and initiator of a new age. It is an odd fact of history that, decades after Jesus' crucifixion and resurrection, critics of what became known as the Way appear to have coined the term *Christian* to denigrate someone who took Jesus to be the Messiah. These critics seem to have viewed Christians as belonging to an aberrant Jewish sect or cult.

God and Human Existence

Connecting with God is the central business of life. Although it may not seem so when we are ill or worried about paying the bills, making this connection is even more important than health, wealth, or longevity, and certainly more important than houses, cars, or boats. As a clinical psychologist, I have learned a lot about what makes people tick, and I believe a good deal of this has to do, knowingly or unknowingly, directly or indirectly, with God.

If you find yourself bruised or dented by the skepticism and hardboiled cynicism of our age and find yourself drawn toward Christianity,

---

4. Not all branches of Eastern Orthodoxy accept the entire contents of this creed.
5. See Wright, *How God Became King*.

I invite you to read further. Jesus was more than an itinerant preacher with apocalyptic preoccupations, or an idealistic and impractical rabbi (teacher) who came to a bad end. He provided us with a unique glimpse into the nature of God, an unparalleled disclosure that makes it possible for us to experience a renewed heart and mind. The New Testament writers often use the metaphor of heart to emphasize that God works at the core of our will, affecting what we most desire. Faith in God through Christ can reinvigorate your existence and everything can become new (2 Cor 5:17). There is absolutely nothing you have ever done, however awful or embarrassing, that needs to remain a barrier between you and God. *That* is the gospel, the good news.

Closing Thoughts

Faith without passion is dry and lifeless. Without conceptual clarity, however, it is likely to entail only a vague understanding of the God in whom Christians place their faith. Although it can be difficult to come up with a precise definition of religion, all religions seem to share certain characteristics. Christianity inspires many different forms of worship, from the largely spontaneous to the highly structured. It also involves a wide range of customs, practices, and beliefs. Even if they have never heard or read the statements of faith formulated by the church in the early centuries, Christians share a set of core beliefs captured in these statements. They all center on the worship of God through Christ.

To *worship* means to acknowledge the worth and worthiness of someone else, and to honor and revere that person. We no longer address a distinguished individual as "Your Worship," but in Elizabethan England and before, such usage was common. As used in a Christian context, to worship implies that the being worshipped, in this case God, is of ultimate value. As early as 1325 *worship* carried the meaning of "reverence or veneration paid to a being regarded as supernatural or divine."[6] Many people today have an aversion to the word because to them it suggests groveling, which is not, however, a correct understanding of the term. To worship God is to come to terms with the Creator-Provider-Sustainer of all that exists.

---

6. *Chambers Dictionary of Etymology*, "Worship," 1245.

CHAPTER 1. SENSE AND FIRE

Preview

In the next chapter, we will explore the relationship between belief and faith. We will also ask what it means for a belief to qualify as knowledge. There are two principal modes of reasoning, deductive and inductive. As we will see, both are involved in Christian faith.

Chapter 2. Faith, Knowledge, and the Logic of Belief

You may have wondered how faith relates to reason, and like other thoughtful people, you may also question how a person can know anything about God. Some claim to have irrefutable evidence that God exists, but not everyone finds such claims convincing. In this chapter, we will explore the relationship between faith and knowledge. Faith, as we will see, exists only in the presence of ambiguity. But we will also see that reason is by no means irrelevant to faith. People who read the New Testament, as they might any other set of historical documents, sometimes find its claims about Jesus sufficiently compelling to inspire them to become Christians. When they do, it may have less to do with cold logic than with God's warm Spirit at work in their hearts.

A British historian has written what he calls an emotional history of doubt.[1] In it, he argues that both belief and unbelief are at root intuitive. He does not think much of the philosophically naive pronouncements of public intellectuals who insist that Christianity is on its face irrational, and he suggests that contrary to what these polemicists say, atheism is equally non-rational. Belief and unbelief both reflect deeply embedded sentiments more than they do cold calculation.

Belief is necessary but not sufficient for faith. Although English translations of the Bible often use *belief* and *faith* interchangeably, it is helpful to draw a distinction between them. Christian faith is based on belief, on recognizing Jesus for who he was, but such recognition by

1. Ryrie, *Unbelievers*.

CHAPTER 2. FAITH, KNOWLEDGE, AND THE LOGIC OF BELIEF

itself does not qualify as faith. Theologian Dennis Okholm distinguishes between the content of faith and the act of faith, which seems at least roughly to correspond to the distinction between belief and faith.[2]

You or I can believe something without it much affecting us. People believe all sorts of things that do not matter to them, one way or the other. I may, for example, believe the Red Sox are going to win the World Series, or that Arsenal will win the World Cup. But unless I am an avid sports fan, live in Boston or London, or have wagered on one or both contests, the baseball or soccer team that triumphs will be unlikely to affect my happiness or well-being. Other beliefs, however, matter a great deal because they involve putting ourselves at risk.

Climbing Rocks

Suppose a friend invites you to go rock climbing. Even though you have had no climbing experience, you agree to go, since your friend seems competent and you enjoy spending time together. The idea of climbing sounds adventurous and initially causes you only a small amount of anxiety. "But you'll need your own rope to practice rappelling," says your friend. This may cause you more concern but perhaps not enough to back out.

At a local sporting goods store, the clerk shows you a heavy braided rope used for climbing. She says it will easily hold your weight and would in fact support the weight of many people your size. You ask if it could break under stress, for example if you were to slip off a ledge and fall twenty or thirty feet. "It will hold," assures the clerk. So, you buy it.

When you and your friend reach the parking lot close to the rock he has selected, you notice that it rises almost a hundred feet in the air. Your pulse quickens as it dawns on you that the rope you have purchased has at least some possibility, however small, of breaking. Perhaps there was a flaw in its manufacture. *It had better prove trustworthy*, you mutter to yourself. The two of you approach the rock, which looks like it reaches into the stratosphere. You realize something that, until now, had escaped your notice. You are afraid of heights.

Your heart begins to pound when your friend tells you that you are going to use carabiners to fasten ropes to pitons already hammered into the rock, and then says something about a Prusik knot. "You'll have to

---

2. Personal communication, November 20, 2020.

put your legs in a harness," says your friend, "that I'll make from nylon straps." Not only will you have to trust the rope, but you will also have to entrust your life to metal spikes, oval clips, a few yards of nylon, and a knot you have never heard of. You also have to trust your friend's ability to make a safe and reliable harness.

Life is teaching you with cardiovascular clarity what it means to have faith. It is one thing to assent to the proposition that the equipment will support you, but quite another to stake your life on it, especially if you know that falling from only two or three stories gives you less than an even chance of surviving.

The imaginary incident I have just described is based on an experience I had while in graduate school. My dissertation chairman invited me to join him one Saturday in rappelling down the side of a steep cliff. All went well, until about halfway down the face of the rock, still thirty or forty feet off the ground, and at least that far from the top, the knot tightened up so much that it would no longer budge. That made for an interesting afternoon.

Faith and Knowledge

If we had complete knowledge, if God enabled us to know everything, the idea of faith would be meaningless. There would be no occasion for faith, no reason for it. If, on the contrary, we had no knowledge of God, if God had disclosed nothing to us, there would be nothing in which, or no one in whom, to place faith. Faith only makes sense within the context of ambiguity, which is precisely what God has designed into our existence. The Apostles' Creed begins with "I believe," and the Nicene Creed with "We believe." Neither begins with "I know" or "We know."

Nothing can be true for faith that is false for reason. But it is also the case that if God is who Christians believe God to be, nothing can be true for reason that is incompatible with faith. There is nothing irrational about Christianity, although there is plenty about it that is more than what can be demonstrated by a logical syllogism. Much in life is like that, such as responding to beautiful music, appreciating great art, or falling in love. Many important things in our existence are incapable of logical demonstration.

CHAPTER 2. FAITH, KNOWLEDGE, AND THE LOGIC OF BELIEF

Knowing versus Proving

Philosophers have traditionally defined knowledge as *justified true belief*. Although this definition is probably correct, it has not gone unchallenged. According to "externalists" in epistemology, knowledge can be true belief produced by a reliable source. Thus, according to this view, at least some of our basic beliefs are held without our being able to justify them. In any event, to know something is not always the same as being able deductively to prove it. I may know many things I cannot prove, for example that my wife loves me or my friends look after my interests.

Some thinkers have declared that one can only know what one can show by a concrete experiment, which is a reassuring thesis for the materialist skeptic. I am not using *materialist* here to mean someone with an inordinate love of money, but in the philosophic sense that nothing non-material exists. A materialist assumes science to be the only road to knowledge. But this assumption itself cannot be proved. It does not, therefore, come from within science but outside of it. It is an assertion of belief, not a conclusion reached through empiricism. It properly belongs in the domain of philosophy known as epistemology, which has to do with how to distinguish knowledge from opinion.

Walter Kaufmann points out that many eighteenth- and nineteenth-century self-identified empiricists were anything but empirical, in that they arbitrarily ruled out of court large segments of human experience.[3] Twentieth-century philosophers of language did no better in declaring that, by clarifying how language is used, they had eliminated what others mistakenly took to be philosophic problems, but which these linguistic analysts now diagnosed as ailments. They succeeded in bringing more precision to the examining room but killing the patient. The evidence in support of a philosophic position is different in kind from the evidence in support of a scientific conclusion, such as how gravitational attraction varies with the mass of two bodies and the distance between them.

In science, it is often possible to make observations that tend either to support or weaken hypotheses, and well-trained scientists will eventually agree on what these observations imply. This is not so in philosophy or religion. Different observers often reach strikingly different conclusions. The case for the existence of God bears little or no similarity to a physical or mathematical proof.

---

3. Kaufmann, *Critique*, 34–37.

PART I. FOUNDATIONS

Proving God's Existence

Assume for a moment that two people, each with strong opinions about the existence of God, walk into a country field at night. It is dark and the sky lights up with countless stars. One gazes into the heavens and exclaims, "Behold the beauty of God's creation and how finely tuned the universe is." The other, peering into that same night sky, quips, "All I see is ice-cold space and how alone we are on a doomed planet." If they tried to persuade each other, they might still be talking when the sun comes up.

For every person who marvels at the beauty of a sunset, there may be someone else who trembles in the path of a tornado. Delicately scented breezes may waft over hill and dale, but lethal hurricanes rip through town and country. Calm seas here, raging typhoons there. As Pascal (1623–62) suggested in the seventeenth century, nature is a marvelous proof of God's handiwork to those who already believe, but it can be unconvincing to those who do not. Pascal was an ardent Christian who contributed original work to the study of hydraulics and conic sections, developed the binomial equation, and founded the mathematical discipline of probability.

Arguments for God based on nature end up assuming what they set out to prove, what a philosopher would call *begging the question*. This logical vulnerability flows through all arguments alleged to prove, in an ironclad way, that God exists. Begging the question is what philosophers call an informal fallacy. Often in everyday speech, the phrase is used to mean "raises the question." You may sometimes hear on the news a statement such as "that begs the question," by which the reporter means it suggests a question that should be answered. This, however, is not how I am using the term here.

When a person declares it self-evident that there is no God, he or she is drawing an inference, every bit as much as the person who declares there is a God. In both instances, the individual is moving from what seems certain to what appears likely. The central question, then, has to do with the size of the gap between what one "knows" and what one infers. In the physical sciences, the gaps are generally small, while in matters of religion they tend to be larger.

Psychiatric facilities are filled with people who make huge inferential leaps, cling to them, and insist that others acknowledge the validity of these leaps. It is the public expression of these points of view, these conclusions, that cause the trouble and land them in hospitals. You may,

CHAPTER 2. FAITH, KNOWLEDGE, AND THE LOGIC OF BELIEF

for example, quietly believe yourself to be Jesus Christ. Of itself, such a delusion may not much affect your life. The disruption comes when you start to talk or act as if you were Jesus. As we will see throughout this book, there is an enormous difference between a bizarre belief held by one person and a belief that is not bizarre, based on substantial evidence, and held by many.

Whether you can *prove* God exists, or anything else of a religious nature, depends on what you mean by proof. If you are thinking of a deductive argument, a syllogism that begins with self-evident statements and ends with something that *must* be so, proofs for religious truth-claims are often unconvincing.

The Power of Deductive Reasoning

In framing a deductive proof, you begin with a major premise or general assertion, what logicians call a universal proposition, such as "All men are mortal." To this, you add a minor premise, what they call an existential proposition, such as "Socrates is a man." Stringing these together you end up with, "All men are mortal, Socrates is a man, therefore Socrates is mortal." The conclusion follows inexorably from the premises, which is what makes the argument valid.

Because both premises are true, this argument is also sound. But not all valid arguments are sound. "All dogs have brown fur, Rover is a dog, therefore Rover has brown fur" is valid because if, indeed, Rover is a dog and all dogs have brown fur, Rover would have to have brown fur. The argument is unsound, however, because it relies on the universal proposition that all dogs have brown fur, which is patently false. Some dogs are black, some white, some tan, some brown, and others spotted. We trust the conclusion of a deductive argument only if we accept its premises. Once we do this, the conclusion is undeniable, and it is incoherent to suggest otherwise. This is because the conclusion resides within the premises. Deductive reasoning is immensely valuable because it allows you to determine if arguments involve contradictions.

An Example of Logical Subtlety

Deductive arguments, as we encounter them in real life, are rarely as straightforward as in the example of Socrates. To demonstrate how tricky it can be to ferret out the implications of premises, consider the following problem adapted from a textbook on logic.[4] Assume that all three of the following statements are true:

P1: If John studies, he gets good grades.

P2: If he does not study, he enjoys college.

P3: If he does not receive good grades, he does not enjoy college.

Is there anything we can conclude about John's academic performance?

This is not an easy problem and its solution is not self-evident. It is sufficiently complex, as the authors point out, to puzzle what they refer to as an unschooled intuition. But it would be child's play for a trained logician, who from the above three premises would quickly conclude that John gets good grades.

Assumptions as Sticky Wickets

Deductively proving anything means you have to show that it must follow from something else. The whole edifice of deductive logic stands or falls on the truth value of premises. In the example above, accepting all three premises as true makes it impossible for John *not* to get good grades. But why should we accept these premises? How, for example, do we know that if John studies, he gets good grades?

Challenging the premises of any argument, if pushed far enough, will force the person advancing it to fall back on other premises, which one may then challenge. Often, out of frustration, he or she will say something like, "I just believe it!" Repeatedly asking *How do you know?* will often reveal what the person believes to be self-evident. This is where the trouble lies. What is self-evident to Sam may be far from self-evident to Sally, even if they are both equally intelligent by conventional standards.

Except in certain areas of inquiry, fundamental premises cannot be demonstrated to be true. Philosopher Paul Sharkey pointed out to me that Gödel's incompleteness theorem is an exception to the non-demonstrability of primary premises, since it amounts to a universal proposition that can, it seems, be demonstrated to be true. This is a technical matter for philosophical logicians. For our purposes, we can take fundamental premises to be what both philosophers and theologians

---

4. Kalish, et al., *Logic*, 1.

call "non-demonstrable." Here is how a contemporary philosopher has expressed this: "Arguments to first principles cannot be demonstrative, for demonstration is *from* first principles."[5] Another way to state this is that you cannot deductively prove many basic beliefs because to prove anything deductively means to show how it follows from something else, from other premises that then become a new set of premises, which themselves must be proved.

Suppose Chris tells Sydney, "It's important to take care of your aging parents." Sydney asks, "Why?" Chris answers, "Because they brought you into the world." Sydney replies, "I never asked them to, so why should I even thank them?" Chris asserts, "Because they've given you life," to which Sydney replies, "That was then, this is now." Exasperated, Chris insists, "You should play fair and give something back." Sydney will have none of it and asks, "Why, exactly, should I do that?" Chris, even more exasperated, snaps, "Because it's morally right." The conversation turns awkward and Sydney retorts, "To you, perhaps, but not to me." Such an exchange could go on indefinitely and will likely continue until one of the two ends the discussion in fatigue or frustration, has a pressing appointment, or comes up with something that persuades the other. This *something* could be almost anything, such as "how you treat your parents teaches your children how to treat you," or "people in other societies venerate their elders."

Here is an example of an argument that does not work because it goes in circles: The atheist asks, "Why do you believe God exists?" to which the Christian replies, "Because the Bible says so." The atheist then asks, "Why do you believe what's in the Bible?" The Christian responds, "Because God wrote it." What to one person is evidence for God's existence may to another be evidence that there is no God and never has been.

Inductive Reasoning

Imagine that a friend tells you that there is life on Mars. You might initially wonder if your friend has been in the sun too long. Then, on the evening news, you learn that NASA's scientists are beginning to suspect there is life on Venus and possibly on Jupiter also. You may begin to suspect there might be something in what your friend said. Two days later,

---

5. McIntyre, "First Principles," 161.

you read in a reliable publication that not only is there life on Venus and Jupiter, but NASA just announced that there is also life on Mercury, Saturn, and Neptune. You might now be far more open to the idea that there might be life on Mars after all.[6]

Philosophers evaluate inductive arguments according to their strength, by how reasonable or plausible they are. No inductive argument can ever be as strong as a well-framed deductive proof, since in the realm of induction we are dealing with probabilities. Some find the existence of God probable. Others do not.

The Scottish philosopher David Hume (1711–76) argued that induction can never lead to certainty, which has resulted in over two centuries of debate and no small amount of consternation. Because the sun has come up every day does not guarantee it will come up tomorrow, although Hume well understood that we do not live as if this were the case.

We make predictions all the time about what is going to happen, based on what has already happened. How likely is Y to be true, given that we know X to be true? If, for example, I know motorists routinely slow down when a traffic light turns yellow, how sure can I be that they will continue to do so? In drawing any inductive conclusion, we take into account all the evidence at our disposal, including whatever may be preconscious or unconscious, and then decide what is likely to be the case. We arrive at a great many conclusions in life, perhaps most of them, through inductive reasoning. This is especially true in religion.

Faith as Induction

There is a difference between religious and scientific inferences, but they have more in common than many people think. Embracing Christian faith involves a change in the assumptions we make about the world and where we fit into it. Alteration of assumptions also happens in science, not as high school textbooks often describe it, but as it happens in the real world.

This is how science actually works: Scientists choose the explanation that best accounts for their observations. From observations A, B, and C, they infer X to be likely. From observations A, B, C, and D, they then infer Y to be more likely than X. Sometimes, they can set up a critical experiment designed to demonstrate Y to be incorrect. If the experiment

---

6. Adapted from Skyrms, *Choice and Chance*, 19–20.

CHAPTER 2. FAITH, KNOWLEDGE, AND THE LOGIC OF BELIEF

fails to show this, evidence in favor of Y becomes stronger. Absent such a decisive test, the shift from X to Y can be surprisingly slow.

Theoreticians or experimenters develop intuitive hunches about how things work. Recall how, in the early years of the twentieth century, a disheveled young man who was unable to land an academic position ended up working in a Swiss patent office. He kept ruminating about riding in elevators, thinking about the speed of light emitted from the headlamp of a moving train, and wondering how quickly a person would age while traveling near the speed of light. In one year, 1905, Einstein published three seminal papers that turned Newtonian physics on its ear. It took years, however, for the scientific community to embrace what they took to be his outlandish ideas. These sorts of hunches may revolutionize scientific understanding of the physical world if experimentation or calculation supports them.

Scientists rarely design an experiment to "prove" a hypothesis. They often try to devise an experiment to disprove it, according to the principle of *conservative arrangement*, stacking the deck against that hypothesis. If, over time, repeated attempts to disconfirm the hypothesis fail, it is regarded as increasingly plausible. Eventually it and the theory from which it derives may be accepted as the best available way to understand, explain, and predict observed phenomena.

Thomas Kuhn,[7] however, argues that once the scientific community gloms onto Y, it often resists embracing Z, long after the evidence for Z has demonstrated it to be superior to Y. Kuhn stresses how advances in science, particularly on the theoretical front, come about through *paradigm shifts*. Such shifts often occur gradually, and scientists can be strikingly reluctant to make them, even in the face of what might seem like compelling evidence. Coming to faith in God through Christ involves a paradigm shift, a change in worldview and the assumptions that flow from it.

We formulate many of our views of the world inductively, drawing conclusions based on experience, whether these come from walking down the street, reading a book or magazine, talking with another person, or experiencing a crisis. Does this or that inference, we ask, continue to seem reasonable? Can we trust it? Is it likely to be true? Our answers to such questions reflect what we assume we already know. Because knowledge is often flawed or incomplete, it amounts to an

---

7. Kuhn, *Structure of Scientific Revolutions*; Kuhn, *The Road Since Structure*.

amorphous blend of true and false beliefs, which is why people reach such different conclusions about religion.

Adopting a religion of any kind often involves rethinking basic assumptions and conclusions. We may question what we thought we knew when we cobbled together our view of life; we may decide we paid too much or too little attention to something, and as a result came to a faulty conclusion. Coming to any worldview, secular or Christian, involves assigning greater or lesser degrees of confidence to what we assume we know, which will always remain in part a matter of induction. Our individual estimate of a statement being true in the face of uncertainty goes by several names, such as *subjective probability*, *personal probability*, and *epistemic probability*. We can therefore speak of its *epistemic value*.

Sociologist Peter Berger has advanced an idea that he suggests should not be confused with the idea of worldview, namely "plausibility structure." McGrath defines such a structure as "assumptions and practices, reinforced by institutions and their actions, that determines what beliefs are persuasive."[8] Whichever of these terms we use, they refer to foundational premises about the world and our place in it.

Altered Premises

If there is an underlying pattern to the universe, an order to it with a personal God at the center, authentic faith implies reckoning with that pattern, with the way the world *is*. The acquisition of faith, if reality-based, therefore amounts to the attainment of insight, to closing the gap between what we assumed to be true and what is in fact the case. It is to come in from the cold and the dark. Christians believe that, without God having revealed God's nature to us in Christ and through the ongoing work of God's Spirit, such insight would be beyond our reach. They also believe we come to such insight because of what theologians call grace, which is a gift from God that we neither earn nor deserve.

Developing faith in God through Christ involves acquiring a new set of premises. These involve both the heart and the head because in matters of existential importance, the two are inseparable. Inner transformations occur when people are moved, captivated, and perhaps shaken. What the new Christian had assumed to be true turns out not to be, and what he or

---

8. McGrath, *Christianity's Dangerous Idea*, 21.

CHAPTER 2. FAITH, KNOWLEDGE, AND THE LOGIC OF BELIEF

she once deemed ridiculous is now believable. One way to describe this change in fundamental premises is *ontological shock*.

God works through feelings as well as thoughts. Emotions in our society, as in many others, tend to be suspect. The ideal, for many of us, would be to live without them, or so we think. "If only these feelings of mine didn't get in the way" or "The trouble with me is I'm too emotional." If we had no feelings, we might as well trade places with robots and we would have no capacity to form and enjoy relationships. It is our nature as thinking-feeling-acting creatures that makes us human. Some people, to be sure, have too little emotional control and allow their feelings to rule them. But lack of emotional control, a deficit in self-regulation, does not turn emotion into a culprit. Renouncing all emotion in your life would be like refusing to board a train because of the occasional run-away locomotive.

What we think, feel, value, do, want, and believe are all interrelated. Reflect for a moment on how different people spend their time and energy, and what this says about how they view life: (1) The man who devotes his discretionary time to watching football enjoys the game, believes it to be worth watching, and derives happiness from it. (2) The woman who uses her free time reading good literature, instead of watching TV, deems that to be a better use of her time and no doubt feels gratified when she chooses to read. (3) The student who majors in sociology, rather than oceanography, because he or she values and enjoys the study of social systems more than the study of aquatic ones.

We spend our time on what we care about. When it comes to drawing conclusions in the face of uncertainty, our intellectual judgments are colored, to one degree or another, by non-rational processes, including emotional ones. In seen and unseen ways, conscious and unconscious sentiments and feeling-tones shape what we think about and find ourselves drawn to. What I referred to above as ontological shock is like what happens when you hear the punch line of a good joke. There is an abrupt shift in frame of reference. You thought it was one thing, but it turned out to be another.

Arguments from Benefits

Although Christianity may provide benefits, such as joy, hope, and peace, these do not guarantee Christian beliefs to be true. Ever since the late nineteenth century, there has been a growing tendency in Western Society to define truth as whatever works. Such an approach blended nicely with the practical bent of American society during the rise of industrialization. It was formalized in the philosophical doctrine of pragmatism, expressed in the writings of William James (1842–1910) and later promoted as the central tenet of education by John Dewey (1859–1952). Philosophers Charles Sanders Pierce (1839–1914), originator of the "pragmatic maxim," and to some extent George Santayana (1863–1952) were also key figures in the development of pragmatism. That faith can be useful, for example in making someone feel better, has no direct bearing, however, on whether its underlying beliefs correspond to reality.

Christians sometimes point to the deep satisfaction they experienced when they came to believe that Christ was their reconciler with God, their rescuer from anguish, and the one who lives and has not abandoned them. As Unamuno suggests, relief from the anguish of life is not the same as release from its agony.[9] Coming to belief in Christ creates for many Christians something like the satisfaction Copernicus must have felt when he first realized that the earth revolves around the sun. Copernicus, who was a Polish monk, might have felt something like, "Ah, yes, God . . . I see it now." A person coming for the first time to faith in Christ often feels much the same way. Some Christians in the past have retained their theological certainty even if they went to the gallows for it, and in some part of the world today, identifying yourself as a Christian is likely to get you shot.

To challenge the validity of religious belief, Karl Marx (1818–1883) and Sigmund Freud (1856–1929) pointed to religion's psychic benefits. Marx described it as the opium of the masses, while Freud viewed it as a comforting illusion based on the infantile wish for a powerful father.[10] Both attempted to explain away religion by reducing it to something else. They offered *eliminative* rather than *explanatory* reductions. Philosophers distinguish between the two. An explanatory reduction reduces something to simpler or more basic parts or elements, without denying either its existence or unique nature. An eliminative reduction, on the contrary, insists that something is *nothing but* something else. It is an explanatory reduction to attribute rising temperature to increased kinetic energy, which in turn reflects increased excitation of molecules.

---

9. See Unamuno, *Tragic Sense of Life*; Unamuno, *Agony of Christianity*.
10. Freud, "Obsessive Acts," 25–35.

CHAPTER 2. FAITH, KNOWLEDGE, AND THE LOGIC OF BELIEF

It is an eliminative reduction to argue that human consciousness is nothing more than the firing of neurons in the brain, or for that matter, that the mind is nothing more than the brain. Although consciousness depends on activity in the brain, it appears to be a different kind of thing. To define consciousness as merely the firing of neurons is to miss its fundamental nature

Attempting to *disprove* religious truth-claims by pointing to religion's psychological benefits suffers from the same weakness as trying to *prove* religious truth-claims by pointing to these same benefits. If there is anything to Christianity, one would surely expect it to provide psychological benefits, but of themselves these benefits do not amount to anything close to incontestable proof.

Arriving at Faith

God changing the direction of our lives, away from the default modes of selfishness and egocentricity, lies at the heart of what it means to become a Christian. This happens only when, nudged and enabled by God's Spirit, an individual comes to recognize the nature, identity, and significance of Jesus, which is the starting point for Christian faith.

We perceive God only with spiritual eyes (John 4:24). "The heart has reasons," wrote Pascal, "that reason knows not of."[11] As useful as analytic reasoning can be in matters of religion, it has limitations. All the well-thought-out and finely crafted theology in the world may never, of itself, bring anyone to faith. Becoming a Christian entails more than analytic reasoning. It also involves intuition and imagination enlivened by God's Spirit. The Augustinian philosopher Dietrich von Hildebrand wrote about the centrality of the heart and its relative neglect by traditional philosophy: "When we read anything philosophical dealing with the heart and the affective sphere . . . [the heart] is presented as less serious, less deep, and less important than [the] intellect or will." He labels this "a philosophical approach which must inevitably fail to do justice to reality."[12]

How, we might wonder, could anyone decide between competing religious truth-claims? Are we left completely adrift on the raft of the arbitrary? Perhaps not. More than any other religion, Christianity has

---

11. Pascal's *Pensees*.
12. Hildebrand, *The Heart*.

historical data to support its claims.[13] Becoming a Christian takes place in a region of knowing that involves both the objective and the subjective, the explicit and the tacit (see chapter 7).

What follows is an example of what it might look like for a reflective person to become a Christian. Early in his career as an Oxford don, and long before he accepted the Chair of Medieval and Renaissance Literature at Cambridge, C. S. Lewis (1898–1963) became a Christian. Here is one account of how his conversion came about:

> After many years of slowly moving toward Christianity . . . he now confessed on his knees in his rooms at Magdalen that "God is God." It was two years later that he and his brother set out by motorcycle for a visit to Whipsnade Zoo, about thirty miles east of Oxford. "When we set out I did not believe that Jesus Christ is the Son of God, and when we reached the zoo I did."

God touched Lewis at his core, and for the rest of his life Lewis wrote book after book about Christianity. He had always wanted to write more poetry and occasionally lamented that God kept nudging him in a different direction. Because of something invisible nudging Lewis, he introduced countless readers to the possibility that Christianity might be true after all, and cooperated with God to persuade many of them to become Christians.

Heart Surgery

We may risk little by acknowledging God's existence, perhaps only the awkwardness of our friends, family, and colleagues possibly labeling us as oddly religious. But if we are fully open about our faith, the risk could be substantial, perhaps losing a job at the hands of a supervisor who loathes religion. In some parts of the world, admitting to being a Christian could trigger our execution. Whatever the price of becoming a Christian, the transformation is likely to be radical. It involves allowing God to perform heart surgery on us.

Almost anything might prepare you for this surgery. Without your awareness, God may prompt you to go to church, open a Bible, or strike up a conversation with a Christian. Regardless of how God accomplishes this, you will never be the same. The truly great part is that you will experience a sense of purpose that absent this surgery you

---

13. See Kreeft and Tacelli, *Handbook*.

would never even know existed. This purpose involves partnering with God to bring the light of Christ into the world and so help advance the kingdom of God on earth.

Through human reason alone and without God's help, no one may come to recognize Jesus for who he was and continues to be. Theologians have long debated how far reason alone can take us, how much it can reveal without God's assistance. Few theologians have ever argued that reason can take us the whole way, and some have insisted that autonomous human reason will not even allow us to begin the journey.

When Newer Is Not Better

The idea of a God who wants to give us life beyond the grave and invites us to become brothers and sisters of Christ may seem antiquated. It is worth noting, however, that the contemporaries of Democritus, who lived five centuries before Jesus, probably thought he had lost his mind when he claimed that the world consisted of atoms. We tend to assume that because X, belief in a supernatural creator, came before Y, belief that there was no creator, Y is correct and X misguided. This is not necessarily a good operating principle in philosophy or religion.

Secular motifs in contemporary Western Culture suggest that we have moved beyond primitive belief in God. Note the pejorative tone of *moved beyond* and *primitive*, which seem to imply that if you believe in a creator, you must be uneducated, unenlightened, and unsophisticated. Or, maybe just stupid. The existence of a divine creator may not be preposterous after all.

Imponderables

We are dangled between two eternities, past and future, and two infinities, large and small. When did time start? Whenever you claim it started, was there not a moment before? Where does time end? When, precisely, is the day after never? As for space, if we halve or double the size of anything, might we not, in principle, do so endlessly? It does not help to say there is no such thing as time, although I suspect something of that sort will turn out to be the case. Or, that space folds back on itself. We can say those words, but few if any of us have the capacity to understand them. I certainly do not. Without the chance to look back from the vantage point of eternity, we may remain incapable of making sense of time or space.

Might these be creations of God for our benefit? God may someday choose to enlighten us about such mysteries and thus enable us to make sense of what now seems imponderable. Given the intricate structure and organization of our world, it may be odd *not* to suspect that there is some purpose and a creator behind it all. I have not lost sight, here, of *stochastic process*, a fancy word for randomness. But I suspect that what now seems random may ultimately turn out to be ordered.

Closing Thoughts

Faith depends on belief. But faith goes beyond belief to include trust and reliance. Knowledge can be defined as justified true belief. For Christianity to make sense, its claims about God and Jesus must be true, and there must be good reasons for accepting them. The validity of deductive reasoning depends on having sound premises, which in the domain of religion remain largely unprovable. Even God's existence cannot be demonstrated with logical syllogisms because the premises of such syllogisms can always be contested. Faith, therefore, relies in part on inductive reasoning. Arriving at faith in God through Christ implies a fundamental change in perspective, a paradigm shift. We are suspended between two eternities, past and future, and two infinities, large and small. Both are hints of God's existence.

Preview

Religions, at a minimum, reflect belief in a supernatural being, or at least in powers or processes that transcend human existence. Sincerity is no guarantee of the validity of religious beliefs, so it is important to determine, as best we can, which beliefs are likely to be true. Because it is difficult if not impossible to love someone you fear, God refuses to intimidate us and wants our love to be freely given. For reasons we will explore, God keeps some things hidden.

Chapter 3. Why Beliefs Matter

THEOLOGY IS THE STUDY of God and God's ways with us. The term *theology* may conjure up images of Gothic cathedrals and medieval monks, and theological reflection may therefore seem outmoded, impractical, and irrelevant. Good theology is none of these. It is thinking through the implications of religious beliefs, exploring how these beliefs fit together, and pondering their significance for human life. Theologies of one kind or another determine much of what religious leaders proclaim in churches, mosques, shrines, synagogues, and temples all over the world.

Those whose opinions we respect, whether inside a church or out of it, influence our beliefs, sometimes without our awareness. We may not recognize, for example, how our worldview is constantly changing, subtly nudged either toward or away from God. It is therefore to our advantage to be as reflective as we can about our beliefs, to sort out what we do and do not believe and why.

It has been argued that everyone has a religion. Whether this is true depends on how you define religion. Not all religions involve belief in a God who acts, much less in one who acts intentionally. Some systems of belief, such as certain strands of Buddhism, do not include the idea of God, and yet they are commonly regarded as religions. Confucianism is sometimes said to be a philosophy rather than a religion. If you think of religion as whatever is most important in a person's life, such a definition may be uncontestable, since everyone regards *something* as most important. Some would argue that such a definition of religion is trite and tautological. If you conceive of religion as entailing belief in an invisible power(s), some form of structured worship, and an organization or group that prescribes morality, the whatever-is-most-important definition of religion may be excessively loose. But it is still worth pondering.

The Need for Theological Humility

It is easy to understand why many people are leery of intolerant religionists, who while often wrong, are never in doubt. If those whom Eric Hoffer derisively calls "true believers"[1] are conservative Protestants, they will likely insist that the Bible unambiguously and unarguably supports their beliefs, whatever these happen to be, and if they are Roman Catholics or Eastern Orthodox, they may insist on appealing to the authority of the church. Triggered by the Reformation, Catholics and Protestants were so vehemently at odds over the role of tradition, among other things, that from the late sixteenth to the early eighteenth centuries, European wars of religion prematurely ended hundreds of thousands of lives. Of these wars, the most horrific was the Thirty Years War (1618–48).

Soon after the start of the Reformation in Germany in the early sixteenth century, and soon thereafter in Switzerland, England, and Scotland, it became painfully clear that some reformers had been unduly optimistic. Presuming, as Martin Luther did, that everyone was competent to read and interpret the Bible turned out to be unrealistic. It was a presumption grounded in hope for the common person, as well as in Luther's passionate belief in the power of scripture, but it quickly proved to be naïve. There was no doubt about the need for reform within the Western or Latin Church, and many Roman Catholics were aware of that. But how far should this go and what form should it take? Perhaps most important of all, how independent of church authority should people now become?

The Bible is a heterogeneous collection of books that were composed over the course of about a thousand years, ending in the first century. No attempt is made anywhere in the Bible to present a coherent system of religious belief, a systematic theology. As an example of the kinds of controversies that arose when Luther and the Vatican were unable to come to terms, a debate quickly arose among Protestants over what, exactly, was going on during mass. Although there is still controversy about what Luther believed, he seems to have held a position that was close to the traditional Catholic one. Roman Catholicism maintained, as it still does,

---

1. Hoffer, *The True Believer*.

that the bread and wine, while retaining the outward appearance of bread and wine, were *transubstantiated* into the actual body and blood of Jesus. Lutherans usually subscribe to a doctrine known as *consubstantiation*, that the body and blood of Christ are present alongside the bread and wine. Calvinist reformers in Geneva took communion to be a sign and a seal that did not involve a physical change in either the bread or wine.

There were also other issues on which Protestants could not agree, such as whether adults who came to newfound faith, having been baptized as infants, needed to be baptized again. Some known as anabaptists insisted they did, while most reformers, including Luther, maintained they did not. As with the controversy over the nature of the Eucharist (Communion), both factions insisted that they based their beliefs on the Bible. These examples illustrate the nature of the relatively intransigent problems that emerged, and perhaps highlight the need to remain open-minded and balance the quest for theological correctness with humility.

Theology As Inescapable

To the extent that any religion assumes the existence of a higher power, it develops a theology. Religious thought-leaders often go to great lengths to express what they take to be the nature of this power, and where humanity stands in relation to it. The most important question to ask about any religion concerns the extent to which its affirmations correspond to reality.

Because the stakes are high, the pursuit of religious truth is important, especially since different religions make incompatible claims. Open-mindedness does not make questions about the soundness of religious truth-claims trivial or irrelevant. It only requires that, in attempting to converge on correct beliefs, it is important to weigh the evidence fairly and not prematurely close one's mind. Few if any religions are completely wrong, but neither can they all be right, especially about Jesus.

If, as Christianity teaches, loving God in response to God's love sits at the center of Christian faith, it is important to understand who, exactly, God is, and what God expects. "We love because he first loved us" (1 John 4:19, NIV). The English word *love* has several meanings, ranging from affection to sexuality.[2] What kind of love, we need to ask, is it that God desires?

2. See Lewis, *The Four Loves*.

PART I. FOUNDATIONS

Sincerity as the Criterion

Some people believe that the principal benefits of religion derive from membership in a religious community, in which case its benefits would not depend on its truth claims but on participation in a group that believed those claims. Authentic religion cannot, however, be based on false beliefs, regardless of how sincerely such beliefs are held or what communal benefits they provide.

All religions have sincere adherents. Recognizing this, some people jump to the conclusion that it does not matter what you believe, as long as you believe something. This, however, makes no sense if the claims of different religions contradict each other. Mutually exclusive assertions cannot be true, and unless you so water down the definition of truth that its presence or absence loses all meaning, sincerity cannot serve as the criterion for a religion grounded in truth. Members of the Flat Earth Society insist that the earth is flat, but this does not make it so.

Taking earnestness to be the earmark of sound religion turns sincerity itself into a kind of religion: one religion is as good as another and the specific contours of a person's beliefs are irrelevant. What difference, ask the advocates of this quasi-religion, do beliefs really make? If you assume that what you believe might make a difference, however, either in how you live or your eternal outcome, it is naïve to endorse the gospel of sincerity. Embracing it may allow you to sleep better at night, but it reflects confused thinking to anyone who understands how much world religions differ.

Christianity insists that God revealed the divine nature in Jesus and gives us the chance to use our hearts and minds to recognize Jesus for who he was. Jesus spent three years showing us, by word, deed, and example, the nature of God.

Ideas about God

The word *God* means different things to different people, which can make answers to questions like "Do you believe in God?" almost meaningless. Surveys indicating that eighty-six percent of people say they believe in God provide little or no insight into what *God* meant to the respondents. An individual indicating a belief in God without further elaboration provides no information about the sort of God in whom, or in which, that individual believes. There is also the fact that how people respond to survey questions may not truly reflect what they believe.

Does the person mean the God of the pantheists, comprising everything from turnips to tigers? The God of many eighteenth-century deists, a divine clockmaker who created the world but is no longer involved in it? Of some nineteenth-century Protestant theologians who did not much care how a person conceived of God, so long as he or she was kind, saw the creator as benevolent, and had oceanic religious sentiments reflecting a sense of the cosmic without reference to a personal God? Perhaps the God of some twentieth-century preachers who suggested or insisted that if you did not believe God created the world in six calendar days, you were going to hell? Would it be the God of prosperity evangelists who continue to claim God wants us all to get rich, and while we are at it, to send in money?

Conceptions of God are not all the same. As an example of how beliefs about God matter, when I was still practicing as a clinical psychologist, I saw a woman whose life changed substantially for the better when she realized that God was not a punitive tyrant, waiting to zap her, but a loving sustainer. If you conceive of God as a stern dictator who commands you to punish unbelievers, you will think, feel, and act differently than if you conceive of God as a benevolent creator who desires a relationship with human beings and wants them in turn to love others. A theology that portrays God as a punitive judge to be appeased is different from one that portrays God as a nurturing parent who is deeply concerned with human hearts, stands ready to welcome people into his eternal family, and desires to give them joy and peace.

A person who thinks of God as a harsh judge may be inclined to try to earn God's favor by such acts of misplaced religiosity as killing people in God's name. A person who thinks of God only as a loving parent, however, may be inclined to minimize the idea of divine justice. Someone with the former view runs the risk of failing to appreciate God's grace, while someone with the latter view runs the risk of trivializing our duty to do what pleases God.

A friend once asked me how it was possible to love an idea, adding that in his judgment God was only that. I now believe he was on to something and that he was partly correct. I use the modifier *partly* because God is a real existence to whom I hope my ideas accurately correspond, but I would never go as far as to suggest that God is nothing but my ideas or anyone else's. People move in and out of my awareness, and when I am awake, I experience them through my senses. As soon as they walk out of the room, stop sending messages, hang up the phone, or disengage in some other way, however, I am left with my mental representations of them. Everyone I know is, in this sense, a set of ideas—immediate impressions, memories of these impressions, and the inferences I draw from both. Some characters in novels are more real to me than people I have actually met. In the parlance of philosophy, they seem to have more "ontological status." Because of how these fictional characters have been portrayed by the authors who created them, I know more about their inner lives, their hearts and minds, than I do about many people who exist.

The states of mind of fictional characters, as they are depicted, are based on states of consciousness that their creators have either experienced or imagined, and what they imagine is creatively based in part of what they have experienced. Whatever dispositions I attribute to the characters based on their words and actions may or may not be those the author intended. Regardless, the characters as I experience them are persons. Although I have not met them, I know them better than the man or woman ahead of me in line at the theater.

My wife and I have been married for decades. If a good marriage is like a long and rich conversation, it is also one in which there are few secrets, and each party comes intimately to know the other's mind and heart. My wife is now upstairs, but I vividly remember what she looked like last evening sitting across from me at dinner. Yet, right now, she is only a set of images and memories. When I think about some acquaintances, I realize that all I really know about them is what they look like. I cannot even recall the sounds of their voices, much less what they said. We have had no conversations that would allow me to infer anything meaningful about their inner dispositions. In the end, we know others by listening to what they say, observing their actions, and noting how others respond. The question becomes whether these inferences are accurate, whether I know people as they actually are. This suggests the most relevant question for our purposes, which has to do with how well I know God and whether my ideas of God are accurate.

Seeing through the Mist

God is not ordinarily detectable by our physical senses. Whatever impressions of God we acquire through these senses typically come from

CHAPTER 3. WHY BELIEFS MATTER

ambiguous clues to a hidden dimension of existence. It is as if we peer at God through a fog or a mist. There is an image off in the distance, so indistinct at times that we are uncertain if it is real. There may also be a voice, so faint that we are unsure we have even heard it. Some people quickly recognize God's image and voice because, owing to a rich spiritual life, they know God well. Many recognize God because they have learned about God through the Bible, and others because they have heard statements about God from Christians. For reasons that are too elaborate to explore here, *kerygma*, proclamation of the gospel, and personal expressions of faith have always been primary modes of summoning people to God.

Some people fail to perceive God at all and are inclined to disparage those who do for what they take to be gullibility. Those adamantly opposed to religion sometimes think of Christians as naïve, likely to interpret an illusion as reality, or given to delusions. But this is how one translation renders Jesus' words in John's Gospel (5: 37–38, REB): "His voice you have never heard, his form you have never seen; his word has found no home in you, because you do not believe the one whom he sent."

In the face of great misfortune, insurmountable adversity, or devastating loss, peering into the mist may seem futile, an idle pastime best left to unrealistic dreamers who have yet to encounter life's harsh realities. Given the adversity some people experience, it is easy to understand such cynicism. Nonetheless, the One in the mist is still there and continues to beckon us. But God has chosen not to terrorize us into belief. Putting on dazzling displays of power, like Zeus or Thor, would only intimidate us into submission, the antithesis of what God wants. Coercion precludes love. No one, not even God, can be loved and feared at the same time.

People will sometimes ask what this means in the Bible: "the fear of the Lord is the beginning of wisdom" (Ps 111:10; Prov 9:10, KJV). Properly understood, in this context fear means something like *reckoning with the existence and reality of*. It implies reverence for God and recognition of our accountability and has nothing to do with being terrified.

How we respond to the image and voice in the mist depends on how we think about God, if indeed we think about God at all. Because of God's desire not to terrorize us, it is as if each of us has a receiver. Some people never turn theirs on. Others tune in to transmissions they quickly recognize as fanciful or fraudulent and so switch them off. Still others, frustrated by the bewildering array of what is coming at them, try for a while to find God but then give up. But what if God has already appeared? What if two thousand years ago, Jesus explicitly revealed the character, in human terms the personality, of God? What if, by subjecting himself to politically ambitious people who valued power over truth, and allowing them to execute him on a cross, Jesus demonstrated God's love, not only for humanity in general but for each of us as an individual? What if this act of God in the person of Jesus happened only once, at the crossroads of history, when civilization had progressed far enough to make sense of what was happening? And, what if God continues to summon us? What if, despite the static that can distort the signal, God is still broadcasting?

Christianity teaches that when Jesus died on the cross, it was no accident of history but an intentional act of sacrifice. The cross demonstrated the nature of God's love for us, what living in communion with God actually looks like and how our natural bent is not to live that way. By deliberately submitting himself to crucifixion, and therefore to the will of God, Jesus made possible the repair of our fractured relationship with God and implanted the Holy Spirit in those who, in responding to Jesus, understand to whom they are responding. Through and in Jesus, God revealed the deep structure of existence (see chapter 6), and without him, our knowledge of God would have remained incomplete and inaccurate.

Why God Keeps Some Things Secrets

Life would be so much simpler if only it could be demonstrated to everyone's satisfaction, not only that God exists but also what he expects from us, and what our reward would be for doing it. There are good reasons, however, why God has chosen *not* to provide humanity with a detailed instruction manual.

First, such a manual would prompt us to do the right things for the wrong reasons. We would be incapable of putting aside notions of reward and punishment, and we would behave largely in the expectation that the Emperor of the Cosmos would look favorably on us. Our focus would be on ourselves and only secondarily on God. We might scurry about and turn into creatures resembling high-strung animals, locked in a cage called earth and pressing levers of goodness for what we expected them to yield. Human freedom of choice would be curtailed and life as we know it would not exist. We would be in a human

CHAPTER 3. WHY BELIEFS MATTER

Skinner Box, a cage inhabited by a laboratory rat that must press a bar to obtain a reward or avoid a punishment.

Second, consider the relationship between faith and knowledge we explored in the last chapter. Faith in God implies trust in God's goodness. We are suspended between having no knowledge and having complete knowledge. If we knew everything about God, faith would be meaningless since there would be no opportunity or need for it. But if we knew nothing, we would have no notion whatsoever of a creator in whom to place our faith. Human beings exist in the middle ground between knowing everything and knowing nothing. As suggested in the last chapter, for faith to be meaningful there must be ambiguity.

Third, for almost anything to become part of us, including faith, we often have to work to internalize it. It must become ours through effort, because what we receive passively tends not to stick. Having to rely on God, as we work to figure things out, gives us the chance to internalize such reliance. Uncertainty brings with it not only the occasion for faith but also the chance to fortify it.

Fourth, at the end of the Gospel of John, we read, "There is much else that Jesus did. If it were all to be recorded in detail, I suppose the world could not hold the books that would be written" (John 21:25, REB). This is hyperbole, of course, but it hints at how understanding God is not a closed-end endeavor, something codified in a book or posted on the internet. In this life, there will never be a comprehensive understanding of God. Human needs and circumstances change, and so do the theological questions we raise and the answers we come up with in response. This requires us to struggle with issues that have spiritual implications. If God made everything explicit, we would not have to struggle at all. Nor, as indicated above, would we confront morally ambiguous dilemmas[3] that present us with opportunities to trust God.

Finally, the Bible contains much that is more like an analog than a digital radio signal. Instruction manuals are by nature digital. Although Jesus sometimes teaches explicitly, for example in the Sermon on the Mount (Matt 5–7), he also tells parable after parable, to the point that his followers sometimes had to ask what he meant. The British New Testament scholar A. E. Harvey writes, "To see what a parable is one must look at the parables of Jesus: it was he who made the form immortal. But the word itself did not necessarily mean anything so extended and

---

3. For examples, see my *Street-Smart Ethics*.

elaborate as most of Jesus' stories. In Greek it meant any 'comparison' or 'simile'; and the Hebrew word to which this corresponded had an even wider range of meanings—proverbs, riddles, illustrations and stories."[4] Ever since brain research took off in the twentieth century, people have tended to describe themselves as predominantly left- or right-brained. The left hemisphere majors in analytic and sequential reasoning, while the right hemisphere supports intuition and pattern recognition. This is an oversimplification, but the metaphor is useful. It may be that, to transform our minds and hearts, God must communicate with us analytically *and* intuitively, through modes of consciousness that are both digital and analogic. Providing us with a compendium of beliefs that appealed only to the left hemisphere would be unlikely to draw us toward God. Consciousness is God's gift to us, and it is perhaps the way in which we are most like God. Neither God nor we could have intentions or purposes without it.

Christianity's Unique Claims

If there is a divine being, a creator-provider-sustainer, not engaging with that being may be to miss the best life has to offer. We human creatures need a relationship with God to complete ourselves, and not thinking about God may be like swearing off food. We cannot do it for long without starving. Eating the wrong food, however, might sicken or kill us. As mortals, we require a specific kind of spiritual nourishment, which we can only obtain by communing with God. Such communion centers on establishing a relationship with the living Christ. As Paul eloquently states in his letter to the Christians in ancient Colossae, God has entrusted the universe into Christ's hands, the hands of his Son Jesus.

What, then, does a person have to believe to establish this relationship, to become a Christian? No one has it all figured out, which is why humility is in order when trying to come to an understanding of God and our obligations to God. As intimated above, in this life there will always be mystery, since we will continue, at best, to see images in a smoky mirror or through a darkened prism. We will return to this question in detail, but the simple answer is to acknowledge Christ as one's supreme authority. Theologians have argued that the virgin birth and physical resurrection of Jesus are major clues to understanding

---

4. Harvey, *New English Bible Companion*, 128.

CHAPTER 3. WHY BELIEFS MATTER

Christ's nature and significance. You may already believe God brought the world into existence. If so, the virgin birth and the resurrection may be easy for you to accept, since if God was able to create the world, he could also have performed these miracles. But if you cannot accept either of them right now, that need not stop you from moving toward God and continuing to explore Christianity.

Although I appeal to the Nicene and Apostles' Creeds as defining documents of Christianity, I am uneasy about declaring that to become a Christian a person must, at the outset, believe every part of them. Only God knows who is and is not a Christian. Although I accept them, you may not. I recall one of the theologians at the seminary where I taught speaking of an umbrella line, by which he meant that, unless one thinks that God will grant everlasting life to everyone, all theists who believe in an afterlife have some notion, however well or poorly articulated and however arrogantly or humbly maintained, about who will and who will not be granted such life. Some are under the umbrella, protected from the rain of separation from God, while others are not. I approach the drawing of such lines cautiously. Christians believe that the overarching truth is captured in Heb 11:6: "And without faith it is impossible to please him, for whoever would approach God must believe that he exists and that he rewards those who seek him" (NRSV).

The central question for anyone thinking seriously about Christianity is whether Jesus was related to God in a way we are not, and what this implies about the divinity of Jesus. Because *divinity* can be an ambiguous term, I want to make clear that by using it I do not mean Jesus merely reflected more divine light (John 1:4). He did that, but also much more. If Jesus was only an intensified reflection of the divine, he might have been little more than a gifted teacher who, like Socrates, came to a bad end. This, however, is not the claim of Christianity. It is Jesus Christians see through the mist referred to above and whose voice they hear. This may be an even more shocking claim than the virgin birth or resurrection, since it implies that God, in the person of Jesus, died on a Jerusalem cross.

Coming to believe in the significance of the virgin birth and resurrection amounts to more than going to church and reciting a creed. It suggests that you appreciate the singular significance of Jesus. But even this is not enough to turn you into a Christian, which requires coming to terms with your frailties and failings. Grasping our lack of holiness, in contrast to Jesus' exemplification of it, is what in Christian theology amounts to coming to grips with the fact that one is a sinner, someone who resists God. Becoming a Christian means accepting the transformation offered through Christ. It is to understand your need for rescue from self-centeredness and to be willing no longer to serve as your own god. If you do this, you may start to feel like a stranger in a strange land, which is what Abram, later renamed Abraham, learns he is about to be (Gen 15:13). A Christian is exactly that. In Christian theology, spiritual rehabilitation is called *regeneration*, a renewed and more vigorous existence.

Jesus represented a transcendent order of existence. The Jewish people grasped this order, and their history reflected how inconsistently they were faithful to a God who remained shrouded. In the person of Jesus, God abandoned that shroud and could now be seen, heard, and touched. His disciples encountered the divine in the form of a man, which drove them to the confession voiced by Thomas: "My Lord and My God" (John 20:28, ESV).

This confession is striking because the early disciples of Jesus were all Jewish and therefore staunchly monotheistic. The Greek word translated in the Bible as *disciple* means student, follower, or apprentice. If there was anything about which Jews were adamant, it was belief in only one God. Christians did not view Jesus as a second God and such a suggestion would have horrified them. Nor did they regard faith in Jesus to be a departure from Judaism.

These first believers in Christ reached the astonishing conclusion that Jesus was the one to whom the Old Testament pointed, and more astonishingly that he was the God they had been worshipping all along. Their newfound faith was a continuation and fulfillment of Judaism, the second act of a two-part drama. The last thing in any of their minds was the founding of a new religion. Christianity was and remains rooted in Judaism, and attempts to sever it from its roots diminish it.

The Apostle Paul's Realization

It is instructive to reflect on Saul's (Paul's) early adult life as a devout Pharisee, and the colossal shift in consciousness he experienced when he finally encountered the risen Christ. A Pharisee was not necessarily a hypocrite, even though this is what the term suggests today. As a group, they were intent on keeping Jewish laws as well as the ritualistic

CHAPTER 3. WHY BELIEFS MATTER

superstructure erected by devout rabbis on the foundation of the Torah (first five books of the Bible).

The world into which Paul was born was saturated with Hellenistic culture and Greek philosophy. Educated Greeks understood God to encompass abstract Platonic forms and the triad of goodness, truth, and beauty. Paul, although exposed to such thinking, grew up in an orthodox Jewish home in accordance with strict Jewish law, which laid great stress on holiness. This no doubt meant observing the rituals spelled out in the Old Testament, including its dietary requirements, and also what rabbis in the centuries leading up to Christ added.

People in contemporary society tend to think of God, if they do so at all, as a vaguely benign and remote presence. This can make it difficult to appreciate the gravity of humanity's problem as Paul eventually conceived it. According to Jewish religion, only a person who obeyed the Jewish law would be free of moral blemish and someone God would accept. Paul understood that no one had been able to keep the law, or even to follow the dictates of conscience. This raised the troubling question of how the chasm between God and humanity could be bridged, especially because it was central to Jewish belief that no one tainted by spiritual or moral imperfection, what they termed *sin*, could approach God and survive. Ritual sacrifice may have begun to feel insufficient to the well-educated, urbane, and sophisticated Paul, which may have been why he zealously hounded Christians. He may have regarded persecution of the new sect as a more profound expression of his faithfulness to God.

More than one New Testament scholar[5] has argued that it is a mistake to assume that the Jewish people were so focused on keeping the law that they remained oblivious to their need for grace, God's undeserved favor, mercy, and pardon. To the contrary, they were painfully aware of it, and that was precisely Paul's problem. The law, which Jews believed God gave to humanity as a guide and requirement, stood as a nagging accuser. What, then, could remove its accusation?

A few years after the crucifixion, Paul was traveling from Jerusalem to Damascus, in modern-day Syria. His mission was to stomp out the new heresy. A heresy is a stubbornly maintained departure from traditional beliefs, and in the eyes of Paul, Christianity was certainly that. But God, he reports, appeared to him as a blinding light and a voice asking, "Saul, Saul, why are you persecuting me?" In response,

---

5. See Wright, *Paul in Fresh Perspective*.

Paul asks, "Lord, who are you?" to which the voice answers, "I am Jesus, the one you are persecuting." God shocked Paul into the realization that Jesus was the promised one. The resurrected Christ, he now understood, was God's appointed agent. Paul further came to see in Jesus that God had already solved our problem, which is what he and other newly transformed Jews called the *Good News*.

It is customary to refer to this experience as Paul's conversion, but that term can be misleading because, in contemporary English, it suggests something akin to checking a different box on a religious-preference form. What Paul experienced was far more than that. It dramatically changed his life and altered his entire perspective on Judaism. Paul realized that, although God had been intimately involved with creation from the beginning, it was as if God suddenly crashed into history. Or, as we might say today, as if Jesus came from another dimension. Even more astonishing, through Jesus God married humanity and paid an inestimable price to establish the means by which to rehabilitate and restore it. God would now reside in the spirit of those who gave God their allegiance through Jesus, and if they were faithful would show the world God's love and grace.

This is Paul's message in the letter he wrote to Christians living in Rome, what we have in our Bibles as the Epistle to the Romans. It is also the main theme of Colossians and Ephesians. Jesus lived and died to make plain the nature of the creator, and in the words of Paul to the Christians living in Corinth, to show us "a more excellent way" (1 Cor 12:31, KJV). This is not the only reason Jesus allowed himself to be executed, but it is an important one. In these and his other letters, Paul urges us to abandon our rebellion and embrace Christ as the only one willing and able to rescue us from death and give us unending life.

God continues to send out this message, the invitation to participate in God's divine existence and agenda. If we accept this invitation, participation starts now. God's Spirit can and will live within us if we respond to God's invitation, which is wonderful news of incomparable value. It is, in fact, central to the Christian Gospel, that God in some mysterious but nonetheless real way can dwell in our hearts through faith (Eph 3:17).

Closing Thoughts

Few if any religions operate without an explicit or implicit theology, or at least a sense of cosmic power or process. Some religions depict God as an impersonal force or principle. Christianity, by contrast, portrays God as personal and intimately involved in human history. Different religions make contradictory truth-claims. Sincerely holding a belief is no guarantee that it is true, so it is important not to mistake sincerity for truth. God refuses to frighten us into faith because coerced belief makes faith impossible. We must rely, therefore, on a kind of sixth sense to perceive God, who is the reality behind appearances. The Apostle Paul was a Jewish Pharisee who, soon after the crucifixion, began to persecute Jesus' followers. Because of a profound religious experience with Christ, he came to the astonishing conclusion that the resurrected Jesus was his Lord and God.

Preview

We turn next to how religion, culture, and values interact. It is important to recognize the difference between religious tolerance, on one hand, and imprecise and muddled thinking on the other. It is also important to distinguish between realistic and arbitrary biases.

Chapter 4. Religion, Culture, and Values

PERHAPS YOU LEARNED IN school, as I did, not to assume that any culture is automatically superior to any other. Because I took courses in anthropology, I appreciate the value of cultural neutrality as a working assumption for anyone doing field work. But a few of my professors went further by insisting that it was unenlightened, narrow-minded, if not glaringly foolish to conclude that any set of values was preferable to any other. I am not sure what they would have made of how, in the neighborhood where I grew up, delinquents settled their differences with bicycle chains. Something was off in what I was hearing in the lecture hall. Rather than encouraging students to think for themselves, these professors were encouraging them not to think.

A tendency toward logical inconsistency afflicts a good many otherwise intelligent people. They advocate a live-and-let-live philosophy and are quick to point out the merits of other groups, cultures, and civilizations. Unreflective open-mindedness, however, can lead to faulty conclusions. Tolerance is a beguiling word. It has a definite cachet, a kind of fashionable appeal. To many people in the West, it seems inherently noble to be tolerant, and in certain areas of life, it most certainly is. But whether tolerance is noble depends on what one is tolerant toward.

Those who most vocally promote tolerance sometimes show themselves to be strikingly intolerant toward anyone who disagrees with them. They can, for example, become stridently hostile toward those they regard as unenlightened. The failure to notice the inconsistency

CHAPTER 4. RELIGION, CULTURE, AND VALUES

between their expressed value of tolerance and such uncharitable behavior reflects muddle-headedness that is rooted in simple-mindedness. Among the more entertaining stories to make its way into the history of philosophy was when Alfred North Whitehead allegedly said that his former student Bertrand Russell regarded him as muddleheaded, while he in turn thought Russell simple-minded. Even people who are consistent in their tolerance and place a high value on others' freedom can end up confused. This happens when they do not distinguish between tolerance of belief or opinion, on one hand, and tolerance of bad behavior or shoddy thinking on the other.

Some people utter such one-liners as, "Each of us has a different reality." If by reality one means a mental state, this is uncontestable. We all, for example, have personal tastes and preferences. This, however, does not mean there are different *objective* realities. Truth is that which is, and a truthful statement is one that accurately reflects the way things are. The thesis that all versions of truth are tenable is itself untenable. This is because "all ideas have merit" has to include "all ideas do not have merit." If all beliefs are equally worthy, does that include the belief that they are not? If all values are equally noble, does that include the ones you do not endorse and possibly abhor?

Until the end of the twentieth century, a liberal education meant becoming conversant with the Western Canon, emblematically enshrined in Britannica's *Great Books of the Western World*. Today, many people do not regard this as essential or even important. Those who are professors at institutions of higher education increasingly jettison what used to be called cultural literacy for something far different.

Commenting on subjectivism and its close relative perspectivism, the authors of a book on Nietzsche write, "The position that every outlook is relative to the perspective in which it is formulated has infiltrated the intellectual climate, such that even those who still insist that there are absolute and universal values nevertheless tend to avoid [saying so]." Worse, "Perspectivist assumptions provide the underpinning of several scholarly disciplines."[1]

---

1. Solomon and Higgins, *What Nietzsche Really Said*, 223.

Behavioral Tolerance

All societies have formal and informal rules of conduct. They establish and enforce standards of behavior that are widely understood, including a criminal code of one kind or another, which tells people what they may not do. Such codes specify actions toward which a society is intolerant. The English philosopher Thomas Hobbes suggested that without laws and a government with the power to enforce them, life would be "solitary, poor, nasty, brutish, and short."

Some societies, such as ours, grant people a wide berth in terms of what they may do without punishment. Because in the West we value freedom and self-determination, we permit citizens to do almost anything that does not injure or deprive others of their property. Nor do we punish people for even the most perverse inclinations, provided they do not act on them.

The man down the street can fantasize all he wants about burning down my house, and he can even share these fantasies with his buddies, as long as he does not try or conspire with them to do so. He may also choose to pray to a wooden idol. Although I do not believe his idol has any more power to affect the course of affairs than the rocks in my backyard, neither you nor I may be inclined or allowed to interfere with his preferred mode of worship. He can pray in any manner he chooses.[2]

Advantages and Limits of Privilege

It is not as if society uniformly enforces its norms. Regardless of the ideal of equal justice and the principle that no one is above the law, the consequences of failing to live up to society's standards tend to be less severe for those who inhabit the higher, as opposed to the lower, social strata. King Henry VIII notoriously demonstrated that it is both convenient and profitable to be king. He got away with beheading two of his six wives, divorcing two others, and confiscating the English real estate holdings of the Roman Catholic Church. High status provides a person with an invisible bank account against which he or she can draw, if necessary, to offset violating society's norms, whether the society in question is a nation or a neighborhood. Social psychologists refer to the currency in such an invisible account as *idiosyncrasy credits*. Those who have fallen from the high

---

2. See Murray, *Religious Freedom*.

perch of life, or never managed to reach it, enjoy less tolerance of their bad behavior than those who dwell at loftier altitudes.

There are limits, however, to how far any of us can go. In the United States, even the President can be impeached for flagrantly breaking the law, and in the United Kingdom, depending on political party, a Prime Minister may be turned out of office by a simple vote. Ancient Israel appears to have been the first society consistently to hold that everyone, regardless of rank, was at least in theory subject to the same code of conduct. Prior to this cultural advance, the punishment attached to a crime had to do with one's social station, such as whether one was a slave. Universal application of the Jewish law is why David, after having impregnated Bathsheba, was so worried that he arranged the murder of her husband Uriah.

Many societies, including our own, took major steps backwards in relation to both the institution of slavery and its treatment of women. With respect to the latter, I recall once having conducted a psychological evaluation of a man who, concluding that his wife was "untrue," murdered her and then shot himself. He survived, albeit with a limp. The courts in his state decided "he had suffered enough" and did not prosecute him for the murder of his wife.

Cultural Savvy

The ancient Greek Herodotus observed how human beings tend to hold that the beliefs and customs of their own societies are best. In *Histories*, Herodotus wrote that if anyone were asked to choose, based on merit, which set of beliefs and customs were best, that individual would choose those of his or her own group and geographic area. The way we do things here is better than how you do things there. It is important to be aware of this bias, and therefore to guard against taking some aspect of one's own culture to be necessarily superior. It is ethnocentric, for example, to assume that anything other than Western styles of dress are inferior. There are ways, however, in which certain cultures are superior to others, and it is disingenuous to ignore this.

Given that the center of gravity for Christianity has shifted from the Northern to the Southern Hemisphere, North American and European Christians need to be especially wary of religious provincialism. Western churches and their missionaries finally realized that for

Christianity to thrive, it must adapt to local culture, and church services in other regions of the world could not remain Eurocentric. This was not, however, a lesson learned quickly by those who first attempted to transplant Christianity. Until the twentieth century, spreading Christian faith meant promoting Western customs. This changed in part when it became increasingly clear that the majority of Christians live in the Global South, in Africa, South America, or parts of Asia. There are, for example, far more Anglicans in Nigeria than the fourteen thousand in the United Kingdom. It is telling that South Korea is now sending Christian missionaries to the United States.

Not long ago, I called an executive of a corporation for which I consulted. The following week, I was scheduled to conduct a psychological evaluation of a candidate he was thinking about hiring, so I asked, as I usually did, if he had concerns to which he wanted me to pay special attend. During our conversation, I mentioned that I was taking a world history course at a community college and that I had recently become familiar with the Mughal Empire. This, I thought, might interest him, since he was born on the Indian subcontinent. I also told him I had been listening to a series of lectures by a history professor from his *alma mater*. With considerable passion, he expressed how regrettable it was that students, even at prestigious universities like the Ivy League one he had attended, remained relatively ignorant of other lands and languages. He was right in calling this regrettable because learning about other civilizations and cultures can reduce the bias to which Herodotus referred.

When Methodology Becomes Ideology

Beginning in the twentieth century, anthropologists claimed they were merely promoting a methodology when they insisted that, to study another culture effectively, one had to transcend cultural bias. They warned against unthinkingly believing in the inherent superiority of one's own ethnic, geographic, or social group, as reflected in its values, beliefs, and societal structures. There is much to commend in this warning. But it turned out to be easy for some within their ranks to slide sideways and turn this principle into an ideology. Fine books such as Mead's *Coming of Age in Samoa* and Benedict's *Patterns of Culture* perhaps unwittingly encouraged the idea that all cultures, and the values they reflect, are equally meritorious. The legacy of such thinking remains with us in the social pressure to be politically correct, which makes it rude to say anything that might make someone else uncomfortable. To the extent all of this diminishes insensitivity and callousness, it is desirable. To the extent it inhibits people from thinking clearly or engaging in sincere, open, and honest debate, as it sometimes does, it is undesirable.

Over the past century, it has become increasingly popular among the well-educated to regard all cultures and the values they reflect as equally desirable, or at least to talk as if this were so. We have no right, goes the argument, to conclude that any of our ways of thinking or acting are better than those of any other group. There is nothing inherently noble, they admonish, about Western Civilization or its most prevalent religion, Christianity.

What can seem at first glance to be admirable open-mindedness, however, can turn out on closer inspection to be superficial thinking that dulls the mind and prevents a person from distinguishing between and among alternatives. An excessively open mind is a sieve. It can impair the ability to detect the difference between sense and nonsense, truth in contrast to its absence, and good versus bad.

From the vantage point of Christianity, no person is worth more to God than anyone else. Nor is one person, regardless of geographical context, less accountable. Because someone grows up in one part of the world rather than another, for example, does not make that person more or less valuable or accountable. For whatever reasons, however, civilizations and cultures embrace and institutionalize different customs and values, and these are not equally admirable.

If you embrace cultural relativism and the ethical relativism that often comes with it, you end up having to draw some awkward conclusions: (1) Hitler was merely expressing the values of the German people in the 1940s, and it is therefore unreasonable to object to his execution of millions; (2) African societies that perpetuate female genital mutilation are simply expressing the values of their cultures, and we have no right to decide it is wrong; or (3) agrarian societies whose inhabitants value male over female children, and sell their daughters into prostitution, are not to be criticized, since such behavior merely reflects their cultural *milieu.*

On the last of these, I recognize that parting with a child in such a fashion may be far from easy and that parents in impoverished societies may feel they have little choice. Selling children into prostitution, morally egregious as it is, may involve a complex ethical dilemma. In his novel *Sophie's Choice*, William Styron depicts a Polish woman during WWII who has to decide, at gunpoint, which of her two children to sacrifice. How far any country should go to influence how another country treats its citizens is open to debate. In addition to issues of national sovereignty, there are the practical costs of imposing standards of human rights on another nation state. These include the potential risk and high price of military intervention, and the even greater risk of all-out war.

Thomas Jefferson suggested that law is but the codification of public opinion. Yet, probably few of us sincerely believe that our cardinal values are mere artifacts of current social thought and in that sense arbitrary. We defend many of our moral judgments as sound, and rightly so. Not only do we recognize that the values of our culture differ in significant ways from those of other cultures, but we also believe that aspects of our culture are decidedly better. People in Western Society are unwilling to approve of genocide, mutilating women, or selling young girls into prostitution.

We insist that a lot of things are wrong, not simply because they violate rules within our culture, but because they are intrinsically so. Who among us is going to argue that it is morally defensible to molest children, or for children to murder their parents to speed up the process of inheritance? If the culture in which we grow up conditions our values, it also reflects them. We generally believe that the rules of our society, on sum, make ethical sense and reflect what it means to be civilized. Even allowing for the evils embedded within the West, such as the inequities arising from capitalism, there is much about Western Civilization that we regard as inherently desirable. Consider the protection of freedoms articulated in the Bill of Rights, and centuries before that, the *Magna Carta*. These emerged out of Christianity, as we will discuss in chapter 18.

Although political events, such as the slaughter of innocent civilians by terrorists, have sanded some of the edges off naïve and muddle-minded tolerance, many well-educated people are still embarrassed to proclaim the virtues of Western Culture or Christianity, as if to do so were *prima facie* evidence of ignorance. It is, rather, the failure to understand and appreciate the virtues of our civilization and its religious heritage that demonstrates ignorance. Such a failure sometimes reflects intimidation by pseudo-intellectuals who shame others into a version of tolerance that even a thoughtful high school student would deem ridiculous. What some pass off as sophisticated thought is often little more than a refusal to examine the absurd notion that all ideas, values, and social structures, including all forms of government, have equal merit. They do not.

CHAPTER 4. RELIGION, CULTURE, AND VALUES

I do not write this to argue in favor of narrow-minded provincialism. Nonetheless, as we will discuss, Christianity has influenced much of what is best about American and European life, including the political traditions that undergird it. It makes no sense to ignore or deny this. To do so is unworthy of a reflective person.

Logical Coherence, Values, and Two Kinds of Biases

Intellectual precision has to do with clear thinking and therefore with what we are willing to conclude *is the case*. Because God's universe is orderly, few of us would claim, for example, that 2 + 2 = 5, and if we did, we would know we were talking nonsense. In 2 + 2 = 5, a 2 is no longer a 2 and a 5 is no longer a 5. The rules of logic lie at the core of sound reasoning: A and not-A cannot both be true at the same time in the same way. Philosophers call this the *law of the excluded middle*. We cannot argue that infanticide is always wrong but also insist that our condemnation of it is provincial. If we believed ourselves to be unable to make judgments that transcend culture, all meaningful political debate would stop, and so would all serious discussion of values.

To hold any value is to deem one thing better than another. It is to choose among options, some of which may be incompatible. Values, as I am using the term, tend to be emotionally charged *pre*judgments. To embrace a value is to discriminate, in the sense of seeing the difference between one thing and another. Words like *prejudice, bias, discrimination,* and *judging* can be ambiguous. When used to refer to disadvantaging subgroups within society because of the color of their skin or their religious beliefs, they point to unconscionable policies or practices. When, however, they refer to making sound judgments based on experience, such as having the good sense not to place one's hand on a hot stove, they are beneficial. We often hear that it is undesirable to judge, to the point that "do not judge" has become a mantra in our society. This thought-form, when it appears in the New Testament, specifically in the Sermon on the Mount (Matt 7:1–3), means we should not condemn. This, I believe, is because we can never really know another person's heart. Because we cannot avoid making judgments, it is important to know in what specific sense we should and should not judge. Do not judge is sometimes used to forbid others from thinking.

PART I. FOUNDATIONS

None of us could survive long without prejudgments. A dog growls and we know to stay away. Milk smells sour, so we pour it down the drain. We do these things because our past experiences, or the experiences of others, have equipped us with judgments that guide our behavior. Another name for a prejudgment is a bias, which is the predisposition to perceive and act in a specific way toward something or someone else.

The problem is not in forming prejudgments but in clinging to arbitrary ones, those based on bad information or unwarranted inferences. Arbitrary prejudgments, stemming from faulty information or bad inferences, are misguided. Whether grounded in race, ethnicity, religion, nationality, cultural subgroup, or a host of other characteristics, arbitrary prejudgments have triggered untold amounts of murderous conflict between individuals, groups, and nations. Philosophers distinguish between *accidental* and *dispositional* properties. The former are superficial characteristics unrelated to the basic nature or character of a person, while the latter are those that reflect this nature or character.

But there is another kind of prejudgment. It is data-based and therefore grounded in reliable information and sound reasoning. We have already noted two such biases, to stay away from threatening dogs and throw away spoiled milk. Without data-based prejudgments, we would perish. Few of us would argue that it makes sense to ignore traffic signals.

When biases develop because of what other people think and say, there is always the chance that what we take to be data-based may, in fact, be arbitrary. And when these people comprise a large segment of society, arbitrary biases can be difficult to recognize, counteract, or change. Many people find ridiculous the claim that God appeared two thousand years ago on earth in the person of a man. They insist that no reasonable person could believe such a thing and cite science as the justification for this opinion. In chapter 15, we will discuss the relationship between science and religion, but I want to anticipate that discussion by stating here that appealing to science in this way is completely illegitimate. More to the point, automatically rejecting Christianity without bothering to examine it is an arbitrary bias.

Becoming a Christian tends to shape a person's biases. These include the willingness to love[3] rather than hate, prefer peace to war, respect others and their property, forgive rather than indulge in payback, and choose truthfulness over duplicity. What Christians appeal to as reasons

---

3. See Smedes, *Love Within Limits*, in which he writes, "Love . . . is the power to endure," 110.

CHAPTER 4. RELIGION, CULTURE, AND VALUES

for these biases are not the sorts of things that come out of a physics lab. They come from encountering God or at least ingesting societal values bequeathed by Christianity.

Getting Clear

There is nothing wrong with believing that religions comfort their adherents. That much seems obvious, since if they did not, religions would likely vanish. But there is a lot wrong with accepting competing and contradictory religious truth-claims. As noted in chapter 3, different religions make contradictory assertions, and the beliefs embodied in the world's major religions are, at pivotal points, incompatible. This may not be politically correct to say at a party, but that does not alter the reality, as any honest comparison of religious claims will attest. No amount of rosy sentimentality will change this. Whether there is something special about Christianity, something that merits serious consideration, may remain an open question for some. What is not on the table is whether Christianity makes distinctive and unique claims.

A key challenge for many people is to formulate a spiritual perspective that reasonably corresponds to the way things are. If the God of Christianity exists, such a perspective would have to be based on what we can discover about that God, which in turn might depend on what God has chosen to reveal to us. Christians typically insist that such a perspective is attainable. They also affirm that the life and teachings of Jesus, as recorded in the New Testament, provide the best glimpse we have into the character of God and the ultimate nature of the universe. Christian faith involves an intellectual choice. Any individual must decide, when reading the New Testament, if its assertions are credible. This implies approaching it as you might any other collection of books to decide if its claims are true. Is it possible that God, in the person of Jesus, came to rescue us, and if so from what?

There are many answers to this question. An obvious one is to save us from the awful implications of death. Another answer, not mutually exclusive with the first, is that Christ came to deliver us from ourselves and what we might become without a relationship with God. If we believe these answers, we confront a potentially life-changing decision. Will we ask God to change us, grant us the gift of eternal life, and enable us to help change the world for the better? Or will we reject God's offer?

PART I. FOUNDATIONS

In Oscar Wilde's *Picture of Dorian Gray*, the young Dorian, having been enlightened by Lord Henry Wotton of the inevitability of his physical decline, longs to change places with a portrait of himself. Crafted by artist Basil Hallward, it fully captures Dorian's perfection. "If the picture could change, and I could be always what I am now!" Which is what, for a time, happens. However unwittingly, Wilde has captured something of what God offers. No one knows what form we will assume in eternity, and speculations about how old we will be—twenty, thirty, or fifty—border on the absurd. That Christians will continue to exist after death, however, is a belief central to Christianity. Because you are reading this, God may be calling and offering you eternal existence. Jesus assures us that if we trust him, the hope of existing forever is not in vain.

Closing Thoughts

Some people suggest that the values of all groups are equally worthy. They confuse the proper methodology of cultural anthropology with cultural and ethical relativism. All people, especially Christians, ought to remain open and sensitive to other cultures. But the subculture of a street gang committed to violence does not deserve the same respect as the subculture of a group of nuns devoted to charity. Few ideas are subject to more misunderstanding than tolerance. Insisting that everyone is entitled to individual religious beliefs, for example, is distinctly different from insisting that society ought to tolerate criminal behavior. People are also confused when they claim that we each have our own truths, as if perceptions determined reality. And, they can confuse two kinds of bias, one based on fact and the other rooted in prejudice.

Preview

There are two kinds of philosophic activity, critical thinking and speculative philosophy. Some forms of speculative philosophy are incompatible with and antagonistic toward Christianity. Christian theology, unlike speculative philosophy, necessarily presupposes the existence of God. Good theology, like sound philosophy, reflects rigorous reasoning.

Chapter 5. Philosophy, Theology, and Rigorous Thinking

I ONCE THOUGHT OF philosophy as interesting but impractical, and of theology as remote and irrelevant. Then, I began to spend time with philosophers and theologians. Philosophy, I discovered, is eminently practical, at least in one of its two forms. As for theology, if God exists, it makes sense to try to understand as much as we can about God's nature and work. In this chapter, I want to discuss similarities and differences between philosophy and theology, and in the Addendum outline what scholars regard as the principal subdivisions within each.

Philosophy is the discipline most explicitly concerned with clear thinking. William James defined it as "the unusually stubborn attempt" to do just that. It is not by nature obscure, although the writings of some philosophers certainly have been. Nor is it inherently impractical. If our ability to make our way in the world depends on how well we think, philosophy may be a good deal more practical than many people believe. *Philosophic reasoning* is, in fact, decidedly useful because by insisting on careful definitions and watching out for inconsistencies and unwarranted inferences, it promotes clear thinking. *Philosophic speculation*, on the other hand, may or may not be useful, which is why people call it speculative. Exactly how helpful a given bit of speculative thinking is hinges on the nature of the speculation.

Some Christians disparage philosophy, arguing that Christianity has made it obsolete or supplanted it, but they fail to distinguish between these two kinds of philosophy. They also seem not to understand that some forms of speculative philosophy are distinctly Christian. Origen (ca. 184–253/254), an important early church father, argued that Christianity is the supreme expression of philosophy, adding, "No one can do true duty to God who does not think like a philosopher."[1] A church father is an influential thought leader in the ancient world who contributed significantly to the development of Christian thought. Far from forbidding his students to study the works of philosophers, Origen encouraged it.

Speculative Philosophy

When non-philosophers refer to Plato's philosophy, or for that matter to that of any other thinker, they often mean the philosopher's assertions about the reality behind appearances. It is usually the case that neither the philosopher, nor anyone else, has been able to demonstrate such pronouncements to be true, except by appealing to other pronouncements that themselves need to be demonstrated to be true (see chapter 2).

To cite just two examples from the ancient world, Thales, commonly regarded as the first philosopher, lived during the early sixth century BC at the western edge of Anatolia, in what is now the part of Turkey in Asia. At the time, it was known as Ionia. Thales suggested that the universe came from water. Heraclitus, who lived in the same region a hundred years later, claimed fire to be the primordial substance. Neither Thales nor Heraclitus produced a convincing proof for their conjectures. The most they accomplished was to come up with weak inductive arguments and to suggest that, based on these, they knew the nature of the original material.

We expect any competent philosopher to reason rigorously and therefore to make statements that are consistent. Even if they satisfy this condition, all speculative systems entail propositions, the truth of which can rarely, if ever, be demonstrated to everyone's satisfaction to be true. Other philosophers will often critique these conceptual edifices, including the premises on which they rest and whatever conclusions they believe to be incorrectly drawn from those premises. So, of course, may theologians. Although few contemporary philosophers speculate about the origin of the universe, many continue to advance

---

1. Quoted in Holland, *Dominion*, 122.

CHAPTER 5. PHILOSOPHY, THEOLOGY, AND RIGOROUS THINKING

philosophical assertions that bear, for example, on theories of justice,[2] law,[3] or the human mind.[4]

Reasoning in Religion and Philosophy

Critical thinking is as central to theology as it is to philosophy. Although careful reasoning does not guarantee good theology, without it such theology could not exist. Such thinking is a necessary but not a sufficient condition for reaching the right theological conclusions. This is because, as discussed in chapter 2, not all valid arguments are sound. If we begin with false premises, we are likely to reach faulty conclusions. If our premises are flawed, our conclusions will probably be also. It is possible, however, to reach the right conclusions, by accident or coincidence, based on the wrong premises.

If Christian theology purports, however imperfectly, to capture what is true of God, it must hold up under close examination. It has to make sense, which at a minimum means it must be free of contradictions. The competent theologian views rigorous thinking as foundational. In both philosophy and theology, it is the *fundamental method*. One can reason poorly and so remain oblivious to imprecision, inconsistency, or ambiguity. But one cannot avoid reasoning altogether. Even the most uneducated and unsophisticated Christian embraces some form of theology, however primitive, which encompasses beliefs about God and the universe.

The paths of theology and philosophy may quickly part when it comes to basic content. This is because the assumptions and conclusions of a given speculative philosopher do not always harmonize with Christianity. Heinrich Heine, the nineteenth-century poet, wrote in *Religion and Philosophy in Germany*, "As soon as a religion seeks help from philosophy, its doom is inevitable." If Heine meant that religion does itself a disservice when it succumbs to the idea that reason alone will get us to God, he was right. Or, if he intended to argue that religion forfeits the game when it tries to prove its affirmations deductively, he was right again. But even a romanticist like Heine hardly believed that theologians could ignore thinking about the basic questions of life.[5]

---

2. See Rawls, *A Theory of Justice*.
3. See Habermas, *Between Facts and Norms*.
4. See Searle, *Intentionality*.
5. Quoted in Wood, *Broken Estate*, 242

PART I. FOUNDATIONS

A theologian grapples with many of the same issues addressed by a speculative philosopher, and when the two disagree, as they sometimes do, both cannot be right. These issues include the nature of reality, whether freedom of choice is an illusion, what sense if any to make of human pain and suffering, the possibility of life after death, and the purpose and meaning of existence, if indeed as Christianity teaches there is purpose and meaning.

When Ideas Replace God

God has endowed us with the capacity to think conceptually, which allows us to make ethical and moral decisions, investigate the world scientifically, and commune with other spiritual beings. This capacity also enables us to reflect on life's most important questions, the theologic and philosophic ones, whether or not we realize we are even doing this. Philosophy in Greek means *love of wisdom*, and perhaps most people have at least some desire for wisdom. Thinking about these questions, when approached with humility and reverence, may well increase our understanding of and appreciation for God. Such thinking is also likely to increase our faith, unless of course we turn the virtue of intelligence into the vice of intellectualization.

A kind of spiritual deterioration occurs when the quest for correct theology replaces genuine worship. It would be primitive to think of God as the same sort of person as our spouse, friend, or next-door neighbor. But it is far more primitive to conceive of God as an impersonal abstraction. God, Christians affirm, is intentional, and the best we can do as humans is to think of God as having a mind, what we understand to be consciousness.

Having taught for a decade at a seminary, I am familiar with how faith can become over-intellectualized. For a while, I became so invested in forming the right ideas *about* God that I temporarily lost sight *of* God. My ten years at that seminary were priceless, but there was still that subtle erosion of my faith. This can sometimes travel with developing more theological sophistication, but living in the head can sometimes crowd out worshipping from the heart.

Nearly two thousand years ago, the author of the last book in the Bible lamented that Christians living in Ephesus had lost their initial love for God (Rev 2:4). Ephesus was a thriving commercial port on the coast

CHAPTER 5. PHILOSOPHY, THEOLOGY, AND RIGOROUS THINKING

of Asia Minor, but because of two thousand years of silt deposits, it is now over five miles from the Mediterranean Sea. Strabo, a geographer, historian, and philosopher born about sixty years before, regarded it as second only to Rome in prestige and population. The ruins at Ephesus remain impressive, with its famous Temple of Artemis, one of the seven wonders of the ancient world. Artemis in Greek religion became Diana in Roman religion. She had long been a focus of religious devotion, and a small industry developed in Ephesus to produce replicas of her. It was a significant challenge, therefore, to introduce Christianity into this predominantly Greek culture. Nevertheless, some early Christian evangelists succeeded. For a long time, Christians living in Ephesus endured hardship, ridicule, and perhaps persecution, but they persevered in their faith and were not inclined to look the other way when someone in their community behaved badly. Nor were they quick to ignore the corrosive influence of those who promoted a distorted Christian message. Eventually, however, they seem to have lost the passion they once had for God. Because Ephesus was urbane and its populace well educated, the faith of Christians living there may have lost its luster under the influence of itinerant philosophers, who were likely to be either Epicureans or Stoics. The Apostle Paul tells us that Greeks were fond of listening to the latest ideas afloat in the marketplace (Acts 17:21). This inclination may have helped dilute the religious fervor of Ephesian Christians and allowed their love of novelty to overshadow their love for God.

Learning can become idolatry. When its subject matter is God, such idolatry can be insidious and so subtly entrap a person that he or she might not realize what is happening. There is no merit in loving theology so much that it causes us to forget or ignore the God to whom good theology points. This would be like becoming so engrossed in a recipe that we neglect to cook.

Assumptions of Philosophers and Theologians

The key difference between Christian theology and speculative philosophy often has to do with foundational assumptions. Christian theologians presuppose that God exists and that the Bible provides unique insight into God's nature. Unless theologians occupy themselves with certain types of apologetics,[6] defenses of the faith, they are not much

---

6. *Apologetics* is sometimes classified under the category of *prolegomena*, critical

concerned with proving God's existence, since this is their starting point, their rock-bottom premise. Theologians sometimes call this a *point of departure*. Some, but by no means all, experts suggest that even the philosophical theologian Thomas Aquinas (1225–74), whose five proofs of God Christian thinkers have cited for eight hundred years, did not address his arguments so much to agnostics or atheists as to believers. He offered his proofs as ways to enrich and strengthen faith that already existed.

A central concern of theology is to clarify what we are to understand by the term God. What is God like? Some so-called theologians render God so impersonal that they seem to be expounding certain strands of European or Eastern philosophy, rather than deepening our understanding of the God of Christianity. It has been claimed that the late Paul Tillich, for example, was more of a German Idealist than a Christian theologian, despite the fact that his three-volume tome is entitled *Systematic Theology*.[7] This is not to argue that Tillich ignored scripture, only that he seems to have gone beyond anything that can be tightly derived or even inferred from the Bible or mainline Christian tradition. Nor is it to suggest that reading Tillich is of no value, only that he is not offering Christian theology as this has been traditionally understood.

Some philosophers suggest that their personal beliefs have nothing to do with their professional work, and in areas such as advanced logic this may be true. In certain domains of philosophy, however, such a claim is untenable. Whenever a thinker develops a metaphysical system for making sense of the world, he or she has erected that system on the scaffolding of basic assumptions, and no philosopher who has ever developed such a system has done so without them. A philosopher may be a devout Christian, a practitioner of another faith, a staunch atheist, or an avowed agnostic. Only in the first case will the philosopher's metaphysics align with those of the Christian theologian. Many philosophers, especially over the past several centuries, have either denied the existence of God or depicted God in a way that no Christian theologian would endorse. The good news is that a renewed interest in questions relating to God has emerged in departments of philosophy at colleges and universities.

A second difference between the theologian and the philosopher has to do with what they allow onto the stage as evidence. Even

---

introduction.

7. Tillich, *Systematic Theology*.

CHAPTER 5. PHILOSOPHY, THEOLOGY, AND RIGOROUS THINKING

philosophers who are passionate Christians do not grant special authority to the Bible when they work strictly as philosophers. Peter Kreeft, an eminent philosopher at Boston College, is an example of a Christian who, when working strictly as a philosopher, does not start with the assumption that scripture is inspired. Two other examples of noteworthy Christian philosophers who approach their work in a similar way are Alasdair MacIntyre and Alvin Plantinga. All three have been profoundly influential thought leaders within Christianity.

Christian theologians assume that the Bible is authoritative, and they attempt to ensure that their theological assertions faithfully reflect its overall content. This is so, whether these theologians are Eastern Orthodox, Protestant, or Roman Catholic. Fulfilling this condition is not always easy, which is one reason theology exists, to identify and highlight the implications of biblical themes. The Protestant Bible contains sixty-six books, while the Roman Catholic Bible includes secondary books, called the Apocrypha, defined as those of less importance and possibly of uncertain authenticity. About two thirds of the Bible are the Hebrew Scriptures, the Old Testament, and the other third the New Testament. They were written over a period of about a thousand years. It can be challenging even for theologians, therefore, to identify and harmonize its various streams of thought.

It is a central thesis of Christian theologies that, however disparate the biblical books may appear, God was involved in their development and preservation, and that collectively they convey an increasingly clear message. In what exact manner the Bible is inspired remains a matter of debate. No one with any religious sophistication believes God dictated the Bible. But neither does anyone with theological insight believe that God had nothing to do with it. It is possible for different theologians to emphasize certain biblical themes at the expense of others, and in fact doing so may be inevitable. At the same time, the Bible contains foundational assertions that no theologian can soft peddle and still claim to be faithful to its message. Christian theologians tend to regard the Bible as its own best commentary, so it is important to view anything that appears in it through the lenses of everything else it contains.

Christian theologians assert that Jesus was more than a man, that Christ is and always has been begotten of the Father. The idea that a single divine begotten offspring of God has always existed may be difficult to accept. It is probably the case that no mortal has ever truly grasped the meaning of eternal. We can say the word, but that is different from getting our minds around what it means. It may be harder to believe that the Son has always existed than that God has always existed, and yet there is no obvious reason why this should be so. If we can accept the eternality of God, we ought also to be able to accept the eternality of the Son, and for that matter also of the Holy Spirit. Augustine (354–430) developed seven propositions in support of the doctrine of the Trinity, that God exists in three persons, Father, Son, and Holy Spirit. The first of the seven is that there is only one God, and the other six state that the three persons are distinct from each other.[8]

There is an important difference between *beget* and *create*. We beget beings like ourselves, such as children, but we create (design, build, manufacture, synthesize) everything else, from tables and chairs to satellites, ships, skyscrapers, symphonies, poems, and paintings. That Jesus was both divine and human is the basis for the claim that he was God's unique self-disclosure, God in the form of a man, which is what Christians mean by *Incarnation*. A theologian who slips and slides when it comes to the incarnation of God in the person of Jesus or Jesus' physical resurrection is "straining at a gnat while swallowing a camel" (Matt 24:12). Christianity centers upon the incarnation and resurrection, which along with the crucifixion are defining events.

Philosophers, as a class, make no necessary assumptions about the Bible or Jesus. Some embrace him as their ultimate authority, while others regard him either as an ethicist, deluded martyr, or shadowy figure about whom we know little. Some view Jesus as a charismatic charlatan. As with the existence of God and the primacy of the Bible, a philosopher can deny the preeminence of Jesus and remain a philosopher. A theologian who denies Christ's preeminence is, at the least, stretching what it means to be a Christian.

An assumption that runs through a great deal of Eastern Orthodox, Protestant, and Roman Catholic theology is the need for humility vis-à-vis the history of Christian thought. Theologians are characteristically hesitant to issue pronouncements that fly in the face of what the church has maintained for two thousand years. Their instinct is to treat earlier theological work with respect and to give it the benefit of the doubt. This reluctance to run counter to centuries of Christian teaching is rooted in the deeply held belief that, despite its failings and controversies, God continues to guide the church. Some religious sects

---

8. Augustine's logic has come under scrutiny, for example by Martinich, "Identity and Trinity," 169–81.

CHAPTER 5. PHILOSOPHY, THEOLOGY, AND RIGOROUS THINKING

claim that soon after the disciples died, the church degenerated into apostasy, meaning that it renounced and abandoned true faith in God. Mainline Christian theologians deny this.

Theological Similarities and Differences

Christian theologians characteristically treat the creeds of the Christian church, such as the Apostles' and Nicene, as definitive, although there is some variance in how they understand the nuances, such as exactly what substance or essence mean. Unless a person wants to intellectualize them away, however, their core affirmations seem straightforward. Once you go beyond such basic creeds, you enter the realm of confessions of faith. These serve as constraints within which theologians within particular tradition work. Every form of Christianity explicitly or implicitly embraces a confession that reflects its theology and shapes it practices.

Within the Protestant communions, those theologians inclined toward a literal view of scripture accept it as exclusively authoritative. Such theologians may refrain from making any affirmation or endorsing any practice not explicitly commended in the Bible. Others of a less restrictive persuasion feel comfortable making any affirmation or endorsing any practice not biblically contradicted or prohibited. Still others do not regard the Bible as authoritative or controlling at all. Taking such a stance can become so extreme that, as intimated above, it calls into question the theologian's claim to be a Christian.

A Roman Catholic theologian would hesitate to put forth anything at variance with the Bible and would also acknowledge the authority of Papal encyclicals, official teaching documents. By definition, a Catholic theologian is one who submits to the authority of the Vatican, and those who do not tend to be regarded as renegades. Partly because of the vast numbers all over the globe who identify themselves as Catholic, there is considerable variation between and among Roman Catholic theologians, with some resembling evangelical or charismatic Protestants and others advocating a return to the Latin mass.

An Eastern Orthodox theologian, like a Protestant one, gives no special deference to the Bishop of Rome (Pope), nor grants authority to any individual for a private interpretation of the Bible. Granting such authority has, to greater or lesser extent, been the bane of many Protestant communions. Roman Catholicism recognizes twenty-one *ecumenical* councils that guide its interpretation of scripture, while Eastern Orthodoxy emphasizes the authority of scripture as interpreted by the seven ecumenical councils it recognizes. Ecumenical councils are taken to be those that are universal and worldwide. Orthodox theologians are inclined to give special honor to such church fathers as John Chrysostom, Basil the Great, and Gregory of Nyssa.

Once a theologian embraces a specific tradition within Christianity, that theologian implicitly agrees to work within its broad conceptual boundaries. Such constraints generally meet the condition of what philosophers of science refer to as *consensual validation* within that tradition, but they fail the other principal test philosophers insist on, *public verifiability*. Neutral observers outside a tradition would not necessarily agree that its constraints were undeniable, and nothing objectively observable would be able to show such constraints to be correct or incorrect. Like religious truth-claims in general, there is no way deductively to demonstrate the logical necessity of spiritual beliefs, which are largely but perhaps not exclusively matters of personal conviction reached by induction.

Evaluating Theological Options

Different theologians excel in different ways. It is nonetheless possible to assess the value of what any theologian publishes by asking how well it fares in three areas: creativity, coherence, and soundness. *Creativity* in theology means providing new insights into the nature of God, the cosmos, and where we stand in relation to both. Creative insight is not, however, the same as untethered invention. *Coherence* has to do with the extent to which a theology is free of inconsistency, of self-contradiction. Theologies that contain affirmations violating basic principles of logic are suspect. *Soundness* concerns whether the presuppositions of a given theology are true and whether the arguments derived from them are valid. As we have seen, no line of reasoning can be sound if it is based on flawed premises. Because many religious premises cannot be objectively demonstrated, this is the stickiest wicket of the three. Theologies are valuable only to the extent that they accurately depict the way things are.[9]

The works of some religious thinkers are not tied in any obvious way to biblical studies, while those of others reflect a concerted attempt to

---

9. See MacIntyre, "Truth as a Good," 197–215.

CHAPTER 5. PHILOSOPHY, THEOLOGY, AND RIGOROUS THINKING

anchor theological assertions in the Bible. I am bypassing, here, the question of just how far a given thinker can move away from reliance on the Bible and still legitimately claim to be a Christian. This is the question of whether a thinker who self-identifies as a Christian theologian continues to function as one, in contrast to becoming a philosopher who simply uses religious language. Although it may make a great deal of difference to where they end up theologically, whether a specific thinker takes a high or low view of scripture is not, of itself, a matter of logic. How competently he or she reasons from scripture most definitely is.

Confusions and Misunderstandings

Theology is an ever-evolving enterprise, and theologians today concern themselves with matters that were unheard of a century ago. Consider the debates that have flared up over cloning and stem cell research. Theologians have always had to address such new and emerging issues. Their work is, nevertheless, by nature conceptual. When William Wilberforce (1759–1833), an English politician and philanthropist, led the movement to end the slave trade in Great Britain, he was theologically aware and religiously enlightened. But he was not developing or advocating a new theology. To the contrary, Wilberforce was advocating the application of an existing and widely accepted theology to an abhorrent practice that was inconsistent with Christianity. Christian theology may have strong implications for social action, but theology is not at root such action. Theologians who label activism as theology are either unenlightened, confused, or disingenuous. They may engage in political activism and believe themselves to be called by God to do so. But when they do, they no longer function as theologians.

Nor are theologians staying within the bounds of their discipline when they offer amateur opinions about science. Unless a theologian is also a trained scientist, he or she has no legitimate basis on which to render summary judgments about the merits of scientific findings, hypotheses, or theories. There are Christian theologians, such as Alister McGrath and John Polkinghorne, who were already accomplished scientists before becoming theologians, but they are rare.

Considerable damage has been done to the reputation of Christianity by sincere but misguided religionists who failed to understand that the Bible is not a textbook of science. Some Christians seem on occasion to worship the Bible more than the God to whom it points, to turn the Bible into a proxy god. Onlookers, reacting to what they see as bibliolatry, sometimes dismiss the claims of Christianity without examining them. This is unfortunate. If you ask if they have ever read a single book from the New Testament, even the brightest among them may answer no. They have never taken the time to read Christianity's primary documents because they instinctively associate the Bible with a rigid lack of intellectual sophistication.

Confronting the Issues

Paul in the New Testament argued that in this life we see through a glass darkly (1 Cor 13:12). The Greek word often translated as *glass* can also be translated as *mirror*, which was an apt metaphor for Paul to use, since a major industry in ancient Corinth was the manufacture of mirrors made of polished silver or bronze. Older New Testament commentaries indicate that the images reflected by these mirrors were cloudy, but more modern commentaries point out that Corinthian mirrors were well polished. The metaphor of looking in a mirror is nonetheless a good one, since even the best mirrored image can be fragmentary and distorted. Paul's notion of a reflected image as an imperfect rendering puts one in mind of Plato's allegory of the cave. We have, at best, partial knowledge. Until God brings down the curtain on human existence, much about the universe will remain a mystery to Christians and non-Christians alike.

But what if, as Paul suggests, the most important questions in life are not only addressed but answered in and by Jesus? What if the documents in the New Testament reveal a great deal about how Christ stands at the center of the universe, as both its owner and Lord? What if the works of Augustine in the fourth and fifth centuries, such as his *Confessions* and *City of God*, provide us with insight into the nature and purposes of God? Or, if the works of Thomas Aquinas in the thirteenth century, such as his monumental *Summa*, point us to that same God? What, in other words, if the affirmations of Christianity are true.

Closing Thoughts

Although rigorous reasoning is central to philosophy and theology, speculative philosophers are not bound by assumptions about the

CHAPTER 5. PHILOSOPHY, THEOLOGY, AND RIGOROUS THINKING

existence, nature, or activity of a supernatural being. Christian theologians may differ in their secondary beliefs, but they all begin with the assumption that a personal God exists. Speculative philosophies must be able to stand up to critical examination and so must theologies. Theologians who are not scientists do not operate within their domain of expertise when they write or speak as if they were.

Preview

In the next chapter, we will ask if there might be an underlying structure to human existence, and if there is, how anyone can claim to know about it. We will also ask how belief in that structure, as Christians perceive it, is the basis for their hope.

Addendum: Modes of Philosophy and Theology

Philosophy

DIFFERENT PHILOSOPHERS DIVIDE THEIR discipline into different categories, and certain domains of philosophy lend themselves, more than others, to speculative system building. Here are what some regard as philosophy's major subdivisions: Aesthetics (nature of beauty and what causes us to respond to something as beautiful); Epistemology (nature of knowledge and how we come to know anything); Ethics[1] (nature of goodness and what it means to lead a moral life); Logic (careful analysis of arguments); Metaphysics (ontology, the nature of being, and cosmology, the nature of the universe; cosmology includes cosmogony, the origin and development of the cosmos); and Philosophy of Science (nature of scientific inquiry and verification). The areas in which differences between philosophy and theology are most likely to arise are metaphysics and ethics.

Some philosophers prefer simply to point to the general domains in which they work or to the types of questions addressed within them, such as these: Education (how pedagogy ought best to be conducted); History (what drives historical development, whether history is headed in a particular direction, and if so what this direction might be); Jurisprudence (basic principles that laws embody and how different judicial protocols do or do not reflect them); Language (its nature and limits,

---

1. Ethics and aesthetics are the two branches of *axiology* or *value theory*.

and how language relates to thought); Mathematics (nature of numbers, axioms, symbols, and proofs, and their respective significances); Mind (what it is and its relation to the body, other minds, and artificial intelligence); Politics (study of government institutions and duties of citizens); Religion (nature of religious questions and truth-claims); and Social Behavior (nature of communal action and ethical values embedded within different social institutions).

Rigorous thinking is necessary in all these areas. Well-trained philosophers are concerned with logical precision, including tightly framed arguments and unambiguous definitions. They are wary of grand inferential leaps, of what we tend to think of as jumping to conclusions. Logic, therefore, sits at the center of all philosophic activity.

Theology

Theology is the study of God and God's ways with us. Christian theology is the attempt, based primarily on the Old and New Testaments, and secondarily on longstanding interpretations of these documents, to develop and articulate the nature of true beliefs and proper practices. Its methods include, but are not confined to, biblical analysis and the study of the history of doctrine. Biblical analysis primarily centers on *exegesis*, which in its general sense refers to drawing from a text its deeper meanings and so involves interpretation and practical application. In its narrower sense, exegesis may include lexical analysis, study of grammar and syntax, exploration of literary forms and genres, attempts to ferret out an author's intent, and making sense of how audiences might have been inclined to understand a particular text.

Well-thought-out Christian theologies comprise a set of navigation charts that point us toward God and keep us from losing our way or crashing onto the shoals of faulty assumptions or questionable inferences. Such navigation charts are not religion *per se* but its conceptual underpinnings. At its best, theology is a guide to sound religion. Throughout its history, the church has had to sort out many questions, and theologians have done much of this sorting. Political ambition colored and occasionally corrupted the process, and from time to time the ship of faith veered off course and the best answers failed to emerge. Christian theology has typically been able to self-correct and regain its bearings.

PART I. FOUNDATIONS

Just as there are different domains within philosophy, there are different domains within theology. Seminaries organize their faculties and course offerings into what these institutions consider to be of primary importance. Although this differs from school to school, here are some of the subdivisions of theology offered by one or more of the major Eastern Orthodox, Protestant, and Roman Catholic seminaries, albeit sometimes listed with different names in their catalogs: Biblical or Exegetical Studies (meaning and implications of specific biblical texts); Biblical Theology (what these texts, considered together, teach on various subjects); Church History (development of doctrine, theological conflicts, and church traditions): Canon Law (rules observed and enforced within certain traditions); Ecumenical Studies (areas of agreement and disagreement across church bodies); Hermeneutics (methods of textual interpretation and how best to approach the Bible); Homiletics (principles of effective religious communication and discourse); Historical Theology (how different theological affirmations developed and what they imply); Missiology (missions, missionaries, and missionary practices); Moral Theology (principles of ethical decision-making); Patristics (study of the writings of the church fathers); Pastoral Theology (approaches to providing ministerial comfort, counsel, and guidance); Systematics or Dogmatics (construction of an organized, comprehensive, and integrated theology); and Liturgy and Sacraments (modes of structured worship and nature of sacraments).

Pastoral Theology today involves the interface between approaches to spiritual formation, on one hand, and advances in psychiatry and psychology on the other. The effectiveness of pastoral counseling can be much enhanced by a rudimentary knowledge of clinical psychology.[2] Systematic Theology or Dogmatics is the attempt to construct an integrated series of assertions about God and divine action. Such system-building has earned a bad name in some quarters, reminiscent of Søren Kierkegaard's (1813–55) battle with both the Danish church and the German Idealist Georg Hegel. For systematic theology to be worth serious attention, it must be philosophically informed and logically sound. Systematic theologians attempt to present coherent, which is to say logically consistent, accounts of God's nature and works. It is helpful to distinguish between the philosophy of religion, which in its pure form does not rely on revelation, and religious philosophy, which characteristically

---

2. See McLemore, *Clergyman's Psychological Handbook*.

ADDENDUM: MODES OF PHILOSOPHY AND THEOLOGY

does. Sacraments are rites, solemn acts or ceremonies believed to confer divine grace or serve as a sign, symbol, or seal of a deeper spiritual reality. Eastern Orthodox, Roman Catholic, and some other churches recognize seven sacraments: baptism, confirmation (called chrismation in the Orthodox church), the Eucharist (communion), anointing of the sick or if appropriate extreme unction, holy orders (ordination), marriage, and penance. Most Protestant churches recognize as sacraments only baptism and communion.

As in philosophy, certain areas of theological study cut across one or more of the specialties listed above. A few of the more common are Anthropology (as used in theology, nature of the human person), Christology (nature and work of Christ), Ecclesiology (nature of the church), Eschatology (humanity's destiny), and Soteriology (means of rescue from death and what the Bible calls sin, and increasing conformity to the mind of Christ).

Regardless of how we divide up the categories of philosophy or theology, the purpose of all critical thinking, from a Christian point of view, is to move ever closer to understanding, standing under, God and God's love for us.

Chapter 6. The Deep Structure of Existence

SOME HAVE QUIPPED THAT the only trouble with Christianity is that no one has ever tried it.[1] To this, G. K. Chesterton replied, "The Christian ideal has not been tried and found wanting; it has been found difficult and left untried." What if there is an underlying order to the universe, one that encompasses and extends beyond what we know as the laws of physics? What if there is a deep structure to the cosmos, and the purpose of life is to align with it and the God who created it?

In this chapter, I want to discuss three different approaches to knowledge and how we acquire it. I also want to discuss the relationships between and among assertions, beliefs, and knowledge. When we acquire knowledge, our thoughts reflect reality, which shapes these thoughts, and when someone makes an assertion, we expect it to be true. Truth is beneficial. So is understanding, which amounts to more than acquiring information. Understanding fosters sound judgment and sound judgment enables us to survive and live well.

Anyone who thinks much about the universe may eventually brush up against the question of whether, beyond the physical, there is an underlying order to it, and if there is, what kind of order. Most people assume that the universe operates according to physical laws, the natural order. Even if we allow for a certain amount of randomness at the molecular level, as physicists seem to do, there is the expectation that much of what now appears random will, someday, turn out to have

1. Chesterton, *What's Wrong with the World?*

CHAPTER 6. THE DEEP STRUCTURE OF EXISTENCE

been predictable. The rub may come if we begin to entertain the possibility of a non-physical or trans-physical order, and to ask whether there is any meaning or significance to life beyond what we create. Is there a purpose to which we can and should commit ourselves, related perhaps to a being above and beyond us who desires and deserves our attention and allegiance?

The question of a universal moral order, and the question about the meaning or significance of life, are not logically identical. Nor does one necessarily follow from the other. There might well be an overarching moral order, but in relation to it one's life may have no meaning or significance. And, there might be meaning or significance, as atheistic existentialists assert, devoid of any overarching moral order. For a Christian, however, the two are related.

Correspondence, Coherence, and Pragmatic Perspectives on Knowledge

Truth is the aim of knowledge, which raises two important questions. The first is what do we know and the second is how do we know it. Some philosophers include both in proposing a theory of knowledge, while others include only the first, choosing to address the second under a separate category, theories of justification.

Many philosophers distinguish between and among *correspondence*, *coherence*, and *pragmatic* theories of knowledge. A correspondence theory of truth posits that true beliefs or true statements accurately describe (correspond to) reality. Less popular among philosophers as a principal approach is a coherence theory of truth, which requires only that a given set of statements be internally consistent, that they do not contradict each other. Finally, a pragmatic theory of truth holds that a statement is true if it is useful for prediction, solving problems, or guiding action. These three definitions are over-simplifications, but they will do for our purposes. Most people subscribe to the correspondence view and assume that their ideas and perspectives mirror the way the world is. They will often admit that no one can be right about everything and allow for errors and inaccuracies, but they tend to believe that their perceptions *correspond* to how things are. Correspondence approaches to knowledge can be difficult to defend. This is partly because primary premises cannot be shown to be true, something we addressed in chapter 2. How could anyone possibly demonstrate to everyone's satisfaction that he or she holds true beliefs about the nature of the world and our place in it?

The claim that ideas correspond to reality becomes less of a problem if we are concerned with things that are publicly observable and verifiable, as they often are in the physical sciences. But as soon as we wander into speculative territory, differences and arguments arise, and the issue becomes whether a person has good reasons for holding his or her beliefs. One person may believe in the superiority of democracy, while another may believe in the merits of monarchy, theocracy, or socialism. One may believe in the redemptive power of God, while another may believe that the state, properly organized and governed, will provide us with everything we need. They may all claim to *know*, but the question remains of how they can justify their beliefs.

Some philosophers have chosen, therefore, to retreat from correspondence theories to the more modest idea of knowledge as coherence. So long as my beliefs do not contradict one another, either directly or in their implications, they are coherent. There is, however, a troubling limitation to a coherence theory of knowledge. The person whose ideas match the way things are tends to do better in life than the one whose ideas, however consistent, do not. People on psychiatric wards who claim to be Napoleon Bonaparte or the Virgin Mary may be entirely consistent, but they can hardly be said to know who they are. Competent philosophers acknowledge the virtues of coherence, but most seem to insist that, while coherence is necessary, it is not sufficient for knowledge. Perfectly coherent beliefs can be false and misleading.

According to a third definition of knowledge, it is not that true beliefs are useful but that useful beliefs are true. Although this idea receives support from only a minority of philosophers today, many people unwittingly endorse it. "It's true if it works for you" expresses a sidewalk version of the pragmatic theory of knowledge, whose best-known exponent was the Harvard physician, psychologist, and philosopher William James (1842–1910). James' pragmatic theory of truth is more nuanced than I have suggested, and what I have written is a bit of a caricature, but the problem with any pragmatic approach to truth is that, like a coherence one, it does not always hold up.

Some functional beliefs are patently false. A wife may believe that her philandering husband is faithful and so continue to bask in the happiness of what she mistakenly believes to be their honest relationship. An unpopular teenager might falsely conclude that he is popular and

CHAPTER 6. THE DEEP STRUCTURE OF EXISTENCE

so act more confidently, which might then increase his popularity. Or, a person might falsely believe that the tyrannical government under which he or she lives is noble and just, which might render non-existent any self-destructive inclination toward dissent. In all three instances, the erroneous belief *works*, but it is not true and therefore does not qualify as knowledge.

Not all knowledge comes from sense experience, and a good deal of it derives from trust in expert opinion or established tradition. Such trust allows us to know that the earth revolves around the sun, even though this is contrary to sense experience, which clearly indicates that the sun rises in the east, sets in the west, circles the earth, and returns the following morning.

Christianity and the Pragmatic

Some Christians try to persuade others of the truth of Christianity by arguing that it will make them prosperous or healthy. It is true that many people who become Christians experience increased peace and joy, the blessedness alluded to in the first verse of the first psalm. When I was teaching at a seminary, I attended a chapel service in which the speaker was the late Australian scholar, Leon Morris. He pointed out that "Blessed" should not be translated as "Happy." Happiness and blessedness are different things. Because of adverse circumstances, those who are blessed are not always happy. Nothing in the Bible suggests that becoming a Christian will lead to happiness, much less to prosperity or health.

More money may flow to a new Christian because he or she acts more lovingly, responsibly, and honorably, or for a reason unrelated to Christianity. Statisticians sometimes speak of *spurious correlation*, which is when one thing appears to cause another, when in reality both are caused by something else. The number of wool hats sold is correlated with the amount of snow on the ground, but neither causes the other. Both are caused by cold weather, which prompts people to purchase wool hats and also fosters meteorological conditions favoring snow. Nowhere in the New Testament will you find anything to suggest that placing your faith in Jesus will make you rich. To the contrary, many passages warn that wealth can be a trap. The gospel of Christ is not the gospel of prosperity.

Nor is there any guarantee that becoming a Christian will make you healthier. There are accounts in the Gospels of Jesus healing people, but there is nothing in the New Testament to support the notion that when you become a follower of Christ, God will cure your cancer, mend your bones, or stop your pain. Although much of what gets passed off as miraculous healing is a combination of hope by the needy and victimization by the greedy, miracles of healing do seem to happen today, usually when and where we least expect them.

If a person embraces Christ and both understands and accepts what it means for Christ to be our *savior*, it ought not to be because of an expected or hoped for practical benefit, but because that person grasps, perhaps for the first time, the deep structure of existence and who is behind it. People who genuinely place their faith in God ordinarily do so because they recognize who God is, not because of what God can do for them. I use the word *ordinarily* because there may be exceptions. Those in dire straits, such as soldiers surrounded and outnumbered, might be focused on getting out alive, and in the process come to sincere faith in the hope that God will save them.

Belief, Insight, and Knowledge

To say you know the truth about something means that a certain relationship exists between you and that something. To draw a true conclusion about it, you must be receptive and responsive. Knowledge comes only when your judgments align with reality, with how things are. Insight is the path to knowledge, and you acquire insight when the gap narrows between what you *believe* and what *is*.

When you were eight years old, your Aunt Mildred told you that lightning never strikes twice in the same place. Because she was an adult and you were a child, you believed her. When a grade-school teacher later tells you that, during the last storm, lightning hit a tree on the outskirts of town several times, you may begin to doubt what Aunt Mildred said. Even though you are not fully convinced by your teacher, you move in the direction of believing her and so begin to develop insight. You do not yet have knowledge, but you have narrowed the gap between what you believe and what is the case. Next, you learn from a college professor that in bad weather lightning can repeatedly strike tall structures, and that it zaps the Empire State Building about a hundred times a year. This provides you with enough justification to conclude that your aunt was wrong. You began with a false belief, gained insight from your teacher, and under the tutelage of a professor acquired knowledge. Acquiring knowledge involves having your thoughts conform to what is true. It is your mind, not the objective world, that must do the conforming. Those who argue that reality conforms to our perceptions turn the concepts of truth and knowledge inside out.

The Swiss psychologist Jean Piaget (1896–1980) pointed out that learning and adapting to our environment involves two complementary processes: *assimilation* and *accommodation.* When we have an experience that is consistent with what we already believe, with our exiting mental templates, we assimilate it. The experience provides additional support for what we assume we know. When, however, we have a credible experience that is inconsistent with one of our mental templates, what Piaget called a *schema*, we revise it to align better with the new experience. Gaining insight and acquiring knowledge are products of accommodation. To major in assimilation to the exclusion of accommodation is to live in your own world. It implies an inability to learn.

When we accept an assertion as true, for example that stepping off a cliff will likely kill us, we believe our thoughts reflect what is the case. Perhaps we have thrown a stone into a ravine and, through a kind of empathic identification, realized we could have been that stone. Or, we may have listened to a news report of what happened when someone strayed too close to the edge and experienced what psychologists call vicarious learning. We accept the existence of a *causal* relationship between the external world, on one hand, and what we believe on the other. Our ideas are often what they are because the realities about which we have those ideas are what *they* are.

My conclusions may be correct, however, only because reality accidentally conforms to my wishes. Suppose at a distant beach the waves are small. But I am home, have no access to a surf report, and choose to believe that big waves are rolling in at that beach. Knowing nothing about what is going on there, off I go. By the time I get to the beach hours later, eight-foot breakers are pounding the shore. Could I legitimately claim to have *known* the waves were big? Guessing correctly is not the same as knowing.

Or, starting from incorrect premises, I may draw a correct conclusion. Suppose I bet that a particular football team is going to win tomorrow's game because it has a spectacular quarterback, an incredible running back, and a gifted pass receiver. The team wins the game, even though the quarterback was injured during practice and had to be replaced, the running back failed to show up, and the pass receiver had to leave suddenly to visit his father who needed emergency surgery. Although I correctly predicted the winner, can I claim that I *knew* which team would win? To the extent that a person arrives at truth either by accident or from false premises, that person has no legitimate claim to knowledge. Most people seem to regard truth as desirable and wisdom as worth pursuing.[2] When they think about spiritual matters and the meaning of life, the issue is not whether they are sophisticated philosophers but whether their ideas correspond to reality.

The Norm of Dependability

If a person states something we know to be false, perhaps that Florida was once owned by Germany, we conclude that the statement lacks credibility. In deciding that a statement is not credible, we implicitly appeal to a norm governing belief and judgment, and any claim that violates this norm we deem false. The questions arise, what is this norm or standard, and why is this important? Why is the absence of truth problematic?

To decide a statement is true is to decide we can rely on it. It is true not because it works, but it works because it is true. False claims, when we accept them, can get in the way of responding effectively to the world. Because we are inclined to act according to what we believe to be true, such claims can lead us down wrong paths and impair our effectiveness. To conclude that a statement is false is to suggest that it might cause harm by distracting us from seeing things as they are. False assertions can disrupt effective living, and it is therefore to our advantage to get things right. Useful true beliefs far outnumber useful false ones. If they did not, our lives would be chaotic.

Information and Understanding

The value of truth consists in more than its ability to correct harmful false beliefs and so protect us. True judgments contribute to understanding. The person who understands is more inclined to make good judgments than the person who does not. It is possible to hold true beliefs about

---

2. See MacIntyre, "Truth as a Good," 197–215.

CHAPTER 6. THE DEEP STRUCTURE OF EXISTENCE

something and yet not understand it well, if at all. I know, for example, that rapidly rotating wheels will keep a bicycle from tipping over, which has to do with something called the gyroscopic effect. That much I remember from physics. But I do not really understand why a two-wheeled vehicle does not fall over when it is moving. I vaguely recall this having to do with forces of some kind. Using the term *gyroscopic effect* does not help my understanding one bit. All it does is convey the impression that I know more than I do. Creating the illusion that you understand something simply by giving it a name is an example of what philosophers call the *nominal fallacy*. If I once understood why a moving bike does not tip over, I lost that understanding long ago.

Accumulating information does not necessarily increase understanding, since to understand something requires that we comprehend not just what, but why, it is as it is. To understand means to grasp the attributes of a thing, place it within a matrix of other things, and see the principles that operate in connection with it. We must create a mind-map so that we know where it fits into a larger framework. To be able to explain something depends not only on knowing its nature but also on being able to articulate its position in this framework, pointing out where it sits in relation to other things, and noting its function or purpose. A monkey pounding on a keyboard might randomly produce an intelligible sentence, just as a distracted high school student scribbling on a pad might accidentally write out the second law of thermodynamics. But neither the monkey nor the student would have any understanding of how what they just produced fits into the overall fabric of knowledge.

Christianity asserts that there is an overarching framework that includes all others within it and exists quite aside from whether you or I pay it any attention. They also believe there is an inseparable connection between that overarching framework and how well we understand the world, a connection that is neither random nor arbitrary but factual and causal.

Christian Hope

At the center of Christianity is the conviction that the deep structure of existence reflects the work of a benevolent creator, and that this creator offers life beyond the grave. The love that God has for us is intended to be reflected in the love we have for each other. A novelist wisely wrote this:

"You could eat in the finest restaurants, you could partake in every sensual pleasure, you could sing [in front of] twenty thousand people, you could soak up the whole thunderstorm of applause, you could travel to the ends of the earth, you could be followed by millions on the internet, you could win Olympic medals, but all this would be meaningless without love."[3] That author also wrote, "death is the opposite of possibility."[4]

For us to accept that God loves people, and indeed loves each of us as individuals, we have to acknowledge who and what God is. This implies that we no longer participate, actively or passively, in the Great Rebellion, the refusal to yield our allegiance to God. It involves giving up the illusion of self-sufficiency. Theologians speak of human beings as *contingent* beings, since our existence depends on a host of things working together, such as physiological processes. In the end, Christians believe, we are contingent on God. Because we all pass through the portal of death, we will eventually be anything but self-sufficient. Separated by rebellion from God and God's love, we may find ourselves unable to enter what the Bible describes as the kingdom of heaven.

Our rebellion hinges on believing that we can set up on our own without God. Efforts to do this may bring pleasure, and even the Bible acknowledges there can be pleasure in this (Heb 11:25). But setting ourselves up as gods tends to bring with it an unquenchable thirst for reassurance. Even though in sober moments we know better, we want other people to persuade us that we are immortal, and if they cannot, to help us cultivate the fantasy that we will be. Many people try to console themselves with the hope of leaving a legacy. Their legacies do them no good, however, after they are dead. Leaving a legacy is no substitute for everlasting life. Whatever momentary reassurance of immortality others provide turns out in the end to be empty. This is because, deep down, we know better.[5] We know that we are going to die. Christians claim to know that dying without a relationship with God gives them no legitimate basis for hope.

Consider how long it can take for some people to achieve the celebrity they long for, perhaps in the semi-conscious hope that fame will confer this immortality. They may come to the stark realization that they do not know most of the people who idolize them, and they can no longer walk into a coffee shop without someone invading their privacy.

3. Haig, *The Midnight Library*, 248.
4. Haig, *The Midnight Library*, 69.
5. See Muggeridge, *Chronicles of Wasted Time*.

CHAPTER 6. THE DEEP STRUCTURE OF EXISTENCE

Unless they are famous, these same celebrities may reach middle age, only to discover that others do not care enough about them even to ask for an autograph. You cannot practice as a clinical psychologist in the Los Angeles area without at least a few celebrities asking for your assistance. I have worked with several actors, whose faces you might recognize but whose names you would be unlikely to recall. Because of its proximity to Hollywood, there are thousands of such people in Southern California. You may have seen some of them in films or on TV. If so, you may never have suspected that they suffered from depression. Loss leads to depression, and the vanishing hope of achieving stardom can be a colossal and corrosive loss.

Having joy for more than a few hours can be difficult if we do not also have peace. The Bible contains many references to both. We read of joy coming in the morning (Ps 30:5), Jesus telling his disciples that their sorrow will turn to joy (John 16:20), and Paul referring to other Christians as his joy and delight (Phil 4:1). It also contains references to the God of Peace and Prince of Peace (Isa 9:6), and Jesus saying to those close to him that he was giving them his peace (John 14:27). He is telling them to allow his peace to envelope them. Unable to know how much of our life remains, we may worry about time running out. *Bind yourself to me*, God beckons, *because I have an infinite amount of time, and connected with me, so do you*. The promise of Christianity is that by embracing Christ we will forever have joy and peace.

Closing Thoughts

There are three common approaches to knowledge and they are not mutually exclusive. To qualify as knowledge, ideas must correspond to reality, be devoid of contradictions, and capture something that can be relied on. Internal consistency is not enough to guarantee knowledge. Neither is usefulness, since false beliefs sometimes turn out to be useful. Insight narrows the gap between belief and the way things are. Understanding, as it turns out, is more than acquiring information. It means grasping how and why something behaves as it does, its place in relation to other things, and the principles that operate in connection with it. Christianity insists that there is a deep structure to human existence, this structure has to do with a loving creator, and confidence in that love is the foundation on which hope is built.

PART I. FOUNDATIONS

Preview

Christian faith is by nature interpersonal. Both objective analysis and subjective intuition bear on faith. Human beings operate with two languages, one private and the other public. Both are related to faith. Jesus used parables, short vignettes, to maximize their spiritual impact.

Chapter 7. Spiritual Knowledge as Interpersonal

FAITH, ALTHOUGH INFORMED BY objective knowledge, is personal and subjective. This does not relegate it to the trash bin of disruptive emotions, intrusions into consciousness that get in the way of clear thinking. To the contrary, it elevates faith to the treasure chest of what makes life meaningful and worthwhile. It places faith alongside such other intangibles as love and trust, which are at the heart of human fulfillment and at the center of Christian faith.

We exist at the intersection of two worlds, the inner and the outer, the subjective and the objective. Many thinkers have taken exception to the idea that there is an objective world. Some have gone as far as to posit that only their own mind exists, which raises the question of why they even bother to communicate this to anyone else. Others have assumed that we all create our own realities, a thesis that makes a certain amount of sense if not taken too far. Still others have argued that there are innate structures in our minds, templates we are born with, according to which we arrange our experiences, a thesis that also makes sense within limits. I have assumed throughout this book that you are open to the idea that there is an objective world and, further, that it makes sense to align yourself with it. I am not suggesting that any of us does this perfectly. But, we do well in life to the extent that the contents of our minds are shaped by reality rather than fantasy.

Whether awake or dreaming, we experience an ongoing flow of ideas, moods, images, emotions, motives, attitudes, sensations, perceptions, and dispositions. It is as if a motion picture, sometimes well-organized but often not, runs continuously in the screening room of our consciousness, a montage of objective realities and subjective impressions. We live in a universe that exists independently of our minds. But we interpret and make sense of that universe according to mental patterns that are uniquely our own and can be distorted. We think both analytically and intuitively, and we rely on some beliefs that are correct and others that are incorrect.

Christian faith is by nature interpersonal. It is between two beings, one human and mortal and the other divine and eternal. Groups, by nature, cannot have faith. Only individuals can. Except as a metaphor, no such thing as a group mind exists. Christian faith depends on what an individual perceives about God through Jesus. But it also hinges on whether he or she grasps that God loves us and ought, therefore, to be loved and trusted in return. Without having arrived at that conclusion, faith is frail or nonexistent.

Philosophers sometimes divide knowledge into three categories: procedural, propositional, and personal. It is the last two of these that I want to discuss in this chapter. Your inner life, like mine, is private. It will never be another person's and the best we can expect from even our closest friends is mutuality, the sense that we are in it together, whatever *it* happens to be. Mutuality grows out of self-disclosure, and if there is no self-disclosure, there can be little or no sense of shared experience, of being companions on a common journey.

Our friends can often empathize with us. They can imagine how they might feel if they were in our shoes, and part of being human is to have a capacity for this. Empathy amounts to a kind of educated guess, and empathic people have a talent for accurately guessing what others think and feel. Regardless of how comforting it may be to believe that someone else understands us, no one else can fully inhabit our consciousness. We are ultimately alone with God.

First-Order Data and the Spiritual

First-order data for any of us is that to which we alone have direct access. Such data comprise the contents of our minds. Your first-order data will never be mine. Nor will mine be yours. To every other human being,

CHAPTER 7. SPIRITUAL KNOWLEDGE AS INTERPERSONAL

our minds will never be more than second-order data and will therefore remain something of a mystery.

The way two people experience life may be strikingly similar, which is what we mean when we say they are intimate. Couples in love share thoughts and feelings, and celebrate their ability to enter into each other's mental universe. Contrary to the impression fostered by textbooks in general psychology, there is no concrete wall between thoughts and feelings. It might therefore make more sense to speak of intimates as sharing thought-feeling constellations, or something of that sort. How, they marvel, could their minds be so alike, so connected? What miracle, they wonder, has allowed them to develop what seems like a single meta-mind to which they both believe themselves to have access? They share what some have called the *numinous*, the sublime.

But such mutuality is fragile. Each person remains an individual and is therefore capable of psychologically separating from the other. If and when such separation occurs, as tends to happen from time to time, it can trigger anxiety. Both had assumed they would remain one, but now the other person has pulled away. Even before the disconnection, however, their experiences would rarely be identical. Would there be any way to know that when they used the same word, they meant the same thing? To her, *love* might mean understanding but to him it might mean sex. Is there any way to be certain that the color she sees and refers to as *blue* is the same as what he sees and calls blue?

Based on what another person says, we may conclude that he or she enjoys a rich spiritual life. But such a conclusion will always remain an inference, and the true nature of another person's heart will always remain in part a secret. Among God's merciful gifts is that we cannot read minds. This is because if we said everything that came into our heads for even a day, we might well lose friends. In relation to God, however, there are no secrets. Everything we have ever done, thought, or felt is known.

Objectivity and Sanity

Knowing how to distinguish between the objective and the subjective is part of what it means to be intelligent. It is also what it means to be sane. Intelligence and sanity are what allow us to separate fact from fiction and reality from fantasy. No one does this perfectly, of course, but an intelligent and sane person evaluates information with a degree of caution grounded in wisdom, what has been called the educational value of doubt.

Complete objectivity in everyday life is rarely achieved, which has led at least one writer to highlight what he calls the "myth of objective consciousness."[1] To insist, however, that we are imprisoned in tight mental vaults with no knowledge of the objective world is untenable. Without reasonable objectivity, connecting with the world as it is and other people as they are, we would be overwhelmed and confused, unable even to find our way home.

Consciousness is always an amorphous combination of objectivity and subjectivity. Without the former, we would inhabit an imaginary world, akin to those poor souls who wander the streets talking to themselves. Without the latter, we would resemble robots. To be human is to view the world through our own unique prism, which consists of vast arrays of inseparable thoughts, feelings, and attitudes. Depending on the translation, the Apostle Paul characterizes those who defiantly refuse to respond to God as heartless, without pity or conscience, and lacking in natural affection (Rom 1:31).

Personal Knowledge

Michael Polanyi (1891–1976) delivered the prestigious Gifford lectures in 1951–52. Adam Gifford (1820–87) established the Gifford Lectureships, each of which is hosted at one of four Scottish universities: Aberdeen, Edinburgh, Glasgow, or St. Andrews. The first Gifford lectures were delivered in 1888, and since then, many celebrated thinkers have given them and many books flowing out of them have become classics. Polanyi had already achieved eminence in several fields, including physical chemistry, economic theory, and most relevant here, epistemology, that branch of philosophy having to do with the nature and scope of knowledge.

His Gifford lectures have been revised and published as *Personal Knowledge*. In that book, he points out that the personality of the scientist plays a critical role in discovery, and that the mind of the scientist is therefore of central importance. Much of the knowledge by which individuals and societies advance is what Polanyi calls *tacit*. Such knowledge cannot be codified or explicitly communicated because it is largely unconscious.

---

1. Roszak, *Making of a Counter Culture*.

CHAPTER 7. SPIRITUAL KNOWLEDGE AS INTERPERSONAL

The notion that scientific truth comes from the mechanical application of a single method reflects naiveté about how science actually works. Copernicus, for example, developed the heliocentric theory, not by following a prescribed method but because thinking about the movement of heavenly bodies from the vantage point of heliocentricity was intellectually satisfying and harmonized well with the understanding he had already achieved. Previously acquired knowledge is what psychologists call *apperceptive mass*, meaning that an individual tries to make sense of new experience by assimilating it to his or her existing ideas.

Polanyi points out how many people have been taught that Albert Einstein developed his theory of relativity in response to the experimental findings of Michelson and Morley. Einstein never mentions the Michelson-Morley experiments, and in fact conceptualized relativity before he had even heard about them. He stated that the idea originated "from a paradox upon which I had already hit at the age of sixteen."[2] Polanyi writes, "When Einstein discovered rationality in nature unaided by any [empirical] observation that had not been available for at least fifty years . . . our positivistic textbooks promptly covered up the scandal by an appropriately embellished account of his discovery."[3] Polayni uses the term *positivism* as shorthand for what is usually called *Logical Positivism* or *Logical Empiricism*, which underestimates the importance of conceptual thinking and overestimates that of machine-like empiricism. Emphasizing how people bring their own modes of intelligence to anything they do, and how there is always a subtle interplay between the objective and the subjective, Polanyi stresses the importance of judgment and, by implication, of intuitive reasoning.

Meaningful advances in knowledge of any kind hinge on intuitively sensing which questions to ask. Many Christians believe that a person asks the most important questions only as God, perhaps through other Christians, moves that person to do so. When this occurs, he or she (a) draws on tacit knowledge, (b) intuitively develops a sense of what might be the case, and (c) invests the time and energy to investigate. While in science a reputation may be on the line, in Christianity it is the whole fabric of a person's life, including how he or she views and values other people.

---

2. Polanyi, *Personal Knowledge*, 10, quoted from Schilpp, *Albert Einstein*.
3. Polanyi, *Personal Knowledge*, 11.

To become a Christian, a person must know about Jesus, who he was and is, and what this implies about the nature of the universe. But coming to believe in and trust the resurrected and living Christ rests on what Polanyi calls *personal knowledge*. It is rarely, if ever, exclusively the result of detached reflection. Knowing a person, in this case God, is different from knowing about a person. The difference between knowing a person and knowing an object or subject matter is captured by two different verbs in some other languages, including French (*savior* and *connaître*), German (*wissen* and *kennen*), and Spanish (*saber* and *conocer*). In English, however, we have only one verb, *to know*.

Languages of Thought

Jacob Bronowski (1908–1974) was a mathematician, scientist, and historian. He was also the writer-presenter of the 1973 BBC TV series *The Ascent of Man*. In Bronowski's *Identity of Man*, he highlights two different kinds of language.[4] The first, the language of *communication*, is what we use when we write a letter, send a message, or talk with a friend. It is usually well-organized and follows accepted grammatical rules. There can be some flexibility in these rules, which allows for variation, so nearly everyone understands "I feel well" and "I feel good" to mean the same thing. Communication is the establishment of an invisible link, a mental bridge, between and among people.

The second is our *thinking* language. It is what we use when we talk to ourselves or engage in imaginary conversations with other people.[5] A thinking language is by nature more chaotic and random than a communication language. People can edit out a great deal of thinking language, so that this deleted material never makes it into their conversations. One's thinking language is akin to the language of dreams, and a sign of a serious mental disorder is that, even while awake, the person is unable to stop a kind of dreaming. Thinking languages are actually the media in which creativity grows, and it is most likely to emerge when the two languages, inner and outer, converge.

These mental languages are heavily colored by Polanyi's tacit knowledge. They reflect not just preconscious and unconscious understandings, but also what Bronowski calls knowledge of the self. This

---

4. Bronowski, *Identify of Man*, 24.
5. Bronowski, *Identify of Man*, 82.

CHAPTER 7. SPIRITUAL KNOWLEDGE AS INTERPERSONAL

includes awareness of where a person stands in relation to the world, including his or her impact on it and other people. Bronowski points out that it was this kind of knowledge that led Charles Darwin to postpone publication of *Origin of Species* because Darwin knew that its publication would embarrass his wife. Higher mammals may use primitive thinking languages, but they do not reflect on themselves as *selves* or see far into the future. Walker Percy (1916–90) makes the same point.[6] Only humans are spiritual creatures.

A person's thinking language may or may not include awareness of God. If it does, such awareness is likely to facilitate more accurate knowledge of the self, so that we see ourselves more as we are, rather than as we imagine or would like ourselves to be. The sixteenth century Protestant theologian John Calvin emphasized how knowledge of God is intimately connected with knowledge of self. Such intuitive knowledge allows us to begin to grasp where we stand in relation to our creator. We are not our own but God's, who is not only Lord of the cosmos but also the one who holds title to everything that exists, including us. Among the most poignant statements by Jesus appears in John 14:18: "I will not leave you as orphans" (NIV). The REB renders this as, "I will not leave you bereft."

Like Polanyi, Bronowski insists that we do not passively connect with objective reality. We are personally involved and "get a false picture of the world if we regard it as a set of events we merely watch."[7] This, Bronowski suggests, is what Einstein demonstrated "as a plain matter of fact" with his theory of relativity. "Nature is a network of happenings that do not unroll like a red carpet into time, but are intertwined between every part of the world; and we are among its parts." He then adds, "In this nexus, we cannot reach certainty because it is not there to be reached; it goes with the wrong model, and the certain answers ironically give the wrong answers." Genuine understanding does not come from robotically observing a series of events or, relevant to our interest here, learning dry facts about the life of Jesus.[8] It comes by developing specific understandings about his significance. You do not have to be an accomplished conceptual thinker to become a Christian, but you do have to be willing to open your mind and heart.

---

6. Percy, *Lost in the Cosmos*.
7. Bronowski, *Identity of Man*, 38.
8. Bronowski, *Identify of Man*, 49–50.

Human existence is conceptual, insists Bronowski, and has to do with ideas, however primitive. "There is no descriptive language that does not consist of general words, that is, of concepts." He alludes to how a young English philosopher, Frank Ramsey, demonstrated "sharply" the deficiencies of the "operational and positivist attitude." Science, and indeed all understanding, involves intuitive leaps, not just as a matter of practice but by nature. Ramsey died in 1930 at the age of twenty-six. Before he died, he constructed an example in mathematical logic that, according to Bronowski, demonstrated how the concepts of a science that was still expanding had to be more elastic and, to quote Ramsey's words, "richer . . . than any logical construction from the sum of its known facts."[9]

Analysis, Intuition, and Faith

Thinking involves both analysis and intuition.[10] When you approach a problem analytically, you identify the options, decide along which dimensions to evaluate them, and determine how much weight to give each rated dimension. This is how researchers at a think-tank approach some of their work. Suppose, for example, you wanted to choose between two job offers, one in Boston and the other in Atlanta. You might evaluate them on many dimensions, but for the sake of simplicity, I want to consider only three: potential growth of the company; level of the job; and salary. Let us assume that for you, job level is twice as important as salary, and potential growth of the company is twice as important as job level. If the position in Boston paid slightly more, the level of both jobs was about the same, but the potential growth of the company in Atlanta was substantially greater, you would probably accept the job there.

Intuitive reasoning, by contrast, involves taking into account many things you might not even be aware of and therefore could not name. And, if you cannot even name them, there is no way you would be able to say which of these things were more important and which less. Such preconscious and unconscious considerations heavily influence thinking and decision-making, which is what people mean when they say things like, "I don't know why, but I have a hunch this is going to happen." Or, "I'm not sure I can explain it, but I believe this is what we should do." As much as we might like to believe that we approach most

---

9. Bronowski, *Identity of Man*, 50.
10. See Gladwell, *Blink*.

decisions analytically, we probably do not. A complicated mixture of thoughts, feelings, preferences, attitudes, and desires play into many of them. In the case of highly personal decisions, such as deciding whom to marry, intuition often trumps analysis. This is also the case when we decide whether to accept or reject God's offer of love. Or, even to sense that such an offer exists.

Evaluating the claims of Christianity involves holding them up to the light of reason, and doing our best to view them objectively. Did Jesus exist? Was he more than a man? And so on. Becoming a Christian, however, involves more than this. It involves Jesus coming to indwell your mind, what the Bible sometimes refers to as your heart (see Phil 2:12; Eph 3:17). This implies that you grasp intuitively, not just analytically, who Jesus was. Acquiring Christian faith implies undergoing a spiritual transformation based on both analysis and intuition, which results in bonding with Jesus, or as the Bible puts it, living *in Christ*. When Christians say they are "in Christ," they mean that Christ, in the person of the Holy Spirit, guides and enlightens them. This is why the Apostle Paul claimed, "for me, to live is Christ" (Phil 1:21, ESV).

The New Testament is about the gospel, the good news. This news is that Jesus came to restore our relationship with God. Christians have the privilege of serving as God's ambassadors to others. In analyzing how people act toward one another, psychologists who study social relationships distinguish between *focus on self* and *focus on others*. As much as possible, God intends Christians to focus on others, to be the salt that brings out their flavor, and also to contribute to society. They are also to care for and about the physical environment, God's creation.

Theology and Faith

One of my former doctoral students emphasized that Jesus taught in parables. He questioned whether anything other than metaphors, symbols, and stories could be used to communicate the Christian faith. He was reacting against dry intellectualism in theology that reduces faith to mere words on a page. Perhaps without realizing it, he was calling into question the entire theological enterprise. That some people substitute doctrine for faith seems beyond question. It makes no sense, however, to stop eating because you have had a bad meal.

Theology is by nature propositional, which means it consists of declarative and upon occasion imperative sentences. To deny this is to run the risk of having a religion based on inconsistent, unrecognized, or faulty premises. When I was teaching at a seminary, I saw how at least one theologian, who was a fine person and excellent pastor, could gloss over conceptual sloppiness with vague terms and catchy phrases that he claimed to be non-propositional. The students, impressed by what they considered to be his profundity, concluded that he was so brilliant that they could not understand him. Much of what he said, however, was unclear, ambiguous, and imprecise. Non-propositional theology does not exist. It is a *non sequitur*.

You can formulate theological beliefs as propositions, and if you cannot, the beliefs may be so hopelessly muddled that they are barely coherent. "Sally is trustworthy" is a proposition. So are "Harry is generous" and "Alan is self-centered." These statements may or may not be true, and it may take some work to determine exactly what the terms *trustworthy*, *generous*, and *self-centered* mean. But all three are propositions reflecting beliefs. It is impossible to think in more than a primitive way without words, which when strung together in meaningful sentences often amount to propositions. You can have a sense, an instinct, that something is true, which may amount to tacit knowledge. For such knowledge to become a belief, it will have to be capable of being expressed as a proposition. "I want a Christianity free of propositions" implies "propositional theology is without value," which is itself a proposition.

Theology provides the scaffolding for faith. It is a kind of skeleton. Just as the human body could not exist without bones, neither can Christian faith exist without theology, whether explicit or implicit and primitive or nuanced. As suggested above, however, regardless of how erudite, theology should not be confused with faith. A skeleton without living tissue to nourish it is dry, brittle, and dead. God may be happier with a person who has a simplistic theology but much faith than one who has an erudite theology but little faith.

Why Jesus Spoke in Parables

The essence of communication is connecting with your audience.[11] Regardless of how eloquent the words or polished the delivery, if you

---

11. See McLemore and McLemore, *Staying One*, 27.

CHAPTER 7. SPIRITUAL KNOWLEDGE AS INTERPERSONAL

have not connected, you have not communicated. You will therefore be unlikely to facilitate change. Jesus came to expand the imagination of his audience, whether farmers and shepherds two thousand years ago or people living today. God has granted us the freedom to decide what we will or will not accept as knowledge. Jesus used parables to increase what people could understand, stories most likely to bring about a change of mind and heart. To communicate an idea that can bring about change often requires the use of a story, simile, or metaphor.

If you wanted to convey how difficult it was to get something across to an unreceptive audience, you might say, "I felt like a blind man in a room full of deaf people." To describe an excessively detail-oriented person, perhaps you could say, "he has an instinct for the capillary." And, to characterize an especially persuasive person, maybe you would say, "She could charm the fur off a cat."

You can communicate some truths through abstractions. Most people have no trouble accepting that it is wrong to defraud a bank, extort money, or betray a friend. But you can better convey other truths through a story. A truth will have more impact if people can grasp it with their hearts as well as their heads, if they can viscerally connect with the point of the story.

One of Jesus' parables depicts two men who go to the Temple in Jerusalem to pray (Luke 18:9–14, NIV). The first is a devout religionist who, after boasting of his piety, thanks God that he is not like other men—adulterers, thieves, scoundrels—or like the other man, a tax collector. At the time, people despised their fellow Jews who worked as tax collectors and viewed them as collaborating with the Romans, in whose name they sometimes extorted additional money for themselves. In the parable, the tax collector stands far off, will not lift his eyes to heaven, and is so remorseful that he beats his chest and prays that, despite his sin, God will treat him mercifully. Jesus declares that the tax collector, not the religionist, went home "justified." He adds, "Those who exalt themselves will be humbled, while those who humble themselves will be exalted." Without the parable, his words would likely have had less impact.

Principles are by nature digital, while stories that illustrate and exemplify them are analogic. For some truths to seep into our souls, we must comprehend them with both sides of our brain. This seems especially to be the case with spiritual truths. Jesus communicated through vignettes to which the average person in his day could relate. His audiences may have included some who appreciated and were comfortable with abstractions, such as Pharisees, Sadducees, and Scribes, but they mostly comprised fishermen, housewives, bakers, beggars, and herdsmen. They would have been most at home with images of fig trees, builders who failed to plan, suffering debtors, overbearing administrators, desperate widows, and roadside victims.

The Importance of Clarity and Precision

Surprisingly, some intelligent people do not worry much about the clarity or consistency of their beliefs, which can therefore be contradictory or fraught with ambiguities, confusions, and unexamined nuances. As I argue throughout this book, striving for clear and consistent beliefs is important, and I would go as far as to suggest that for any Christian it is a responsibility. The Bible contains three-quarters of a million words, two thirds of them in the Old Testament. Christians believe that the Bible points to what is true about God and the world. Yet, nowhere in its pages does it contain a carefully laid out and interrelated set of religious propositions. God has left that to us. Many Christians believe that the Bible is not only a record of God's self-disclosure, but also God's ongoing inspirational Word, such that the Holy Spirit influences them through its words.

As social conditions change and new challenges arise, theologians respond to them. As an example of a change in society that forced theologians to face a new problem, the Bird Universal Medical Respirator (ventilator) appeared in 1955. It was a small green box that not only allowed society to get rid of the iron lungs that kept polio victims alive, but it also forced society to decide when, if ever, to "pull the plug"? Should physicians continue to sustain the life of a person who shows no signs of brain activity and is unlikely ever to do so? Bird Respirators and its successors are still used around the world.

Theology, therefore, is ever evolving. But the essentials of Christian theology do not change. By immersing themselves in the thought-forms of the Bible, Christian scholars have labored for two thousand years to understand God's nature, work, and purposes. They have painstakingly mulled over biblical similes, analogies, types, and images.[12] By wrestling with all of this and more, theologians have attempted to draw out the implications of these thought-forms for how created beings ought to relate to their creator and each other. They have attempted to express

---

12. See Farrer, "Images and Inspiration," 20–36.

CHAPTER 7. SPIRITUAL KNOWLEDGE AS INTERPERSONAL

these implications in their native languages, without compromising what was originally written almost entirely in Hebrew (Old Testament) or in Greek (New Testament). Always, the product has been a set of statements intended to reflect true beliefs. Because faith without sound theology carries with it the risk of running off the rails, the statements theologians make are important. Through frontline members of the clergy, theologies radiate out and shape the thinking of millions of people in the pews. We may never be able to come up with the complete and perfect theology and may always remain at least a little misguided. But this does not mean we should not strive for it.

An example from history of why clear and precise theology is important has to do with the nature of Christ. Christianity rises or falls on what we make of Jesus, and Christian scholars worked hard during the fourth and fifth centuries to arrive at a satisfactory answer to what became known as the Christological question. This has to do in large part with the relationship between Christ and God, and by implication with the nature and work of Jesus as Messiah. Some maintained that, because of his obedience to the Father, Jesus was adopted as God's Son and that he had not existed prior to his birth in Bethlehem, six miles southwest of Jerusalem. Others argued that God took on different modes or forms in different historical periods: Father in the Old Testament, Son in the New Testament, and Spirit thereafter. Still others insisted that Jesus only appeared to be human, his body was a kind of illusion, and he remained always and only God. Many Gnostics held this *docetic* view. Docetism comes from the Greek, meaning "to seem." Even if we accept that Jesus was both divine and human, we still face the question of how these two natures interact.[13] The view of the Latin or Western Church is that Jesus had two co-existing natures, that he was simultaneously divine and human.

Some, however, have suggested that both natures blended into one. The notion of the two natures blending is held by some Eastern Orthodox groups. This view stands in contrast to the pronouncement contained in the Chalcedonian Creed (AD 451), which was embraced by the western Christian communions. The Chalcedonian Creed endorses the doctrine of *hypostatic union*, by which is meant that the human and divine natures of Christ, though each is distinct and complete in itself, co-exist. Some branches of Eastern Orthodox Christianity, such as the

---

13. See introductory comments, Appendix II.

Assyrian Church as well as Coptic, Ethiopian, and Syrian Orthodoxy, reject the Chalcedonian formulation.

Sometimes there is no single word in the Bible that represents a principal belief in Christianity, so to make explicit what is implicit in the New Testament, theologians had to come up with one. An example is the word *Trinity* and another is *Incarnation*. *Trinity* refers to the idea that one and only one God exists in three persons—Father, Son, and Holy Spirit—and that God, therefore, is an eternal fellowship or communion. Christian thinkers came to this understanding after struggling for centuries. The trinitarian concept was embraced only after much study, reflection, and debate. Viewed through this conceptual framework, passages in the New Testament illuminate parts of the Old Testament and reflect what Jesus' disciples came to believe and proclaim. See, for example, how Heb 1:8 interprets Ps 45:6,7 in relation to Jesus. *Incarnation* refers to the idea that God, through the agency of the Holy Spirit, came upon Mary, who then miraculously conceived Jesus as the unique child of God. We mortals, while resembling God in important ways, are not God's children in the same sense. The phrase *begotten of God* applies only to Jesus. To use a technical term, we do not share God's *ontological status*.

Both concepts, *Trinity* and *Incarnation*, carry implications for belief and practice. They suggest, for example, the answer to the question of whether a Christian can legitimately pray to Christ. Theologians reasoned that since Christ is God, it is appropriate to worship and pray to him, who as Jesus was the God-Mortal and remains the third person of the Trinity. For the same reason, they maintain that it is also legitimate to pray to the Holy Spirit.

Necessary Subjectivity

When it comes to beliefs, we are at the mercy of what some thinkers call a *subjective point of departure*. If we define knowledge as justified true belief, the noun is *belief* and the adjective is *justified*. You and I must decide what constitutes enough evidence for a given belief to qualify as knowledge. The basis for deciding the truth or falsity of a Christian belief, therefore, depends on our judgment of how well the evidence supports it.

Philosophers have devoted considerable time and energy to exploring the nature of justification as it relates to knowledge. Here, I merely want to point out the danger of going down either of two

CHAPTER 7. SPIRITUAL KNOWLEDGE AS INTERPERSONAL

divergent paths: fideism and skepticism. With *fideism*, you reach a closed-minded insistence that everything you believe is beyond question and that no one has the right to question or doubt it. And so, it is the belief that demonstrable truth is either unrelated to or opposed to faith. With *skepticism*, you reach the equally dogmatic insistence that you can never know anything, especially about God. It is the assertion that knowledge is either strikingly uncertain or impossible to attain. The ultimate form of skepticism is *solipsism*, the doctrine that you can never be sure that anything other than your own mind exists, and that it might be the case that you or I are disembodied minds in bell jars. Few philosophers take such extreme skepticism seriously. I have confidence that the chair in my kitchen will support my weight, the brakes on my car will work, and the sun will come up in the morning. Even though I cannot be sure of any of this, I am willing to say in each instance *I know*, and so my skepticism has limits. As discussed in chapter 2, in many cases, the point at which one has enough justification to decide that a belief qualifies as knowledge can be unclear.

Not all knowledge may come through the physical senses. But to qualify as knowledge, something must have an impact on a person's consciousness, even if on the subliminal level where tacit knowledge finds its home. To speak of knowing something is to assert that it is understood in the mind. Because *mind* is by nature subjective, subjectivity remains central to belief. This does not mean that there is no objective reality to which a given belief corresponds, only that believing anything entails subjectivity. The objective reality of stubbing my toe leads to the subjective sensation of pain, which in turn causes me to conclude that it is best to wear shoes. Subjectivity and truth are often compatible.

Some philosophers, such as Dietrich von Hildebrand, have suggested that knowledge is an ultimate datum, by which I take them to mean that one can have direct and immediate knowledge of reality, of the objective world, and that you cannot reduce this knowledge to something else or explain it away. Because I am not a professional philosopher, I will leave the evaluation of this claim to those who are, and simply suggest that personal subjectivity always conditions what goes on in our minds.[14] Religious knowledge is personal indeed, and unless God gets hold of and transforms our minds, we will never *see* Christ.

---

14. See Evans, *Subjectivity*, 74–123.

PART I. FOUNDATIONS

Is Religious Knowledge Possible?

As noted in chapter 2, both the Apostles' and Nicene-Constantinopolitan Creeds begin with assertions of belief rather than knowledge and therefore reflect epistemic humility. But it is important to recognize that embracing these creeds implies personal commitment to the ideas they contain. Countless people who continue to recite these creeds in church do so in the conviction that what they are reciting has the status of knowledge. Still, thoughtful Christians will acknowledge that because of how faith loses all meaning if it rests on absolute certainty, "we believe" feels a lot more authentic than "we know."

It just might be, however, that those things of which you or I can be the most certain in this life have to do with God, and that such certainty comes only when God's Spirit works in us. This is what some theologians refer to as the *inner testimony of the Spirit*. Loving God may turn out to be the only thing that is enduring and substantial. Yet, even our love of God is less enduring and substantial than God's love for us.

In Graham Greene's WWII novel set in London, *The End of the Affair*, Bendrix and a married woman named Sarah have just been intimate. Minutes later, a German bomb kills Bendrix. On her knees, Sarah promises that if God will bring him back to life, she will end their relationship. Bendrix, injured and bleeding, suddenly staggers into the bedroom. Stunned, Sarah wonders if Bendrix believes in anything he cannot see. "People go on loving God, don't they, all their lives without seeing Him?" she asks, to which Bendrix replies, "That's not our kind of love." Sarah responds, "I sometimes don't believe there's any other kind."[15] All through the story, God tugs at Bendrix, but when Sarah dies, he becomes hard and bitter. Greene, a deeply committed Catholic, ends the novel with Bendrix uttering these chilling words: "I wrote at the start that this was a record of hate . . . O God, you've done enough. You've robbed me of enough, I'm too tired and old to learn to love, leave me alone forever."[16]

God may be tugging at your mind and heart through Jesus, who issues this invitation: "Come to me, all who are weary and whose load is heavy; I will give you rest" (Matt 11:28, REB).

---

15. Greene, *The End of the Affair*, 69.
16. Greene, *The End of the Affair*, 192.

Closing Thoughts

Although total objectivity is rarely if ever achieved, Christian faith is not arbitrary. It is informed by objective realities. But it is also subjective. Awareness of God involves tacit knowledge based on intuition. People have a thinking language and a communication language. When Christian faith is alive and well, a person's thinking language includes a private ongoing conversation with God. We do not passively connect with reality but actively engage with it. Jesus used similes and metaphors to impart spiritual insight. Theology guards against unsound beliefs and fosters tacit religious knowledge.

Preview

Although Nietzsche was not the first to announce the death of God, he most blatantly gave people permission to serve as their own gods and define their own moralities. He regarded Christianity as toxic to the human spirit. As we will see in the next chapter, his thinking was both insightful and flawed.

Part II. **COMING TO TERMS**

Chapter 8. Reports of God's Demise

FOR WELL OVER A century, intellectuals in the West have told us God is dead. By this, some mean that no intelligent person could continue to take religion seriously. They point to the sad condition of humanity and from it conclude that we are alone in the cosmos and not even well suited to it. Few in the death-of-God camp mean that God once existed but no longer does. Most mean there never was a God and the idea of such a being is, on its face, absurd. Nineteenth-century philosopher Friedrich Nietzsche (1844–1900) was not the first to announce God's demise, but his name is most closely associated in popular culture with the notion that Christianity is dead as a meaningful option. In this chapter, I am going to discuss his thinking in some detail.

Deep within us is the potential for rebellion against rules, regulations, norms, laws, and most significantly God. We just do not like to subordinate ourselves. I take no joy, for example, in having to wait minutes at a traffic light, stand in a long line, or receive a summons for jury duty. Even yielding to the demands of my body, for example having to visit my dentist, can feel like an interruption. Much of the time, I secretly resent life's inconveniences, large and small, and it is difficult to accept that, rather than serving as intrusions into my life, they are my life.

It can be hard to keep in mind what C. S. Lewis included in a letter to his friend Arthur Greeves on December 20, 1943, when the U.K. was anything but a resort. Bombs were dropping on London at a ferocious pace, ultimately killing almost 30,000 people, demolishing over 70,000 buildings, and damaging another 1.7 million. Oxford, where Lewis lived, is only fifty miles away. Lewis wrote to Greeves, "The great thing, if one can, is to stop regarding all the unpleasant things as interruptions of one's 'own' or 'real' life. The truth is of course that what one calls interruptions are precisely one's real life—the life God is sending one day by day." I am so fond of these lines that I made them into a bookmark to give to my friends.

When in the Ten Commandments I read, "Thou shalt have no other gods before me" (Exod 20:3, KJV), or in a more modern translation, "You must not have any other god but me" (NLT), I realize that this is not just warning me against turning wealth, fame, or pleasure into a god. It is also warning against *hubris*, the pride involved in acting as my own god. In my worst moments, however, I lose sight of this and want to be even greater than God because God has limits. The idea of God's omnipotence must allow for these limits or it is nonsense. There are certain things, for example, that by nature God cannot do, such as lie or engage in self-contradictions. I, on the other hand, want to be unrestrained and do whatever I want without consequence.

When Thomas Hobbes (1588–1679) insists that, without a government to keep people in line, life would be savagely brutal, he may be on to something. Hobbes was born several months premature, probably because the Spanish Armada, sitting off England's southern coast, terrified his pregnant mother and the rest of the country. Hobbes later lived through the bloody British civil war. As historian Trevor-Roper points out, according to Hobbes we do not so much move toward positive ends as away from negative ones. It is fear that propels us toward what Hobbes calls a "perpetual and restless desire of power after power, that ceaseth only in death."[1] Nietzsche embraces the Hobbesian idea of the lust for power, but unlike Hobbes regards fear as the earmark of the weak.[2]

Permission to Be One's Own God

Although during his lifetime many regarded Nietzsche as peculiar if not deranged, he continues to have influence. More than any other thinker, Nietzsche gives people permission not only to rebel against God but to revel in that rebellion. His writings stand in blatant defiance of the divine.

---

1. Trevor-Roper, "Thomas Hobbes," 566–71.
2. See Benson, *Pious Nietzsche*.

CHAPTER 8. REPORTS OF GOD'S DEMISE

To declare God dead in the way Nietzsche does is to assert that people no longer believe in an objective ultimate order. Anything that appears to be such an order is born of an infantile wish and misguided need to believe in some rational and higher purpose to life. Like fish dying on a dock in the sun, gasping for whatever oxygen they can extract from a medium to which they are ill-suited, we attempt to discover meaning in chaos. When we cannot find it, we invent the myths, superstitions, and moral codes of religion.

Nietzsche's writings can leave you reeling. They haunt and challenge. But they also fail to offer a coherent view of the world. His works, sometimes impassioned to the point of the borderline bizarre, contain ambiguities and inconsistencies. Yet, *not* to read him and so confront his barbs and assaults is, for a reflective person, to miss an opportunity for stark self-examination. Such self-examination may prove disturbing, particularly to those who have never struggled to sort out their beliefs, but in the end this can be beneficial. To study Nietzsche and the two-track nature of his thought—creative disruption on one hand and head-spinning incoherence on the other—might actually invigorate one's faith. As Nietzsche famously puts it, "What doesn't kill you makes you stronger." If nothing else, to square off with Nietzsche on his own turf can be to escape the pretentiousness of self-proclaimed Nietzscheans who, perhaps having read little of Nietzsche, invite us to attend God's funeral.

Themes and Paradigms

The core of Nietzsche's thought, as it concerns us here, reflects these themes: aggressive rejection of Christianity and the announcement of its demise; disparagement of democratic values; disdain for all things egalitarian; exaltation of the person who creates his or her own morals; and celebration of the will to power.

Two intellectual paradigms inform Nietzsche's writings: what he regards as the relentless quest for truth, and a headlong dive into an abyss whose emptiness cries out that truth, in any ultimate sense, cannot be found. Nietzsche starts out striving for understanding, for something in which to believe, then doubts his grasp of truth, and eventually denies the possibility of truth itself.

PART II. COMING TO TERMS

Iconoclasm, Ambiguity, and Antipathy

The Nietzsche of popular culture often bears little resemblance to the Nietzsche of serious study. One is a sensationalist who majors only in acerbic wit and merciless invective. The other is an astute but tormented scholar who, in his quest for truth, explodes with aphorism after aphorism on the way to concluding that there is no truth beyond what he proclaims. Nietzsche judges most harshly those who have the temerity to judge, and he is especially intolerant toward those he regards as intolerant, in particular Christians.

Nietzsche's philosophy, to the extent it holds together, is almost entirely critical. Perhaps intentionally, his concepts of the quasi-superhuman Overman (*der Übermensch*)[3] and the will to power remain imprecise and ambiguous. As for the unrestrained Dionysian versus the restrained Apollonian distinction he outlines in *The Birth of Tragedy*, admiration for the former may come mostly from adolescent frat-house boys who embrace its bacchanalian motifs. Free of parental oversight and nudged on by whatever remnants of Nietzsche's utterances they have picked up at parties, they taste the intoxicating wine of emancipation.

For those who care enough to read his works and reckon with their provocations, Nietzsche shatters clichés and conventions. Several of his books, including the widely read *Also sprach Zarathustra* (*Thus Spoke Zarathustra*), consist of aphorisms that sometimes seem contradictory. It is possible, therefore, to find support in his writings for a broad spectrum of ideas, which partly accounts for their appeal. His books are an intellectual Rorschach blot. Nietzsche is sometimes liberating, often spicy, rarely comforting, characteristically imaginative, and routinely goading.

It may be that Nietzsche turned against religion because his father died when he was a child, which may have left him feeling abandoned. In 1938, Karl Jaspers (1883–1969) delivered a series of lectures on Nietzsche in Hannover, Germany, that are reproduced in a short but powerful book, *Nietzsche and Christianity*. In it, he argues that Nietzsche's unrelenting war on Christianity was spawned in the waters of the very religious tradition he attacks. It is not only that Nietzsche came from a long line of ministers against whom he seems to have rebelled (his father and both grandfathers were Lutheran pastors) but that his writings seem driven by values inherited from Christianity itself, such as relentless intellectual honesty. Nietzsche seems inconsistently aware of how much Christianity

---

3. Overman is sometimes less accurately translated as superman.

CHAPTER 8. REPORTS OF GOD'S DEMISE

contributed to his personal quest for truth. Ironically, he ends up repudiating the very quest for truth that derived from, and impelled him to go to war against, Christianity.

Even before turning to philosophy, Jaspers had achieved prominence as a psychiatrist and developed considerable respect for Nietzsche. He concludes that Nietzsche's attacks on Christianity were, in the end, inseparable from Nietzsche's personal connection to it through his family and broader cultural heritage. Jaspers was not, however, engaging in a cheap *ad hominem* argument, one that tries to counter an idea by discrediting the person advancing it. Jaspers was not attempting to discount Nietzsche's thought by psychologizing it away, just trying to make philosophical and psychological sense of Nietzsche's complexity and inconsistencies.

Contrary to Nietzsche's view that Western religion is detrimental, a scourge that has all but ruined the human spirit, Christianity substantially paved the way for, and actively encouraged, unfettered inquiry and therefore the emergence of modern science. Few people fully appreciate the pivotal role played by Christianity in the development of Western Civilization, particularly in its valuation of the search for truth, not only in physical science but in other domains of inquiry as well. We will discuss how much Christianity contributed to civilization in chapters 18 and 19.

Nietzsche does seem to understand his quest for truth as the indirect product of a Christian ethos. He concedes, forthrightly enough, that with the advent of Christianity, the Western World came to embrace and eventually cherish the systematic accumulation of knowledge. Freely granting this, however, Nietzsche concludes that the pursuit of truth has nothing to do with God. Nowhere does Nietzsche appear to entertain even a smidgen of doubt about his atheism, and it is sometimes the dogmatically certain who become famous. There is brilliance, erudition, and urbanity in much of what he writes. But there is no spiritual or intellectual modesty, no humility, and no genuine openness, the kind that leads an agnostic to suspend judgment about the existence of God.

He argues that the truthfulness fostered by Christianity will eventually lead to its decline, and that this decline has already started. The loss attending the abandonment of the Christian faith will plunge humanity into an abyss, the likes of which it has never experienced. Out of this abyss of nothingness, Nietzsche's Overman will emerge. The Overman appears to be everything that the sickly, isolated, and tormented Nietzsche would like to have been but was not.

Nietzsche may have been in search of a kind of meta-Christianity, or perhaps a deeper one, and some of what he writes hints at this. But the Jesus he finds in the New Testament is more a function of his fantasies than of the one a responsible scholar would discover. This is astounding, given that Nietzsche was a philologist, a student of languages and manuscripts. Reminiscent of Thomas Jefferson, who through his deletions created his own New Testament, Nietzsche has no qualms about cutting and pasting, excising anything in the Gospels that does not suit him. The Jesus he ends up with is hapless and weak. Even a casual tour of those Gospels indicates that Jesus was neither. Philosopher C. Stephen Evans pointed out that Nietzsche viewed Jesus as a "decadent," but as the only honest decadent, and regarded the history of Christianity, beginning with Paul, as a record of its attempt to gain power. Nietzsche respected Jesus for not doing this.[4]

In *Joyful Wisdom*, Nietzsche writes, "The greatest event of recent times—that God is dead, that belief in the Christian God has become unworthy of belief—already begins to cast its first shadows over Europe ... At last the horizon lies free before us, even granted that it is not bright; at least the sea, *our* sea, lies open before us. Perhaps there has never been so open a sea."[5] This is how Jesuit philosopher and historian Frederick Copleston decodes this passage: "Decay of belief in God opens the way for man's creative energies to develop fully; the Christian God, with his commands and prohibitions, no longer stands in the path; and man's eyes are no longer turned towards an unreal supernatural realm, towards the other world rather than towards this world." Copleston continues, "This point of view obviously implies that the concept of God is hostile to life." Nietzsche reaffirms this in several other works, including *The Twilight of the Gods* and *The Antichrist*. Like Edward Gibbon (1737–94) in *The History of the Decline and Fall of the Roman Empire*, Nietzsche sees Christianity as having substantially contributed to bringing it down.

You have to wonder what version of Christianity Nietzsche is so adamantly against and what sorts of Christians he encountered. Perhaps, akin to Kierkegaard, he was surrounded by those for whom Christianity had become little more than a cultural artifact. When he goes on the attack, he seems to have in mind the kind of nineteenth-century

---

4. Personal communication, November 30, 2020.
5. Copleston, *History of Philosophy*, 403.

Chapter 8. Reports of God's Demise

Protestantism that was long on platitudes but short on passion. Nietzsche is brutally critical of the lack of transformation he sees in the lives of Christians.

Nietzsche's Approach to Politics

Nietzsche sees in democracy the remnants of an eviscerated Christianity, and he takes a similar stance in relation to any form of egalitarianism. It repulses him that we assist the weak and that the ineffective receive benefits rightfully due, in his judgment, only to those who are superior. He argues how the struggle for supremacy that routinely goes on between and among people lies hidden beneath claims of entitlement, buttressed by the erroneous belief that everyone is talented. All persons are not created equal, he insists, and to say they are is to suppress greatness.

When, according to Nietzsche, people finally realize the foolishness of egalitarian aspirations, they will fully embrace life. Nietzsche seizes on the will to power as especially ennobling. He never claims that the quest for power explains all human behavior. But he does insist that residing within the human psyche is the drive to ascend, rule, and dominate, and that often this drive, however well camouflaged, becomes all-consuming.

Nietzsche may be on to something. Power strivings play more of a role in behavior than many people in the nineteenth century were willing to concede. It is Nietzsche's genius that he is able to penetrate deeply enough through the veneer of socialized conduct that he is able to see the importance of the power motive. This was well before Alfred Adler (1870–1937) imported the idea into psychiatry and psychology. Nietzsche is also prophetic in predicting that nationalism would become an ominous force, which it did a few decades later with the ascendance of the National Socialist German Workers' Party in Nazi Germany.

The will to power is recognizably close to what Christians call sin, and in the eyes of some theologians the lust for power is central to it. How Nietzsche evaluates the compulsive quest for power is markedly different, however, from how theologians view it. What Nietzsche takes to be an important determinant of advancing humanity, the Christian theologian regards as the very thing that hinders such advance. To the Christian, it is pride and the desire to live untethered to God, expressed in the desire for power, that lies at the root of moral evil. There may be little difference, in the end, between the lust for power, however well disguised, and rebellion against the creator. In some of Nietzsche's writings, however, the highest and best expression of the will to power is self-restraint, and what the noblest Overman overcomes is himself. Self-overcoming, he insists, is foundational to artistic creativity, a value dear to Nietzsche. For him, the greatest work of art one can ever create is oneself as an Overman.

Nietzsche's View of Truth

Truth, Nietzsche informs us, is fiction, and what we take to be truths are mere interpretations. There is no objective truth, only individual perspectives, personal points of view. His *perspectivism*, as some have called it, leads to the notion that no fixed rights or wrongs exist and that moral codes are mere conventions, habits, and customs of the mind. In offering this conception of truth, Nietzsche seems to presuppose that he sits in a tower from which he alone can objectively perceive the relativity of all truth and its arbitrary nature. We are to view everything that, until now, we have believed true as arbitrary and subjective. What Nietzsche expounds, however, we are to take as objective and absolute.

Viewed through one set of spectacles, there is no such thing as immutable truth. Viewed through another, Nietzsche is forever making assertions that he puts forth as immutable. It is difficult, for example, to regard ideas like the Overman as one among many perspectives when he asserts such ideas so dogmatically and uncompromisingly. Despite what he sets forth as his official position—perceptions of truth and statements of value are personal interpretations—Nietzsche makes claims and espouses values with such ferocity that it is all but impossible to avoid the conclusion that he intends them as absolutes. Jaspers suggests that Nietzsche writes in two different media, ink for his views and pencil for everyone else's.

No reasonable person would debate that the pursuit of truth, so central to Christianity, has resulted in tensions between and among Christians. This has prompted constructive debate, but it has also left Christianity vulnerable to critiques of it as a social invention. It has also invited well-deserved denunciations of uncharitable, hypocritical, and combative Christians. But, such tensions have rarely prompted Christians to doubt that, however imprecisely they may grasp it, there is such a thing as objective truth.

CHAPTER 8. REPORTS OF GOD'S DEMISE

When you get to the end of the line with Nietzsche, there remains only provocation, iconoclasm, and despair. Likening his writings to Zen *koans*—"What is the sound of one hand clapping?"—may bring comfort to his devotees but does little to help anyone who still regards truth as potentially discoverable, coherent, and communicable. With Nietzsche, there is never a finished product, only a kind of manufacturing plant specializing in turning out works-in-progress that foster petulant self-assertion. It is always nice to have someone convince us of the rightfulness of our selfish actions, if for no other reason than neutralizing the sting of conscience. If I want to take advantage of my neighbor, it is convenient to be assured that morality is a device promoted by the weak to disadvantage the strong.

Nietzsche's Self-Insight

Nietzsche claims to be ruthlessly committed to self-reflection and self-examination. One of his claims, which deeply influenced Freud, is that we are ignorant of most of what motivates us and generally do not understand the will, a non-rational instinctive force. But Nietzsche seems oblivious to any possible connection between his ideas and his own psychodynamics. He occasionally pens self-effacing aphorisms, but there is little in his writings to suggest that he understands or takes seriously the existence of such a connection. He can be insightful about the workings of others but less insightful about his own. No matter how hard we try to be honest with ourselves, there is always the possibility of introspective distortion. Of this, Nietzsche seems oblivious.

He informs us, for example, that the concept of sin, which he holds to be irrelevant to life and the enemy of progress, is a potent toxin that courses through the veins of Judaism and Christianity. Rarely if ever does it occur to Nietzsche that, like the rest of us, he has frailties and failings. Or, that he may be a rebellious creature at odds with God. He seizes on some of the worst qualities in himself, such as arrogance, and puts them up for veneration. Syphilis may have resulted in mental deterioration during the last decade of his life, but this does not earn him a pass because he finished his major works long before then. His syphilitic dementia appears only to have strengthened his attachment to the conclusions with which he began.

PART II. COMING TO TERMS

Nietzschean Futures

It is foundational to Christian hope that eternal life, in union with God, is a gift God gives to those who respond to divine love, ask for forgiveness for their failings, and acknowledge Jesus for who he was and continues to be. Over against this hope, Nietzsche proposes a doctrine of eternal recurrence: our lives repeat endlessly. This might seem to suggest some moral significance to existence, but for him it does not. Underneath Nietzsche's doctrine is the unwavering declamation that there is nothing in the universe to endow our lives with meaning. Perhaps, as some have suggested, Nietzsche intends the idea of eternal recurrence as a test, a measure of willingness to live one's life over again and embrace it. Nietzsche balks at eternal life but embraces reincarnation. Most Christian theologians find the idea of eternal recurrence incompatible with Christian faith.

What happens if, like Nietzsche, we eliminate God and are left with creation devoid of a creator? The world is then without moorings, and beneath whatever joy we derive from life may be a dull sense of lostness that silently lurks at the margins of consciousness. Many people therefore try to turn science into a philosophy or quasi-theology. If we put our faith in science alone,[6] however, we are left without a way to make large-scale sense of human existence. The theories and findings of science, ever subject to revision and reinterpretation as they are, cannot substitute for God.

Nihilism

Harvard philosopher George Santayana (1863–1952) suggested that a fanatic is someone who, having lost sight of his purpose, redoubles his efforts.[7] By this measure, Nietzsche seems a bit like a fanatic. He is at different times a naturalist, perspectivist, or existentialist. Nietzsche seems to recognize the danger of nihilism and seems to want to turn it on its head. Yet, we find him crafting this anarchistic affirmation, reminiscent of Dostoevsky: Nothing is true; everything is permitted.[8] Nietzsche intends this to encompass ideas, however contradictory, as well as actions. He is

---

6. See Barrett, *The Illusion of Technique*.

7. "Fanaticism consists in redoubling your efforts when you have forgotten your aim." Santayana, *Life of Reason*, 13.

8. Dostoevsky, *The Brothers Karamazov*.

the prototype of the person who, instead of striving to reach closure on the truth of a thing, falls back on the idea of alternative truths. To follow Nietzsche to the bitter end is to obliterate all norms and values, and inevitably to renounce all truth and objective reality. Nothing remains.

He is determined to question, challenge, and debunk just about everything, with the result that it is impossible for him either to prescribe an emotionally satisfying mode of living or promote an intellectually satisfying philosophy of existence. Nietzsche is unable to realize the former for himself or formulate the latter for anyone else. His writings are stirring because they prompt us to blow out the walls of conceptual prisons, but such explosions can leave behind only rock and rubble. Nietzsche advocates the repudiation of established laws and social institutions, the rejection of all norms and conventions, and a sympathetic stance toward anarchy. He is, in short, an intellectual terrorist.

Advancing in the Wrong Direction

Nietzsche, as I have suggested, inherited much of his predilection for the pursuit of truth from Christianity. But in pursuing truth, he repudiates what, to the Christian, lies at the heart of healthy human existence, a loving connection with God and other people. He seems lost but rejects the idea that the remedy is divine rescue and redemption. One meaning of *redeem* is to take back whatever has been placed on hold or confiscated. As C. S. Lewis puts it,[9] we must lay up our arms and come to see God as a loving parent, thereby putting an end to our rebellion. Nietzsche, however, insists that we are not rebellious enough and that humanity's only hope consists in ever more rebellion. What he defines as hope, beyond romanticized self-inflation, is unclear.

Some people take Nietzsche's words as profound analyses of the human condition. A hundred years ago, however, what Nietzsche wrote was regarded as the ravings of a madman. One contemporary author, while acknowledging Nietzsche as "the most powerful of atheistic philosophers,"[10] cites his *Beyond Good and Evil* as one of ten books that have proved detrimental to society, ranking right up there with Hitler's *Mein Kampf*.

---

9. Lewis, *Mere Christianity*.
10. Wiker, *10 Books*, 99.

PART II. COMING TO TERMS

Nietzsche performs a service for Western Culture by pointing to the lifeless corpse that much of Christianity had become in nineteenth-century Europe. This condition has only worsened across much of the Continent. Like Kierkegaard, Nietzsche has little use for systems of philosophy or institutionalized religion. Similarities between Kierkegaard and Nietzsche do not end there. They are both passionate in their writings and focus attention on psychology as well as religion. But they begin with vastly different premises and reach strikingly different conclusions. While Kierkegaard promotes the rejection of fossilized religion in favor of passionate Christian faith, Nietzsche promotes its disparagement and repudiation.

Closing Thoughts

Nietzsche encourages people to discard conventional morality along with belief in God, particularly the God of the Christians. He argues that Christianity has become a lifeless corpse. Nietzsche exalts the self-determining Overman, disparages egalitarianism, and focuses on the will to power. He denies the existence of objective truth, which he regards as a matter of perspective, but nevertheless views himself as in possession of it. He demonstrates insight into the minds of others but seems to demonstrate little insight into his own.

Preview

Death is inevitable. We all have what Somerset Maugham calls an appointment in Samarra. We flee death only to find ourselves staring it in the face. The terrible thing about death is loss. God, however, promises those who love him everlasting life.

Chapter 9. Appointment in Samarra

Perhaps, like me, you are keenly aware of time. Even as a teenager, I was acutely conscious of it, and for many years I took this to be the result of having spent three years in a military academy, where no one survives without an eye on the clock. Contrary to popular opinion, delinquents do not last in military boarding schools. On those rare occasions when they are admitted, they usually manage to get themselves expelled before Thanksgiving. My time-consciousness, I now realize, is rooted in something deeper, the awareness that life is finite and will someday end. We are on a journey to a destination we would prefer to avoid.

The end of life is not something you can usually talk about in polite society. It is just not the sort of subject you bring up, unless of course a friend or acquaintance has recently died, and then you might speak only in whispers. Although the inevitable hangs above our heads like a sword, we tend to do everything possible not to think about it. But, regardless of how much we enjoy life, the end comes, and when it does, whether painfully or peacefully, we go to sleep. Eventually, so does everyone else. If there is no God, we sleep forever.

We appear to be the only creatures on the planet who realize that someday we will die. Presumably, unlike dogs, cats, chimps, or dolphins, we are conscious of our mortality and live with the gnawing awareness that life will end. If there is no escaping death, knowledge of our own mortality may be our most private haunting nightmare.

PART II. COMING TO TERMS

Existential Dread

When the starkness of human finitude hits us, not just intellectually but viscerally, we may experience dread, which can be mild or intense and continual or intermittent. Such dread is neither the anxiety of the child who worries about being loved, nor the insecurity of the adolescent who is concerned about being sufficiently intelligent, attractive, athletic, or popular. It is the awareness that we are engaged in a lethal game of survival in which the odds are stacked against us and the house always wins.

To a small child, the idea of death is difficult to grasp. It may just mean something bad. To a teenager, the idea is more comprehensible, but its finality may still seem remote. "I'll die someday," muses the typical teen, "but that's a long way off, so I need not concern myself with it." By middle age, the implications of death begin to dawn. They may appear suddenly, perhaps triggered by the death of a friend or surviving a serious accident. Or, they may creep up on us slowly, as we notice the looming decline of our bodies and how sags and wrinkles begin to invade and despoil our once youthful appearance. In whatever way such awareness comes, and however much we try to suppress it, around the edges of consciousness lurks the knowledge that we all have an "appointment in Samarra."

This phrase comes from a play Somerset Maugham wrote in 1933 and crafted around an old Arabic tale. It was used a year later as the title of a bestselling novel by John O'Hara.[1] Here is the essence of the tale: One morning, a merchant sends his servant to shop in the Baghdad marketplace. The man returns in great distress and reports that he has just met Death, who informed him that they have an appointment that very day. The servant asks the merchant to lend him a horse so he can flee to Samarra. He rides until dusk and, exhausted, enters the marketplace. To his astonishment, he again meets Death, who informs that, because he rushed off so quickly that morning, he had misunderstood. Death, in fact, had been surprised to run into him earlier that day in Bagdad, since their appointment was that night in Samarra. Regardless of how much we involve ourselves in career development, wealth building, social positioning, sports, hobbies, recreation, family, or the pursuit of pleasure, we ultimately keep this appointment.

Some people do a good job of blocking out all thoughts of it. They may compulsively accumulate like Egyptian pharaohs, as if they could

---

1. O'Hara, *Appointment in Samarra*.

CHAPTER 9. APPOINTMENT IN SAMARRA

take their possessions and prestige with them when they die. Or, they may strive to leave legacies, as if symbolic immortality could substitute for the real thing. They strive, toil, worry, amass, and compete, all the while dimly haunted by the lurking specter of death and disintegration, avoiding as best they can all conscious awareness of their inevitability.

Death and Loss

People fear death for all sorts of reasons. Anxiety about the unknown. Dread that, once in the grave, they will turn out to be no more than a collection of desiccated chemicals. Concern that, even if there is life after death, they will no longer be the same persons or recognize people they know. Worry that they will no longer have the same minds, or even if they do, that they will never again on earth enjoy sunsets, oceans, mountains, or sitting in front of a fireplace. Fear of death is, for many, rooted in the *Angst* of annihilation and the foreboding expectation that, when they cease to exist, everything they have spent their lives building will vanish. They may dread ending up like gyroscopes that slow down, wobble, and fall, or like smoke that evaporates into the air.

The most emotionally painful part of death for many of us is that it ends all human conversation. It brings with it separation and puts an end to affection and closeness. Death stops any chance we have to give and receive love, iron out differences, reach understandings, achieve resolutions, or make amends. It makes it impossible to utter that special something we planned to say, to offer that hug we intended to give, or enjoy those moments of happiness we wanted to share. Even if you are a Christian and believe those you love will live on in a realm or dimension you cannot now see, and into which you may only occasionally glimpse, the anguish of separation remains. Death is the enemy, the destroyer.

Death also brings with it another loss. It marks the end of any opportunity to cooperate in this life with God in the transformation of ourselves and the betterment of the world. The displays on the arcade game of life flash *tilt* and *game over*. Death ends all chance of collaborating with the One who granted us life in order to transform us. It also brings to a close our opportunity to help change even a small part of the world into something that pleases and delights God (see Rom 8:28).

PART II. COMING TO TERMS

Days of Wine and Roses

In a wistful scene from the film *Days of Wine and Roses*, the wife in a couple struggling with alcohol dependence looks down into a river and recites these lines by Ernest Dowson:

> They are not long, the days of wine and roses:
> Out of a misty dream
> Our path emerges for a while, then closes
> Within a dream.

In the same poem, Dowson minted a phrase that novelist Margaret Mitchell used as the title of her post-Civil-War novel, which the entertainment industry memorialized in a film with the same title: *Gone with the Wind*.

Dowson knew what he was talking about. His parents committed suicide in 1895, before he reached the age of thirty, and for the next few years the melancholic Englishman drifted around Europe. In 1900, at the age of thirty-three, he died from complications associated with alcohol abuse. That, ironically, was the year Margaret Mitchell was born. But her life, too, ended prematurely and tragically. A motorist ran her down before her fiftieth birthday. Both Dowson and Mitchell, gone with the wind. Our days of wine and roses, however satisfying, do not last, and our paths indeed emerge only for a while. Like bubbles from a child's wand, whatever moments of happiness our days bring fade quickly. For most of us, all awareness in the minds of others that we once existed fades away within a few generations, until no one on the planet even remembers us.

The Big Freeze

Astrophysicists generally agree that at some point in the future, somewhere around five billion years from now, the sun will burn out. In less than one-and-a-half billion years, it will have expanded so much that the oceans will evaporate and life on earth will no longer be possible. Humanity at best will have had a good run. As with even the most successful of Broadway shows, the curtain will finally come down, ushering in an eternal eon of ice. Absolute zero. Science and technology will likely prove unable to alter these events, in which case our world will cease to exist. Even if humankind does not destroy itself before then,[2] and figures out a way to escape the frozen horror by traveling to another solar system, this does nothing to help us now as individuals. What is to become of you and of me?

Without God breathing eternal life into us, we may go the way of all flesh and become, against the backdrop of infinity and eternity, insignificant. What good did it do Alexander the Great of Macedonia to have once dominated the known world? Of what worth is all that to him now? Of what personal value have been the accomplishments of any other military, political, scientific, artistic, or intellectual leader? Even if the ancient greats, such as Plato and Aristotle, had lived another two or three or even five hundred years, where would they be today? In Graham Greene's *End of the Affair* to which I referred in chapter 7, Bendrix, struggling against God, says, "If we are extinguished by death, as I will try to believe, what point is there in leaving behind any more than bottles, clothes or cheap jewelry?"[3] Absent a relationship with a God who exists, we are doomed to become, at most, a memory. Humankind has managed, in a mere twelve to thirteen thousand years, to climb out of the nomadic pit of hunting and gathering to become builders of skyscrapers, masters of microcircuits, and creators of masterpieces. This changes nothing of individual personal relevance. To dust we will all return.

Empty Hope

There is little merit in the idea that we should believe in God because belief without faith leaves us vulnerable to despair. Religion, some believe, is like chicken soup, good for the soul. Or a pick-me-up when the chips are down to make us feel better, bring us cheer, and set us on our way again. Such religion may indeed lift one's spirits, but that alone is unlikely to cause anyone to develop faith. Hope in the absence of any underlying reality on which it is based turns out in the end to be hollow and completely without substance. You might as well put your trust in the tooth fairy. People cannot believe in and place faith in a God they think does not exist.

Trumped up belief may be comforting in the face of a temporary setback, but it does little for someone *en route* to Samarra. Exhortations

2. See Kahn, *On Thermonuclear War*.
3. Greene, *The End of the Affair*, 148.

to see the brighter side only make sense if there is a brighter side. Improving your state of mind is actually detrimental if it prevents you from seeking and finding the one true God. Realistic hope, by definition, must be based on something real, and spending time to contemplate and revere a non-existent God is futile. A prisoner on death row may place his faith in an attorney filing an appeal, but if the attorney is incompetent and the appeal flawed, there can be no realistic hope. Unfounded hope is no hope at all. There may be positive illusions,[4] such as believing that your untalented child is musically gifted and so provide that child with opportunities to become a better musician. Or, that you will succeed at something, which absent that belief you would fail at. False religion is not one of them.

If there is no God, we have to wonder why people all over the globe have developed religion. Perhaps it is because they have a psychological need to come up with a reason to live that is greater than themselves. But if so, where did that need come from? How and why did it develop? Maybe the human inclination toward religion resulted from random changes in DNA, so that people have a genetic predisposition toward belief. If so, what survival or other benefit results from this? Could it be, as Freud suggested, that people have an infantile need for a father? Might it just be, however, that millions if not billions of people intuitively know that God exists but do not know how or where to find God? Like the Athenians in the Apostle Paul's day, they may continue to worship the unknown god Paul refers to (Acts 17:23) and to whom Christianity points.

Christian Hope

Many people appear to live with a low level of existential despair. They may find life flat, empty, and without purpose. Like our need for air, food, and water, we have an inner void that can only be filled by God's Spirit. This is another of God's gifts because, knowing as we do of our upcoming appointment in Samarra, awareness of this void may be how God summons us.

Death is part of what Christianity promises he will set right. God has disclosed through Jesus, and before Jesus in the Old Testament, God's desire for communion with people. It is to have this communion with God and each other that we exist in the first place. This means

---

4. See Taylor, *Positive Illusions*.

CHAPTER 9. APPOINTMENT IN SAMARRA

that, if Christianity is true, our minds and what makes us unique will continue after death. Such hope is part of what Christians mean by the good news. They believe God will give them new and resurrected bodies, akin to what Jesus had after his resurrection. The Bible refers to these bodies as incorruptible (1 Cor 15:52).[5] No one knows exactly what this means, although from reports in the New Testament it appears that Jesus was able to walk through walls.

Why not? When we see teleportation depicted in science fiction, do we not find ourselves imagining that, someday, such a thing might be possible? Prior to the twentieth century, scientists viewed the conservation of matter and of energy as two distinct principles, and no scientist took seriously the idea that mass and energy were interconvertible. Then, in a 1905 article written for a physics journal, Einstein published $E = mc^2$. Prior to the discovery of nuclear fission, such interconvertibility would have ranked right up there with teleportation as fantasy.[6]

Might God, after having already giving us life, someday equip us with capacities of which we now have no inkling? Perhaps we will penetrate barriers. Matter is primarily empty space anyway. Maybe two objects can occupy the same space if they have the right molecular structures. Instead of heaven turning out to be an endless state of mindless boredom, might it turn out to be, for those who love and give God their allegiance, a life of increasing joy and everlasting fulfillment?

Closing Thoughts

Many people go through life with low-grade existential dread. Some go to great lengths to persuade themselves and others that they will live forever. Regardless of how much celebrity, wealth, or power an individual achieves, nothing protects even the most favored among us from keeping our appointment in Samarra. Death ends human relationships and so precludes further experiences of love and affection. But it also ends the opportunity in this life to love, worship, serve, and obey God.

---

5. Wright, *Surprised by Hope*.
6. See Bodanis, *E=mc²*.

PART II. COMING TO TERMS

Preview

Many people develop ingenious maneuvers to block out of awareness whatever they find unpleasant. Early in the twentieth century, psychoanalysts described these maneuvers in detail. Defense mechanisms can be, are often are, used to keep out of consciousness all thoughts of God and of death and its implications.

Chapter 10. Psychologically Defending Against Death

PEOPLE HAVE MANY WAYS of preventing themselves from confronting questions about the meaning of life or the existence of God.[1] At one time or another, I have used many of them, and there are still moments when I live as a functional atheist, as if my life were entirely my own and the word *God* a religious abstraction. Our two principal ways of sidestepping life's most important questions, the existential ones, are defenses and distractions. In this chapter, I want to discuss defenses that people seem most to use to keep such questions at bay. In the next chapter, we will examine how people rely on distractions to avoid facing them.

Many people seem to understand the general nature of unconscious process: statements or actions that appear to mean one thing turn out to mean something else. Among the more helpful insights to keep in mind about unconscious process is that there are no jokes. This is not literally true, of course. But, when people say something hostile, and then excuse it by saying they were only kidding, it is wise to ask yourself whether they might have meant what they said. Slips of the tongue, what psychologists and psychiatrists call *parapraxes*, can also betray what a person thinks, feels, wants, fears, or intends. Consider the tired hostess who says to her departing guests, "Come back when you can't stay longer."

Twentieth-century psychoanalysts paid considerable attention to understanding, describing, and writing about defense mechanisms,[2]

1. See McLaughlin, *Confronting Christianity*.
2. See Fenichel, *Psychoanalytic Theory of Neurosis*; Freud, *Mechanisms of Defense*.

ways we prevent unwanted thoughts from becoming conscious. Whether people are completely unaware of such thoughts remains a matter of debate, and one philosopher has taken up this question in detail.[3] When a psychologist or psychiatrist refers to *unconscious process,* he or she often means that the individual is blocking something out of awareness. If it were to become conscious, it would trigger anxiety. Our interest in this chapter is in those defenses people seem to use to block out questions relating to God.

According to classic psychoanalytic theory, defense mechanisms only operate unconsciously. If you know you are using it, it is not a defense. Consider the woman who stops at a green light on the way to the rehearsal for her wedding. Although this could be because she is mentally preoccupied or distracted, it could also be because she is ambivalent about getting married or unsure she has picked the right husband. Stopping at the green light at least raises the question of what she truly wants. But such a definition may be excessively restrictive. Some defenses appear to be conscious deliberate efforts to avoid the unpleasant. People who are afraid of heights, for example, may refuse to look down from a bridge.

Other defenses, however, fall somewhere between conscious and unconscious. Think of the man who habitually forgets to bring his wallet when dining out with friends, and so repeatedly avoids paying his share of the check. The extent to which such forgetfulness is conscious or unconscious can be ambiguous. Defenses that start out as intentional may eventually become ingrained and automatic. Refusing to think about God can be like that.

The Trivialization of Human Choice

Among the achievements of modern psychiatry is that, beginning in the nineteenth century, it began to promote the view that seriously troubled people require medical attention. This had the admirable effect of protecting disturbed individuals from a great deal of persecution at the hands of the ignorant or malicious. Along with reducing the moral stigma associated with mental disorders, however, came the unfortunate consequence of increasingly defining bad conduct as the result of psychiatric ailments. Psychiatrists and psychologists became secular priests

---

3. MacIntyre, *The Unconscious.*

CHAPTER 10. PSYCHOLOGICALLY DEFENDING AGAINST DEATH

who ever more broadly told society which modes of behavior warranted clinical attention.[4]

It is true that many people suffer psychological damage because they have had to live through hellish experiences, such as a civil catastrophe, physical or emotional abuse, or the trauma of war. Or, because faulty genes have left them with little resilience in relation to the buffeting and battering of ordinary life. Other people, however, suffer because of bad choices they have made, sometimes throughout life, and only a strict determinist would argue that they *had* to make those choices, and therefore that they bear no responsibility for them. Determinism is the philosophic position that everything is the inescapable result of all that preceded it. Applied to people, this means choice is an illusion. One implication of this view is that if people have no free will, it makes no sense to hold them accountable for their actions.

Training in psychiatry, psychology, and other mental health professions encourages people to think as determinists, sometimes without sufficiently introducing them to points of view that leave room for human choice. Determinism is the proper foundation of science, defined as the systematic search for observable and measurable causes and effects, and mental health professionals rightly strive to approach their work scientifically. There is a difference, however, between being scientifically informed and insisting that all behavior is scientifically explainable. While psychotherapy at its best is a scientifically informed art, it will always remain an art and never, in the strict sense, be a science

An excessively narrow understanding of why people act as they do has contributed significantly to defining more and more psychological disorders as medical ailments, even in the absence of demonstrated physical causes. As an example of medical overreach, the current edition of the 1,000-page psychiatric diagnostic manual contains scores of pages devoted to personality disorders, which are medical only in the loosest sense. No identifiable physical disease process underlies them and they typically require no medication. Psychiatrists and clinical psychologists have long used the diagnosis "Antisocial Personality Disorder" or its predecessors. To warrant this diagnosis, the person (patient) must exhibit at least three of the following: significantly unlawful behavior; chronic deceitfulness; impulsiveness or failure to plan; irritability and aggressiveness; reckless disregard for the safety of self or others; consistent

---

4. See London, *Modes and Morals*.

irresponsibility; and lack of remorse. Medicalizing or psychologizing away such human behavior has led many mental health practitioners to minimize the existence of personal choice.

How Defenses Can Anesthetize Us

Denial is refusing to recognize something outside of ourselves. It often operates in conjunction with *Repression*, which is refusing to acknowledge something within. As an example of how the two can operate together, some people refuse to read, watch, or listen to any news that involves crime. This allows them to avoid acknowledging its existence (denial), while also enabling them to block out of awareness all thoughts of personal vulnerability (repression).

Through much of the film *Ordinary People*, the husband fails to recognize that his wife does not love their son (denial), whom she holds responsible for his brother's accidental drowning. By refusing to come to terms with her coldness, the father is able to wall off from his awareness the distressing thought that she is a toxic mother (repression). He also minimizes or refuses to acknowledge what he sees going on (denial).

Denial and repression enable people to avoid thinking about death and its implications. Society has so institutionalized the denial of death that people often euphemistically refer to it as *passing* and try to keep their distance from anything that reminds them of it. Refusing to think about mortality struck such a note of recognition in readers that Ernest Becker's *Denial of Death*[5] became a bestseller, and Evelyn Waugh's fictional parody of the funeral industry, *The Loved One*,[6] became a successful film. We sometimes treat the inevitability of death like the man who, experiencing pressure in his chest, shortness of breath, and pain down his arm, concludes he is suffering from indigestion. Death is what it means to be mortal, and thinking about death can bring up religious questions. Denial and repression working together make this less likely to happen.

Reaction Formation is an awkward term that refers to the defense of consciously expressing, and at least half-believing, what is contrary to one's deeper thoughts, feelings, or desires. An example is the eleven-year-old boy who, alarmed by his budding erotic impulses and newfound interest in girls, insists that he hates them.

---

5. Becker, *The Denial of Death*.
6. Waugh, *The Loved One*.

CHAPTER 10. PSYCHOLOGICALLY DEFENDING AGAINST DEATH

More than a few strident atheists seem to defend against fear of death by developing a fascination with it, perhaps by watching films in which there is a great deal of it. Some who represent themselves as atheists seem unconsciously to replace their awareness that God exists and loves them with the belief that God either does not exist or does not love them.

Counterphobic Behavior often shows up in people afraid of death. They may engage in behaviors that paradoxically move them closer to it, such as participating in high-risk activities like skydiving or racecar driving. Surviving danger brings them a kind of temporary comfort, which they sometimes describe as feeling fully alive. By outwitting death, they are able to persuade themselves that they are invincible and death therefore is irrelevant. This also provides them with the questionable benefit of not thinking about religious questions, and by implication not thinking about God.

Rationalization is reinterpreting reality by explaining it away or minimizing its significance, often with the goal of reframing desires, justifying bad behavior, or coming up with self-reassurance. In Aesop's fable of the fox and the grapes, the fox concludes that the desirable but out-of-reach grapes are sour anyway, so the fox does not want them after all. The teenager explains to the judge that he only stole the car because the owner, who is really at fault, left the keys in the ignition. A middle-aged man comforts himself with the illusion that, in his lifetime, medical science will discover a cure for any life-threatening ailment that might befall him.

The last of these can do nicely to take the sting out of death by rationalizing that it is too far in the future to worry about. Thoughts about death and consideration of religious questions, once again, can conveniently be set aside. People can also rationalize away all thoughts of dying, perhaps by reassuring themselves that God, if they believe God exists, can be put off. They can always explore religion later. Like Augustine in the fourth century, they want God to make them holy, but not yet.

Isolation is separating normal reactions from whatever would typically produce them. An example would be a person who witnesses a horrendous and bloody traffic accident in which several people die, and yet has no particular emotional response to it. The person blocks out or walls off potentially disturbing thoughts and feelings. This is what some people do in relation to death and the religious questions it can lead to. They underreact to it and their emotions remain flat. Isolation underlies many post-traumatic disorders. Stress disorders that result from the trauma of combat are often perpetuated by this defense mechanism. But to keep strong feelings at bay is to keep them unresolved.

Intellectualization is isolation with a twist. Instead of decoupling feelings from thoughts, intellectualization replaces feelings with thoughts. A happily married person unexpectedly served with divorce papers would likely feel some combination of anxiety, depression, anger, betrayal, grief, self-doubt, or devastation. Instead of feeling any of this, an accomplished intellectualizer might start to think about what RV to buy next or sit down to open the mail. Some people who appear to be intellectually preoccupied with death may, in reality, feel almost nothing in relation to it or its inevitability. Instead of encountering God, they may become lost in abstract academic questions about religion. Some become theologians. If fear of the Lord is the beginning of wisdom, both isolation and intellectualization can foster a lack of wisdom by blunting ordinary human responses.

Projection. Alan becomes consumed with anger and jealousy toward Ted, who bears him no ill will. Through projection, Alan convinces himself that it is Ted who is angry and jealous. We project onto others what we find difficult to acknowledge in ourselves.

Projection is not so much ignoring as indicting God. Our anger becomes God's anger. If I am unhappy about my life, it is because God is punishing me. When I have experienced adversity, God should have helped me. God should have prevented my supervisor from firing me, stopping me from losing all that money in a bad investment, and dropping out of school. If my unhappiness and frustration in life is because I made bad decisions, God should have caused me to make better ones. Thus, I project responsibility that belongs to me onto God and blame God for whatever prevents me from having the life I believe I justly deserve. In taking such a stance, I blind myself to the incredible gift God has given me, free will, a gift God rarely if ever overrides. Projecting onto God the responsibility for choices I, or for that matter the ones any other human being makes, prevents me from perceiving God's goodness. As suggested in "The Hound of Heaven," a late nineteenth-century poem by Francis Thompson, God nonetheless pursues us.

We have reviewed a few of the ways people defend against reckoning with death, the deep structure of existence, or our creator. There are many more, but since this is not a clinical textbook, we will end our discussion of them here.

CHAPTER 10. PSYCHOLOGICALLY DEFENDING AGAINST DEATH

Defenses and Reality

If there is no life beyond the grave, there may be little point to thinking about existential questions, and certainly no merit in dwelling on them. Defenses may therefore be functional, since they can help us avoid coming to terms with terrible realities. What good could possibly come of thinking about the guillotine if we are destined for it, if life is without any meaning or purpose beyond what we invent? If, however, our existence is meaningful and we have a God-ordained purpose, facing our mortality and confronting questions about God may be tremendously important.

Defenses come at a price. If there is no God, that price amounts to little more than the psychic energy needed to maintain them, and the benefits may outweigh the cost. If, however, there is a God who will eventually call us to account, the price of defending against asking these questions may be high.

In Plato's dialogue *Euthyphro*, Socrates asks, "Does not every man love that which he deems noble and just and good, and hate the opposite?"[7] Christianity makes a different claim, that we tend by nature to love darkness rather than light and instinctively to do what is in our interest rather than the interest of others. Think of the times you have thought, felt, or done things you would prefer others never to know about. Christianity may be in the best position to help us understand why we do these things.

Closing Thoughts

We have examined how people can avoid facing the inevitability of death and the existence of God. Among these ways are denial, reaction formation, counterphobic behavior, rationalization, compartmentalization, isolation, intellectualization, and projection. Defense mechanisms are, at root, ways we lie to ourselves, the most basic lie of which is that there is no personal God.

Preview

There are other ways people prevent themselves from thinking about mortality. These are not so much defense mechanisms as avoidance

7. Plato, *Euthyphro*, 15.

strategies. All of them can be convenient distractions. In the next chapter, we will consider how people use distractions to crowd out of consciousness all thoughts about death, dying, and a creator to whom they owe their existence.

Chapter 11. Avoidance Through Distraction

PASCAL NOTED CENTURIES AGO that people dread doing nothing. To avoid facing the most important questions in life, they occupy themselves with distractions. These fill up the time and ward off the anxiety that can come from gazing up into what may seem like a lifeless void. In the last chapter, we considered defense mechanisms people seem to use to avoid facing existential questions. In this chapter, we will discuss how distractions serve the same purpose, and how becoming distracted—getting on the wrong track—may take on the character of a religion.

Distractions are ways of filling up free mental space. They may leave little or no room for much else, including thinking about what most matters. Distractions, like defenses, may keep us comfortable but only at the price of making us numb. Here are some of the more common objects of pursuit that can become distractions: power; money; status; pleasure; arrogance; intellectualism; and utopianism. This chapter is addressed primarily to God-avoiders.

Power

This is the ability to influence or compel the actions of others. Money and status, which we will take up next, often operate in the service of power, but the need for power can also express itself in other ways. Although some theologians, such as Augustine, have argued that pride is the root of what theologians call *sin*, others have suggested that it is power.[1] What is it about power, we might ask, that makes it so much a part of life? What is the motivation behind the drive to have and use it?

Power provides access to resources. The powerful, for example, can enact laws and regulations that benefit them to the disadvantage of others. They can also determine who does and does not have medical care, freedom of movement, or even food and water. Or, who will remain safe and secure or be put at risk. We share with animals the tendency to dominate when we can and defer when we cannot. This inclination differs from person to person, and in some it is little more than the benevolent desire to lead rather than follow. For others, however, it is predatory.

Perhaps what most fuels the power motive in some people is that power allows them to feel like a god, and the more power they have, the more godlike they feel. The heady wine that comes with power is the illusion of feeling almighty and all-knowing. Like high-proof liquor, power can dull the senses and make it harder to see things as they are or recognize the One who is forever trying to get our attention, the One who both deserves and demands it.

Money

In an interview about his years in the White House, former President Nixon remarked that money is only important if you do not have it. For many people, this is true. But for others, the more they get, the more they want and believe they need. Few people care nothing about money. This may be because society often defines success in terms of it. But it is also because money enables us to obtain goods and services. John Kenneth Galbraith (1908–2006) suggested that, although economists differ in their analyses of money, they all agree that a unit of money, whether a dollar, euro, pound, yuan, or peso, represents a unit of stored labor.[2] Most of us would not know how to build a house, but if we have the money, we can buy one someone else built. Few of us know how to repair a car, but money allows us to hire a mechanic. Money is a powerful motivator. Although we can debate whether the love of money is the root of all evil (1 Tim 6:10), greed has certainly caused a huge amount of it.

---

1. See Shuster, *Power, Pathology, Paradox*.
2. See Galbraith, *Money*.

CHAPTER 11. AVOIDANCE THROUGH DISTRACTION

There are at least two significant difficulties with devoting your life to accumulation. The first is that once a person rises much above the poverty level, the psychological benefits of having more money fade quickly. Studies of the correlation between wealth and happiness have repeatedly yielded the same result: A positive relationship between money and happiness holds only for those at the economic margins of society, the relatively poor. Money does not satisfy us for long because we quickly adapt to whatever standard-of-living it enables us to attain.[3] When, for example, people suddenly come into money because they win a lottery, they quickly establish what psychologists call a new *comparison level*. If I earn thirty dollars an hour today and a week later find myself earning fifty, the latter becomes my new expectation and the standard against which I measure the value of my time. The same would happen if I woke up one morning and discovered that my bank balance was five million dollars. After I got over the shock, I might begin to feel sorry for someone with only a hundred thousand.

The second and more significant problem with unrestrained acquisition is that the motive to acquire money can crowd out thinking about the intangibles in life. A compulsive accumulator may rarely reflect on what matters most in a friendship or a marriage, and fail to notice that close friends or a loving spouse may be drifting away. See the parable in Luke 12:16–20, about a wealthy landowner whose fields are so bountiful that his barns cannot contain their yields. He decides to build even bigger ones and take his ease, to eat, drink, and be merry. To this, God replies, "You will die this very night. Then who will get everything you worked for?" (NLT).

Christianity regards the material world as good. But it affirms that it is important to see beyond the material, to the God who created and sustains it. Two of the four Gospels have Jesus saying that a person cannot serve God and money (Matt 6:24; Luke 16:13). There is nothing wrong with earning money, and pretending there is has fostered a lot of hypocrisy. Money can be a great blessing. It is not, however, when its pursuit becomes all-consuming and distracting.

A Harvard professor, social scientist, and columnist, commenting on the title of a popular song, "I Can't Get No Satisfaction," points out how this is "the greatest paradox of human life."[4] He writes, "We crave

---

3. See Myers, *The Pursuit of Happiness*.
4. Brooks, "The Satisfaction Trap," 22–30.

it, we believe we can get it, we glimpse it and maybe even experience it for a brief moment, and then it vanishes. But we never give up on our quest to get and hold on to it." It is endemic to our nature as persons, he suggests, always to want more, and more after that. He then advises, "we can beat this affliction . . . if we're willing to make some difficult changes to the way we live." I would add, also to the way we think.

Status

Just as few people can sincerely claim not to care about money, the same is true of status. Think of the jockeying for position that goes on in many corporations or the half-polite struggle for importance that occurs between customers in a high-end department store. Under competitive conditions, people can behave like territorial primates, only humans are smarter and can better disguise their need to feel superior. Having what others want enhances status. Consider the social value of net worth, educational pedigree, professional achievement, advanced degrees, celebrity, youthfulness, good looks, or a well-toned body.

There is a large literature in psychology on *social comparison*, the tendency to judge how we are doing by how others are doing. For many people, it is not enough to have money, be attractive, or take expensive vacations. They must have and do more, and other people have to recognize this. It is not enough that I win. Others must lose. I once heard a speaker quip, "What's the use of having a big house if nobody envies it?" Inspiring jealousy is the central motif in some people's lives.

Basing your sense of worth on provoking envy leaves you, in turn, vulnerable to envying other people. There is always someone else who has or does more. This can turn your everyday existence into an endless competition that allows little time off, a life in which happiness, contentment, and subjective well-being depend on the admiration of an ever-changing audience. In the fourth chapter of the Epistle to the Hebrews in the New Testament, the writer suggests that only in God through Christ can one find true peace and genuine rest. The biographies of some of the most accomplished people on earth describe their petty and sometimes bizarre preoccupations with eminence.

The Victorian novelist William Thackeray (1811–1863) wrote *Vanity Fair*, the title of which came from John Bunyan's (1628–88) *Pilgrim's Progress*. At the beginning of Thackeray's novel, he writes of "a world where everyone is striving for what is not worth having." When you are consumed with the need for others to worship you, it is hard to recognize the worth of anyone else, including God.

Pleasure

Some have suggested that increasing pleasure and decreasing pain drives all human behavior. There is little doubt that they shape much of it.[5] People do, however, sometimes demonstrate forms of altruism that would be difficult if not impossible to explain as hedonistic, at least not without so stretching the definition of pleasure that it loses all meaning. Firefighters, for example, knowingly sacrifice their lives to save strangers. Still, we listen to music, go to movies, take in plays, watch TV, dine out, attend sporting events, or buy tickets to concerts because such activities bring pleasure. We also brush our teeth to prevent cavities, pay our bills to avoid penalties, and refrain from staying in the sun too long to avoid burns, blisters, or skin cancer. If you are fond of the ocean, you may go to the beach, and if you like the snow, you may go to the mountains. *Yes* to lobster, steak, and pizza, if you like them, *No* to liver, tripe, and lima beans if you do not. Different people have different pleasures, but there is little doubt that we tend to be drawn toward whatever we find pleasurable or prevents or ends pain.

By first studying laboratory rats and then extrapolating his findings about positive and negative reinforcement to people, B. F. Skinner (1904–90), mentioned in chapter 3, demonstrated the extent to which rewards and punishments influence behavior. Human action is far more influenced by consequences than people typically realize. Because of what Skinner and his colleagues discovered about partial reinforcement schedules, we now understand why some people run to gaming casinos, even when they know the odds are against them and the house wins more often than it loses. A schedule of reinforcement specifies how often and under what conditions reinforcement is given for a certain behavior, such as inserting a coin and pulling down the arm of a slot machine.

As we grow older, our capacity for pleasure declines. We cannot get around like we used to, which limits the joy we can derive from a simple walk around the block. Our sense of smell diminishes and with it the ability to appreciate complex and subtle flavors. Even sex, which for many

---

5. See MacFarquhar, *Impossible Idealism*.

is the grandest pleasure of all, is not at age seventy-five what it was at thirty-five. If a person lives long enough, there may be little pleasure left in anything. Pleasure is often short-lived. Years ago, when I was chatting with a woman at RAND, we began to talk about how we spent money. "What's the half-life of pleasure?" she mused. "What will it mean the next morning to have eaten at an expensive restaurant the night before?"

The concept of half-life originated in physics and refers to how long it takes radioactive material to become half as radioactive. The half-life of 240U, an isotope of uranium, is a little more than half a day, while the half-life of 42Ar, an isotope of Argon, is thirty-three years. Geologists use the phenomenon of half-life to date rocks, and pharmacists also use it. Pharmacologists, for example, point out that the half-life of a low dose of aspirin is two to three hours, and of a large dose up to a day or more. Very few pleasures have the half-life of argon, some would do well to rival that of uranium, and many do not even equal the half-life of an aspirin. To dine at a fine restaurant with friends or family may give us lasting memories, but these are likely to come more from having spent time with them than from the quality of the food or ambiance. Many pleasures are good. But an obsessive preoccupation with any pleasure can turn life into an increasingly desperate search for ever more pleasurable stimulation, which, like the compulsive quest for power, money, or status, crowds out consideration of life's important questions.

Arrogance

Do we not, at times, want to proclaim ourselves extraordinary? What can make such desires seductive is their appeal to our sense of the heroic. Some people, too self-aware to retreat into denial, and too conscientious to become hedonists, turn arrogance into a strategy of sophisticated despair and themselves into modern stoics. Due perhaps to the human capacity to carry on against overwhelming odds, some people live in fatalistic defiance, which can be an effective distraction. They resist reckoning with the universe on its own terms, and how without God they are bereft (John 14:18, REB). They reconcile themselves to eventual obliteration, arrogantly claiming to be captains of their fates and masters of their souls.

William Ernest Henley (1849–1903) achieved enduring fame with his poem "Invictus" (Latin for *unconquered*), which he seems to have

CHAPTER 11. AVOIDANCE THROUGH DISTRACTION

written from a hospital bed. It may come as no surprise that the 1995 Oklahoma City bomber Timothy McVeigh invoked "Invictus" as his final pre-execution statement, or that Eric Robert Rudolph, the terrorist responsible for the bombing at the 1996 Summer Olympic Games, also alluded to it. Here it is:

> Out of the night that covers me,
>   Black as the Pit from pole to pole,
> I thank whatever gods may be
>   For my unconquerable soul.
>
> In the fell clutch of circumstance
>   I have not winced nor cried aloud.
> Under the bludgeonings of chance
>   My head is bloody, but unbowed.
>
> Beyond this place of wrath and tears
>   Looms but the Horror of the shade,
> And yet the menace of the years
>   Finds, and shall find, me unafraid.
>
> It matters not how strait the gate,
>   How charged with punishments the scroll,
> I am the master of my fate:
>   I am the captain of my soul.

I find these words as stirring as I did when my high school English teacher proclaimed them as his philosophy of life. There are few lines better suited to appeal to *hubris*, excessive and self-defeating pride. I sometimes wonder if, in Henley's final moments, he pulled back from defiance. After writing the last line of the second stanza—"My head is bloody, but unbowed"—did he ever question if, in fact, there was a God in relation to whom it would be appropriate to bow?

Young men and women, caught up in such sentiments, can be eager to join the military and go into combat, unconcerned about the prospect of death or the pain that can precede it. Their fearlessness may be a good thing for the nation, but it is unrealistic. William Tecumseh Sherman (1820–91), a highly decorated Civil War general, graphically describes the horrors of battle in his *Memoirs*, published in 1875. Ten years earlier, in a personal letter to James E. Yeatman, he observed that those clamoring for "more blood, more vengeance, more desolation" have "have never heard a shot" or "the shriek and groans of the wounded and lacerated." It was Sherman who coined the phrase, "war is hell."

We may infuse our stance toward life with self-congratulatory heroism, a motif captured in Tennyson's poem *Ulysses*.[6] The mythic Greek figure sets off on a last voyage, "To strive, to seek, to find, and not to yield." But, what precisely is Ulysses striving for or hoping to find? What, or whom, does he seek? In the face of what will he not yield? Perhaps we are all striving for something Christians call *salvation*. But we will never find it if we decide, beforehand, that we cannot, and insist on dying with misplaced valor, all the while disregarding God and what he offers.

Intellectualism

Living in the head to the exclusion of the heart is a wonderful way to distract ourselves from facing the big questions. Although there are many worthwhile forms of intellectual pursuit, from learning about the history of art to studying the tactics of chess, any of them can be so all-consuming that they distract a person from thinking about God.

Existentialism is among the more philosophical forms of intellectualism and it comes in two varieties, both originating in the nineteenth century. One, according to some, traces its roots to the Christian philosopher Søren Kierkegaard. The other is atheistic and traces its roots to Nietzsche. Atheistic existentialism illustrates how intellectual pursuits can begin to resemble a religion. Some of the twentieth-century's best-known literary figures, such as Jean Paul Sartre, became darlings in highbrow French and American circles after World War II. Proudly proclaiming themselves atheists, they informed the rest of us that life had no objective meaning and there was nothing beyond ourselves to give it purpose. We are on our own to create such significance and purpose as we can out of the chaos of everyday life. In the face of fundamental emptiness, we are to make up for what is missing by inventing it.

Atheistic existentialism is a kind of nihilism, the philosophical-political position that all values are without foundation and, in the extreme, nothing can be known. It is the repudiation of established beliefs

---

6. See Bloom, "Alfred, Lord Tennyson," 591–638.

CHAPTER 11. AVOIDANCE THROUGH DISTRACTION

and conventional morality, an intellectual demolition derby conducted on the playing field of skepticism peppered with cynicism. This derby requires each person to devise a one-off philosophy of meaning. You invent yours and I invent mine. Sartre captured the imagination of countless university students and professors. No sideline player, he had been actively involved in French resistance movements during WWII.

Few contemporary philosophers promote his once trendy doctrine and most never did. Sartrean existentialism, popular in the salons but less so in departments of philosophy, has gone the way of classical Marxism. Apart from a few remaining pockets of interest scattered here and there along the corridors of English departments, it is all but dead. I mention atheistic existentialism to highlight how philosophies that become quasi-religions can be comforting, but only as long as you do not hear the word *malignancy* from a physician.

Christianity insists that life has a purpose, our significance lies in fulfilling that purpose, and anything short of doing so leaves us spiritually bankrupt. By embracing this purpose, we become persons who endure rather than shadowy ones who may not. Jesus pointed to the great paradox of existence. To find your true *self*, and with it the fulfilling life God intends, you must first lose it (Matt 10:39, 16:25), which I take to mean abandon the artificial props we mistakenly take for genuine life.

Utopianism

Some who long for a better world become so consumed with perfecting it that they think about little else. God, according to Christianity, summons us to contribute to the enhancement of society. Wanting to improve it, however, is different from trying to perfect it. We may be able to assist God in facilitating the good, just, and noble, but we must ultimately leave to God the business of fully bringing them into existence.

Since belief in the existence of God seems to be going out of fashion in much of the Western World, people look for something in which to believe. The British journalist and late-life convert Malcolm Muggeridge (1903–90) suggests that, for a contemporary Westerner, there are only two reasonable alternatives: Christianity and utopianism.[7] In addition to being a journalist, Muggeridge was a literary pundit, media

---

7. See Muggeridge, *Jesus Rediscovered*; Muggeridge, *Jesus: The Man Who Lives*; Muggeridge, *Chronicles of Wasted Time*.

personality, and sharp-tongued satirist. As Muggeridge well knew, *utopia* means *no place*. It comes from the Greek *ou* (not) and *topos* (place). Thomas More (1478–1535) used the term as the title for his well-known sixteenth-century masterpiece.

Utopianism involves unshakable faith in the idea of progress, which has a long history.[8] Contemporary utopian movements often center on education, population control, forms of government, technological advance, wealth redistribution, environmental management, food and water supplies, medical care, or applications of behavioral science.[9] Many of these pursuits are noble. At issue is whether any of them is capable of perfecting human nature and by implication society, especially given that the predatory drive to control others and their resources is powerful and resilient.

When we hear of modern atrocities, we tend to view them as the actions of the uneducated and unenlightened. The Nazi Holocaust, however, took place in what was arguably the most educated and enlightened culture in history. It was the land of Gutenberg and Luther; of Bach, Beethoven, Brahms, and Wagner in music; of Goethe, Lessing, Mann, and Hesse in literature; of Hegel, Heidegger, Kant, and Husserl in philosophy; of Duerer, Ernst, Holbein, and Klee in art; and as just a small sampling of Germany's contributors to science, of Kepler, Koch, Wegener, and Heisenberg.

Sophie Scholl is a German film about a twenty-one-year-old Christian and her brother who were arrested in 1943 for distributing anti-Nazi leaflets. During her trial, Sophie insists that Germany is going to lose the war ("just look at the map") and that Hitler was insane to send 300,000 German soldiers to the eastern front. Her statements so outrage the judge that he orders her executed. In the film, even high-ranking officers in the military, who ought to know better, remain convinced that the Third Reich is destined to become Germany's longed-for utopia.

It is simplistic to explain the emergence of Nazi ideology and the inhumanity to which it led by blaming them on the economic inflation caused by the punitive Treaty of Versailles. Massive inflation was no doubt a contributing cause, as was Hitler's desire to acquire more land on which to produce food for the Reich. These are secondary to a more

---

8. See Nisbet, *Idea of Progress*; McCord, *Voyages to Utopia*; Manuel and Manuel, *Utopian Thought*. The last of these contains an excellent introductory essay, "The Utopian Propensity," 1–29.

9. See Skinner, *Walden Two*.

fundamental cause, however, which is flawed human nature. As unlikely as it may seem, some version of Nazism, directed against one group or another, could emerge again.[10] The Holocaust took place within the lifetime of some who may read this book.

The hope of improving human nature is admirable and everyone, especially Christians, ought to strive for constructive social change. Who among us would not like people to act more virtuously? How many of us would vote against curtailing crime, imperialistic war, or reducing the threat of nuclear annihilation? But incremental improvements offer little protection against the resolve of persuasive leaders who pander to the masses. Horrors taking place today are every bit as barbaric as what happened in ancient Rome or medieval Europe. Vlad the Impaler, the fifteenth-century Romanian prince known for mounting the heads of vanquished foes on stakes, was no worse than contemporary zealots who behead their victims on TV or kill thousands of innocent civilians by crashing planes into skyscrapers. In 2001, the terrorists who attacked the World Trade Center were well-educated. Scientific and technological progress has advanced more rapidly than moral progress seems to have. The ever-widening gap between the two may bring an end to civilization long before the sun burns out. Unless, of course, God continues to preserve it. Even our most gifted philosophers have failed to explain why people act altruistically when they do, why they sometimes take incredible risks for others when there is nothing in it for them.[11] Nor have our best psychologists demonstrated *how* to increase an individual's inclination to act altruistically. This leaves open the question of just how close society can come to perfecting itself. We sometimes act like beasts and other times like angels. Christianity suggests that the tendency to act like beasts will remain in the gene pool of the human heart.

Authentic Living

Living authentically cannot be based on mistaken religion or a counterfeit god.[12] Insofar as we derive our sense of well-being from a false religion, life is likely to be off-kilter. Many widely touted strategies for living, including self-improvement programs, appeal to the desire

---

10. See Sinclair, *It Can't Happen Here*.
11. See Rachels, *Moral Philosophy*.
12. See Keller, *Counterfeit Gods*; Keller, *The Reason for God*.

to control outcomes and therefore place us at the mercy of circumstance. It does not make sense to allow our states of mind to depend on something so fraught with unpredictability.[13] We may someday find ourselves working for a hostile supervisor, or during a routine physical exam learn we have a terminal disease. We may be prosperous today but on the financial ropes tomorrow. Even the young and beautiful, if they live long enough, become old and decrepit.

Poorly educated or psychopathic religious leaders may promise that becoming a Christian will give you a comfortable life. Embracing Christ is more likely to give you an uncomfortable one. If you live in certain parts of the world, it might even kill you. Many Christians have forfeited their lives for refusing to renounce Jesus, and while some have marched to the stake with joy, far more probably went to it in anguish. Nothing can preserve and protect us from the unforeseen or inevitable. But a living relationship with God may enable us to see beyond both.

Whatever gets in the way of God becoming an ongoing presence in your life is a distraction, and whatever encourages you to move toward God is a blessing. Life presents us with many imitation heavens that will not, and indeed cannot, enable us to avoid our appointment in Samarra. The saga of history is the story of people trying to find something in place of God that will bring them happiness. But none of it does for long, not wealth, wars, cruelty, ambition, empires, or enslaving others. No lasting joy comes from avoiding God.

Closing Thoughts

People can distract themselves from reckoning with life's big questions in many ways. One is a preoccupation with acquiring power. Another is the consuming love of money. For some, it is striving for status, social standing, and position. Others build their lives around the quest for pleasurable experiences. Some develop a self-absorption that precludes attention to anyone or anything else, and some distract themselves with obsessive intellectual pursuits or engrossing hobbies. Still others throw themselves into one or another form of utopianism through social action. There is also compulsive gambling, the oblivion of alcohol and drugs, or other mind-numbing addictions. All of these are false religions that crowd out thoughts of God.

---

13. See Gladwell, *Outliers*.

CHAPTER 11. AVOIDANCE THROUGH DISTRACTION

Preview

Christianity is rooted in Judaism, to which it owes a considerable debt. Although the ancient Israelites occasionally adopted religious beliefs and practices of the surrounding tribes, they ultimately embraced monotheism, which we will discuss in the next chapter.

Part III. **PIVOTAL QUESTIONS**

Chapter 12. What Does Christianity Owe to Judaism?

FOR MANY YEARS, I failed to appreciate the importance of Judaism to Christianity. Christians sometimes distance themselves from the roots of their faith and the significance of the Old or First Testament.[1] Whenever people in the Western World think of God, however, they tend automatically to conceive of a single God. For this and much else, they are indebted to the Jews.

Some scholars suggest there is evidence that humanity started out believing in a single god. Even if this is true, from the dawn of recorded history, about six thousand years ago, polytheistic religion was the norm until the ancient Hebrews embraced monotheism. Belief in only one God is a counterintuitive idea, and Hebraic insistence on it made the Israelites distinctly unpopular with the other tribes in the ancient Middle East. It also raised a problem that continues to challenge theologians.

Imagine that you lived 5,000 years ago in Thebes, 500 miles south of the Mediterranean Sea, on the east bank of the Nile. As summer approached, it would be natural to pay homage to Hapi, the god of the annual flood that deposited rich silt along the Nile's banks. Without enough silt, the autumn harvest would be sparse and famine would follow. If you were a pregnant Egyptian woman, you might also petition Hathor for protection when you came to term.

If you lived in Athens 2,000 years later, 1,000 years before Jesus, and found yourself smitten, you might appeal to Aphrodite, goddess of love,

---

1. See Nirenberg, *Anti-Judaism*.

asking her to prompt your beloved to return your affection. And, if you were about to address a group of citizens to enlist their support, you might pray to Hermes, the god of eloquence. For a sense of what it might have felt like to live at that time, see Mary Renault's *Last of the Wine*.

At the time of Christ, if you were a Roman commander about to go into battle, you might ask Mars, deity of war, to smile favorably on your campaign. And, if you were a sailor, you would likely address your petitions to Neptune. But the "whim of a god was a variable thing"[2] and you could not count on the goodwill of any of the gods because they could be capricious.

Westerners often view polytheistic religions as primitive. This, however, is not necessarily the case, as would be obvious to anyone raised as a Hindu. Moreover, many Hindus, especially in the West, tend to view Hindu gods as incarnations or reflections of a single deity. Belief in at least two gods appears to be easier on the human psyche than belief in only one. Jewish and Christian theologians still struggle with the question of how an omnipotent God could also be benevolent.

Of any of the arguments available to an atheist, the existence of evil may be the strongest, and it suggests why polytheism can prove attractive. Whether you believe in two gods or many, as long as you imagine them in a struggle between good and bad, right and wrong, the problem of evil does not arise. If you believe in only one God, however, you face the challenge of trying to explain why a loving God allows horrible things to happen.

Monotheism introduced the problem, which may be partly why ancient polytheistic peoples seem to have regarded the Jews as narrow-minded and intolerant. Global patterns of religious belief are strikingly different today than they were two thousand years ago, when only a tiny fraction of the world's population believed in a single God. Of the eight billion people now alive, roughly a third identify themselves as Christian, about a quarter as Islamic, and under one percent as Jewish. All three are Abrahamic religions because they trace their origins to Abraham in the book of Genesis. Each is decidedly monotheistic, and together they represent well over half the world's population. Two-thousand years ago, Christianity was non-existent, Islam would not appear for 600 years, and much of the world remained polytheistic or embraced cosmic principles as religions.

---

2. Holland, *Dominion*, 30.

CHAPTER 12. WHAT DOES CHRISTIANITY OWE TO JUDAISM?

Monotheistic Religion as Interpersonal

Thomas Cahill points to an important byproduct of monotheism: "Out of an age of tall tales of warriors and kings," he writes, "comes this story of a skeptical, worldly patriarch's [Abraham's] trust in a disembodied voice. This is becoming, however incredibly, the story of an interpersonal relationship."[3] Cahill highlights the close connection between monotheism and a developing sense of personal identity.[4] Each human being now bears responsibility for his or her own sin, and a new sense of individual accountability emerges. Many students of religion are so accustomed to emphasizing the corporate nature of Jewish worship that they miss the Old Testament concern with individual worship.

With the prospect of a deeper and more intimate relationship with God also came the possibility of deeper interpersonal connections among people. Because human beings are both biological and spiritual beings, such connections are always in part spiritual. It is not as though no one had ever thought about how people related to each other. But prior to the emergence of monotheism, there was less of what Martin Buber in the twentieth century called "I-Thou" in contrast to "I-It."[5] The importance of this to human development and the advance of civilization was tremendous.

The Interpersonal Covenant

Both Christians and Jews believe God established a covenant with the ancient Hebrews. A covenant differs from a contract, which is an exchange of promises supported by what attorneys call consideration, something of value. It takes the form of "I will *do* something for you, such as repair your roof, and you in turn will do something for me, such as pay this amount of money." A covenant, by contrast, takes the form of I will *be* something to you, and you will be something to me.

As with many religious beliefs, there is no reason automatically to dismiss the idea of a covenant as wishful thinking by the ancient Israelites. Why God chose them is unclear, but it would have been equally unclear if God had selected any other group. The Old Testament

---

3. Cahill, *The Gifts of the Jews*, 70.
4. Cahill, *The Gifts of the Jews*, 72.
5. Buber, *I and Thou*.

contains the record of their struggle to believe in only one God and the promises contained in the covenant. It is also a strikingly candid record of their failures to honor it.

Contemporary Jews often react negatively to the suggestion that Christianity is the continuation and fulfillment of Judaism. Christians take the Old Testament, and by implication Judaism, to be a prelude to the appearance on earth of the God-Mortal, Jesus.

How Monotheism Emerged

Belief in one God came out of the Middle East from Hebraic religion. Both Jews and Christians believe God nurtured this belief within the Hebrew tribes, whose prophets repeatedly called them away from polytheism. Without what Jews and Christians believe to have been God's involvement with these tribes, perhaps no religious person today would be monotheistic. Unwavering belief in a single God took a long time to solidify and early Hebrew writings mention other gods. The early Israelites lived within and reflected the views of a polytheistic world, and even after they realized there was but a single God, they periodically defaulted into old patterns. God, however, shaped their thought-forms. It took centuries for them to settle on belief in one and only one God, and to move beyond trying to hedge their bets by paying homage to multiple deities.

Monotheistic belief set the Hebrew tribes at odds with others, whose members found the Hebraic claims both arrogant and insulting. The resulting conflicts were often hostile and sometimes lethal. Hebrews insisted not only that their God YHWH was superior, but that there were in fact no competing gods. YHWH appears to be related to words that have to do with *being* and *becoming*. Believing in other gods, they insisted, was idolatrous. Challenging the existence of these gods would have been like insulting the Monarch in an English pub on a Saturday night. Because the history of Judaism as narrated in the Bible is foundational to Christianity, I want to summarize it.

Early Monarchy

Almost two centuries after the death of Moses, which seems to have occurred in the thirteenth century BC, the Hebrew tribes installed Saul as their first king. Nearly every school-age child knows the story of how David, a young shepherd, killed Goliath with a slingshot. An ancient rock-and-sling, however, was a weapon of war that should not be confused with what we tend to think of as a slingshot. It included a rock, weighing perhaps five pounds, that was rotated rapidly within a sling. It could easily prove fatal. David eventually succeeded Saul as king and Solomon succeeded his father, David. The lands the Hebrews controlled lay along major trade routes, and what had once been twelve loosely confederated tribes became a wealthy kingdom. This wealth enabled Solomon around 966 BC to build an impressively opulent Temple. Solomon's taxation measures became increasingly onerous, but the people put up with them during his lifetime.

When Rehoboam succeeded his father Solomon, the leaders of the ten northern tribes petitioned him for tax relief. Heeding the counsel of his young friends, rather than of older and wiser advisors, Rehoboam threatened the people with even heavier tax burdens. In response, the northern tribes seceded, which left two kingdoms, each governed by its own monarch, the Northern Kingdom of Israel and the Southern Kingdom of Judah. This division occurred between 931 and 920 BC. It is from Judah, not Israel, that contemporary Jews trace their ancestry and from which the word *Jewish* derives. The terms *Kingdom of Israel* and *Kingdom of Judah* can be confusing. Both comprised Israelites, but even in the Bible, for example in Isaiah, Israel sometimes refers only to the Southern Kingdom. What further lends to this confusion is, first, that the name for the modern Jewish country in the Middle East is State of Israel, not State of Judah. Second, whether they later belonged to the Northern or Southern Kingdom, all members of the Hebrew tribes called themselves *Israelites*, for which they had good reason. According to the Old Testament, Abraham was the father of Isaac, who in turn was the father of Jacob. Genesis informs us that God gave Jacob the new name *Israel* (see Gen 32:28 and 35:10). This word can mean either "striven with God" or "saved by God."

The Northern Kingdom

Early Hebrew worship frequently included homage to the image of an animal, or worship of the storm and fertility god Baal. As it appears in ancient texts, *Baal* can also refer to other gods, one of which may have been the sun god of the Canaanites. It is an imprecise term that means *lord* or *master*. The worship of Baal sometimes included worship of fertility deities and encouragement of sexual license. Against this backdrop of the blending together of heterogeneous religious beliefs and practices, what is technically called *syncretism*, the Hebrews believed that as long as they continued to make ritual sacrifices, God would uphold and protect them. They prospered materially for two centuries but declined spiritually. The Old Testament writer Hosea provides this sobering commentary on conditions in the Northern Kingdom after its secession: "There is no truth, nor mercy, nor knowledge of God in the land" (Hos 4:1, KJV).

Assyria, which was becoming the dominant power in the region, threatened the Northern Kingdom, which inconveniently stood between Assyria and the Mediterranean. Israel eventually became a vassal state on which the Assyrians intermittently imposed deportations. The only power capable of limiting Assyrian imperialism was Egypt, so it was to Egypt that the ruler of the Northern Kingdom turned. As would also happen with the Southern Kingdom more than a century later, the Egyptians proved to be a disappointment. Israel was on its own.

Patriotic and nationalistic sentiments continued to run high in the Northern Kingdom, and following many years of placation, it finally revolted. The Kingdom held out in Samaria against an Assyrian siege for three years, until in 723/722 BC Sargon II succeeded in conquering it. His troops annihilated the forces of Israel, which would never again be a political entity.

The Assyrians deported tens of thousands of Israelites, relocating them to Mesopotamia, Persia, and areas south of the Caspian Sea. Sargon then began to replace the deported Israelites with people brought in from other territories. These immigrants intermarried with the remaining Hebrews, forming a mixed population that remained under Assyrian rule. They became known as Samaritans. Many Israelites from the Northern Kingdom seemed to have little desire to return to their homeland, perhaps because they had become rooted in their new regions.

The Southern Kingdom

The Southern Kingdom continued to stand between Assyria and Egypt. It was therefore subject to whichever of these two formidable powers was currently dominant. Sargon's son and successor, Sennacherib,

CHAPTER 12. WHAT DOES CHRISTIANITY OWE TO JUDAISM?

moved against the Kingdom of Judah and carried off large numbers of its citizens who lived outside the protective walls of Jerusalem (2 Kgs 18:13). The full conquest of the Southern Kingdom, however, would not come for another century. Solomon's Temple and the Jewish dynasty temporarily remained intact.

Under successive monarchs, the Kingdom of Judah slowly recovered from Assyrian savagery, but as in the Northern Kingdom, the people lapsed into the worship of *Baalim*, the plural of the Semitic *Baal*, which as noted above means an idol or false god. Regional religions, such as the child-sacrificing cult of Moloch, continued. Although there were brief periods of reform under Kings Hezekiah and Josiah, the reforms did not last. Prophets, such as Isaiah, issued warnings, but mostly without effect. Annihilation loomed. Egypt was threatening a weakened Assyria, and the Kingdom of Judah was in danger of becoming collateral damage. The Assyrian Empire finally surrendered, not to the Egyptians but to the Medes and Babylonians, who divided the former Assyrian territories between them. No longer worried about Assyria, the Egyptians began to concern themselves with the Babylonians, whose king, Nebuchadnezzar II, had already defeated them once, in 605 BC.

The Southern Kingdom at first subjugated itself to Babylon, but once again nationalistic impulses boiled over into revolt. Reminiscent of the Northern Kingdom, the people clung to the belief that ritual sacrifices, along with Solomon's Temple, would protect them. The prophet Jeremiah warned the people to turn from idolatry and excess, but his warnings only infuriated them, and they nearly succeeded in murdering Jeremiah. He found asylum, first in Mizpah, north of Jerusalem, and later in Egypt, where he died.

For four or five years, Judah was able to stave off total defeat at the hands of Nebuchadnezzar, but Jerusalem capitulated in 597 BC, when the Babylonians carted off thousands of its citizens to what is today Iraq. The Babylonians installed Zedekiah as vassal ruler over what remained (2 Kgs 24:18). After nearly a decade of further religious and moral decay, rebellion once more flared up, encouraged by the familiar hope that Egypt would come to the rescue. The Egyptians temporarily forced Nebuchadnezzar to lift his siege of Jerusalem, but the Babylonians again closed in on the city, which despite famine held out for more than a year.

PART III. PIVOTAL QUESTIONS

In 587/586 BC, through a breach in the city wall, the Babylonians entered Jerusalem.[6] This time, they meant business.

Perhaps because its mere existence seemed to encourage rebellion, the Babylonians demolished Solomon's Temple, the centerpiece of Jewish hope and worship. Its destruction proved psychologically devastating to inhabitants of the Southern Kingdom. The Babylonians transported its sacred vessels to Babylon and distributed them among pagan shrines. Only a shadow of its former self, Jerusalem's major buildings no longer existed and its walls lay in ruins. The conquerors relocated perhaps 50,000 Jews into regions close to the Chaldean capital of Babylon, leaving behind the maimed or decrepit to tend the land and prevent it from turning fallow. This geographic dislocation contributed substantially to the Jewish sense of devastation. The straight-line distance from Jerusalem to Babylon is about 500 miles, but because of the terrain, the journey on foot was considerably longer. Those who survived were impressed into slavery, and as the prophet Amos had predicted, they would become the *remnant*. The Jews were not subjected to overly harsh treatment and it seems that some were able to obtain their freedom.

The Babylonians were astute enough to recognize that a local government was necessary to maintain order in what remained of the Southern Kingdom, so they installed Gedaliah to oversee those not relocated. His capital was Mizpah, which triggered the return from nearby territories of Jewish exiles who had managed to avoid deportation. Another ethnic Jew, in league with the Ammonites from the east side of the Jordan river, led a small band in the assassination of Gedaliah and began to force a migration to Ammon. A Jewish military commander managed to thwart this, but many Jews feared retaliation by Nebuchadnezzar for the murder of Gedaliah, and in search of asylum left for Egypt.

A crucial development in Jewish history was that the Babylonians allowed the relocated Jews to settle in colonies comprising their own clans and families. This tribal continuity helped sustain their ethnic identity and religious ethos. Without it, both would likely have vanished, which is what had happened in the north.

For centuries, a fierce nationalism had prevented the Jewish people from heeding the warnings of their prophets against idolatry and excess, but now the proclamations of Ezekiel and Jeremiah returned to haunt them. The principal meaning of *prophet*, as used in much of the Old

---

6. See Humphreys, "Historical Contexts of the Biblical Communities," 41.

CHAPTER 12. WHAT DOES CHRISTIANITY OWE TO JUDAISM?

Testament, is not one who predicts events but one who expresses the desires and intentions of God. The term *prophecy* took on the meaning of prediction later. Through a long series of painful lessons, they concluded that, far from having abandoned the Jews, God intentionally brought them to despair and used the Assyrians and Babylonians to drive them toward undiluted monotheism. God, they believed, forced them to learn what it meant to be faithful, and as Jesus put it centuries later, to worship God in spirit and in truth (John 4:23).

Prior to the destruction of the Temple, the Jews had largely concerned themselves with ceremonial observances. Like people today who believe that regardless of what they think, feel, or do, they need only show up now and then at church, many in the Southern Kingdom had comforted themselves with the crude conviction that carrying out concrete rites, such as animal slaughter, was all God required. With impunity, they could continue their involvement in syncretistic cults, peppered with whatever erotic indulgences struck their fancy. Now, however, Jews had become clear about the force and significance of the First Commandment. They were not to put anyone or anything before God.

The Spiritual and the Ritualized

After the conquest of the Southern Kingdom, the Babylonian Empire slid into decline. In 539-538 BC, the Persian Empire, which now encompassed the Medes, overran it. Cyrus, the Persian King, allowed the Jews to return to their homeland, gave back the sacred vessels confiscated by Nebuchadnezzar, and helped fund[7] the rebuilding of the Temple. Cyrus may have recognized that a restored Jerusalem would have been inconceivable to the Jews without it, and he was keen on fostering loyalty and stability. Some of the Jews from Samaria, whose ancestors had been exiled from the Northern Kingdom, tried unsuccessfully to participate in the rebuilding of the Temple. The resulting tensions still existed when the New Testament was written five or six centuries later. See, for example, the discourse between Jesus and the Samaritan woman in John 4:1-38.

Precisely why, in human terms, Cyrus allowed the return of the Jews has been a matter of conjecture and debate. It may have been that he was astute enough to recognize that it was undesirable to have large numbers of dispossessed and potentially disgruntled people in his realm, which

---

7. See Humphreys, "Historical Contexts of the Biblical Communities," 40.

remained under threat of an Egyptian assault. The many kindnesses he afforded the Jews surely built into them a debt of gratitude, which he could cash in for loyalty if needed. Astute Jewish observers had not, however, missed the connection between spiritual decay in the Northern Kingdom and its geopolitical fate. The Persian Empire lasted over two centuries, until the successors of Alexander the Great divided it up.

The half-century without a temple and the rituals that went with it cemented in monotheism and made Jewish worship decidedly more spiritual. This was a remarkable step forward, a stunning achievement, in that virtually all religion, as it then existed in the region, centered on sacrifice. The Jewish people would come to understand that true religion involves more than parting with a valuable animal. It had to do with the reorientation and commitment of one's entire being. See Rom 12:1–2 for how the Apostle Paul carries this theme forward.

Jews had been through a thousand years of nationalistic preoccupation and syncretistic religion, punctuated only by brief periods of genuine worship. They had failed to be the light of the world, which was what many Jews believed God intended. Now, through adversity, they became committed monotheists. The Babylonian Captivity was the beginning of what scholars call the *diaspora*, a term that means any dislocation and dispersion of a people from their place of origin. But the Jewish diaspora refers to what happened to the Jews after the conquest of the Southern Kingdom, and secondarily after their large-scale revolt against the Romans. This revolt lasted on and off for sixty-five years, from before AD 70 to AD 135, when Emperor Hadrian put a decisive end to a rebellion led by the charismatic Bar-Kokhba.

The diaspora after the Babylonian conquest paved the way for more spirituality. The five decades during which they no longer had a temple, and probably offered few if any animal sacrifices, made all the difference. Jewish worship now came even more from the heart and the Jewish people developed a new resolve to obey the commandments. One New Testament scholar suggests that this stress on following the law is reflected in "reading the 'book of the law of Moses' before all the people" as recorded in the eighth chapter of the book of Nehemiah in the Old Testament.[8] This was admirable in that it reflected their renewed dedication to holiness and living in communion with God.

---

8. See Hagner, "Paul, Judaism, and the Law," 367.

CHAPTER 12. WHAT DOES CHRISTIANITY OWE TO JUDAISM?

It was not long, however, before a redoubled focus on obeying the letter of the law surfaced in what is known as Second Temple Judaism. It is called *Second Temple* because the Babylonians razed the original one built by Solomon. Second Temple Judaism expressed itself in the emergence of groups like the Pharisees, who slowly developed ritualistic observances that could become burdensome. As noted in chapter 3, many Pharisees were sincere in their efforts to honor God. Paul himself was a Pharisee, who prior to his experience on the road to Damascus was relentless in doing what he believed God wanted.

Significance of the Ten Commandments

The term Law, as used in the Old Testament, can mean different things, from dietary injunctions to codes of morality. Christians who recognize their debt to Judaism face the question of which specific parts of the Law remain in force. If my brother dies, for example, am I obligated to marry his widow to perpetuate his hereditary line? Students of comparative religion recognize that the Ten Commandments resemble other codes that existed at the time, but only the Jewish Law explicitly centered on monotheism. Both Jews and Christians regard them as the enduring centerpiece of morality, and some believe that the human heart contains an indelible impression of them. Christians also believe that the Ten Commandments have an educational purpose, which is to demonstrate that we are unable or unwilling to live up to them. According to Christianity, this paved the way for humanity to recognize its need for salvation.

Jesus did what we could or would not do. He kept the Law by loving both God and people as they were meant to be loved. "If you love me, keep my commands," says Jesus in the Gospel of John (14:15, NIV), and Christians believe this means loving God without reserve and treating others as we want to be treated. The Jews did not live out the Ten Commandments, and neither has anyone else except Jesus. In the third book of the Old Testament (Lev 19:18), we read, "love your neighbor as yourself," and in the fifth (Deut 6:5) quoted by Jesus, "You must love the Lord your God with all your heart, all your soul, and all your mind" (Matt 22:37–39, NLT). When asked which commandment Jesus took to be the greatest, he quotes these imperatives, adding "on these commandments hang all the law and the prophets" (Matt 22:40, KJV).

That we do not do what Jesus taught tells us a great deal. Our deficiency lies not so much in what we do or do not do, but in what it reveals about who and what we are and are not, about the *dis*-ease of our inner beings. We have a serious condition that only God can fix. The Law exists, in part, to make clear that we need God through the Holy Spirit to give us a change of mind and heart.

Christianity and Personalized Monotheism

Without monotheism, there could have been no Christianity. Christian faith rests on belief in a single God, and Christianity would have made no sense to anyone who did not already share this belief. For Christianity to take hold, God first had to implant within the Jewish psyche the idea embodied in the *Shema*, which remains the focal point of Jewish worship: "Hear, O Israel, the Lord our God, the Lord is one" (Deut 6:4, ESV).

Most Christians today are not ethnic Jews, and therefore many Christians are unaware of the debt they owe to Judaism. The worldview of these Christians often includes, explicitly or implicitly, the assumption that Christianity began as a new religion. This is true in one sense but not in another. They may recall, at the margins of consciousness, that Jesus' early followers were Jewish, as he was, but they quickly move on to insist that, because most Jews rejected Jesus, Christianity has nothing to do with Judaism.

Human history centers on a two-part drama. The Old Testament reveals what happened in Act One. Act Two begins with Jesus and is carried forward by Peter and Paul, who were both ethnic Jews and figured prominently in the early church. The book of Acts contains this history. In Bibles, it appears as Acts of the Apostles, but it could also be called Acts of the Holy Spirit. Over the past few decades, scholars have paid increasing attention to their Jewishness, especially Paul's, and prominent among them is N. T. Wright.[9] Paul remained a Jew until he died, and his beliefs about Jesus came from the vantage point of his heritage. Christianity, according to Paul, was a continuation of the faith in which he was raised.

Like Judaism, Christianity existed in a religiously hostile environment. Through a puppet regime, the polytheistic Roman Empire

---

9. See Wright, *Paul in Fresh Perspective*; Wright, *Paul: A Biography*; Wright, *Paul and the Faithfulness of God*.

CHAPTER 12. WHAT DOES CHRISTIANITY OWE TO JUDAISM?

occupied and ruled what later became known as Palestine, where most events in the New Testament took place. For decades, the Romans regarded Christianity as a Jewish sect and for a long time tolerated it. This greatly concerned those Jews who had not embraced the New Way. As the number of Christians grew, they became increasingly worried that they would lose the exemption the Romans had given them *not* to have to worship the emperor. This sense of threat may have motivated some Jews to encourage Roman persecution of Christians.

Jesus reaffirmed the monotheistic belief that God had created the universe and continues to uphold it. Reinforcing the spiritual turn the Jews had taken five hundred years earlier after their return from Babylon, Jesus stressed that worship of God begins in the heart. He highlighted the understanding that monotheism had begun to reach, that each individual could enjoy a personal relationship with God. It is one thing to say we believe in God, but quite another to say we have a relationship with God. God is not a person in the sense you and I are, but describing God that way may be the best we can do. At root, the question is whether God is a conscious being with intentions. Someone *in* Christ could now act, think, and pray as God's true child. Even for Jews, who regarded themselves as God's chosen people, this was new.

For polytheists, it would have been extraordinary. Imagine an Egyptian in 3,000 BC trying to have an intimate relationship with the flood god. Or, a Greek in 1,000 BC establishing one with the goddess of love. Or, a Roman soldier 2,000 years ago communicating in a similar way with the god of war. Such gods might or might not care, and people at the time would probably have found it odd to call them loving. It would have been strange indeed for people in the ancient world to try to establish anything like the close relationship with their gods that Jesus taught we could have with the one true God.

The Gift of Faith and a New Nature

Christians view faith as a gift from God given through the Holy Spirit. With this gift comes an additional nature, with desires and capacities that are new. The two natures will always remain in conflict. The two are what Paul in the New Testament calls *spirit* and *flesh*.

Under extreme conditions, our primal nature may quickly emerge, as evidenced by what happened in 1820 when an enormous sperm whale rammed and sank the eighty-seven-foot whaling ship *Essex*.[10] The crew of the *Essex* abandoned ship and in whaleboats soon suffered from dehydration, starvation, and exposure. They began to consume the bodies of deceased colleagues but eventually were driven to draw lots to decide who among the survivors they would sacrifice as food. The sinking of the *Essex* helped inspire Herman Melville to write *Moby-Dick*, first published in 1851. Members of the Donner (Donner-Reed) Party also resorted to cannibalism, eating the bodies of those who died, but unlike survivors from the *Essex*, they seem not to have sacrificed anyone. The Donner Party comprised eighty-seven pioneers who became stranded during the winter of 1846-1847 in the Sierra Nevada mountains. Only forty-eight survived. I have no evidence to prove that a Christian, under such conditions, would be less likely than a non-Christian to act like a cannibal. But I would like to think this might be the case.

Although the Holy Spirit nudges a person in the direction of altruism, God does not override human freedom, and even the most devout Christian can yield to primal instincts. It does not always take much to peel away the veneer of civilization. In 2021, my wife and I were following directives to remain indoors, not socialize in large groups, keep a safe distance if we did, and wear masks to prevent catching or transmitting the new virus. In a warehouse store, we saw people ready to assault each other over a few rolls of toilet paper. Again, I would like to believe that few if any of them were Christians. It is important to recognize, however, that although the Holy Spirit pulls a Christian in the direction of goodness, God does not override that Christian's freedom of choice. Even the most devout Christian is at risk of reverting to the ways of the jungle.

Faith enables us to recognize Jesus for who he was, God come to earth, and who he still is. Jesus was from another realm. Christians view him as the embodiment of the *logos*, a Greek word that suggests order and rationality, the antithesis of chaos and disorder. The New Testament contains many passages suggesting that God is forever seeking us, ready to give us faith. Neither you nor I can will ourselves into believe anything, since beliefs are always attempts to decide what is true. We simply cannot persuade ourselves of something our reason rejects. Christians through the ages have insisted that if you earnestly search, you will find God, sometimes when and where you least expect to. It is unlikely that you are reading this book if you are not open to Christianity and perhaps

---

10. Philbrick, *Heart of the Sea*.

CHAPTER 12. WHAT DOES CHRISTIANITY OWE TO JUDAISM?

part-way down the road to believing there is a God who might honor such a search. If you are beginning to suspect that Jesus was who and what the New Testament claims, you may be surprised one day to discover that he has become your Lord. Philosopher Peter Kreeft refers to this as installing Christ as one's Supreme Commander. Christianity teaches that Jesus overcame humanity's great enemy, death, and that our long-term hope, as individuals and as a species, is in him. This is why Christians use the term *savior*. Jesus began the rescue of flawed and frail humanity from the stark consequences of rejecting God.

Imagine a cruise ship on which all passengers and crew are infected with a fatal bacterium, but most remain unaware of it. Some are in first-class cabins and take their meals at the officers' tables in the best dining room. Members of the crew dwell in cramped quarters below deck, and rush through meals on the way to their next chore. To live, passengers, officers, and members of the crew all need an antibiotic. There is a doctor on board who runs through passageways frantically warning everyone of the urgency. But most believe the doctor is overreacting and put off going to the health center.

There will be an *omega point* in human history,[11] a climactic destiny when Christ will summon to everlasting life all who have given their allegiance to God. I am borrowing this term from the Jesuit paleontologist, Teilhard de Chardin. In the person of Christ, God may be standing at the door of your heart, ready to give you that gift (Rev 3:20) and hoping you will recognize his voice. As one theologian put it long ago, God beckons us to surrender what we cannot keep, to gain what we cannot lose. Although many have probably used this phrase, to my knowledge it was John Calvin who first used it.

Monotheism and the Trinity

The Christian assertion that Jesus was God in the flesh was revolutionary. It must have astounded many when they first heard it. Yet, however mindboggling the idea may have been, those who embraced the Way reached that very conclusion, supported by such events as one of Jesus' skeptical disciples declaring, "My Lord and my God" (John 20:28, NIV).

One of Paul's letters in the New Testament reports that over 500 people saw the *risen* Jesus, and that many of them were still alive when

---

11. Teilhard, *The Phenomenon of Man*.

Paul wrote it (1 Cor 15:6). We need not quibble over the exact number, but it must have been considerable. This and much else propelled them to proclaim a reality that seemed at odds with monotheistic Jewish teaching and was certain to turn them into outcasts, at a time when a person's family and community established his or her identity, and were therefore extremely important. Many Jewish traditionalists no doubt wondered what these renegades were up to. Were they reverting to polytheism? To a first-century Jew who did not even accept Jesus as the Messiah, the claim that he was God was blasphemous, and the Gospels contain many accounts of how outraged Jews were at claims even hinting at the divinity of Jesus. What made matters worse was that these renegades claimed that the Holy Spirit, the same one to whom the Old Testament prophet Joel referred, now did such things as enabling people to speak in other languages (Acts 2:5-12).

Not even Paul had a vocabulary to express in philosophic terms how God, Christ, and the Holy Spirit related to one another, yet with the help of God's Spirit he intuitively grasped their interrelationships. There is no hint in Paul's writings that he doubted how everything in the universe belonged to and converged on Christ, its ultimate ruler. He was also convinced that the Holy Spirit at times guided what he said and wrote. He knew what it meant to live in, and with, the power of that Spirit, but it took centuries for the church to conceptualize and capture in words the idea of one God in three persons, what theologians came to call the Trinity. The African theologian Tertullian, who was born a century after Paul, seems to have been the first to begin to formalize this, and the church attempted to express it in contemporary philosophic terms during the fourth and fifth centuries.

Many years ago, I was sitting with the philosopher Geddes MacGregor in his study, discussing the miracle of the loaves and fishes, and how Jesus transformed a small quantity of food into enough to feed thousands. Geddes suggested that, taking the text at face value, even a skeptic would have to grant that Jesus must have been extraordinary to get so many people to bring out and share whatever food they had hidden away. Personally, I believe Jesus miraculously multiplied the food and that this was more than a trick or an instance of mass suggestibility by a charismatic rabbi. Whatever the precise explanation for this event and others like it, something of a singular nature happened. It also happened to those who became true followers of Jesus.

CHAPTER 12. WHAT DOES CHRISTIANITY OWE TO JUDAISM?

Christianity rests on the fundamental insight that there exists one and only one God. Christians, therefore, should neither forget their debt to the Jews nor how their spiritual heritage derives from Judaism. God chose the Jews to help elevate humanity and then sent Jesus to demonstrate how people needed to live in order for this to happen. The Gospels portray Jesus as the culmination of Israel's story, as launching this new humanity and building a bridge over which people could walk on their return to God. The New Testament is not about a different religion but the fulfillment of an existing one.

Christians who disparage Jews are like teenagers who rebel against their parents. One theologian writes, "There already was a 'people of God' . . . [and the Gospels tell us] the story of Jesus as the climax of that people's story." This climax "ushered in a new world order," which arrived through a Jewish redeemer who was the representative of Israel. "This new order pitted the ways of God against the ways of Caesar, and replaced the love of power with the power of love."[12]

The Old Testament portrays the history of the Jews, along with poetic prayers, startling prophecies, and other writings that record how God brought the Israelites to the realization that God was the one true God. Although scholars continue to debate how literally or figuratively to interpret different parts of the Old Testament, Christian theologians refer to the overall arc of what the Bible portrays as *salvation history*. It culminates in Jesus and what he revealed to us about God, whose essential nature he shares.

The Prophetic in the Old Testament

Christians see in the Old Testament unmistakable signs pointing to Jesus. There is no question that the Jews looked forward to the coming of a Messiah, a Christ. From its texts and the events surrounding Jesus, it is clear that they were expecting a new Moses, someone to do what Moses had done, liberate them from foreign oppression.

Although there are passages in the Old Testament that allude to the Messiah as more than human, the Jews in early first-century Palestine were focused on a political leader. Jesus was both more and less than they expected. He was less by having no interest in leading a revolt against the Romans. He was more by being both divine and human.

---

12. Wright, *How God Became King*, 112, 118, 187, 239.

PART III. PIVOTAL QUESTIONS

Closing Thoughts

The Bible tells the story of the tribes of Israel, whose members became increasingly committed to belief in a single God. This belief is counter-intuitive because it renders it more difficult to make sense of evil. One of the byproducts of monotheism was the development of the belief that faith is interpersonal, between the individual and God. We have reviewed the history of the Israelites, how and why monotheism emerged, and the difference between spiritual and ceremonial religion. Without monotheism, there would have been no Christianity. The history of Israel led to, converged on, and culminated in Jesus.

Preview

Without the Old Testament, Christian faith would never have been possible. In the next chapter, we will explore some of the criticisms that have been leveled at the New Testament, asking whether it even makes sense to base a religion on it. How much we can trust the documents in contains?

Chapter 13. Can We Trust the New Testament?

AMONG THE THEMES IN the Bible is that God has been, and continues to be, involved in history. Its overarching theme is God's offer to rescue us from the destructive self-centeredness to which we are naturally inclined. Christians take the Bible to be the record of how God, through Christ, calls human beings out of the prison of egocentricity, to become God's true children and participants in a new humanity initiated by Jesus.

In this chapter, I want to address issues and problems that have been raised about the Gospels. When we talk or write about biblical inconsistencies or mistakes, it is important to specify exactly what we mean by these terms. From the point of view of many Christians, to claim the Gospels are accurate means that, by reading them, a reasonable person will form an accurate picture of the kinds of things Jesus said and did. Viewed in this light, many of the difficulties and disputes highlighted in this chapter become trivial, irrelevant, or meaningless.

The Challenge Presented by Jesus

To the degree we are human animals, we tend to place our survival and well-being, and perhaps that of our loved ones, above the survival and wellbeing of others. To the degree we are spiritual beings, we have the God-given ability to do evil or good. How much to take care of ourselves and how much to take care of others is therefore a pivotal issue.

We have the freedom, at one extreme, to behave destructively, especially if such behavior furthers our interests. But we also have the freedom, at the other extreme, to act altruistically, placing the survival and well-being of others above our own. Most of us live in the middle, between the two extremes, balancing the welfare of others, including the wider society, with the welfare of ourselves. Even at our best, we may not always persist in altruism for long, and regardless of how well we cover it over in polite society, our primal nature takes over, especially if our life or property is threatened.

God's offer of rescue, if we accept it, is that if we persevere, God will enable us to become increasingly like Jesus. This means that we will tend, over time, to care more and more about the welfare of others, to be transformed into what the New Testament refers to as the image of Christ.

God's Self-Disclosure and the New Testament

God has at least two modes of self-disclosure. The first is through nature, which includes not only its beauty that we can appreciate but also what it suggests about God. This is what the Apostle Paul was getting at in the first chapter of his letter to Christians living in first-century Rome, that God's invisible attributes are self-evident to anyone willing to see them (Rom 1:19). God's other mode of self-disclosure is through scripture, writings the church regards as inspired and sacred.

To allow ourselves to become wrapped around the axle of debate about whether the Bible contains errors or inaccuracies brings with it the risk of pulling us away from trusting God, which is the essence of faith. The function of the Bible is to help us to get beyond it, so that we can focus on and grasp the character of God. This is hard to do if we spend too much time trying to defend the Bible against assaults on its veracity. Such defenses yield little that is productive. They may be useful to scholars, but for the rest of us, they can prove sadly distracting.

The Bible contains many different literary genres and their functions vary. The Book of Psalms, for example, is a prayer book and ancient hymnal. It is not a theological treatise. But the Letter to the Romans is. The last book in the New Testament is a metaphoric visualization of Christ's return, not a secret code to be mapped onto human history by those clever enough to have deciphered the code. All of the books in the Bible, over sixty of them, reflect the cultures, customs, and

CHAPTER 13. CAN WE TRUST THE NEW TESTAMENT?

conventions of when and where they were written, so it is important to ask who wrote them and why.

Inspiration and Composition of the Bible

Christians regard scripture as inspired. To some, this means God dictated the words of the Bible, or at least the words in the original documents, what scholars call lost *autographs*. To others, it means God prompted the biblical writers to express in their own style and vocabulary what God revealed to them. To still others, it means God was on the minds of the biblical writers who, prompted by God's Spirit, wrote down their own insights, experiences, and points of view. The church has never developed a universally accepted definition of inspiration. Rather than worrying about arriving at a precise definition, it may be more fruitful to ask whether the Bible, and particularly the New Testament, reflects what God intends us to know. This chapter is about what the New Testament is and is not.

"We can read the Bible," writes Thomas Cahill, "as a jumble of unrelated texts . . . But this is to ignore not only the powerful emotional and spiritual effect that much of the Bible has on readers . . . but also its cumulative impact on whole societies. The Bible's great moments . . . are hard to brush aside as merely human expressions."[1] Something beyond such expression seems to have been at work in the creation and preservation of its documents.

Although different Christian traditions include different books in their Bibles, most accept the books of the Old Testament and some also include those in the Apocrypha. Nearly all include the entire New Testament, which consists of four biographical narratives (Gospels), a history of the early church (Acts), twenty-one letters (Epistles), a theological essay (Romans), a sermon (Hebrews), and a symbolic vision of the end of the world (Revelation or Apocalypse). These documents make up what scholars call the New Testament *canon*.[2]

When theologians refer to the New Testament *canon*, they use that term to mean rule or standard. It derives from the Greek word *kanon*, which in turn comes from the Hebrew word *kaneh*. To say a document is

---
1. Cahill, *The Gifts of the Jews*.
2. See *Cambridge History of the Bible*; MacGregor, *Literary History of the Bible*; Nicholson, *God's Secretaries*; McGrath, *In the Beginning*. For a colorful and scholarly book, see Hamel, *The Book*.

canonical, therefore, means it is accepted as authoritative, which implies that its contents are sound and consistent with the rest of scripture. Contrary to the position held by some nineteenth and early twentieth century theologians, research has shown that the church accepted the books in the New Testament much earlier than those theologians believed. Many Christians believe God provided the Bible to the church and ensured that it remained available through the ages.

Many ancient manuscripts written after the time of Jesus, such as the Gospel of Thomas, are not regarded as authoritative. Although such books may interest scholars, it is apparent why the church never embraced them. The Gospel of Thomas, for example, is principally a hodgepodge of miscellaneous and unrelated aphorisms.

Character of the New Testament

Because Christianity centers on the New Testament, the issue becomes how much to trust it. Do its depictions of Jesus and his teachings reflect what Jesus said and did? Did Paul encounter the risen Jesus on his way from Jerusalem to Syria? Are the ideas captured in the New Testament coherent, meaningful, and relevant to contemporary society?

Had only one person written the New Testament, we could more easily categorize it as a religious invention. But at least ten different authors contributed to it. They had their unique slants, and most had specific audiences in mind. Matthew, for example, wrote his Gospel to persuade his fellow Jews that Jesus was the promised Messiah. Regardless of these differences, all the books in the New Testament contain the same message: Christ is Lord.

It is highly unlikely that the authors of its documents colluded. Some probably did not even know each other. Most, if not all, suffered persecution for their beliefs, and some gave up their lives. People do not pay such prices to maintain a conspiracy. And, if they were spreading a set of delusions, they devoted an enormous amount of time and energy doing so.

Many scholars believe the Gospel of Mark appeared before the Gospels of Matthew or Luke. Both these authors seem familiar with Mark's text and to have fleshed it out with additional details. This is hardly collusion. Most believe both Matthew and Luke had copies of Mark's gospel, and that they used it as source material. They also believe that they relied on a lost document ("*Q*") that supposedly contained sayings of Jesus. The letter Q stands for the German word for source, *Quelle*. It is worth noting that people in the ancient world seem to have had excellent memories for oral material, perhaps because so many of them were unable to read or write. If Q existed, it is likely that whoever wrote it did a pretty good job of setting down what Jesus, in fact, said on different occasions

John's Gospel is substantially different from the other three, in that it opens with a philosophically oriented prologue. Its opening verses, centered as they are upon the idea of the *Logos* (Greek for "Word"), seems decidedly Hellenistic. Much of what the other Gospels contain is missing in the Gospel of John and vice versa, which is why experts call Matthew, Mark, and Luke *synoptic*, meaning viewed from the same perspective and having similar contents. Unlike the authors of the Old Testament, nearly all those who wrote books in the New Testament lived at the same time. Something of earthshaking significance happened in Jerusalem. The question becomes to what extent we can depend on the New Testament to enlighten us about it.

Languages Behind the New Testament

Jesus probably spoke Aramaic, a Semitic language related to Hebrew, but we cannot rule out the possibility that, like many of his contemporaries in the Middle East, he was multi-lingual. Although some of the earliest manuscripts in the Bible may have been written in other languages, such as Syriac, Coptic, or Latin, these were soon translated into Greek. *Koine* Greek was "known and used by most of the peoples of the Roman Empire."[3]

The New Testament contains different grades or levels of Greek. In terms of sentence structure and vocabulary, its three most literary books are Hebrews and the two-part work by Luke, his Gospel and Acts of the Apostles. Mark and Revelation (Apocalypse), the last book in the Bible, are the least literary. They are in colloquial or conversational Greek.

God did not turn human authors into mindless automatons who took dictation. Each book in the New Testament reflects the culture and character of its author, which makes these books feel refreshingly human. Christianity teaches that Jesus was a unique marriage of God and humanity, and in a sense so is the Bible.

---

3. "Introduction to the New Testament," *New Oxford Annotated Bible*, iv.

PART III. PIVOTAL QUESTIONS

Objectivity and Subjectivity

"No interpretation (of *any* text) takes place without presuppositions, of which we are often unaware."[4] Whether you are an avowed atheist or a committed Christian, you may not be able to remain completely objective when you approach anything of personal significance. Whenever we see, hear, or read something important to us, we perceive it through filters that allow us, correctly or incorrectly, to make sense of it. We continually live in the tension between the objective and the subjective.

We noted in chapter 6 how we tend to move between *assimilation* and *accommodation*. Daily life involves the continual interplay of fitting new information into existing cognitive frameworks, and modifying existing cognitive frameworks to adjust to new information. To assimilate means to *integrate* new data into what you already know, while to accommodate means to *revise* your beliefs so they are consistent with new data. You may never have heard of San Marino or Liechtenstein. Suppose that by watching the evening news, you learn that both are tiny countries in Europe. You would then assimilate this new information into your mental picture of Europe. On another night, you watch the news and discover that, although you had always assumed Angel Falls to be in Africa, it is actually in South America. Through accommodation, you modify your understandings of Angel Falls, Africa, and South America to align better with this new information. Genuine assimilation or accommodation only occurs when the new data correspond to reality. Otherwise, knowledge and understanding decrease rather than increase. If the claims about Jesus in the New Testament are true, our existing cognitive frameworks may have to be modified.

Objectivity can be difficult to achieve, especially when it comes to religion. It is the rare individual who can open a Bible with no preconceptions. Some people immediately discount it. They will likely find support in its pages for their skeptical preconceptions. Others, positively disposed toward Christianity, are just as likely to find support for their beliefs.

It seems reasonable to approach the New Testament on its own terms. Some Christians go to great lengths to insist that its original documents were without error. This, however, is not helpful because we no longer have those documents. What we do have are English translations of copies of Greek texts. Christians view the books in the New Testament

---

4. "Modern Approaches to Biblical Study," *New Oxford Annotated Bible*, 391.

CHAPTER 13. CAN WE TRUST THE NEW TESTAMENT?

as examples of what attorneys refer to as *res ipsa loquitor*, Latin for *the thing speaks for itself*. That, however, does not mean that we have a complete understanding of everything in the Bible.

The author of a preface to a series of commentaries on the New Testament suggests, "the vision of 'objective scholarship' (a vain chimera) may actually be profane . . . When God speaks to us through his Word, those who profess to know him must respond in an appropriate way, and that is certainly different from a stance in which the scholar projects an image of autonomous distance. If the text is God's Word, it is appropriate that we respond with reverence, a certain fear, a holy joy, [and] a questing obedience."[5]

Solidification of the New Testament

Although no one knows exactly when the church first regarded the documents in the New Testament as inspired, Christians accepted them as authoritative by the end of the second century and probably much earlier. In the first and second centuries, individuals copied New Testament documents for personal or communal use.

From the beginning, Christians regarded the words of Jesus as on a par with the Torah, the first five books of the Old Testament. In a single verse (1 Tim 5:18), for example, the writer quotes two passages, one from the Old Testament, "You are not to muzzle an ox when it is treading out the grain" (Deut 25:4, REB) and the other from one of the Gospels, "A workman is worthy of his hire" (Luke 10:7, KJV). He describes both as scripture. Long before calling them that, Christians regarded the teachings of the Apostles as authoritative. Thus, in 2 Pet 3, the author criticizes "false teachers who twist the words of Paul as they do with the rest of scripture."[6]

Some New Testament scholars believe Paul's associates wrote certain letters attributed to him, such as Colossians, Ephesians, 2 Thessalonians, 1 and 2 Timothy, and Titus. This does not challenge the trustworthiness of these letters, since it was common practice in the ancient world to invoke the authority and endorsement of one's teacher by using his name. This is evident in how difficult it is to know whether in some of Plato's dialogues the ideas are his or those of his mentor Socrates. Dictation was

---

5. Carson, *Gospel According to John*, 6.
6. Hagner, *The New Testament*, 713.

also common, and Paul appears to have used a secretary for at least some of the letters that bear his name.

How to Read the Gospels

The authors of the Gospels portray Jesus in different ways, which should not surprise us. Like shining a light on a precious gem from different angles, each writer illuminates facets that the others do not. Some who identify themselves as Christians do not regard what the Gospels contain as factual and are inclined to view Jesus as a gifted teacher, ethical model, or both. They tend to read the events recorded in them as mythical and to interpret what Jesus taught about the kingdom of God as metaphorical. And, rather than regarding the Holy Spirit as a personal presence in their lives, they tend to think primarily of God's Spirit as a general impetus to improve the world. Such people may sincerely strive to promote human well-being, but they seem to do this with only a vague sense, at best, of actively collaborating with God as ambassadors of his kingdom.

Others are inclined to regard the Gospels as historical but tend to downplay Jesus' claim that, through him, the kingdom of God had already arrived. They believe the crucifixion and resurrection made it possible to have eternal life, but they do not always come to terms with how Jesus launched a new humanity two thousand years ago in the form of the church.[7] They have a strong future orientation focused on heaven, treat their time on earth as a holding pattern, and are not much concerned with improving human existence or caring for the planet.

Because there has been so much unproductive controversy around how literally to interpret scripture, I would like to offer a few suggestions on how to read the Gospels. Because they report the ministry, death, and resurrection of Jesus, which together form the foundation of Christianity,[8] knowing how best to approach them is important. This implies taking them seriously but not spending inordinate amounts of time defending what it would be better to internalize.

Here is the introductory passage of the Gospel of Luke (1:1–4, NRSV):

> Since many have undertaken to set down an orderly account of
> the events that have been fulfilled among us, just as they were

---

7. See Wright, *How God Became King*.
8. Hagner, *The New Testament*, 59.

CHAPTER 13. CAN WE TRUST THE NEW TESTAMENT?

> handed on to us by those who from the beginning were eyewitnesses and servants of the word, I too decided, after investigating everything carefully from the very first, to write an orderly account for you . . . so that you may know the truth . . . .

This suggests how conscientiously Luke went about his task, which seems also to have been the case with the other authors of the New Testament.

The Gospels all tell the same story, only with different emphases. In the second century, Justin Martyr referred to them as "memoirs of the Apostles." That there are four instead of one Gospel is a source of enrichment, not a reason to worry about their trustworthiness. We "have the same story told with trivial variations."[9] The authors based their accounts on what they observed and eyewitnesses told them,[10] but they "exercised considerable freedom in constructing their narratives,"[11] which are more like portraits than photographs.

What we now have as Gospels contain deeds and teachings that each author believed to be especially important. They are neither works of fiction nor biographies in the modern sense; they are historical narratives within a biographical framework. They tell us nothing about Jesus as a small child or what he did from when he was twelve to about thirty. Nor do they present a uniform chronology we can use to create a single timeline, although there can be value in what are called *harmonies* whose authors attempt to do this. Except for Jesus' trial and crucifixion, the order of events was relatively unimportant to the Gospel writers. What *was* important was their significance.

It makes little sense to require the Gospels to reflect the kind of unfolding of events you would find in a modern history textbook. "The Evangelists group materials together in whatever way seems compelling to them." Thus, to come to their accounts "with expectation of a degree of exactness or accuracy that they do not intend to provide is to misuse them and misunderstand them . . . we must accept the Gospels as God gave them to us."[12]

---

9. Hagner, *The New Testament*, 63–64.
10. See Bauckham, *Jesus and the Eyewitnesses*.
11. Hagner, *The New Testament*, 63.
12. Hagner, *The New Testament*, 62–63, 65.

PART III. PIVOTAL QUESTIONS

Inconsistencies and Inaccuracies

Certain questions arise in relation to several passages in the New Testament. Such questions do not come up because of a single translation but occur in widely used and well-regarded translations. In alphabetical order, these include the English Standard Version (ESV), New International Version (NIV), New Jerusalem Bible (NJB), New Revised Standard Version (NRSV), and Revised English Bible (REB). These translations accord well with each other, and in those instances when there is uncertainty about a passage, the translators usually add footnotes that highlight alternatives. The scholars who produced these works labored hard to give us translations that reflect honest scholarship. Rather than weakening confidence in the New Testament, their work should strengthen our confidence in it.

Textual criticism or textual analysis is the discipline of comparing alternative versions in various copies of manuscripts, to determine the text as it left the hands of the original authors. Noting that a "perfectly reconstructed text" of the Bible is important to many Christians, one expert remarks on the extraordinary diligence that has been exercised in the pursuit of this reconstruction. He adds that one should not assume "that the results often radically change the traditionally 'received' text. On the contrary, the changes are usually much less fundamental than is popularly imagined."[13]

In many of the passages about which scholars have raised questions, it seems as if they are nitpicking. Documents now lost might well supply good explanations. In most instances, the difficulty is minor. Mark 14:12, for example, indicates that Jesus died the day after the Passover meal. John (19:14), however, writes that the Romans crucified Jesus the day before it. Theologian Anthony Thiselton notes, "From the standpoint of John's chronology, this must have been 'their' Passover, even if it was technically a day earlier, just as today some families enjoy 'their' Christmas not exactly on December 25."[14] Even if Thiselton is wrong, the difference is hardly enough to discredit the New Testament. Differences such as this only add to its historical credibility, since no one bothered to smooth them over.

In Luke (2:39), Joseph and Mary return to Nazareth, whereas in Matthew (2:19–22) they flee to Egypt. Might one event have preceded the

13. MacGregor, *Dictionary*, "Textual Analysis," 607.
14. Thiselton, *Life After Death*, 42.

CHAPTER 13. CAN WE TRUST THE NEW TESTAMENT?

other? How much does this detail matter? And in Acts (9:26), the second half of Luke's account, Paul leaves Damascus for Jerusalem, whereas according to Galatians (1:16–17) it seems he did not. Both could be accurate and refer to events occurring at different times.[15]

In Mark (2:26, GNT) we read, "When Abiathar was the high priest." But David did the act in question when Abiathar's father Ahimelech was high priest (1 Sam 21:1–6). This could be an honest, though trivial, mistake, either by Mark or a copyist. Some translations render the phrase as "in the time of Abiathar." Might Mark's reference to Abiathar be because Abiathar was more prominent in the Old Testament and remained in office for many years during David's reign? Or, because of this prominence, might the phrase refer to a general section of scripture? Once more, does it matter? We also read in Mark (4:31, NIV) that the mustard seed is the "smallest of all seeds on earth," which it is not. Then again, the Bible is not a biology textbook, and the church has ended up in difficulty whenever it has lost sight of this. Is it possible that Jesus was simply using a metaphor that his listeners would understand?

This suggests the question of what Jesus knew and when. There is no necessary reason to believe Jesus was omniscient during his life on earth, although he may well have been. Was he all-knowing as an infant? If he became omniscient as an adolescent or adult, when did this happen? Was it gradual or sudden, perhaps at his baptism? We do not know the answers to these questions.

The Gospels, I believe, give us an accurate picture of the kinds of things Jesus said and did, which is especially important when we read what they indicate about the end of his life. If we approach the Gospels with this in mind, many of the issues and disputes I highlight in this chapter will be unimportant or irrelevant to their principal message. Worse, they can become distractions.

Passages of Uncertain Authenticity

Although it mirrors the thought-forms of the rest of the Gospel of John, there is a question about whether chapter 21 is original, since John's Gospel seems to end naturally with chapter 20. Some scholars have also raised questions about the book's prologue (1:1–18), which is in a poetic style that does not occur elsewhere in John's Gospel. And although

---

15. See Wright, *Paul: A Biography*.

the ideas contained in the prologue also appear in the main body of the text, much of its vocabulary does not. They therefore conclude that the prologue was an add-on. Yet, both it and chapter 21 appear in our earliest manuscripts. At a minimum, these passages are probably close to what the author wrote.

There are passages in John that some critics insist were not part of the original documents. One is the story of the woman caught in adultery (7:53—8:11), an account that does not appear in the other Gospels. This, of itself, is inconclusive. Of more significance is that several of the words and phrases, as well as the overall writing style of this account, do not match the rest of John's Gospel. Most telling of all is that the story does not appear in the best and oldest manuscripts. There is no reason to conclude, however, that the incident never happened. Some scholars believe it was a widely circulating story about Jesus and that someone added it to John's Gospel as a marginal note that eventually made its way into the text. Certain manuscripts place it elsewhere in John, after 21:25, while others put it in another Gospel altogether, after Luke 21:38.

Another passage some believe a later scribe added occurs in Mark 16:9–20. Jesus appears to Mary Magdalene, who reports his appearance to the disciples. He then appears to two others. Next, he shows himself to the eleven remaining disciples (Judas Iscariot had already committed suicide). Chastising them for their unbelief, Jesus commissions them to announce the good news. He speaks about belief, baptism, and salvation, and tells them that in his name they will cast out demons, speak new languages, pick up snakes and be immune to poison, and heal the sick. Finally, Jesus ascends to heaven, where Mark reports him now sitting at the right hand of God. The disciples then set about proclaiming the gospel and having their proclamations validated by "signs."

Some scholars believe all twelve of these verses were added to Mark's Gospel because (1) they are missing in the oldest and best manuscripts, (2) many of the words and phrases do not appear anywhere else in this Gospel, (3) the transition between Mark 16:8 and 16:9 is awkward (Mary Magdalene is mentioned in verse 9 as if she had not been mentioned before, when in fact she had), and (4) the writing style in verses nine through twenty is inconsistent with the rest of Mark.

That Mark's Gospel seems to end abruptly if we snip out this passage has led some scholars, but by no means all, to suggest that we are missing the original ending. It may be that Mark's manuscript did end with the eighth verse of chapter 16, since such an abrupt ending would

CHAPTER 13. CAN WE TRUST THE NEW TESTAMENT?

bring the reader up short, encouraging serious reflection. Ending Mark's Gospel at 16:8 would further strengthen a central motif in Mark, that those closest to Jesus repeatedly failed to grasp his significance. According to Mark, they never seemed to "get it," not until Pentecost (Acts 2:1–13), which occurred after the close of Mark's narrative. None of this is certain, and such speculation can substantially divert attention away from the key message of the New Testament.

Another passage that poses problems for some occurs in the first epistle of John (5:7–8), called the "Johannine Comma." These two verses are the most explicit statement in the Bible of the Trinity, the idea that God subsists in three persons. This passage appears in manuscripts of the Latin Vulgate. The Vulgate was principally the work of Jerome (340–420), who began it at the request of Pope Damascus in 382. For over a thousand years, it was the most widely used Bible in the Western church, and it was this that Gutenberg printed around the year 1450, seventy years before Luther kicked off the Reformation and translated the Bible into everyday German. The Vulgate went through many competing editions. Jerome translated the New Testament from the Greek, and then took up the study of Hebrew so he could complete his work with an accurate translation of the Old Testament. In 1546, the Council of Trent declared it to be the authentic and official translation of the Bible, and a revised edition appeared in 1592. The title Vulgate is from *vulgata edition*, meaning the popular or common translation. Work on updating it continues to this day.

The Johannine comma does not appear in many Greek manuscripts, including those that the great Rotterdam scholar Desiderius Erasmus (1466–1536) used for his Greek New Testament. Because of the pressure brought to bear on Erasmus by incensed theologians, he later included it. Erasmus' Greek New Testament came to be known as the *Textus Receptus* (received text). Although it was based on nothing close to the number of manuscripts available today, it continued to be reprinted for over three hundred years and served as the principal foundation for the King James Bible (1611). Some translations still include the Johannine Comma without a qualifying footnote, but most include one.

PART III. PIVOTAL QUESTIONS

Differences Among Manuscripts

A *variant* is a discrepancy between or among manuscripts, ancient translations, or quotations of biblical passages by early church fathers. In 1707, Oxford fellow John Mill (1645–1707) published a densely annotated Greek New Testament in which he pointed to about 30,000 variants in the manuscripts available to him. John Mill, the theologian, is not the same person as Scottish philosopher James Mill (1773–1836) or his more famous son, John Stuart Mill (1806–1873).

Mill's publication, the result of thirty years of scholarship, caused considerable consternation among the devout at the time. This was unfortunate because the more variants available, the better scholars are able to determine what the earliest manuscripts contained. The 30,000 variants cited by Mill did not impugn the integrity of the New Testament but rather enabled scholars to establish it more firmly. Bart Ehrman writes, "the thirty thousand variants uncovered by Mill do not detract from the integrity of the New Testament; they simply provide the data that scholars need to work on to establish the text, a text that is more amply documented than any other from the ancient world."[16]

Contemporary scholars estimate the number of variants to be at least 200,000, with some estimates ranging as high as 400,000. Mill relied on about 100 Greek manuscripts, while contemporary scholars have access to around 6,000. How many manuscripts we now have depends on how one defines *manuscript*. If, for example, one counts fragments, the number is appreciably larger than if one counts complete books of the Bible or collections of such books. "At last count, more than fifty-seven hundred Greek manuscripts have been discovered and catalogued."[17]

The oldest manuscripts are on material made from papyrus reeds, but the latter ones are on animal skin (parchment or vellum). Some date from early in the second century and differ considerably in how much of the New Testament they contain. Besides these roughly 6,000 Greek manuscripts, there are about 10,000 copies of the Bible known as the Latin Vulgate, which Jerome and his associates translated from Hebrew, Greek, and Aramaic between AD 382 and AD 405. We also have manuscript versions of the New Testament in other languages, such as Coptic and Syriac. And, there are writings in Greek from church fathers, such as Origen and Athanasius, and in Latin from other church fathers such

---

16. Ehrman, *Misquoting Jesus*, 87.
17. Ehrman, *Misquoting Jesus*, 88.

CHAPTER 13. CAN WE TRUST THE NEW TESTAMENT?

as Augustine and Tertullian, all quoting portions of the New Testament. Biblical scholars, therefore, have at their disposal a wealth of resources from which to draw conclusions.

Christians sometimes worry that scholarship will erode the authority of scripture, that it will lead to a cascade of crumbling beliefs. If we allow textual critics to call a single biblical passage into question, they insist, there will be no end to their efforts to shred the Bible and eventually little will remain of it. To dismiss textual scholarship because of what it might reveal does not suggest much confidence in the New Testament. God gave us minds and we ought to use them, not spend our time fretting over what good research may reveal.

Not all research is good however, and some scholars approach their work with anything but objectivity. They seem to come to the study of the Bible with glaring biases and go to great lengths to garner evidence in support of them. An example of what appears to be biased scholarship is put out by the Jesus Seminar.[18] Albert Schweitzer once quipped that the nineteenth-century quest for the historical Jesus looked down the long wall of history and saw its own reflection. These scholars display what psychologists call *confirmation bias*, the tendency selectively to search for whatever appears to support their preconceptions. Such biases may be rooted as much in the heart as in the head.

Inadvertent and Intentional Alterations

Two kinds of changes crop up in biblical manuscripts, inadvertent and intentional. The former occurred when a scribe copied the wrong vowel or mistook one word for another. In Rom 12:11, for example, Paul exhorts Christians to *serve the Lord*, which is how the New Revised Standard Version (NRSV) renders that verse. Because of a copying mistake, however, some manuscripts have it as *serve the time*. Similar accidental alterations occur in manuscripts for other parts of the New Testament. Examples are 1 Cor 12:13, Rom 5:1, and Rev 1:5. The New Revised Standard Version (NRSV) treats these passages correctly. Biblical scholars call such accidental alterations *primitive*.

Intentional changes may have occurred because the copyist wanted to add interpretive clarity to a passage or for polemical reasons. Origen, a third-century church father of prodigious learning, quotes

---

18. Funk and the Jesus Seminar, *The Acts of Jesus*.

Celsus as accusing Christians of "altering original texts of the gospel," either to prevent heresies or to facilitate agreement with their doctrines. Some scholars view Celsus as honest but jaundiced, and he may have had only a superficial knowledge of Christianity. Virtually everything we know about Celsus comes from his words, which are quoted almost in their entirety by Origen. Celsus castigates Christians for welcoming the outcast and downtrodden, rather than those whom he regards as virtuous, thus missing the central themes in Christianity of grace and reconciliation. If there were scribal alterations, Origen did not believe them to be intentional.

At the beginning of Mark (1:23), the quotation used is not from Isaiah, as it incorrectly indicates, but from a blend of two verses, one in Exodus (23:20) and the other in Malachi (3:1). Some scribes, recognizing this, changed the text in some manuscripts to read, "As is written in the prophets . . ." The reference to Isaiah, however, occurs in our earliest and most reliable manuscripts, and therefore, however inaccurate, it belongs in any good translation.

In Matthew (24:36), where Jesus says that no one, not even he, knows when the end of the age will come, some scribes deleted the phrase "nor even the Son." How, they may have wondered, could Jesus not know something like this? So, they changed it. Another example occurs in Mark (9:29). Possibly to reflect his own religious practice, a scribe changed "only by prayer" to "only by prayer and fasting." In Luke 11:2–4, some copyists appear to have lengthened the Lord's Prayer by borrowing from the parallel passage in Matthew (6:9–3). And, in John 5:3–4, oral tradition may have prompted scribes to add a few lines in some manuscripts about an angel disturbing the waters of the pool of Bethesda.

In each of these instances, good translations get it right. This implies that, although we do not have the original documents, what we do have brings us encouragingly close. Christians generally believe that God not only prompted these authors to write what they did, albeit in the idiom of their own personalities, but that God also protected their writings so that we still have access to what is very close to what they wrote and therefore to their ideas. God bless the Irish monks for preserving the many documents they did.[19]

---

19. See Cahill, *Irish Saved Civilization*.

Other Possible Alterations

Luke 24:12 has Peter running to Jesus' tomb and finding only linen clothing. Some manuscripts do not contain this verse. The NRSV adds the note, "Other ancient authorities lack verse 12." This, and reasons relating to style, have led critics to conclude that these lines were not part of Luke's original Gospel. Since a parallel account in John's Gospel (20:3–10) presents the same incident in more detail—Peter and the "beloved" disciple rushing to the tomb, only to find it empty and linen clothing on the ground—the conclusion, once again, seems of minor practical importance.

A phrase that appears in many modern Bibles, but is missing in some of the earliest manuscripts, comes at the end of Luke. Soon after the resurrection, Jesus was "carried up into taken" (24:51, ESV). What makes this passage especially challenging is that in Acts 1:9–11, which Luke also wrote, we read that the ascension of Jesus occurred weeks after the resurrection. Some scholars believe the disputed sentence in Luke was not part of his original Gospel. There is no easy way to harmonize the two accounts.

Another disputed passage has to do with women. In his first letter to Christians living in the cosmopolitan Greek city of Corinth (1 Cor 11:2–16), Paul seems to indicate that women routinely spoke in church. Yet in that same letter (14:34–35), he forbids them from speaking. It is possible that in the first of these passages, Paul is referring to private versus communal worship. Some scholars, however, suggest that he was inconsistent, perhaps because of ambivalence about the role of women. A third possibility is that, from the vantage point of the male-centered ethos of antiquity, women in the Corinthian church were becoming so vocal that they were causing disruptions and discord. Paul may have been concerned to preserve the peace, since his primary goal was to advance the gospel.[20] Fourth, some textual critics believe someone other than Paul inserted the latter passage, and that these verses were not part of Paul's original epistle. Finally, from the syntax, it appears that in the second of the two statements, Paul may have been quoting something he intended to refute.

Luke tends to depict Jesus as unflappable, while Mark portrays him as intermittently angry, anguished, and bordering on despair. It seems possible, therefore, that some scribe, intending to harmonize the

20. See Jewett, *Man as Male and Female*.

two Gospels, added verses to Luke that have to do with Jesus praying ever more earnestly and his sweat becoming "like great drops of blood" (Luke 22:43–44, NRSV). Our earliest and best manuscripts omit these verses. Such issues can puzzle us. In the end, however, they do not amount to much, and in no instance are they central to the message of the New Testament.

The beauty of an honest and open-minded approach to biblical scholarship is that it allows us to entertain such possibilities, which do not however call into question over ninety-nine percent of the New Testament. As with findings in science, conclusions of biblical scholars will sometimes remain tentative. None of this constitutes a legitimate threat to faith in God through Jesus, to the reality of who Christ is. Although passages in the New Testament raise questions, none of them subverts the core affirmations of Christianity.

The New Testament as Its Own Commentary

Christian theologians long ago realized that the Bible serves as its own best commentary. To make proper sense of any part in the Bible, it is important to view it in the light of the rest. Clearer passages shed light on more ambiguous ones. As an example, some textual critics are quick to suggest that sections of Luke (22:17–19) contain words borrowed from Paul's first epistle to Corinthian Christians (1 Cor 11:23–25).[21] The words in question have to do with the Lord's Supper, with what Christians call Holy Communion or the Eucharist. Perhaps these critics are right. Because we no longer have the original manuscripts, we cannot be sure. But this does not change the significance of Communion or what either Luke or Paul wrote.

Why should Luke not have quoted Paul if that helped express what he, too, believed? In raising the possibility that Luke may have relied on Paul, rather than the other way around, I am honoring the timeline most New Testament scholars suggest, that Paul's epistles were written earlier than Luke's Gospel. What matters most is that we understand the significance of the Eucharist, rejoicing and expressing gratitude, which the rest of the New Testament affirms. For those of us who are not New Testament scholars, fretting over whether Luke quoted Paul may be yet another distraction.

---

21. See footnote to Luke 22:20 in the NRSV.

CHAPTER 13. CAN WE TRUST THE NEW TESTAMENT?

It seems odd that people who rarely question the authenticity of ancient books are instinctively skeptical about the New Testament, even though the number of extant biblical manuscripts or fragments of manuscripts undergirding it substantially exceeds those for all others. What if the New Testament is trustworthy after all? If so, failing to read it with an open mind may be to miss something of great importance. Although each writer had his own perspective, the themes running through the New Testament are remarkably consistent. That its authors converged on these themes is striking, and in the view of Christians no accident. The Bible, as we have it, contains all we need to know to approach God. It tells us about God's character, our natures, who Jesus was, and what he did on our behalf. It also tells us, individually and as a global population, where to find rescue and deliverance from the evil that human beings have inflicted on each other from the dawn of time. We are wanderers who have lost our way. The Bible points to how we can find it again.

Closing Thoughts

We have examined the New Testament and various criticisms directed at it. The New Testament has far more documents in support of it than any other ancient text or set of texts. We have looked hard at inconsistences and inaccuracies, passages some have concluded to be inauthentic, differences between and among the manuscripts on which the New Testament is based, and inadvertent or intentional alterations. All of them are trivial. None of the sentences or passages that have been questioned amount to more than a small fraction of the twenty-seven documents it contains.

If you have never read the New Testament, try reading the Gospel of John. Then, move on to Ephesians. Don't worry about the details. Just look for major themes. If you do this with an open mind, you may discover, to your surprise and joy, that God exists, loves you, and has been pursuing you all along. I close this chapter by quoting the words of a chorus by Paul Baloche that thousands of Christians sing every Sunday:

> Open the eyes of my heart, Lord,
> open the eyes of my heart,
> I want to see you . . . I want to see you.

PART III. PIVOTAL QUESTIONS

Preview

Having explored the trustworthiness of the New Testament, we will next take up the question of what we can conclude about Jesus. We will examine what authors of books in the New Testament say about him. Their claims were extraordinary.

Chapter 14. What Can We Conclude About Jesus?

CHRISTIANITY RISES OR FALLS on beliefs about Jesus. This raises important questions. Did Jesus exist? Was there a teacher by that name who once walked the hills of Galilee? If so, what might we conclude about him? If Jesus existed, was he more than a flesh-and-blood human being? These questions are central to Christianity. If Jesus was only a man, Christianity in any meaningful sense falls apart.

No one in history has generated more controversy than Jesus, a Jewish rabbi whose public life lasted three years. People have long debated who he was. The New Testament contains accounts of his actions and teachings. It shows his intellectual adeptness, such as when those intending to trap him asked if they should pay Roman taxes. Jesus replied, "Pay Caesar what belongs to Caesar, and God what belongs to God" (Mark 12:17, REV). Had he replied *yes*, they would have labeled him a collaborator with the Roman occupation forces. And had he said *no*, they could have reported him to the Romans as an insurrectionist. If the biblical record stopped at reports of his cleverness, there would be little controversy about Christ's nature. But they do not. All through the New Testament, there are accounts of Jesus causing events that, in the ordinary course of things, would be impossible. Even more astonishing, its authors claim that, after his execution, Jesus came back to life and spoke with his disciples. A person living today would not readily accept such a claim, and neither did those alive at the time.

Austin Farrer was an astute mid-twentieth-century theologian, biblical scholar, and Oxford chaplain. On the back cover of one of his books, the publisher describes him as "independent and orthodox, intellectual and devout, Catholic and Reformed, impossible to pigeonhole." On its front cover, Rowan Williams, Archbishop of Canterbury from 2002 to 2012, refers to him as "Possibly the greatest Anglican mind of the 20th century."[1]

Farrer offers some penetrating comments on what we know about Jesus and how we know it. Commenting on the Gospel of Mark,[2] he challenges those who reason that since the only biographical documents we have about Jesus are the Gospels, and since the authorship, nature, date, and precise origins of these documents are open to dispute, nothing about him can be known. "Such reasoning is entirely false," suggests Farrer, because "our primary witness to a historical Christ is not any of the Evangelists, but St Paul . . . himself a historical character of flesh and blood; his great letters are genuine beyond doubt, and can even be accurately dated." Most if not all of them appeared before any of the Gospels.

Jesus, Farrer points out, was about five years older than Paul. According to Paul, Jesus died and was buried, rose from the grave—and here's the telling part—"conversed with many people" Paul knew. Farrer adds, "about the facts of Christ's wonderful life, death and resurrection there is no disagreement among the Apostles." He goes on to say, "It is through St Paul, then, that our faith is rooted in history; and a firm root it is. And so it is not necessary, even if it were honourable, to press the evidence about the authorship, date or sources of the Gospels further than it will go." Farrer is not challenging the authenticity of the Gospels, and to make this clear he states they were composed, "under the double control of memory and inspiration." He adds, "to those of us who have already believed the Apostles and become Christians, the Gospels carry conviction; for the Christ we believe in speaks to us as a real person from the gospel pages."[3] The Gospels do not so much inform us about "a different kind of human, but a different kind of God . . . [one who] having made humans" appeared on earth as one of us.[4]

It is important to let the New Testament speak for itself and not force our own interpretations on it. This means refusing to insist on

---

1. Farrer, *The Truth Seeking Heart*.
2. See Farrer, *The Truth Seeking Heart*, 60–64.
3. Farrer, *The Truth Seeking Heart*, 62.
4. Wright, *How God Became King*, 104

literal readings of passages that might better be understood symbolically (e.g., streets of gold), as well as refusing to explain away passages intended to be taken literally (e.g., love your neighbor). Those who press for extreme literalism border on turning the Bible into an idol, worshipping the scriptures instead of the God toward whom they point. Those who prefer to rationalize away the force of the New Testament convert it into a disjointed guide to a vague and ill-defined spirituality.

Christians typically believe that God communicates through the words of scripture more often, reliably, and powerfully than in any other way. Van Gogh once suggested, "All the world's a song, the symphony of nature."[5] Some people hear God's voice when they walk through a forest or stroll by the seashore. Others sense God when they attend a play or read a novel. And, still others feel God's presence when they visit a beautiful library or take in the paintings in a fine museum. Christians have always held that God connects most explicitly with human beings through the Bible.

The Idea of Salvation

Christianity sometimes becomes so watered down that there is little to distinguish it from any other religion. This is especially true of feel-good versions that do not take seriously the idea of a creator who is involved in our lives and has every right to call us to account. It is also true of versions of Christianity whose adherents discourage theological discussion, lest someone disrupt their sense of well-being by putting them in the awkward position of having to say what it means to be a Christian.

Those who take traditional Christianity seriously inevitably talk about salvation. That word may conjure up images of people who ask, "Are you saved?" Some who ask this question might find it difficult to explain what exactly they mean by it. Throughout the history of Christianity, theologians have offered different definitions of salvation, and if Christianity is more than a weak sentimental religion, the question of what salvation means is important. Theologians routinely face these questions: Who is or has been saved? From what, how, by whom, and why? They call this the study of *soteriology*.

A Roman Catholic dictionary, noting that salvation derives from a Latin word meaning "making safe" or "rescuing," defines it as, "A

---

5. Quoted in *Civilisation*.

comprehensive term for being delivered from personal or collective suffering and evil," adding, "The New Testament stresses liberation from sin and death (Mark 1:5; Rom 5:12—7:25; Heb 2:14–18)."[6] A Protestant dictionary defines salvation as, "The divine act of delivering a believer from the power and curse of sin and then restoring that individual to fellowship with God for which humans were originally intended."[7] And, a philosopher of religion writes, "salvation signifies rescue or release from an imperfect or evil state . . . In Christianity, the conditions for salvation are provided through the Atonement, by which Christ has reconciled God and man (at-one-ment)."[8]

Because of the centrality of Christ to this reconciliation, to our reconnecting and making peace with God, basic questions arise about Jesus. Recall that when many people use the word "Christ," they treat *Christ* as a last name, when in fact it is a title. Christ is the Greek translation of the Hebrew word *Messiah*, which means, among other things, *Anointed* or *Sent One*. Christianity teaches that Jesus was the one toward whom the Old Testament points. What it means to be the Christ is therefore pivotal.

Six Important Questions

1. There is, first, the question of whether Jesus existed. Was he a historical person or a figment of imagination, perhaps a mythic figure like Hercules or Odysseus? We know that Socrates, born five centuries earlier, existed. But did Jesus? Are there sources outside the Bible that mention him?

2. How much can we rely on the claims made by the authors of the New Testament? What caused them to make these claims?

3. Was Jesus more than a man? Even atheists are willing to concede that Jesus was a gifted teacher. If he was more than a man, who and what was he?

4. What about miracles? Are they possible? If so, might Jesus have performed some?

---

6. O'Collins and Farrugia, *Concise Dictionary of Theology*, "Salvation," 233–34.
7. Erickson, *Concise Dictionary of Theology*, "Salvation," 175.
8. MacGregor, *Dictionary*, "Salvation," 553.

CHAPTER 14. WHAT CAN WE CONCLUDE ABOUT JESUS?

5. Then there is the challenge of making sense of what the New Testament claims Jesus said about himself. Some of these claims are astonishing. Were they false, and if you believe in only one God, were they blasphemous?

6. Finally, there is the resurrection. For many, this remains the stickiest wicket on the path to Christianity. Is such a thing possible, and if so, did it actually happen?

Question # 1: Did Jesus Exist?

Historians believe a man named Jesus lived, walked the hills of Galilee, and spent time in Jerusalem. The earliest reference to Jesus outside the New Testament seems to come from the late first-century writings of the Jewish historian Josephus (died ca.100). He reports that Jesus was a "wise man" who was "good and virtuous" and a "doer of wonders." Josephus further writes that Jesus recruited many disciples, Jewish and non-Jewish, and was crucified at the hands of Pilate. He also reports that Jesus' followers claimed he appeared to them three days later, that they believed he was the Messiah, and depending on which version of Josephus you consult, either that "the tribe of Christians, so named from him, are not extinct to this day" or "those who had become his disciples did not abandon their loyalty to him."

Based on textual analysis, scholars seem to agree that Josephus was a dispassionate reporter who had no particular religious agenda to promote. His stance seems neutral and there is no indication that he was especially sympathetic to Christianity. It therefore seems reasonable to trust what he wrote. Some have argued that later Christians added phrases to the writings of Josephus to make Christianity sound better. I have not included any of these phrases in the quotations above, and it is highly likely that Josephus wrote what I have quoted. In the improbable event that the writings of Josephus someday turn out to be inauthentic, the New Testament itself consists of a small library of sources, all certifying that Jesus existed.

The four Gospels are selective or episodic biographies. They are not biographies in the modern sense of narrating events over the full course of a person's life. There is nothing about the childhood of Jesus in Matthew, Mark, or John, and only Luke provides information about him as a boy. None of the Gospels tells us anything about Jesus as a late adolescent or young adult. Nonetheless, it is clear to scholars that Jesus was a real person.

Question # 2. How Much Can We Rely on Claims Made by the New Testament Authors?

It is natural to wonder if the writers of the New Testament colluded, but as discussed in the preceding chapter, there is nothing to suggest that they all knew each other. Paul certainly knew Peter and Luke, but it is unlikely that he ever laid eyes on the author of the Gospel of John. Why would anyone, much less a group, spend all the time and energy required to conspire? And, if they did not even know each other, how could they have done that? What would have been the advantage of joining such a conspiracy? If they wrote to further belief in the resurrection, it was because they already knew it had happened. Even a cursory look at the New Testament makes clear that Jesus did nothing to encourage political or economic intrigue.

There are other problems with the conspiracy theory. At least some of the authors of the books in the New Testament, such as Peter and Paul, were almost certainly martyred. Why would anyone choose to risk death to keep up a charade? Why would they have continued to insist on the resurrection if belief in it failed to give them compelling hope? Their claims surely made it more likely for their fellow Jews to ostracize them or for the Romans to do far worse.

It takes considerable time and effort to write a narrative even as short as Mark's Gospel. There is also the challenge of writing one as tightly crafted as all the Gospels are, which makes such a task even more daunting. If what they wrote never happened, they jointly invented the genre of biographical fiction. The paradox of the Gospels is that, if the claims about Jesus are deceptions, the writers must have been uncommonly clever to dream up such interesting material. Add to the four Gospels the other twenty-three books in the New Testament, and the argument that their claims are credible becomes even stronger. It is difficult to fathom why anyone, much less a group, would go to all that trouble and take all the chances they did to promote a fable. What would have been the payoff in becoming, at a minimum, a social outcast, or later in the first century, taking the risk of being crucified,[9]

---

9. Latourette, *A History of Christianity*, 85.

CHAPTER 14. WHAT CAN WE CONCLUDE ABOUT JESUS?

getting turned into a human torch, becoming food for ravenous animals, or having to square off with a veteran gladiator?

What made crucifixion so horrendous is that victims sometimes survived on crosses for a day or more, and scavenger birds would feast on them before they died. Emperor Nero (AD 37–AD 68) supposedly doused Christians in oil and set them on fire, although the source for this is Tacitus in his *Annals*, written half a century later and therefore regarded by some but not all scholars as questionable. Other Christians were dressed in animal carcasses and turned over to packs of hungry dogs. As for facing gladiators, Christians sometimes refused to fight.

When I read the New Testament, I sometimes think of the Chinese proverb, "The wise man can play the fool, but the fool cannot play the wise man." There is great art in its documents, and that art resides in its ideas. It is fruitless to spend time worrying over whether Jesus spoke the exact words we read in the New Testament. It is certain, in fact, that he did not because Jesus probably spoke Aramaic, the texts on which scholars rely are in ancient Greek, and we read them in English. Jesus never said a word that appears in an English Bible, nor in a Chinese, Dutch, French, German, Japanese, or Spanish one. What we have in the New Testament are concepts. Translations, if they are well done, are sincere attempts to convey what these concepts would have meant to the original audiences.

Some translations are more literal and others more figurative, but all are influenced by the biases of the translator(s). Any translator faces the perpetual challenge of conveying, in another language, meanings contained in the original one. Some translators strive to do this literally, word-by-word, aiming for *formal equivalence*. Others strive for translations that are less literal, more sense-by-sense or thought-by-thought, aiming for *dynamic equivalence*. A problem with formal equivalence is that, at times, there may be no synonymous word or phrase in the target language for a word or phrase in the source language. The power of metaphors and similes in the source language may be lost through literal translation, forcing the translator either to forfeit meaning by sticking to word-for-word translation or render the passage more figuratively. A problem with dynamic equivalence is that it allows the translator to stray further from the original and to produce translations that may turn out, decades later, to be incorrect. The more any two languages resemble one another, the easier it is to rely on word-for-word translation, which does not, however, solve the problem of accurately conveying the true meaning of metaphors and similes. All translations are to some degree interpretations, and as such are vulnerable to preconceptions and presuppositions, whether theological, philosophical, or scientific. The better the translation, the less this is a problem.

It is not as if the Gospels describe the existence of an itinerant rabbi who, against his will, met a tragic end. To the contrary, they report that Jesus intentionally submitted himself to the horrors of crucifixion. But long before he did, he told instructive stories (parables), ministered to the poor and marginalized, shared teachings about a higher morality, revealed the nature of God, and performed miracles,[10] all of which point to Jesus as a one-of-a-kind being who initiated God's kingdom on earth. The whole story, from beginning to end, is extraordinary.

There is no rigorous proof of the resurrection, nor could there be. Even if we had a video record of Jesus walking out of the tomb, skeptics would likely insist it was a trick, perhaps something put together by artificial intelligence on a computer. In the worst case, allowing for the most egregious alterations by irresponsible scribes, and removing from the New Testament every book or passage whose authorship or authenticity has been questioned by honest scholarship, we still end up with a narrative that is startling in its claims, dazzling in its teachings, and stunning in its implications. How, indeed, could so many fools become so many wise men?

Question # 3. Was Jesus More Than a Man?

All four Gospels present a remarkably parallel, though not identical, narrative of Jesus' death and resurrection. Although each writer adds his own emphasis, the four are strikingly consistent in what they report about the last days of his life. By the time the Gospels appeared, Christians were dying for their beliefs, so it is impressive that their authors dared write them at all. Turning to the rest of the New Testament, Paul wrote or dictated much of it. Thirteen of its twenty-seven books are attributed to him, some with certainty and others probably written by close associates. These writings and the rest of the New Testament resound with statements about the implications of the resurrection.

Although Paul knew of Jesus and may even have witnessed the crucifixion, in all likelihood he had not met Jesus prior to what happened

---

10. Lewis. *Miracles: A Preliminary Study*; Brown, *Miracles and the Critical Mind*.

CHAPTER 14. WHAT CAN WE CONCLUDE ABOUT JESUS?

en route to Syria. Prior to that, Paul devoted considerable time and energy trying to suppress belief in Jesus by those he considered heretical Jews. Paul's outrage in response to the claim that Jesus had come back to life was considerable. On his way to Damascus to continue the harassment, Paul had an experience that caused him to conclude that God had resurrected Jesus (Acts 9, 22, 26). But Paul had questions. What if the risen Jesus had been far more than a man, which now seemed likely? What if Jesus was some never-before-encountered combination of God and humanity? What if he revealed God's nature as never before and showed the world what God is like as a flesh-and-blood being? Paul's letters capture answers to these questions that he had worked out after up to a decade of careful reflection.

Paul had been a Pharisee and continued throughout his life to identify himself as one, albeit with a revised view of where he and his fellow Christians stood in relation to the Jewish law. As mentioned above, the title Pharisee did not mean then what it does today. Pharisees belonged to a devout sect that advocated meticulous observance of the law. After encountering Christ on the road, Paul began to present reasoned arguments for faith in the risen Messiah and to proclaim the good news. This news was "about God coming back in person to rescue his people."[11] Instead of attempting to eradicate the Way, Paul now promoted it. He had become steadfastly convinced that Jesus was who and what the disciples claimed, and that only by faith in God through Christ could a person triumph over evil, including his or her own, and death. Paul realized that the claims about Jesus, if true, carried with them momentous implications for what matters most in life and whom we ought to worship. If Jesus was more than an ordinary mortal, as Paul now believed, human beings faced choices on which everything of ultimate significance depended.

There might have been no other way for God to get through to humans than to live among us and demonstrate what it looks like to love as God loves. Not the sappy love depicted in low-budget three-hankie movies, but a boundless love, grounded in absolute and eternal truth. Sacrificial love. The incarnation, crucifixion, and resurrection may have been the only way to get skeptical and self-absorbed creatures with free will to understand God's character. And, to get us to ponder the deep structure of existence discussed in chapter 6.

---

11. Wright, *How God Became King*, 93.

PART III. PIVOTAL QUESTIONS

Question # 4: Are Miracles Possible?

If miracles are impossible, Christianity is in trouble. Worse, the two great miracles on which it hinges, supernatural birth and physical resurrection, never happened. Skeptics are inclined to argue that miracles are impossible and so never happen and never could have happened. But how do they know this? Some insist the resurrection never happened because the New Testament is unreliable. How do they know this? Because it contains references to the resurrection. Circular reasoning.

Miracles are unpredictable events we consider unnatural (supernatural) because they violate what we take to be immutable laws of nature. Three thinkers are especially well known for doubting their occurrence. Baruch Spinoza (1632–77) in the seventeenth century was the first major philosopher to challenge theistic religion. The German dramatist Gotthold Lessing (1729–81) in the eighteenth century wrote that, regardless of how hard he tried, he was unable to make it across an "ugly, broad ditch" to belief.[12] And Scottish philosopher David Hume in that same century dismissed miracles on probabilistic grounds.[13]

The prejudgment that miracles are impossible is an assumption, not a demonstrable truth. If there is a God, miracles may be more common than people think, and from the vantage point of eternity, we may come to the startling realization, "that was you, God, there, there, and there, and all the while I never knew." I find this phrase touching and first heard it used by David Allan Hubbard, president of Fuller Theological Seminary, in a commencement address. It is akin to the well-known poem "Footprints," whose central metaphor is that, as we look back over our lives and see only one set of footprints, it is because God was carrying us.

Many who subscribe to the deistic position that God, having created the world, no longer has anything to do with it, have already made up their minds. Their claim is that miracles are impossible because God does not involve himself in human affairs. Fair enough, so long as they do not advance their opinion as the product of logic or science. We have already noted how conclusions based on deductive logic are only as good as their premises, and that only arguments based on true premises yield sound conclusions. As we will see in the next chapter, science cannot demonstrate conclusions of a nonscientific nature to be true or false. It cannot, by its nature, render judgments about the existence of God or the possibility

---

12. See *Lessing's Theological Writings*, "On Proof of the Spirit," 51–56.
13. See Hume, *Enquiry Concerning Human Understanding*.

CHAPTER 14. WHAT CAN WE CONCLUDE ABOUT JESUS?

of miracles. Page after page, through a quarter of a million words, we read in the New Testament of healings and lives changed. Might at least some of them have happened? If so, why not others?

Question # 5: What Did Jesus Say About Himself?

In the sixth chapter of John's Gospel, Jesus says, in essence, "I am the way, the truth, and the life; no one has access to the Father apart from or without me." Some scholars believe John was written late in the first century, and that its author put words in Jesus' mouth that reflect the beliefs of late-first-century Christians. Such a view is hard to defend when throughout Paul's epistles he makes essentially the same claim for Jesus. John certainly reflects a mature and well-developed theology, but it is a theology consistent with the rest of the New Testament.

Elsewhere in the Gospel of John we read that Jesus also said, "I am the resurrection and the life. Those who believe in me will live, even though they die" (John 11:25, GNT). He claims, "Before Abraham was, I Am" (John 8:58), which may be the most astounding of all, since in the Old Testament God uses "I Am" as a unique self-reference (Exod 3:14).

It is important to keep in mind just how recently Jesus said this, when compared to the age of the earth and the history of humankind. Two thousand years is the blink of an eye in geologic time, given that the earth is almost 4.5 billion years old. It is even shorter when compared to the age of the universe, since the Big Bang occurred 13.8 billion years ago. Anthropologists believe that human beings, *Homo sapiens*, have existed for between one and two hundred thousand years. Viewed against such vast expanses of time, all human history is contemporary.

Perhaps Jesus was delusional, but this seems unlikely in view of the rest of the New Testament. Maybe he was a fraud, a confidence man, a sociopath. If so, it is difficult to account for his teachings about morality, which are unlikely to have come from someone with a defective conscience. There remains the possibility that Jesus was what he said, and what the authors of the New Testament take for granted.

The belief that Jesus was both divine and human sits at the center of Christianity. To construct a Christianity devoid of this metaphysical affirmation, portraying Jesus as merely an ethicist, is to end up with no Christianity at all. Stripping out the divinity of Christ leaves you with a religion, but it is not Christianity, and it will not support your claim to be a Christian, at least not in the sense that the church has affirmed for two millennia.

Question # 6: Did the Resurrection Happen?

The power of the Christian faith rests on the claim that Jesus, having died at the hands of the Romans, came back to life. To deny the physical resurrection is to miss the true nature of Jesus and his relationship to our creator. Because the resurrection is so central to authentic Christianity, I want to discuss it in detail.

No other ancient text, as noted in the last chapter, comes close to having as many source documents, or stands up as well to textual scrutiny, as the New Testament. Its authors presuppose his resurrection. From what the Gospels indicate, Jesus' post-crucifixion encounters with his disciples persuaded them, beyond any doubt, that he had resurrected and deserved their worship (John 20:19). The New Testament tells us that many other people also saw Jesus after his resurrection.

It is almost certain that Paul never met Jesus prior to his crucifixion, but Paul later became immovably convinced that Jesus had resurrected. He also claimed that hundreds of people still living attested to this. Stripping the resurrection out of Christianity to make it more palatable destroys it. Attempts to explain away the resurrection come in many forms, but they do not hold up. All of them, in one way or another, gratuitously assume that the physical resurrection could never have happened.[14]

Perceptual Distortion and Mental Aberration

Perceptual errors take three forms: illusions, delusions, and hallucinations. An illusion is misidentifying something that exists, a delusion is rigidly holding on to a bizarre belief in the presence of contrary evidence, and a hallucination is perceiving something for which there is no physical cause.

Illusions fool many people, and not just during magic shows. Thirsty people lost in a desert can mistake sand for water, just as many of us on a hot summer day see water on the road ahead where there is only asphalt.

---

14. See Kreeft and Tacelli, *Handbook of Christian Apologetics*, "The Resurrection," 176–98, and in their shorter *Pocket Handbook of Christian Apologetics*, "The Resurrection," 69–78.

CHAPTER 14. WHAT CAN WE CONCLUDE ABOUT JESUS?

Perhaps those who saw Jesus after the resurrection were subject to an illusion. Maybe they believed they were talking with the risen Jesus but were actually conversing with someone else.

A skeptic might cite the incident on the road to Emmaus to suggest how this might have happened (Luke 24:13–32). The Gospel of Mark (16:12–13) contains a similar passage. Both recount a post-resurrection appearance that Rembrandt memorialized in one of his paintings, *Christ at Emmaus*. Luke reports that on the evening of the resurrection, a disciple named Cleopas and another disciple are walking toward Emmaus, seven miles from Jerusalem. They are discussing what they had heard earlier that day about an empty tomb. A stranger joins them and asks what they have been discussing. Perhaps because "their faces were downcast," they do not recognize him and ask with surprise whether he is the only person in Jerusalem who is unaware of what has happened. Jesus asks, "What things?" and after they answer, he chides them for their superficial grasp of the Old Testament. As they near the village, they press Jesus to remain, and as he breaks the bread during the evening meal, they recognize him for who he is. This is reminiscent of Jesus breaking and distributing bread at the last supper.

His appearances, however, went far beyond this one. He spoke with many people on different occasions, and it is a stretch to conclude they all mistook someone else for Jesus. Even a close look-alike would have had to persuade them of his identity (Luke 24; John 20–21; Acts 1). Although his resurrected body seems to have been a mixture of physical and transphysical properties, there was no mistaking that it was Jesus.

Delusions and hallucinations, in contrast to illusions, occur only in those with serious mental disorders. As noted above, a delusion is a rigidly held bizarre belief. When I was practicing as a clinician, I treated people who insisted that the CIA was eavesdropping on their conversations. Maybe the disciples developed bizarre beliefs about Jesus, his resurrection, and their encounters with him after the resurrection. But if this was the case, how and why did such delusions develop? As any psychiatrist will tell you, when people become delusional, they are seriously disturbed. They often feel humiliated, may make statements of being extraordinarily gifted or important, and tend to be hypersensitive to slights and offenses. There is nothing to suggest that any of this characterized the disciples, including the women who first discovered the empty tomb.

It seems improbable that the disciples would have simultaneously developed the same delusional belief in a resurrection that never occurred. There must have been some objective basis for so many people reaching the same conclusion. Two people sometimes enter into a single delusional system, the technical term for which is *folie à deux*. One person may conclude, for example, that she is the Virgin Mary, while another may decide he is Mary's son Jesus. Such shared delusions rarely involve more than two people.[15]

Delusional people tend to voice the belief that they are extraordinary, persecuted, or both. People with delusions of grandeur are self-absorbed, as are those suffering from delusions of persecution. The disciples, however, focused on Jesus, the one they believed to be their divine Lord. The statements in the Gospels affirming Jesus' physical resurrection are so clear, strong, definitive, and above all worshipful that it would be an enormous jump to treat them as delusional. No other major religion has people attesting to how the person at its center died, came back to life, and conversed with others. Not Buddha, Moses, Mohammed, Shiva, or Zoroaster.

But what about a hallucination, perceiving something that does not exist? People in whom chemicals, tumors, or systemic diseases have assaulted their brains may experience visual hallucinations. For those who are organically impaired, these can be terrifying, for example in heavy drinkers who, when they stop drinking, may develop delirium tremens (DTs) and on rare occasions perceive spiders or insects crawling on them. But, by far, the most common type of hallucination is auditory. The individual may hear a voice that is persecutorial ("you deserve to die") or malevolent ("kill your uncle"). Maybe those who saw Jesus drank the same water containing hallucinogenic substances or fever-producing bacteria, so what they reported seeing never happened. But how likely is this? When people appeal to hallucinations as explanations, they are rarely familiar with what hallucinations are or the mental states of those who experience them. What we read of in the New Testament are face-to-face encounters, such as when Jesus challenges Thomas to do what he had earlier insisted he would have to do before believing, which was to thrust his hand into Jesus' side (John 20:21).

The trouble with conjectures that revolve around mental disorders is that they are hard to square with the nature and quality of everything else in the Gospels. The disciples engaged with a real person, not a phantom, and they had this experience on multiple occasions. Paul, as mentioned

---

15. On rare occasions, more than two people can develop the same delusional identity, which happened in the late 1950s. See Rokeach, *Three Christs of Ypsilanti*.

CHAPTER 14. WHAT CAN WE CONCLUDE ABOUT JESUS?

above, indicates that Jesus appeared to hundreds of people at the same time, many of whom were still alive (1 Cor 15:3–8). It can be difficult for someone living in the twenty-first century to believe that Jesus came back from the dead. There is no reason to suppose that people at the time were much inclined to believe it either. Some passages in the New Testament indicate how unlikely it was for people in the first century to admit the possibility of physical resurrection. At the time, for example, there existed a group of elite Jews called Sadducees, who were well known for denying that anyone could ever experience resurrection. And yet, countless people concluded that Jesus had been resurrected.

Jesus Only Seemed to Die

Given the details of the crucifixion, such as the actions of the Roman soldiers during his execution, the so-called swoon theory requires a huge intellectual leap. The Gospels indicate that a wealthy man (Mark 15:43; John 19:38; see also Matt 27:57) who had become a disciple asked Pilate for Jesus' body. He interred it in a rock cavern, a sepulcher, sealed with a large stone that would have been difficult, if not impossible, for a healthy person to move from the inside. Jesus had been beaten and hung on a cross for hours, so if he was still alive, he would have been profoundly weak. Even if Jesus had somehow managed to move that stone, he would still have had to overpower or slip by the soldiers guarding it.

Roman soldiers were proficient at crucifixion, and given the uproar surrounding Jesus, his executioners were unlikely to have bungled the job. Pilate was nervous about the possibility of Jewish insurrection. There was the ever-present potential for seditious revolt, led by zealots, who were ready to put their Roman overlords to the sword. Pilate no doubt made it clear to the soldiers that they were to be certain Jesus was dead. He also sent a centurion, an officer in charge of up to a hundred soldiers, to supervise. People crucified typically died of asphyxiation, and to speed the process along, Roman soldiers could break a victim's legs to prevent him from boosting himself up. That the soldiers did not break Jesus' legs, as they had the legs of the other two, attests to his death (John 19:34–35). The writer of the Gospel of John provides evidence of asphyxiation by noting that blood and water flowed out of Jesus.

Before his entombment, Jesus' body was wrapped in sheets, which would have made it difficult for even a healthy person to escape from such wrappings. If Jesus survived the crucifixion, he would have been on the brink of death. The Romans hardly sterilized the spikes they drove into the hands and feet of those they crucified, and neither tetanus immunization nor antibiotics would exist for another two-thousand years. A half-dead, hobbled man with massive systemic infection would have, at best, required weeks, and more likely months, to heal. Yet, soon after his resurrection, Jesus appears to the disciples. There is nothing in the record to suggest that he needed medical attention (John 20:19–29). Finally, if Jesus survived and revived, where did he go?

According to the Gospel of John, Pilate ordered a notice, written in Hebrew, Greek, and Latin, posted on the cross, "Jesus of Nazareth, King of the Jews." Because the crucifixion occurred near the city, there can be little doubt that many of those in Jerusalem would have read it, including the Jewish leaders who had incited the crowds to clamor for his crucifixion but objected to what appeared on the sign. They would have been especially keen to make sure Jesus was dead.

It Was a Conspiracy

According to this explanation, the claim that Jesus had risen from the dead was the product of a clandestine plot. It is possible to combine this idea with the swoon theory by suggesting that the disciples made off with the body and nursed Jesus back to health. If the New Testament reports are anywhere near accurate, the disciples would have had to be medical practitioners of extraordinary genius to get Jesus ready for his immediate post-resurrection appearances. There is no question that Jesus died by crucifixion. And if he did, there is no possible way he could have survived, after having suffered such massive trauma.

This raises the question of how the disciples, devoid of military training, could have overpowered the trained soldiers guarding the tomb and taken Jesus away. There is also the problem of why, if there was such a conspiracy, no one involved in it ever cracked, sold out the others, and recanted, especially since there would have been strong pressure to do so. Neither the Jewish authorities nor the occupying Romans looked kindly on the idea that Jesus had risen, since this would have strengthened the belief that Jesus was the Jewish Messiah and mocked the Romans for their incompetence as executioners. The disciples became outcasts and were in some cases tortured and executed. Who among us is going to

CHAPTER 14. WHAT CAN WE CONCLUDE ABOUT JESUS?

suffer, much less die, for a hoax, especially since Jesus had made it clear that he had no intention of serving as a political leader?

Perhaps naïve people simply wanted to believe they had encountered the risen Christ. If so, like Paul who almost certainly died for his beliefs, they might have paid dearly for clinging to this belief, first in the face of the Jewish power structure and later the Romans. One or two people might risk persecution and death, but would so many? If as Samuel Johnson quipped, nothing focuses the mind like a hanging, it is also true that nothing encourages recantation like the prospect of martyrdom. Inventing the story of Jesus' resurrection and its aftermath would also have required great creativity. The disciples, however, were "simple, honest, common peasants." In the face of rumors about a resurrection, both Jews and Romans would have been eager to find and produce the corpse. They never did.

The Resurrection Is a Myth

Nothing in the New Testament may be as difficult to believe as Jesus having come back to life. Some theologians insist on the significance of what they call the *Christ event* but deny the physical resurrection. It seems odd to argue for the significance of something that never happened. The New Testament describes the announcement God made to humankind *through* the resurrection. The most compelling testimony to who Jesus was occurred when he died and returned from the grave. By this, he defeated our ultimate enemy, death, so that when we die, we need not cease to exist. Because Jesus was the son of God in a sense none of the rest of us are, we may well say that Jesus is of mythic proportions. But this is entirely different from saying his resurrection is a myth. Nothing about it resembles one. Were it not for the vivid, first-hand accounts in the New Testament of the discovery of the empty tomb, and of people soon thereafter seeing and talking with Jesus, it might be reasonable to assume that, over time, a myth of the resurrection emerged. These encounters were personal, physical, and poignant. What had been the disciples' pre-resurrection timidity now became their bold proclamation.

Even after the resurrection, Jesus demonstrated the supernatural qualities that came with a post-resurrection body, such as the ability to walk through walls. This is not the stuff of myths. There was little time for a myth about the resurrection to develop because his interactions after the resurrection happened quickly. It was women, moreover, who first reported the grave to be empty and the stone rolled away. Society at the time only recognized men as witnesses, and the writers of the Gospels would surely have omitted this awkward fact if it were not true.[16]

What the Church Concluded About Jesus

The Christological question, as it is called, is actually a series of questions having to do with the nature of Jesus, his relationship with God, and his significance for us and our standing with God. I have taken the Apostles' and Nicene Creeds as principal outlines of Christian belief. Much of the motivation for Emperor Constantine convening the Council of Nicaea in AD 325 was the need to resolve contentious issues that the church at the time was confronting. Crafted in a city located in what today is northwestern Turkey, it affirmed that Jesus was of the same nature, essence, or substance as God. Jesus, the Nicene Creed claims, was God in the person of the Son. This was not arrived at without struggle, controversy, and debate.

Those who attended the later Council of Chalcedon in 451 affirmed that in Christ the human and divine fully but distinctly co-existed. This is called *hypostatic union*. The majority of Christian traditions continue to endorse Chalcedonian Christology. These include but are not limited to Anglicans, Baptists, Eastern Orthodox, Lutherans, Methodists, Presbyterians, and Roman Catholics. The proximate cause of the Council at Nicaea was the controversy that had arisen between Arius (ca. AD 250–336), a priest in Alexandria, and Athanasius (ca. AD 295–373), its bishop. Arius argued that the Son of God was created, did not always exist, and is distinct from and inferior to God, who alone is *unbegotten*. Recall that the difference between creating and begetting is that we create things that are different from ourselves, such as musical scores or pieces of machinery, but we beget beings like ourselves (children). Arians acknowledged Jesus as Lord and believed that he was born before time began and created the world on behalf of God. Christ was divine, they conceded, in that his nature resembled God's, but he was not equal to God, who sent him to earth for our salvation. Against these notions, Athanasius argued that all three, Father, Son, and Holy Spirit, were uncreated and had always existed. His

---

16. See Bauckham, *Jesus and the Eyewitnesses*.

CHAPTER 14. WHAT CAN WE CONCLUDE ABOUT JESUS?

view was trinitarian, according to which Christ was a distinct being of God, which the Latin fathers rendered as one God in three persons.

Arius appears to have been exiled around 325. Ten years later, Athanasius was exiled because Emperor Constantine regarded him as an obstacle to peaceful reconciliation within his empire. The Arian missionary Ulfilas successfully brought *Arianism* to Germanic tribes across the Danube. These tribes, therefore, included many Arian Christians when they put an end to the Roman Empire in the fifth century.

Another proposed resolution of the Christological question appeared even earlier. From late in the first century, there were *Gnostic* sects comprising those who believed they had secret knowledge. Gnostics maintained that matter was evil, intentionally created by a lesser and sinister god or demiurge to derail us, and that our physical bodies were impediments to recognizing the divine light within. Many Gnostics espoused *Docetism*, a term that derives from a Greek word meaning *to seem*. Thus, they argued that Jesus had been a spiritual being who only appeared to have a physical body, to die, and to have resurrected. He was pure spirit and everything physical about him was an illusion. Some first-century Christians may have developed docetic doctrines to make Christian teachings more palatable to pagans, and in one form or another such beliefs endured until at least the thirteenth century, when the Albigensian Crusade (1209–29), initiated by Pope Innocent III, suppressed them. The title Albigensian comes from Albi, the city in southern France where the movement took hold, and their beliefs are referred to as *Catharism*. Some sources suggest such beliefs continued into the fourteenth century. A related movement was *Marcionism*, dating from the second century.

Still another approach to the Christological question was *Sabellianism*, so named for its founder Sabellius who lived in the third century. This is a non-trinitarian belief, also known as *Modalism*. It maintains that the Father, Son, and Spirit are three modes, aspects, or manifestations of God, rather than three distinct co-equal and co-eternal divine persons. The early church father Tertullian (ca. AD 160–AD 220) applied the label *Patripassianism* to this movement because it suggested that God suffered on the cross in the mode of the Son.

Adoptionism emerged as a form of *Monarchianism*, the belief that God is one and only one person. Its central thesis was that God adopted Jesus as the Son when Jesus was baptized by John in the River Jordan, and it was only from that moment, after the Spirit descended on him, that

Jesus performed miracles. Some Adoptionists, however, maintained this happened either at Jesus' resurrection or ascension into heaven. Adoptionists suggested that God chose Jesus because of his sinlessness and pietistic devotion. They denied the pre-existence of Jesus but affirmed that he was divine, albeit subordinate and unequal to God. Some medieval theologians, such as Abelard (1079–1142) and Dun Scotus (1265–1308), may have promoted some version of Adoptionism.

The last approach we will consider is *Socianism*, originated by Lelio Sozzini (1525–62) in the sixteenth century. He was an Italian antitrinitarian who, like the Adoptionists, went beyond Arianism to deny the pre-existence of Christ. Sozzini and his followers also seem to have denied the divinity of Jesus, except in a metaphoric sense.

These are some of the proposed answers to questions about the nature of Christ and his relation to God. Some theologians emphasize *Christology from above*, which means they begin with the divinity of Christ as the pre-existing *logos*, translated in the Gospel of John as *Word*, and work down to his nature as Jesus the man. Others emphasize *Christology from below* and begin with the humanity of Jesus, including his miracles and teachings, and move up from there toward his incarnation and divinity. Among the more contentious issues was whether Christ embodied one nature, two natures merged into one, or two co-existing natures. The last of these was the position adopted by the Western church.

Suggestions for Seekers

Skeptical questions are often sincere. An assumption within Christianity, however, is that because of our self-oriented bent toward rebellion, none of us is naturally inclined toward seeking, loving, or serving God. Or even toward recognizing spiritual truth. Questions about God are well worth asking, and with the help of God's Spirit, anyone who sincerely wants answers is likely to find them. When trying to determine if Christianity makes sense, it may help to begin with the assumption that the conclusions arrived at by Christian theologians through the centuries are probably correct. When it comes to the claims of Christianity, the crux of the matter is whether only a divine Jesus would be able to "save" us. If Jesus was only a philosopher, regardless of how insightful, it would make little sense to build your life around him.

CHAPTER 14. WHAT CAN WE CONCLUDE ABOUT JESUS?

Closing Thoughts

No serious scholar, even an atheist, doubts that Jesus existed. He was not a figment of imagination. There is no good reason to conclude that the authors of the New Testament colluded or engaged in a conspiracy. They all reached the same conclusion, insisting that Jesus was not only their savior but also their Lord. That miracles are possible can be denied, but not without presupposing that they are impossible. Because of the nature miracles, their possibility or impossibility can never be demonstrated. Jesus also made extraordinary claims about himself, such as being the only path to God. That we may own a New Testament should not cause us to take its contents for granted, certainly not without reading it.

Preview

We will now turn to the contention that science and religion are at war. This belief was promoted in the nineteenth century by two public intellectuals who should have known better. Considerable mythology has developed around the unfounded assumption that a benighted church victimized the scientists.

Chapter 15. Are Science and Religion at War?

MANY PEOPLE ASSUME THAT no rational person could be a scientist and still believe in God. Science in their view has debunked religion, and the two will always stand opposed to one another. Until the nineteenth century, the idea of any serious incompatibility between science and Christianity would have seemed strange. There were skeptics and cynics during the eighteenth-century Enlightenment, but even prominent intellectuals like Voltaire had limited impact on mass public opinion.

For reasons we will discuss in this chapter, the incompatibility thesis became popular in the nineteenth century, and in the twentieth disputes between biblical literalists and evolutionists reinforced it. In the present century, celebrity scientists have again fueled the fires of controversy by stridently arguing against theism.

The warfare that has been alleged to exist between science and religion is popularly assumed to have had a long history, going back at least as far as Copernicus and Galileo. The former was a Polish monk whose book advancing the heliocentric contra geocentric theory was only published on his death in 1543, while the Galileo affair, ending in his relatively benign punishment, lasted a full twenty years, from 1613 to 1633. For the most part, this imagined warfare has only existed in its polarized form for about a hundred and fifty years, with atheists and fundamentalists raging at each other from extreme positions on both sides of the issue. The alleged war was triggered by the publication of two books, John William Draper's (1811–1882) *History of the Conflict*

CHAPTER 15. ARE SCIENCE AND RELIGION AT WAR?

between *Religion and Science* (1874) and Andrew Dickson White's (1832–1918) *Warfare of Science* in (1876), later expanded into *History of the Warfare of Science and Theology in Christendom* (1896). Although the general public is familiar with contemporary fundamentalists who argue, for example, that the earth was created 6,000 years ago in six calendar days, it is less aware that scientists railing against God's existence also deserve to be regarded as fundamentalists.

Science, at its best, is the self-correcting advance of knowledge about the physical world in the interests of benefiting humankind. At its worst, it becomes camouflage for scientists posing as philosophers, for which they have often had little or no training. Although scientists who stick to the business of science can be humanity's great benefactors, those who misunderstand or hide the difference between a scientific and a philosophic question may do it considerable harm. Their pronouncements on non-scientific questions in the name of science are at best amateurish and at worst fraudulent. The difference between fraud and simple misrepresentation is that fraud implies intent. As mentioned in chapter 2, *epistemic* means relating to knowledge, and such boundary violations are what philosopher Nathan Ballantyne refers to as *epistemic trespassing*.[1]

Options

People tend to understand the relationship between science and religion in one of three ways. First, they may believe that science and religion are incompatible, an idea promoted with equal vigor by strident atheists and reactionary believers. The atheists insist that science has so discredited Christianity that only a narrow-minded dolt, mentally living in the Middle Ages, would embrace it. Insecure Christians, for their part, insist that modern science threatens faith at every turn and is therefore Christianity's enemy.

A second understanding is that science and religion have nothing to do with each other because they operate in entirely different spheres, separated from each other by a wall border. When the two appear to be in conflict, it is because one has strayed into the other's territory. This was the position taken by the late Harvard paleontologist and

---

1. See Yong, "COVID-19 Manhattan Project," 55.

evolutionary biologist Stephen Jay Gould.[2] He proposed "a simple resolution to the supposed conflict between science and religion." Each, he suggested, has its own *magisterium*, its proper domain of authority, and the two do not overlap. The magisterium of science is empirical—what the universe consists of (facts) and why it works as it does (theory)—while the magisterium of religion has to do with questions of values, morality, and ultimate meaning.

The third understanding is that through the ages people of science and people of faith have mostly respected each other, even when the implications of science and religion seemed to differ. When they do, both must live with the tension this produces. Galileo's discoveries are an example of how discoveries of science and beliefs of the church can conflict. Scientists and Christians have often been the same people. Johannes Kepler (1571–1630) is an example. He believed that in doing science he was able to think God's thoughts and in that way share God's mind. If you search for a list of Christians in science and technology, you will find many people who have identified themselves as Christians. An excellent source for this is the International Society for Science and Religion (ISSR). The number may surprise you, not just from prior centuries but also by those living today. Christianity and science have had a nuanced and complex history, and the relationship between the two has occasionally been tense. Contrary to popular opinion, however, it has usually been irenic and rarely oppositional.

Although the idea of independent domains fosters a live-and-let-live tolerance, it tends to minimize or ignore that science can influence religious belief. Sometimes, to the surprise of many, science turns out to support such believe. As an example, the thesis that God created the universe at a specific point in time has been around for thousands of years and is a basic tenet of Christianity. It turns out to be consistent with the Big Bang.[3] Science also touched on religion with the discovery from skeletal remains and artifacts that *Homo sapiens* have been around at least 40,000 years and perhaps for hundreds of thousands.

---

2. Gould, *Structure of Evolutionary Theory*.

3. Fred Hoyle (1915-2001) coined the term "Big Bang" as a term of derision during a BBC broadcast in March, 1949.

CHAPTER 15. ARE SCIENCE AND RELIGION AT WAR?

Getting Clear

Some people, aware that science cannot substitute for philosophy or theology, find this intolerable, and the resulting despair and disillusionment leads them, as it led Nietzsche, to nihilism. In its ethical form, nihilism regards all values as without foundation. As it relates to truth, it is profound skepticism toward the possibility of knowledge. Concluding that there is no fixed, reliable, and ultimate truth, nor any underlying order to the universe, people can lose interest in truth and retreat into dogmatic assertions that reflect nothing more than personal opinion. If pushed far enough, there remains only taste, and as we have seen, the idea of truth then devolves into my truth versus your truth but never *the* truth. The attending absence of an appeal to objective reality encourages some to impose their values on the rest of us and so paves the way for tyranny.

Others pass off their opinions on the unsuspecting as if these opinions were scientific, and more than a few atheistic scientists promote a false dichotomy between evolution and God, when in fact a person may believe in both without inconsistency. They speak as philosophers, and if in any legitimate sense they are philosophers they seem to be either uninformed or disingenuous ones. Like Nietzsche, these scientists renounce the concept of God and assert not only that there is no God, but worse for its philosophical naivete, that the very idea of God is illogical or absurd. What is, in fact, illogical and absurd is a scientist promoting philosophic views as if they were science, much like celebrities posing as experts on soap. Christianity holds that we became human beings, with all this implies, because God made it so. Exactly how God did this is of secondary importance.

When society embraces science and technology as a quasi-religion, as it has done in fits and starts since the seventeenth century, it is destined to be disappointed. Expecting empirical discovery to enable human beings to make sense of life, to illuminate its significance and guide moral decisions, is like trying to get orange juice from a mushroom. Science as science *cannot* reveal significance or provide ethical guidance without straying beyond its borders. Such matters are the proper province of philosophy and, if the existence of an intentional God is granted, of theology. When the bankruptcy of science masquerading as philosophy finally hits home, as it may someday do, society is likely to oscillate between clinging to whatever hope it manages to retain in the power of scientism and caving in to cynical irrationalism.

Seeds of the latter already appear in some forms of postmodernism, a term that has been around since the nineteenth century and appears first to have been used by Arnold J Toynbee (1889–1975) to describe a historical movement. People use terms like *postmodernism* and *postmodernity* in a variety of ways. These labels are sometimes applied to the intellectual position assumed by those in Western Culture who are disenchanted with empirical science, find their belief in progress wavering, and may question the soundness of reason itself. To the extent that it is a coherent movement or mindset, its central thesis seems to be that reality is a social construction. This skepticism toward rational inquiry and logical thought is largely what leads to, "your truth is not my truth." Such a stance is reminiscent of the sense of futility that can develop when religion becomes so watered down and secularized that it turns into a loosely thought-out doctrine of cozy comfort and political correctness.

Geologic Science

Five cataclysms have occurred during the earth's nearly five-billion-year history.[4] The first was 444 million years ago, when almost all multicellular organisms that had begun to develop two hundred million years earlier became extinct. In the second global catastrophe, 372 million years ago, all but a quarter of the wildlife that recovered from the first cataclysm perished. Over the next 100 million years, reptiles, enormous dragonflies, giant millipedes, and plants with seeds emerged. The third catastrophe occurred 252 million years ago. It is what paleo-biologists call the "Great Dying." About ninety-four percent of marine species vanished, along with seventy percent of terrestrial vertebrates. Those that remained flourished until the fourth cataclysm, 201 million years ago, killed off half of them. After the fourth cataclysm, what had been a single landmass (Pangaea) began to break up into what would become our continents. The waters between them teamed with "sponges, sharks, snails, corals, and crocodiles."[5] Earth's climate was substantially subtropical. Some 150 million years ago, stegosaurs lived, and sixty-seven million years after its extinction, tyrannosaurs reigned. The fifth great catastrophe caused the elimination of the dinosaurs, which occurred about sixty-six million

---

4. Bosker, "What Killed the Dinosaurs," 44–55.
5. Bosker, "What Killed the Dinosaurs?," 47.

years ago. Scientists still debate what caused their extinction. Not all of them agree with Bosker.

I mention these cataclysms to suggest that, in misguided attempts to defend Christianity, it makes no sense to pretend they never happened. We should not read the opening chapters of Genesis as alternative science, which it is not, much less as an injunction to avoid scientific inquiry. One purpose of Genesis, among others, is to highlight the majesty and dominion of God. This, incidentally, inspired some of the wonderful poetry we find in the book of Psalms.

Human beings are more than animals. We are biological creatures and in that sense share with the animals the desire to survive, to live rather than die. But we are also beings that, by the will of our creator, share such divine attributes as the ability to develop long-range intentions, enjoy interpersonal relationships, and know right from wrong. The universe has existed over thirteen billion years, but humans have existed for only a couple hundred thousand. It seems significant that in the twelve and certainly no more than eighteen thousand years since the development of agriculture, humankind has made such enormous strides, which suggests that something occurred to turn the genus *Homo* into true human beings.[6] Against the backdrop of geologic time, it is as if this just happened.

If you calculate how long *Homo sapiens* may have been around, 200,000 years, as a percentage of the age of the earth, 4,500,000,000, you will see that this percentage is infinitesimally small. If you calculate it as a percentage of 13,800,000,000 years, the age of the universe, the percentage is even smaller. Think of how, depending on geographic location, the Stone Age ended between 8,000 and 3,000 years ago, when people first learned to make tools and weapons out of metal. Look at how far we have come. Perhaps our emergence as *Homo sapiens* is what Genesis refers to as God breathing life into Adam, Hebrew for man.

Reason and Faith in Science and Theology

Some people claim that science works through cold logic but theology only by faith. This reflects a misunderstanding. Science and theology both represent collections of knowledge-claims and a set of prescribed methods for

---

6. See Porter, *Creation of the Modern World*.

acquiring new knowledge. Through careful reasoning, both scientists and theologians strive to move from premises to conclusions.

Science rests on assumptions such as a belief in physical causation and the lawfulness of nature. The validity of these assumptions may seem self-evident, but prominent thinkers such as Scottish philosopher David Hume points out that such beliefs are only probabilistic inferences. Hume goes even further by arguing that, in fact, we have no sound basis whatsoever for placing our confidence in inductive reasoning. Because B follows A, and always has in our experience, does not imply that A causes B, and because the sun rose this morning does not mean it will rise again tomorrow. We can respond to Hume's skepticism by dismissing it in the name of common sense, but this does nothing to change how, from the vantage point of logic, he is right. Hume well knew that we could not navigate through life without a belief in material causation and the regularity of the physical world.

Although Hume's logical point stands, modern science is based on being able to predict how one thing reliably follows another. Scientific inquiry also rests on the assumption that there is a world outside our minds, and few if any scientists take this world to be a figment of imagination. Although we may have trouble discerning the true nature of things, there is little doubt on the part of scientists that nature objectively exists.

Scientists assume, too, that they can potentially make sense of their observations, that whatever they discover through empirical methods will contribute to a coherent understanding of the world. They may have to check and recheck measurements, or amplify incoming signals with instruments like microscopes and telescopes, but once they perform such checks and amplifications, such measurements and signals enable increasingly precise data gathering, which in turn facilitates understanding. Although understanding amounts to more than prediction, the ability to note that A and B tend to occur together, and more powerfully that B routinely follows A, are minimum criteria for a scientific advance.

All three beliefs—predictable causation, objective reality, and the value of empirical observation—are foundational to science and travel well with a pragmatic view of truth (see chapters 2 and 6). In light of the enormous contribution science has made to human life, especially in medicine,[7] nearly everyone in the modern world shares these beliefs.

---

7. See Porter, *Greatest Benefit to Mankind*.

CHAPTER 15. ARE SCIENCE AND RELIGION AT WAR?

Theology, like science, rests on the scaffolding of careful reasoning. But it is not principally concerned with studying the concrete visible world. Christian theology does this based on the assumptions that God exists, the Bible contains the history of God's dealings with humankind, and Jesus was both God and human. Without these assumptions, there can be no legitimate Christianity. Like science, theology is the quest for knowledge, for justified true belief.

For theology to be sound, it cannot categorically reject the conclusions of science, and if these conclusions turn out to be *robust*, theology must attempt to accommodate them. For a scientific finding to be robust, it must be replicable. This is akin to how, in philosophy, only those valid arguments based on true premises are sound. Theology depends as much on rigorous reasoning, and therefore on principles of logic, as even the most exact science. Just as there can be sloppy science, there can be sloppy theology. But sloppy theologies, like mediocre works of art, do not diminish the value of great ones.

There are uncertainties in both science and theology. Light, for example, behaves as both waves and particles, but it may not be entirely clear how or why. As another example, there are ways in which the opposing ideas of Albert Einstein and Niels Bohr both seem true and are each explanatorily superior. In both science and theology, scholars search for understanding, try to penetrate mysteries, and attempt to reduce ambiguity and confusion. Good science and good theology have more in common than many people think.

If you define science as an empirically verifiable body of knowledge, along with a set of procedures that yield observable physical results, theology is not a science. Throughout most of the Middle Ages, theology was regarded as the queen of the sciences, a claim later applied to philosophy. Starting with the Modern Period, which began in the middle of the 1400s, *science* became synonymous with systematic empirical investigation of physical phenomena. If theology and philosophy had each been queen, science was now king.

People sometimes claim that Christianity is unscientific, as if this were a startling new discovery, and they may go on to say that theology is therefore ridiculous. What may be ridiculous, however, is not theology but a worldview that defines only the tangible as real. When they are consistent, people who hold such a view have trouble regarding love, affection, bravery, patience, tolerance, justice, fairness, loyalty, truthfulness, or any other kind of goodness as real.

PART III. PIVOTAL QUESTIONS

Two Kinds of Materialism

Attacking Christianity as unscientific is often rooted in philosophic materialism, the doctrine that you can explain everything that happens with physical laws. We may not know all the material causes for a given phenomenon, such as human consciousness, but these causes are believed, in principle, to be discoverable. The issue of causation is complicated, with a long history going back at least as far as Aristotle. But even if we knew how every neuron in the brain fired when someone reported a specific thought or feeling, this would not explain the nature of consciousness itself.

Philosophical or metaphysical materialism asserts that there was, and in fact could not have been, a nonmaterial being behind creation. Nor could such a being uphold the world, much less interact with it. There is no God, certainly no personal God. Among the reasons for denying the existence of God may be that people are reluctant to grasp their own natures as spiritual. This kind of materialism is closely related to causal determinism, which is the thesis that, however else it may seem, everything that occurs, including thought, is the necessary result of whatever preceded it. Given what went on before, whatever happens in the future *must* happen. According to metaphysical materialism, there exists only a chain of physical events that is the product of activity at the atomic and subatomic level. When you last went to a vending machine, put in the money, and made your selection, you had no alternative, even if you thought you did. That you made a choice was an illusion, what philosophers label as *epiphenomenal*.

It is important to distinguish *metaphysical materialism*, on the one hand, from *methodological materialism* on the other. Metaphysical materialism, or as it tends now to be called *physicalism*, posits that everything in existence is material. The closely related idea of *metaphysical naturalism* is the thesis that everything can be explained by nature. Some metaphysical naturalists, however, are willing to acknowledge that not all natural entities, such as thoughts, are material.

When they work within the confines of science, all scientists are, by definition, *methodological* materialists, but they are not all *metaphysical* materialists. The decision of scientists to think and act according to the principles of methodological materialism implies nothing other than their willingness to conduct their professional activities according to the commonly understood dictates of natural science. The decision to

CHAPTER 15. ARE SCIENCE AND RELIGION AT WAR?

embrace metaphysical materialism, however, has nothing logically to do with the scientific method or knowledge that has come from its application. It is to decide in favor of one among many ways of making sense of life, and for some it functions as something akin to religion. Because of the ambiguity of the term *God*, it is difficult to determine what percentage of scientists believe in a transcendent God. But it appears that a substantial percentage do.

Philosophical Confusions

Confusion results when scientists fail, knowingly or unknowingly, to distinguish between their scientific work and their personal beliefs. Metaphysical materialism is a philosophic stance, an assumption some researchers layer on top of their science. And if they are polemically inclined, they may use their scientific credentials to promote that stance. Some well-known scientists pass their anti-religious views off as science, which such views most certainly are not.

When a well-respected scientist makes a pronouncement within the province of his or her discipline, it is fitting to give that scientist the benefit of the doubt. Unless we also have expertise in the same area, we know far less than the scientist does about the subject. A given scientist may be wrong, of course, but he or she is far more likely to be right than we are. If it turns out that the scientist erred, other researchers or theoreticians will eventually point this out, based on more systematic observations or mathematical calculations.

In the physical sciences, systematic observations are collected whenever possible by doing controlled experiments. In some branches of science, including medicine, it is not ethical to carry out certain experiments. We cannot, for example, test the efficacy of a new drug by dividing people into two groups, infecting only the members of one group with an infectious pathogen, and comparing the results. In the softer disciplines, such as sociology and economics, it is rarely possible to devise and carry out anything even close to a question-settling experiment, or even a series of them. This has at least two implications.

First, social scientists usually rely on correlations, which has the defect of not always revealing causation. To use a variation of an example from chapter 6, on any particular day the amount of ice cream sold is highly correlated with the number of drownings. Although it is a simple matter to predict one from the other, neither causes the other, and in fact hot weather causes both. When it is hot, more people go to the beach, enter the water, and may therefore drown, and when it is hot more people buy ice cream. Second, biases based on ideology are more likely to color the interpretation of results in the softer disciplines. Theology and speculative philosophy are the softest disciplines of them all.

Expertise in one discipline does not suggest, much less guarantee, competence in another. When a scientist without training in philosophy makes a pronouncement that is expressly philosophical, there is no reason to accept or even pay it special attention. There are a few scientists, such as John Polkinghorne[8] and Alister McGrath,[9] who have achieved eminence in both science and theology, and their opinions in both domains therefore merit attention. Most scientists are neither trained philosophers nor knowledgeable theologians, however, and they are disingenuous when they posture as if they were.

It is one thing for a scientist to offer an opinion about the existence of God. Anyone can do that. It is quite another for a scientist to state, intimate, or allow others falsely to believe[10] that such an opinion is based on science. A doctorate in particle physics from the finest university in the world does not guarantee any expertise in, say, literature. Such a physicist may have never heard of Claude Simon, French winner of the 1985 Nobel Prize in Literature, or V. S. Naipaul, a Brit who won it in 2001. Neither does it guarantee any expertise in philosophy. To characterize Christians as unenlightened is to resort to a level of argument unworthy of any educated person, much less a world-class scientist. Name-calling is neither a legitimate nor robust form of argument, but unfortunately it can persuade people who are not attuned to differences between and among disciplines.

A section of Hyde Park in London known as Speaker's Corner is where anyone can hold forth on just about anything and find an audience. When I encounter strident critics of Christianity waxing eloquent in the name of science, I recall standing around Speaker's Corner one chilly Sunday afternoon. Predictably, not everyone in the crowd took a given speaker seriously, and one or two listeners occasionally heckled. Other speakers addressed attentive audiences, but their members did not always

---

8. See Polkinghorne, *Faith, Science and Understanding*.

9. McGrath, *Christian Theology: An Introduction*.

10. Lies of omission can be just as damaging as lies of commission. See McLemore, *Street-Smart* Ethics, 23–23, 154, 159, 162–63.

recognize unsound arguments when they heard them. This is the sort of uncritical attention sometimes paid to the statements of scientists who are anti-religious polemicists in the name of science.

Some years ago. a celebrated Oxford biologist caused quite a stir when he penned a book claiming that religion is unscientific and superstitious.[11] His intention was not only to call into question such religious practices as attending church, but also to debunk beliefs supporting such practices. Matters became even more confused when reviewers described his book as *bold, groundbreaking,* and *courageous.* His work may have been bold, but it was not bold science, and in fact it was not science at all. Such efforts can be little more than barroom opinion, the sort of bombast that might be delivered by someone after having downed a few pints of lager. As for breaking new ground, this ground is not new at all. People have been promoting atheism in one form or another for a long time, but until recently they have rarely included well-known scientists. Courageous? In what sense and in relation to which audience? Certainly not the Western World, which is now filled with religious skeptics.

For a reputable scholar to hold forth as an expert in an area in which he or she has no recognized expertise is like a pianist who plays by ear, cannot read music, but decides one day to compose a symphony. Such a pianist might eventually be able to do it, and even do it well, but not without a great deal of study. The scientists I have in mind are inclined to take up arms against caricatures of Christianity, rather than the genuine article.

Origin of the Warfare Thesis

The thesis that science and religion are in mortal combat has a peculiar history, and if you are interested in learning more about the relationship between the two, I recommend the lectures given by Johns Hopkins University Professor Lawrence Principe.[12] Widespread belief that there is a war between science and religion has existed for only about a century and a half, but it has become entrenched in contemporary culture. Except among members of the *avant garde* during the eighteenth-century Enlightenment, there was little tension between science and religion.

---

11. Dawkins, *The God Delusion.*
12. Principe, *Science and Religion.*

Then, as noted above, two men of letters introduced into American culture the idea that science and religion are, and always have been, at war. Both had backgrounds that should have caused them to be more careful and perhaps also more honest. John William Draper was a physician, accomplished chemist, and pioneer in photography—"In 1840, he made what may be the oldest surviving photographic portrait, a picture of his sister, which required an exposure of 65 seconds."[13] Andrew Dickson White was a professor of history and literature, a diplomat, and a polyglot. Each served as head of a prestigious academic institution and president of an important professional association.

Draper, the son of an English clergyman, attended University College London and emigrated with his widowed mother to the United States, where he completed medical school at the University of Pennsylvania. He taught, among other places, at New York University and eventually became president of its medical school, which he had helped found. He later became president of the American Chemical Society. Draper published books on such diverse subjects as the intellectual development of Europe and the history of the American Civil War.

White,[14] younger than Draper by a generation, was by any measure extraordinary. Born in rural New York, he attended Yale, then studied at the Sorbonne and the University of Berlin. He served for a while as translator for the American ambassador to Russia and returned to Yale to earn a Master's degree in history. He taught at the University of Michigan and became a New York State senator, where he befriended fellow senator Ezra Cornell, a wealthy captain of the telegraph industry who had founded Western Union. With the assistance of a sizable donation from Cornell, the two co-founded Cornell University in 1865, the year the Civil War ended. White served as its founding president. Later, after doing work for President Grant, he accepted diplomatic posts, including United States Minister to Russia and Ambassador to Germany. He was also president of the American Historical Society.

Their Popular Works

In 1874, Draper wrote *A History of the Conflict between Religion and Science*, a widely read book that remains in print. And in 1876, White

---

13. *Chambers Biographical Dictionary*, "John William Draper," 556.
14. *Chambers Biographical Dictionary*, "Andrew Dickson White," 1940.

CHAPTER 15. ARE SCIENCE AND RELIGION AT WAR?

came out with *The Warfare of Science*, followed in 1896 by his two-volume *History of the Warfare of Science with Theology in Christendom*. Both Draper and White had agendas that were compelling enough to ensure that, when it came to writing about science and religion, neither bothered much with accuracy. They pulled quotations out of context and used them to support points that were sometimes the opposite of what the original authors intended. Their portrayals of events were often skewed, their interpretations biased, and their comprehension of religion unnuanced.

It may be easier to understand the historical sloppiness of Draper than of White, since Draper was a scientist and not a historian. Giving him such an easy pass, however, is unwarranted. He was fervently anti-Catholic, and in line with anti-immigrant prejudices of the time, Draper accused the Catholic Church of everything from hindering scientific inquiry to preventing desirable population growth, on its face an astounding claim. Only nineteenth-century liberal Protestantism, which had backed away from anything supernatural, enjoyed his unqualified favor. Professor Principe indicates that, in the course he teaches on the history of science and religion at Johns Hopkins University, he has been unable to find a single passage from Draper's 1874 book that does not provoke laughter from his students.[15] Principe writes, "Although Draper's work is easy to dismiss as cranky and ahistorical, his theme and many of his anecdotes have entered the common consciousness, where they have remained hard to remove."[16]

White was a trained historian from whom we might have expected better. But, like Draper, he had another agenda, perhaps crystallized in part because there was substantial opposition to co-founding Cornell without a religious affiliation, a dramatic move in the middle of the nineteenth century. As an example of White's superficial fact-checking, he promoted the idea that, prior to Columbus and Magellan, people believed the world was flat, an assertion that continues to show up in secondary school textbooks. Believing the earth to be flat may have been characteristic of some uneducated people, but it certainly was not for the learned, who even in the Middle Ages understood the earth to be a sphere and disagreed only about its size. Neither did the medieval church forbid dissection, as White mistakenly asserted, or condemn science as

---

15. Principe, "The Warfare Thesis," *Science and Religion*, Lecture 2.
16. Principe, *Course Guidebook*, 6.

the handiwork of the devil. Principe writes about White's book, "His methodological errors are collectivism (the unwarrantable extension of an individual's views to represent that of some larger group of which he is a part), a lack of critical judgment about sources, arguments by ridicule and assertion, failure to check primary sources, and quoting selectively and out of context."[17] Many of these criticisms also apply to Draper's book, on which White appears in places to have relied.

Good Drama, Bad History

Aside from their scholarly flaws and socio-political motives, Draper and White seemed to believe that scientists and religious people occupied two antagonistic worlds and that their only interactions consisted of the latter oppressing the former. Influenced by the interpretations of history that Draper and White suffused into popular culture, film makers glommed onto the warfare thesis and produced good drama based on bad history. Prior to the modern era, scientists tended to be theists of one stripe or another who took for granted a Christian worldview. With few exceptions, the church has traditionally embraced the work of scientists, who in turn embraced the church and what it stood for.

The greatest of the church fathers, Augustine, laid great stress on the need for clergymen to be knowledgeable about science, lest they make fools of themselves, and worse, create the impression that Christianity was only for the simple and therefore unworthy of respect. The Polish monk Copernicus (1473–1543) advocated a model of the universe that his friends warned him might be unpopular. Yet, some of his fellow clergymen pushed him to publish it immediately, and the church had earlier obtained his help in reforming the calendar. Johannes Kepler (1571–1630), a German astronomer and mathematician, viewed his scientific contributions as a form of worship.[18] He openly declared that in working out of the laws of planetary motion he intended to unravel the mysteries of God's creation and, thus, to bring glory to its creator. As for the complex matrix of facts surrounding the trial of Galileo Galilee (1564–1642) and the events that led to his spending years under house arrest, that drama too has been misunderstood and misrepresented. There was far more to the Galileo affair, politically and

---

17. Principe, *Course Guidebook*, 6–7.
18. Kepler's life brings to mind Rom 12:1–2.

philosophically, than is commonly recognized, and we cannot reduce it to ecclesiastic suppression of science. Plays and movies do not always major in political subtleties or intellectual nuances, and what occurred between Galileo and the church reflected both.

Natural Theology

Natural theology is the attempt to establish God's existence and divine attributes by inferring them from nature, often from its complexity or beauty. One version of this argument was that since creation resembles the inner workings of a watch, there must have been a watchmaker. Aside from whether a mechanical timepiece is a suitable metaphor for nature, a problem with all such arguments is that they do not necessarily point to, much less prove, the existence of a god, much less the Christian God. They are just as likely to support deism, the belief that God created the world, then left it to its own devices. Classical deism stands in contrast to theism, whose personal God is intimately involved in human affairs. Setting aside whether *arguments from design* point to theism, or at least to deism, there is still the issue of whether such arguments are convincing.

As we saw in chapter 2, Pascal suggested five hundred years ago that proofs of God from nature are most persuasive for those who already believe. Yet, there are passages in the New Testament that suggest God is self-evident to anyone who cares to notice. Paul, for example, writes, "From the foundation of the world, God's sovereignty and power, while invisible to the natural eye, have been obvious to the receptive and discerning heart."[19] But he also suggested that this knowledge is corrupted by sin. Natural theology has much to recommend it, provided it is not advanced as a rigorous proof of God's existence. It may, however, contain probabilistic hints.

Fundamentalists and Darwinists

A major impact of what Draper and White promoted was the polarization of atheistic scientists and reactionary Christians. Those in both camps were quick to take up the cudgel. Strict biblical literalists feared that if they allowed scientists to pick away at the Bible, beginning with the creation narratives, nothing would remain of Christianity. They worried about

---

19. Paraphrase of Rom 1:20.

what has come to be known as the *domino theory*, the notion that when the first domino falls, it knocks down the second, which in its turn knocks down the third, and so on, until all the dominos have fallen.

This was not an issue for those Protestants who no longer took scripture seriously and showed little patience with the supernatural, apart from a kind of diffuse spirituality. Nor was it of focal concern to Catholics, who had the authoritative pronouncements of the Holy See in Rome on which to rely. But for some conservative Protestants, the implications of reading the creation stories in Genesis as anything other than concrete narratives were ominous, and they worried that science was pulling society in an atheistic direction. From the public atheism of outspoken scientists, they began to see science as inherently atheistic, which it most certainly is not.

During the early part of the twentieth century, the conflict between evolutionary theory and literalist religion came into sharp relief with the publication between 1910 and 1915 of a series of documents intended to set forth Five Fundamentals of the Faith. Among them was the assertion that the Bible contains no errors, contradictions, or inconsistencies. If discrepancies arose, it was either because we no longer had the original biblical manuscripts or we had not yet discovered how to reconcile apparent discrepancies. Protestants who believed in biblical inerrancy and modernists who disparaged that idea soon drew their battle lines.

Darwin (1809–1882) followed his 1859 *Origin of Species* with an even more controversial volume in 1871, *The Descent of Man*. Especially inflammatory was Darwin's proposed mechanism of evolution, natural selection, by means of which animals as well as people evolved into what they now are. Organisms with characteristics favoring survival enjoyed the privilege of mating and passing on whatever had given them a survival advantage.

The belief that giraffes have long necks because they once had to stretch to reach food, and then passed their stretched necks on to succeeding generations, is not Darwinian but Lamarckian. Jean-Baptiste Lamarck (1744–1829) was a proponent of the inheritance of acquired characteristics. In the nineteenth century, there was heated controversy between those who subscribed to Lamarck's ideas and those who subscribed to Darwin's. Although the genetic basis of evolution (DNA) was not discovered until long after their deaths, Darwin's thesis was that giraffes had long necks because those with long necks could reach scarce food better than giraffes with short necks. This allowed long-neck

CHAPTER 15. ARE SCIENCE AND RELIGION AT WAR?

giraffes to survive and mate, thus passing on to their offspring whatever gave them long necks to begin with. According to Darwinian theory as it exists today, parents *only* pass along the DNA they were born with, which they acquired from *their* parents, and there is no inheritance of acquired characteristics. There has been a resurgence of interest in Lamarck's ideas in the form of *epigenetics*, although without the suggestion of changes in DNA.

Ideas contained in Darwin's books spread across Western Society, which troubled many conservative Christians. To them, Darwin was not only challenging the God-given dignity of a human being as the pinnacle of creation, but also disparaging the Bible. As they understood Genesis, the idea of evolution taking place over vast reaches of time was unthinkable. That human beings might have evolved over time, even from lower animals, was an idea that had long existed within Christianity, and allusions to this possibility go back at least as far as Augustine. Many of Darwin's early advocates were educated Christians who were open to his ideas and defended him.[20]

Some Christians believe God could not possibly have used evolution in the creation of human beings. The anti-evolution position has come down to us in certain forms of *creation science* and, more recently, *intelligent design*.[21] But there are others, among them highly respected scientists, who subscribe to *theistic evolution*, the idea that God used evolution to achieve divine purposes. Battles over evolution continue, which only encourages people to think that science and faith are incompatible, which they are not. As I have tried to show, nothing in well-executed science makes it the enemy of faith. Nor does anything within Christianity make it the enemy of science.

The Scopes Trial

In 1925, the American Civil Liberties Union (ACLU) decided to set the fundamentalists back on their heels by arranging a trumped-up test case, the purpose of which was to allow the ACLU to appeal the predictable decision. With the help of John Scopes, a part-time schoolteacher who agreed to violate Tennessee's law against teaching evolution, they triggered what turned out to be a well-attended spectacle, replete with

---

20. See Livingstone, *Darwin's Forgotten Defenders*.
21. See Behe, *Darwin's Black Box*.

political and legal luminaries. Scopes' trial was the first courtroom proceeding broadcast on radio. Earlier that year, the Butler Act had made it unlawful for a teacher in a publicly funded school "to teach any theory that denies the Story of the Divine Creation of man as taught in the Bible." Inglehart, cited in the Introduction to this book, writes, "It once was generally assumed that religious beliefs shaped political views . . . But recent evidence indicates that the causality can run the other way . . . many people change their political views first and then become less religions."[22] It is difficult to determine the direction of influence, if it existed, in the Scopes affair.

It had been the ACLU's intention to focus the trial on constitutional issues. But when famed defense attorney Clarence Darrow joined Scopes' legal team, he redirected the focus toward the Bible as a scientific textbook. In response to Darrow's arrival, former Secretary of State and three-time failed Democratic presidential candidate William Jennings Bryan joined the prosecution. He did so with flair but without distinction. The courts found Scopes guilty, but later overturned his conviction on a technicality that had to do with the fine imposed. In 1968, the U. S. Supreme Court struck down the Butler Act and all similar statutes.

Not a Scientific Textbook

Jews and Christians have long pondered the nature of the opening chapters of Genesis, trying to decide how best to understand them. Genesis contains two accounts of creation, the first having to do with the creation of the world (Gen 1:1—2:4a) and the second with the saga of Adam and Eve in the Garden (Gen 2:4b–25). Are *days* in the first creation narrative literal or might they refer to periods like eras or epochs? Should a Christian take these narratives literally, or treat them as religious poems? Or something in between, like a powerful myth? Perhaps the Christian, while reading Genesis, might picture Adam and Eve and think of them as actual people, yet believe on another level that they might not have existed as individuals. Then again, perhaps they did.

Christians run along the wrong tracks when they defend the Bible as if it were a scientific or technical manual. Worse, they run the risk of missing the overarching trajectory of the Bible, which culminates in the

---

22. Inglehart, "Giving Up on God," 114. See also Douthat, *Bad Religion*.

CHAPTER 15. ARE SCIENCE AND RELIGION AT WAR?

appearance on earth of the Son of God.[23] When a new scientific discovery or well-supported theory emerges, it is important for Christians to ask whether they need to revise their previous understanding. The discovery or theory may be wrong, and if it is, this will eventually come to light. But, if it stands up to scrutiny, Christians are duty bound as honest thinkers to grapple with its implications. Christians use the same tool, reason, to study what Augustine called God's two great books, nature and revelation. When these books appear to disagree, Christians have an obligation to try to figure out why.

Biblical Criticism

Fundamentalists bridled at the emergence in the nineteenth century of so-called *higher critics* who increasingly emphasized source criticism. They studied texts to determine literary origins, historical contexts, cultural influences, authorial intentions, and literary nuances. Rather than welcoming such research, some Christians worried that opening the door to it would invite the wholesale discrediting of the Bible. It does not behoove Christians, however, to cling rigidly to an unexamined set of beliefs, as if these were desiccated twigs about to disintegrate. Some Christians were also suspicious, although perhaps less so, of the work of certain *lower critics*, textual specialists who partly concerned themselves with how the biblical documents were preserved and transmitted, with a view toward reconstructing the originals.

What alarmed many conservative Christians was that many of these critics were part of an academic movement whose stated mission was the militant deconstruction of the Gospels. They were in quest of the real Jesus, which they had determined, quite arbitrarily, could not be the Jesus portrayed in the Gospel narratives. Critics insisted the Gospels contained a great many inaccuracies and distortions. Over the past century and a half, several theologians have stridently pushed this position. Although we do not have space to go into the subject in detail, here are some of the weaknesses of such efforts:

1. They typically begin by assuming what they are supposed to prove, thus falling victim to *confirmation bias*, selectively searching for information that supports one's preconceptions. Confirmation bias is related to begging the question (see chapter 2).

23. See Enns, *The Evolution of Adam*.

2. The books in the New Testament were written between AD 50 and AD 85 with one or two possibly later.[24] These critics tend to rely heavily on documents from the second or third century.

3. Even atheistic scholars deem some of the key manuscripts these critics rely on to be manifestly inferior.

4. They sometimes test the authenticity of events in the biblical documents by the curious and questionable criterion that a given account is most likely to be false if it supports traditional belief.

Among the more dangerous enemies of reasoned and evidence-based argument is hard-heartedness and the calcification of thought-forms to which such hardness can lead.

Where This Leaves Us

The thesis that science and religion are at war is grounded in misunderstandings about both. There is certainly a legitimate if not indispensable role for the philosophy of science, which has to do with the nature of science, how science operates, and the logic behind acquiring scientific knowledge. But science in itself is not philosophy, and for a scientist to suggest that it is embroils that scientist in the sort of intellectual trespassing mentioned near the beginning of this chapter.

Nor is religion science, and pretending it is invites questions about a Christian's intellectual competence. The Bible is not a book of scientific facts, principles, or findings, and legitimate science can only enrich Christianity. If God made the world and everything in it, how could it not? Christianity, for its part, can only enrich the minds of scientists by giving them a deeper appreciation for the universe and a larger conceptual framework into which to fit whatever they discover.

The poet Alexander Pope (1688–1744) crafted this epitaph for Isaac Newton: "Nature and Nature's laws lay hid in night: God said, 'Let Newton be!' and all was light." Although Newton seems not to have believed in the Trinity, he spent considerable time reading and writing about the Bible, and he funded the distribution of Bibles to the poor. These things were unknown to the general public until the auction of his nonscientific papers in 1936.[25]

---

24. See Bauckham, *Jesus and the Eyewitnesses*.
25. Hummel, "Isaac Newton," 38–41.

CHAPTER 15. ARE SCIENCE AND RELIGION AT WAR?

Newton, however, was clear about disciplinary boundaries. When he was president of the Royal Society, for example, he prohibited the publication of any document touching on religion and wrote, "We are not to introduce divine revelations into [science], nor [scientific] opinions into religion." It would be a major step forward if scientists and Christians today observed the same boundaries.

Closing Thoughts

Science and religion are not at war and never have been. Through the centuries, science and Christianity have usually gotten on well. Scientists who denounce religion in the name of science are either unaware of the difference between scientific and philosophic questions or deceptively promote atheism in the name of science. John Draper was a physician who became head of the medical school at New York University, and Andrew White was a historian who co-founded Cornell University. Both wrote books promoting the warfare thesis. The flawed claims in their books were reinforced by conflicts in the early twentieth century.

Preview

In light of atrocities that continue to this day, including the murder of thousands of innocent Americans in 2001, it seems naïve to dismiss evil as an outdated idea. Though some are uncomfortable with the use of the word, evil as an object of study has been given renewed attention by contemporary philosophers. In the next chapter, we will consider two kinds of evil, and I will argue that evil is far from an antiquated idea.

Chapter 16. Is Evil an Outdated Concept?

How a person uses, or fails to use, the word *evil* suggests how that person thinks about atrocities and disasters. Since words convey ideas, the question becomes whether an individual's conceptual apparatus includes the category evil and if it is part of that person's thinking language. This may, in turn, reveal the difference between a worldview that is exclusively materialistic and reductionistic and one that includes the spiritual. We live in a world of physical causation. Air, water, and food sustain us, for example, and without them we die. Accidents kill and so do bullets and viruses. But might there be another dimension to existence that goes beyond the physical? Are some actions so destructive and malicious that we may properly call them malevolent?

Philosophers speak of two kinds of evil. *Natural* or what some philosophers call *surd* evil is part of the physical world and happens without human beings causing it. Examples include typhoons, earthquakes, tsunamis, droughts, volcanoes, diseases, avalanches, and forest fires. Because they are part of the natural order, no individual or group is directly responsible.

Moral evil is the direct result of human action or inaction. Examples include genocide and murder for financial gain. Others examples are refusing to protect a child from a predator, not warning someone about to fall over a cliff, or stealing drugs from a person who needs them to stay alive. The Addendum to this chapter contains an abbreviated list of moral evils that have occurred throughout history.

CHAPTER 16. IS EVIL AN OUTDATED CONCEPT?

The difference between *morality* and *ethics* is worth noting. Some philosophers use the terms synonymously. Others, although acknowledging that the two can blend into each other, distinguish between them. They understand morals to be whatever an individual has internalized as right and wrong, which therefore guides and influences that person's behavior. Morality, therefore, carries with it a kind of subjective undertone and may reflect religious or secular values. They define ethics, by contrast, as whatever a society or subset of society prescribes, proscribes, and often enforces. Corporate codes of conduct are codifications of ethics that may or may not reflect moral values. Morality and ethics sometimes stand in conflict. If a defense attorney, believing that a cold-blooded murderer should be convicted, announces to the jury that his or her client is guilty, that attorney may be following an inner moral compass. But the attorney would likely be disbarred for violating the ethical principle that, in a criminal case, lawyers have a duty to provide a client with the best possible defense.

A Sobering Experience

On a Saturday morning in March of 2019, my wife and I were on a ship anchored near the New Zealand port of Akaroa, which has served as the port for Christchurch since an earthquake destroyed the pier at Lyttleton in 2011. We intended to visit Christchurch that day, but this turned out no longer to be possible. The previous afternoon, a white-supremacist assassinated fifty-one Muslims and wounded dozens more. Animals kill for food, territory, mating rights, or to defend against aggression. Only humans commit hate crimes or mass murder.

People, including many who have not personally encountered Christ, may be hesitant to recognize evil for what it is. To acknowledge moral horrors, yet lack the hope that everything will somehow make sense in the end, can lead to demoralization. Some people, therefore, avoid thinking about such horrors, or they manage to explain them away by framing moral evil as the result of adverse circumstance.

Intelligence, Enlightenment, and Benevolence

Humankind has been capable of obliterating the planet and annihilating itself for over three-quarters of a century. Dwelling on the possibility of nuclear winter might plunge us into despair, so most of us do not think much about it, perhaps because we do not want to believe it could happen. To get a sense of what it might be like to live for months, knowing that radioactive clouds were drifting in your direction and bringing with them certain death, read the 1957 novel *On the Beach*. In it, nuclear war has destroyed civilization in the northern hemisphere, and those who live in Australia now await their fate.[1] For over twenty years, I consulted for a think-tank that emerged out of WWII to assist national defense and security. The human reasons such a catastrophic event has not happened are surely complex.[2] It may be that, behind the scenes, God has had a lot to do with this.

Some attribute our avoidance of nuclear winter to human intelligence. When you consider that many smart people are willing to die in the service of evil, you have to wonder about what leads them to this. Intelligence does not always restrain evil. Out of every ten thousand intelligent people, at least one may be willing to commit suicide on the altar of fanaticism, and in the process bring down civilization. An intelligent terrorist might conclude that large-scale homicide is reasonable if this conclusion follows from the premise that God would look favorably on it.

People sometimes attribute the restraint of evil to enlightenment, by which they often mean education in the western liberal tradition. I grew up in this tradition, value it, and wish everyone on earth did. But equating education with enlightenment is fraught with difficulties. It potentially conflates learning to think and mastering academic content, on one hand, with changing values, beliefs, and attitudes on the other. Some see enlightenment as getting people to support democratic forms of governments, based on the assumption that once people understand democracy, they will embrace it. This is not always the case. People in other parts of the world do not routinely view Western values as superior and are often astute enough not to confuse its material benefits with these values. They may, for example, regard the welfare of the family, clan, or tribe as more important than the welfare of the individual, regard capitalism as corrupt, and view democracy as *unenlightened*. Enlightenment only restrains evil when people adopt certain values.

The argument that benevolence prevents evil is also hard to defend. There are many virtuous and admirable people, but there are also some

---

1. Shute, *On the Beach*. For a realistic and horrifying account of the death and devastation brought about by the explosion of a nuclear bomb, see Hersey, *Hiroshima*.

2. See Haass, *World: A Brief Introduction*.

CHAPTER 16. IS EVIL AN OUTDATED CONCEPT?

who are willing to cut off peoples' heads in the public square. Good can triumph over bad and it often does. But malevolence can also triumph over benevolence, and when it does, the lion devours the lamb. In "Why We Fight—and Can We Stop?" Robert Wright asserts, "We seem designed to twist moral discourse—whatever language it is framed in—to selfish or tribal ends, and to remain conveniently unaware of the twisting."[3]

Defining Evil

Evil is a mystery and it makes little sense to treat it as only a social problem. It is clearly that, but it is also something more, something spiritual. Moral evil involves moral choice, which only a human being can make. Many people become uncomfortable if in a conversation you use the word evil. They view such usage as anachronistic and may believe the concept should be tossed onto the rubble of the Middle Ages, when monks occasionally taught parishioners to fear witches. Few depictions of demonic work are more vivid than the paintings on the inside walls of the cathedral of Santa Maria del Fiore in Florence, its duomo (cathedral). Ascending it, you see fiendish creatures doing unmentionable things to the wicked. With such imagery bequeathed to us by Renaissance artists, it may be understandable that some people shy away from the word. Evil as a category seems so closely associated with superstition that it can be hard to take it seriously.

Most philosophers appear to think in terms of a continuum of evil, rather than a dichotomy, ranging from the minor to the horrific. Some define evil as the opposite of good. Others define it as whatever is intentionally harmful. Still others argue that evil is only what goes well beyond everyday immorality or malice. It is something horrendously malevolent.

By this last definition, a married person engaging in a series of clandestine affairs is a regrettable and immoral betrayal of trust, but it is not evil. Neither is punching your neighbor in the face, which could get you sued or a night in jail, but again there is nothing inherently evil about this. It is indisputably evil, however, to fill syringes with poison to kill patients in a hospital, shoot people at random in a theater, order mass executions, or engage in ethnic cleansings. What such acts have in common is that they are *surrealistically unfathomable*, and it is this

3. Wright, "Why We Fight," 115.

above all that makes them evil. Evil is shockingly perverse, grotesquely inhuman, and morally ineffable.

Even if we adopt a loose definition of evil, it may make sense to distinguish between broad and narrow categories. Included within the broad category would be any bad state of affairs, character flaw, or harmful action, so even a toothache is evil. Evil in this sense can be natural or moral. Included within the narrow category would be morally reprehensible acts, which can only be committed by moral agents. An article on evil by a philosopher ends with, "It seems that we cannot capture the moral significance of these actions and their perpetrators by calling them 'wrong' or 'bad' or even 'very very wrong' or 'very very bad.'"[4] These are "the most *morally* despicable sorts of actions, characters, events, etc." Marcus Singer states, "evil [in this sense] . . . is the worst possible term of opprobrium imaginable."[5]

Like the boundary between natural and moral evil, the one between seriously immoral and horrifically malevolent is hazy. Evil is difficult to define precisely, and we find ourselves once again thrown onto the sands of family resemblances (see chapter 1). That we cannot come up with a clear line of demarcation between the morally deplorable and the genuinely egregious does not mean we cannot recognize clear cases of horrific evil when we encounter them. That a boundary is fuzzy does not mean that it is useless to reflect on it. Think of France and Germany and their many conflicts over Alsace-Lorraine (Moselle), territory that has been tossed back and forth between them for a long time. Its annexation by either of the two does not preclude thinking about either France or Germany. It is possible that, in a given society, moral depravity can be so extreme and pervasive that few within it recognize horrific evil for what it is.

Increased Lethality

With the kinds of technological advances increasingly available, small groups of determined fanatics can murder ever larger numbers. A thousand years ago, one warrior was roughly equivalent to another warrior on the opposing side. What made the difference between victory and defeat was physical size, athletic prowess, martial skill, and extraneous events like weather and terrain. Even a knight with good armor on a horse was

---

4. Calder, "The Concept of Evil." s.v.
5. Singer, "The Concept of Evil." Quoted in Calder, "The Concept of Evil." s.v.

CHAPTER 16. IS EVIL AN OUTDATED CONCEPT?

equivalent to perhaps thirty soldiers on foot. In the modern era, when automatic weapons first became available, a soldier firing down from a well-fortified position might, on average, kill fifty soldiers before one killed him. A soldier using a Gatling gun, introduced in 1860, might mow down a hundred or more before he succumbed. In the middle of the twentieth century, these ratios changed dramatically, and by the latter part of that century a few technically savvy terrorists with a lunch pail of high-grade plutonium became theoretically capable of annihilating an entire city or port. If that terrorist used what is known as a dirty bomb, he or she could render it uninhabitable for a very long time.

Given that so much nuclear material is *in commerce*, which is a euphemism for *unaccounted for* and perhaps therefore available to the highest bidder, it is close to astonishing that no city or harbor has become radioactive waste. Years before the attack on the World Trade Center in 2001, I asked the late Carl Builder, a senior researcher at the RAND Corporation, why no terrorist had ever used a nuclear device. He had once served as Director of Nuclear Safeguards for the Nuclear Regulatory Commission. In the 1950s, while a midshipman at the Naval Academy, Builder invented a new jet engine and spent the rest of his life either at RAND, teaching at one of the war colleges, or serving as a senior-level advisor on nuclear weapons to the U.S. government. In answer to my question, he replied, "If in 1900 I told you to pick up that soda bottle on my desk, fill it with gasoline, stick a rag in it, and light it, you would have told me I was crazy and had just given you a recipe for blowing off your hand. Someone had to show that doing so would create an effective and inexpensive incendiary device. People have been throwing Molotov cocktails ever since. Someone had to demonstrate feasibility." A terrorist may someday demonstrate such feasibility, and if this happens the idea of evil may once again gain currency.

Technological and Moral Progress

Tribalism and nationalism have reemerged as strong global trends. We have mastered the atom but cannot seem to unite people in a benign social order. Technological progress has moved ahead geometrically, while moral progress seems to have moved forward only arithmetically. We may have improved morally in some ways but gone backwards in others.

PART III. PIVOTAL QUESTIONS

Malcolm Muggeridge, mentioned in chapter 11, suggested that the darkness overtaking civilization is not the result of an energy crisis, overpopulation, monetary challenges, or unemployment. It is the result of confusing good and evil and the lack of a sense of moral order, without which no lasting societal, economic, or political stability is achievable. He further argued that God entered visibly into history in the form of Jesus, the Sent One, and that to turn our back on God now would be to nullify two thousand years of human history and social advance. To the degree that we in the West believe in an objective moral order, we tend knowingly or unknowingly still to accept, and rely on, the bequest of Judaism and Christianity.

Explanatory Science and the Effects of Choice

It seems unlikely, and may in principle be impossible, for science, including behavioral science, completely to understand the actions of such depraved individuals as Jeffrey Dahmer, who sexually assaulted, murdered, dismembered, and cannibalized at least sixteen male victims. Or Ted Bundy, who was charming and good-looking but turned out to be a serial killer. Or Dennis Rader, who specialized in "BTK," binding, torturing, and killing. Some people, regardless of intelligence, education, social status, income, or net worth, are worse than wild beasts and act with enormous perversity. They make moral choices of which dolphins, apes, and tigers are decidedly incapable.

We begin life with a wide range of moral options, but as we grow and develop, our freedom to choose increases or decreases. Career choices influence our options but in themselves do not determine whether we choose the good or the bad, the right or the wrong. A plumber as much as a surgeon must decide to what extent to behave ethically. The consequences vary but not the basic nature of the decision. The moral and ethical decisions we make today flow from the ones we made yesterday, the day before, and the day before that. In theory, anyone can act differently and sometimes people do. But bad moral choices crystallize into bad habits of the heart,[6] and these become increasingly difficult to change. Good moral decisions increase freedom of choice, or at least do not diminish it, while bad moral decisions decrease such freedom.

---

6. See Bellah, et al., *Habits of the Heart*.

CHAPTER 16. IS EVIL AN OUTDATED CONCEPT?

Limitations of Choice

Criminals may have less freedom of choice than we think. I remember watching the *Sopranos*, a TV series about a crime family in New Jersey, and I remember thinking, this is Tony Soprano's life and occupation. He has kids who talk back, a therapist treating his panic attacks, and a wife who wants him out of organized crime. But the only thing Tony knows how to do is run numbers, sell protection, steal, defraud, extort, launder money, bribe officials, and occasionally kill other bad guys. The lack of alternative skills does not justify such criminal behavior, but it can help us better understand why some people act as they do.

A few years ago, I was talking with a man in his twenties who was fixing something in my house. He told me that he had become a Christian and how faith changed his life. He showed me a picture of his kids. "I never thought I'd have a job, a wife, or a child." In his teens, he had used and sold drugs, been involved in potentially lethal battles with rival gangs, and done time in prison. "I was arrested for violating parole and told the judge to [expletive deleted] himself and do whatever he wanted with me, I didn't care." He continued, "The judge sent me to a Christian program, and for some reason I stayed. I even ran into a guy who once tried to shoot me." Then he said something I will never forget. "They say people have choices . . . they don't."

For a variety of reasons, including prior decisions and life circumstances, doing the right thing is not as easy for some people as it is for others. The man telling me his story was not making excuses, and he had obviously chosen to move toward God. He simply meant that some people feel trapped, and in certain ways they are. If there is no freedom to choose, there is no morality, and moral responsibility becomes untenable. Some freedom of choice always remains, but it may be greatly diminished.

Even if we understand some of the reasons people do terrible things, this does not make their actions any less evil. Bad behavior is bad behavior, regardless of who does it or why. But limits on their choices, whether caused by parents who have failed them or tumors in their brains, suggest it is wise to avoid thinking in terms of *us* and *them*. Some limits come from bad habits of the heart formed by repeatedly choosing wrong over right, bad over good. Others, however, stem from circumstances. In looking at the behavior of someone else, we can never know for sure the extent to which bad behavior is due to genetics, experience, or choice. Or, how our life, under sufficiently adverse circumstances, might have come to resemble theirs.

Evil and Psychopathology

Some people believe that what looks like evil is *merely* the expression of psychopathology. Those who back away from the idea of evil seem to believe that psychology and psychiatry have made short work of it. These disciplines, the argument runs, have discovered that what society once regarded as evil is nothing of the sort, and that we must understand how even those who inflict grievous harm on others are victims of psychiatric disorders.

Thomas Szasz (1920–2012), a professor of psychiatry and distinguished lifetime fellow of the American Psychiatric Association, wrote a celebrated book[7] in which he argues that a great deal of mental illness is not illness in the usual sense, a physical malady, but rather a problem in living. He points out that, except in cases of organic brain disease, no physical test results support inclusion of these problems in a medical diagnostic manual.

Concluding that a sadistic murderer *only* needs psychiatric treatment rests on two questionable assumptions. First, there is the mistaken idea that labeling something explains it, what we pointed to in chapter 6 as the nominal fallacy. In this case, it is assuming that putting a psychiatric label on aberrant behavior enables you to understand its nature and removes it from the arena of ethical discourse. Medicalizing evil promotes the illusion that we understand and can therefore eradicate it. But, what if we cannot? What if some acts are inexplicable and will forever defy explanation? To insist that we will eventually understand the workings of the mind enough to stop the evil of which some people are capable is to assume something without evidence to support it. The second assumption is subtler. Words like *merely* and *only* suggest that what murderers do, for example, is not so bad after all. Inhumane acts are *nothing but* manifestations of misfiring neurons, excesses of a neurotransmitter, or deficiencies of a regulating hormone. This can make horrific actions seem ordinary. In the next chapter, we will note Freud's point of view, which was different from what one might have expected.

---

7. Szasz, *Myth of Mental Illness*.

CHAPTER 16. IS EVIL AN OUTDATED CONCEPT?

The Sticky Wicket

Some have argued that the existence of evil, whether natural or moral, is the strongest argument against the existence of a personal God. We noted in chapter 12 how it is possible to frame the problem of evil as a question: How can an all-powerful God also be benevolent? If God can do anything, why does he allow terrible things to happen? Why, for example, do thousands perish each year from natural disasters or busloads of children plunge into ravines?

George Mavrodes (1926–2019), late Professor Emeritus of Philosophy at the University of Michigan, suggested that evil only becomes a problem when we encounter it personally.[8] Until then, the problem of evil is likely to remain an abstraction. It is when pain or loss overwhelms us that we are most likely to cry, "Why me?" and insist on the unfairness of life. Whether the pain or loss comes from a debilitating illness, intractable pain, or the suffering and death of a loved one, this is when we are most likely to launch our protest.

The agony becomes a crisis point. A Christian can soldier on, trusting in God's goodness and continuing to take on faith that God is just and merciful, even in the absence of understanding how. The person can say with Job in the Old Testament that regardless of what God does or does not do for me, or what God allows to happen to me, I will bless and not curse God (Job 13:15a). The entire book of Job, in fact, centers on the question of why the righteous suffer. God's ways are not ours and Job insists on giving God the benefit of the doubt. The book ends with evil remaining inexplicable. A faithful Christian can identify with Jesus who in the Garden of Gethsemane prayed, "Thy will be done" (Matt 26:42; Luke 11:2). Alternatively, a person may decide, in the face of evil, that he or she had it all wrong. God is not the God he or she once thought. God either lacks compassion or the power to change things. He or she may reject the God of Christianity and in helpless rage declare, "I will no longer believe." God designed human existence such that no mortal will ever be able to "solve" the problem of evil.

A theodicy[9] is an attempt to harmonize belief in God with the existence of evil. Gottfried Wilhelm von Leibniz (1646–1716), who was the first to use the word theodicy in his native German, devoted his only full-length work to the problem of evil, which troubled him most of his

8. Mavrodes, *Belief in God*, 90–111.
9. Wikipedia, "Theodicy." https://en.wikipedia.org/wiki/Theodicy.

life. Leibniz's theodicy was a response to the philosopher Pierre Bayle (1647–1706), who had concluded that since the problem of evil was unsolvable, but the Bible affirmed the coexistence of both God and evil, we must accept both and reason no further. Leibniz argued that what we have is the best of all possible worlds.

Some contemporary philosophers devote considerable time and attention to evil and the challenges it presents. To them, evil is not a trivial problem and they do not dismiss the concept as anachronistic. Thinkers, before and after Leibniz, have tried to reconcile the presence of evil with the existence and nature of God. Some draw a distinction between a *defense*, which attempts only to demonstrate the possibility that God exists in the face of evil, and a *theodicy*. A *defense* is an attempt to show that evil is not incompatible with God's existence, that both are logically possible, but a *theodicy* goes further by trying to answer the question of why God allows evil.

Among many attempts to address the problem of evil are those that turn on free will, such as these:

- To be a full human being entails the possibility of free will and therefore of moral evil.
- The existence of evil is necessary for human choice and thus for human development.
- Evil is necessary for people to understand and choose the good.

Such attempts often fail to satisfy critics. Like arguments for the existence of God, they are most persuasive for those who already believe.

More than one Christian thinker has taken exception to the construction of any defense or theodicy, with a few characterizing both as destructive. Some suggest that trying to come up with justifications of God in the presence of evil can lead to trivializing suffering and fostering cold clinical detachment. Karl Barth (1886–1968) has been the most prominent theologian to insist on the impossibility of a theodicy that establishes God's goodness. To Barth, the crucifixion conveys this goodness and everything else is irrelevant.

Austin Farrer's Views

Of all the attempts to make sense of evil, I find two the most compelling. One comes from Austin Farrer (1904–68), mentioned in chapter 14, and the other from French philosopher Simone Weil. Farrer was an Anglican theologian, philosopher, and penetrating thinker of the first rank who suggested an intriguing approach.[10] He argues that human life would not be what it is, were it not for the existence of natural evil, *accidents*. Reminiscent of Barth, he argues that any true understanding of the universe must begin with God's self-revelation. Farrer offers the perspective that we live in a physical world consisting not of a single system but of many interacting systems, and that evil occurs when two or more of these systems collide. An example of systems colliding is when the human body is invaded by a bacterium. The body is a system and so is the world in which bacteria live. Thomas Aquinas had already suggested in the thirteenth century that evil is the result of one thing flourishing at the expense of another. According to Farrer, if God removed the "mutual interference of systems," life would not be what we now know it to be.

Farrer rejects any attempt to justify moral evil, for example by arguing, as John Hick (1922–2012) does, that it builds virtue, or as Richard Swinburne (b. 1934) does, that it is necessary for the emergence of higher-order goods. Farrer classifies such attempts under the category of *philosophical treatments*. Farrer finds philosophical treatments deficient because they rely on two anthropomorphic presuppositions. The first is that in designing creation God acted like a human being building a world, and the second is that such attempts appeal and subscribe to secular standards of morality, according to which we judge and perhaps in our hearts condemn God. He will have nothing to do with any attempt to vindicate God by rationalizing evil as good. The other category is *theological treatments*, and it is the one to which Farrer subscribes. His view of moral evil begins with the Augustinian thesis that evil is the absence or corruption of good, and that it has no independent existence. If there were no good, there could be no evil. Such a view has the benefit of upholding God as the creator of only what is good, even though we cannot fathom why God allows its degradation.

This is precisely Farrer's point, that we cannot fathom it. For Farrer, making sense of evil begins with God's self-revelation and a person's Christian conversion. Apart from such conversion, he suggests, it is impossible for a human being, blinded as he or she is by sin, to think clearly about spiritual matters. The unconverted soul is always

---

10. Oliver, "Theodicy of Austin Farrer," 280–97.

vulnerable to succumbing to the view that the following three propositions cannot co-exist:

- God is all good.
- God is all powerful.
- Evil exists in the world.

The person drawn to God through Christ, and responding to God's call, lives with this apparent inconsistency, refusing to fall into the pit that Farrer sees some philosophers jumping into. A thoughtful Christian will regard these three statements as paradoxical but not contradictory.

Views of Simone Weil

Simone Weil (1909–43) advanced an interesting perspective that may shed light on the problem of evil, especially when combined with Farrer's suggestion that the nature of human existence would be unrecognizable, were it not for seemingly random events including accidents of nature. By creating the universe, Weil argued, God engaged in an act of renunciation. Instead of remaining the sole reality and power, God brought into existence other realities and powers. Although everything ultimately exists by God's power, for good reasons God has chosen strictly to limit this power.

God created nature so that everything in it functions as it does because it cannot do otherwise. Weil likens this to the workings of a machine. According to the characteristics God has assigned them, all things in nature are compelled to act as they do. Nature, according to her, is indifferent to us, and we are ambivalent toward it. In response to nature's indifference, some people insist there is no God. Nature can be beautiful and its beauty tells us about God. But it can also be dangerous.

To find it credible that God is good and loves us, we must overcome the barrier between us and God that nature represents. God has deliberately placed nature's indifference in our path to ensure that our devotion would be to the good that God *is* rather than to the pursuit of the benefits God's creation *provides*. The true significance of nature's indifference only appears if we grasp that such benefits will never be enough to satisfy us.

All human beings, whether noble or base, are vulnerable to suffering, and there is no obvious association between human goodness and human outcomes. Bad things happen to good people and good things to bad people. God did not want our obedience to be the means by which to obtain rewards, such as good health or good fortune, toward which, if such payoffs were predictable, we would principally and inevitably be motivated. Nature therefore provides a context in which we are able to exercise freedom of choice, which God has granted to no other created beings. People have purposes but exist in a universe that operates by material causes and in itself has no purposes.

Christians have traditionally believed that God can and does sometimes intervene in nature temporarily to override what we take to be its laws. But not even the most devout Christian can predict if and when this will happen, which is why we remain uncertain whether God will grant us anything for which we pray. There is always uncertainty, which is what the Bible means when it refers to Christians as walking by faith and not by sight (2 Cor 5:7). God acts in history, in relation to individuals as well as groups, but ambiguity exists and God remains partially hidden.

Weil is correct in affirming that nature is indifferent. She is also right in suggesting that how we respond to nature's indifference has everything to do with whether we believe God to be good. The problem of evil is not some intellectual inconvenience with which Christians must reckon on the way to faith. It is a primary test of faith.

Utopias and Scorpions

Additional education, that should do it. Or, perhaps redistributing wealth and raising standards of living. Even a cursory glance at the backgrounds of those who crashed planes into the World Trade Center, the Pentagon, and an empty field, challenges both beliefs. The perpetrators were educated and from well-off, middle-class families. There will never be a perfect society without Christ completing the redemptive work he began two thousand years ago. In large regions of the globe, existence may feel more like a yard overtaken by weeds than a well-tended garden, and regardless of how much people try to tidy it up on their own, weeds remain. Utopian approaches to evil suffer from a signal defect, captured in the story of the frog and the scorpion.

Together they face fast-rising floodwaters. The scorpion asks the frog to carry it to dry land, but the frog fears the scorpion, which insists that if it stung the frog, they would both die. Halfway across, the scorpion stings, and in amazement the frog asks why. To which the scorpion replies, "It's my nature." We are all frogs and scorpions. However much we or others aspire to act benevolently, and may in the main succeed, there is always the possibility that a malicious impulse may surface. If it does and we act on it, we may find ourselves astonished because we never imagined ourselves capable of whatever it is we did. Even the best of Christians, those with radically transformed lives, retain the capacity to sting. As noted above, they will always have two natures, referred to in the New Testament as *flesh* and *spirit*. The flesh has less to do with sensuality than with the poison of selfishness and self-absorption.[11] If we have embraced and given our allegiance to Christ, God's Spirit lives in us and we have an antidote to the toxin of egocentricity and the baseness to which it can lead. But the poison lies dormant, and on earth we will never be completely free of or immune to it.

Another review in *The New Yorker* includes the statement, "the desire to maim and murder has its roots in a disease of the mind so powerful and passionate that to call it political . . . hardly seems to capture its nature."[12] To label it political or anything of the sort only refers to its mode of expression. The primary cause of human evil is what Christians call sin, the refusal to acknowledge God as God and the responsibility we have toward our neighbors. If evil is the strongest argument for the atheist, it is also the strongest argument in favor of our need for God. We require a reconstruction of who we are and how we think. Without a relationship with God through Christ, we can only gaze into the sky and realize that we are temporary inhabitants of a supersonic spaceship from which we will soon depart. If, however, we have such a relationship, we may look into that same sky with hope and gratitude, believing that God will eventually transport us to another dimension.

Writing only a few years after the end of WWII, Christopher Dawson suggested, "We have learnt that barbarism is not a picturesque myth or a half-forgotten memory of a long-passed stage of history, but an ugly underlying force whenever the moral authority of a civilization loses its control."[13] The age of evil has not passed. Totalitarian regimes still exist and the ambitious lust for power, wealth, and prestige continues to motivate dictators.

---

11. Theologians refer to this as the ethical use of *sarx*, the Greek word for flesh. See Ladd, *New Testament Theology*, 469–70.

12. Gopnik, "Blood and Soil," 103.

13. Dawson, *Religion and Western Culture*, 24.

CHAPTER 16. IS EVIL AN OUTDATED CONCEPT?

Digital Disappointments

An article on the relationship between electronic communication and dictatorships recently appeared in the flagship publication on international relations.[14] In it, the authors demonstrate how, because of technology, totalitarian regimes have become increasingly effective and efficient at discouraging and punishing opposition, through incarceration, torture, or execution. Experts used to believe that the availability of digital resources, from cell phones to social media, would hasten the spread of democracy and democratic values.[15] In the early 1990s, this optimism seemed justified, and it increased during the Arab Spring, when dictatorships in Egypt, Libya, Tunisia, and Yemen came crashing down. The Arab Spring began in 2010 and lasted only two years. The authors suggest, "this wishful vision of a more democratic future proved naïve."

It took years for dictators to harness technology for nefarious purposes, but once they did, it proved much easier for them, and far less costly, to keep an eye on citizens. By monitoring emails, voice messages, and posts on social media, together with the use of face and gait recognition, autocrats became able to use algorithms to track physical movement, who associates with whom, expressions of political opinion, and most important of all plans to gather, protest, and rebel. It was indeed naïve to expect technology to usher in respect for individual rights and freedom of expression. In parts of the world today, Orwell's *1984* is a reality, and apart from God's kingdom supplanting this reality, evil will endure and possibly increase.

Closing Thoughts

In this chapter, we distinguished between natural evil, which has no human cause, and moral evil, which results from intentional acts by individuals or groups. We considered the nature of choice and how psychological and psychiatric disorders may or may not be implicated in evil. How to account for evil poses a significant challenge to theologians, and this challenge is perhaps the strongest argument of the atheist. We discussed two of the more intriguing approaches to the problem of evil. Utopian hopes to the contrary, human effort is unlikely to put an end to evil. What

---

14. Kendall-Taylor, et al., "The Digital Dictators," 103–15.
15. See Fukuyama, *The End of History*.

initially appeared to offer hope, such as social media, later turned out only to make the commission of evil more effective and efficient.

Preview

Next, we turn to an exploration of how well-known philosophers have addressed evil. Some speculated on its causes and proposed remedies, while others merely lamented its presence in the world and paid little attention to what human society might be able to do to eradicate or ameliorate it. One gave himself over to evil and celebrated it.

Addendum. A Brief Compendium of Evil

I HAVE LISTED BELOW just some examples of egregious barbarity. It may seem as if these things never happened. But they did. Had it not been for Judaism and the Christianity that grew out of it, some of these examples would likely have been worse. Contrary to aiding and abetting evil, Christianity often restrained it. Atrocities have taken place in the name of Christ, but acting in Christ's name never meant that those so acting necessarily had Christ in their hearts. A recent history of Christianity[1] demonstrates how some well-known examples of evil done in the name of Christ are far more nuanced than many people assume. Here are the examples:

1. Over the course of six and a half centuries, beginning in 264 BC, Roman gladiatorial games cost the lives of over 1,000,000 prisoners, slaves, and dissidents; this estimate is almost certainly low; few combatants survived and many were forced to fight without armor against wild animals or well-equipped, trained professionals.

2. Between AD 9 and AD 23, the Xin Dynasty brought about the deaths of 10,000,000 Chinese during the breakup of the Han Dynasty, and from 184 to 280, during the Three Kingdoms War, the final overthrow of the Han resulted in the deaths of an additional 35,000,000 to 40,000,000.

---

1. Holland, *Dominion*, 304–6.

3. The Fall of the Roman Empire, which took over fifty years, beginning in 395, directly or indirectly resulted in the deaths of at least 5,000,000 and perhaps as many as 7,000,000 people.

4. Slave trading in the Mideast, which began around 700 and continued for well over a thousand years, caused the deaths of over 15,000,000.

5. The An Lushan Revolt in China (755–763) killed 35,000,000.

6. Genghis Khan and the Mongol Conquests, which lasted from the early thirteenth to the mid-fourteenth century, brought about the slaughter of between 30,000,000 and 40,000,000 people; Tamerlane was a Mongol conqueror who, during his reign from 1370 to 1405, killed as many as 17,000,000.

7. In the Hundred Years War (1337–1453), in which England and France battled for control of France, 2,000,000 and possibly 3,000,000 died.

8. Between the fifteenth and early nineteenth centuries, because of the Atlantic slave trade, around 10,000,000 men, women, and children never made it to the auction block but perished on slave ships; over 15,000,000 died in the perpetuation of this perverse institution.

9. Although on the scale we have been considering, the number of the deceased was small, among the more bizarre and hideous examples of evil occurred in the early seventeenth century, when serial killer Countess Elizabeth Báthory of Transylvania, along with her accomplices, murdered hundreds of young women.

10. The Thirty Years War (1618–1848) in Europe resulted in the deaths of 8,000,000 people, either as a direct result of the war or as a side effect, for example from famine; estimates run higher.

11. In 1638, as a result of the Shimabara Rebellion during the Edo period of the Tokugawa shogunate, the Japanese feudal government executed, typically by beheading, at least 10,000 Christians.

12. The Qing conquest (1635–62) of the Ming Dynasty resulted in the deaths of 25,000,000 people.

13. Perhaps 100,000 people, maybe more, died in a 1738 uprising in Delhi.

ADDENDUM. A BRIEF COMPENDIUM OF EVIL

14. In 1792, frenzied mobs killed over 1,000 French citizens without mercy; in the ensuing years, many of the 300,000 to 500,000 people caught up or imprisoned during the Reign of Terror died of brutality or disease. Ironically, the guillotine was adopted to ensure a swift and less painful death.

15. During the Napoleonic wars (1799–1815), over 4,000,000 and perhaps as many as 7,000,000 perished.

16. Turkish Sultan Mahmud II executed over 20,000 members of his own elite guard in 1826.

17. The Taiping Rebellion in southern China lasted from 1850 to 1864, when its homicidal leader, Hung, fearing defeat, committed suicide, taking with him almost 100,000 of his troops; the fourteen-year rebellion claimed over 20,000,000 lives.

18. In the "Bloody Week" of Paris in 1871, there was another French struggle for political control; fighting and mass executions left 17,000 dead.

19. Our topic suggests mention of Henri Landru, the French "Blue Beard," who from 1915 to 1919 murdered, dismembered, and incinerated at least ten women at his villa in the French countryside; to list all known serial killers and their victims would take volumes.

20. Beginning in 1915, Turks began the genocidal eradication of the Armenian minority, at first deporting large numbers to Syria and neighboring lands; estimates vary, but it appears that about 600,000 of the deported were either murdered or died of starvation, and estimates of the total number killed run as high as 1,500,000.

21. More than 1,000,000 French and German soldiers died or suffered debilitating wounds at the Battle of Verdun in 1916, and in the Great War (WWI), at least 15,000,000 people lost their lives.

22. During and immediately after the Russian Revolution of 1917, millions died, either from famine brought about by inept collectivist reforms or as a result of executions by Red (communist) or White (anti-communist) Russians; between 1917 and 1953, at least 8,000,000 (low estimate) and possibly as many as 61,000,000 (high estimate) were killed, with the average estimate hovering around 20,000,000, most during Stalin's regime; in response to Polish resistance to the Soviet invasion, Stalin had what seems to

PART III. PIVOTAL QUESTIONS

have been over 4,000 prisoners executed in the Katyn Forest—one bullet for each—and it is suspected that another 10,000 were killed on Stalin's orders.

23. During WWII, the lowest estimate from any reputable historian is that at least 40,000,000 people died, with most estimates running to considerably more; this does not include those who lost their lives in the Holocaust.

24. The Holocaust (1941–45) resulted in the deaths of roughly 6,000,000 Jews, and if we count them as Holocaust victims, of another 3,000,000 non-Jewish Poles and Slavs; estimates of all racially and politically motivated killings during this period run as high as 15,000,000. Philosophers and historians continue to debate the ethics and necessity of the United States having used nuclear weapons in that war.

25. From 1949 to 1975, under Mao Zedong, at least 45,000,000 and possibly as many as 75,000,000 Chinese were executed or died of starvation due to agricultural mismanagement.

26. Genocides have continued, resulting in the death of millions, including what happened in Rwanda in 1994, which claimed the lives of up to 1,000,000 Tutsis.

27. In 2001, roughly 3,000 innocent people died in the World Trade Center, the Pentagon, and on hijacked planes.

Evil is not an outmoded concept. It is very much alive. Shortly after what happened in 2001, I had separate conversations with two high-level corporate managers. To my surprise, both took exception to my using the word evil to characterize it. They thought I was going too far. What else, I wondered, could they possibly call it?

Chapter 17. How Have Philosophers Addressed Evil?

THE ENTRY ON EVIL in the *Stanford Encyclopedia of Philosophy* opens with this sentence: "During the past thirty years . . . philosophers have become increasingly interested in the concept of evil."[1] Its author goes on to note that atrocities, such as the Holocaust, Rwandan genocide, obliteration of the World Trade Center, and the actions of serial killers have fueled this revival of interest.

Few threads in the fabric of intellectual history provide more insight into the minds of major thinkers than how they approach evil. Although the Christian faith stands in tension with any system of thought that denies the existence of God, an analysis of atheistic systems can prove informative. Such study also provides insight into contemporary currents of thought. In this chapter, we will look at how major thinkers have defined, tried to make sense of, and attempted to come to terms with evil. It contains only a small and perhaps arbitrary number of examples. Those I have chosen to include are intended to be representative but by no means exhaustive.

In her book on the history of modern philosophy, Susan Neiman writes, "the problem of evil is the guiding force of modern thought."[2] She regards responses to that problem as a fruitful lens through which to view its history. It therefore seems worth the time and effort to explore how prominent thinkers have treated evil. Neiman makes no

---

1. Calder, "The Concept of Evil," s.v.
2. Neiman, *Evil in Modern Thought*, 2–3.

attempt to define evil, but those who use the term typically believe they know what it means.

As suggested in chapter 12, it is far easier to make religious sense of the problem of evil if we conceive of ourselves as caught between warring supernatural forces, which contributed to how ancient Greeks and Romans made sense of life. Some Christians today see themselves in the middle of a struggle between God and the devil. Christianity, however, regards God as supremely powerful and has never accepted a conception of the two as equal-but-opposite. Many Christians live as though evil were as powerful as good, but if pressed, most would probably agree that God is ultimately in charge.

Augustine and Irenaeus

Augustine, whom many think of as the most influential theological philosopher in history, initially embraced Manichean thought and therefore reasoned dualistically. But on becoming a Christian, he developed an understanding that was more akin to Neo-Platonism, which denied that evil was a substance or property. To Augustine, evil has no independent existence but is instead the absence or corruption of a good. It is a privation that God did not create, and without good there would be no evil. Evil entered the world through disobedience, and it is a just punishment for our having inherited and acted on a disposition toward disobedience. Humans, according to Augustine, are inclined toward evil because they no longer possess their original goodness. Yet, they remain potentially good because God created them. If people were completely evil, they would cease to exist. This understanding does not solve the problem of evil, which confronts us with the challenge of explaining why God allows such corruption, but many theologians through the ages have embraced this Augustinian conception. It can be difficult to think of the evil of physical agony, which feels distinctly tangible, with the *absence* or *corruption* of the good of physical well-being. Or to think of a sadistic murderer as simply lacking the virtues of empathy, kindness, and compassion

Augustine argues what has come to be known as the free will defense. Although God does not desire moral evil, he allows it to enable us to make moral choices. This is a necessary condition for freedom, God's great and ennobling gift. We are neither machines nor mere animals, since we were created in God's image. To be free, we must have the power to choose between good and evil. For Augustine, however, Christians will have complete freedom only in heaven, when they will no longer be able to sin. Free will is not the condition for obedience but its result.

Irenaeus (ca. 130–ca. 202), who preceded Augustine by two centuries, views the existence of evil as necessary for moral development. Because human beings were created in the image of God, they have the potential to reach moral perfection. Attaining that perfection involves coming into the likeness of God, and to do this we must have free will. For free will to exist, however, there must be suffering, and God therefore maintains a certain distance from humanity.[3] Evil exists to allow us to develop as moral agents.

Machiavelli

Niccolò Machiavelli (1469–1527) was a theoretician and diplomat, who in the early part of the sixteenth century wrote *The Prince*, a short but power-packed treatise. It became a bestseller and remained so for centuries. Machiavelli had served as an advisor to the infamous political figure Cesare Borgia (1475–1507), who was possibly the illegitimate son of Pope Alexander VI. The book reflects a keen understanding of what it sometimes requires for rulers to acquire and retain power. *The Prince* was innovative. For the first time, a thinker unambiguously distinguished between virtue and practicality, the noble and the necessary, idealism and principles determined by expediency.

For over five-hundred years, scholars have debated the nature of Machiavelli's motives. Some have suggested he was indulging in irony. Others have suggested he was trying to curry favor with the Medici family, who had imprisoned, tortured, and deposed him from his post as a Florentine ambassador. Scholars have also differed on whether the book is prescriptive or descriptive, whether Machiavelli intended it as an instruction manual or a description of how effective rulers behave. Perhaps he intended it as both.

Some rulers, he argues, act ruthlessly. They may reason that, since the two primary functions of government are to promote stability and security, a leader must sometimes resort to deception and violence to ensure them. Lying, cheating, stealing, misrepresentation,

---

3. The term for this is *epistemic distance*, which means that God does not allow us to have complete knowledge, an issue addressed in chapter 2.

incarceration, and assassination, therefore, are fair game if used in the service of higher objectives, including the goal of remaining in power. Christians have traditionally regarded such actions as wrong, although some make allowances of how, in the interest of a greater good, one or more may be necessary. Sometimes a leader faces a *tragic moral choice* and must therefore choose between the lesser of two or more evils,[4] each of which has undesirable consequences. An example resulted in the decision to drop an atomic bomb on Hiroshima and three days later on Nagasaki. Such choices touch on *just war theory*, which concerns the moral basis for going to war, ethical duties during war, and responsibilities toward the vanquished once war has ended.

An issue I once heard discussed with considerable expertise and humanity, at a meeting of the International Society for Military Ethics, is the tolerable level of collateral damage in military actions. Suppose an enemy sniper, shooting from the top of a building, is killing soldiers. Assume that the only way to stop him is to fire a rocket into an apartment building with civilians inside. How many civilians would be likely to die before you decided it was immoral to fire the rocket? Two? Five? Ten? Twenty? How many soldiers would have to die before you decided it was immoral not to? Machiavelli is unconcerned with any of this.

No one before Machiavelli had explicitly told the Western World that unethical actions are sometimes necessary, and by implication that a ruler who is not up to the challenge stands a diminished chance of succeeding or even surviving. Traditional morals, he argues, are unrealistic and trumped by pragmatism. It is still important for a leader to appear virtuous, and hypocrisy has its place in affairs of state. Rather than trying to raise the real to the level of the ideal, Machiavelli is willing to treat the real as the ideal, to turn fact into value.

Running all through Machiavelli's thought is the assumption that we are fundamentally selfish, and to this extent he aligns himself with the Christian thesis that all of us are flawed. Yet, he is no fan of Christianity, which he believes will eventually cease to exist. Nor is he a fan of the virtuous, and anticipating Nietzsche three centuries later, he regards the righteous as weak. Machiavelli seems to be the first thinker to redefine evil. He simply defines it out of existence.

---

4. See McLemore, *Street-Smart Ethics*.

CHAPTER 17. HOW HAVE PHILOSOPHERS ADDRESSED EVIL?

Bayle

Few people today have ever heard of Pierre Bayle (1647–1706), a seventeenth-century French philosopher. But many people in the eighteenth century read his *Historical and Critical Dictionary*, which began to appear in 1696. The *Dictionary*, which amounted to a six-million-word encyclopedia, was a bestseller and became a key text of the Enlightenment. Bayle was "the most important and most influential skeptic of the late seventeenth century."[5] The son of a pastor, Bayle was a Huguenot, a French Protestant, at a time when France openly persecuted Protestants. He escaped to Geneva, returned to France for a time, and then moved to Rotterdam, where he spent the rest of his life. One of his brothers died in a French prison because of Bayle's subversive publications.

In addressing the problem of evil, he briefly flirts with Manichaeism, according to which two powers or principles, God and Satan, struggle for supremacy. Such dualism conveniently dispenses with having to confront the problem of explaining how, given that evil exists, God can be both benevolent and all-powerful. Bayle refuses to take this easy way out.

For Bayle, there can be no reasoned solution to the problem of evil. Any attempt to harmonize God's omnipotence and benevolence, he argues, ends in a blind alley. Bayle seems to have retained at least some allegiance to Calvinism throughout his life, which was the form of Protestantism in which he grew up. He argues that the problem of evil is cloaked in mystery, and that philosophical objections to such mysteries need not prove troubling, since they merely confirm that God's ways infinitely surpass our ability to understand them. Reason, he insists, is not only useless but pernicious as a foundation for belief, so it must yield to faith. One of Bayle's best-known critics, the theologian and biblical scholar Jean Le Clerc, accused him of undermining religion, and by implication Christianity, since it was impossible to believe what he had already admitted is fraught with insurmountable difficulties.

Bayle points out that philosophers often accept these sorts of propositions, such as those enshrined in the debate over whether one could infinitely double a line or endlessly reduce it to a series of points.[6] Contrary to endorsing irrational fideism, Bayle insists that he is simply

---

5. Popkin, "Pierre Bayle," 257.

6. Bayle advanced these ideas in his posthumous *Entretiens de Maxime et de Thémiste* (*Conversations between Maximus and Themist*). Problems such as this appear in what philosophers refer to as Zeno's paradoxes.

recommending a retreat from labyrinthine debates about evil that go nowhere. Whatever Bayle's true beliefs, his books ignited a firestorm of controversy. His argument for our inability to solve the problem of evil had broad implications, since it appeared to call into question the power of reason itself.

Leibniz

Gottfried Wilhelm Leibniz (1646–1716) and Voltaire (1694–1778) have come to symbolize two opposing views about God and the world. Leibniz was a German philosopher-mathematician. His only book, *Theodicy*, is an attempt to harmonize faith and reason, something Bayle believed impossible. Bayle had advised us to abandon reason and fall back on faith.

Leibniz is convinced that the connection between sin and suffering, as well as how and why God arranges everything for overall optimization, will eventually become clear. Leibniz comes close to denying that evil is, in fact, evil. Many, accepting Leibniz's thesis, continue to believe that evil serves a higher purpose. Leibniz argues that, because of God's wisdom, of all the possible worlds God could have created, the one we have is the best.

Voltaire

Considering the amount of carnage nature is forever inflicting on the human race, it may be surprising that even a catastrophic earthquake would have triggered an intellectual crisis for Voltaire (François-Marie Arouet). But it did. In 1755, the Great Lisbon Earthquake leveled much of Portugal's capital. This brought into stark relief a question that had haunted philosophers, which was whether they could make any sense of natural disaster. This, at a time when some of the best thinkers in the Western World, albeit small in number, were already leaning toward or had committed themselves to atheism. Intellectuals, especially the French *philosophe* Voltaire, were much troubled by this devastating event. *Philosophes* were eighteenth-century French thinkers who became minor celebrities long before the advent of social media. Educated and affluent Parisians would meet to exchange ideas in *salons*, which were centers of socialization. Although *philosophe* can be rendered in

CHAPTER 17. HOW HAVE PHILOSOPHERS ADDRESSED EVIL?

English as *philosopher*, at the time the term applied to any thought-leader within French society.

The quake occurred about twenty minutes before 10:00 a.m. on Sunday, the first of November. Churches all over Portugal were packed with those attending mass. The ground began to shake and roofs crashed down on worshippers. Those who were not crushed ran into the streets, and fire broke out everywhere. The earthquake approached 9.0 on the Moment Magnitude Scale. Its epicenter seems to have been 200 miles southwest of Lisbon, where fires also broke out. Three-quarters of an hour after the quake, monumental waves from a tsunami killed thousands, and it is likely that somewhere around 50,000 people died in Portugal, Spain, and Morocco. What made the Lisbon earthquake particularly ironic was that November first is All Saints' Day, and both Portugal and Spain were devoutly Catholic countries. The number of fatalities associated with the Lisbon catastrophe, coupled with the devastating property damage inflicted on over 80 percent of the city and its surrounds, pointed the spotlight back to the book Leibniz had written decades earlier, in 1710. Before the Lisbon quake, Voltaire had insisted that, regardless of what happened, he would not turn against God. The quake seems to have changed that. Four years after the tragedy, his novella *Candide* appeared.[7]

Young but naïve Candide lives a happy and contented life. He embraces the teachings of Professor Pangloss, according to which everything is for the best. Candide's sheltered existence soon deteriorates, however, and he becomes slowly disillusioned by the hardship he witnesses and experiences. The book is a scathing critique of the views of Leibniz, who had died almost four decades earlier.

Voltaire decides that any attempt to harmonize Christian belief with natural evil is absurd if not ridiculous. He takes the position that if evil is necessary, as some Christians believe, we have grounds for despair, for such a belief crushes all hope of an ideal or even a better world.[8] Voltaire clearly recognizes the nature of evil, and despite his reputation as the quintessential Enlightenment thinker, he does not suggest that reason will ever enable us to make sense of what happens in the world. Natural evil, he argues, ought to prompt us to work hard for humanitarian causes and shed the manacles of narrow-minded religion whenever and wherever it hinders such work.

---

7. Voltaire, *Candide*.
8. Neiman, *Evil in Modern Thought*, 136.

Rousseau

Prior to Jean-Jacques Rousseau (1712–78), public intellectuals tended to adopt the view that evil will, someday, turn out to have served a greater good. Some, echoing Leibniz's optimism, believed we will eventually understand exactly how and why evil can serve such a purpose. Others agreed that evil can stand in the service of the good, but like Bayle, do not believe such understanding will be forthcoming.

Although his contemporary David Hume distinguishes between moral and natural evil, Rousseau appears to be the first thinker to draw a sharp distinction between the two, and he focuses on the former. He insists on labeling evil for what it is and refuses to rationalize away its ugly character, or to regard it as an illusion. He is suspicious of the passivity to which the denial of evil can lead, and he lauds the freedom people have to combat it. We no longer have the option, according to Rousseau, of blaming God. It is our job to remedy moral evil where it exists, and doing so is the responsibility that rests squarely on our shoulders. Rousseau believes the antidote to evil is knowledge, imparted through education based on proper instruction. Evil, he believes, will disappear because of pedagogical advances. This view aligns with a shift that was taking place in society toward faith in the inevitability of progress.

Some philosophers, going back to Leibniz, refer to *metaphysical evil*, which is taken to be the result of finitude or limitation, such as blindness or deafness. There is also another type of evil, but it is not metaphysical but societal. It is structural or institutional evil. It occurs when social systems so institutionalize moral evil that it becomes a self-perpetuating part of it. Evil is carried out in such a society by flawed people who have either come to see themselves as acting nobly or for whom evil actions become more or less unthinking and automatic. As we will see below, this is what Hannah Arendt may have been getting at in her analysis of Nazi war crimes. What struck her was the *banality* of it all.[9]

It is Rousseau's conviction that the choices people made from the dawn of history changed human nature. He insists that human beings are essentially good, the capacity to make the world better is in our hands, and we need not appeal to the supernatural. Rousseau maintains that moral failure leads to suffering and that nobility promotes well-being: evil leads to pain and virtue to contentment. God made the world good, but humanity spoiled it. Once the process of spoilage began, it gained

---

9. See Arendt, *Eichmann in Jerusalem*.

CHAPTER 17. HOW HAVE PHILOSOPHERS ADDRESSED EVIL?

momentum. The luxuries we have come to believe we need, for example to make ourselves attractive, carry with them greater potentials for loss than gain. Since losing a luxury is more painful than acquiring it is pleasurable, acquiring a luxury only increases the potential for pain.

Rousseau insists that it is hard enough to make sense of and correct the evil we are responsible for, so there is no point worrying about the evil we are not. He has almost nothing to say, therefore, about the Lisbon earthquake. Some have suggested that in focusing so much on moral as opposed to natural evil, Rousseau lets God off the hook.

Many people mistakenly believe Rousseau advocates a return to nature and the pristine condition of the noble savage. Rousseau may never have actually used this term, although it is most often associated with him. Such a return, in his view, is impossible. Properly educated and reared, a child will grow up empowered to resist the corrupting lures of society and will therefore likely contribute to its betterment. This is the theme of *Emile*, which also goes by the title *On Education*.[10] In it, Rousseau outlines how innate human goodness can be cultivated and retained. Central to a child's education should be the development of self-insight, and therefore the ability to distinguish between genuine and false needs. This, in turn, will lead to an adult with the ability to be an independent thinker. The path to such insight is for the child to learn, through experience, how virtue leads to happiness.

Like many other thinkers, theory and reality in Rousseau do not always converge. When he was still a teenager living in Switzerland, he seems to have become what some have described as the boy-toy of a Swiss-French noblewoman. When he eventually made his way to Paris, he took up with a near-illiterate laundrywoman who bore him five children, all of whom he remanded into the custody of an orphanage.

Advances in the education of a child do not, in Rousseau's view, come about through coddling, and pain can be an effective teacher. A child who touches a hot stove is unlikely to touch it again. Rousseau promotes a kind of indoctrination for pupils. His repudiation of consumerism fits well with motifs in Christianity, but as a remedy for the selfishness and acquisitiveness that afflicts many human beings, his prescriptions seem unrealistic. At very least, their value as a remedy for evil remains undemonstrated. Excessively structured education, which

---

10. See Rousseau, *Emile or On Education*.

Rousseau argues will foster free independent thinking, may paradoxically do little to promote it.

Hume

David Hume, a contemporary of Rousseau, was a congenial Scottish philosopher who provided the world with a blast-furnace critique of inductive reasoning, which he held to be unable to come to conclusions about God, causation, or existence beyond the grave. Many Enlightenment thinkers wanted to abandon Christianity, and in its place install a universal natural religion. This, they believed, would put an end to quarreling between and among religious factions and ground religion in self-evident truths. In place of revealed religion, they advocated what they believed to be a religion based solely on reason. They espoused Deism and the lip-service worship of a far-off Creator-God, based in some cases on admiration of an exquisitely designed universe. Hume would have none of it.

He attacks the idea that experience provides proofs of God or his goodness, and he suggests that subscribing to natural religion is as much motivated by fear and superstition as subscribing to theism. Hume rips to shreds the hope of a new religion devoid of revelation. He also points out that all arguments from design rest on inferences, from effects to presumed causes. Why not, he asks, just as reasonably conclude that something as intricate as the human body came from nothing? No ironclad principle of logic impels us to believe effects always have causes, certainly not divine ones.[11]

Causation, argues Hume, is merely constant conjunction, and we have no good reason to assume it is anything more. One billiard ball collides with another and the second ball moves. Perhaps that is all there is to it. If an event happens only once, say the bodily resurrection of Jesus, surely there can be no logical grounds for concluding God caused it. Hume goes on the attack against all inductive reasoning and undermines any presumed certainty that similar causes yield similar effects.

In attacking the argument from design, Hume suggests that if you paid to have a building designed that turned out to have serious defects, as our world does, you would promptly fire the architect. The argument from design is that since the world is so fine-tuned and perfectly ordered,

---

11. Yitzhak and Lin, "Sufficient Reason." s.v.

it must have had a designer. Neiman writes, "For all . . . Voltaire's patent rage, a touch of awe endured. God remained a sovereign against whom one might with reason rebel. He had not yet become a contractor whom one might decide to fire."[12] With Hume, skepticism comes into full bloom. He is the first major thinker to be thoroughly secular.

Neiman adds, "Hume's prose exudes a ghostly sort of calm that conceals the ferocity of his attack."[13] Hume aligns himself with Bayle, at least as far as their shared distrust of reason, which both insist to be fallible or at least limited. In his 1738 *Treatise of Human Nature*, Hume suggests that it is in the face of the problem of evil that reason stumbles and skepticism prevails. He also suggests that if you desire to hold onto your belief in God's benevolence and omnipotence, you are certainly free to do so. But it is illegitimate to base your belief on reason. You can maintain it only by faith. There is more than a hint in Hume that the existence of evil calls into question the existence of a loving creator.

Hume does not much concern himself with the nature and causes of moral evil. He is more interested in arguing that the widespread presence of evil, both natural and moral, makes the existence of a benevolent and omnipotent God unlikely. Certainly, suggests Hume, a God who exists could have designed and created a better world than the one we have. In his view, there are no good evidential arguments, based on life as we know it, in favor of theism.[14] Hume acknowledges that the existence of evil is not logically inconsistent with the existence of God, only that belief in the existence of a good God cannot be based on observations of nature.

Kant

The German philosopher Immanuel Kant (1724–1804) argues that there is an insuperable gulf between *is* and *ought*, which in principle we can never cross, an idea that is today more associated with Hume than Kant. Indeed, even the terminology is Hume's. We are stuck with the gulf and must therefore live with a certain level of ignorance. All the intellectual paraphernalia involved in trying to address the problem of evil, such as grasping God's intentions and the nature of creation, are in Kant's mind

---

12. Neiman, *Evil in Modern Thought*, 160.
13. Neiman, *Evil in Modern Thought*, 162.
14. See O'Connor, *Hume on Religion*; Flew, ed., *Hume: Writings on Religion*.

off limits and over-reaching. The desire to disregard these limitations amounts to posturing as God. Among Kant's principal theses is that we cannot know things in themselves but only things as they appear. God alone knows things as they are.

For Kant, morality is grounded in reason. When we say an event should never have happened, he suggests, we are implicitly saying that virtue and happiness ought to go together. Every instance of empathy is rooted in the unconsciously held belief that the world should work according to moral principle. Think of how we use the phrase *innocent suffering*. It is meant to suggest that so-and-so did not deserve what happened. Kant's mission is to foster a world in which a systematic connection can be seen to exist between happiness and virtue. The notion that we are free to choose between good and evil is central to his thought. So is the assertion that, by nature, we are inclined toward both. It was Kant who coined the term *radical evil*.

There are times when we either fail to do what we ought, or the world does not cooperate with our nobler efforts. This can lead to despair, which only a rational faith, grounded in reason, can overcome. Such faith is not empirically verifiable, however, and so does not qualify as scientific knowledge. We are inclined to believe that God will ultimately put things right, and Leibniz had even argued that progress in science will someday make it possible for us to understand the relationship between natural and moral evil. Kant holds that, in this life, we will never understand this relationship. Nor should we try, since the quest for such understanding is hopeless and only causes frustration. Nieman writes that according to Kant, "Solving the problem of evil is not only impossible but immoral."[15]

Suppose we knew that every noble action is certain to produce a reward and every base one a punishment. How moral could we then be? Would we ever be able to do something solely because it is ethically right? All intentional acts would become instrumental, designed to obtain desired and predictable outcomes on which we would focus our attention. A morally transparent world would make morality impossible. To behave honestly because honesty is the best policy, in business for example, does not reflect great moral virtue. It would not, according to Kant, be virtuous at all. At the heart of morality is human freedom, which according to Kant requires limitation, and to behave freely implies acting with incomplete knowledge. Not knowing if noble actions will lead

---

15. Neiman, *Evil in Modern Thought*, 69.

CHAPTER 17. HOW HAVE PHILOSOPHERS ADDRESSED EVIL?

to gain is a necessary condition for morality. In view of clearly foreseen consequences, everyone's behavior might improve, but it would not be more moral. It could not, in fact, be moral at all.

Elsewhere in this book I have suggested that God may have intentionally built ambiguity into our lives. Kant explains that such ambiguity is necessary if life is to have meaning beyond the pleasure-pain principle. For Kant, even praying for salvation is unworthy of human beings and demeaning to God. To rid ourselves of superstition, we must recognize God as infinitely beyond whatever we can know or imagine. In pointing to God's unfathomable nature, Kant echoes the thinking of Bayle and anticipates that of the Swiss theologian Karl Barth (1886–1968), who like Kant emphasizes the incomprehensible distinction between us and God, what Kierkegaard (1813–55) termed an *infinite qualitative difference*.

If we cannot know things in themselves, how do we know there is anything or anyone, such as God, causing us to have the sense experiences we do? Can we ever know evil in itself? Kant argues that we have access only to the *phenomenal*, things as they appear through the senses, and never to the *noumenal*, things in themselves. According to Kant, because we can only know what is empirically verified, God cannot be understood through the senses. Yet, Kant insists that reason requires us to believe in God.

Hegel

Georg Friedrich Hegel (1770–1831), another philosopher of the Enlightenment, was born nearly half a century after Kant, to whom Hegel acknowledged a considerable intellectual debt. Even before Nietzsche, Hegel informed us that God is dead, although what he meant by God is unclear.

Hegel insists that his entire philosophy is "about God and nothing but God." Kierkegaard spent half his short life trying to debunk those he called "system builders," chief among them Hegel. In Kierkegaard's view, Hegel was worse than a heretic because of his denial of the immeasurable difference between us and God. Kierkegaard had attended lectures delivered by Hegel's one-time friend and roommate, Friedrich Wilhelm Joseph Schelling (1775–1854). It is possible that Schelling's criticism of

Hegel fueled Kierkegaard's,[16] although in Kierkegaard's journals he appears to dismiss if not disparage Schelling's lectures.[17]

Hegel believes it was a mistake for Christianity so dramatically to distinguish between human and divine nature, and it appears he intends to provide us with ways for the former to become more like the latter. Among these is to accept responsibility for evil rather than trying to palm it off on God, a view reminiscent of Rousseau's. Before Hegel, major philosophers had tried to suggest at least a tentative link between philosophy and theology, and the language of philosophers often sounded quasi-religious. Up until the modern era, in fact, it tended to be explicitly religious. Hegel is the first to try to account for evil in purely secular terms. The world is precisely as it ought to be and nothing can subvert God's purposes. As suggested above, however, it is doubtful that what Hegel intends by the word *God* is anything like what Christians do.

According to Hegel, "God's will" prevails in history, which amounts to the working out of providence. Hegel once described history as a slaughterhouse. He is clear-minded, therefore, about the existence and nature of evil, and there is nothing in Hegel to suggest that evil is an illusion. But he believes history will eventually right itself. It is not the existence of evil that Hegel questions, only its significance. Instead of making the argument that God will someday enable us to understand how evil exists in the service of a higher good, Hegel argues that history itself will make this clear. In place of traditional theism, Hegel posits *Geist*, the German term for spirit. Hegel's *Geist* should not be confused with what Christians mean by Holy Spirit.

He sees history as moving toward an end goal, and for this reason his philosophy is teleological. History moves with purpose toward a culmination point. *Geist* or world spirit pushes history forward "with the right combination of freedom and necessity."[18] The evolution of human consciousness, and the emergence of human freedom, are natural and inevitable, and Hegel's ideas align nicely with the growing optimism of the nineteenth century. Our world is getting better, he believes, a motif challenged in the twentieth century by two world wars. Hegel tries to get behind what Peter Kreeft characterizes as the garbage of history,[19] to the

---

16. Paul Redding, "Hegel." s.v.
17. Personal communication, November 30, 2020.
18. Neiman, *Evil in Modern Thought*, 97.
19. Kreeft, *Essays in Christian Apologetics*.

progress he believes to be latent within it. Humans can and will come up with remedies for the evil they have caused.

Hegel believes that wherever we find ourselves in time, a later point in history will negate it, and a point beyond that will improve it. Because of this thesis-antithesis-synthesis paradigm, the gap is slowly narrowing between *is* and *ought*. Hegel was not the originator of this repeating three-stage paradigm, the German idealist Johann Gottlieb Fichte (1762–1814) was, but Hegel made it famous.

His optimistic thesis that humanity is on an inexorable path of progress may seem unrealistic in view of all the destruction that continues to take place in the world. It is therefore reasonable to ask on what basis Hegel arrives at this conclusion. He certainly does not try to idealize human existence and its horrors. Hegel does not so much explain evil as reinterpret it. According to Hegel, civilization will inevitably advance and the present carnage will turn out later to have been beneficial. His is a strange form of optimism. Progress, he argues, requires death and destruction, and the triumph of the spirit is rooted in the absolute necessity of suffering and despair. Hegel redefines the significance of evil and argues that, in the end, it will turn out not to have been evil at all.

Schopenhauer

Arthur Schopenhauer (1788–1860), who like Kant and Hegel was a German philosopher, was born in Poland into an aristocratic family. As a teenager, Schopenhauer attended an English boarding school when such schools were known for merciless brutality. During these years, he developed an antipathy toward Christianity, and he was the first major thinker to discard its tenets for those more aligned with Buddhism. Schopenhauer rejected theism and the pantheism inherent in some forms of Hinduism. He was among the earliest philosophers to challenge the assumption that the world is rational. Significantly influenced by Kant, Schopenhauer reckoned squarely with the strife and conflict in human existence. His thought-forms anticipate trends within contemporary culture, such as an interest in eastern religion, a proclivity toward cynicism, and a fondness for vague spirituality. Because of his eastern bent, Schopenhauer was out of step with Enlightenment themes, and he shared none of the optimism reflected in later Romantic thinkers. It is no wonder that his early-nineteenth-century contemporaries, living as they did in an age that embraced the idea of inevitable progress through reason, shunned him. Many Enlightenment thinkers deemed progress to be inevitable and self-evident. The two world wars in the twentieth century encouraged many educated people to abandon the optimism of Hegel in favor of the pessimism of the previously neglected Schopenhauer.

He opposes the faith in reason so characteristic of his peers. From a Christian perspective, he seems close and yet far. Schopenhauer understands what introduces so much misery into human existence. Reckoning with evil as acutely as he does, he conveys a bleakness shown by few other intellectuals. He decries abstraction and conceptualization, yet writes abstract and conceptual material because he believes this to be necessary for effective communication. Schopenhauer is a western man trying to describe an eastern attitude of mind, a mode of contemplative consciousness that is by its nature ineffable. Rational description is alien to the thing described. Some argue that Schopenhauer ultimately became a Stoic.

Schopenhauer insists we can make life more bearable by limiting our natural desires, and if we cannot do that, by living aesthetically. Schopenhauer insists that life itself is a form of suffering and that our goal ought to be to escape the painful wheel of existence. This approach to life, he believes, will at least increase our awareness of just how ugly human existence actually is. The aesthetic attitude, which he conceives of as a kind of hypnotic trance, will at least enable us to transcend the egocentric and ruthless inclinations of the will.

In discussing Schopenhauer, as with Rousseau and Nietzsche, it is difficult to avoid argument *ad hominem*, dismissing his ideas because of his disposition and behavior. Given that he provides little evidence or systematic argument in support of his infamous pessimism, it is difficult not to reflect on the realities of his life and wonder if these might not have spawned or at least contributed to his despairing outlook.

Schopenhauer came from an unstable family whose instability he seems to have inherited. While living in Berlin, Schopenhauer became embroiled in a lawsuit filed by another tenant in his rooming house, who accused him of assault and battery. He lost the suit and the court ordered him to make payments that ended only when the woman died twenty years later. With a servant, he parented an illegitimate daughter, who was born in 1819. In that same year, he refused to settle another suit relating to the family business. Two years later, in his thirties, he fell in love with a teenage singer, continued a relationship with her for

CHAPTER 17. HOW HAVE PHILOSOPHERS ADDRESSED EVIL?

years, and then refused to marry her. Schopenhauer's epithets about marriage are memorably cynical. He quips, for example, that marriage cuts one's rights in half, while doubling one's obligations. He also opined that getting married is like being blindfolded and putting your hand in a sack, hoping to extract an eel from among the snakes. His relationship with his widowed mother also became strained, as did his relationships with colleagues. He launched vitriolic attacks on the philosophies of Fichte, Schelling, and Hegel. His arrogance, which early in life caused his failure as a lecturer at the University of Berlin, showed itself in Schopenhauer having deliberately scheduled his lectures at the same time as those of the immensely popular Hegel. Reflecting a continuing inability to establish and maintain congenial relationships, Schopenhauer moved to Frankfurt, partly in response to a cholera epidemic in Berlin. For the remaining twenty-seven years of his life, he lived alone with only a succession of small dogs as companions.

Schopenhauer's most famous work is *The World as Will and Representation*.[20] Although Fichte had already focused on Will, Schopenhauer's originality lies in stressing that Will is neither rational nor intellectual. It is without mind, the raw urge at the heart of instinctual drives, indeed at the heart of everything. Anticipating Nietzsche, Schopenhauer sees will, the blind desire to dominate, as a kind of ultimate ruler, the acting out of which, true to his ever-present theme of despair, inevitably causes unhappiness. Schopenhauer, like Kant, insists that the real is not what is known (representation). Nor is will, which also cannot be known. Like Hegel, Schopenhauer believes we can acquire metaphysical knowledge, and both claim in different ways to understand the deep nature of reality. Hegel believes all thought to be contained in an absolute thought. Schopenhauer believes all will to be contained in a universal will. But unlike Hegel, Schopenhauer is convinced that the universe is moving inexorably toward self-destruction, and further that there is nothing we can or should do about it.

We delude ourselves, first with hope and then by attaining what we hope for. We are unhappy in a state of desire and bored in a state of fulfillment. The only happiness we experience is based either in the past, on memory, or in the future, on expectation. The present is but a "small, dark cloud." According to Schopenhauer, "Knowledge that the objects of desire are illusions—that the distinctions and honors we prize, the goals

---

20. Older English translations use *Idea* instead of *Representation* in its title.

we aim at, the self on which we insist, are illusions—acts as a quieter of the will..."[21] For Schopenhauer, the essence of human existence is suffering. He assumes this to be so self-evident that he has little need to supply any semblance of a proof.

According to Schopenhauer, two stages on life's way are open to us. The first involves realizing that other people are also centers of desire. This enables us to rise above Hobbesian egotism, all against all, toward camaraderie and a sense of justice and equality. The second stage is to grasp that all centers of desire are manifestations of a single overarching will. We are all one. Ancient Hinduism, according to Schopenhauer, attained this stage long ago, while Christianity remained primitive. In this second stage, the individual no longer draws a distinction between self and other, which enables sympathy and compassion to emerge. At its peak, such sentiments might dispose someone to lay down his or her life to save others, although as noted above, Schopenhauer did not seem much inclined toward altruism.

Dying for others, ironically, is precisely what Christians insist Jesus did. Even more ironically, Schopenhauer disparages Christianity for embracing the crucifixion as a central motif and symbol. How he moves from an understanding of our instinctive self-centeredness to the idea that everything in the world, from rocks to napkins, has *will*, and further to the notion that this will is moving purposefully toward its own destruction, is unclear.

In *Mere Christianity*,[22] C. S. Lewis takes pains to stress how people generally hold to some standard of justice. Despite Schopenhauer's pessimism, he never abandons the idea of ultimate justice and in fact embraces it, but he believes justice works itself out in the present. Human wretchedness and moral turpitude get us exactly what we deserve. The world's built-in natural tribunal ensures it. Humanity is diseased. Its will is infected and it is getting its just desserts. Although it remains unclear how Schopenhauer reaches this conclusion, he believes natural evil helps even the score and balance the scales between malfeasance and misery. The innocent cannot be said to suffer because, in fact, no one is innocent.

Each of us lives with an unrestrained desire to survive, propagate, and thrive, even at the expense of our neighbor. If wanting someone or something brings pain, therefore, why not put an end to desire?

---

21. Jones, *History of Western Philosophy*, 154.
22. Lewis, *Mere Christianity*.

Renunciation, Schopenhauer insists, is in fact the route to freedom from anguish and anxiety. The only treatment, according to Schopenhauer, is not the proper channeling of desire but its eradication. He is like a man in a dark room, groping around to find the light switch, and after that the door. Unable to find either, he decides to resign himself to living the rest of his life in the despair of the dark. If hell is diagnosis without treatment, Schopenhauer dooms us to it.

Schopenhauer recognizes that the renunciation of sexual impulses would result in the extinction of humanity, but this is fine with him. He correctly observes that even a small change in temperature would be enough to upset the delicate balance of life on earth and plunge us into the abyss of annihilation. Never, it seems, does he suspect that a creator might be in the business of sustaining it. He is a man in need of rescue from his unvarnished awareness of the futility and meaninglessness of life, a man without God. Perhaps more than any other philosopher, he personifies the pathos of life without Christ, a phrase I first heard used by my college classmate William Devlin. Despite references to sympathy and compassion in his writings, Schopenhauer's thought, his mentality, is misanthropic, and existence to him is without hope.

Marx

Many governments and movements over the past hundred years have claimed to be Marxist. It is worth noting, however, that although countries like China and Russian have institutions known as Communist Parties, these countries are in reality capitalist societies with extensive government intervention in economic affairs. Only a small number of countries, including North Korea, seem to have governments that Marx might recognize as faithful to his principles.

Karl Marx was born in Prussia and became a prodigious reader early in life. He spent enormous amounts of time as an adult in the reading room of the British museum, primarily devouring the works of political economists. As a result, Marx ended up with hundreds of pages of notes and essays on such topics as capital, labor, property, trade, markets, and the state. He was determined to understand how capitalism worked, so he studied the writings of scholars such as James Mill, David Ricardo, and Adam Smith, who in 1776 had written *The Wealth of Nations*.

Marx studied for a PhD at the University of Berlin but earned his doctorate from the University of Jena. He came from an affluent family, but from time to time he and his wife subsisted on loans from friends. Marx was therefore able to spend much of his life as a professional student. Ever the polemicist, he combined intellectual interests with activism, serving at times as a writer, editor, or publisher. Before rounding the corner on thirty, he had become acutely critical of philosophers, who to him favored thought over action. Marx quipped that philosophers interpret the world. The point was to change it.

He is known for historical or *dialectic materialism*, the thesis that the world undergoes change, not through abstractions but because of material events. Apparently, Marx never adopted this term, which seems to have been coined by his friend and sometime collaborator Friedrich Engels. The ideas of French socialists and English economists influenced Marx, and so did the thought-forms of Hegel, who however put greater emphasis on ideas than did Marx.

Whereas Hegel views *Geist*, which can be translated into English as spirit, mind, or intellect, as propelling history forward, Marx regards this concept as a superfluous mystification that obscures the harsh realities of life. Marx sees history as the unfolding of class struggle and is convinced that capitalism will eventually destroy itself. Materialism, he concludes, is the driving force in human events. Hegel points to an abstraction as the impetus for change. Marx points to the concrete desire for wealth and property. People act according to their tangible interests.

Like Hegel, Marx believes history will ultimately transform human nature. He also believes that the advance of human consciousness begins with coming to terms with alienation. In Marx's view, this centers on understanding that the urban worker no longer has a direct connection with what he or she produces. Through the evils of capitalism, large numbers of people had changed from indispensable craftspeople into replaceable cogs in the implacable machinery of the factory. To Marx, again like Hegel, progress is not only possible but certain. But, to Marx, it will only come about through political action, which will triumph when economic forces make progress inevitable. He is a relentless fomenter of revolution by the working class against the affluent middle-class *bourgeoisie*.

Marx devotes little attention to *natural* evil, except perhaps to blame it on a God he does not believe to exist. To get the flavor of Marx's atheism, recall his quip, "religion is the opium of the masses (people)." His focus is on *moral* evil and how one class (capitalists or

CHAPTER 17. HOW HAVE PHILOSOPHERS ADDRESSED EVIL?

owners) oppress another class (proletariat or workers). Marx is keenly aware of the nature of such evil, and among major thinkers he may actually best understand it.

According to Marx, beyond the money to buy machinery and materials, capitalists contribute little or nothing to the production of goods. Workers, by contrast, give blood, sweat, and tears, and they do it for a pittance, under the domination of the wealthy who take rapacious advantage of them. Marx pays little attention to the economic value of innovation, capability, or financial risk-taking. The last sentence of *The Communist Manifesto*, which he wrote with Friedrich Engels (1820–95), published in 1846, is "Workers of the world unite."

Marx does not view capitalists as inherently evil, and although this seems a stretch, some have suggested he does not believe true evil exists. Capitalists, he argues, oppress workers because the economic system requires them to. They have no choice because, like workers, they are caught up in the capitalist system. If you correct economic inequality, you eliminate abuse based on social class. Classical Marxism exists today mostly in the halls of academia, but it does not take a Rhodes Scholar to see that, in the spirit of Marx, materialist solutions to the world's problems are alive and well.

Some who look to material solutions as the way to eliminate evil shy away from private ownership in favor of state control, which when coupled with the restriction of markets characterizes communism. Although no thoughtful person can deny that evils attend capitalism, Winston Churchill once quipped, "The inherent vice of capitalism is the unequal sharing of blessings; the inherent virtue of socialism is the equal sharing of miseries."[23] Although democracy and capitalism are not identical, they tend to be associated. This brings to mind another of Churchill's comments, one delivered to the House of Commons on November 11, 1947: "Democracy is the worst form of Government except for all those other forms that have been tried from time to time." Adam Smith argues that free (capitalist) markets do a better job than governments in fostering the economic well-being of a society.[24]

Communism is not a monolithic entity and it can take many forms. China, as mentioned above, operates with a hybrid of communism and capitalism. Although avowedly communist in its policies, it fosters and

---

23. See Langworth, *Churchill by Himself*, 574.
24. Smith, *Wealth of Nations*.

underwrites a considerable amount of entrepreneurial capitalism. It was only when China moved in a capitalist direction that it became prosperous. There are problems with communism devoid of capitalism, which does not much seem to help ordinary citizens.

First, today's luxuries become tomorrow's necessities. The definition of *enough* is therefore elastic. Although the homes of many people in the Western World do not have central heating, the majority do. Every winter morning, millions of household heaters automatically start when a thermometer, connected to a timer, turns them on. Even if residents do not have an automatic thermostat, they can usually flip a switch to heat their residences. Two hundred years ago, no one enjoyed that luxury, much less an integrated system that turns on the furnace when it is cold. It is difficult and perhaps impossible to translate the Marxian ideal of "each according to his needs" into a policy that effectively defines needs and minimizes human acquisitiveness. People compare what they have with what their neighbors have. The desire to have ever more is the nature of greed.

Second, there is a clear relationship between goods and services, on one hand, and what it takes to produce or provide them on the other. Some person or group has to design, manufacture, and distribute every good, or organizes the provision of every service. It takes effort to do all this, not to mention intelligence, creativity, and a tolerance for risk. People naturally regard it as unfair when the lazy benefit as much as the industrious. The lack of incentives, of a positive correlation between effort and outcome, seems to cause those in Marxist societies who might otherwise be creative and hardworking to lack motivation. It can also lead to resentment toward colleagues who are slackers and party officials for whom it is difficult to see the connection between what they contribute to the state and the benefits they derive from it.

Third, within Marxism there can be a neglect of flexible economic policy. In response to changing conditions, governments must make decisions, such as when to raise taxes and whether to increase or decrease the national debt. Neglecting to modify economic policy when needed can trigger runaway inflation, the negotiation or renegotiation of terms for loans, or default on the nation's debt. Contemporary Marxist governments spend a lot of time arguing about economic policy, but because decisions must conform to ideology, the results sometimes diverge from sound economic practice.

CHAPTER 17. HOW HAVE PHILOSOPHERS ADDRESSED EVIL?

Fourth, according to Marx, workers must be given power, and if they are not, owners will continue to oppress them. Marx appears oblivious to how, once workers become leaders and represent their fellows, they can also become oppressors. People in power ride in limousines, while those they putatively represent ride bicycles. High-ranking leaders often find ways to rationalize their privileged lifestyles and Swiss bank accounts. Marxist societies seem to have an abundance of racketeers who collude with corrupt governments to further terrorize and oppress citizens. As noted above, human beings tend naturally to be acquisitive—Marx had that right—and those with power frequently use it to increase their individual economic outcomes. This is no surprise to Christians, who have a more realistic and less sanguine view of human nature.

In reading the *Communist Manifesto*, you can palpably sense Marx's seething resentment toward the wealthy. He is astute enough to highlight the adverse consequences of driving a wedge between the worker and what he or she produces, and how factories can hinder individual creativity. The scope and depth of what Marx wrote is impressive, but he seems to assume that human nature, free of class constraints, will magically become virtuous. History has demonstrated this to be a gratuitous and flawed assumption. Regardless of where we draw the lines separating different classes, or how fuzzy and imprecise they may be, there will always be distinctions between and among people, and therefore something resembling a class structure. In communist countries, a few belong to the central committee or politburo and live in splendor. Most do not and live in relative poverty.

Nietzsche

Friedrich Nietzsche sees the whole idea of evil as pernicious because he believes it pampers the weak and discourages the strong. In *Genealogy of Morals*, he suggests that the powerless promoted the concept of evil because of their feelings of hate, envy, and resentment, which for emphasis Nietzsche substitutes the French *ressentiment*. Resentment is central in Nietzsche's thought. Slave morality is passive, reactive, and negative, while master morality is active, assertive, and life affirming.

The slave sees the master as evil, as he does the master's attributes. To the slave, the good are the meek and the weak, who are also likely to be the poor. Nietzsche believes the slave revolt began with the Jews, but

"Nietzsche's anger at Judaism is really fueled by his anger at Christianity."[25] Slave morality smothers initiative rather than encouraging it, and love as Christians define it, is dangerous because it is life negating.

Since I devoted most of chapter 8 to Nietzsche, I will not rehearse more of his ideas here, except to repeat that Nietzsche is the consummate iconoclast. His writings are nearly always *against* something or someone. Many people feel liberated when they read Nietzsche because he gives them the sense that, finally, here is a philosopher who thinks the unthinkable and speaks the unspeakable.

Although in his lifetime many saw him as a madman, that changed in the twentieth century. Students and professors found themselves attracted to how Nietzsche upended the notion of evil by arguing that evil, as traditionally defined, is not evil at all. It is the expression of Übermenschen (superhumans), who refuse to allow conventional morality to act as straitjackets. Such superior people invent their own morality, without regard to lesser mortals who cling to effete values like charity, mercy, and humility. It is no surprise that Nietzsche regarded Christianity as his enemy and quipped in *The Antichrist*, "there was only one Christian, and he died on the cross." This is more pithily expressed in the misquote, "The last Christian died on the cross."

The Marquis de Sade

Donatien Alphonse François (1740–1814), the legal name of the Marquis de Sade, died thirty years before Nietzsche was born. He had already acted out Nietzsche's program in his strange and chaotic life, much of which he spent either in prison or an asylum. It is from him that we get the term *sadism*.

For Sade, morality means pursuing your darkest passions and most destructive impulses as far as you can, no matter what the cost to others. Many regard his life and writings as perverted and indicative of a psychotic disorder. While Nietzsche is an armchair philosopher, Sade demonstrates the courage of his convictions through sexual extremism. In Nietzsche's words from *The Birth of Tragedy*, Sade exhibits the unrestrained and uninhibited Dionysian in contrast to the restrained and disciplined Apollonian. Dionysus was the Greek god of wine, fertility, excess, abandon, emotion, and festive merrymaking. The corresponding

---

25. See Evans, *History of Western Philosophy*, 544–45.

CHAPTER 17. HOW HAVE PHILOSOPHERS ADDRESSED EVIL?

Roman god was Bacchus, associated with intoxication, ecstasy, and freedom, from which we get the term bacchanalian. Apollo was both the Greek and Roman gods of rationality, order, knowledge, logic, medicine, poetry, and restraint. It was Nietzsche, not the ancients, who most pointedly set Dionysus and Apollo in opposition.

For Sade, the only evil is self-restraint, and vice becomes virtue. This inversion may be what writers in the New Testament refer to as the unforgivable sin (Luke 12:10; Mark 3:29; Matt 12:31–32; 1 John 5:16). Sade wants to do what society defines as evil, especially in the realm of sex. Nietzsche also shuns traditional morality, but rather than inverting it on principle, as Sade does, Nietzsche believes the Overman can and should construct a new morality. Sade's and Nietzsche's attitudes toward Jesus and Christianity are similar. Neither seems to consider the possibility that he is rebelling against God. I once heard a faculty colleague say, "To become famous, you have to shock someone!" Sade and Nietzsche shocked nearly everybody.

Freud

Sigmund Freud (1856–1939), although not a professional philosopher, may have had more influence on ideas flowing through Western Culture than anyone else in the twentieth century. He made some striking statements about evil in an interview that took place in 1930,[26] years before WWII. He first tells the interviewer that he does not believe in existence beyond the grave and that he has no interest in prolonging his own life. The interviewer then shifts gears. Because of Freud's deep psychological understanding, the interviewer suggests, a practitioner of psychoanalysis would have to be tolerant of everything, so that the analyst could show "genuine charity." With the depth of insight into the workings of the mind achieved in the consulting chamber, he suggests, the analyst would have to suspend all moral judgments. *"Tout comprendre c'est tout pardoner,"* quips the interviewer, to understand all is to forgive all.

"On the contrary," replies Freud. "To understand all, is not to forgive all. Psychoanalysis teaches us not only what we may endure, it also teaches us what we must avoid. It tells us what must be exterminated. Tolerance of evil is by no means a corollary of knowledge." Note Freud's

---

26. Viereck, *Glimpses of the Great*, 263–72.

uninhibited use of the word *evil* and how he is not reluctant to declare war on it, as evidenced by his use of *exterminate*.

Freud seems to be getting at what philosophers refer to as the difference, noted in chapter 2, between eliminative and explanatory reductions. Because we can make partial sense of evil, perhaps by pointing to its biological or developmental precursors, does not mean evil is nothing but the product of such precursors. We may understand the neurological correlates of a person becoming a vicious criminal, but this does not change that person's nature or the depravity of the crimes. The criminal is a conscious being who makes choices. Even if we deem retributive justice to be undesirable, or acknowledge that because of genetics, personal history, or circumstances people have less freedom of choice than we sometimes assume, this does not mean we should turn loose on society those who, unless incarcerated, would probably again kill, rape, or maim. Nor should we set them free because we have correctly concluded that prisons rarely rehabilitate and frequently help perfect criminality by putting novices together with veterans.

The interview with Freud took place years before Hitler (1889–1945) reminded the world of what radical evil looks like. Freud would never have explained away Hitler's actions as a lack of education or the failure of his parents to teach him good manners. Or, with some far-fetched conjecture that his mother had improperly toilet-trained or breast-fed him. How you regard Hitler hinges, in the end, on whether you see him as a free moral agent, making at least partially free choices, or as the passive victim of biological conditions and developmental events. "If only he'd been admitted to art school, he might have behaved better." Not likely. It was the sinister nature of Hitler's character and actions that show us exactly what we are dealing with when we look evil in the face.

Arendt

Hannah Arendt (1906–75) was a German-born Jewish political theorist who escaped from Europe during the Holocaust. In 1961, *The New Yorker* dispatched her to attend and report on the trial of Otto Adolf Eichmann. He had been a Lieutenant Colonel in the SS and a key figure in the Nazis' "final solution." A Jerusalem court sentenced him to death in 1962.

CHAPTER 17. HOW HAVE PHILOSOPHERS ADDRESSED EVIL?

In 1963, Arendt published her controversial, *Eichmann in Jerusalem: A Report on the Banality of Evil*.[27]

In it, Arendt asserts that, contrary to being radical, evil is the result of ordinary people thoughtlessly carrying out orders and fecklessly aligning with mass opinion. Her apparent trivialization of evil triggered a firestorm among Jewish intellectuals, who viewed her as cold, unfeeling, and devoid of sympathy. Arendt concludes the book with the odd statement that, since no member of our species would want to share the planet with Eichmann, it made sense for him to hang.

Perhaps Arendt was overly influenced by Eichmann's façade of ordinariness and dull impassivity. Another observer might have come to a different conclusion about him, especially when his malevolent statements came to light. What she wrote appears to some as a striking example of denial. Many believe that she was simply shutting her eyes to the horrific nature of what happened and the role Eichmann played in it. At a more conceptual level, Arendt's denial appears to be backing away from the nature of radical evil itself.

It makes sense to ask whether Arendt is right about the nature of evil. Is it routine, maybe even boring? She seems to accept Eichmann's argument that he was only doing what he was told, the so-called *Nuremberg defense*. This still leaves us with the job of accounting for the actions of Goering, Himmler, and ultimately Hitler. Calling evil banal may have been more indicative of Arendt's need to shut her eyes to the awfulness of what had occurred than of any psychological, philosophical, or theological insights.

Evil in Contemporary Thought

Some contemporary thinkers argue that we should stop using the word evil, while others argue that society ought to resurrect the concept. Among the arguments for continuing to use the term is that only evil can properly describe the moral significance of such horrendous acts as abducting, torturing, and murdering children. By placing evil in its own category, we can more accurately understand it in relation to other kinds of wrongs. Yet, what we think of as perverse evil may only be a matter of degree, since evil invades all of our lives in one way or another. Under

---

27. Arendt, *Eichmann in Jerusalem*.

certain circumstances, we may all be capable of evil, and depending on how you define it, we are all guilty.

The words "lead us not into temptation but deliver us from evil" from the Lord's prayer may mean little to someone who is happy, contented, without pain, and devoid of need. Given adverse enough circumstances, however, those words might express a raging battle of conscience inside a person who is desperately unhappy, massively discontented, in excruciating pain, or so racked with hunger that obtaining even a morsel of bread would seem miraculous—if, for example, he or she were captive in a concentration camp and had to decide whether or not to steal that morsel from another famished inmate. Evil lurks just inside the gate of temptation, and some conditions in life may make it easy to open that gate.

We have been able to discuss only a small number of thinkers who have published their views on evil. There was insufficient space to discuss the ideas of the French novelists and philosophers Albert Camus (1913–60) or Jean-Paul Sartre (1905–80). Or, the Russian novelists Fyodor Dostoevsky (1821–81) or Lev Nikolayevich Tolstoy (1828–1910). Nor have we touched on the more contemporary work of John Rawls (1921–2002) and his idea of justice as fairness.

Whenever you read anyone's writings, consider pondering the question of what he or she makes of evil. The answer may reveal a great deal about that person's approach to life. It may also suggest where he or she stands in relation to Christianity, what that individual makes of evil, and how human beings might best respond to it. The existence of evil is likely to remain a significant problem in philosophy and theology as long as human beings inhabit the planet and retain the ability to think.

Closing Thoughts

Philosophers have become increasingly interested in evil. Its place in the history of ideas provides a window into the minds of thinkers who have addressed it. Included in the list of those we discussed are Augustine, Irenaeus, Machiavelli, Bayle, Voltaire, Leibniz, Rousseau, Hume, Kant, Hegel, Schopenhauer, Marx, Nietzsche, Sade, Freud, and Arendt. Fewer than half had ideas about evil that were compatible with Christianity. Those whose ideas we had insufficient space to discuss, but who published important views on the subject, include Camus, Dostoevsky, Sartre, Tolstoy, and more recently Rawls.

CHAPTER 17. HOW HAVE PHILOSOPHERS ADDRESSED EVIL?

Preview

In the next chapter, we will review some of the many ways Christianity contributed to the development of civilization. Many in the Western World are unaware of this, or give it little thought. The scaffolding of democracy rests on values and virtues that originated in, or were promoted by, Christianity.

Chapter 18. What Has Christianity Contributed to Civilization?

LIKE MANY PEOPLE, YOU may have wondered what Christianity contributed to civilization. Has its influence been constructive or corrosive? In a celebrated television series on the history of civilization,[1] Kenneth Clark argues that for any civilization to develop, there must be leisure, movement, and independence. There must also be intellectual energy, freedom of mind, a sense of beauty, and perhaps a craving for immortality. Clark notes that civilization "suddenly appeared" about five thousand years ago,[2] adding that it "could be convincingly argued that Western Civilization was basically the creation of the Church." This raises the question of the extent to which non-western parts of the world, such as China, also developed civilizations. In this chapter, we will focus our attention on the West, asking if Christianity fostered or hindered the conditions to which Clark refers?

It is fashionable in some quarters to argue that Christianity discouraged creativity, degraded culture, and prevented people from thinking for themselves. This may have been true at times, but as I will try to show, Christianity's overall impact has been to encourage innovation, enhance culture, and promote independence of thought. Over the past two thousand years, Christianity has exerted more positive influence on the development of Western Civilization than any other force in history.

---

1. Clark, *Civilisation*, 163.
2. *Civilisation*, Episode 2, "The Great Thaw."

CHAPTER 18. WHAT HAS CHRISTIANITY CONTRIBUTED TO CIVILIZATION?

A few years ago, I told a friend with a doctorate in philosophy that I had just read a short book on the history of ideas.[3] "I wouldn't read a book like that," he said, "because anyone who claimed to cover such a vast subject in a couple hundred pages would have to do so superficially, so it wouldn't be worth reading." I thought for weeks about what he said but eventually decided there might still be merit in a brief treatment of this complex subject if its focus were restricted to the relationship between Christianity and civilization.

Although it is often impossible to prove direct causal links between Christianity and specific cultural advances, many historians believe such links exist. In his classic work *Christianity and the Rise of Western Culture*, Christopher Dawson writes, "If . . . we study a culture as a whole, we shall find . . . an intimate relation between its religious faith and its social achievement."[4] This book is based on his Gifford Lectures delivered at the University of Edinburgh. Dawson studied at Oxford, taught for several years at Harvard, and believed religion to be the axis on which history turns. In *Lessons of History*, Will and Ariel Durant write, "even the skeptical historian develops a humble respect for religion . . . in every land and age." They cite Napoleon as having remarked that religion "has kept the poor from murdering the rich."[5] By religion, he meant Christianity.

How were a small number of people who had faith in God through Christ able to transform Western Society? This transformation ultimately freed humanity from its dependence on nature, in large part because it reinvigorated the desire to think clearly and deeply, a desire that had lost momentum when the Roman Empire eclipsed Greek culture. Apart from a few abstract thinkers like Emperor Marcus Aurelius (121–80), Romans were primarily builders and administrators. Although the Roman Empire had philosophers who continued in the Greek tradition, for example Epicureans, Platonists, Stoics, and Skeptics, once it absorbed the Greek city-states, interest in Greek philosophy declined in favor of the practical. The Romans admired the Greeks but failed to perpetuate their love of wisdom.

---

3. Ferry, *Brief History of Thought*.

4. Dawson, *Religion and Western Culture*, 14. See also Schmidt, *Christianity Changed the World*; Stark, *Victory of Reason*; Woods, *Catholic Church and Civilization*.

5. Durant and Durant. *Lessons of History*, 43.

PART III. PIVOTAL QUESTIONS

Two Modes of Thought: Concrete and Abstract

How did it happen that Western Society returned to abstract thinking? What caused this? To begin with, those in the West were not captive to unbending social tradition, as they often were in the East, where people tended to believe that no one could improve on established custom. This, however, does not fully explain the return to conceptual thinking, nor the ideals of personal and social freedom that emerged as a result.

Like Judaism out of which it grew, from the beginning Christianity embraced language. Words embody ideas, and without sufficiently nuanced words to capture and communicate ideas, thinking remains primitive. The link between ideas and the *written* word is especially important because writing allows the storage of ideas in a permanent form, which in turn facilitates the passing down of ideas from generation to generation and their ongoing refinement. Written language existed long before Christ. Its use by the Romans tended toward the concrete rather than the conceptual. Christianity picked up where Greek philosophers left off, only its ideas, unlike those of the Greeks, were rooted in theism.

The tendency in Western Civilization to value words, symbols, and the concepts they reflect has come to us largely through Christianity, and contrary to popular stereotypes openness to innovative thought-forms characterized it from the beginning. A quick tour through Paul's epistles will reveal his intellectual power. It took Christianity to reestablish the value of the conceptual coupled with the tangible. Civilization needs theory and practice to advance. The Greeks had the first and the Romans the second. Christianity had both. In modern terms, ideas without application remain on the whiteboard or in the laboratory, while technology without science stagnates.

Before the modern period, most people in the West could not read, but they understood language, and Christianity encouraged them to think in abstract terms. If a culture demands that you think along specific lines, thinking will remain constrained. All cultures promote some thought-forms and discourage others, but even in the so-called Dark Ages, Christian civilization was relatively less thought-restricting. The Italian scholar Petrarch (1304–74) seems to have coined the term *Dark Ages*. That term was used by those who assumed that, with the fall of the Roman Empire in the fifth century, little or no progress had been made in Europe until the Italian Renaissance in the fourteenth century. Later scholars defined the Dark Ages as ending in the tenth century. Because it is inaccurate and misleading, many contemporary historians avoid its use altogether. Lacking knowledge of the technological and social advances that ensued during these centuries, many people continue to think of the Early Middle Ages as benighted, and in that sense not only dark but culturally dead. It was neither.

The Western World was in ruins after the fall of the Roman Empire in the fifth century, and it was the church that rebuilt it. This was the result of the value it placed on ideas and innovation. There was no shortage of narrow-minded clergy who forced their ideas on others—there never has been—but clerical imperialism was limited. Authoritarian priests could compel people to say the right words, but they could not force them to stop thinking. People began to wonder and then ask *why* and *how*.

As noted above, Clark points out that civilization requires leisure. People who work twelve hours a day, wresting a living from reluctant or unforgiving soil, have little time or energy to plan, tinker, and invent. This was the case immediately after the fall of Rome, and it was also the case during several succeeding periods. Here are a few examples:

In 536, a volcanic eruption in Iceland produced massive quantities of smoke and fog, leaving much of Europe, China, and the Middle East in round-the-clock darkness for eighteen months. This launched the coldest decade in the past two-thousand years and led to catastrophic crop failures and starvation. Harvard historian and archaeologist Michael McCormick suggests that 536 was "the beginning of one of the worst periods to be alive, if not the worst year."[6] It was not 1349, he suggests, when bubonic plague killed off half of Europe, or 1918 when flu caused between 50 and 100 million people to die. In 540-541, there was a second volcanic eruption, and in 547 a third. These eruptions caused temperatures in Europe to drop by up to 10 degrees Fahrenheit, which caused further famine. If this was not bad enough, from 541 to 543 plague killed off up to half the population of the Mediterranean.

Despite these events and the ensuing economic stagnation that lasted a century, innovation eventually began again under the ethos and auspices of the church. The resumption of silver mining in 640 marked "the earliest stirrings of [a] new medieval economy."[7] By 660, there was a switch from gold to silver coinage, which further advanced this economy and enabled some to have the leisure to which Clark refers. This allowed

---

6. Gibbons, "Worst Year," 733–34.
7. Harper, quoted in Gibbons, 733.

abstract ideas to motivate concrete action. The church had always valued both. It placed a high value on words, such as could be found in the Bible and the creeds framed in the fourth and fifth centuries, but it also valued translating those words into charitable action.

Both Judaism and Christianity have been, and continue to be, religions of the book. Although the ability to read and write in the medieval world left much to be desired, this did not prevent people from thinking and talking. The fabric of Western Culture has always centered on texts, whether heard in church or, far more rarely, read by the hearth. Western Civilization's love of words mirrored its love of concepts, two loves that resulted in a disposition toward exploration and discovery.

Intellectual and Other Freedoms

Among the salient features of contemporary Western Civilization is open access to information and the free exchange of ideas. Both reflect a civilization nurtured in the arms of Christianity. Refusing to imprison itself in unbending tradition, Christianity exerted subtle but unrelenting pressure in favor of intellectual freedom. Although autocratic clergy sometimes tried to restrict it, such attempts bucked the long-term trend. Intellectual autonomy was necessary for sustained and creative cultural advance.

Cherishing Human Life

Prior to Christianity, society tended to neglect or abuse the infirmed. From texts in the New Testament, it is obvious that first-century Christians looked after each other. "In the third century, malaria epidemics helped drive people to a small, much persecuted faith that emphasized healing and care of the sick, propelling Christianity into a world-altering religion."[8] Its benevolence served as a model throughout Europe and the Middle East. Arabs, for example, having observed how Christians cared for the sick and dying, began in the eighth century to establish their own hospital-hospice facilities.[9]

One outcome of the ecumenical Council that Emperor Constantine convened at Nicaea in AD 325 was that cities with cathedrals were

---

8. Jarvis, "Buzz Off," 69.
9. Schmidt, *Christianity Changed the World*, 157.

CHAPTER 18. WHAT HAS CHRISTIANITY CONTRIBUTED TO CIVILIZATION?

required to care for the sick and shelter the poor.[10] The first hospital in Christendom seems to have opened during the late fourth century, in what is now central Turkey, and others soon followed in both Eastern and Western Christendom. The term *Christendom* has been used in a variety of ways. I use it in this book to mean the worldwide community of Christians, regardless of subgroup affiliation and whether they describe themselves as Eastern Orthodox, Protestant, Roman Catholic, or none of the three. Monasteries increasingly became centers, not just of spiritual formation but also for healing, and religious orders arose for the express purpose of providing health care. These orders, comprising knights, drifted increasingly toward military action, although they also continued to care for the sick and dying. One example was the Order of Knights of the Hospital of Saint John of Jerusalem. This change in society elevated the value of life, which endured in the West. In the service of political and economic struggle, people continued to die in war, but once Christianity took hold, only sociopathic leaders trivialized life. Our cultural heritage has imbued all but the worst of us with a deep sense of the individual's worth.

Some people firmly dedicated to humane causes mistakenly assume that their compassion has nothing to do with the legacy of Christianity infused into them by Western Culture. They may believe and sometimes say that we are past all that now, with *that* referring to religion in general and Christianity in particular. But, in some parts of the world, a human life is still worth less than the price of a bullet. Such differences across regions tend to be correlated with the presence or absence of Christianity. Totalitarianism may be the inevitable result of a society made up of people without an awareness of or relationship with God.

The Western Mind

The history of modern Europe can be, and often has been, interpreted as one long record of imperialism and exploitation. Both have always existed and therefore cannot explain why European civilization turned out as it did. Something else had to be going on, and it was the development of the western mind. It had been developing along two lines from the beginning of Christianity. These were technical innovation, on one hand, and exploration on the other. The former, as noted above, married

10. Schmidt, *Christianity Changed the World*, 155.

ideas to their applications, theory to practice, abstract conceptualization to concrete expression. The latter conceived of the earth as God's creation and the study of its workings as an expression of reverence.

Both were products of a long educational tradition intimately associated with Christianity, a tradition that encouraged the dual ideals of understanding and improving the world. It was a Franciscan friar, Roger Bacon (1214–94), who first successfully promoted the idea of combining scientific and philosophic knowledge, encouraging a synthesis that strongly propelled Western Civilization forward.

Development of Technology

European history, if you examine it closely, reflects a series of renaissances, some small but others large, and it was criticism and change that fostered them. These renewals mostly occurred independently of each other and spread spontaneously, but in one way or another they encouraged intellectual advances. Because medieval Western Society was expressly Christian, the early renaissances did not push people away from God. This was not true of later ones, some of which moved technology forward but encouraged either the neglect of God or a tacit denial of God's existence.

Most of us would probably agree that humanity is better off because of science and technology. In the Western World, for example, people live longer than they did a century ago. Life expectancy data are heavily skewed by the rate of infant mortality, which has decreased markedly. But even allowing for this, life expectancy has substantially increased. In 1900, a male in the United States who reached the age of sixty could be expected to live another twelve to fourteen years, to an age between seventy-two and seventy-four. A female who reached that age would probably live another fourteen to fifteen years, to between seventy-four and seventy-five. Today, a male age sixty is expected to live another twenty to twenty-two years, to between eighty and eighty-two, and a woman age sixty is expected to live another twenty-three to twenty-five years, to between eighty-three and eighty-five.[11] Two hundred years ago, few people had indoor running water or sanitary waste disposal.

Technology is not always beneficial. Nuclear energy generates electricity, but it also threatens the continued existence of civilization.

---

11. Infoplease, 2023.

CHAPTER 18. WHAT HAS CHRISTIANITY CONTRIBUTED TO CIVILIZATION?

Medical advances prolong life, but in some parts of the world people live longer only to undergo the slow agonizing death of dehydration or starvation. Given that civilization has not destroyed itself, technology so far has been mostly beneficial.

Sacred-Secular Tension

The advance of Western Civilization reflected a strain between the two cultures out of which it emerged. One was the warrior culture of the barbarians, with its focus on heroism and aggression. The other was the peaceful culture of the church, with its focus on charity and spirituality.

Western culture, from the start, embodied tensions between the sacred and the secular. Augustine had drawn a distinction in the fifth century between the City of God and the City of Man, and Christian thinkers took for granted the existence of a fundamental difference between the two. This recognition made political realism possible and paved the way for modern science. The tension between ecclesiastical and secular power ensured that a thoroughgoing theocracy never developed in Europe. It also encouraged criticism and change.

Monasticism

For over seven hundred years, from the decline of classical civilization to the emergence of European universities in the twelfth century, the influence of Christianity on society often came via monasteries. It may be difficult to shed the stereotype that throughout the Middle Ages clergy were uneducated and superstitious. This, however, was hardly the case. Many of them were among the most learned people around. An example of someone who does not fit this stereotype is Sylvester II (946–1003), the first French pope, who was among the most intelligent and urbane thinkers of his age. "It was only by the Church and, particularly, by the monks that the tradition of classical culture and the writings of classical authors . . . were preserved."[12]

This is the theme of Thomas Cahill's *How the Irish Saved Civilization*.[13] A new Christian culture arose, early on, out of the monasteries in the British Isles, and it gradually spread across Western Europe. Central to

12. Dawson, *Religion and Western Culture*, 45.
13. Cahill, *Irish Saved Civilization*.

this culture was the sanctification of work, so that even the peasant found his labors regarded as valuable. Although historians sometimes credit Luther with having introduced the idea of work as worship, that understanding had been developing for centuries in the monasteries.

Cities as such were nonexistent during the Dark Ages, and the center of European urban life remained the monastery. In addition to serving as centers of intellectual life, by the ninth century the monastery became the source of medieval culture and remained so for centuries. Taken together, monasteries provided society with "churches, workshops, storehouses, offices, schools, and almshouses, housing a whole population of dependent workers and servants."[14]

During the Carolingian Empire in the ninth century, people came to regard the king as having a sacred responsibility, including to the monasteries. He was the head of Christian society, and both he and those he ruled were bound by complementary duties. The king was the protector of the people, guardian of justice, and a *de facto* sacred-secular minister. The people were therefore duty-bound to serve the king. This amounted to a theocratic constitutionalism. Dawson notes the close connection between the contemporary understanding of a constitutional monarchy and the medieval tradition of kingship. People viewed both king and priest as ordained by God, and society viewed the divine right of kings through much of the Middle Ages as conditional and revocable.

Evangelism and Civilization

Among the achievements of Christianity was the civilizing of large barbarian populations. They were barbarian because of their warrior traditions and cultures, and their exemplars could be ruthless in their disregard for the lives or property of others. The medieval chronicler Adam of Bremen tells us that, in contrast to the former piracy of Scandinavian tribes, "after their acceptance of Christianity, they . . . learned to love peace and truth . . . even to distribute what they have stored up . . . Of all men they are the most temperate both in food and in their habits, loving above all thrift and modesty."[15] Adam of Bremen was a German ecclesiastical historian who lived in the eleventh century.[16] He

---

14. Dawson, *Religion and Western Culture* 63.
15. Dawson, *Religion and Western Culture*, 98.
16. *Chambers Biographical Dictionary*, "Adam of Bremen," 11.

CHAPTER 18. WHAT HAS CHRISTIANITY CONTRIBUTED TO CIVILIZATION?

was a canon at Bremen Cathedral at the time of the Norman Conquest of England in 1066, and he used as source material church archives and personal interviews. His work "is the most important source for the history, geography and politics of northern Europe between the 8th and 11th centuries." Regarding those in Iceland, he writes, "they have now all put on Christianity. There is much that is remarkable in their manners, above all Charity."[17] Even allowing for exaggeration, Christianity had a profoundly civilizing effect on the barbarity that characterized the age of the Vikings. After the decline of Anglo-Saxon culture and the Norman Conquest in 1066, Iceland spawned many of the scholars of the twelfth and thirteenth centuries, to whom we owe much for our knowledge of life at that time.

Byzantium was the center of a second realm of Christendom, and until the formal split between Eastern and Western Christianity in 1054, the two coexisted in an uneasy peace. Christianity had been struggling with barbarian tribes for centuries. In the twelfth and thirteenth centuries, nomadic hoards such as the Mongols began to disrupt Byzantine Christianity significantly, but until its overthrow in the fifteenth century, Eastern Orthodoxy, centered in Byzantium, exerted its own evangelistic and civilizing influence.

Corruption and Reform

By the tenth century, corruption had spread through much of the monastic system. In Odo's view, the church and its monasteries tolerated and at times condoned immorality, materialism, and oppression of the poor. Odo was a forerunner of the ecclesiastical reform that would begin in the next millennium. He showed keen awareness of how the potential for injustice and abuse is ever-present, and how no amount of social engineering would completely eradicate it. This insight, which had always been central to Christianity, has come down to us in the form of representative government with checks and balances.

During the tenth century, the Papacy suffered scandals and stood as much in need of reform as the monasteries. A century later, the demand for change no longer came from isolated groups of idealists but became official policy for the church, which had become a cross-national unifying force. Along with this came an increasing tendency to challenge the divine

---

17. Quoted by Dawson, *Religion and Western Culture*, 99.

right of kings and replace it with more representative forms of government. Temporal rulers generally supported and acknowledged the church's authority, which meant that if they erred grievously in the performance of their duties, the church called them to account.

Feudalism and Its Consequences

From the ruins of the Carolingian dynasty, rebellious nobles established independent and often warring feudal states. Western Civilization became increasingly militaristic and the only adhesive holding a fiefdom together was the bond of loyalty between warrior and chief. There were similarities between the new feudal states, as they existed for example in Normandy, and both the earlier Greek city-states and the later Italian Renaissance principalities.

Societal reform began in the eleventh century, and the crusades began just before the end of that century. Crusades of one kind or another in the name of Christ continued to the end of the 1600s. While they no doubt expressed the greed of some, especially later-born nobles who were subject to primogeniture, the crusades unified the West, which had long suffered from weakness, a sense of inferiority, and victimization by Muslims. Feudal society, which had evolved considerably, spread the French ideal of chivalry throughout Europe. Dawson points out, "the First Crusade was an achievement of the highest magnitude, which marked a turning point in the history of the West: ending the long centuries of weakness and isolation and cultural inferiority and bringing the new peoples of Western Christendom back to the old centres [sic] of Eastern Mediterranean culture." He adds, "The revival of religious, intellectual and artistic life was connected . . . with these feudal states," and while the noble was "the lineal descendent of the barbarian warrior," he was also a knight "who possessed a certain loyalty to the wider society of Christendom, and a certain fidelity to the Church."[18]

Despite its ethos of military values, the feudal system, as it began to exist in the year 1000, ironically gave rise to considerable gentility and opened the way for increased literacy. As feudalism developed, the knight became increasingly chivalrous. He pledged himself to show fidelity to his lord and to defend the church, the widow, and the orphan. Along with the priest and peasant, the knight became an indispensable

18. Dawson, *Religion and Western Culture*, 141, 143, 150.

CHAPTER 18. WHAT HAS CHRISTIANITY CONTRIBUTED TO CIVILIZATION?

agent of society, as he moved further away from his pagan and warlike roots and more toward the center of Christian culture. Although this shift may have had little impact on the conduct of a given warrior, it established a new code of morality for medieval society.

One distinctive feature of this enhanced morality was its emphasis on affection and courtesy. The new code increasingly concerned itself with refinement, and a complex system of manners developed that centered on chivalry and romantic love. It was "sophisticated and subtle even by modern standards, and . . . stood out in abrupt and startling contrast to the brutality and violence" that remained in segments of feudal society. There had been no precedent for it in the West. But another version of chivalry developed out of the first. It was distinctly more hedonistic, reflected the culture of much of the Southern Mediterranean, and left behind the more noble motifs of the crusades. This second form of chivalry amounted to a secular aristocratic culture that stressed erotic love, honor rooted in wounded pride, acquisitiveness, the wealth to which this led, and above all pleasure. Such a conception of chivalry has come down to us as consumerism and a preoccupation with youth and beauty.[19]

From the early 1200s, both altruistic and selfish understandings of chivalry existed side by side. They slowly blended together and promoted confusing ideals. The long-term result has been enduring tension in Western Culture between two sets of values and their associated prescriptions for action. To lessen this tension, society moved in the direction of redefining selfishness, first as inevitable and later as necessary and even desirable. Altruism, however, continues to be an ideal in Western Culture, and this is the direct result of Christianity. The origins of this ideal go back to the Old Testament and more explicitly to the teachings of Jesus.

Cities as Social Structures

Even more important than chivalry to the development of civilization was the reemergence of the city, which changed the economic fabric of Western Europe. During the Dark Ages, the West had become almost entirely agrarian. From the twelfth century on, however, life revolved around cities, as it had in the ancient world. There was a revival of civic spirit that worked against the crudeness and aggression of feudalism.

19. Dawson, *Religion and Western Culture*, 53, 155.

PART III. PIVOTAL QUESTIONS

The medieval city was based on voluntary economic associations and therefore tended to be a locus of peace, which made the emergence of the city a high point in the history of medieval Europe. Its citizens shared common interests, revolving around the efficient production of goods. The freedom to work and acquire property was increasingly based on industriousness, which made the city a model for Christian society. From the vantage points of politics and economics, the civic culture that began in the eleventh century laid the foundations for the modern world. Some cities, such as several in Renaissance Italy, would later become anything but oases of peace, plagued as they were by conflict and treachery. But the typical medieval city was a domain of security and prosperity, where people could live under the protection of the church. Without modern medicine, few lived beyond the age of fifty, and many suffered from debilitating pain and disease. As much as any place could be at the time, cities were havens of comfort.

With the rise of the new merchant class in the tenth and eleventh centuries came the founding of guilds. As merchants and trade associations became increasingly powerful, both started to play important roles in municipal government. And, as their power grew, they developed stronger desires to control those political, juridical, and military functions that had previously been the sole province of the bishop, count, or lord. Communes emerged, based on a compact among inhabitants to "keep the common peace, defend the common liberty, and obey the common officers."[20] These communities were by no means anticlerical, and in Italy, Northern France, and Germany they were closely associated with the church and its attempts at reform.

Powerful guilds developed in the thirteenth century, and they increasingly wrested control from the nobles, who in some regions became ostracized, prohibited from holding office, or as in Tuscany exiled. Resentment toward any person or class that claimed special privilege helped control magistrates. Increasing prosperity, growth of trade, and expanded personal freedom fostered an expansion of Christian culture. This began in France in the twelfth century, and over the next century and a half spread across Western Europe. The Cathedral of Notre Dame, tragically damaged by fire in 2019, is testimony to this culture. Spiritual-cultural trends facilitated social change, which in turn fostered economic development. For roughly two centuries, beginning in 1150, medieval Europe

---

20. Dawson, *Religion and Western Culture*, 164.

began to resemble one great society in which people had a defined place in the hierarchy, identified with a vocation, and felt important.

Work, conceived as service to God and neighbor, was no longer viewed as slavish drudgery but had a higher meaning. Unlike feudal society, which never escaped strife and discord, the medieval city, centered on its cathedral, was an orderly and self-contained unit enclosed within walls and towers. It was a "community of communities" in which people defined liberty not as the license to do what they wanted but the privilege to participate in the city's life and, for some, in its governance. In allowing such participation, it rivaled if not exceeded the Greek *polis*. Towns were increasingly able to send elected representatives to advise the king, an advisory structure that had its origins in the church.

Emergence of Universities

From the seventh to the twelfth century, what historians call the Benedictine Age, monasteries were the centers of learning. By the eleventh century, intellectual leadership was beginning to pass to cathedral schools. Finally, it moved to the universities, such as those established in Bologna,[21] Oxford,[22] and Paris.[23] An important intellectual shift was taking place in late medieval society, reflected in part by the transition from Augustinian to Thomistic theology. The traditional Christian view of life had included a clear division between the church and the world. What now emerged was an effort to integrate the two, which increased the tension between them. When the church pushed the integration too far in its direction, the threat of theocracy rose up, and when the state pushed it too far in its favor, the threat of it co-opting the church arose.[24]

Tenure in contemporary academic settings is intended to ensure the intellectual freedom of a professor, and unless he or she is grossly incompetent or acts egregiously, it amounts to guaranteed lifetime employment. Its roots reach back to the twelfth century, when its purpose was to protect medieval scholars from losing their jobs if they irritated a priest, took the wrong side in a dispute, or published an unpopular treatise.

---

21. Founded in 1088.
22. Founded in 1096.
23. Founded in 1150.
24. Dawson, *Religion and Western Culture*, 178–79.

PART III. PIVOTAL QUESTIONS

Having once held tenure on the faculty of a doctoral program, I recognize how controversial a practice it is, especially in light of changes to labor laws in the United States. Universities and colleges no longer have the right to compel a professor to retire at age sixty-five, which had been their right until 1978, when the mandatory retirement age increased to seventy. In 1986, compulsory retirement became illegal. This has had the unfortunate result of leaving in place tenured professors whose information is out of date, who do as little work as possible, and who prevent their tenure-track positions from being offered to younger professors.

It is important, however, not to miss how crucial tenure was in medieval European universities. The tenure system may have made the single most important contribution to establishing free speech and open inquiry in Western Society, and it developed as a byproduct of Christianity's commitment to freedom of thought. The rise of the university system represented the desire to embrace new learning, and tenure was a way to prevent the church from placing restrictions on that. It could no longer fire those whose views it found troublesome. Christians laid the foundations for modern science. Roger Bacon believed God to be the ultimate source of knowledge, and his intellectual heirs built the infrastructure for modern science. William of Ockham (1288–1347) also believed God to be the ultimate source of knowledge. He was an English Franciscan Friar and philosopher who is best known for "Ockham's Razor," the principle that, in choosing between or among competing explanatory hypotheses, one should favor the most parsimonious.

Universities encouraged healthy skepticism. Such skepticism encouraged medieval debates called *disputations*, which had been going on long before the controversy kicked off by Luther. For better or worse, the Reformation reflected a concern with autonomy that had been gaining momentum in the West for over three hundred years. To the extent disputations devolved into logic chopping, they were a poor use of time and energy. Scholastic logic chopping is a derogative phrase sometimes used to criticize medieval arguments about trivial or meaningless questions. Some have derisively suggested that such arguments were the equivalent of asking how many angels could dance on the head of a pin. This should not obscure the salutary effects even esoteric debates had on sharpening the mental acuity of scholars. Public debates encouraged rigorous reasoning and cognitive complexity, the capacity to perceive connections between and among ideas. The extent to which students at good universities today continue to learn to see such connections is a modern expression of the intellectual habits these disputations fostered.

Although the emergence of the universities might have promoted the development of an integrated Christian culture, by the fourteenth century there was considerable division, strife, and conflict between church and state. The East-West or Great Schism had been the formal separation in 1054 between Eastern (Orthodox) and Western (Roman) churches. A second schism, known as the Western or Papal Schism (1378–1417), began in the fourteenth century. It was the result of the removal of the papacy from Italy to France and the election of two rival popes, one in Avignon and the other in Rome. In 1409, a third pope was elected in Pisa. This was also the time of England's devastation of France and of the Muslim invasion of Europe. Through the ensuing centuries, fewer and fewer people in Europe would embrace Christianity. But the Christian faith, embedded within Western Culture by the church and its universities, established a set of ideals that remain central to many of its practices, formal documents, and the humane aspirations these documents express.

The Reformation

In the fourteenth and fifteenth centuries, society was still very much Christian, but pressure for a separation of church and state continued. However indirectly, this made Protestantism (pro-test-ism) more acceptable than it might otherwise have been. If the second half of the thirteenth century was the high point of medieval culture, it was also a time of developing crisis. For centuries, Western Europe had been edging toward a unified Christendom. It would now begin to move in the opposite direction. Reform had long been smoldering and was finally ignited by Martin Luther in Germany. It was further fueled by Huldrych Zwingli in Zurich and John Calvin in Geneva. The less radical English Reformation soon followed.

Efforts to reform the church had been going on for centuries, and several well-known figures died as a result. As one example, Jan Hus (ca.1369–1415) was burned at the stake for promoting the doctrines of John Wycliffe (ca. 1320–84), who died from a series of strokes. The church exhumed Wycliffe's corpse in 1428 and burned it along with his books. Wycliffe and Hus were forerunners of the Protestant

Reformation. The impulse toward reform finally reached a critical point in the early 1500s. Tradition has it that on October 31, 1517, Luther posted ninety-five theses or propositions on the door of the castle church in Wittenberg, seventy miles south of Berlin. As we have seen, he seems to have wanted to invite other scholars to a debate, which invitations had become common practice and ordinarily amounted to little more than challenges to intellectual fencing matches.

Luther's theses, however, contained scathing criticisms of the pope and the selling of indulgences. Representatives of the Roman Catholic Church at the time claimed an indulgence decreased time in purgatory, either for the purchaser or a relative. The term *purgatory* comes from Latin and means purging or cleansing. Thesis eighty-six asks why the pope did not rebuild St. Peter's with his own money, rather than using the money of the poor raised by what he regarded as fraudulent sales. Luther had visited Rome in 1510, where he witnessed ecclesiastical opulence and clerical corruption. He was never the same after that, and criticisms of the church began festering in him. By nature, Luther was intense and tended to go all-out in anything he did. Provocative as his theses were, he underestimated the powder keg he ignited or the backlash that would ensue, including his excommunication in 1521. The printing press, invented in the middle of the prior century, contributed substantially to the conflagration, since copies of Luther's theses began to appear throughout Europe. This made them impossible for Rome to ignore. Local German princes, who found it a financial strain to continue to support the church, were happy to unite in endorsing Luther's anti-papal views. This had economic implications for Rome.

Of political importance is how Luther responded to the imperial Diet of Worms, convened to examine him by the Holy Roman Emperor, Charles V. When his interrogator, Johann Eck, required Luther to retract his views, Luther asked for time to think through his response. Legend has it that when he returned, Luther replied, "Here I stand . . . I can do no other . . . God help me." Regardless of whether Luther uttered these words, it is clear that he publicly refused to subordinate himself or his views to the two greatest powers on earth: church and state. This was the first time a public figure insisted on complete freedom of speech, and promoting such freedom may have been the greatest contribution of the Reformation to Western Culture.

CHAPTER 18. WHAT HAS CHRISTIANITY CONTRIBUTED TO CIVILIZATION?

The Infusion of Christian Values into Western Culture

The forces behind the spread of any ideology, religious or secular, are complex and multifaceted. Such forces are the special concern of scholars who study intellectual history, the sociology of ideas, and political movements.[25] Whatever the fine-grained character of these forces, once an ideology reaches critical mass, it embeds itself in the cultural ambience. This is what happened early in the fourth century, when Constantine converted to Christianity and took the Roman Empire with him. In AD 312, Constantine reported having seen a cross in the sky on the eve of the Battle of Milvian Bridge, and he credited his ensuing victory to Christ. It has been suggested that, since many of his soldiers had already become Christians, Constantine's conversion was a political maneuver. Perhaps he anticipated the Machiavellian dictum to find out where the crowd is going and lead them there. Whatever Constantine's motives, a little over forty years after his death, the Eastern Emperor Theodosius and his Western counterpart Gratian declared in 380 that Christianity was the official state religion.

Western mores continue to reflect the values of Christianity. From the beginning, Christianity advocated charity toward one's neighbor and an ethical duty to look out for that neighbor even at personal cost. Some deride its self-sacrificial tenor. But such derision would likely evaporate if they found themselves in a dark alley facing muggers, and their only hope of rescue was by a Christian bystander who, instead of hurrying by, decided to help. The imperative to love others as we love ourselves has had a profound influence on our culture.

By showing mercy to those who might not deserve it, we have transcended eye-for-an-eye retributive justice. We also have a constitutional amendment outlawing cruel and unusual punishment. Originally written into English Bill of Rights in 1689, this prohibition became the eighth amendment in 1787. Regardless of how terrible a crime, committed by the most merciless psychopath, we tend as a society not to respond in kind, which reflects the institutionalization of Christian values. From the beginning, Christians have been in the business of extending love and forgiveness. Living according to "the more excellent way," Christians have often furthered the kingdom of God and tried to live out the phrase from the Lord's prayer, "Thy will be done on earth as it is in heaven."

---

25. See Collins, *Sociology of Philosophies*; Watson, *Ideas: Fire to Freud*.

PART III. PIVOTAL QUESTIONS

It took many centuries for the idea of individual freedom to emerge, but when it did, it was because Christianity promoted it. To the extent people try to impose their religious beliefs on others, they fail to grasp that God so values human freedom that God does not impose the divine will on people but instead grants them the right of self-determination. The early settlers in New England appear to have been in quest of a holy society, but their theocracies were misguided because they insufficiently valued the freedom to choose and missed how it is a mistake for any government to discourage people from exercising that freedom.

In an overview of what was going on in Europe in comparison with other cultures, Niall Ferguson argues that what amounted to domination by the West for 500 years was due to six cultural trends: competition fostered by relatively small political units; science and technology; increasing effectiveness of medicine; property and the rule of law; the work ethic; and consumption/consumerism.[26] But he also points out, "Europe's path to the Scientific Revolution and the Enlightenment . . . had its origins in the fundamental Christian tenet that Church and state should be separate," adding, "It was Christ's distinction between the temporal and the spiritual, adumbrated in the fifth century by St Augustine's *City of God* . . . that enabled successive European rulers to resist [ecclesiastical control]."[27]

People in the West also place a premium on human dignity, another product of its Christian heritage. An increasing number of people in America are moving away from, and out of, organized religion. This is nothing new in Europe, where it has been going on for a long time. Although people can distance themselves from churches, it is more difficult for them to shed the values that Christianity reflects and endorses.[28] Christ calls his followers to advance the kingdom of God on earth, but Christians also understand that violence will continue until God brings the curtain down on it. Theologians refer to the kingdom of God as *already and not yet*.

---

26. Ferguson, "Rasselas's Question"; Clark, *Civilization*, 1–18.
27. Ferguson, *Civilization*, 60.
28. See Lewis, *The Weight of Glory*, 1–15.

CHAPTER 18. WHAT HAS CHRISTIANITY CONTRIBUTED TO CIVILIZATION?

Closing Thoughts

Christianity combined the practical know-how of the Romans with the intellectual astuteness of the Greeks. Early on, Christians embraced the importance of the written word. Except for periods in the Middle Ages, access to information and the free flow of ideas were central to Christianity, which also promoted high regard for human life and dignity. Christianity fostered the development of the western mind, with its ever-expanding curiosity, and also encouraged the emergence of universities. These paved the way for science and technology. There were formidable tensions between church and state, which eventually led to their separation. Religious reforms repeatedly reinforced morality and integrity. Towns, revolving as they did around monasteries, evolved into cities with strong civic spirit resembling that of monasteries. The Protestant Reformation, together with the printing press, promoted literacy.

Preview

In the next chapter, we will consider the contributions of individual Christians to the modern world. As society moved through the Renaissance and into the modern period, Christians were central to the emergence and growth of civilization. We will review some of their contributions and note how Christianity often motivated them.

Chapter 19. How Have Christians Contributed to the Modern World?

As suggested in the last chapter, establishing causal links between Christianity and cultural advances will always remain in the domain of probability and never of certainty. This is the nature of inductive reasoning,[1] which is the only kind often available to the historian. It seems a considerable stretch, however, to deny the connection between the vast number of cultural advances and the Christian ethos out of which they emerged. Even those who view the Protestant Reformation as an unfortunate historical event often agree that it moved civilization forward. Among its influences was that it helped more firmly to establish modern freedoms, such as those captured in the First Amendment to the United States Constitution and the Bill of Rights.

The Enlightenment increased religious skepticism in Western Culture, but Christianity had left an indelible imprint on it. Through its many cultural bequests, Christianity continues to have an enormous impact on Western Civilization. Throughout much of the modern period, Christian faith inspired gifted and learned people to make contributions to civilization, either as acts of worship or with a keen awareness of God as creator. In this chapter, we will discuss the influence on civilization of individual Christians during and after the Reformation.

Over the past few centuries, society has moved in a secular direction, in part because of scientific and technological advances for which Christianity laid the foundation in the Middle Ages. Most people in the

1. Skyrms, *Choice and Chance*.

CHAPTER 19. HAVE CHRISTIANS CONTRIBUTED TO THE MODERN WORLD?

West continue to identify themselves as Christians, although many use the term simply as a synonym for gentile. This is both unfortunate and confusing because many gentiles are atheists and many ethnic Jews are Christians.

Regardless of what a person may say about what motivated him or her to contribute to society, it is impossible to know for sure how much to attribute to personal faith. This is doubly true for someone who died centuries ago. To argue, for example, that Leonardo da Vinci (1452–1519) was a Christian in anything more than a cultural sense is debatable. Schmidt suggests that Leonardo was a Christian. Who among us today can affirm or deny this? Certainly, he seems to have been a gracious man.[2] From historical records, it appears that he was good-hearted and generous. But so are many atheists. I will mention in this chapter only those whose faith in God through Christ appears significantly to have influenced what they contributed.

Science

Astronomy had been invented by the Greeks, but Johannes Kepler (1571–1630) revolutionized it. He also regarded science as "thinking God's thoughts after him." As noted in chapter 15, Isaac Newton (1643–1727), who based his work partly on Kepler's, spent considerable time reading the Bible and thought of himself as a Christian, although he recognized that he was not an orthodox one and may have been what today we would call a Unitarian. Gottfried Leibniz (1646–1716) who, parallel to Newton, invented calculus was a devout Lutheran. Blaise Pascal (1623–62) is famous, not only for the penetrating classic in Christian thought known as *Pensées*, his also for his pioneering work on conic sections, hydraulics, and probability. Michael Faraday (1791–1867), who discovered electromagnetic induction and invented the generator, was a passionate Christian who read the Bible every day. Lord William Kelvin (1824–1907), who gave us the concept of absolute zero, insisted that Christianity and science were fully compatible and believed deep thinking in science inevitably led to belief in God.

The science of genetics began with Gregor Mendel (1822–84), a monk from the same Augustinian religious order as Luther. Still alive and contributing today is the eminent Francis Collins (b. 1950), who oversaw

---

2. Schmidt, *Christianity Changed the World*, 223.

the successful mapping of the human genome and became Director of the National Institutes of Health in 2009. He is an outspoken Christian.

Robert Boyle (1627–91) is best known for his gas law, that the pressure of a gas is inversely proportional to its volume. He helped found the Royal Society, wrote theological essays, and provided money for Bible translations. Antoine Lavoisier (1743–94) demonstrated the conservation of energy, performed quantitative experiments in chemistry, and helped develop a system for classifying chemicals; guillotined during the French Revolution, he appears to have died confessing his Christian faith. Alessandro Volta (1745–1827), who invented the electric battery, wrote in one of his letters that, like Paul, he was "not ashamed of the gospel" (Rom 1:16). George Washington Carver (1864–1943), who became the most celebrated agricultural scientist of his day, remained a devout Christian until he died. These are just a few examples of people who have made monumental contributions to science while also professing their Christian faith. Wikipedia contains an extensive "List of Christians in Science and Technology."[3]

Medicine and Health Care

Care of the sick and dying has always been central to Christianity. A complete list of health care professionals who in the past have been committed Christians would fill a book, so I will mention only a few. Ambroise Paré (1510–90) made pioneering contributions to surgery, pathology, and the treatment of wounds sustained in battle. He is known to have said, after he tended the wounded, "God healed them."

Louis Pasteur (1822–95), a chemist and biologist who pointed to microbes as the origin of infectious diseases, introduced inoculation into medicine and developed what we know as pasteurization. "Posterity," he stated, "will one day laugh at the foolishness of modern materialistic philosophers. The more I study nature, the more I stand amazed at the work of the creator. I pray while I [work] in the laboratory."[4] There was also Joseph Lister (1827–1912), who building on Pasteur's work, vigorously promoted the use of antiseptics, sterilization of surgical instruments, and the practice of hospital staff washing their hands. He was serious enough

---

3. Wikipedia, "Christians in Science and Theology." https://en.wikipedia.org/wiki/List_of_Christians_in_science_and_technology.

4. *Literary Digest*, "Louis Pasteur." n.p.

about God to have suffered bouts of religious melancholy. It may be of interest that about ten years ago, a nationally prominent physician told me that the mortality rates of two comparable wings in a hospital with which he was familiar differed substantially, in his opinion because of how often their respective staffs washed their hands.

In the mid-1800s, many physicians contributed to the discovery of anesthetics like nitrous oxide and ether, among them the eminent and devout Scottish doctor James Young Simpson (1811–70) who demonstrated the properties of chloroform. The United States Civil War was the bloodiest in American history. Imagine what it would have been like without morphine, which by that time was available to soldiers. An unfortunate byproduct of this in many veterans was *soldier's disease*, morphine addiction, but the use of anesthetics was nevertheless a major breakthrough in medicine. Florence Nightingale (1820–1910) was the English Christian who established modern nursing, and her Swiss contemporary Jean-Henri Dunant (1828–1910) co-founded the Red Cross.

Education

The Christian focus on texts goes back to Paul's letters, some of which circulated among the early churches. New Testament scholars believe he penned his earliest epistles in the 50s. By the second century, the church had established schools to provide religious instruction, regardless of social class, for both men and women. The matriculation of women deteriorated in the Middle Ages, when men began to outnumber them in schools. There were some successful efforts to recruit female students, but even among men, the literacy rate remained low. The Reformation changed that.

When Luther toured churches in Saxony in the late 1520s, the level of ignorance appalled him, and in response he produced a small manual to provide basic instruction in Christianity. Luther endorsed the idea of educating both sexes, argued for state supported schools, and advocated compulsory school attendance. John Calvin, the leader of the Reformation in Switzerland, also believed in the education of both sexes. Luther's greatest contribution to Western literacy was his insistence that the Bible be available in the language of the people, and to that end, just one year after his excommunication at the Diet of Worms, he translated the New Testament into everyday or what is called vernacular German.

A byproduct of his work was standardization of the German language, which before Luther varied from region to region. Translation of the Bible into contemporary languages was a key motif of reform movements throughout Western Europe.

Although as early as the seventeenth century there were sporadic instances of education taking place on Sunday, Robert Raikes (1735–1811), a Scottish printer and devout Christian, launched the Sunday School movement in the 1780s. Raikes primary interest seems to have been prison reform, and he believed in discouraging future crime by educating the young. Because children typically worked long hours on the other six days of the week, he used Sundays for this purpose. Raikes used the Bible as the primary textbook for teaching students to read. Sunday schools greatly advanced literacy, especially among the poor.

In 1817, Thomas Gallaudet (1787–1851), a Congregational minister, opened the first school for the deaf in America. Twenty years later, Friedrich Fröbel (1782–1852), a committed Christian, gave the world its first kindergarten in Germany. And, in the 1820s, the dedicated Christian Louis Braille produced an alphabet for the blind consisting of embossed dots.

We have already seen how monasteries were forerunners of universities, which became centers of research. For the first few centuries, this research focused on theological study. But by the fourteenth century, empirical research was underway, for example at the University of Bologna in Italy, where professors were dissecting cadavers. The modern research university might never have come into existence had it not been for its medieval predecessors. Our most revered educational institutions, such as Cambridge, Oxford, and the University of Paris on the Continent, and Harvard, Princeton, and Yale in the United States, were all founded either to educate clergy or in close association with them.

Architecture

The Christian Emperor Justinian (ca. 482–565) built the Hagia Sophia ("Holy Wisdom") in the 530s as a cathedral, in what is now Istanbul. It was the world's largest building at the time, and its massive dome remains an engineering marvel. The Hagia Sophia, along with Gothic cathedrals in Europe, such as those in Chartres (1220), Durham (1093–1133), Exeter (1400), and Paris (Notre Dame, 1345), are spectacular

CHAPTER 19. HAVE CHRISTIANS CONTRIBUTED TO THE MODERN WORLD?

tributes to the grandeur of Christian architecture. So is the Doge's Palace in Venice (1340) and St. Peter's in Rome (1626).

As additional examples of architectural achievement, there is the early Renaissance Cappella Pazzi (1442) and Duomo (1436), both in Florence and designed by Fillipo Brunelleschi. In Cambridge, there is King's College Chapel (1446),[5] in Venice the Biblioteca Marciana (1588), and in Rome the Church of the Gesù (1580). From the seventeenth century, there is Sant'Agnese (1653) in Rome's Piazza Navona, and from the eighteenth century, Melk Abbey in Austria overlooking the Danube (1736).[6] St. Paul's Cathedral (1711) in London was built at roughly the same time as Melk Abbey. All of these are examples of magnificent structures designed and built in the service of Christianity.

Once again, it is impossible to establish irrefutable causal links between personal faith and architectural advances, but the case for such a link seems strong. One art historian points out that, as recently as 1976, the design for a New York skyscraper was "faintly reminiscent of Leone Battista Alberti's [church] façade of about 1460."[7] He is referring to Alberti's façade for his Renaissance Basilica of Sant' Andrea in Mantua. The grandeur of the United States Capitol building in Washington suggests the rich architectural heritage that has come down to us from Christian churches, and so do the British Houses of Parliament in London's Palace of Westminster. Because of their destruction by fire, the Houses of Parliament were demolished in 1834 and rebuilt between 1840 and 1876.

Other religions have also produced great architecture. Islam, for example, inspired hybrid styles that often integrated those already existing in lands to which it spread. The opulent Taj Mahal in India reflects an Indo-Islamic style, while the Alhambra in Spain mirrors a Hispano-Islamic one. It would be provincial to claim to have an objective reason to proclaim Western architecture as superior. My purpose here is only to suggest that architecture in Western Culture owes a considerable debt to Christianity.

---

5. See Gombrich, *Story of Art*, 203.
6. Wikipedia, "Melk Abbey." https://en.wikipedia.org/wiki/Melk_Abbey.
7. Gombrich, *Story of Art*, 492–93.

PART III. PIVOTAL QUESTIONS

From Medieval to Modern Painting

"The Great Roman Empire was in decline by the early 2nd century AD, and by the 3rd century its political life had degenerated into chaos."[8] The Empire in the West was approaching collapse at the hands of nomadic tribes from northern Europe, who finally finished it off in the fifth century. We can debate whether they deserve the pejorative term *barbarian*, but when they vanquished the Romans, they had not yet embraced Christianity. They were ruthless in mentality and behavior. Art within Latin Christendom, therefore, came to a temporary halt.

This, however, was not the case in Byzantium. In the decades preceding the collapse of Rome, art in the Eastern Empire began its first golden age. Then in 726, Emperor Leo III publicly opposed, and in 730 officially outlawed, human images in painting. The Emperor's decree was the result of the iconoclastic controversy, with the iconoclasts (image breakers) arguing that any realistic representation of Jesus, his mother Mary, saints, or angels violated the commandment not to worship "graven images." The final revocation of Leo's decree in 843 launched a second golden age of Byzantine painting. "The importance of Byzantine art is seen in its profound influence on Gothic art . . . the first part of a tradition that was to remain predominantly Christian, and was to run right through the Middle Ages."[9]

Over time in the West, many more invaders from northern Europe became Christians, and when they did, they introduced into it a highly decorative form of art. This made its way into the monasteries, which produced hand-copied manuscripts, meticulously adorned with Christian signs and symbols. The most celebrated illuminated manuscript is the *Book of Kells* created around AD 800 and housed in Trinity College, Dublin. In addition to smaller works, it contains the four Gospels and gets its name from the Abbey of Kells, which housed it for centuries. It is among Ireland's greatest national treasures. The significance of such manuscripts is not only their high art but also the attention they drew, through the centuries, to words and therefore to ideas. Christians, as noted above, have always been people of the book.

Beginning late in the thirteenth century, artists began to paint scenes of events in the Bible, or those the Bible suggested or implied. The Dutch artist Hieronymus Bosch (ca. 1450–1516) is an example of a painter who

8. Beckett, *Story of Painting*, 34.
9. Beckett, *Story of Painting*, 3.

CHAPTER 19. HAVE CHRISTIANS CONTRIBUTED TO THE MODERN WORLD?

depicted scenes he believed the Bible to suggest or imply. His paintings contain hideously elaborate depictions of people suffering in hell. "The Garden of Earthly Delights" is his most celebrated work. Artists began more accurately to portray three-dimensional space. Their work shows the residual influence of Byzantine art and also reveals a move toward realism. By the beginning of the fifteenth century, this move had progressed to the point that paintings began to resemble photographs. Artists engaged in close study and appreciation of the world as it was.

This trend away from the stylized toward the actual, which took many centuries to mature, reflected the longstanding motif within Christianity of embracing reality rather than fantasy. You can see this in the expressions on faces. By the time of the Renaissance, realism had won the day, and it would not be until the late 1800s that art would begin to move away from realistic representation. Terms for art can be confusing because they tend to be general characterizations rather than precise definitions. Imitative or realistic representational art is sometime called figurative art.

One can argue that the development of art in the Renaissance reflected secular more than sacred concerns. But the move toward realism mirrored the deeply ingrained disposition in the western mind toward discovery and exploration. Muslims outdistanced medieval Christians in some areas of mathematics and science, as exemplified by their invention of algebra, work in astronomy, and relatively advanced approaches in certain domains of medicine. I cannot do justice in this book to the many contributions of the Muslim world to civilization, but during the Middle Ages they were considerable.

It took until the nineteenth century for Impressionism to emerge, reflected in the works of Édouard Manet (1832–83), Edgar Degas (1834–1917), Claude Monet (1840–1926), and Pierre-Auguste Renoir (1841–1919). It bridges the gap between Romantic-era painters, such as William Turner (1775–1851), John Constable (1776–1837), Eugène Delacroix (1798–1863), and the Post-Impressionists. These include Paul Cézanne (1839–1906), Georges-Pierre Seurat (1859–91), Vincent van Gogh (1853–90), Henri de Toulouse-Lautrec (1864–1901), Paul Gauguin (1848–1903), Pablo Picasso (1881–1973), Henri Matisse (1869–1954), Salvador Dali (1904–89), and Jackson Pollack (1912–56). They are often identified by the schools they represent, such as Fauvism, Expressionism, Cubism, and Abstract Expressionism. School, as used here, refers to a group of artists whose style reflects a common origin or artistic conviction. The Impressionists, and many artists after them, turned their attention to what they experienced as they looked at the world.

This inward turn was not new to Christianity, as evidenced by Augustine's *Confessions*. The shift toward the subjective is desirable if it occurs in someone who understands that he or she is subject to a creator. It is less desirable when it suggests that the person has turned himself or herself into a substitute god. There is no space here to explore the roots of other movements in art, but this may be enough to dispel the idea that our civilization and its art spontaneously arose with no enduring debt to Christianity.

Music

As with architecture, there may be no reason to conclude that Western music is superior to that of another culture, but we should at least note the rich history of classical music. Just about all Western music, from ballads to heavy metal, relies on the same musical scale and harmonic structures that come from late medieval music. This scale is known as twelve-tone diatonic, which divides an octave into twelve parts. An octave is the interval between a given pitch (cycles per second) and one that doubles or halves it. A piano, reflecting the diatonic scale, has twelve keys between Middle C and the C immediately above it. Music from other cultures is often based on a different scale, which divides an octave into larger or smaller intervals.

For almost the first thousand years of Christian history, music was monophonic, a single melodic line without harmony. Gregorian chants are well-known examples. In the tenth century, polyphony emerged, which is two or more simultaneous lines of independent but (usually) related melodies. Harmony has to do with how these lines relate to each other. Polyphony enabled the development of such musical forms as sonatas, symphonies, and concertos.

I have already mentioned several of the West's most celebrated composers. These include Bach, Beethoven, Brahms, Chopin, Debussy, Handel, Haydn, Liszt, Mendelssohn, Mozart, and Schubert. If we include Russia, there was also Rachmaninoff, Stravinsky, and Tchaikovsky. Some of these composers may have had little or no interest in religion, while others were devout. Regardless of their religious convictions, all profited from what Christianity bequeathed to them by way of monastic music and the contributions of earlier composers who wrote music to glorify God and support the work of the church.

Literature

Christianity has always been a religion of the word. A culture can embody great ideas and insights that it never expresses in words, but it cannot express great ideas and insights in words without first having developed the ideas they embody. This is similar to how you can be a good thinker without being a good writer, but you cannot be a good writer without also being a good thinker. Both the Old and New Testaments contain an abundance of insights, and if you reflect on them carefully, you may find yourself wondering where these insights came from.

Two pre-Renaissance works that significantly influenced the development of Western literature are *The Divine Comedy* by Dante Alighieri (ca. 1265–1321) and *Canterbury Tales* by Geoffrey Chaucer (1343–1400). The Reformation in the sixteenth century triggered an explosion in literature, aided by the printing press. As noted above, this explosion, which greatly facilitated the growth of literacy, was in part triggered by Luther's translation of the Bible into German. Luther published his translation of the New Testament in 1522 and of the complete Bible twelve years later, in 1534. His New Testament was based on the Greek New Testament produced by Desiderius Erasmus (1466–1536). At about the same time, William Tyndale (1494–1536) completed his partial translation of the Bible into English. Less than a century later, in 1611, the King James Bible appeared, and it had a profound effect on English literature for centuries. Some argue it still does.

It would be foolish to try to summarize the vast influence Christianity had on the development of literature. There is no doubt, however, that the centrality of the Bible in Western Culture influenced many of its greatest works of literature.

Human Life and Dignity

We noted in the last chapter how Christians set an example of care and compassion for the infirmed, but Christianity had an even greater impact on morality. It had been common practice in many cultures, including throughout the Roman Empire, to abandon children if they posed a liability. Christianity opposed and ultimately brought this to an end, as it also did with infanticide. Pagan societies had often condoned both practices. Another contribution of Christianity to the ancient world was stopping the gladiatorial games. Christian emperors in both Eastern and Western Empires finally put an end to them in the fourth or fifth century.

In modern times, few would deny that Christians played key roles in the abolition of slavery. William Wilberforce successfully led the effort in Great Britain to end the slave trade, and Christians in the United States comprised the backbone of the Underground Railroad that smuggled escaped slaves into the North.

The Rule of Law

Under the influence of Christianity, Western Culture moved significantly in the direction of embracing the principle that everyone, king and commoner, is subject to the same laws. Although legal equality does not always work out in practice, it is far more the case in Western Society than anywhere else.

John Locke (1632–1704), who regardless of differing views on the matter, insisted he was a Christian, significantly shaped the thought-forms that flow through England's Bill of Rights (1689) and later the U.S. Constitution and the American Bill of Rights. Although some of America's founding fathers, such as Jefferson (1732–1826), were not Christians in any recognizable sense, many were. Jefferson is known to have taken a Bible and excised from it whatever he found objectionable. Even those who want nothing to do with Christianity have grown up and lived in a culture heavily influenced by it.

There are many other domains in which Christianity appears to have positively influenced society, including its support of private property. When we ask whether Christianity has been more constructive than destructive, I believe the answer is clear. Much of what is admirable in our culture can be traced to it.

Closing Thoughts

Astronomy and mathematics were substantially advanced by Christians, some of them impressively devout. Kepler codified the laws of planetary motion, and Newton his three laws and the nature of gravity.

CHAPTER 19. HAVE CHRISTIANS CONTRIBUTED TO THE MODERN WORLD?

Both Newton and Leibniz developed the calculus. Pascal worked on hydraulics, conic sections, and probability, Faraday on electromagnetic induction, and Kelvin on absolute zero. Mendel established the science of genetics. Boyle is known for his gas law, Lavoisier for chemistry, and Volta for electricity. Carver greatly enhanced agriculture. Paré contributed to surgery, Pasteur to inoculation and pasteurization, Lister to antiseptics and sterilization, Simpson to anesthetics, Nightingale to nursing, and Dunant to the founding of the Red Cross. Luther promoted compulsory schooling, Raikes Sunday schools for the poor, Gallaudet a school for the hearing impaired, Froebel the first kindergarten, and Braille an alphabet for the blind. Christian architects were central to the design of countless churches, monasteries, and cathedrals, many of them stunningly beautiful, such as Notre Dame in Paris and St. Paul's in London. Christians contributed innumerable works of art well into the modern period. Music might never have evolved into what it is today, whether in concert halls or on rock stages, without the many centuries that Christians wrote sacred music and worked out principles of harmony. The same can be said for Christians and their influence on literature. Of primary importance to the development of civilization, Christians contributed to the high regard Western Society has for human life and dignity as well as the rule of law.

Preview

People sometimes say that violence carried out in the name of Christ prevents them from becoming Christians. In the next chapter, we will explore how well this objection holds up.

Chapter 20. What of Violence in the Name of Christ?

NO ONE CAN CREDIBLY deny that considerable brutality has been done under the banner of Christianity, which raises the question of why people who call themselves Christians could do such things. The crusades lasted from the late 1000s to the late 1200s and resulted in enormous loss of life. Inquisitions began as early as the twelfth century, expanded considerably in the 1400s, reached their peak in the 1500s, and continued in diminished forms for centuries thereafter. Beginning in the 1500s, there were the Conquistadors and what they did in Central and South America, and as late as the 1690s New Englanders burning women at the stake for witchcraft. There was also slavery perpetrated by self-identified Christians, both in the Caribbean and the American South, and support of the Nazis by clergy in Germany. We could include the "troubles" in Northern Ireland between Catholics and Protestants, but these were more nationalist conflicts than religious ones.

In addition to drawing attention to some of the psychological processes that often lead to religious violence, there are at least three reasons for addressing it in this chapter. First, I want to demonstrate that a Christian is willing to recognize the evil done over the past two-thousand years in the name of Jesus. Second, I want to view and interpret this evil within broader historical trends. And, third, I want to place it within what I believe to be an appropriate theological context.

Zealots of many faiths, including Christianity, have often believed their appointed mission to be defending God against doctrinal

CHAPTER 20. WHAT OF VIOLENCE IN THE NAME OF CHRIST?

corruption, and at times they have annihilated those whose beliefs differed from theirs. Fanatical religionists have been determined to persuade others of the love of God, even if they had to kill them. They have beheaded heretics, suspended some in cages for rats to consume, and stretched still others on the rack until maimed, dismembered, or dead. It is a macabre bit of historical irony that if a person was sentenced to die at the stake but merited favorable treatment, the executioner might first use a garrote. Otherwise, it might take days for charred, blistered, and infected flesh to finish the job. William Tyndale, whose translation of the Bible into English earned him the death penalty, was granted this magnanimous courtesy by Henry VIII. Tyndale (1492–1536) was the first person to translate most of the Bible into English. He translated directly from Hebrew and Greek.

Anatomy of Religious Violence

It would take more space than we have to explore in detail the psychodynamics of how and why violence occurs in the name religion, but I would like to suggest some of the psychodynamic processes that can fuel this. Because of the need to protect their social standing, some people have difficulty acknowledging undesirable motives in themselves, so they clothe them in trappings of righteousness. Textbooks on psychopathology sometimes use the example of the lecherous clergyman who, unable to acknowledge his lechery, campaigns against pornography. This allows him to indulge in the forbidden content while enhancing his status in the community. Rage at one's father, mother, spouse, or sibling may turn into rage against heretics onto whom such rage is displaced. A misanthropic disposition can become zeal for compelling conversions at the point of a sword. A colleague of mine, Dr. Patrick Sullivan, demonstrated in his doctoral dissertation the close association between racism and misanthropy. Although his work does not prove a causal connection, it certainly suggests one. If sex and aggression have fused together, sadistic impulses clothed in religious garb may inspire truly horrific acts. Finally, some people channel their mental disturbances into religious causes. Regardless of the specific religion, psychopathology is an equal opportunity motivator.

The need to participate in a cause greater than oneself can also be a powerful incentive for violence in the name of religion. Distorted ideas about God appeal to those in search of whoever or whatever offers to give their lives significance. The arrogant thesis that one's beliefs, whatever they are, are complete and infallible has, throughout history, promoted many fundamentalisms that turned violent. People drawn to charismatic leaders are often unsophisticated and may not realize with what or whom they are involving themselves. All they know is that the cause, whatever it is, feels pure and noble and provides them with a sense of purpose. Under deranged religious leaders, followers have done all sorts of unconscionable things, which in their more rational moments they would never have done. These can range from allowing spouses to engage in sexual relations with the leader to poisoning their own children. Perhaps the most poignant recent example is what happened to those who followed Jim Jones to Guyana, Africa. In November of 1978, after killing a congressman and four others who had come to visit their camp, members of Jonestown, as it was called, administered cyanide to over 300 children and themselves. All told, over 900 people died. Sociopaths are skilled at using religion to further violent purposes. They have little empathy and inflict pain without remorse. Psychopathic religious leaders may drive expensive cars and shop at opulent stores without a twinge of conscience over misappropriating donated funds. Recall Elmer Gantry in Sinclair Lewis' 1926 novel of that name. Like Gantry, sociopaths may embrace religion because it allows them to prey on the gullible. And, if they do in some sense believe what they say, they so compartmentalize these beliefs that they exert little or no influence on how they act. History has also had its share of paranoid religious leaders who have been adept at teaching followers to see other groups, from Jews to Romani ("gypsies"), as personifications of evil. In the Preface to a series of essays on religion and race, a former colleague of mine at the seminary where I taught writes, "Racism is at bottom a religious phenomenon." Within the precincts of Christianity are religionists who rationalize away their hateful conduct by clinging to the belief that since they are Christians, God will forgive whatever they do. God, they believe, does not much care, since they are "saved." They abuse their "freedom in Christ" to do what is the antithesis of what Jesus taught. It appears they have forgotten Paul's question, should we sin more to enable God's grace to show itself more (Rom 6:1)?

    I have provided this overview of the psychodynamics of religious violence to suggest that no religion, including Christianity, is immune to abuse by the warped, deranged, conscience-deprived, or ethically

CHAPTER 20. WHAT OF VIOLENCE IN THE NAME OF CHRIST?

challenged. Christian language can be impressed into the service of any cause, however inhumane, because it is flesh-and-blood, imperfect, and occasionally diabolical individuals who use it for unworthy purposes. No pursuit of an immoral cause is consistent with Christianity. Nor can it be by nature Christian. The idea of Christian evil is a *non sequitur*.

What Christianity Does and Does Not Do

Nothing in Christianity promises to make a person's psyche instantly healthy or perfect his or her character. It is reasonable to expect Christianity to make a constructive difference, but not that it will make saints of devils who have little or no interest in sainthood. A mind transformed by Christ reflects a transformed heart, which when faith is genuine results in a renewed life. There is little doubt that a given Christian may remain irritable when tired or say uncharitable things when provoked. But if the Spirit of God lives in that person, which is what it means to be a Christian, such behavior is likely to occur less often than it otherwise would. John Newton, who had been captain of a slave ship, experienced such a rebirth and was dramatically changed because of it. In collaboration with William Wilberforce, who had also undergone the sort of Christian transformation I am writing about in this book, Newton helped end the slave trade in Great Britain and wrote the hymn, "Amazing Grace."

Even after what the late Catholic philosopher and theologian Dietrich von Hildebrand calls *transformation in Christ*,[1] a Christian always remains a delivered, redeemed, and rescued sinner. The Holy Spirit may reside within, but there will always be the struggle and conflict to which Paul alludes: "For I do not do the good I want, but the evil I do not want is what I do" (Rom 7:19, NRSV). Complete restoration to health and holiness comes only at the end, when God claims all who are Christ's for their final destiny.

It is important to avoid dividing humanity into two classes, good and bad, sacred and profane, us and them. There is nothing that makes Christians ontologically different, nothing that changes their essential nature as human beings. How we think, feel, and act is the complex result of genetic endowment, developmental history, and prior choice. It has to do with where we start, what happens to us, and what we choose to do along the way. We will always remain a mystery even to ourselves, a

---

1. Hildebrand, *Transformation in Christ*.

puzzling mixture influenced in unseen ways by what we have and have not allowed God to do with us.

Before I review some of the violence done by self-proclaimed Christians, I want to suggest that whatever harm people have done in the name of Christ is, on sum, far less than what others have done in the absence of that name. Even a cursory glance at the Addendum to chapter 16 may convince you of this.

The Great Schism and Its Aftermath

About fifty years before the first crusade, the inevitable happened in 1054. Five centuries before the Reformation, the Eastern (Byzantine) and Western (Roman) branches of Christendom officially separated. Prior to this, nearly every Christian was part of the Holy Catholic Church. But Latin and Greek Christians had been moving toward separation for centuries. Theological differences and tensions around governance formalized it. Controversy over how much authority the Bishop of Rome (Pope) was to enjoy over other bishops triggered the split. But there were also other reasons.

Arguments had existed for centuries over which church councils were ecumenical and therefore authoritative (fewer in the East) and the relationship between the Son and the Holy Spirit, as expressed in two different versions of the Nicene-Constantinopolitan Creed. There had been longstanding disagreement over a single Latin word (*filioque*), which Eastern Orthodoxy denied ever having approved or authorized. According to the Western arm of the church, the Holy Spirit proceeded from the Father and the Son (*double procession*), whereas the Eastern arm insisted that the Spirit proceeds only from the Father (*single procession*). This difference continues to this day. Eastern and Western Christianity now peacefully coexist, but this has not always been the case, and there were times when the relationship turned violent. Illustrative of how the Eastern and Western arms did not always coexist peacefully, in 1204 participants in the Fourth Crusade sacked Constantinople, looting several key Orthodox sites and turning them into centers of Latin Catholic worship. The crusaders carried off to the West various holy artifacts, and established a number of vassal crusader states in the eastern region. And, there were attempts by knights in northern Europe to capture states that were decidedly Russian Orthodox. Some historians believe that the fracture of the

CHAPTER 20. WHAT OF VIOLENCE IN THE NAME OF CHRIST?

Byzantine Empire contributed to its eventual conquest by Islam, which was decisively accomplished with the fall of Constantinople to the Turks in 1453. Much like what was going on in Northern Ireland, Christians killed other Christians. They also killed people for leading or participating in what church officials regarded as heretical sects.

The Crusades

The crusades began as what those in the West considered a *just war*, a concept introduced into Christianity by Augustine in the fifth century. There is little doubt that many who participated in the crusades were sincerely motivated. For almost two hundred years, beginning near the end of the eleventh century and ending near the end of the thirteenth, Western nobles led armies to the Middle East, sometimes with the avowed purposes of recovering relics, recapturing the Holy Land centered on Jerusalem, converting Muslims to Christianity, and retaliation. The customary dates of the crusades are from 1095 to 1291. Converting Muslims through aggression was never a principal purpose of the crusades because Christians tended to believe that forced conversions were suspect. Muslims had already been waging *jihad* (holy war) against Christians.[2]

For some in the upper tiers of society, a major motive for leading or joining a crusade related to *primogeniture*, the principle that the eldest son inherits most or all of his father's estate. Some later-born sons reasoned that an expedition into Islamic territory offered the hope of a workaround, a way to circumvent this by confiscating Islamic wealth. If this required the shedding of innocent blood, so be it. It mattered little that Jesus would never have approved of that.

Reading Arab accounts of the battles in the twelfth and thirteenth centuries is enlightening,[3] in part because it demonstrates what Paul pointed out in several of his epistles. We are all cut from the same cloth and ethnicity does little to change that. At the hands of the Crusaders, the Arabs suffered considerably. And, so did the crusaders. During the crusades, at least 1,000,000 people died. Some estimates run considerably higher.

---

2. Ferguson, *Civilization*, 50. See also Stark, *God's Battalions*.
3. Gabrieli, *Arab Histories*.

PART III. PIVOTAL QUESTIONS

Papal Failings

Some Protestants believe Christianity became dormant after the first century, what church historians call the Apostolic Age, and that it reemerged only in the 1500s. They believe there were few, if any, Christians before Luther sparked the Reformation. It is true that the church in the West during the late Middle Ages had its moral failings. But throughout the past two thousand years, there have been countless sincere and passionate followers of Jesus who had their theological heads screwed on right.

It is a paradox of virtue that although noble behavior may help an individual ascend within the sacred or secular realm, once having acquired power, that individual may become selfish or ruthless. A line from John Emerich Edward Dalberg (Lord Acton) is often repeated in the truncated form, "Power corrupts and absolute power corrupts absolutely." The original sentence, from a letter written in 1887 to Bishop Mandell Creighton, is "Power tends to corrupt and absolute power corrupts absolutely." This was certainly the case with several popes and their families. The ascent of the Borgias, for example, is among the more infamous examples of how homicidal treachery can infect ecclesiastical leadership, which has occasionally been more about power than religious devotion.

Among the more noteworthy developments of the medieval church was its transformation into a major political power. By the fifth century, the West had become fractured into disorganized regional entities, and what was left of the Roman Empire needed a unifying force. For a thousand years, the church functioned in that capacity. It proved to be a serious and sometimes superior rival to the military and social hegemony of European princes. Power is an intoxicating elixir, and by embracing the wealth that often comes with it, the church at times lost its way. To this point, well over 250 men have been Pope. At times, instead of serving as a beacon of light, the papacy became a labyrinth of intrigue. Although many popes through the ages were exemplary Christians and astute theologians, a few were scoundrels and philanderers.[4] Clearly, there was need for reform.

The requirement of celibacy for ordained clergy in the Catholic Church was formalized by the Second Lateran Council in 1139, although it seems to have been practiced from at least the eleventh century and often well before that. For an enlightened analysis of the depths to which some pontiffs fell, one can do no better than to read

---

4. See Wills, *Papal Sins*.

the impressively honest account by Northwestern University historian, Garry Wills. He remains a Roman Catholic and has addressed why he remains so.[5] Wills has also written an interesting commentary on Luther and the North German Reformation.[6] The pressure for renewal in the church had been building for a long time, and with varying degrees of success reform had been going on for centuries.

Europe in the Run-up to the Renaissance

With the fall of the Roman Empire and the social deterioration that ensued, progress in the West proceeded slowly and trailed advances in the East. The Byzantine Empire, with its capital in Constantinople (Istanbul), had already become a hub of cultural and scientific advance, especially after Emperor Constantine in the fourth century moved his capital from Rome to the isthmus joining Europe and Asia. It is not as if, from the fifth century on, there was no progress in the Latin West, which is what many people assume when they hear the term *Dark Ages*. Inventions occurred, there were impressive architectural innovations, and some members of the clergy worked hard to preserve literacy. But there was insufficient leisure, economic development, or social coordination to allow rapid cultural advance. Several other regions and cultures were far more developed than Europe's, including the Byzantine Empire, Arab world, dynasties in India, and Ming China.

Life in Europe remained harsh for the better part of a millennium, with most people dedicating their waking hours to mere subsistence. Death came early. In the year 1,000, the average life expectancy in Europe was about thirty years, and at times it was decidedly lower. There were devastating plagues, such as the Black Death that reached the British Isles in 1348,[7] widespread disease because of abysmal sanitation practices, and frequent victimization at the hands of the unscrupulous, who were themselves at the mercy of the even less scrupulous. The rule of law was late in coming, and it was not until King Henry I agreed to the *Charter of Liberties* in 1100 that limitations on royal power began to take hold. The *Magna Carta* of 1215 further strengthened these limitations. Nevertheless, medieval Europe lagged behind other major civilizations.

---

5. Wills, *Why I Am a Catholic*.
6. Wills, "Renaissance and Reformation," 154–64.
7. See Herlihy, *The Black Death*.

PART III. PIVOTAL QUESTIONS

The Reformation and Violence

Papal corruption reached its zenith during the Renaissance, and by the late fifteenth century the Latin Church sank to its all-time low. We have already noted how disputations were common among the learned in medieval Europe and were ordinarily amicable, with the worst outcome amounting to no more than embarrassment for the losing party. But no matter. The outwitted person might prevail next time. Arm-in-arm, off they all went to the *Ratskeller* for a brew. Luther's posting of his theses, however, seems to have been altogether more serious and provocative.[8]

Peculiar twists of history turned his lighting of a match into a forest fire. As alluded to in chapter 18, Pope Leo X was determined to rebuild St. Peter's Cathedral, and to help finance this massively expensive project, the church sold indulgences. An indulgence is a kind of spiritual credit, used to shorten one's own or a loved one's time in purgatory. The church dispensed these credits out of what it held to be a treasury of merit, an invisible bank account stored up by Jesus and the saints. Luther, having visited Rome, had become reactive to clerical abuse and took exception to how Johann Tetzel moved from town to town selling these indulgences. The young Augustinian monk insisted that Jesus' death on the cross was sufficient for salvation, and that it made no sense to add additional grace to what was already complete and perfect. The sale of indulgences, he believed, was theologically misguided and suggested ecclesiastical corruption.

Few Catholic theologians would deny that the church in the sixteenth century needed reform, but most would disapprove of the course the Reformation took. Among its less desirable side effects was that it helped incite the Peasants' Revolt (Great Peasants' War) of 1524–25. This resulted in the slaughter of over 100,000 people, causing Erasmus of Rotterdam acerbically to quip to Luther, "We now reap the fruits that you have sown." The Lutheran Reformation led to over a century of violence and bloodshed and contributed substantially to the wars of religion, most famously the Thirty Years War between Catholics and Protestants. Depending on the source you consult, that war appears to have caused the deaths of at least 3,000,000 and perhaps more than 6,000,000 people. The total number of dead and debilitated in Europe during the seventeenth century because of such conflicts is astonishing. Neither side could legitimately claim its conduct to be Christian.

8. See Naphy, *The Protestant Revolution*.

CHAPTER 20. WHAT OF VIOLENCE IN THE NAME OF CHRIST?

This exercise in human devastation also reflected economic issues and political tensions that had little or nothing to do with religion. Protestants allied themselves with Catholics against other Protestants, and vice versa. Some of the underlying reasons behind the Thirty Years War had to do with the development of strong monarchies and nation states.

The Counter-Reformation and Spanish Inquisition

When people hear the term *inquisition*, they often think of dungeons, torture, and perhaps its first Grand Inquisitor, the Spanish Dominican friar Torquemada. Tomás de Torquemada died in 1498, when Luther was not yet fifteen. He therefore predated the Reformation and was not part of the Catholic response to Protestantism. The inquisitors initially focused on Jews and Muslims, but after the Reformation they turned their attention toward combating what they feared would spread throughout the Iberian Peninsula. Catholicism's response to Protestants was swift and severe.

The Roman Church was prepared to take extraordinary measures to ensure popular allegiance to it, the litmus test of which was loyalty to the Pope. It was technically the state, rather than the church, that carried out the sentences prescribed by inquisitors, but the church played the judicial role. Because of the spotty and unreliable nature of historical records, it is difficult to determine precisely how many people became victims of the Inquisition. It seems to have resulted in the death of between 3,000 and 5,000 people and the maiming of many others.[9] Estimates run as high as 10,000. Many more died in prison due to torture and mistreatment. There were also Inquisition-related deaths in neighboring Portugal, but these were fewer in number.

The Inquisition also encouraged a strong response to Protestantism by the Council of Trent (1545–63), which took place in northern Italy. Inquisitions of one kind or another had been going on for centuries, and they would continue in lesser forms for several more. Such counter-reformation efforts reflected, in part, the desire to promote the loyalty of Catholic populations, but they also highlighted the need to stop the hemorrhaging of money away from the Catholic Church. Funds that formerly flowed toward Rome now made their way to Protestant groups in Germany, England, Switzerland, and Scandinavia. Where would it end? The

9. See Pérez, *The Spanish Inquisition*.

Reformation, while inciting the spiritual fervor of common people, also served the material purposes of secular authorities, especially the nobles. Opportunistic princes, delighted by the chance to weaken the power of Rome, added political accelerant to Luther's expanding conflagration. But it would be mistaken if not disingenuous to argue that materialism was the exclusive or even the primary motive for the Inquisition. Ideas are powerful motivators for which people will lay down their lives, and in no domain of life is this more evident than religion.[10]

Colonial Imperialism

The lure of gold has always been tempting to religious organizations, in part because it can be easy to justify the quest for it by pointing to all the good its acquisition might enable. When the *conquistadors* invaded Middle and South America, they did so with the blessings of the church. Some were honest about their desire for money. Others, such as priests and friars, were sincerely on a Christian mission. Still others combined the two motives. In addition to a desire for wealth, they wanted to proclaim the gospel to native populations and actively supported the work of the clergy.

Whatever their motives, the invaders damaged or destroyed indigenous culture, much of which is now gone forever. The Aztec Empire in central Mexico reached its maximum power in the early 1500s, just prior to the arrival of Hernán Cortés, who by forming alliances with enemies of the Aztecs managed to conquer them. Like what happened to Native Americans, the outbreak of smallpox among the Aztecs, who had built up no immunity to it, also played a key role. As inappropriate as colonialism may seem, the importation of European values to the Americas had its salutary side, for example by putting an end to human sacrifice. From the fourteenth century to their fall, the Aztecs ritually sacrificed perhaps 3,000 people each year. Estimates of sacrificial deaths over the centuries exceed 1,000,000. Smallpox also played a role in the conquest of the Peruvian Incas, whose empire was the largest in South America. Francisco Pizarro began this conquest in the 1520s and the Spanish completed it within fifty years.

After an arduous campaign that lasted almost two centuries in Mexico and Central America, the decentralized Mayan civilization

---

10. See Kirsch, *The Grand Inquisitor's Manual*; Huntington, *Clash of Civilizations*.

ended in the late 1600s. This was after initial defeats of the Mayans in 1523 and 1524 by Spain's Pedro de Alvarado. As elsewhere, many conquistadors combined evangelistic fervor with self-serving avarice. There were priests who condemned enslaving Indians, and the issue ultimately reached Rome. In the end, however, nationalism, the desire for gold, and the quest for a larger empire trumped religion.

Protestant Violence

Luther's doctrine of the priesthood of all believers and rejection of *sacerdotalism* supplied the theological rationale for the Reformation. Sacerdotalism is a religious system built around the concept that a propitiatory sacrifice for sin must be offered by priests. We have already noted the large number of deaths that resulted from the Great Peasants' Revolt, also known as the German Peasant's War. The mystic-leaning Anabaptist and eventually executed Thomas Müntzer (1488–1525) was among its leaders. The term *anabaptist* refers to someone who believes that, even if a person was baptized as an infant, he or she must be baptized again after professing faith in Christ.[11] Its contemporary successors include Mennonites, Amish, and Hutterites. Müntzer was a member of the movement known as the Radical Reformation that soon parted ways with Luther, insisting that the Reformation had not gone far enough in repudiating Roman Catholicism, and had gone too far in aligning itself with secular authorities.

Puritans, whose theologies generally followed the Reformed tradition crafted in Switzerland by French lawyer-in-exile John Calvin (1509–64), came to North America in search of freedom from oppression. English Roman Catholics, under the protection of Bloody Mary (1516–58), who ruled England from 1553 until her death in 1558, were not kind to them. Neither were members of the state-sponsored Anglican Church, who enjoyed the protection of English rulers before and after her. Religious passion seems to have been the principal driving force behind their emigration out of Britain in the seventeenth century, but the hope for a better material life also played a role.

If the various inquisitions became an embarrassment to Catholics, the witch trials in New England during the late seventeenth century

---

11. The technical term for this is *credobaptism*, in contrast to *paedobaptism*, the baptism of infants.

became an embarrassment to Protestants. Such trials were not the exclusive province of Puritans. There was precedent for them in Europe, beginning in the late fifteenth century, and it was only with the Witchcraft Act of 1735 that "sorcery" ceased to be punishable by law in Great Britain. Germany later passed a comparable statute. The last execution for witchcraft in the United States took place in Salem, Massachusetts, in the early 1690s. A noted church historian writes, "the entire clerical cause was embarrassed by the infamous witchcraft hysteria, particularly in Salem during 1692 . . . it did lead to chagrin and public remorse, which in turn reduced respect for the colony's religious leadership."[12]

It seems inconceivable that, only three centuries ago, people could suffer execution on the meager strength of a neighbor's accusation that they were in league with the devil. This, however, is more believable than it might initially appear. One spring evening years ago, my wife, daughter, and I attended a mock witch trial in Williamsburg, Virginia. Although it was a tourist attraction, the trial turned out to be chillingly realistic. Members of the audience were invited to provide testimony in support of the prosecution, and during the trial, self-righteous anger seemed quickly to rise to the surface. Several "witnesses" quickly became so caught up in the proceedings that it reminded me of the Stanford Prison Experiment, first carried out in 1971. In it, students acting as guards so completely immersed themselves in their roles that they became shockingly harsh toward other students acting as prisoners. Contemporary witch-hunts of one kind or another are by no means inconceivable, and in fact we saw one in the United States during the McCarthy era (1950–54), when thousands of Americans stood accused of being communists or communist sympathizers.

Many books address the treatment of Native Americans by European settlers, most of whom identified themselves as Christian. Well before the emergence of the genus *Homo* two million years ago, groups displaced other groups, and *Homo sapiens* have been no exception. It is no surprise, therefore, that having vanquished indigenous peoples in North America, Europeans confiscated their land. Indigenous peoples had migrated across the Bering Strait perhaps 13,500 years ago. A minority opinion is that this migration could have occurred as long ago as 40,000 years. What is surprising about the westward expansion was the ethnic prejudice developed by the settlers, who often seemed to view

12. Ahlstrom, *Religious History*, 161.

CHAPTER 20. WHAT OF VIOLENCE IN THE NAME OF CHRIST?

Native Americans as less than human, anticipating how some but by no means all plantation owners would later see African slaves.[13] There was also disregard for existing cultural mores and confinement of tribes on reservations. The survival impulse of settlers no doubt surfaced under the threat of an arrow or a tomahawk, so these attitudes and impulses may, to some extent, be understandable. As often happens in armed conflicts, escalation led to escalation, as settlers used muskets, rifles, and eventually machine guns against more primitive weapons. As a result, millions of Native Americans died.

An indelible blot on the record of Christians in both the United Kingdom and the United States was slavery. Slavery of one kind or another had been around throughout recorded history. What was new was its abolition. The British Parliament passed the Slave Trade Act in 1807, which outlawed the importation of slaves. The United States passed a comparable act that same year. Thanks mostly to the tireless efforts of William Wilberforce, Great Britain passed its Slavery Abolition Act in 1833, which put an end to slavery in most of the British Empire. America trailed in this, and slavery in the United States continued for another thirty years, until the middle of the Civil War. President Lincoln issued the Emancipation Proclamation on January 1, 1863. The Civil War began two years earlier, in 1861, and did not start out explicitly in the service of abolition, but rather to prevent secession by slavery-supporting states. There were economic reasons for the persistence of slavery in the South, where its agricultural economy had grown dependent on forced labor. This, however, does not change the moral horror of depriving human beings of freedom without just cause or due process. The justification for slavery became so comingled with Christianity that some living in the South believed it their spiritual duty to uphold it. Worse still, some became convinced that it was their Christian duty to mutilate or murder any black man believed to have offended the honor of a white woman.[14]

The Holocaust

In the twentieth century, there was complicity by many Protestants in the Holocaust. In addition to active involvement in, or at least passive acquiescence to, the Nazi cause by many German citizens, some

---

13. *Sub-speciation* is the term for regarding other groups as less than human.
14. See Humphries, *Letters of the Century*, 223.

German pastors supported Hitler's regime. Geddes MacGregor once told me how, prior to WWII, a German theologian had suggested to him the correctness of *kenotic* theology.[15] The Greek word *kenosis* has to do with emptying, and kenotic theology centers on the concept, suggested in one of Paul's epistles (Phil 2:5–8), that through the incarnation Jesus emptied himself of his divine attributes. This pro-Nazi thinker told MacGregor that Jesus had indeed fully emptied himself, as evidenced by his having come to earth in the form of the absolute nadir of human existence, a Jew. No doubt some German clergy wanted to end up on what they believed would be the winning side when the war was over. They were, however, deluding themselves. Hitler was no friend of Christianity and wanted to eradicate it because it protected people he wanted to sterilize or euthanize, among them those with physical deformities, intellectual deficiencies, or psychiatric afflictions. Like plantation owners a century earlier and the theologian who offered his interpretation of kenosis, some members of the German clergy accepted or embraced the Nazi insistence on the superiority of Aryans. They, too, have been an embarrassment to the church.

The Roman Catholic Church also engaged in suspicious behavior relating to WWII. Some have suggested that it facilitated, or at least did not oppose, confiscation of Jewish property by the Nazis. On the other side of the ledger, hundreds of Jews were given shelter in the Pope's summer residence at Italy's Castel Gandolfo. Priests in Hungary worked frantically, at great personal risk, to issue bogus baptismal certificates, and papal representatives in Romania implored government officials to avoid deporting Jews ("bad weather" subsequently halted the trains). It can be argued that Pope Pius XII was not more vocal in his renunciation of Nazism, despite having previously criticized National Socialism, because he was concerned that doing so would make things worse. There was also the Roman Catholic Oskar Schindler (1908–74), whose story provided the scaffolding for the 1993 film "Schindler's List." Schindler saved well over a thousand Jews by employing them in his enamelware and munitions factories. Years ago, while walking down a street in Regensburg, Germany, I came across a plaque on a house indicating that Schindler has lived there briefly after the war. He then moved to Munich, then to Argentina, and finally returned to Germany. He died in

---

15. Personal communication, 1983.

CHAPTER 20. WHAT OF VIOLENCE IN THE NAME OF CHRIST?

poverty. Tom Holland has written an enlightening discussion of Christian responses to the Nazis.[16]

Like Christians who operated or supported the Underground Railroad that smuggled escaped slaves into the North before the Civil War, some German Christians set themselves against the Nazi cause. For this, many paid dearly. As an example, the Nazis imprisoned and executed Lutheran pastor and theologian Dietrich Bonhöffer (1906–45) for his involvement in a failed attempt to assassinate Hitler. The bomb, hidden in a briefcase, exploded under a conference table, but Hitler emerged unscathed. Bonhöffer, whose influential books remain in print,[17] decided to participate in the assassination attempt only after much soul-searching.[18] He reached the conclusion that ending Hitler's life was the lesser of two evils.

Bad Actors

We all have the potential to behave badly, and perhaps most of us occasionally experience tension between impulse and restraint. "The heart is deceitful above all things, and desperately wicked: who can know it?" (Jer 17:9). As noted in chapter 13, we face the ever-present challenge of deciding how much to take care of ourselves and how much to take care of others. Those completely given over to evil, however, live without much conflict. They experience little or no ethical or moral tension, perhaps because they have deficient moral compasses.

Human populations have produced countless individuals who were unsavory if not reprehensible, and all cultures spawn sociopaths skilled at hiding their unscrupulous purposes beneath cloaks of imitation virtue. Many sociopaths are skilled at *virtue signaling*, publicly voicing opinions or sentiments to demonstrate their nobility. The church has no built-in immunity from this. Within it, there have been evangelists caught embezzling funds, rationalizing that since they brought in millions of dollars, they deserved to live in grand mansions, drive expensive cars, and take extravagant vacations. Their actions have done economic violence to those who contributed the funds they embezzled. Some deeds by Christian clergy have been far worse, from acting out perversions on children

---

16. Holland, *Dominion*, 476–87.
17. Bonhoeffer, *Ethics*; Bonhoeffer, *The Cost of Discipleship*.
18. Metaxas, *Bonhoeffer*.

to murdering fellow priests or pastors who they worried would expose them. The Christian world will continue to have its share of wolves masquerading as lambs. Their behavior should never be attributed to the faith they betray and may never have embraced to begin with.

The Personal Nature of Christian Transformation

Many people have concluded, along with Nietzsche, that Christians behave no differently than everyone else. Whether this conclusion is warranted depends on what you mean by *everyone*. If you mean the sum of all those people on earth who do not claim to be Christian, it is false. Claiming to be a Christian on a survey form, as noted above, may indicate nothing more than that the questions were insufficiently precise and that the respondent came from a family that was Catholic, Orthodox, or Protestant. This is different from relating to Christ as one's Lord.

Few Christians deny the corporate dimension of Christianity. At the same time, in the language of the Bible, arriving at Christian faith involves a kind of death and rebirth (John 3). Placing faith in Christ often occurs within, and is supported by, a community of Christians, but it is ultimately a solo sport, a transaction between the individual and God. Becoming a Christian is the establishment of a new relationship with God, who remains invisible but is very much present. A Christian is someone who may have once lived in tension with God but now lives in harmony with God.

Even when a country, such as the United States, has a governance structure that reflects the residual values of Christianity, this does not ensure its long-term health or survival. A nation and its government are only as good as its citizens. Cultures shape people, but people also shape cultures. Human beings carry out this shaping based on what, and more pointedly who, resides in their hearts.

To recognize God in and through Christ, and internalize that Jesus is both Lord and savior, is the result of the Holy Spirit acting on an individual's mind and heart. When we grasp that God is our creator, provider, and sustainer, the one who gives us every good thing, including consciousness and the next breath we breathe, we begin also to realize that it is God to whom we owe our most profound duties. We also owe it to all other human beings not to use violence as a means of furthering selfish ends. That imperative is fundamental to Christianity, and when

CHAPTER 20. WHAT OF VIOLENCE IN THE NAME OF CHRIST?

individuals, groups, or societies abrogate it, they are not only turning away from Christ but turning against him.

Closing Thoughts

Violence has been carried out under the banner of many religions and Christianity is no exception. Skeptics often cite the Medieval Crusades as examples of violence carried out in the name of Christ. Motives underlying the crusades included payback, greed, reconquest of the Holy Land, recovery of relics, regaining the diminished prestige of the church, and passionate faith. Rarely if ever were they motivated by the desire to convert Muslims to Christianity. The church was riddled with corruption and its clergy were not always above extortion and violence. Although the Protestant Reformation was in part an attempt to correct this, the Reformation inadvertently fostered violence. It also triggered the counter-reformation and intensified the violence of inquisitions that had long been underway. Colonialism was motivated by the lust for gold, and priests tried hard to mitigate or eliminate its ruthlessness. Protestant clergy were ineffective in discouraging and reducing violence against native Americans within what would become the United States. Some in the twentieth century were complicit in the Holocaust. All of this demonstrates the flawed nature of humanity. Looking back through history, however, Christianity has mitigated violence, encouraged benevolence, and advanced human rights more than *any* of the alternatives. What has helped make this so, perhaps, is that Christians usually understand that we are all part of the same humanity. They do not fool themselves about their capacity to behave like angels under the right circumstances or beasts under the wrong ones.

Preview

Many people regard the physical resurrection of Jesus as impossible and find the hope of existence beyond the grave improbable. We turn next to some of the questions that Jesus' resurrection poses, including the possibility of life after death.

Chapter 21. Is There Life After Death?

MANY PEOPLE WITHOUT RELIGION are skeptical about the possibility of life after death. Such skepticism has been increasing for centuries. Before Spinoza in the 1700s, no major philosopher in the West had publicly challenged religious belief or the possibility of an afterlife. A century later, Hume believed he had driven a stake into the heart of anything beyond what we can observe and demonstrate, and by implication into the idea of miracles. If Jesus did not come back to life after his crucifixion, however, the Christian hope of everlasting life is pointless. It becomes but a hopeless fantasy shrouded in rosy sentiment.

A person who insists that such a thing is impossible is also likely to deny the existence of a God who created the world and acts in history. Miracles[1] do not prove God's existence, since a miracle might occur for reasons having nothing to do with God. But if they have ever happened, they at least suggest God's existence. If there is a creator, it seems reasonable to believe that such a creator is capable of overriding what we think of as immutable physical laws.

Another Dimension

Some people freely speculate about other dimensions of reality, different modes of space and time, or the existence of parallel universes. Such speculation hints at a realm of reality we may sometimes sense but that remains beyond our ordinary grasp. It is a dimension that Christianity

---

1. See Brown, *Miracles and the Critical Mind*.

teaches is all around us, which is why Paul, quoting an ancient poem, writes, "In God we live and move and have our being" (Acts 17:28). This dimension may, in fact, be part of what we tend to think of as the miraculous. The Christian hopes and expects, at some future time, to have a resurrected body and to enjoy what the Bible refers to as a new earth, both of which would qualify as miraculous. Properly grasping the miraculous may require a more penetrating perception of this dimension than, as mortals, we typically have.

Christians believe that life, both before and after death, has to do with existing in this dimension, which is closer to us than the air we breathe. They also believe the resurrection of Jesus was a prototype, the template for what those *in Christ* will experience. Belief in resurrection after death is the Christian hope, the confident expectation, that we too will experience this miracle. This expectation hinges on the resurrection of Jesus. If that never happened, Christianity becomes at most an ethical system. Denying the resurrection disconnects Christian belief, and therefore Christian faith, from flesh-and-blood history and leaves in its wake only the dead skeleton of empty aspiration.

Understandable Skepticism

Skepticism about the resurrection of Jesus implies doubts about the reliability of what is reported in the Gospels or the chain of custody for the New Testament. Some wonder, if for polemical purposes, copyists embellished what the original authors wrote, or if they unintentionally introduced errors. These concerns are certainly understandable, and we addressed them in chapters 13 and 14.

That someone has never witnessed a miracle, something that at present lies beyond explanation, does not mean miracles never happen. Absence of evidence is not evidence of absence. Only a small number of people witnessed Jesus changing water into wine (John 2:1–11), but that does not mean it never occurred. If we tried to set up an experiment to determine if miracles exist, we would run into an insurmountable problem. The resurrection of Jesus was an act of God that we can neither explain nor replicate. Asking for empirical proof of a one-time event is like trying to count grains of sand with a ruler. We would be using the wrong instrument. "Science studies repeatable phenomena; an experiment can be replicated on the other side of the world. History studies unrepeatable phenomena . . . 'Proof' in history must therefore reside in the balance of probabilities."[2]

Christians believe these probabilities come down in favor of the resurrection, but if they are honest and clear thinkers, they also acknowledge that probabilities offer only soft evidence. When it comes to the resurrection of Jesus, what a person believes the evidence points to is never a question of raw intellectual power but of the disposition of the heart.

From Skepticism to Faith

Many people assume that those living in the first century were more gullible than we are, an assumption that reflects what social scientists call *temporocentrism*, automatically and arbitrarily favoring the present over the past. There were certainly physical ailments that residents in Jerusalem attributed to unseen spiritual forces. But from the New Testament records, it seems clear that people at the time were decidedly skeptical toward claims of anyone coming back to life. Jesus' disciples were a handpicked group with whom he spent three years. Even after all that time, they initially found his resurrection incomprehensible. If we can trust the eleventh chapter of John, their skepticism is even more noteworthy because at least a few of them had been with Jesus when he summoned Lazarus out of the tomb and restored him to life.

In John's Gospel, we read an account of the resurrection of Lazarus, the brother of Martha and Mary. Lazarus becomes ill and dies. The two sisters send a message to Jesus, who announces that the illness has occurred to bring glory to God and God's Son. Jesus remains where he is for two days, then declares his intention to go to Judea. The disciples remind him that some there want to stone him to death, but apparently led by Thomas, they resign themselves to dying. When they near the village of Bethany, Jesus learns that Lazarus has been in the tomb for days.

As he approaches the village, Martha meets him on the outskirts of town, and ever the conscientious one, chides Jesus for not having shown up earlier. If he had, she insists, her brother would still be alive. Mary then arrives and echoes Martha's disappointment (John 11:21). When Jesus sees Mary and others weeping, it troubles him deeply. He proceeds to the tomb and orders the men to remove the stone at its entrance. Martha reminds Jesus that Lazarus has been dead for days,

---

2. Wright, *How God Became King*, 108.

CHAPTER 21. IS THERE LIFE AFTER DEATH?

adding in the vivid language of the King James Bible, "by this time he stinketh" (John 11:39). Jesus then prays and, in an angry voice, roars, "Lazarus, come forth!" With his face wrapped in cloth, and his hands and feet bound in linen, Lazarus stumbles out.

Despite his raising of Lazarus, the disciples were not inclined to accept the possibility of Jesus' resurrection. That the Romans had executed Jesus was too much for them. They could not fathom how the long-awaited Jewish Messiah would die on a cross as a common criminal, in disgrace and humiliation. They expected a Messiah like Moses, one to deliver them from foreign oppression. Their response to reports of Jesus' resurrection was disbelief in the wake of disillusionment.[3]

The women who first go to the tomb discover that Jesus is missing and come to the astonishing, though tentative, conclusion that he had risen from the dead (Matt 28:6; Mark 16:6; Luke 24:6). The Gospel of Mark tells us they flee the tomb, so distressed that they say nothing. They then remember how Jesus had predicted his arrest, crucifixion, *and* resurrection, which prompts the women to share what they had discovered. Most of the disciples dismiss their reports as nonsense, but Peter and another disciple run to the tomb, find only grave clothes, and return stunned and befuddled (Luke 24:8–12).

We read that Jesus first appears in his resurrected body to Mary Magdalene. She seeks out the grief-stricken disciples and tells them she had encountered Jesus, but they do not believe her. Jesus next appears to disciples in the country who then return to the city, but no one believes them either (Mark 16:9–13). Later that day, we find Jesus approaching two disciples walking toward the nearby town of Emmaus (Luke 13:13–32). But they, too, fail to recognize him. This appears to have been because Jesus' post-resurrection body was somehow different and yet the same. One can only speculate about how Jesus looked after his resurrection. When Jesus asks what they have been talking about, they are amazed that he seems to be the only person in the vicinity of Jerusalem who is unaware of what happened, how earlier that day women found the tomb empty and claimed Jesus was alive. The two urge him to remain, and Jesus explains the meaning of Old Testament passages relating to him. They then recognize him.

Jesus later appears to the disciples. They are astonished and afraid, and he chides them for their unbelief and hardness of heart (Mark

---

3. See Bauckham, *Jesus and the Eyewitnesses*.

16:14). Even when Jesus stands among them and wishes them peace, this does not settle them down. They remain terrified and assume they are seeing a ghost. To verify who he is, Jesus invites them to examine his hands and feet, and he points out that ghosts are not flesh and bones. But they continue to miss the significance of who is standing in front of them and remain flummoxed, caught in a swirling mixture of hope and confusion (Luke 24:36–41).

The disciples later tell Thomas, who was not with them when Jesus appeared. He cynically snipes that unless he puts his hand in Jesus' side and his fingers in the holes of his hands, he will not believe (John 20:24–25). A week later, Jesus appears again, and this time Thomas is present. Inviting Thomas to place his fingers in the wound and examine his hands, Jesus sternly tells him to stop doubting and start believing. Overwhelmed, Thomas blurts out, "My Lord and my God!" The unfathomable hits Thomas with the force of a hurricane. After Jesus physically showed himself to his disciples, they no longer questioned whether he had resurrected. Wright refers to this as "bursting upon them."[4] The experiences of these first-century Christians recorded in the New Testament comprise strong evidence of it.[5]

We can proceed down the path of indirect proof by examining how well arguments against the resurrection hold up. Kreeft and Tacelli write, "The greatest importance of the resurrection is not in the past 'Christ rose'—but in the present, 'Christ is risen,'" The promise of Christianity is that those who follow Jesus will experience what he did, resurrection from the grave. These accounts are too detailed and realistic to dismiss out of hand. There is no good reason to doubt them, since with admirable candor they portray the reactions of the disciples, and how skepticism turned first into belief and then into faith. What these companions of Jesus experienced two thousand years ago was once again a shift in their fundamental assumptions, which resembles what happens to people today when they become Christians. The Holy Spirit moves them from skepticism to faith.

---

4. Wright, *How God Became King*, 197.
5. Kreeft and Tacelli, *Handbook*, 177.

CHAPTER 21. IS THERE LIFE AFTER DEATH?

Atheism and Agnosticism

To arrogate means to lay claim to something without warrant, without the right to do so. We have noted how the major creeds of Christianity begin with affirmations of belief rather than knowledge. Although countless Christians through the ages have recited these creeds, convinced that they not only believed but *knew*, well-crafted Christian confessions reveal a certain humility. Atheism reflects none of this, and when atheists promote their beliefs as incontrovertible knowledge, they show themselves to be irrationally biased.

Like Christianity, atheism involves a leap of faith. While the atheist may argue against God because of the existence of evil, the Christian may argue for God because of the existence of good. Few atheists prudently suspend judgment. An agnostic, by contrast, is someone who believes nothing is known or perhaps can be known about the existence or nature of God, a person who affirms neither faith nor disbelief. Judgment is suspended. Since the seventeenth century, an increasing number of thinkers have professed atheism. Two have been especially influential, and many people who argue against the existence of God and the reality of the resurrection, knowingly or unknowingly, echo their thought-forms.

Spinoza on Theism and Miracles

Baruch (Benedict) Spinoza (1632–77) was a Dutch thinker of Portuguese descent. He paved the way for the rationalism that thinkers like Voltaire later promoted. I refer here to the period known as the Enlightenment, but I shy away from using that term because it was, in some ways at least, a time in history when reason eventually fell short of fulfilling its promises. Reason alone proved unable to deliver such benefits as uninterrupted moral progress and lasting peace. The two world wars in Europe during the twentieth century made this clear.

By all reports, Spinoza was uncommonly virtuous. No one seems to have had an unkind word to say about him. He had no known vices and never married. Spinoza worked much of his short life as an independent scholar. He spent time and corresponded with friends, among them the noted mathematician and scientist Christiaan Huygens. Huygens was a renowned Dutch mathematician, astronomer, and physicist, who among other things promoted the wave theory of light. Spinoza lived frugally and made a modest living as a lens grinder and instrument maker. His skill at lens grinding was superb and he applied it primarily to lenses for telescopes and microscopes. He died at the age of forty-four from lung disease, and his early death may have been related to breathing in fine glass dust.

In his youth, Spinoza had attended a *yeshiva*, a Jewish school devoted to the study of *Torah* and *Talmud*. *Torah* has a variety of meanings, including simply instruction. At a minimum, it refers to the Pentateuch, the first five books of the Bible. It may also include references to additional biblical books and rabbinic commentaries, or even to the whole of Jewish culture, teaching, and practice. *Talmud* consists of two parts, the *Mishnah*, a compendium of rabbinic teaching as of about AD 200, and the *Gemara*, assembled a few hundred years later. It comprises interpretations of the Mishnah and other Jewish writings.

Spinoza ended his formal education at age seventeen to work in the family's import business. Until his father's death four years later, he appears to have been an observant Jew. But Spinoza had been moving away from orthodox Judaism for some time, and he came to his adult beliefs after what he reports was long and patient study. For some time, Spinoza had been socializing with a sect of rationally inclined, anti-Calvinist thinkers. Some of his closest friends were dissident Christians who rejected the authority of established churches.

He took issue with major tenets of the Jewish religion, among them that Moses had written the Pentateuch. As a result, leaders of his congregation summoned Spinoza to examine him. He seems to have answered their questions with a bit of swagger, and a knife-wielding assailant, shouting "Heretic," attacked him on the steps of the synagogue. In 1656, two years after his father's death, the congregation, which had become increasingly aware of his unorthodox views, excommunicated Spinoza. By then, he had rejected the idea of a providential God, denied the possibility of life after death, and refused to accept the Ten Commandments as something God had given to the Hebrew people.

Spinoza concludes that God is abstract and impersonal, and that what we refer to as *God* is only nature by another name. Debate continues about whether Spinoza is a pantheist or panentheist. "Panentheism considers God and the world to be inter-related, with the world being in God and God being in the world . . . [but] seeks to avoid . . . identifying God with the world, as pantheism does."[6] He is surely atheistic in the sense of

---

6. John Culp, "Panentheism." s.v.

not subscribing to theism. Spinoza is a staunch determinist who regards whatever happens as the necessary consequence of everything before it. Free will, he maintains, is an illusion, and human behavior reflects only natural impulses, which are but the playing out of prior conditions. Ideas of blame and praise are therefore misplaced. Nothing we do happens either by choice or chance, and even our thoughts are determined.

Both *mental* and *physical* are two ways of describing the same thing, two manifestations of a single underlying substance, however difficult it may be to say precisely what that substance is. This metaphysical view is called *neutral monism*, to be distinguished from dualism (mental and physical are each fundamental), physicalism (physical is fundamental and mind derivative), and idealism (mind is fundamental and the physical derivative). Neutral monism maintains that both mind and body are ways of depicting the same underlying elements, which are neither exclusively mental nor physical. To Spinoza, nothing happens in violation of natural laws, which are universal and immutable. Miracles are therefore impossible.

Three questions arise in relation to Spinoza's thought. First, how does he know laws of nature are universal, that they apply always and everywhere? Second, what leads him to conclude that any, not to mention all, such laws are immutable? Third, might it be possible that miracles reflect higher laws we may never in this life discover?

Hume's Skepticism

In preceding chapters, I have mentioned the ideas of the Scottish philosopher David Hume. Similar to Spinoza, Hume was a congenial soul whose conviviality belied the strident opinions reflected in his writings. Spinoza was a rationalist and Hume an empiricist. Many philosophers shy away from terms such as these because they are potentially inaccurate. Since, however, they are still widely used and can be useful, albeit simplistic intellectual reference points, I will provide a brief definition of each. Rationalism is a belief in reason as the ultimate criterion for truth, but it also usually reflects a belief in innate ideas and an emphasis on deductive reason. Empiricism, by contrast, is a belief in sense perception as the sole source and basis of truth, an emphasis on inductive reasoning, and the repudiation of innate ideas.

Spinoza is comfortable proposing the metaphysical thesis that mental and physical events are manifestations of the same underlying reality. Hume, however, refuses to engage in such speculation. He prefaces his comments about miracles by stating how he "flatters himself" that he has discovered an argument, which if it holds up will "with the wise and learned, be an everlasting check to all kinds of superstitious delusion, and consequently, will be useful so long as the world endures."[7] He asserts that his argument is a "direct and full proof, from the nature of the fact, against the existence of any miracle." By "full proof" he has in mind probabilities, to what he regards as overwhelmingly likely.

Like Spinoza, Hume affirms that a miracle is a violation of the laws of nature. He further argues that unwavering experience has led to our formulation of these laws. Hume then submits that, if we are wise and reason soundly, we will believe something only to the extent that the available evidence supports it. Since, he asserts, the weight of evidence is clearly on the side of the operation of natural laws as opposed to their violation, it makes no sense to believe in miracles. It takes little discernment to detect a hint of derision in Hume's words. As gracious and affable as he may have been with friends, he was unrelenting in his attack on religion.

A key point in Hume's thought is his insistence that "firm and unalterable experience has established these laws," which are based on repeated observations. This reflects a subtle difference between Spinoza and Hume. For Spinoza, because scientific laws are immutable and universal, miracles are impossible. For Hume, since our experience of the operation of natural laws is uniform, miracles may in theory be possible, but the evidence we have should strongly incline us not to believe in them. As a strict empiricist, he remains unconvinced of anything not confirmed by sense observation. Hume's thought is closely aligned with how some but not all scientists think about the world. Note the difference pointed out in chapter 15 between methodological and metaphysical materialism.

Because miracles are exceptions to what otherwise would happen, Hume regards them as improbable. Yet miracles, by definition, are non-repeatable evens. By insisting that the sole criterion by which a miracle can be verified is repeatability, Hume rules out the possibility of miracles and, in so doing, begs the question by assuming what he is obliged to prove. Implicitly if not explicitly, he also denies the existence

---

7. Hume, *Inquiry Concerning Human Understanding*, Section X, Part I, para. 86.

of a creator who, having crafted nature and transcends it, can at any time intervene in its workings.

Hume's reasoning seems to suggest that any one-time event is so improbable that it would be irrational to believe it happened. Astrophysicists, however, find convincing the evidence in favor of the Big Bang, the quintessential one-time event, and I suspect Hume would also. This raises questions about what he allows as credible evidence. Unlike the water-to-wine miracle, no one was around to witness the Big Bang, and only a small number of people even pretend to understand how or why it occurred.

Alternatives

Long before Jesus, people debated what happens when we die, and prehistoric drawings on the walls of caves suggest that such musings go back a long way. Is there an afterlife, and if so, what is its nature? Do we end up as nothing but desiccated chemicals, or are we more than our physical properties? Are we, as Plato taught, souls indwelling bodies that are released when we die, a view that continues to influence many Christian thinkers? Or are we indissoluble combinations of minds and bodies? This relates to why Christianity offers the hope of resurrected bodies. Most Christians appear to believe that if a person stubbornly resists and rejects God, whatever happens is not good. I want to highlight a few possibilities that some have suggested might happen to us after death.

Annihilationism asserts that once you die, it is game over. You cease to exist. Regardless of how fondly others may remember you, and even if you have made it into the history books, existence in any personal sense ends when your body, and by implication your brain, gives out.

If you assume that all mention of the spiritual is sentimentality, you are likely to conclude that annihilationism makes sense, perhaps because it has the appeal of being simple. Many people are familiar with the principle from the philosophy of science that the best theory is the one that is least complicated and therefore, from a conceptual point of view, most parsimonious. To believe babies come from a fertility god visiting a woman's womb is far simpler than thinking about ova, spermatozoa, gamete motility, vaginal acid-base balances, and chromosomal sorting. The latter view has the disadvantage of being more complex. But it has the overwhelming advantage of being true.

People who believe death ends human life usually also believe we are only material beings. This still leaves unanswered the question of how the material can generate the mental, how bodies (brains) create consciousness. The issue becomes whether materialism is up to the job of explaining everything, of whether philosophic materialists can make sense of life as we know it. For a theory to be robust, it must account for all available data, and hardcore materialism seems to ignore or explain away such intangibles as love, joy, and justice. There is no need for God in annihilationism, and its emotional appeal may be that it allows people to avoid thinking about whether there even is a God. In its thoroughgoing form, materialism renders questions about God meaningless, and if you believe your inevitable destiny is to return to dust, it might make sense to eat, drink, and be merry on the way to oblivion. There is no necessary connection between annihilationism and the idea that only the physical world exists. It is possible to believe we are spiritual beings but also that some or all people do not survive death. The term *spiritual* is used so loosely in our culture that, for this sentence to make reasonable sense, we would have to define what we mean by the word.

Some Christian theologians suggest that those who have rejected God's love cease to exist after death, and such theologians therefore accept a version of annihilationism that does not derive from materialism. By their lights, those who align themselves with God inherit eternal life, while those who reject God perish when they die. What the Bible refers to as hell, therefore, amounts to death as the final curtain. The implication of annihilationism for these theologians is that people only enjoy eternal life if God gives them that gift, and God does this because they recognize who Jesus was and believe what he has done. One virtue of this view is that it carries with it the implication that whatever is opposed to God, in this case hell, does not exist forever. When the last human being dies, and the forces of evil have been vanquished, hell will be no more.

Universalism is the belief that every human being will enjoy eternal life. Because God created and loves us, everyone from Adolph Hitler to Mother Teresa will survive death and spend eternity with God. Many universalists are well aware that people have bad desires, intentions, and behaviors, but they insist that God sees what causes them. God eventually forgives evil, including what Jesus' contemporaries did to him. We will all enjoy *continued personal identity* and the ability to recognize ourselves and others, and we will experience everlasting bliss. Philosopher

CHAPTER 21. IS THERE LIFE AFTER DEATH?

C. Stephen Evans points out that it is theoretically possible for someone to have continued personal identity but not be recognizable.[8]

A variation of universalism is that after we die, God will find a way to perfect even the worst of us if we allow it. Regardless of what they have done, or how many others they have tortured, maimed, or murdered, God will accept them, but only if they end their evil ways. Theologian Dennis Okholm points out that some, such as Gregory of Nyssa (ca. 335–395), believe that, prior to salvation, people undergo punishment, not so much to mete out divine retribution as to cleanse them from sin.

To the street-corner evangelist's question, "Are you saved?" the universalist replies, "Of course, and so are you." Many universalists suggest this is because Christ died for everyone. Such a stance can be comforting, since it is pleasant to think of God as all-accepting and all-loving, a God who, regardless of how egregious our actions, imposes on us no final judgment or lasting penalty. Believing in a God who treats everyone with unconditional positive regard is also emotionally appealing. If you have ever experienced anything like this from another person, you know how validating and affirming it can be. I remember how, when I practiced as a clinical psychologist, some people who came to see me would experience significant positive change because someone listened empathically. It was not the brilliance of my psychodynamic insights, behavioral prescriptions, cognitive reframings, or anything of the sort that brought about change, but simply providing a safe interpersonal context in which to feel heard and understood. This is the closest some people may ever get to sensing what it feels like for God to love them.

Universalism is difficult for many Christians to accept because it seems to trivialize ethics and our obligation to live as God intends. The foremost Protestant theologian of the twentieth century, Karl Barth (1886–1968), seems to have died before he was able to resolve the tension between his belief in universalism and the principle of divine justice. That God might rescue diabolical human beings seems to fly in the face of what we think of as this justice.

Metempsychosis, a synonym for reincarnation, is a third possibility. Belief in it is central to Hinduism. It is the belief that, when we die, we come back to life in a different form, a better one if in our previous existence we had good intentions and behaved well, or a degraded one otherwise. Many people in the West do not seem to take the possibility

---

8. Personal communication, November 20, 2020.

of reincarnation seriously. A notable exception is Nietzsche, but it is an open question whether he intends others to take literally his thesis of eternal recurrence. Reincarnation is not a foolish idea,[9] but most Christian theologians regard it as incompatible with Christianity.[10]

According to the traditional belief in reincarnation, death brings with it only *samsara*, living one's life over again, potentially an endless number of times until we get it right. Without any memory of our past lives, however, it is hard to see how learning could carry over from one incarnation to another. If we view Jesus as a man who was on his way to another human life, we miss the significance of his crucifixion and resurrection. We also trivialize the incarnation, the idea that God appeared on earth, once and only once, in the form of a human being.

A Haunting Possibility

Hell is an uncomfortable subject. Even committed Christians may skip over references to it in the Bible and never take the time and trouble to think through what these references might mean. But there are too many such references to allow any responsible Christian blithely to dismiss hell as an outdated concept.

Biblical literalists conceive of hell as a place where fires burn and people suffer. They may picture a pit near the center of the earth to which God remands the unrepentant. A friend of mine, taking exception to this once said, "I can't imagine God forever taking a blow torch to anyone." Notions of eternal pain and suffering may be primitive, but it is equally unenlightened to refuse to consider what hell might be. To conclude that it refers to something spiritual rather than physical, which it may, is not however to render the idea trivial. When Jesus refers to himself as the Good Shepherd (John 10:11–14), people generally understand that he was using a metaphor, an image first-century Palestinians would immediately grasp. Maybe we need to think of "fire and brimstone" as metaphors also.

Perhaps to make it into hell, you must put yourself there. There are many kinds of principles at work in the universe, such as social, physical, and spiritual ones. Although some criminal convictions require mandatory sentences, penalties for violating societal laws can be

---

9. See MacGregor, *Reincarnation as a Christian Hope*.
10. See MacGregor, ed. *Immortality and Human Destiny*.

flexible, and so in a criminal trial the judge may be able to show leniency. Those for violating physical laws, by contrast, are non-negotiable, and jumping off a cliff will likely kill you. Christianity teaches that there is a third kind of principle, a spiritual one. Whatever hell is, it may reflect the operation of that principle.

Some theologians believe that, even after death, the possibility of redemption will remain. With God, all things are possible (Matt 19:26). Because of their hardness of heart, however, even after death some people may refuse the love God offers, and so condemn themselves to everlasting solitude. Hell may turn out in the end to be inconsolable loneliness. If you have ever lost a loved one, especially a cherished spouse or beloved child, you know the indescribable pain such loss brings. There is nothing you can do to fix it, no way to bring the person back. You live thereafter with a raw wound. The pain may decrease, but the wound may never entirely heal, and the residual loneliness can be a kind of hell.

A psychiatrist long ago observed, "Loneliness [is] such a painful, frightening experience that people will do practically [anything] to avoid it." Loneliness is "one of the least satisfactorily conceptualized psychological phenomena, not even mentioned in most psychiatric textbooks."[11] This is no longer true, but it was throughout most of the history of modern psychology and psychiatry.

In Conor McPherson's play *The Seafarer*,[12] Sharky has placed a wager, and if he loses, Lockhart, the Devil, will own him. Here is an edited version of their conversation:

> LOCKHART: Your brother . . . He's a real believer, isn't he? [Pause.]
>
> I hate these stupid insect bodies you have. What are human beings? Two balloons—that's your lungs and an annoying little whistle at the top where the air comes out—that's your voice. And He became one of you so He could see what pain was and what fear and death were . . . What a mess! I mean what have you got that I haven't?! You all age and wither before me like dead flowers in a bright window! You're nothing! Me? . . . I'm the very power that keeps us all apart! Aren't I worth saving? Evidently not. No, He loves you. He loves all you insects . . . figure that one out.
>
> SHARKY: What'll happen to me? If I lose.

---

11. Fromm-Reichmann, "Loneliness," *Psychiatry*, 1–15.
12. McPherson, *The Seafarer*.

LOCKHART: You're coming to Hell.

SHARKY: What is . . . ?

LOCKHART: Hell is . . . when you're walking round the city, and the street lights have all come on and it's cold . . . And you see all the people who seem to live in another world, all snuggled up together in the warmth of a tavern or a cozy little house, and you just walk and walk and walk, and you're on your own and nobody knows who you are. And you're hoping you won't meet anyone you know because of the blistering shame that rises up in your face, and you have to turn away because you know you can't even deal with the thought that someone might love you . . . Well, that's a fraction of the self-loathing you feel in Hell, except it's worse. Because there truly is no one to love you. You're locked in a space that's smaller than a coffin . . . And it's so cold that you don't even feel your angry tears freezing in your eyelashes, and your very bones ache with deep perpetual agony . . . You never even sleep because every few minutes you're gripped by a claustrophobic panic and you get so frightened you squirm uselessly . . . and your heart beats so fast against your ribs you think, "I must be going to die . . . " But of course . . . you never will . . . Oh, you'd have loved Heaven, Sharky. It's unbelievable! Time just slips away in Heaven. But not for you. No. You are about to find out that time is bigger and blacker and so much more boundless than you could ever have thought possible.

Many people think heaven is desirable and hell undesirable, but they would be hard pressed to say much more. Thoughtful Christians understand pearly gates and streets of gold to be metaphors. They may also understand the metaphoric nature of references to unquenchable thirst. Metaphors point to something beyond themselves. If Christianity is what it claims, heaven and hell must refer to *something*, if for no other reason than Jesus having stressed their significance.

God's Kingdom on Earth

The New Testament refers to a new heaven and a new earth, and some theologians believe there will someday be a transformed and revitalized planet. They stress that Jesus inaugurated the kingdom of God on earth two thousand years ago, and that the mission of the church has always been to further that kingdom. When Jesus prayed that God's will be done on earth, he implied that God's purposes remain at least partly unrealized. Christians, therefore, ought to be in the business of making life on earth better. This is a helpful corrective to the belief that life *here* is a waiting room for life *there*, that Christians have no duty to contribute to society or care for the planet, and that their sole obligation is to get into heaven when it is their turn.

If there is to be a new heaven and earth, what happens when the sun burns itself out? Will God prevent this? For the earth to undergo a permanent transformation, God would have to halt the self-destruction of the sun and with it the extinction of life on earth. As argued throughout this book, if God created the universe, surely God could do these things. Heaven, however, may turn out not to be a physical place but a state of existence in which God's intentions prevail. Theologian Dennis Okholm suggests that since God is omnipresent, existing everywhere, heaven may be omnipresent now as another dimension.[13] In the end, it may matter less where heaven is than what it signifies.

Musings About the Afterlife

It is difficult to know much about life after death, although at least one prominent philosopher has written a book about heaven.[14] Whatever it is, it is not going to be old people in white togas playing lyres. Eternal life must bring with it three things, without any one of which it might not be as attractive as Christianity implies. First, Christians must enjoy continued personal identity and continuity of consciousness. They would be able to recognize themselves as the persons they are. Some believe that in heaven they will no longer be able to sin. Others believe that, although they will retain the capacity to sin, they will not exercise it, preferring instead to enjoy the flow of God. Whichever is the case, *selves* in heaven must involve continuation of selves on earth.

Second, heaven must involve interpersonal relationships. This implies that Christians will not only retain their individual identities but also relate to others who retain theirs. Distinctions between and among people, what psychologists call individual differences, will likely recede into the background. Heaven may be the dimension of existence in which the unfiltered essence of each person, as an *I*, communicates

13. Personal communication, November 20, 2020.
14. Kreeft, *Everything About Heaven*.

with the unfiltered essence of every other person as a *You*, or in Martin Buber's terms, a *Thou*.[15] Heaven may be both private and social, perhaps with a kind of restorative and rehabilitative leveling. Introverts may be more comfortable around others than they are now, and extraverts may be more comfortable being alone. I believe we will enjoy what I will discuss in chapter 27 as *holy intimacy*.

Third, for those aligned with God, eternal existence will be joyful. This is the Christian hope. Whatever else, heaven will not be boring. Peaceful yes, plagued by *ennui*, no. Heaven will not be what it feels like now to sit through a mind-numbingly dull church service. It is likely to inspire Christians to express joy, to celebrate their freedom from pain, suffering, want, loss, and abandonment, and to praise God for their absence of anxiety. In heaven, Christians will encounter God in an ultimate relationship and bask in what the Bible refers to as God's glory.

But God's thoughts are not ours, and God may have something in mind for Christians that will be different from all of this. Heaven may turn out to be more fulfilling than anything we could ever imagine. As suggested at the end of chapter 9, heaven may bring with it capacities of which we can only dream. We may become telepathic, able to read each other's minds, which in this life might horrify us. And, we may be able to teleport from one region of the galaxy to another, or turn water into wine and perform all sorts of other miracles. Who knows?

Perhaps in heaven each Christian will be able to do what he or she most enjoys, provided it honors God. It might be playing a grand piano, reading great books, learning to paint landscapes, or spending time with loved ones at the seashore. Maybe it will be cooking gourmet meals, restoring vintage cars, or playing videogames. Heaven may involve serving others in a way that is devoid of egocentricity, self-absorption, or expectation of return. All this too is speculation. For now, we live by faith with only partial knowledge. Depending on our fates, if heaven turns out to be eternally desiring that which we already have, hell may be not having what we should never have desired in the first place.

Christians believe God will not let them cease to exist and that God created human beings for their joy as well as God's. In the fable of Pinocchio,[16] a woodcarver named Geppetto longs for a child. He creates a marionette who, at the end of the story, becomes a real live boy. Like

---

15. Buber, *I and Thou*.
16. Collodi, *The Adventures of Pinocchio*.

CHAPTER 21. IS THERE LIFE AFTER DEATH?

Geppetto, God wants us to become real live *persons* who will spend eternity with Christ. It is for this purpose that Jesus went to the cross.

Closing Thoughts

Producing vast quantities of energy by splitting atoms in a small amount of radioactive material seemed like science fiction a hundred and fifty years ago. So did the idea that viruses cause disease. Although these two examples have to do with physical phenomena, the line between the physical and the spiritual may be less a wall than a curtain. Absence of proof for the resurrection is not proof it never happened. Some theologians believe those who reject Christ will cease to exist after death. Others believe everyone will end up in heaven. Still others insist there is a hell, although they disagree about its nature. Heaven, Christians believe, will bring with it continuity of consciousness and personal identity, interpersonal relationships, and above all joy.

Preview

The substructure of faith are those beliefs on which it is based. We next turn our attention to an outline of some basic affirmations to which Christians subscribe.

Part IV. **TRANSFORMATION IN CHRIST**

Chapter 22. Important Christian Beliefs

CHRISTIANITY IS EXPANDING RAPIDLY in Asia and the Southern Hemisphere, to which its center of gravity has shifted.[1] Its modes of expression in that hemisphere often differ from what you are likely to find in Europe or North America. The forms Christianity take continually change, and it is not always easy to tell, among groups of professing Christians, which differences are significant. Nor is it possible to determine with certainty that someone is or is not a Christian, since only God knows anyone's heart.

Sin is humanity's serious affliction. Christians understand it to refer to offenses against God and other people. Because the word sin can sound stuffy and perhaps bring to mind self-righteous Pilgrims in Hawthorne's *Scarlet Letter*, it is tempting to substitute for it terms like *wrongs* or *misdeeds*. Such alternatives, however, run the risk of trivializing the seriousness of sin and the extent to which it affects human behavior. Christians believe we need a way to remove our responsibility for sin and something to equip us with the power to resist it in the future. This something is Jesus and God's Spirit.

Before reviewing beliefs that are at the heart of Christianity, I want to discuss a major change that has occurred in Western Society. From nearly everyone taking Christian beliefs to be self-evidently true, large segments of society now view them as irrelevant, ridiculous, or harmful.

---

1. See Marty, *Protestantism*.

The Erosion of Belief in Western Culture

As people over the past few centuries began increasingly to back away from the church, secular alternatives to Christianity emerged. During the transition from the Middle Ages to modernity, in the fifteenth century the European Renaissance took place. It spawned a rapid uptick in artistic activity. In Italy and beyond, it also sparked a desire to revive the glory of ancient Rome. One would have to try hard not to feel awed by the beauty of paintings produced by Renaissance masters like Leonardo, Michelangelo, or Caravaggio. The Renaissance was a time of creativity and prosperity that brought with it the wealth and leisure necessary to further civilization. But it caused some to back away from the church, and even if they continued faithfully to attend mass, they began to take religion less seriously.

The Renaissance led to three overlapping developments that helped move society even further away from faith. The Scientific Revolution in the seventeenth and eighteenth centuries demonstrated the capacity of human beings to understand and predict physical phenomena. The Enlightenment, most of whose thought leaders were distinctly either non- or anti-religious, occurred at roughly the same time and focused attention on secular intellectual activity. Some of its leading figures were vocal in rejecting theism, with its belief in a God who acts in history and interacts with people, in favor of deism with its belief in a creator who does neither of these things. The Industrial Revolution that began in the late eighteenth century demonstrated the power of technology applied on a grand scale, from its ability to produce massive quantities of cloth in mechanized factories, to transporting hundreds and soon thousands of people in railroad cars across large swaths of the country.

No reasonable person would deny the enormous benefits that have come to us because of science, technology, and industrialization. Or the long-term value of the focus on reason that began to be disseminated widely in the seventeenth century. As just one example, consider the advances in medicine that led to the powerful infection-fighting power of antibiotics. All of this was heady wine that produced the intoxicating idea that people no longer needed to rely on or have anything to do with God. Millions still attended church, and many continued to have passionate faith, but the trend away from religion was accelerating.

As more fine-grained examples of how rigorous reasoning has immensely benefited humankind, but perhaps also subtly pulled it away from Christianity, consider ideas about disease and its prevention. We now take for granted the "pathogenic theory," according to which microorganisms cause diseases from tetanus to typhoid. The history of the germ theory of disease is fascinating, especially since many of the 100,000 or so unnecessary deaths occurring annually in United States hospitals are still attributable to hospital staff not washing their hands.

Conjectures consistent with modern germ theory actually go back to ancient times, and more recently to the Persian physician Avicenna in the eleventh century. The Italian entomologist Agostino Bassi (1773–1856), based on his studies of a disease that lethally infected silk worms, seems to have been the first to state the modern germ theory and to provide empirical support for it. The discovery of microorganisms had been made earlier by Antonie van Leeuwenhoek (1632–1723) of Delft.

John Snow (1815–58), who also introduced the use of ether as an anesthetic into English surgical practice, demonstrated in 1854 that cholera, which had become epidemic, was transmitted by contaminated water coming from its Broad Street pump in London. Louis Pasteur (1822–95) put to rest the notion of spontaneous generation, according to which life forms emerge from non-life forms. He did this, in part, by demonstrating that no bacterium grows unless what it grows on is exposed to air-born microbes. German physician and bacteriologist Heinrich Hermann Robert Koch (1843–1910), who won the Noble Prize for physiology or medicine in 1905, had achievements too numerous to mention here, including isolation of the anthracis bacillus that causes anthrax, the bacillus that causes cholera, and the one that causes tuberculosis.

A story of great pathos surrounds the life of Hungarian-born obstetrician Ignaz Philipp Semmelweis (1818–65), who correctly deduced that physicians who had participated in autopsies immediately prior to attending their maternity patients triggered the often-fatal puerperal (childbed) fever. This is a form of septicemia, a systemic infection caused by pathogens or related toxins in the bloodstream. Semmelweis, who was in charge of keeping the relevant statistics, posited that the young doctors carried, on their hands, minute cadaverous particles. As head resident of a maternity ward in Vienna General Hospital, he insisted in mid-May of 1847 that physicians wash their hands in chlorinated lime. Although the germ theory had not yet been accepted, Semmelweis was clearly on the right track. The mortality rate on his ward declined dramatically. In April of that year, it had been over eighteen percent. In each of the months,

June, July, and August, it was two percent. Although these findings, largely publicized by his students, were well received in some quarters of medicine, they were misinterpreted or rejected in others, to the extent that even today you may come across use of the term Semmelweis reflex as a metaphor for the automatic rejection of new ideas because they run counter to prevailing wisdom. He was not hesitant to label his medical colleagues as murderers, and perhaps because of his aggression, he was dismissed from his position, committed to a psychiatric facility in 1865, and ironically died two weeks later of septicemia, probably caused by a severe beating received at the hands of attendants. It was left to the English surgeon Joseph Lister (1827–1912) to promote the practical application of pathogenic theory to surgical procedures, namely by insisting on sterile practices. All of these discoveries had the cumulative effect of causing some to trust science to the relative neglect of religion.

Loss of a Unifying Authority

The gradual turn away from religion during the Enlightenment morphed into spiritual Bewilderment for many. But something else was going on during the preceding centuries that also contributed to the erosion of religious belief. Although it went largely unnoticed, a slow tectonic shift had been taking place within the western psyche. Alec Ryrie, an Anglican historian at Durham University in England,[2] points out that prior to the Reformation, the church instructed people in what to believe. They might not believe all of it, but at least they lived without much religious or existential uncertainty.

That changed with the Reformation, which began in North Germany and soon spread to Switzerland, England, and Scotland. In the wake of the theological debates that ensued, and perhaps more significantly the Catholic-Protestant conflicts of the Thirty Years War, Christians could no longer look to a single institution to tell them what to believe. This, suggests Ryrie, led to religious anxiety and smoldering anger over the loss of certainty. I do not intend by this to impugn the Reformation. The church clearly needed reform. But the damage that came as an unintended consequence of the Reformation was considerable and contributed substantially to the change in western consciousness from focus on God to focus on self.

2. Ryrie, *Unbelievers: History of Doubt*.

CHAPTER 22. IMPORTANT CHRISTIAN BELIEFS

Creeds, Confessions, and Catechisms

Large groups of Christians continue to rely on creeds, confessions, and catechisms to crystalize the most important features of their beliefs. It may be helpful, therefore, to define what each one is and point to their similarities and differences. Creeds are short formal statements of what a person must believe, and be willing to declare, to be a Christian. Believers throughout the world hold that a Christian must subscribe to the Apostles' and Nicene Creeds. As mentioned in chapter 1, the contents of this book are consistent with both. Creeds highlight *in whom* a Christian believes. They have to do with the nature and work of God, Christ, and the Holy Spirit. Not intended to be exhaustive, creeds are taken to formalize what is taken to be essential.

Confessions are statements that express the distinctive beliefs and emphases of specific groups, traditions, or denominations, and in that sense are secondary to creeds. They highlight what one must believe to be a member in good standing among a particular group of Christians. Examples are the *Catechism of the Catholic Church*, the *Thirty-Nine Articles of Religion* for Anglicans, and the *Westminster Confession of Faith* for Presbyterians.

Catechisms are instructional materials based on the creeds and a particular confession, typically in question-and-answer formats. They are efficient ways to teach what those in one branch of Christianity believe and are usually well-suited for use by both adults and children. Many churches encourage, and some require, members to memorize the answers to questions contained in their catechisms.

The Undeserved Gift

God, Christians believe, is both just and loving. Because God is just, God cannot simply turn a blind eye to human detachment or rebellion. Something had to be done to absolve us of denying, neglecting, or defying our creator. Because God is loving, God gave humanity the undeserved gift of Jesus, who by taking its sins on himself, cleared the way for human beings to approach and reconnect with God.

Theologians use the term *justification* for what happens in salvation. It is important not to misunderstand this. In Christian theology, justification does not carry with it the sense that the Christian now has adequate reasons or excuses. Christians are not exonerated or acquitted, as if the judge declares that they never committed a crime or bear no responsibility for whatever damage they caused. It is more as if someone else served the time, paid the damages, and secured a pardon. That someone, of course, is Jesus.

During the Middle Ages, theologians maintained that *justification* is the result of God and the individual working together, a belief reaffirmed by the Roman Catholic Church through the eighteen-year-long Council of Trent (1545–63). This remains the official position of both Roman Catholicism and Eastern Orthodoxy. Leaders of the Reformation insisted, by contrast, that Christ's death and resurrection were enough for Christians to be justified. Martin Luther, in fact, regarded justification by faith alone as the doctrine by which the church stands or falls, and John Calvin argued that it was the hinge of the Reformation. Although different branches of Christianity disagree on whether faith alone is sufficient or exactly how Christ's death removed the consequences of sin, they all agree that through his death Jesus enabled reconciliation with God.

Christians view Jesus as the embodied or incarnate *Logos* (Word), by which they mean he was both God and human, and the usual language for this is "Word made flesh." They do not mean God inhabited a body that only appeared human, one without feet that ached or fingers that bled, but a totally human one. The God-Mortal Jesus experienced life like any other human being.

The Bible

The foundation of Christianity has always been the New Testament, which Christians take to be a continuation and fulfillment of the Old Testament. Without a Bible and theological affirmations based on it, Christianity would either disintegrate or morph into something unrecognizable. God, Christians believe, continues to communicate through the Bible, and the ideas it contains are in that sense alive. Muslims believe the *Koran* in Arabic alone to be the word of God, which is why Islamic students are taught this language. No translation is deemed suitable. Christians, on the other hand, have produced a large number of translations of the New Testament, all intended as much as possible to convey the intended meaning of the original Greek. Jews, like Christians, have also continued to translate and retranslate the Old Testament, with the same intent, to penetrate the meaning of ancient languages in order to ascertain meanings contained in the original documents. Christians take the Bible to be unlike any other set of documents and they claim it provides insight into God's nature and relationship to humanity. They believe the Bible to be the record of divine revelation and further suggest that if we come to its pages with an open mind, it will help us see the deepest realities of human existence.

Christians sometimes refer to the Bible as the written Word of God, although theologians continue to debate in what sense this is so. Few believe God dictated the Bible, as if its human authors were transcription machines. It is therefore ideal to approach each biblical document by knowing something about its context and purpose.[3]

I recall once having attended a performance of "The Physicists," a comedy by Friedrich Duerrenmatt in which there is talk of a theory of all possible discoveries. Some Christians seem to believe that the Bible contains all possible knowledge. It certainly contains all we need to know for our salvation, but few Christians believe the Bible contains everything we need to know. The Bible is not, for example, an archaeology textbook. It is pointless and off-putting for religious people to carry on about how God created the world in six calendar days, which only serves to alienate educated people who might otherwise be open to Christianity.

As we saw in chapter 15, the notion of an irresolvable conflict between science and religion emerged only in the late 1800s. It was promoted by two men in the nineteenth-century, Draper and White, and later by early twentieth-century Christians who called themselves fundamentalists. Some of the early fundamentalists believed there was no conflict between scientific and religious truth, and several accepted a version of Darwinism. It was later fundamentalists who gave the term its contemporary connotations.[4] Principe points out that the revered early-fifth-century theologian Augustine argued for both *Credo ut intellegam* ("I believe in order to understand") and *Intellego ut credam* ("I understand so that I may believe"). The church has traditionally held that there are two *books*, scripture and nature, and that Christians must study both.

Primacy, according to Christian theology, is to be given to scripture, but this assertion is not meant to support rigid biblical literalism, much less *fideism*, blind faith without regard to or even disparagement of reason. In 1998, Pope John Paul II issued a much-publicized

---

3. The discipline having to do with methods of interpretation is *hermeneutics*.
4. See Principe, *Science and Religion*, Lectures 2 and 3.

encyclical entitled *Fides et ratio* (Faith and Reason), which emphasizes the importance of both faith and reason. In a treatise written in 1615 to the Dowager Grand Duchess Christina, Galileo quipped that the Bible shows us how to go to heaven, not how the heavens go.

Reflective Christians believe that the Bible, while neither a biology, geology, nor astronomy textbook, is a trustworthy guide to the nature of God and what God desires of us. This is what they mean when they claim the Bible to be scripture. To call something scripture means, at a minimum, that it is sacred writing. But what this means is open to interpretation. Perhaps a good sidewalk definition is that scripture is whatever, in written form, God played a direct, in contrast to an indirect, role in crafting. This does not mean that God dictated the words, only that the Holy Spirit actively guided the thoughts of the writer as he set down those words. Although they differ among themselves regarding what parts of the Bible to take literally and what parts metaphorically or allegorically, thoughtful Christians usually agree on the essentials. There are interpretive differences, but these are of secondary importance.

When they read Genesis, for example, some Christians take the story of Adam and Eve literally. Others may picture two concrete individuals, but if pressed would allow that they are probably symbolic. As another example, some take the conversations between God and Satan in the book of Job to have taken place as written, while others read them as poetry containing important truths relating to God's sovereignty and the problem of evil. As a third example, some insist Jonah survived three days in the belly of a large sea creature, while others take the book of Jonah to be a parable. None of this is central to the principal message of the Bible: God in Christ redeeming people. It may be best to refrain from dogmatically insisting that none of them happened. When I read these portions of the Bible, I visualize real people and events, but I spend no time worrying about whether they are literal or figurative.

Scripture and Tradition

Central to much of Protestantism is Luther's insistence on the principle of *sola scriptura*, that we understand God only through scripture, which is taken to be the sole guide to faith and practice. For Luther, the central message of the New Testament is clear enough for anyone to see. A corollary is that people need no ecclesiastical authority to explain the gospel.

Luther does, however, insist that the church needs well-trained clergy to interpret the Bible properly and therefore to get doctrine right.

Within a few years of Luther's trial in 1521, it became apparent that Protestants did not always agree on what the Bible taught. Some of their differences were of minor importance, but others led to major controversies, and eventually to the fractionation still glaringly evident within Protestantism. A joke with some truth to it is that, as soon as two people in a Protestant congregation disagree, one of them starts a new church on the next corner.

Although many Protestant associations and denominations have ruling bodies to mediate disputes, there is no overarching Protestant authority to bring all of them into alignment and agreement. Because some groups within Protestantism are closely affiliated but not formally part of an official denomination, the term association is more appropriate for them. The freedom of the individual to make sense of scripture, guided only by the Holy Spirit, is what British scientist-turned-theologian Alister McGrath refers to as Christianity's "dangerous idea."[5]

All groups of Christians have traditions, and to a great extent these determine what someone belonging to these groups can affirm without censure. The suggestion that only Roman Catholicism and Eastern Orthodoxy appeal to tradition is therefore inaccurate. Some informal traditions are more powerful than formal ones, although because formal tradition are explicit, they are more binding.

Although the Bible as sole authority for faith and practice has always been a cardinal Protestant doctrine, virtually all Protestants formally or informally recognize secondary authorities that provide eyeglasses through which congregants view scripture. Such authority is embedded within their cultures. Sometimes the secondary authorities are confessional statements, such as the Anglican *Thirty-Nine Articles* or the Presbyterian *Westminster Confession*. Depending on the sub-denomination or specific congregation, these confessions function as strong or weak authorities. Such authority is explicitly formalized in Roman Catholicism.

Differences Related to Papal Authority

There has always been a disagreement between Roman Catholicism and Eastern Orthodoxy over the Holy Spirit (see chapter 20). But the biggest

---

5. McGrath, *Christianity's Dangerous Idea*.

difference between Catholicism and both Orthodoxy and Protestantism has nothing to do with that. It has to do with the Bishop of Rome. Since the late 1800s, the Catholic Church has affirmed that when the Pope pronounces on matters of faith and morals *ex cathedra*, meaning from the papal chair, God protects him from error, and that such proclamations are infallible and operate with something resembling the force of scripture. This understanding had long been implicit within Catholicism, but Pope Pius IX formalized it in 1870 during the First Vatican Council (Vatican I). Papal infallibility does not mean that the Pope never makes a mistake. Nor does it suggest that what he proclaims *ex cathedra* can contradict the Bible. It does mean that on crucial theological matters, the Pope's pronouncements are final. Neither members of Orthodox nor Protestant churches have been willing to accept this.

God's Nature and Standards

If you believe in God, you may be inclined to believe that there is only one God. This may seem to be the only reasonable option. People in other parts of the world do not necessarily think like this. Some Hindus are monotheists who regard Brahma, Krishna, Shiva, and Vishnu as different manifestations of one God. Other Hindus, however, are pantheists who believe God is identical with the universe as a whole, while still others are polytheists and believe in several if not many gods. The precise definition of pantheism continues to be debated, but what I have written is accurate enough for our purposes.[6]

Although Christians, Jews, and Muslims believe in a single God, Christianity teaches that God exists in three persons, an understanding captured in the word *Trinity*. Christians conceive of God as an eternal three-person community or fellowship and therefore believe God to be inherently relational. According to Christianity, God has self-disclosed, through creation, nature, history, scripture, and most explicitly Jesus. Philosopher C. Stephen Evans pointed out to me that the philosopher Alvin Plantinga leaves room for God's self-disclosure via nature, natural theology, but argues that we all potentially know God through the *sensus divinitis*, a term introduced by John Calvin in the sixteenth century. It refers to an innate awareness of God that, according to Plantiga, all humans possess. Because of sin and its distorting effects on our thinking,

---

6. Mander, "Pantheism." s.v.

this sense does not operate in everyone as it should. Plantiga puts stress on the importance of *special revelation*, which is knowledge of God that comes from the Bible and what it reveals about Jesus. Special revelation stands in contrast to *general revelation*, knowledge of God available to everyone through observation and reason alone. In the person of the Holy Spirit, God operates on the human mind and heart to call people to faith. As stated above, to speak of God in personal terms such as this is probably inadequate, but it may be the best we can do as finite creatures.

Although human standards of love and justice vary, they are more alike across cultures than they are different. In whatever way a given culture defines them, its members will usually disapprove of or punish people who fail to act benevolently toward those they are supposed to love, or refuse to act justly toward those they are supposed to treat fairly. Anthropologists have long written about what they believe may be universal, or near-universal, taboos, the most often cited of which is incest. Cannibalism and patricide are also taboo in many if not most cultures. That human beings seem to regard these as fundamental, and apply standards of right and wrong to them, may reflect that God too has standards. Why should this not be so, if God created us as beings who, in the words of the Bible, bear God's image?

Christians believe God expects us to live up to certain standards. It may be impossible for God to ignore our inclination to look out for number one, treat others as objects or means to ends, or idolatrously turn ourselves into objects of worship. God, moreover, is the author of veracity and cannot therefore see us as anything other than who and what we are. Ignoring this depicts God as an over-indulgent parent who does not care enough to treat us as free moral agents who can weigh the moral or ethical implications of our actions.

The Gifts of Life, Time, Consciousness, Freedom, and Deliverance

If you ask Christians what they believe to be God's greatest gift, many will say salvation. That answer overlooks the fact that for salvation to be a meaningful idea, people must first exist. God's first and greatest gift, therefore, is life. Time is also among God's gifts. Without time, there could be no change, in which case the whole idea of choice would be meaningless.

Consciousness is another of God's gifts. The mind depends on the brain, and if the integrity of the brain is compromised, the mind will be also. No one has come up with a credible explanation of how mind (consciousness) and body (brain) interact, what philosophers call the mind-body problem. The brain is like a gyroscope. When the wheel inside the gyroscope spins, consciousness emerges. If the well-being of the brain becomes impaired, however, whether through trauma, malignancy, infection, dementia, drugs, or some other cause, it spins more slowly, and freedom of choice becomes more limited. Eventually, the wheel stops, the gyroscope tips over, and we die. But the gyroscopic effect, which is an invisible force, is not the same as the mechanical gyroscope that creates it. Consciousness remains a gift and a mystery.

Still another gift is the freedom to make decisions. We could be conscious but have no true freedom of choice, no free will. Many psychologists believe that everything we do is determined and that choice is an illusion. If I buy a gray car rather than a blue one, it is because I have been wired to buy the gray one, and if I think otherwise, I only fool myself. Christians have always believed human beings have at least limited freedom. How the gyroscope of my brain enables my mind to make free choices remains another mystery. Without freedom, not only is choice an illusion, but there could be no genuine responsibility, and it would therefore make no sense for God to hold anyone accountable for anything. Nor would it make sense for society to punish even the worse of criminals, or if they had to be incarcerated for the protection of others, not to ensure that life in prison was as comfortable as the average person's.

If we presuppose the gifts of life, time, consciousness, and freedom, we now come to the gift of salvation, which implies that there is something from which we need saving. This something is our alienation from God, other people, and ourselves. Without rescue and deliverance, we remain estranged and adrift. We may sense God exists—nature suggests as much—but without God's Spirit assisting us, we might never know much more. The Spirit enables us to see God and begin to see ourselves for who and what we are, in contrast to who and what we would like to think we are or have others believe us to be.

CHAPTER 22. IMPORTANT CHRISTIAN BELIEFS

Creation, Pre-History, and Supernatural Help

Christians believe God created the world out of nothing. This is wonderfully compatible with the Big Bang. The irony is that scientists had long assumed that matter had always existed, and they either viewed the notion of creation as a religious fantasy or lived with the tension between their religious beliefs and what they scientifically believed to be true. In 1931, however, a Roman Catholic priest, theoretical physicist, and professor at the Catholic University of Louvain theorized that the universe was expanding. He proposed the idea of a primeval atom that he later called the beginning of the world. Although the term "Big Bang" did not yet exist, that is essentially what he proposed. His theory was soon confirmed. The relevant theological point is that God was never compelled to create anything but did so out of love.

Exactly when God brought the first true human being into existence is controversial and hinges on how you define human. Informed estimates range from 40,000 to 200,000 years ago, but some scientists believe it might have been considerably longer. Humans foundered by asserting their independence from God, and we now find ourselves adrift as a species, alienated from but still responsible to a creator who does not take rebellion lightly.

It is not so much that this offends God, as if God's nose were out of joint, but that the path of self-assertion is self-defeating and discordant with the overall harmony of the universe. God cannot compel us to move closer without taking away our freedom. Human resistance to the divine puts things off kilter and disrupts the cosmic order, the deep structure discussed in chapter 6. God cannot ignore this resistance, not because he is rigid or unloving, but because of an unbreakable connection between truth and justice. The truth is that we have offended God, and the justice requires us personally or vicariously to pay for it.

As a species, we are infirmed, and without God's help, there can be no rehabilitation. At some time in the distant past, human beings succumbed to the temptation to reject God and live for themselves. They became estranged from their creator, yet responsible to God. Having become alienated from God, others, themselves, and creation, humanity lost its way and became incapable of returning to God without help. Jesus provided that help. Through his actions, teachings, crucifixion, and resurrection, he revealed God's nature and made possible a renewed connection between God and humanity. God demonstrates both divine justice and, through Jesus, divine mercy.

Justice, by holding Jesus accountable on our behalf for everything we should have done but failed to do, and everything we knew to be wrong but did anyway.[7] This is a paraphrase of Thomas Cranmer's elegant words enshrined in the Anglican *Book of Common Prayer* as, "We have left undone those things which we ought to have done, and we have done those things which we ought not to have done." Mercy, by transferring onto Jesus, who was innocent, the transgressions of we who are not. Having rebalanced the scales on our behalf, Jesus triumphed over death and continues to represent and advocate for all those who belong to him.

The Old Testament, Jesus, and the Church

The Old Testament contains the record of how God brought the world into existence and chose to interact with a given people. Both Christians and Jews believe God did this to reveal the divine nature and draw humanity away from the worship of imitation gods. In the ancient Middle East, these gods were typically primitive nature gods. Today, they can be power, fame, money, status or anything else that entices us away from loving the one true God. It is not fruitful to spend a lot of time debating how much of the Old Testament to take literally and how much metaphorically. Few theologians, for example, take the large numbers that appear in its historical books as concretely true, and tend to regard them as figurative language for something akin to "a large number of people." At the same time, only a minority of theologians regard the Old Testament as a record of Jewish imaginings of how a fantasized God interacted with them.[8]

Christians believe that the Old Testament culminates in God entering history as a man, a one-time event. The joining of divinity to humanity was an irreversible union designed to show us God's love and rescue us from death, which is the destiny of human beings apart from God. In Eastern Orthodox and Eastern Catholic churches, Christians speak of deification[9] and directly participating in God's energy and activity. There are also themes of this running through Western Catholicism.

---

7. See Jacobs, *Book of Common Prayer*.
8. See O'Day and Petersen, eds. *Theological Bible Commentary*.
9. The formal name for this is *theosis*. See Earhart, ed. *Religious Traditions*, 506–13;

CHAPTER 22. IMPORTANT CHRISTIAN BELIEFS

A key teaching of Eastern Orthodoxy is "God became Man, that men might become God." God in the person of Jesus married humanity and is in the process of expanding God's family. A haunting but unanswerable question is why God chose to do this *now*, after an eternity behind us and an eternity before us. There is the possibility that God may have created in the past, or will create in the future, other worlds. But this is blind speculation.

Jesus was the anointed or sent one, to whom the Hebrews had looked forward, the Messiah, the Deliverer. But the Jews in first-century Palestine were under oppression by the Romans. They wanted and anticipated a political leader who would help them throw off the yoke of Roman oppression and taxation, and enable them once again to be self-governing. When Jesus turned out to have no political ambitions, and in other ways to prove troublesome, the Jews and Romans killed him.[10] For a gruesome account of the crucifixion and what led to it, read *Killing Jesus*, which elucidates the political relations among Pilate, Herod Antipas, Caiaphas, and Annas, and highlights the tensions then existing between Romans and Jews. By submitting to crucifixion, Jesus launched a new age and a new order of transformed humanity, the church, and commissioned it to advance the kingdom of God on earth. That the church has at times done a terrible job of this does nothing to cancel that commission. The church, after all, is made up of sinners.

Christ's Life and Work

We are intelligent animals, which quickly becomes evident when we feel threatened. For our long-range survival and that of our species, we need a way to transcend our primal nature and its cunning duplicity. Animals tend to be territorial and predatory, but people can plan and deceive in ways no animal ever could. Even in our finer moments, we retain the potential to lapse into self-absorption, self-centeredness, and ruthlessness. This egocentricity is not just the tendency to talk too much at parties. It is more profound and has more serious consequences.

What Christian theologians call salvation implies coming to see that we have a duty to the one who created and loves us, the one who guarantees that if we accept and respond to what Christ has done, we will

---

Ware, *The Orthodox Way*; Payton, *Light from the Christian East*.
10. O'Reilly and Dugand, *Killing Jesus*.

never again have to worry about looking out for our long-term interests. Love implies caring about the welfare of the beloved. God is in the business of lovingly transforming us into persons who will be comfortable in the presence of unfiltered goodness.

That God requires us to live up to divine standards seems on its face ridiculous, simply because we cannot do it. No self-aware person can legitimately claim even to live up to the Ten Commandments, much less to Jesus' teachings in the Sermon on the Mount (Matt 5–7). Given our frailties and failings, on one hand, and God's insistence that we live up to divine standards on the other, the question becomes how exactly we are to do this. Or if we cannot, how God could accept us as we are. That God can and will is wonderful news.

For two thousand years, theologians have tried to work out exactly how, without flying in the face of divine justice, the crucifixion made it possible for God to see us in Christ, as if Christ were a lens filter that allowed God to perceive our failings as Christ's perfection. Theologians refer to this as the result of *atonement*, which becomes ours when we recognize and embrace God in Jesus. Atonement means righting wrongs and reconciling us, through Christ, to God. By going to the cross, Jesus gave us a new way to live—with a transformed heart. Through his life, death, and resurrection, Jesus became our bridge to God. The existence of that bridge is what Christians call grace, which is what distinguishes Christianity from other religions. Grace means receiving God's favor, even though we cannot claim on moral grounds to deserve it.

Responding to Jesus means, however imperfectly, glimpsing into God's mind and taking on faith that we will someday understand what we now do not. We may be able to understand why God built ambiguity into human existence, but we will never be able to make sense of evil, or as it is sometimes called, the problem of pain. How we respond to God when evil is so palpably present may be the ultimate test of faith.

Two Pivotal Beliefs

The concept of Christ as our savior rests on two important beliefs. This is because being humanity's savior requires a being who is both divine and human. No mere mortal is up to the job. Christians believe the biblical claim that Mary conceived and gave birth to Jesus, whose father was not a human being but God. It can be difficult to believe in the incarnation, but it was just as difficult two thousand years ago. Jesus' identity as the savior of humanity hinges on this miracle. It also hinges on the reality of the resurrection. Because of the horrors of a crucifixion and the result it guaranteed, Jesus was clearly dead, and the ordinary processes of what happens to a human body after death no doubt began immediately. But God reversed all this and brought Jesus back to life, not as a ghostly spirit but as a living person with a transformed body. Biblical accounts of the resurrection are exceedingly detailed, and the entire New Testament certifies the unwavering conviction that Jesus came back to life and that God directly caused this. By embracing the resurrection as something that actually occurred, Christians proclaim Jesus to be the Lord of the dance.

Some theologians, such as the New Testament scholar Rudolf K. Bultmann (1884–1976), attempt to divorce faith from history, and so suggest that only the life and death of Jesus, not his resurrection, is necessary for Christian faith. Bultmann does suggest, correctly, that to demand of anyone acceptance of any secondary belief has the potential to turn faith into a "work." Various bodies of Christians have unwittingly thrown obstacles in the path of those on their way to finding God. Sometimes these obstacles are requirements that state or at least imply that to become a Christian, one must accept some secondary belief. Other times, the obstacles have been demands to change some feature of one's behavior, such as not playing cards, dancing, smoking, drinking, or gambling. Still other times, they have been a demand to change one's sexual orientation or romantic practices, or to engage in a particular religious ritual, such as baptism by immersion in contrast to sprinkling. Although Christians should be as clear and unmuddied as possible in their personal and corporate convictions, they should never impede the progress of those who seek God by placing on them demands that, while perhaps desirable in themselves, such as not smoking or drinking to excess, can amount to a boulder hung around a seeker's neck (see Mark 9:42 and Luke 17:2). But when it comes to the resurrection of Christ, it seems odd to grant central significance to something that supposedly never happened, which is what theological demythologizers like Bultmann appear to do.

The crucifixion and resurrection would have accomplished nothing had Jesus not obeyed God. He asked to be released from what he was about to endure, but his death and resurrection were necessary. In aligning himself with the Father's will, rather than yielding to the human desire to survive, Jesus defeated death. By dying willingly and sacrificially, he demonstrated God's love and the immutability of the justice of God, who shows mercy in the face of our frequent lack of it. The Nicene-Constantinopolitan Creed asserts Jesus to be the "only-begotten Son of God, begotten from the Father before all time, Light from Light, true God from true God, begotten not created, of the same essence [reality] as the Father, through whom all things came into being."[11] Because of Christ, the way is open for us to walk across the bridge that he, in fact, is.

Implications of Reconnecting

Christianity teaches that when a person moves toward God, it is because God's Spirit beckons. The Spirit enables people to begin to understand how, without a relationship with God, they remain covert insurrectionists, and it is this Spirit who motivates the turn-about that theologians refer to as conversion. When people respond to God by grasping who Jesus was, and why, the Spirit takes up residence within their minds and begins to shape their desires. It is the Spirit who speaks through the pages of the Bible and who motivates Christians to share with others the good news of God's love. When a person declares Jesus to be the supreme authority, that person approaches life with new eyes and a new heart.

Reconnecting with God involves the repair and restoration of a disordered relationship. This reconciliation involves giving up the demand that God explain things to us, including why innocent people suffer. It implies giving up our resistance and moving toward God, finally coming home. God initiates this reconciliation by opening our hearts to accept God's offer of adoption and eternal citizenship. If we accept and respond to it, we become Christ's brothers and sisters. We henceforth relate to God in a way we did not before, as creatures who acknowledge and respond to God's holiness. The word *holiness* means many things, such as *flawless moral beauty*. Unless we harden ourselves against the Spirit, we now want to live according to divine purposes, not just our own. We will never, in this life, be free of the tendency to rebel, but those who love God will never again be able to do this without conflict. Old habits die hard, and the journey toward spiritual maturity, what theologians call *sanctification*, may proceed slowly. But those who have met the risen Christ attempt to live as Jesus did and have others see God's presence in them. "Like the lamp, you must shed light among

---

11. See Leith, ed. *Creeds of the Churches*, 33.

your fellows, so that, when they see the good you do, they may give praise to your Father in heaven" (Matt 5:16, REB).

Why Joining a Church Is Important

Christians have always maintained that it is important to be part of a church. Many people have a strong aversion to organized religion, which is understandable, given the scandalous transgressions of some members of the clergy. Because of the widespread availability of news, turbo-boosted by social media, infractions that in prior centuries would have been little known are now widely publicized.

God is continually forming and purifying the church, which consists of every Christian on the planet. As the creed of AD 381 puts it, "one holy, catholic, and apostolic church." The Bible refers to this as Christ's body. No matter how flawed, frail, and feckless, or temporarily hindered by scandal, that body consists of a revitalized humanity made up of those who have acknowledged their need for God and embraced Jesus. Participation in a church reminds us of what God has done for us, in and through Christ, and repeatedly draws us away from our natural egocentricity and toward the creator who loves us.

The Spirit works in and through the church to make God known and help people respond to God's graciousness. It also teaches that we have a duty to meet human needs, relieve misery, and strive for justice. The church has the privilege and responsibility of helping people understand God's nature and work, and to minister to them through its sacraments, which Christians take to be a visible means of invisible grace. Although ecclesiastical bodies differ about which rites qualify as sacramental, most believe that sacraments signify and confer spiritual blessings on those to whom they are administered.

Centuries before Jesus, the Greek word that English Bibles translate as church[12] referred to a gathering of citizens in a city-state such as Athens or Sparta, for the purpose of allowing them to debate and vote on matters of general concern. Just as the Jewish term *synagogue* later referred both to a group of people and the place where they met, *church* referred to those who embraced Jesus as Lord. It only later came to designate a building.

---

12. *Ekklesia*, Latinized as *ecclesia*, is the Greek term translated in English Bibles as *church*.

Paul routinely used the term to refer to a local congregation, and there were likely several congregations in such large urban centers as Jerusalem and Ephesus. Corinth, for example, was located on an overland trade route, between the Aegean and Adriatic Seas, that allowed merchants to avoid navigating the unpredictably treacherous waters around the southern tip of Greece. Today, this trading route is a modern canal through which large cargo ships pass. Corinth was once a thriving and sophisticated port city with easy access to the mainland (Attica) and southern Greece (Peloponnese). Paul recognized that Christians in Corinth remained Corinthians and that they therefore had two identities, one spiritual and the other regional. They would be most at home in Corinthian culture, which would have differed from the culture to the north in Thessalonica. But both groups had more culturally in common than either had with Christians in Rome, Jerusalem, Antioch,[13] or Ephesus. All of them, however, would have made the same key affirmations about Jesus as the Christ, and stood against the immorality that Paul sternly criticized in the lives of some Corinthian Christians.

Christians sometimes insist that anyone believing in Christ must belong to their branch of Christianity. Many people mistakenly believe that, according to Roman Catholicism, a person must be Catholic to have eternal life and go to heaven, which is incorrect.[14] The branches of contemporary Christianity, particularly within Protestantism, often resemble cultural preferences more than theological differences. Certain branches encourage emotional expression, while others discourage it. Some have tightly structured services, while others worship casually. Whether they choose to become Anglican, Baptist, Catholic, Lutheran, Methodist, Orthodox, Pentecostal, Presbyterian, or join another branch may be less important than that they join one. If fixed forms of worship (liturgy) feel too formal, it would be better to join a more casual church than no church at all. If it does not feel quite right for clergy to look like they are about to attend a luau, it might be better to attend a church led by clergy who dress more formally or don vestments. If it feels better to worship by singing choruses, a congregation that makes this central to its worship might be best. The important thing is to affiliate with a congregation that does not deviate from what the church at large has taught for two thousand years, one that proclaims Jesus to be both savior and Lord.

---

13. See "Antioch," *Dictionary of the Bible*, 36–37.
14. Joseph Arsenault, "Catholics and Heaven." s.v.

CHAPTER 22. IMPORTANT CHRISTIAN BELIEFS

Christian Hope

Many people feel stuck, caught between wanting to believe there is a purpose to life and the haunting dread that there might not be. They may sense themselves suspended between the desire for hope and the need to be appropriately cautious. If there is no God, we are forced to face the harsh and inevitable reality that we will die without hope, and our journey on the way to Samarra could be lonely and bleak. Christianity insists that there is a God who is in the process of rescuing people, and that Christ will complete this rescue by bringing the dead back to life, judging them according to what they have done, and enabling those united to him to enjoy an everlasting mode of existence. People who accept God's offer of deliverance through Christ become part of God's everlasting realm. They will someday acquire resurrected bodies and live forever. God adopts all those who commit themselves to Christ, enabling them to call God *father* as Jesus did.

When it comes time to die, the Christian hope and expectation is to be able to face death in the conviction that Christ has cancelled its permanence. Like other Christians, I believe there will be something akin to continuity of consciousness, and that someday I will enjoy a state of existence the Bible calls heaven. Since my sense of who I am depends on my memories of what I have thought, felt, said, and done, and since these memories change over time, the idea of continued personal identity is not without its philosophic difficulties. In some sense I cannot fathom, there might be a new "I" that incorporates all of this. God's Spirit continually works to prompt us to confront our failings and respond with gratitude to what God offers: forgiveness for the sin of pride and self-centered living; acceptance into God's invisible family; and resurrection into a being who is not genetically preprogrammed to die. Christians look forward to heaven, whatever that turns out to be, and to Jesus bringing to perfection everything that has been entrusted to him by God.

Closing Thoughts

We are sinners in need of salvation through a savior who has atoned for our rebellion and defiance, serves as our bridge to God, and equips us with the potential to overcome the curse of self-centered existence. God gave us Jesus as an undeserved gift. Although Christians disagree about the role of good works in salvation, they agree that through his death

Jesus reconciled us to God. Christianity is grounded in the New Testament, which Christians take to be a trustworthy guide to God's nature and what God desires for and from us. They differ, however, in whether the Bible by itself is sufficient or if church tradition is also needed. Questions about the relationship between God and Christ were settled by the fifth century, with the church affirming that God exists as Father, Son, and Holy Spirit. Belief in the miraculous birth of Jesus and his physical resurrection are defining characteristics of Christianity, which without them is eviscerated. Christ inaugurated a new age and launched a new humanity. He commissioned his followers to work together with God, through the church, to make God's kingdom on earth a reality.

Preview

There is an awkward truth flowing through Christianity. It is the need for us to come to grips with what we have done and failed to do, and more fundamentally with who and what we are. Few of us want to do this, but to become and live as a Christian, it is necessary.

Chapter 23. Awkward Realities

IT IS EASY TO offend others by expressing religious beliefs. Many people hesitate to express such beliefs because, like politics, religion can be a touchy subject. When it comes to discussing Christianity, however, not bringing it up deprives others of the chance to respond to God through Christ. The gospel is likely to offend anyone who insists on rejecting God and remaining a rebel, since it requires surrender, and having to do this can wound human pride. We tend to admire people who are self-reliant and refuse to surrender, perhaps because it implies weakness. Surrender, however, is what God requires.

No one ever became a Christian through star-gazing or detached nonchalance. Accepting God's offer to adopt us in Christ is rarely a dispassionate exercise, the sort of thing you might do while dozing off on a blanket in the park or in a beach chair. We are not naturally inclined to accept this offer, and becoming a Christian often involves crisis. *Crisis* comes from a Greek verb meaning to separate, decide, judge, or discriminate. Physicians in the late Middle Ages used it to refer to the turning point in a disease, when the afflicted individual was at the point of living or dying. In the early 1600s, the word took on the more general meaning of a decisive moment. Moving toward God for many people becomes an inflection point. For some, the call to faith extends over years, during which friends or relatives may pray for them. For others, it can be almost instantaneous. Whether gradual or sudden, becoming a Christian opens our minds and brings new insight.

Owning Up

The idea of surrender can seem out of place in the twenty-first century because of its emphasis on autonomy and self-determination. But surrender remains at the center of Christianity. The *repentance* that accompanies it can be difficult. When some people hear that word, they immediately think of people on street corners holding up religious signs. The *Oxford English Dictionary* defines repentance as a "change in one's mind through regret about past action or conduct." The *American Heritage College Dictionary* offers, "To make a change for the better . . . as a result of remorse or contrition."

English Bibles translate two related Greek words from the New Testament as repentance: *metanoia* and *metalomai*. In classical Greek, *metanoia* meant to change one's mind or heart, and when this term is used in the New Testament, it takes on the additional meaning of altering one's purpose and future direction. Repentance means facing who and what we are, which for a Christian entails a change in worldview. It involves a transformation in how we perceive God and other people, and it therefore involves attitudinal, intellectual, and emotional realignments. The Anglican *Book of Common Prayer* includes the statement, we are "truly sorry for our sins."[1] In uttering these words, the focus still remains on God. It is this redirection of focus toward God and away from self that, more than its emotional components, characterizes repentance. Even those with limited mental ability appear to have the capacity for this. Coming to grips with how we have failed to live up to what God desires is, by definition, only something we can do in relation to a being who is conscious and has both intentions and standards. Repentance is only meaningful when we realize we have disappointed and aggrieved a personal God.

God is not a distant scrooge who wants to deprive us of joy, but an involved creator who wants us to come to our senses. Reckoning honestly with ourselves is likely to prompt us to make different choices and act in new ways. We may, for example, refrain from snapping at someone who has injured us, not because we worry that God that will punish us but because we have a new awareness of who we are, who God is, what God has done for us through Jesus, and that the other person is God's creation. Owning up involves looking in the mirror and seeing, not the fine person we have believed ourselves to be, but the rebel we have always been.

---

1. *Book of Common Prayer*, 352.

CHAPTER 23. AWKWARD REALITIES

There are three ways we can orient ourselves in relation to another being: toward, against, and away. Becoming a Christian is to become repositioned toward God and Christ, and it is this repositioning that characterizes Christian life. Acknowledging our faults and frailties is necessary for such repositioning, which means admitting that we have rebelled. It is our rebellion, above all, with which we must reckon. It may be active and defiant, or passive and neglectful, but it nonetheless exists in all of us.

As humans, we prefer to think that, while we may have done a few bad things here and there, we did the best we could. We prefer to believe that whatever wrong we have done fails to reflect our true nature, and that when we behaved badly, we were not quite ourselves. This self-assuring conclusion glosses over our central problem, which is the condition of our hearts. However noble we may otherwise be, we have a built-in disposition toward rebellion.

It is from a relentless focus on ourselves that God's Spirit can rescue us, but only if we allow it, and we will allow it only if we are willing to face ourselves. Christian repentance means coming to terms with how, until now, we have lived disconnected from God. Having gone our own way, we have lived out the self-indicting words of a popular song, "I Did It My Way." Although doing it our way allows us to imagine that we are living heroically, in truth it only accentuates what Unamuno calls the "tragic sense of life."[2] Owning up allows us to make peace with God, and perhaps for the first time to understand our place in the universe. Rather than continuing to live with a gnawing awareness of the inevitability of death, and perhaps resenting that life has not dealt us better cards, we reckon with who we are, and are not, and embark on a new relationship with God through Christ.

We can avoid coming to terms, but not if we want God to transform us into people with fresh eyes and renewed vision. Such avoidance is understandable. Few of us are eager to hop on an operating table. But someone with heart disease would be foolish not to do so, if the right operation by the right doctor would save his or her life. God, as it turns out, is the perfect heart surgeon, in fact, the only heart surgeon.

In a novel about the human heart, the narrator utters these sorrowful words of self-reflection:

---

2. Unamuno, *Tragic Sense of Life*.

I [think about how easily they accepted me into their home] which makes my treachery all the worse. I, who intended... nothing but harm... was welcomed into their lives; and I accepted their hospitality as Judas might have accepted Christ's at the Last Supper: duplicitously, deviously, deceitfully.[3]

I find that passage sobering. It brings to mind the following modified passage from the *Book of Common Prayer*:

> Most merciful God,
> I confess that I have sinned against you
> in thought, word, and deed,
> in what I have done,
> and by what I have left undone.
> I have not loved you with my whole heart;
> I have not loved my neighbors as myself.
> I am sorry and repent.
> For the sake of your Son Jesus Christ,
> have mercy on me and forgive me;
> that I may delight in your will,
> and walk in your ways,
> to the glory of your Name.[4]

It is not just that we have done things for which we may be sorry but that we are flawed. Many people have moments of moral excellence, for example when they stand up for the underdog, speak in favor of an unpopular but worthy cause, or even risk their lives to save someone in danger. Despite such moments, we all tend to lapse back into selfism,[5] into what's-in-it-for-me. Until we come to terms with this, we remain estranged.

Killing Lizards

The Great Divorce[6] is a fantasy about a busload of ghost-like people from hell who take a weekend excursion to heaven. But they find it

---

3. Mason, *The Drowning People*, 223.
4. *Book of Common Prayer*, 79.
5. See Vitz, *Psychology as Religion*.
6. Lewis, *The Great Divorce*, 98–101.

CHAPTER 23. AWKWARD REALITIES

unpleasantly solid. The narrator, who resides in heaven, sees one of the visitors moving toward him. On the visitor's shoulder sits a lizard, twitching its tail and whispering in his ear. An angel asks if the visitor would like the reptile quieted, and the visitor enthusiastically answers that indeed he would. When the angel offers to kill it, however, the ghostly being questions whether such an extreme measure is necessary, whether this is the only way to be rid of it, and he wonders if "the gradual process" might not be better. But the angel informs him that such a process would be no good at all. The ghostly creature then indicates that he would gladly let the angel kill the reptile, only not now, since he is not feeling quite himself, adding, "Why didn't you kill the damned thing without asking me?" To this the angel replies, "I can't kill it against your will." Like that ghost, we may worry about what is to become of us if we decide to ask God to kill our lizards.

What if, when it is all over, I am not the same person? What if I lose my identity, if I end up having to give up everything that makes me who I am, everything distinctive, everything that gives me character and personality? When we identify too closely with our occupations, station in life, or any of a thousand other things that serve as props, we run the risk of ending up empty when life strips them away. Almost anything in which we pride ourselves, from superior opinions to inflated piety, can be a reptile that needs extermination. Central to Christian faith is the willingness to allow God to kill our lizards.

Regardless of how we spend our time, we all run out of it. Every moment is therefore of infinite worth and eternal significance. Most of us live between sixty and eighty-five years, which comes to between 22,000 and 31,000 days. These days constitute a bank account of available moments, around a third of which we spend sleeping. Of the moments that remain, we use many of them trying to survive. We eat, drink, bathe, and attend to personal needs. As we grow up, we may work, go to school, take our car in for servicing, and so on. This still leaves us with a great many discretionary moments. None of us knows how many we have left. Life is like a line of credit that will eventually be called in. People die from heart attacks and strokes. Or, they undergo a routine physical exam, only to discover they have cancer.

Becoming a Christian means risking the valuable resources of time and free mental space. If there is no God, becoming a Christian means committing yourself to a delusion that uses up these non-renewables. Building a life in cooperation with God means paying what economists call opportunity costs. Paying an opportunity cost means foreclosing on other opportunities. A Christian will have less time to accumulate money or increase power, and if Christianity is a dream based on a hoax, paying these costs would be folly.

If, however, Christianity is based on truth, the greatest opportunity cost of them all would be to ignore Jesus' call, "come to me" (Matt 11:28, ESV). If Jesus was but a man, these words are meaningless. But if they embody an invitation from God, saying no is like a starving beggar refusing to attend a banquet. The New Testament confronts us with a paradox. The person who tries to hold on to a life crafted apart from God will find that it evaporates, while the person who lets go of such a life in partnership with God will discover that it endures.

Facing the Awkwardness

Regardless of the words we use, it is with our sin[7] that we must reckon if we are to experience transformation in Christ. The word *sin* comes from the Greek *amartia*, which means to err or miss the mark, as an archer might in shooting at a target. Here are a few definitions of sin: In a Catholic dictionary, we read, "Any thought, word, or deed that deliberately disobeys God's will and . . . rejects the divine goodness and love."[8] A Protestant dictionary defines sin as, "Any act, attitude, or disposition that fails to completely fulfill or measure up to the standards of God's righteousness."[9] Those in the Orthodox tradition stress how sin destroys *koinonia*, communion and fellowship with God, other people, and nature. It reduces the divine likeness of human beings.[10]

Most of us remember when we did the wrong thing or neglected to do the right one. Becoming a Christian demands a penitent heart. It requires that we face the bad we have done and the good we have not, and also requires us to set things right whenever possible. At the core of repentance is coming to terms with how sin operates as a process within us. The idea that, rooted deep within, is a dynamic or process of sin was emphasized by the Chinese evangelist Watchman Nee (1903–72), who

---

7. The study of sin is technically called *hamartiology*. See Berkouwer, *Sin*.
8. O'Collins and Farrugia, *Concise Dictionary of Theology*, 243–44.
9. Erickson, *Concise Dictionary of Christian Theology*, 182.
10. Wikipedia, "Eastern Orthodox View of Sin." https://en.wikipedia.org/wiki/Eastern_Orthodox_view_of_sin.

drew attention to what he called the "sin principle."[11] We are not sinners because we sin; we sin because we are sinners. Sin is a chronic ailment, a condition, a disease.

Where Repentance Leads

Christian transformation involves relating to God through Jesus in a way that leads to an ethical and moral makeover. But it will never change us into angelic beings. In bringing into sharp relief our lust for power, Nietzsche was right, only instead of viewing it as a regrettable flaw, he endorsed it as an attribute of nobility. In the twentieth century, Ayn Rand did much the same thing in her advocacy of the "virtue of selfishness." To see the tragic position in which trying to live this out left her, read the account by a psychologist's wife based on Rand's affair with him.[12] We always potentially remain both beasts and angels. Life as a Christian amounts to falling on our faces, again and again, and getting up each time, once again to see Jesus.

When we face our natures and embrace Christ as Lord, God's Spirit sets us on the road to becoming renewed persons. That Spirit now lives in us and we can henceforth participate in God's ongoing existence. When we ask Jesus to become our Lord, things change, and with God's help the vicissitudes of life become less likely to unravel us. Jesus promised, "I will not leave you as orphans" (John 14:18, NLT).

Some of us imagine ourselves in a stadium, down in the center of the field, with the stands filled with anonymous accusers pointing down and shouting, "God couldn't possibly forgive you for *that*!" No one else can hear them, but we can, and our imaginary stadium can become a torture chamber. One of the names for the devil in the New Testament is Accuser. Jesus stands ready to clear out those stands and evict the Accuser.

Becoming a child of God and a brother or sister of Christ means accepting that God wants to adopt us. The Bible uses the metaphor of God as Father and tells us that without God we remain ultimately alone. When we become a Christian, God begins to change us from what we once were, to what we will someday be. God does this by taking up residence within us. In one of his letters, Paul asks his readers

---

11. Nee, *Normal Christian Life*, 25–26.
12. Branden, *Passion of Ayn Rand*. A film of the same name starred Helen Mirren.

PART IV. TRANSFORMATION IN CHRIST

if they have forgotten that they are temples of the Holy Spirit who now lives in them (1 Cor 6:19).

Embracing God in Christ is not a self-improvement program. It is not like joining a gym or going on a diet. Nor does it amount to trying harder to be nicer, which can be a veiled attempt to feel virtuous and deserving. We are neither of these. Nor can we earn God's grace. Earned grace, by definition, is not grace. God loves us, not because of the good we do, but in spite of the good we fail to do. The gospel is not only that God loves us, but that God loves us anyway.[13] Not only that, but God suffers when we do, which may make it easier to come to terms with the problem of evil.

If you have difficulty believing some part of Christian doctrine, do not let this stop you. Think of the story in the New Testament of the worried father who cries to Jesus, "help my unbelief" (Mark 9:24, NRSV). Another way to render this passage might be, "Lord, I have faith . . . help me have more."

You may have trouble believing that Mary had no sexual intercourse before conceiving Jesus. Or, wrapping your mind around the idea of his resurrection. Maybe the miracles in the New Testament do not seem credible to you. Perhaps there is something in your life that you believe makes you unacceptable to God, something the fine upstanding citizens down the street would condemn you for, something you believe you must first fix. If so, bear in mind how C. S. Lewis suggests that some prostitutes are closer to the kingdom of God than the prigs in church.[14] You do not have to do or be anything, beyond facing yourself and responding to God's love. Do not worry about the rest. The important thing is to recognize who Christ is, which you can best do by immersing yourself in the New Testament. Keep in mind the opening words of a hymn, written by Charlotte Elliot in 1835, "Just as I am, without one plea." You do not have to qualify for God's love, rescue, and deliverance. Nor do you have to be virtuous. You need only accept the divine love. God will take care of the rest.

---

13. See McLemore, *Honest Christianity*.
14. Lewis, *Mere Christianity*.

Closing Thoughts

Repentance, the doorway through which all Christians must pass, involves coming to terms with the wrong you have done and the good you should have done. We all have long lists of both. It means sorrow for past sins, confronting who and what you are, and relying on God to help you become more and more like Jesus. Repentance is turning away from dispositions, attitudes, and actions that pull you away from God. Becoming a Christian involves risk. If Christianity is true, it would be tragic not to take that risk. God has given us the gift of Christ. All we need do is respond in gratitude to that gift.

Preview

In the next chapter, I am going to suggest what it means to become a Christian.

Chapter 24. Becoming a Christian

SOMEONE MAY HAVE URGED you, at some time in your life, to believe in Jesus and accept Christ. He or she may have asked if you have been saved. Such questions may be intrusive. Regardless of the awkwardness of their approach, many such people care. They know Jesus as their Lord and want others to know him too. People sometimes associate phrases like *believing in Jesus, accepting Christ,* and *being saved* with televangelists or backwoods preachers. As primitive as these terms may seem, no one ever became a Christian without grasping who Jesus is, accepting Christ as Lord, and embracing God's offer of deliverance. This offer is part of what the Apostle Paul refers to as the good news.

Paul and his companion Silas are in the Roman colony of Philippi, near the northeast coast of Macedonia (Acts 16). Having angered the owners of a fortune-telling slave girl, they are thrown in jail. Around midnight, an earthquake so rattles the door of their cell that it opens, leading the jailor to conclude that, in the darkness and confusion, they have escaped. The Roman Empire did not deal kindly with negligent guards. To avoid what was likely to be a slow and painful death, he draws his sword and is about to kill himself. Paul cries out to reassure him that he and Silas are still in his custody. The jailor calls for torches by which to see, runs to Paul and Silas who no doubt had already told him about Christ, and asks what he must do to be saved. Their answer: "Believe in the Lord Jesus."

The following morning, city officials send the police to tell the jailor to release Paul and Silas. But much has taken place during the night. The jailor tended to their wounds, which were probably severe because the town's mob had flogged them, and invited the two to his home to feed them. Paul and Silas baptized the jailor and his entire household, and Luke reports they further proclaimed "the word of the Lord to them," (Luke 16:32). For two thousand years, Christians have insisted that to enjoy a relationship with God, a person must respond to that word.

Spiritual Insight

Belief implies affirmation. To believe anything is to affirm it to be true. No rational person would put faith in anything he or she does not believe. For faith in God to make sense, it must rest on knowledge of who Jesus is, what he accomplished, and how this enables us to relate to God as we otherwise could not.

There may be a kind of intelligence, if I may call it that, which is unrelated to performance in school or on tests, a spiritual awareness that God bestows on and nurtures in people through the Holy Spirit. Such intelligence implies grasping what is going on beneath the surface. Psychologists sometimes describe this as an "ah-ha" experience," the sort of thing that happens when you suddenly grasp the solution to a difficult problem. Suddenly grasping the solution to a problem was first defined by a psychologist working with primates.[1] Whether spiritual insight occurs in an instant or over a long time, it is central to becoming a Christian.

Insight, as we have repeatedly noted, is narrowing the gap between what we had assumed to be the case and what we now know it to be. A person who becomes a Christian recognizes that Jesus was no ordinary man. It is not just that Jesus was exceptional. Many people are willing to concede that he was a wise teacher who had a quick wit, told clever stories, and threw out memorable maxims. But his exceptionalism went far beyond this. Jesus was unique, *sui generis*, in a class by himself.

We read in the New Testament that Jesus was without sin (Heb 4:15) and willing to suffer for his friends.[2] Friend in this context means *disciple*, a word borrowed from a Latin term meaning *pupil*. It implies someone willing to accept instruction. The word implies to grasp intellectually and analyze thoroughly. When many of his contemporaries encountered Jesus, he impressed them as virtuous. He maintained his

---

1. Yerkes, *Mental Life of Monkeys and Apes*.
2. *Chambers Dictionary of Etymology*, "Disciple," 282.

purity, not because he never experienced temptation but because he did not yield to it. Unlike Jesus, we give in to all sorts of temptations. This, as the British might put it, is true of bum and barrister alike. Insight into this is at the core of Christian faith and is the antithesis of living without a connection to God.

Sin is like a skin disease. We may be able to hide it, but it is still there. The blemishes it creates may be small or large, tiny flecks on a painting or gaudy blotches. Whatever the nature of these blemishes, from not caring enough to help old people find their cars in parking lots, to committing major crimes, we all have them. When a person realizes that these blemishes stem from a lethal disease, it is because the Holy Spirit prompts that understanding. Unbelief is not a mere difference of opinion in the face of conflicting evidence, but a willful denial of evidence that is clear. Sin has a corrosive effect on the mind,[3] especially when it comes to religion. The most sinister of sin's effects is that it distorts a person's primary premises, and as we noted in chapter 2, these premises condition any conclusion based on them.

Accountability

Some people wonder why, if our creator can do anything, God cannot simply let bygones be bygones, forgive and forget, and ignore whatever wrong we have done. They may go as far as to suggest that if, as Christians claim, Jesus was God's son, to insist that he sacrifice himself was not evidence of love but its absence. Was it not possible for God to find another way? Even if this were possible, God chose *this* way, and it is with it, therefore, that we must come to terms.

There are things, as we have noted, that even God cannot do. For God to ignore our rebellion and estrangement would be to treat what is true as if it were not. In learning of a horrific crime, people sometimes say, "Whoever did this must be brought to justice." As psychological research has repeatedly shown, human beings gravitate toward equity. Built into us is a desire for fairness.[4] If I injure you, I will try to make up for it in some way, and if you injure me, you are likely to do the same. If we as humans expect justice, how much more might this be true of God?

---

3. This is called sin's *noetic* effect, its adverse impact on thinking and the intellect.
4. See Rawls, *A Theory of Justice*; Rawls, *Justice as Fairness*.

CHAPTER 24. BECOMING A CHRISTIAN

People can reassure themselves with statements like, "I'm doing the best I can," "No one's perfect," or "I'm better than Alex down the block." These are all beside the point, which is that we are out of alignment with the universe and the God who created it. It is not as if we are incapable of doing good, or even of doing it for a long time, but that we find it difficult to divorce benevolence from self-interest. That my flaws are greater or less than the next person's does nothing to change that I have some. Nor does it change that I have done things discordant with that objective order. Like a musician playing out of tune in a concert hall, unless someone comes on stage to put my instrument right, I could be banished from the orchestra. Jesus is that someone. He tunes the instrument to the correct pitch, abolishes my responsibility for all the bad notes, and persuades the conductor to disregard them. To become a Christian is to accept that there is an objective order to the universe, recognize that Jesus embodied it, and accept that he can and will wipe away all tears (Rev 7:17, 21:4). The consequences of sin have been folded retroactively into what, to borrow a term from physics, was a *singularity*, a one-time event. It was a transaction between God and the Son that led to the crucifixion and resurrection, to Jesus dying in our place.

Reconciliation and Its Implications

God married humanity out of a desire to commune with us. Moved by love, God addressed the problem of our estrangement by giving us Jesus. We need only acknowledge our need to be reconciled, face our flawed nature, and give God our allegiance. In the seventeenth chapter of John's Gospel, Jesus offers this prayer:

> Father, the hour has come; glorify your Son so that the Son may glorify you.... And this is eternal life, that they may know you, the only true God, and Jesus Christ whom you have sent... I have made your name known to those whom you gave me from the world... the words you gave to me I have given to them, and they have received them and know in truth that I came from you... I am not asking on behalf of the world, but on behalf of those whom you gave me, because they are yours... They do not belong to the world, just as I do not belong to the world ... I ask not only on behalf of these but also on behalf of those who believe in me through their word... Righteous Father, the

world does not know you, but I know you, and these know that you have sent me (John 17:1–25 NRSV).

Jesus was on a mission of redemption. Theologians analyze the work of Christ in terms of his priestly, prophetic, and kingly functions. He lived and died to balance the scales, to set things right with God for those willing to acknowledge Jesus for who he is and their need for him. Through his life and death, Jesus demonstrated what love looks like. It is one thing to expound on the virtues of love when you are sitting safely by a fireplace in an armchair, but quite another to sacrifice yourself for the welfare of others. Jesus put himself through an agonizing and humiliating death. He threw himself on the hand grenade of human turpitude, in order to show us the route home and established a way for us to get there.

The *logos* had been with God from eternity, and without ceasing to be one with God, that *logos* entered space and time as a man and subjected himself to crucifixion. Without Jesus having done this, there would be no restoration or reconciliation. It can be difficult to believe we are accepted as we are and allow God's acceptance to penetrate. There is nothing for us to do to earn it, and if we try, we run the risk of rejecting God's grace.

Evil and the Unseen

A Christian is obliged to concede the possibility that there exists a supernatural being with malevolent purposes. C. S. Lewis was an Oxford Don and later a Cambridge Professor. He became a Christian when he was about thirty. Initially, he did not take the idea of a devil seriously. But, as reflected in his *Screwtape Letters*, he later became convinced that a devil did exist. The existence of the devil is an explicit or implicit part of most Christian statements of faith.

If two hundred years ago, I told you that tiny organisms, and even tinier bits of DNA or RNA encased in proteins, were capable of causing disease, you would have concluded I at least needed a better education. Even physicians in the 1800s insisted that diseases such as cholera were caused by bad air, *miasma*. Today, we would question the education of anyone who refuses to acknowledge the infectious potential of bacteria and viruses. The difference between demonstrating the existence of germs versus a devil is that you can detect germs using an electron microscope. Although I do not understand what these terms mean, there is also immunoelectron microscopy, cryo-electron microscopy, and electron tomography. There is no objective way, however, to prove or disprove the existence of a devil.

Millions of Christians pay lip service to the idea of a devil but privately believe the idea to be a carryover from the Middle Ages. There are other Christians, many of them intelligent and well-educated, who while not quick to mention the devil in conversation, suspect that evil reflects the work of a supernatural being. They take seriously a cosmic conflict between good and evil.

Spiritual Eyes and Ears

When I push God away, I construct a temporary fortress wall. That wall exists because I worry that God is not looking out for me and I must take matters into my own hands. The wall I erect to protect myself turns out to be a prison, incarcerating me in a penitentiary of potential despair. Even when I am not worried about anything in particular, I sometimes feel my muscles tighten. Often without awareness, I am bracing myself against life, against the part God has given me to play in the human drama.

Some having witnessed the resurrection of Lazarus (John 11) recognize Jesus for who and what he is. Others scamper off to report to and curry favor with political-religious leaders, the power people of the day. Oblivious to the significance of what has happened, these leaders begin to fret about threats to their power. Caiaphas, high priest that year, derides them by saying, "you know nothing." Fearing that Jesus might precipitate an insurrection, he insists that it is better for one man to die than to provoke the Romans. Caiaphas and his colleagues worry that the occupying forces might depose them in response to an uprising. Even Jesus' ability to raise the dead was not enough to bring about a spiritual awakening, to prompt those in power to recognize Jesus as the Christ. Ensnared by love of the temporary, they lose sight of the permanent. They remain benighted and develop no spiritual vision.

When Jesus speaks of seeing and hearing, as he often does in the Gospels, he refers to whether a person can see with spiritual eyes and hear with spiritual ears. To be a Christian is to recognize Jesus as the unique embodiment of God and humanity, understand how God's nature differs from yours, believe his death made it possible for you to enjoy a relationship with God, and acknowledge Christ as your Lord.

PART IV. TRANSFORMATION IN CHRIST

Closing Thoughts

Christians have accepted God's offer of salvation through Christ and deliverance from self-centered living. God's offer includes transcendence of death and eternal life. To embrace Christ as Lord means accepting him as one's supreme authority and guide. Jesus achieved for us what we could not do for ourselves and demonstrated what selfless love looks like. We need a restored relationship with our creator. Such a relationship begins with believing God loves and accepts us. Becoming a Christian involves accepting that we no longer stand accused.

Preview

A good indicator of faith is how much a Christian prays. We next take up the subject of prayer. Authentic prayer is that which aligns our will with our creator's, and allows us to think and act in partnership with God (Rom 8:28).

Chapter 25. Authentic Prayer

PRAYER DOES NOT ALWAYS come naturally. When I pray, I often do so in bits and pieces through the day, in a silent conversation with God. Some of my experiences with prayer have forced me to think through what, exactly, we do when we pray. I have also had to think about what prayer is not. God's intent is not to turn us into magicians who use prayer to do tricks, but into disciples. This has profound implications for how we pray and what we ought to pray for. Viewed one way, prayer reflects our acknowledgement of God's benevolence. Viewed another, it is how we participate, in real time, in God's existence.

One of our children wanted to attend a service academy and prayed hard for this. He was fortunate enough to obtain congressional nominations to both the Military Academy at West Point and the Naval Academy at Annapolis. To attend either one, however, he needed a waiver. Early one spring morning, he woke me up to say he had just hung up the phone. "West Point said *no*." He was crushed. Sitting up in bed, I then told him how, in my twenties, I had a cat that became seriously ill. Its condition worsened by the hour, but believing God would restore the cat to health if I had enough faith, I earnestly prayed. "You know what, Kevin?" I asked. "The damned cat *died*!" He burst out laughing, which for the moment ameliorated his sadness.

I sincerely believed the cat would live, and I was devastated. It was not that I doubted God's existence or had second thoughts about who Christ was, only that I was profoundly disappointed in God and confused about why my prayers had not had the desired effect. We do not always get what we pray for. Kevin ultimately got what he prayed for because late that spring a FedEx envelope arrived, instructing him to report to the Naval Academy for plebe summer. He is now a Bird Colonel in the Marine Corps.

Prayer as Alignment

A good way to learn something about a person's faith is to ask if he or she prays. How often, and for what or whom? We may wonder, however, why we should bother to pray at all. If God is in charge of everything, and if as some Christians insist, God ordains everything that happens, what is the point? Is prayer merely a ritual that comforts us but has no real effect?

In the Gospel of Matthew, Jesus cautions against "vain repetition" because God "knows what you need before you ask him" (Matt 6:5–8, NIV). Yet, there are other passages in the New Testament that encourage constant prayer, such as the parable of the relentless widow who, because of her persistence, convinces a judge to act on her behalf (Luke 18:1–6). We also have the example of Jesus who often separates himself from the crowds, including those he could heal, and retreats to a secluded place to pray. As a quick scan of the Gospel of Luke will attest, prayer is vitally important to Jesus.

The primary purpose of prayer is not to ask God for desirable outcomes, acknowledge shortcomings, or express appreciation for good fortune. All of these are important, but they are not its main purpose, which is to communicate with and align ourselves with God. This means sharing God's mind and participating in God's work. Like many other things in the life of a Christian, that we can do this is extraordinary. Alignment means arranging things so they are in proper relation to each other. When we pray as we ought, we want the good to prevail, but we also recognize that, ultimately, only God knows the exact contours of what that will look like. To pray properly is to grasp a key implication of the fifteenth chapter of John's Gospel, which is to remain tethered to God through the Son.

If you do not believe God has intentions, none of this will make much sense. But if you have concluded that God resembles what we mean when we use the word *person*, the idea of sharing God's mind and lining up on the side of God's overarching design may seem more reasonable. Christians sometimes draw a distinction between God's *perfect* and *permissive* wills. The former is what God wants to occur, such as people acknowledging Christ as Lord, while the latter is what God allows, quite aside from whether God desires it. Thus, although it is not God's desire for a person to become addicted to narcotics, God is not going to so restrict human freedom as to make this impossible. The goal of a Christian ought to be to align with God's perfect will.

Alignment is a meta-category of prayer, since it is the proper aim of all prayer. This is how Jesus approached it in the Garden of Gethsemane. Luke reports how, after a final meal with his disciples, they all make their way to the Mount of Olives. There, Luke informs us, Jesus "withdrew from them about a stone's throw" (Luke 22:42, REB) to pray. "Father," pleads Jesus, "take this cup from me" (Luke 22:43, REB). He means, of course, the bitter cup of an impending, unjust, and agonizing death.

Jesus knew what was coming. As a flesh-and-blood being, he desperately wanted *not* to suffer the hideously cruel and painful death of crucifixion. Crucifying criminals and other malefactors, who might take a long time to die, was a common form of execution by the Romans. They had turned crucifixion into an art form, and given its widespread use, Jesus had probably witnessed its horrors. To emphasize his fear of it, Luke adds, "in anguish of spirit he prayed the more urgently" (Luke 22:44, REB).

If we read no more deeply, we have only the account of a good man pleading with God to spare him. A cynic might say that Jesus was superstitiously begging whatever forces there were in the universe to save him in the eleventh hour, to get him out of a jam. It is important, therefore, to feel the full weight of what Luke reports as Jesus' prayer, which includes these additional words: "Father, if it be your will, take this cup from me. Yet not my will but yours be done" (Luke 22:42, REB). Or, as older translations have it, "Thy will be done," This is what it means to align with God. In the face of tragedy, we rarely grasp what God's intends. But like at the end of a mystery story, when everything suddenly falls into place, Christians believe life will turn out to have made sense. As mortals, we remain partly ignorant of God's overarching purposes, of the Grand Design.

Although theologians debate this, in the Garden Jesus may not have been fully aware of God's purposes. This touches on the question of whether Jesus, as he walked the earth, was omniscient, whether he knew everything, from what was in the heart of another person to the laws of thermodynamics. If he did, this raises the further question of when he acquired such knowledge. As an infant in the manger? An adolescent? At his baptism by John? Luke reports in his Gospel that Jesus grew in wisdom (Luke 2:52). Jesus realized that he was different and that he was the Sent One, the Messiah. But in the Garden, Jesus may have been in roughly the same position we would be if a doctor told us we were about to die. Why God, we might ask? Why this? Perhaps all Jesus knew was that he was going to be executed and that this was God's desire. On the cross, Jesus cries out, "My God, my God, why have you forsaken me?" (Matt 27:46, Mark 15:34, NRSV). Did Jesus at that point know that his death would initiate the bridge over which humans could walk to reach God? Perhaps Jesus knew it all, acquiesced to his Father's will, and completely trusted it. Luke reports his final words as, "Father, into your hands I commit my spirit" (Luke 23:46, REB). It is this acquiescence and trust that characterizes holy prayer.

Prayer is essential to our development, to becoming and remaining aligned with God. It is the necessary fuel for the engine of spiritual growth. Just as a car built to run on gasoline, hydrogen, or electricity will not run on air, prayer without allegiance to and alignment with God may accomplish nothing. Although God acts in human affairs, God does not always do this straightforwardly or in ways we deem best. However devout we may be, God is not at our disposal. God is sovereign and can therefore do whatever God pleases, and as long as we walk this earth, God's ways will remain in part unfathomable.

A Distracting Concern

It is not up to us to worry about whether praying for a hurricane to bypass our town might cause it to smash into a neighboring one, as if it had to do one or the other. Nothing prevents God from ensuring that it bypass both towns. Then again, God usually allows nature to take its course. God is not running a zero-sum casino in which one player's win is another one's loss. I try to keep in mind what Austin Farrer points out, that for life to have the character it does, it must include accidents and what may seem like random events. Although accidents follow predictable patterns and physical principles, many Christians believe that God has the power and occasionally uses it to suspend, speed up, slow down, or override what would ordinarily happen according to these patterns and principles. We do not know, of course, if and when this will happen, when our prayers will be "answered," and it is presumptuous to assume we do. We tread on thin ice when we begin to indict God for not doing what we, from our imitation perch of divinity, decide should have happened.

We need to maintain a personal rather than an abstract philosophic focus. What is of primary interest and concern is our relationship with God, which we nourish through habitual prayer, even if only for a few seconds at a fuel station or in a checkout line. Thinking of our relationship with God as interpersonal clearly suggests that God is, in some sense, a person or at least personal. Theologians sometimes say that God is self-aware, has intensions, operates to bring about divine purposes, and so on, but good theologians recognize these as metaphors. God has left us with a lot to work out for ourselves, and although Jesus revealed a great deal, he did not disclose everything. Once again, faith without ambiguity is meaningless.

Prayer as Intimacy

Prayer, at its best, is a two-way conversation, in which we express our thoughts, feelings, and desires, and the creator of the universe occasionally whispers back. Conceiving of prayer in this way may seem to border on hallucination, and psychiatrically disordered people do sometimes hear God audibly talking to them. This, however, should not cause us to shut out God's voice, which would be like refusing to listen to music because the kid next door occasionally bangs on a piano.

As mentioned in chapter 7, the only human who can enter completely into your inner life is you, which is simply to acknowledge that your mind (consciousness) will never be directly accessible to anyone other than God. It will always remain at least a partial mystery to everyone else, a mystery in relation to which even the most gifted psychologist is able to make only educated guesses. To the extent that we can participate in another person's consciousness, we enjoy intimacy with that person. God is the ultimate being with whom we have the astonishing privilege of enjoying intimacy. We can only participate in such intimacy if we listen with spiritual ears to what God is saying. Authentic prayer fosters such listening. Weakness in our ability to listen occurs when we become too enmeshed in and distracted by activities and concerns, which can choke off spiritual interest. Intimacy with God also declines if we neglect what God has revealed in the New

Testament about the person and work of Jesus, the Christ, or what God nudges us to say or do through the Holy Spirit.

Modes of Prayer

Prayer as Worship: Prayer as a mode of worship is instinctively alien to many people. Like the idea of surrender, worship may seem to them like weak if not pathetic sniveling. To people who have grown up to be self-reliant and self-sufficient, as many of us in the West have, anything that resembles placation may seem unnatural. Conceiving of surrender or worship as sniveling, however, is a mistake. As we have noted, the term *worship* stems from an Old English word that meant to acknowledge worth or worthiness. For Christians, it means acknowledging God to be supremely worthy.

Prayer as Gratitude: Some people are thankful regardless of how much they suffer. They are grateful that God has granted them life and remain so to the end. Others are more cantankerous and unappreciative, regardless of how comfortable their lives are. We may express thanks that we have been admitted to a specific school, been offered a desirable job, or landed a big account. Maybe we have avoided a serious accident or earned enough money to pay for a week or two at a resort. Because life is a mixture of pleasure and pain, joy and sorrow, fulfillment and disappointment, there will always be things for which, if we believe there is a God, we can be grateful. A huge step on the way to a holy life is to remain grateful, not only for pleasure, joy, and plenty, but despite whatever pain, sorrow, and disappointment comes our way.

Prayer as Request: These are also called prayers of petition, supplication, or intercession. People who pray sometimes ask God to grant them something, perhaps help with a difficult task, a good outcome on their next series of lab tests, or greater prosperity. There is certainly nothing wrong with asking God for what we want, but when our prayers focus too much on ourselves and too little on others, we are in danger of losing touch with God's Spirit. When we witness a loved one suffer, we may temporarily waiver in our belief that God always desires what is good, and we may cry out to the heavens, "Why?" We are especially likely to think this way when, as is often the case, there seems to be no redeeming value to the suffering. Yet, even when we desire something noble, such as the survival of a child with a ravaging infection, we may not get what we want. The challenge is to continue to believe that God is in charge and that regardless of how things may appear, God is indeed good. In their better moments, Christians believe that even when it looks like evil is winning, they will someday understand why things happened as they did. Maintaining this belief, even when events seem to lead to a different conclusion, lies at the core of faith.

Certain passages in the New Testament suggest that God will do whatever a disciple of Christ asks, from relocating mountains to healing illnesses. Many people pray as if they were able to understand the meaning of such passages without reference to the rest of the New Testament. God may occasionally grant petitions for the miraculous. But the Bible makes clear that Christians are to pray in accordance with God's will, in other words, in the spirit of "Thy will be done." We may or may not know in a specific instance what God's will is, and we skirt the edges of arrogance and pretense to assume we do.

Prayer as Self-Reckoning: What I am calling prayers of reckoning are also called prayers of confession. Anyone with self-insight is aware of personal shortcomings. Once a person accepts the idea that at least some of these shortcomings amount to ethical or moral failure, to an unwillingness to seek the good, the definition of sin as missing the mark may begin to make sense. There is no euphemism for sin that makes it easier to face. It is a nettlesome concept to have to apply to yourself. Coming to terms with the specifics, without excuses or rationalizations, is difficult. "I was ill-tempered and intolerant when I snapped at that old man holding up traffic, and before you, God, I have no excuse." If you have never felt the need for forgiveness, you may not yet appreciate the meaning of grace, and thanking God for it may therefore seem hollow. To appreciate grace, we must first see our need for it, as illustrated in a poignant story from the New Testament.

A Pharisee, a rigorous observer of the Jewish law, invites Jesus to his home for a meal (Luke 7:36–47). The Pharisee is probably curious about the religious teacher who has been causing all the commotion. A woman, who lives nearby, discovers where Jesus is and shows up at the Pharisee's house with a container of ointment. Luke describes her as a sinner, perhaps alluding to promiscuity or prostitution. She stands behind Jesus, weeping, and begins to wash his feet with her tears and dry them with her hair. The woman repeatedly kisses Jesus' feet and then anoints them with the ointment. This prompts the Pharisee to murmur that if Jesus were truly a prophet and saw deeply into the nature of people, he would realize what sort of woman she is.

Knowing the Pharisee's thoughts, Jesus addresses him. "Simon, I have something to say to you," and proceeds to tell him a story about two debtors, one who owes ten times as much as the other. When both debtors confess their inability to pay, the creditor forgives their debts. "Now which of them," asks Jesus, "will love him more?" to which the Pharisee replies, "The one, I suppose, for whom he cancelled the larger debt." Jesus commends him for his answer, then asks, "Do you see this woman?" he asks. "I entered your house; you gave me no water for my feet, but she has wet my feet with her tears and wiped them with her hair. You gave me no kiss, but from the time I came in she has not ceased to kiss my feet. You did not anoint my head with oil, but she has anointed my feet with ointment. Therefore I tell you, her sins, which are many, are forgiven—for she loved much. But he who is forgiven little, loves little" (Luke 7:40–47, ESV). We know nothing about the woman's specific sins, perhaps because Luke does not consider these details important. His purpose is to emphasize the relationship between self-awareness and gratitude, between reckoning with the significance of our sin and loving God for pardoning and embracing us.

Pride can mean healthy self-respect, enjoying an appropriate sense of our worth and dignity. Or, the satisfaction that comes from achieving a worthwhile goal, acquiring something of value, or belonging to a special group such as an honor society. But it can also mean conceit, haughtiness, disdain, and the kind of rigidity that prevents self-insight and deters us from making peace with God. Such pride keeps the blinders on. It can be like the stubbornness of a two-year-old child, stomping and shouting, "I will *not*!" Perhaps, in the end, we either settle accounts with God or God settles them with us.

Prayer as Participation: The notion that prayer has a tangible impact on outcomes runs throughout the Bible, but we can never tell in advance if praying will change an outcome. Nor can we necessarily know afterwards. Alignment with God, nonetheless, amounts to more than passive assent. Earnest prayer allows us to participate actively in God's work, in a sense to partner with God. Physicists have made enormous progress in understanding causal relationships in the material realm. Many Christians believe that such relationships also sometimes occur at the boundary between the spiritual and material.

CHAPTER 25. AUTHENTIC PRAYER

Expressing our innermost thoughts, feelings, and longings to God allows us to assist in the great unfolding of God's plans. Not only do we vote for the good to prevail when we pray for it, but in a given instance we may help bring it about. We have no formula that allows us to predict, in a given circumstance, the extent of our influence, whether it delivers a mere nick or a major assault on evil. But there may be occasions when if we do not pray, the good will not prevail. Prayer is the real-time act of walking alongside Jesus, participating in God's work, and at times helping those who may still live as rebels and therefore as captives to sin. What we pray for is not necessarily arbitrary. God's Spirit may prompt us to pray for certain things without our even realizing it. If in those instances we follow the Spirit's leading, we align our will with God's.

Magic and Prayer

Some people find petitionary prayer troublesome because some religious people, under the guise of asking God to do something, seem instead to be directing God. God may occasionally grant petitions for the miraculous, but we may or may not know in a specific instance what God's will is, and we skirt the edges of arrogance if we assume we do.

Certain Christians pray as if God were their personal emissary. They talk and act like puppeteers pulling strings that make God do whatever they want and decide in advance when and where God will perform the next miracle. Such people are often sincere, but they behave as if they know God's will in every instance, or worse as if they can command it. Resembling witch doctors more than humble disciples, they convey the impression that they enjoy a privileged status with God and that their prayers are uniquely powerful. They fail to understand that the goal is not for us to become more influential with God, but for God to become more influential with us.

Christians who tell gravely ill people that, if only they have faith and refuse medical treatment, God will heal them are making claims in the name of God they have no right to make. By doing so, they trivialize God, treat the creator as their assistant in a magic act, and in that way use God's name in vain. The infirmed, understandably frightened and suffering, may believe God can heal them and may therefore be reluctant to discourage such people, whose implied warnings and forebodings can rival a tribal shaman's. Those afflicted need protection from any would-be healer who becomes spiritually toxic by pressuring those who are ill to choose between faith and medicine. It is worse than misguided to tell anyone to make such a choice, as if faith and medicine stood in opposition.

No sane person in the Western World would want to return to living in an age without modern plumbing, when people routinely died of cholera because sewage ran through the streets and contaminated the drinking water. What folly it would have been if after the introduction of plumbing, devout souls had simply dropped to their knees to pray instead of taking advantage of it. Today, no one with any sense would yearn for life without physicians, antibiotics, analgesics, or anesthetics, and it borders on the criminal to guilt-induce those with a disease into choosing faith alone when medical treatments are also available. Over the past hundred and fifty years, God has given us an enormous amount of common grace in the form of technologies, including increasingly effective medical care. It is our privilege and duty to avail ourselves of it when and where we can.

Liturgical Prayer

There is nothing wrong with using written prayers, such as those in the *Book of Common Prayer* or a *Roman Catholic Missal*. The *Psalms*, after all, are written prayers. But there is everything wrong with mindlessly reciting them. I have heard prayers uttered from the mouths of people who sounded as if they were reading obituaries, and some of them were in pulpits. I have also heard prayers that sounded more like instructing or chiding an audience than communicating with God.

Just as random sounds do not qualify as music, empty recitation does not qualify as prayer. The detached and mindless recitation of printed texts is spiritual sleepwalking, and I suspect God prefers the primitive groanings of a sincere heart. Written prayers can teach us much and may enable us to pray better, but simply reciting them is no substitute for heartfelt communication with our creator.

Prayer, Benevolence, and Humility

In its rendering of 1 Cor 13:13, John Wycliffe's late fourteenth-century English translation of the New Testament used the word *charity*. So did the seventeenth-century King James Version and many others since. But that word has a complex history.[1] As far back as linguistic tracings take us, charity implied good will and a benevolent disposition. It came into English by way of a French term borrowed from Latin. During the transition from early to late Middle English, when Wycliffe produced his translation, charity meant not only almsgiving but also lovingkindness, hospitality, and love for God. Today, the meaning of *charity* is narrower and we often take it to mean philanthropy. To better convey the meaning intended in the New Testament, modern translations often use the word *love*.

Jesus' injunction to love our enemies means praying for anyone who has hurt us or toward whom we feel anger, such as the reckless driver in the other lane who almost crashed into us. Or, the irritating person in a grocery line who only after knowing the total, begins to search for a wallet, purse, checkbook, or bank card. Praying under these circumstances may not be easy, but it is what God desires. It may be difficult if not impossible to pray for someone without also in some sense wishing that person well, since the mere act of praying implies good will. Praying for one's enemies is a corollary to loving and forgiving them (Matt 5:44).

To live a life informed by prayer and the search for truth is, in the language of the Bible, to "seek the face of the Father" who is the "author of truth," and to have what the Apostle Paul refers to as the "mind of Christ." Many Christians believe that when they pray God's Spirit will invariably guide them in what to pray for. But they may be mistaken. This calls for a certain amount of *epistemic humility*. To pray with such humility is to admit that, in any particular instance, one might be wrong about the true leading of the Spirit.

Closing Thoughts

Prayer is a two-way conversation that can align us with God. We can be wrong about what God desires. Since God is no one's personal agent, none of us can guarantee that God will do what we pray for. At times, our prayers may be inspired by the Holy Spirit, but prayer ought always to be undertaken with humility and in the spirit of *thy* will be done. Prayer, at its best, promotes intimacy with God, the chance to become more familiar with the mind of Christ, and the opportunity to act in partnership with God. Prayers can be modes of worship, expressions of

---

1. *Chambers Dictionary of Etymology*, "Charity," 160.

gratitude, moments of self-reckoning, or requests on our behalf or for the good of others. Liturgical prayer can be helpful, but only if it does not become what in the Sermon on the Mount Jesus calls "vain repetition" (Matt 6:7, KJV).

How, it is reasonable to ask, does a life saturated with prayer compare with one passionately dedicated to the pursuit of truth, the philosophic life? Both, I would argue, share the same goal, the acquisition and internalization of *that which is*. The idea of a person sincerely loving God without a desire for truth is an oxymoron. A true philosopher loves truth. He or she is more interested in acquiring insight than demonstrating cleverness. The genuine philosopher would rather write one good book that sells three copies than five bad ones that sell ten-thousand. All Christians, even the least gifted among them, ought to resemble philosophers, lovers of wisdom.

Preview

In the next chapter, we will discuss the gifts God has given us, and what we may or may not do with them.

Chapter 26. Responding to God's Gifts

MANY PEOPLE FIND IT difficult to believe God loves them. But God has given human beings many gifts which express that love. As discussed in chapter 22, among them is time, the medium through which we live and make decisions. Apart from time, there could be no freedom of choice. Through time, we make choices that affect who and what we become. If we were unable to make decisions, there would be no possibility of change, no growth or development, and perhaps no accountability. This touches on whether a person can sin unintentionally. Some theologians believe we sin whenever we do anything contrary to God's will, regardless of whether we realize it or not, while others believe we only sin when we know what God wants but refuse to do it.

Many people live as though God created the world and then forgot about it. They live as functional deists. Such people claim to believe in God and may attend church, but they view God as detached and impersonal, and themselves as having little or no accountability to their creator. Some live with "Moralistic Therapeutic Deism," according to which God created the world and generally looks after people, but there is no need for God unless they need help with a problem. It is God's will for people to be good, nice, and fair, and people who are go to heaven. By these lights, the goal in life is to be happy and have high self-esteem.[1]

Theologians sometimes refer to God's immutable attributes. Divinity students learn that God is omnipotent, omnipresent, omniscient, self-originating, self-sufficient, just, and loving.[2] Focusing too much on

---

1. See Smith and Denton, *Soul Searching*.
2. The attributes of self-origination and self-sufficiency are called God's *aseity*.

God's unchanging attributes, however, can numb us to the reality that God *acts* in and on individuals and history, that God is involved with us. Some conceive of God as so abstract that they cannot comprehend the idea of God acting. Others regard God as pleasant to think about, now and then, but quickly set God aside whenever they have to get on with the serious business of living.

God's Sustaining Energy

God pours out divine energy to sustain life and the world in which we live. Bishop George Berkeley (1685–1753), an Irish philosopher who was a central figure in British Empiricism, suggested something akin to this. He is well known for the Latin phrase *esse est percipi*, to be is to be perceived. The world, according to Berkeley, depends for its existence on God continuing to perceive it.

We now know that matter and energy are interconvertible. This might lead us to conclude that God used up energy during the Big Bang, has done so ever since to keep the universe going, and therefore has become less. Pouring out divine energy, however, does not diminish God, who is not a material being, just as loving another person and using energy in the service of that love does not diminish us. People who do not love are the ones who shrink and become less. Love is God's nature (1 John 4:16) supremely demonstrated by having come to us in the person of Jesus.

A Closer Look at Time

The gifts of life, consciousness, and freedom of choice occur through time and space, the media in and through which we live. Without time, the concepts of choice and change would be incomprehensible. When we make a choice, we settle on a course of action for the future, even if that future is no more than the next minute or two. If there were no future, there would be no choices to make and no possibility of change.

God grants us time to give us opportunities to reason, choose, and help determine who and what we become, which we do throughout life. Of central importance is how we deploy our time, including who and what we spend time thinking about. All of us devote time each day to eating, sleeping, and so on, and to live at anything beyond a subsistence level most of us also work. We spend time with friends and loved ones, attend recreational, social, or sporting events, and may go to church. In all of this, we have the chance to honor (worship) God who is always present.

We cannot think about God every moment, however, because if we did, we might fail to stop at red lights or watch for oncoming traffic at intersections. Loved ones might drift away in response to our neglect, and if we work outside the home, we might well end up unemployed. The key question has to do with how we spend *discretionary* time, which both determines and reflects who and what we are. Discretionary time gives us periods of consciousness that responsibilities do not consume, and it is about these that God may most care.

A Closer Look at Consciousness

For most of us, life includes consciousness. Our existence brings with it awareness. Few people would argue that a person in an irreversible coma without brain activity is no longer human, or that we suspend our humanity when we fall asleep. But having a mind is central to what it means to be a complete person.

Philosophers and scientists have worked hard to understand the relationship between mind and body. How is it that I can raise my arm by deciding to? Researchers can demonstrate the dependence of the body on the brain by stimulating regions of the brain to trigger actions, sensations, or emotional states. We observe the dependence of our minds on our bodies whenever we are unable to think clearly because we have come down with the flu or are excessively tired. The brain is physical and we can touch it. Not so with the mind. Even if we knew everything there was to know about neurons, synapses, and how neural events correlate with mental ones, we would be no closer to understanding what consciousness is. How might we touch an idea? What does it weigh?

People in Western Society have increasingly favored the subjective, especially when it comes to the spiritual. One historian, focusing on what happened in the seventeenth and eighteenth centuries, writes, "Now there began the modern tendency to regard religion as a matter of opinion, as 'subjective,' and essentially a private affair. This profound change has been called 'the turn to the subject.'"[3] This turn has furthered the tendency to treat feelings as trustworthy guides to action and decreased concern with

3. Edwards, *Christianity*.

objective truth. On the other side of the ledger, the shift toward the subjective has not been without merit. It has enriched civilization by getting people to pay more attention to their inner workings. Augustine's *Confessions*, written in the years leading up to AD 400, was groundbreaking. It is a superb example of constructively attending to experience. Unfortunately, many Christians have lost sight of how important our states of consciousness may be to God (Mark 7:21).

The Gift of Freedom

God has given us freedom, respects our decisions, and refuses to override them. Without freedom, not only would we be protoplasmic robots, but moral accountability would make no sense. Because Christians believe God is infinitely loving, it is not reasonable to believe that God arbitrarily puts anyone in hell. Some theologians believe that, before creating the world, God chose whom to save and make part of his eternal family. Others go further in subscribing to the idea that God, in having chosen some to save, intentionally chose others not to save. They insist that such election has nothing to do with human merit, such as how moral a person is. Nor, they suggest, are God's choices based on knowing in advance how a person is going to respond to the gospel. All of this, they insist, is a mystery. Because theologians have often argued that God is not *in* time, that to God all moments are present, it may not be especially helpful for any of us to dwell on when, how, or why God decides such matters. Like the problem of evil, these matters are beyond us. What is not beyond us is that we are accountable. As long as we are alive, everything we do shapes who and what we are, and we tend to become the sum of our choices. Some decisions are trivial, such as whether to drink water or lemonade, but others are highly significant, such as whether to throw in with God or go it alone.

No one has complete free will. Our genes impose physical and mental limits on us, and so does our developmental history. That history includes how others have treated us, which has a lot to do with how we think about and treat ourselves and other people. It also includes the attitudes of people who have served as role models. Despite limits on their freedom, people retain some measure of choice. As the French philosopher Jean-Paul Sartre suggests, we can always say *no*. And in relation to God, so long as our mental faculties are intact, we can also say *yes*. The relationship between free will and brain physiology is an interesting and complicated subject filled with mystery. It is clear that the capacity of the mind to exercise freedom of choice depends on the integrity of the brain, but such freedom, once established, may no longer depend only on the brain. The mystery has to do with what else it might depend on.

Any theological discussion of free will would be incomplete without pointing out that two themes in the Bible appear to be in tension. The first is that people are free to make choices and will be held accountable for the choices they make, themes that run throughout it. The other is that people do what God causes them to do. In Genesis, God hardens the heart of Pharoah (see Exod 4:21; 9:12; 10:1, 20, 27; 11:10; 14:4, 8), and in Ephesians, Christians have been predestined (1:11). Some strands of Christianity insist on the first and others on the second. Perhaps the majority of Christian theologians suggest that, although seemingly incompatible, both are true and constitute a paradox or antinomy, terms some philosophers use interchangeably.[4]

Life with God

Every day, we construct who and what we are, and we may move into eternity as whatever we have helped determine ourselves to be. While we are alive, we can cooperate with God (see Rom 8:28) to help shape us into ever closer approximations of creatures God approves of. When we die, however, the jobsite may shut down and we may remain whatever we have chosen to become. Some in major branches of Christianity believe that even after death there remains the possibility of change. A haunting possibility is that those who reject God's love may forever remain painfully aware that they have. "Now we see things imperfectly, like puzzling reflections in a mirror, but then we will see everything with perfect clarity" (1 Cor 13:12 NLT). They may know they have lost God and that God has lost them. It may be as if those who have died *in Christ*, bonded to God, exist on the other side of a one-way mirror. They see us but we cannot see them. Note the parable of Lazarus and the rich man (Luke 16:19–31).

No one knows exactly what the long-term outcome will be for those who refuse to respond to God's love. As suggested by the excerpt from *The Seafarer* in chapter 21, it may turn out to be irreparable loneliness,

---

4. Cantini and Bruni, "Paradoxes and Logic." s.v.

so that basic human needs for intimacy, contact, and tenderness remain unfulfilled. It may be eternal cut-off-ness and self-absorbed solitude. What may make it especially terrible is that the contours of a person's nature may already have been fixed, with little or no chance to change them. Not because God wants it that way, but because the individual does. Some people may have so given themselves over to selfism that if, even after they die, Christ were to invite them into the kingdom of God, they would refuse his invitation. I have referred above to Jesus' lament over Jerusalem, whose inhabitants also *would not* (see Matt 23:37, Luke 13:34). They may reject all opportunities to choose light over darkness, and spend eternity in a self-created dungeon of isolation. This may be what the Bible refers to as unquenchable thirst. The difference between a life of self and a life of faith is that living for yourself keeps the focus on whatever you believe makes you happy. Being a Christian does not replace the quest for happiness, but it adds another dimension to it, joy. Only a relationship with God will give us enduring joy.

If Christians remain open to the influence of the Holy Spirit, they concern themselves with what makes them holy, more like God. They may not go around talking about holiness, but the awareness of their need for it is always there. Desiring holiness means wanting to partner with God, to have a sacred as well as a secular purpose. Living for God means asking, "What do *you* want?" not just "What do I want?" God offers us salvation from sin and death so that we increasingly become like Christ and wants to give this gift to anyone who desires it.

Closing Thoughts

Our moment-to-moment decisions have enormous influence on what we become. We can use them to allow God to shape us into fit citizens of heaven. Time gives us opportunities to move toward God, who sustains the world, is involved in the arc of human history, and participates in the lives of individuals. Consciousness cannot be reduced to physical events without explaining it away. God is most concerned with the nature of a person's mind—consciousness—since the mind reflects the heart. The questions in this chapter have had to do with how we respond to God's gifts. Do we love God?

Chapter 26. Responding to God's Gifts

Preview

We turn next to three short, more conversational chapters, addressed primarily to Christians. Since they concern everyday relationships, they may also be of wider interest. Every person you meet is a divine creation. This gives the Christian the opportunity to be the face of Christ to everyone from the greeter at Walmart to the barista at Starbuck's.

Part V. **CHRISTIANITY AND OTHER PEOPLE**

Chapter 27. Dynamic Relationships

IN THIS CHAPTER AND the next two, I want to make some suggestions about how Christians can live with the kind of warm and welcoming communion God desires. As you read, imagine that you and I are sitting by a fire and that I am sharing something of what I have learned as a psychologist about the nature of relationships. Whether you are in search of faith or skeptical about ever finding it, these observations may prove helpful. Christianity teaches that we exist to live in communion with God and each other. Many hurting people need the services of a mental health professional, but perhaps far more need the compassionate listening ear of a friend.[1] I want to describe in this chapter what an ideal relationship might look like, and how a certain kind of intimacy characterizes it.

From early in the twentieth century, it became customary to characterize relationships as varying in degrees of healthiness, with some relationships regarded as sick and others as healthy. A woman married to a man who brutally beats her, for example, is sometimes said to be in a sick marriage, while a man or woman happily married is said to be in a healthy one. Such usage feels so natural to us today that we not only take it for granted, but also think of it as descriptively accurate. In one sense it is accurate, if you think of health abstractly, as a kind of all-encompassing biopsychosocial ideal. It is important to recognize, however, that as pointed out in chapter 16, applying medical terminology to psychological phenomena, in the absence of identified physical pathology, is to use metaphoric language.

---

1. See Schofield, *Psychotherapy: Purchase of Friendship*.

PART V. CHRISTIANITY AND OTHER PEOPLE

Life Without Relationships

Simone Weil wrote, "We have only to imagine all our desires satisfied; after a time we should become discontented. We should want something else and we should be miserable through not knowing what to want."[2] It is probably the case that we will never find contentment by striving for things we never needed. My son Kenneth suggested, correctly I think, that our greatest everyday fear is not of failure but of wasting our lives chasing goals that lead nowhere. What, then, are worthwhile goals, and how does this relate to other people?

If you walk into a room and want to make a lot of people uncomfortable, just start talking about intimacy. You will see them stiffen up and the conversation may turn awkward, as if they do not quite know what to say or do. Yet, when Jesus said, "Love one another as I have loved you," he was referring to more than acts of kindness. He was pointing to the sort of life he had been leading with his disciples, to the nature of the relationships he enjoyed with them, to holy or sacred intimacy. I want to focus in this chapter on such intimacy, what Christians call fellowship. Intimacy involves a specific kind of friendship. Establishing and maintaining intimate friendships lies at the heart of what it means to live as a disciple of Jesus.

As indicated in the opening pages of this book, I did not grow up in a religious home, and if it had not been for Christians willing to love me as they knew God loved them, Christ might never have become an active presence in my life. There was a retired Marine who was impressively honest with me and genuinely interested in how I was doing. And a doctoral student in physics at my college. I do not believe he or his wife ever realized what their hospitality meant. They were the faces of Christ to me and related without pretense. I think, also, of the thirty-year-old minister who paid to have a new battery installed in my car and on another occasion a new generator. I was a young graduate student who stumbled into his church one Sunday evening. He was almost as poor as I was—young ministers do not get paid much—but he put up the money anyway. We would talk candidly about our struggles and about Jesus, hour after hour on Sunday nights after the service he led. I learned a great deal from him about God. Like the Marine and the doctoral student, he too was the face

---

2. Quoted in Allen, *Three*. Original source: Weil, "Thoughts on God," *Science, Necessity, and God*.

of Christ to me, in no small part because he spoke from the heart and did not relate through a professional veneer.

Memorable Science Fiction

Years ago, I watched an episode of the science-fiction television series, *Outer Limits*. I have never forgotten it.[3] A scientist shoots a powerful beam from his attic into the heavens. One night, a mummy-like creature comes down the beam, and frightened, encases itself in a large transparent and impenetrable triangle. Nothing will dent or scratch it, neither bullets nor diamonds. For several consecutive nights, the creature descends along the beam, emerges from the glass-like triangle, converses with the scientist, and returns to wherever it came from.

One night, the scientist goes out, leaving his wife, her mother, and the now-trusting creature alone. The woman and her mother realize that if they had the creature's shield, they would be invincible. So, with a handgun they shoot the creature and drag it into the cellar. The wife then races back to the attic, and using a small ball she has ripped from a vein in the creature's wrist, erects the shield around herself. You watch the panic sweep across her face as she realizes that she cannot get out. She will be entombed in it forever.

Meanwhile, the wounded creature has climbed from the basement to the first floor and then up to the attic. With his dying breath, he puts a drop of his blood against the shield and dissolves it, freeing the scientist's wife. Profoundly moved by what the creature has done, she asks remorsefully, "After what we did, how could you? How could you help?" To which the creature replies, "How could I not?" This captures what it is in Christians that often prompts them to move toward others. How could they not? How could they not want to connect with and help those in need? For me, the question has been, how could I not write this book? I would like to believe that the source of my motivation has been the Holy Spirit.

I want to share some thoughts about intimacy, and in the process point out what true communion and holy friendship look like, and what it requires by way of risks and costs. I will close this chapter by offering some suggestions on how best to foster such communion and friendship.

---

3. "The Bellero Shield," *Outer Limits*, aired February 10, 1964.

PART V. CHRISTIANITY AND OTHER PEOPLE

We Were Created for Intimacy

God made us for communion. This is partly what it means to have been created in God's image, to have the potential for intimacy. Christians may be especially able to realize this potential because they know God has addressed and forgiven the flaws that separate them from God and each other. Jesus came to restore, to once again make possible, intimacy between God and human beings and intimacy between and among people. Such intimacy is not optional, an elective in the Christian curriculum. It sits at the center of living in communion with Christ. God wants nothing to separate us from our creator or others. Connecting warmly and closely with other spiritual beings is the primary reason we exist. Without such connections, we will never be complete persons and at best remain caricatures. As suggested in chapter 21, we would remain like Pinocchio before he comes to life and, in a metaphorical sense, wooden.

Be one as I and the Father are one is a theme that runs through much of John's Gospel. It was not an idle musing by Jesus, something on the order of, "it would be nice if you cozied up a bit to your neighbor." It is a direct expression of God's desire for us to have the best in this life and beyond. Intimacy is fulfilling. It is, in fact, the only thing that brings lasting joy. Be one as I and the Father are one reflects what Paul calls the "mind of Christ." Another way to phrase this might be to say that Christians ought to be joined at the heart.

If we lack closeness with other people, we probably also lack it with our creator. Worse, we may not even understand what intimacy with God is. I am not just referring here to the mechanics of everyday friendships but to how God wants us to participate in the divine ongoing existence, how the intimacy we enjoy now is a hint, a glimpse, a look ahead and a practice field for what it will be like in eternity. Intimacy is part of God's nature. This is an implication of the Christian doctrine of the Trinity, according to which God exists in three persons, Father, Son, and Holy Spirit, an eternal fellowship.

We can choose to relate intimately to God or not, and whether to relate intimately to other people. God entrusts others to Christians, who therefore have a special duty toward them. The choices we make in relation to other human beings have spiritual implications, and as suggested several times in this book, they are of great significance. More times than I care to remember, I have made the wrong choice. The task, whatever it was, took precedence over the relationship. There was this to do that I felt was more important or had to take care of first. But sometimes, the task is the relationship.

Intimacy Requires Self-Disclosure

What some Christians regard as community in their churches is but a shadow of what it could be and of what God intends. Genuine communion amounts to more than exchanging pleasantries over a cup of coffee. It is related to the idea of "joining oneself to" God and other people, and it is God's Spirit at work in a Christian's heart who encourages and facilitates such joining. That you and someone else believe the same things does not guarantee that the two of you will experience any communion whatsoever. Holy intimacy may totally elude you, even if you go to church several times a week.

I cannot enjoy communion with you if I do not know you, which is another way of stating I cannot love you if you do not come out of hiding. Nor can you love me if I refuse to share what is going on inside. All of us have petty faults we would prefer to conceal. We may have thoughts we are ashamed of, done things we hope no one ever learns about, or harbor longings that remain locked in the vaults of our minds. I am not suggesting we say everything that comes into our heads. If we did, we might scare other people. You have to be able to edit and filter. But regulating self-disclosure so it is appropriate does not mean eliminating it. By sharing our inner selves with others, we honor God and learn how to have more fulfilling lives. We also learn to be more open about our frailties, which allows others to comfort us when we need it. Another way to put this is confessing our sins. Not a lot of this that goes on in many churches, where impersonal superficiality prevails, often in the form of pretending to be nicer than we are. There is much to commend in churches in which formal confession is a regular part of the Christian life. You may have gone to church as a child or an adult when you were hurting. The person next to you may have been decked out in finery—he or she had it together—while you were in pain. Maybe you tried to participate, but you mostly sat there worried, angry, depressed, or in some other way haunted, preoccupied, and distracted.

But it may also have been the other way around. The person next to you may have just lost a job, found out a friend or family member was gravely ill, or discovered that a spouse decided to leave the marriage.

These are the moments when we have an opportunity to respond to God's call to support our fellow human beings, but we can best do this if we are truthful. Regardless of what you do for other people, you will never enjoy communion with them if you do not shed your armor. Truth and love are inseparable, and if you want others to take off their armor, it is a good idea to shed yours too.

Intimacy Is Costly and Requires Good Judgment

Communion or fellowship is not simply the warm glow of sitting together around a campfire. It is more. Creating intimacy is not easy, nor has it ever been. Developing intimacy requires that we invest time, even when we might not get anything back. It means expending life energy. You have to be wise about how you spend this energy. We ought to cherish every minute God has given us and not waste them. This is important to do, so when we really have to rise to the occasion, when something comes along that demands our all, we have enough left in our emotional gas tanks to respond and be fully present, to do whatever it takes.

For years, a friend of mine would get annoyed because I did not spend more time with him. He would feel insulted when I said I had obligations to meet. Then, some years ago, he and his grown sons were experiencing considerable conflict. I met with them on three separate occasions. Each was a grueling five-hour, non-stop, session that exhausted all of us for the rest of the day. Being a psychologist had little or nothing to do with it. They simply needed a friend to be with them, care enough to listen well and occasionally nudge the conversation along. I did not care what it cost me because I knew it was important, and if I did not give whatever I had to this, my friend might have gone to his grave estranged from his children. I doubt I could have been there for them if I had allowed him or other people to decide how I deployed the time and energy God gave me. Some things are simply worth doing. But not all things are, and it is important to know the difference. Paul the Apostle tells Christians not to live according to the flesh, by which he meant living only for oneself (see Rom 8:3–6, 12–13). Life in the flesh is selfish existence, split off from God's Spirit, the antithesis of Christianity. But each of us must decide what is and is not worth our investment.

CHAPTER 27. DYNAMIC RELATIONSHIPS

Intimacy Takes Courage

Intimacy requires taking risks. These risks would be trivial, were it not for human frailty. As things stand, however, they are anything but trivial because when you reveal yourself to others, you give them the power to hurt you. But it is precisely to this that God calls Christians, who at their best give others that power, partly in the hope of also showing them Christ. This puts me in mind of Peter's statement in Acts 3:6, which one might loosely translate as, "I have no silver or gold, but my heart, Christ's heart, I will do my best to give to you." Holy intimacy means summoning the courage to be authentic rather than artificial.

Self-disclosure and trust go together, but you cannot trust everyone to the same extent. If you disclose too much to some people, all you will get back is superficial advice or a raised eyebrow. We have a responsibility to nurture the well-being of our own hearts as well as to care for other people. In developing a friendship, what typically occurs is that you disclose something personal and the other person discloses something in return. You then reveal a little more. If all goes well, the process continues and intimacy builds. Practicing the art of intimacy is a spiritual discipline.

Recommendations for Fostering Intimacy

Caring and candor are present in all good relationships and both ideally characterize relationships between and among Christians. I want to close this chapter by offering some suggestions on how to be a good friend and therefore how to promote what theologians call *koinonia*, the New Testament Greek word for communion or fellowship with God and other Christians.

Support others. It is a tough world out there. Everyone needs a rooting section, especially when he or she is in the wrong. It is not when I am right that I need support. It is when I have said or done something stupid or uncharitable, and feel self-righteously defensive about it. Even if the whole world says I am wrong, I want to hear, "You're still okay." I am not suggesting that you or I encourage or condone bad behavior or pretend that what is wrong is right, just that we err on the side of dispensing grace rather than law.

Be honest. It is not so much lies of commission that are corrosive. It is lies of omission, in part because they are so much more common and easily go undetected. Say what you think and feel. Just give yourself the time to make sure your thoughts and feelings are not spur-of-the-moment reactions that will pass, such that if you express them, you will later regret it. Allow thoughts and feelings to age a bit. But once you have done this, express what you think and feel. Say it clearly, say it as often as you need to, and make sure you get through. Community, at its best, allows you to know another person and in the process to be fully known. Do not miss it.

Express your resentments. It is hard to be honest when you are seething. That is when you may say to yourself, "I'll fix you, only you'll never know." Resentment is a lethal state of mind. It is when you hope the other person slips on a banana peel, only you do not want to take the responsibility for pushing him or her down. Just before he took his final oral examinations for his PhD, I asked a graduate student, Douglas Pepe, what he thought it took to have a good marriage, or indeed any good relationship. I was his dissertation chairperson so I was especially interested to see what he would say, given that we had spent several years together doing research on interpersonal dynamics. I will never forget his answer, "pulling weeds." Do whatever it takes to work things out, to pull your weeds. And pull them fast, lest they become unmanageable. This is especially important when someone has significantly dented your trust, which is when expressing resentment can be the most difficult. When you believe that someone has failed to honor that trust, do not be passive. Raise the issue, no matter how uncomfortable doing so makes you feel. Even if you do not get the resolution you want, and the other person is defensive or says you are imagining things, this is still worth doing. If you talk it out, you may be able to restore the relationship to its prior level of closeness, and perhaps even to deepen it. If you do not talk it out, I can almost guarantee that intimacy will be impaired. This, unfortunately, is what often happens inside the church and outside it.

Forgive. It is difficult to forgive when you are harboring resentment, which is why I have suggested expressing resentments if they are significant. As I have suggested elsewhere,[4] I am not a fan of superficial forgiveness. Pretending to forgive when you have not done so is to lie, if only to yourself. It may take decades to forgive someone who has inflicted great damage on you or a loved one, and in this life you may never be able to forgive that person. Yet, forgiveness is central to what Christians are

---

4. McLemore, *Toxic Relationships*, 12–13.

summoned to do in the face of evil. One path on the road to forgiveness is to pray, since praying for anyone means desiring good outcomes for that person. If he or she has done something egregious to you or someone close to you, praying will put you in tension, and you will be caught between doing what you know to be right and being unable to do it.

Be gentle. This is not always easy, and there have been times when I wish I had been gentler, a sentiment with which you may identify. When you become genuine friends with someone, you and the other person give each other emotional power. Use that power wisely. You can hurt friends far more easily than strangers.

Stay engaged—connected. As in your relationship with God, you can position yourself in relation to another person in three ways: toward, against, or away. In the beginning of a friendship, there is a lot of moving toward. But this can change. Of the three, moving away is the one to be on guard against. When you detach, there is no hope of working anything out. When those in superficial friendships argue, they may say things like, "I'm so angry, the conversation's over!" Committed friends, on the contrary, are more likely to say, "I'm so angry, the conversation's over—but I will be back later to finish it." Continue the conversation, even if it means sacrificing sleep. If you cannot continue it today or tomorrow, continue it the following day. Hang in there and work hard for resolution and reconciliation.

Enjoy the moment. For many people, life consists of many missed moments. God wants you to enjoy life, God's greatest gift. Savor your moments of friendship and if you can, turn them into moments of magic.

Turn relationships, especially friendships, into adventures. Especially if the friendship is also romantic, for example your marriage. Keep it exciting. Build in surprises. Do something unexpected that brings happiness and joy.

Closing Thoughts

This chapter contained four affirmations: (1) We were created for intimacy with God and other people; (2) Intimacy requires opening up emotionally; (3) Intimacy is costly and necessitates using good judgment; and (4) Intimacy takes courage. It also presented eight recommendations for how to promote intimacy: (1) Support others whenever possible; (2) Be as honest as you can; (3) Deal with resentments and do not let them fester; (4) Forgive when you have it in you, but to do this you may first have to address your resentments; (5) Be gentle; (6) Stay engaged; (7) Enjoy the moment; and (8) Turn relationships into adventures.

Preview

In the next chapter, we will take up the subject of emotional healing, and how you may sometimes be able to bring this about in others.

Chapter 28. Helping Others

NO ONE SAILS THROUGH life without difficulty. It may look as if some people do, especially if they put up a good front. Celebrities on talk shows usually appear as if their lives were carefree, but even a quick glance at the tabloids shows that this is rarely the case. People have enormous power to help or harm others, to lift them up or push them down. Some people get emotional help and support from friends, or even from barbers, beauticians, or bartenders, but many get none at all. For over a century, psychiatrists and psychologists have been doing much of what the church should have been doing all along. If you are a Christian, your face may be the only one in which another person may ever see God.

At the same time, many members of the clergy could learn a great deal from psychologists and psychiatrists, if only they opened themselves to learning from them. I have been surprised by the competitiveness with which some clergy treat psychologists. Despite having taken a course or two in pastoral counseling, they seem to know little about how best to help hurting people. Although they acknowledge that the Bible is not a textbook in physical medicine, they act as if they know all they need to know about how best to respond to psychologically troubled people.

People have failed you. Parents fail their children, children fail their parents, husbands and wives disappoint each other, and friends are not always there when we need them. Even those closest to you may have failed you. In fact, just about everyone in your life with whom you have had a long and close relationship may have, at one time or another, let you down. And, you have probably let them down. You and I, and probably everyone we know, have suffered at least some emotional pain. There have been times in my life when, had it not been for the care and concern of others, I might not have made it. Life would have gone on and I would not have jumped off a bridge, but I might have ended up scarred.

I want to share some of what I have learned about emotional healing and how you can sometimes bring this about in others. What follows are three observations about how healing occurs and how intimacy fosters it. I will also offer recommendations on how best to help others who are in pain.

Everyone Needs Healing

No one on earth makes it through life without struggle. I certainly have not. Many people assume physicians never get sick. They may also assume psychologists rarely experience anxiety, depression, loneliness, irritability, and dread. If so, I must have missed that class during my training, because I have experienced all of them at one time or another.

Sometimes, all we need is a little sleep. Other times, a change of venue will do the trick, perhaps taking a walk, reading a novel, or going to a movie. But there are other times when we need more. Maybe we did not get into the school we wanted or failed to land a coveted job. Or, the love of our life dumped us, or someone devastated us with a withering remark or tore into us with rage. Perhaps, we suffered a financial loss. Whatever it was, we ended up in pain. These are the times when we may need someone else to pick us up off the floor and put us back together again, someone to help heal our wounds.

It Takes People to Heal People

When I was in college, I read a book[1] by Harry Stack Sullivan (1892–1949), a psychiatrist who had figured out something profoundly important: It takes people to make people sick, and it takes people to make people better. He was using sick, of course, as a metaphor for emotional anguish, hidden pain, and mental distress. Many psychological problems are primarily due to our experiences with other people. If you or anyone you know is in emotional distress, a negative encounter with someone else, or a series of them, probably triggered it. Similarly, if you feel happy, contented, and like you can handle anything life throws at you, the odds

---
1. Sullivan, *The Psychiatric Interview*.

are high that others have treated you well and enabled you to feel loved, accepted, valued, and appreciated.

Some people go through horrific life experiences and God seems to heal them, even if they do not get much help from others. We cannot assume this is going to happen, however, and it is important not to miss opportunities to help people when and where we can. God often works *through* us and we may turn out to be the only channel through which healing comes.

As an example of the immense impact people have on each other, it is not primarily hospitals that keep suicidal patients alive, certainly not over the long run. A suicidal person may definitely need to be hospitalized, but this is a temporary measure. The long-term medicine is people who care. I do not deny the role of biology in suicidal ideation or behavior, which can be considerable, just emphasizing the importance of relationships.

Being Present Is Powerful

When I was a young psychologist, I believed that every time someone came to see me I had to say something clever. Was that not my job, to provide new insights and perspectives? I now look back on all this with regret. Helping another human being rarely has anything to do with being brilliant. The important thing is simply to be there in the same room and listen. Attentive presence is powerful. It can also be enormously healing. When people are in emotional pain, they are nearly always lonely. Merely being with someone who is hurting provides the hope of not being alone, the hope of human connectedness.

Over the past few decades, psychiatrists and psychologists have begun to talk about *sitting with* patients and clients. You may not be able to do some of the things a therapist can, but you can sometimes do what may be the most important thing. Just be there and listen. Sit with those who need you. Being available and paying attention can go a long way. Below are a few additional suggestions on how to care for others when they are in pain.

Listen with Your Third Ear

Perhaps most of us want to express ourselves to someone who will understand and see the world through our eyes. We want to tell our story to another human being who will provide us with that scarce commodity known as empathy. But we rarely tell our stories in a straightforward way, which is why it is important to listen closely to what the other person says and does not say.

Empathy is emotional food, a kind of sustenance. It is what our spirits thrive on. Just as pediatricians diagnose some infants as failing to thrive, adults fail to thrive when they experience empathic malnutrition. A lot of people see therapists and counselors because they just want someone else to hear them and understand. I remember a woman many years ago asking me in a plaintive voice, "Don't you understand?" Sometimes I did and sometimes I did not. What you never want to hear is, "You just don't get it."

It is not always easy to understand someone else, which is why empathy is in short supply. Understanding requires listening with what one psychoanalyst called the *third ear*. Not just to the words, but also to what is behind and beneath them, their emotional significance.[2] Understanding fosters intimacy, which in turn often fosters healing.

Focus on the Other Person

To communicate empathy to others, you need to keep the focus *on them*. This means resisting the natural tendency to turn the attention back to yourself. In ordinary conversation, people take turns. You complain about the rain and I complain about the cold. You tell me about your anxieties and I tell you about mine. This is not, however, the nature of conversations that bring about healing. To provide others with the intimacy they may need, you have to care enough to suspend your own needs. When someone is in emotional pain, it is not the time to ask that person to take care of you, not the time for *quid pro quo*.

You may find this difficult to do, which is why being a therapist is harder than it looks. It is not easy to keep the focus on someone else for forty-five or fifty minutes. You do not have to be stiff or rigid in focusing on the other person. There are times when it is helpful to say

---

2. See Reik, *Listening with the Third Ear*.

something about yourself, something self-disclosing. But when you are trying to help somebody, a little self-disclosure goes a long way. It is easy to overdo it.

Take the Pain Seriously

There are several ways to bring emotional healing to an abrupt halt. One is to offer superficial advice. We sometimes do this because we want everything to be all right, and we cannot stand the anxiety of being *with* the other person for very long in their misery. Empathy is taxing and costly. It requires that you tolerate ambiguity, which means living with a certain amount of discomfort. We want to rush in and fix things, to solve the problem, whatever it is, to make it go away. Superficial advice is rarely helpful. People in pain need understanding more than platitudes.

A second way to put an end to intimacy is to offer empty reassurance, to suggest that the other person does not really have a problem and everything will turn out fine. That is not what hurting people want to hear, and if that is what they do hear, they will conclude you are not listening, you have checked out, or you are not interested.

Still a third way to end intimacy is to change the subject. Again, we tend to do that when we cannot tolerate listening to someone else's pain and see no immediate way to alleviate it. If and when you change the subject, it will be for your benefit, not that of the one you are trying to help.

A fourth way to chill the conversation is to crack jokes. Cracking a joke is a sign that you are uncomfortable and do not know what to say. Hurting people rarely want others to humor them out of their pain, which is almost always impossible anyway. When they are bleeding to death, they do not need a court jester.

Lift People Up with Grace

When I was a professor, I joined a group of six or seven colleagues who met every few weeks. I was in that group for months before I realized that one of the other members was the late Bob Munger, the author of a wonderful little booklet entitled, "My Heart, Christ's Home."[3] I remember Bob saying one evening that Christianity is inclusive, that Jesus stands with open arms to receive anyone who wants to receive

3. Available in a volume nicely illustrated by Andrea Jorgenson.

him. I also vividly recall Bob saying, "People are helped more by being lifted up with grace than by being weighted down with law." Bob knew that much of the time the way to help others understand the goodness of God's grace is to show them some.

Act When You Have To

This recommendation may seem contrary to much of what I have written above, but it is important. There are occasions when the other person needs someone to assume responsibility that, for one reason or another, he or she cannot or will not.

If you believe someone needs professional help, say it tactfully but directly. For example, if someone tells you that he or she is having bizarre thoughts or thinking about suicide, that is not the time to worry about whether it is right to give that person advice or direction. It is the time to act, and if time permits, to ask for advice from someone who knows how best to respond, such as a psychiatrist, clinical psychologist, or other mental health professional.

Use Reframing, But Only When Appropriate

Reframing means interpreting whatever happened differently, helping the other person make sense of it in another way. Let me illustrate the power of reframing with a story told to me years ago by a friend who was a professor at Berkeley. He had watched this mini-drama unfold the day before: A mother and her four-year-old son were walking along a beach. She handed the child a helium-filled balloon and attempted to tie it to his wrist. But small children often want to assert their independence. He wanted to hold it and not have it fastened to him. The boy insisted that he was four years old, not three, and only *little* kids needed balloons tied to their wrists. In less than a minute, he loosened his grip and the balloon floated away.

The child put up a fuss, wailing and carrying on terribly. With great intuitive wisdom, his mother said, "Johnny, that was fantastic! What a launch!! That is the best launch I've ever seen. Your balloon might go all the way to China, or Russia, or Japan." The child looked up at the vanishing balloon, stopped crying, and with tears streaming down his face asked, "You really think so Mom?" To which she lovingly said, "Of course!" He grinned from ear to ear. Sometimes it helps to suggest another frame of reference. But you have to be careful about what you say and how you say it, to make sure you are not trying to talk the other person out of the pain.

Here is an example of reframing from the Bible. Near the end of Genesis, as Joseph looks back over what has happened in his life, including his brothers having sold him into slavery, he muses, they meant it for evil, but God meant it for good (Gen 50:20). What makes this a powerful example is that it is saturated with insight, which is what characterizes all meaningful as opposed to superficial reframing. It facilitates a new way of making sense of what happened. In talking with someone in pain, you may be tempted to say, "Life has something better in store for you." Say this only if you have already listened carefully and earned the right to say it, and if you believe the person will benefit from hearing it. Otherwise, it is likely to come off as an expression of your need to trivialize the problem and avoid listening. If an attempt at reframing is ill-timed or ill-placed, it may leave the other person feeling tossed out in the cold while you sit by the fireplace in your overcoat.

Combine Caring with Candor

All deep relationships involve caring and candor. Caring without candor creates a relationship of lukewarm superficiality, while candor without caring can be offensively harsh. I once heard the late psychiatrist Carl Whitaker say in a lecture, "If you're going to use the scalpel of truth, dip it first in the anesthetic of love." This is parallel to Paul's exhortation to speak the truth in love (Eph 4:15). If you are going to say something confrontational, something that might sting, phrase it artfully, gently, and supportively.

These are the seven most useful things I know about how to help other people who are in emotional pain. I am not suggesting you turn your life into a therapy office, much less a Lucy Van Pelt psychiatry booth. Lucy, a character from the comic strip "Peanuts" by Charles Schultz, routinely posts a sign offering psychiatric help. But I am suggesting that you may sometimes be able to bring healing to someone who may get it in no other way. Someone you know may need the help that only you can provide. "Now that I have washed your feet," said Jesus, "wash one another's."

Closing Thoughts

The chapter began with three observations: (1) Everyone has been injured and therefore needs healing; (2) It takes people to heal people; and (3) Being present when someone else is suffering can make all the difference. It also contained seven recommendations for how to help another person: (1) Listen for deeper meanings; (2) Focus on the other person; (3) Do not trivialize another person's pain or rush in with superficial advice; (4) Support and lift people up rather than making them feel responsible; (5) Take action when appropriate; (6) Cautiously, sensitively, and carefully reframe events and circumstances if you have earned the right to do this; and (7) Combine candor with caring.

Preview

In the next chapter, we will discuss how a person may only see Christ in the face of a Christian, who may for that person be Christ's only representative on earth.

Chapter 29. Representing Christ

IN THE GOSPEL OF John, Jesus says, "As I have loved you, you also are to love one another. By this all people will know that you are my disciples" (John 13:34–35, ESV). This is God's call to live a transformed life. An inescapable feature of human existence is that we influence other people, for better or worse, often with little awareness of the impact we have on them. In this chapter, I want to share some observations and musings about impact, and how it can occur in unexpected ways that turn out to be enormously important.

"For more than half a century," wrote the late Malcolm Muggeridge, "I've been a communicator, what Augustine called a vendor of words."[1] This is what we all are, in one way or another, shapers of the minds and hearts of others by what we say and do, and sometimes by what we write, whether in a letter, text, or e-mail message. Below are a few thoughts about what it means to communicate and how communication sometimes happens in unexpected ways. They also contain suggestions on how to communicate effectively and constructively.

Communication Means Connecting

To communicate is to connect with your audience. All the knowledge in the world will not amount to much if you do not connect. We all have the opportunity to connect, regardless of the kind of job we hold

---

1. Muggeridge, *Twentieth Century Testimony*, n.p., quotation under bust of the author.

or whether we even have a job. Parents who do not work outside the home may have the greatest chance of all to connect because God has entrusted children into their daily care. Connecting sometimes requires working hard to achieve it. We must sometimes learn the language of those with whom we want to connect, whether it is a spoken language or just a manner of talking. Communicating requires heart. If you talk to people only from the head, without speaking out of your experience, you will at best connect tenuously. Others may need to hear about your life, including how you are connected to Christ. They may also need to learn about your struggles and failings.

To the degree my conversations with other people have been meaningful to them, it has often been because I opened up about mistakes I made and what I should have done differently. I tell them how, when I was a young psychologist in training, working on an in-patient psychiatric ward of a large hospital, I was too proud to pick up the phone to call a patient's relatives in Canada. That, I assumed, was the social worker's job. An understanding nurse made the call. I also tell them I would have been a more effective professor in my twenties if I had been less concerned with, and protective of, my status and dignity.

But communicating is more than connecting. It is connecting in a way that has impact and brings about change. You have to touch the soul as well as the cerebrum. This is why it is not always teachers who best connect with students. Sometimes it is the person who works in the alumni office, assists an administrator, or delivers the mail. Nor is it always an executive in a company. Sometimes, it is the parking attendant.

Impact Is Unpredictable

Sometimes you know immediately when something you have said or done has been influential. But often, you do not. There is a lot of unpredictability weaving its way through life. Years ago, someone told me that he had recently been on the Washington Metro and saw a woman, across from him, reading an old tattered and yellowed paperback. He then noticed my name on the cover. The book had been out of print for years. That was when I appreciated for the first time that books have lives of their own and sometimes become part of the culture. Spoken words can do that also. What you say can endure for a long time in the minds of those who hear it. Your words linger on and can travel down

CHAPTER 29. REPRESENTING CHRIST

generations. You can never predict that this will happen. But it might. What you say to someone in a store, hallway, office, restaurant, or shopping mall may change a life.

As just one among many examples, this unpredictability reveals itself in the life of Herman Melville, who was born in 1819. He made it big, early on, with stories set in the South Seas. But by the 1850s, his writings had begun to fall out of favor. He died in 1889, having long inhabited the margins of poverty and obscurity. Not only did no one much care for his massive tome about a deranged captain obsessively searching for a whale, but more than anything he had written, that book, published in 1851, turned the reading public against him. Then, in the early 1920s, literary critics rediscovered *Moby-Dick*, which became America's answer to the Great Russian Novel. By the time scholars rescued it from dusty library basements, Melville had been dead for over thirty years.

It may not ultimately matter whether our impact comes now or after we die, not if we expect to spend eternity with God. Paul expressed that he could not even judge his own work, let alone anyone else's, and that he would leave such judgment to the Lord (1 Cor 4:3).

Impact Can Be Unconscious

You may deliver what you consider to be the best work of your life, perhaps the result of a major project, and yet have little impact. On the other hand, you may utter some throwaway line in a hallway that will forever alter the way someone else sees the world. I learned this lesson decades ago, when I was still practicing as a clinician. There were times when I delivered what I thought was a superb therapeutic hour. The following week, I would ask how the client had experienced it. I was trying to find out if my suggestions had been as productive as I had expected and whether what I said led to further insight. Sometimes, I was disappointed. "Last session was fine," the person might politely answer, "but that comment you made in the waiting room as I was leaving... that changed everything." I could not even remember what I said.

This illustrates the difference between explicit and implicit communication. There are the formal messages and there are the meta-messages. People are keen observers. They watch the way you hold your coffee cup and if you get annoyed when things go wrong. You may be trying to put your best foot forward, but without even thinking about it, they are taking the measure of you, processing dozens of implicit messages. I once heard a missionary from India say, "I cannot hear you, for your life out-speaks your message." How you act and what you say matters, more than you may think.

Great Communicators Convey Important Ideas

Ours is a world in which people produce, dispense, and consume facts by the truckload. But if all we do is deliver facts, we are not communicating effectively. To give others the best of what is inside of you, share with them the best ideas you have and do not hold back. If Christ's reign as Lord of the universe is an important idea for you, say it. In one way or another, just about all of us are time-bankrupt and do not need anyone else to give us more to do. Nevertheless, it is worth an hour or so to sit in a chair with a pad and pencil and jot down what you consider to be the most important things you know. If you have never taken the time to do this, you may be surprised by how hard it is. There are so many choices.

Knowing the date of the Norman Conquest, the atomic number of selenium, or the difference between declarative and procedural knowledge may help get you on a quiz show. But, by themselves, such factoids will not make you a great communicator. Great communicators express key concepts in ways others can understand, so it is worth the time to identify, out of everything you know, which ideas you believe to be centrally important. I call these power ideas, the ones with the potential to have major impacts.

The Heart Has Reasons That Reason Knows Not Of

Recall these words from Pascal, cited in chapter 2, and the insight they convey: You influence others by how you treat them and how well you connect with their hearts. A hundred years ago, psychiatrists and psychologists believed that dispensing well-timed insights would automatically bring about healing. This turned out not to be true. Eventually they figured out that how they behaved toward their patients, the nature of the relationship, was far more important. Could they provide the right kind of warmth? Could they be genuine rather than guarded? Could they empathize?

CHAPTER 29. REPRESENTING CHRIST

Regardless of what job you hold, if any, there is one thing you can say to anyone, something they will remember, especially if you mean it: "I believe in you." The people who believed in me along the way allowed me to believe in myself, and that has made a great deal of difference. Maybe it is been the same for you.

God Put You There

You may not always believe God has summoned, much less appointed, you to do what you are doing. Perhaps you harbor fantasies of what else you might have done with your life, notions of what psychologists refer to as other possible selves.[2] You may imagine that if you had entered another profession or taken a different job, you would have been happier or more successful. Maybe you say to yourself, I could have been a lawyer, novelist, veterinarian, dentist, or physician. Or, gone into a different business. Yet, God may have led you to where you are now, doing exactly what you are doing. God may be sending certain people to you, or you to them.

Own What You Believe

There is a Greek word from the New Testament that is dear to Christian theologians. It is *kerygma*, which means proclamation, specifically the proclamation of the good news of redemption. Even people who grasp the significance of Jesus sometimes forget how living as a Christian can put them in tension with secular culture. This will not happen if they never declare themselves to be people with faith, but it can happen quickly if they do. If you are a Christian, share with others what you know of God. And, if you are still in search of God, remain open to the idea that God may also be in search of you.

Closing Thoughts

This chapter contained seven suggestions for how to communicate, and if you are a Christian, how to convey this to others: (1) The essence of communication is connecting with your audience, and if you do not

---

2. Markus and Nurius, "Possible Selves," 954–69.

connect, you cannot communicate anything of value; (2) You can never predict the impact you might have on someone in the future, and this impact may be great; (3) The impact you have on someone may at times be outside your awareness; (4) Give to others those ideas that, to you, have been the most powerful and helpful; (5) Convey to other people that you believe in them, which can have enormous positive impact; (6) Wherever you find yourself, embrace this if you can; and (7) Be open about what you believe.

Preview

If you are thinking about becoming a Christian, in the next and final chapter, I will invite you to take the plunge. Committing your life to God through Christ can make all the difference.

Part VI. **TAKING THE PLUNGE**

Chapter 30. All Things Made New

BECOMING A CHRISTIAN INVOLVES accepting that Jesus, though still divine, accomplished two things. First, he showed us what a holy life looks like. Second, he took on our human nature and went to the cross in order to reconcile us with our creator. God gave Jesus to humanity as an unmerited gift, and through the crucifixion he absorbed our sins within himself.

Tim Keller was known for making the statement that Jesus lived the life we should have lived and died the death we should have died. John Stott was known for saying that sin is substituting ourselves for God, while salvation is realizing that Jesus substituted himself for us.

Approaching God through Christ requires acknowledging that, like every other human being, you have done things you knew to be wrong and failed to do things you knew to be right. At least some of these things were not innocent mistakes and we have all done them. John Calvin suggested that our knowledge of God is intimately connected with our knowledge of ourselves. In Ps 51, King David prays, "I know my transgressions . . . cleanse me from my sin . . . create in me a pure heart." David knew himself.

There have been many attempts to assist people who want to become Christians by recommending specific prayers. The words are not important, but the thought-forms are. Here is one you might use:

> Loving, gracious, and merciful God, I come to you in humility, knowing that I have not been living for you but for myself. I have paid little attention to your desires, and I have not had an ongoing relationship with you. I have often done what was

wrong and failed to do what was right, and for this I ask your forgiveness. I realize what you did for me in allowing your son to be put to death on my behalf. I now call you Father, as Jesus taught, and I ask that your Holy Spirit guide me as I follow you. I acknowledge Jesus as my savior, and I ask you to help me become more like him. And, I ask you, Jesus, to become my Lord.

Fresh Eyes and a Renewed Spirit

Becoming a Christian means seeing God and ourselves more clearly. It also involves viewing other people differently. Regardless of the appearance, ethnicity, or behavior of others, when Christians are at their best, they see them as existing at God's pleasure and having been created in God's image. They may fall back into viewing or treating others with dispositions and prejudices acquired before becoming Christians, but they will usually be aware of it and feel the pangs of conscience.

We love people who love us, care about those who care about us, and feel comfortable with others who resemble us. Few of us are naturally inclined to love those who intend us harm, disparage us, or are distinctly different. Christian conversion begins to change all that. Not only are Christians to love and accept those who are different, but they are to do this even when it is costly and even if they have injured us. This is what Jesus did on the cross when he asked God to forgive his executioners (Luke 23:34). Acquiring the potential to do this is part of what it means in the New Testament to be *born again* (John 3:3).

Growing As a Christian

Opening ourselves to the leading of God's Spirit is central to transformation in Christ, of allowing God to pull us out of the pit of self-absorption. It is not that Christians never behave in self-centered ways. As human animals, we will always tend to put ourselves first. But a Christian, in whom the Spirit of Christ dwells, also has another nature, one that reflects transformation. In the words of Thomas à Kempis[1] in *Imitation of Christ*, the Spirit enables the Christian to *imitate* a life patterned after Christ, to become increasingly like him. Imitate, here, does not mean

---

1. Thomas à Kempis was a fifteenth-century priest and canon regular. According to the entry in Wikipedia, the *a* in his name represents the Latin *from* and is erroneously accented.

CHAPTER 30. ALL THINGS MADE NEW

pretending but emulating. God is not finished with the process of ushering in what the New Testament refers to as God's kingdom. Neither is God done working in an individual Christian's life, of conforming that Christian to the image of Christ. This is also true of Christian communities whose members want to grow spiritually.

Christians may resemble seeds mentioned in the "Parable of the Sower" (Matt 13:3–8; Luke 8:4–15). Some, says Jesus, is sown on rocky ground. These are the people who respond with joy to the message of God's love, but since they have no roots, faith withers and dies. Other seed is sown among thorns. These are people whose anxiety, wealth, and pursuit of pleasure choke off all spiritual growth. Some seed, however, is sown in rich moist soil. These are the ones who develop into mature Christians, show God's love to others, and communicate the good news to them.

Life for a Christian is not without difficulty, and Jesus bluntly tells his followers that it will bring trouble and adversity (John 16:33). There are many accounts of Christians who suffered tremendously at the hands of others but who nevertheless continued to trust God. One was Corrie ten Boom, a Dutch watchmaker and member of the Dutch Resistance who, along with other members of her family, hid Jews from the Nazis. When the Nazis discovered this, they sent her to Ravensbrück concentration camp. Difficulties may take the form of irritations and inconveniences or major misfortunes and losses. As hard as it may sometimes be, Jesus encourages us to see beyond all this. Because Jesus has overcome the world (John 16:33), with its decadence and corruption, he tells Christians to have peace. World, in this passage, can best be understood as *world system*. Jesus did not live and die to insulate us from evil or the struggles of daily existence, but to enable us to transcend them.

When you become a Christian, at least four things happen: First, everything become new (2 Cor 5:17).[2] Second, you are adopted into God's family (Rom 8:15, 23; Rom 9:4; Gal 4:5; Eph 1:5). Third, you become a joint heir with Christ of all that God has given him (Rom 8:17; Titus 3:7; I Pet 3:7). And fourth, you acquire the capacity, if you remain open to the leading of the Holy Spirit, to develop holiness. Protestants can be uncomfortable with the idea of deification or divinization alluded to in Roman Catholicism and emphasized in Eastern Orthodoxy, but it expresses an important truth about what theologians call sanctification.

---

2. See Smedes, *All Things Made New*.

To continue to grow and develop, repentance and conversion have to be ongoing features of your existence. This means owning up to whatever runs counter to God's will, and if you can, turning away from anything likely to make owning up necessary in the future. When Jesus told his followers to be perfect as God is perfect (Matt 5:48), he meant it. We stumble and fall, but the key to growing as a Christian is to return, again and again, to Christ.

How to Remain Focused

Much of what we read in the New Testament happened two-thousand years ago, which at times may seem irrelevant to everyday existence. We have to work, collect paychecks, pay bills, care for loved ones, tend to our health, and meet social and governmental obligations. With all there is to do, how is anyone supposed to have time for religion, to become re-connected with God? But life has always been a struggle. Millions of people who responded to Christ in the past had it no easier and probably worse. They faced different challenges, but like us, they were all working a problem.[3]

To keep believers focused on Christ, many traditions highlight the importance of contemplation, of stepping back and disengaging, emptying our mental file cabinets to make room for God. This is also why what some Christians call "quiet time" is important. A key part of such time ought to be devoted to saturating yourself in the New Testament.

Relating Personally to the Universal Redeemer

Jesus was Jewish. He was not a gentile masquerading as a Jew, but a rabbi, a teacher, steeped in the Old Testament[4] and Jewish culture. That culture can feel alien to a person unfamiliar with the Bible or who has not been raised in a Jewish home. How, therefore, is a non-Jewish person in twenty-first-century secular culture supposed to relate to a Jesus with whom he or she may have little culturally in common?

Because Jesus is the universal redeemer, cultural differences have nothing to do with it. He is the global savior, who lived and died for people all over the world, not just white Americans. Long ago, he

   3. I owe this insight to Debbie Cobo.
   4. See Yancey, *The Bible Jesus Read*.

CHAPTER 30. ALL THINGS MADE NEW

shared the gospel with those who walked the streets of Jerusalem with him. Today his disciples, in partnership with God's Spirit, share it with those who walk the streets of Beijing, Caracas, Moscow, Nairobi, Madrid, New York, Mumbai, Paris, or Sydney. Ethnicity and nationality are contexts, not the good news.

Why Church Is Important

Some people, as we reviewed in chapter 22, say they are Christians but do not belong to a church and have no interest in formal religion. When such people allow clerical scandals to keep them from attending church, they are missing something of enormous value. Church encourages a person toward faith, and without such encouragement, faith is often anemic. Attending a church that is faithful to the gospel allows a person to hear readings from scripture, sermons or homilies based on it, and hymns that promote reverence, all of which nudge a person toward God. Human nature, in concert with secular culture, nudges us to move away from God. Church pulls us in the opposite direction.

A Closing Word

The following quotation, from the book of Numbers (6:24–26, NIV), is sometimes pronounced at the conclusion of worship services. I end this book by addressing them to you:

> "The Lord bless you and keep you; the Lord make his face shine on you and be gracious to you; the Lord turn his face toward you and give you peace."

Appendix I. The Apostles' Creed
(Third Century)

No one knows when the Apostles' Creed was first crafted. Its basic contents go back at least as far as the writings of Hippolytus[1] in the third century, Marcellus[2] in the fourth, and Rufinus[3] (Aquileia) in the fifth. The final version,[4] still recited in contemporary churches, dates to around AD 700. It contains core Christian affirmations.

> I believe in God the Father almighty, creator of heaven and earth; and in Jesus Christ, his only Son, our Lord, Who was conceived by the Holy Spirit, born of the Virgin Mary, suffered under Pontius Pilate, was crucified, dead, and buried. He descended to hell, on the third day rose again from the dead, ascended into heaven, sits at the right hand of God the Father almighty, from thence he will come to judge the living and the dead; I believe in the Holy Spirit, the holy catholic Church, the communion of saints, the forgiveness of sins, the resurrection of the body, and the life everlasting. Amen

---

1. Leith, ed. "Interrogatory Creed of Hippolytus," 22–23.
2. Leith, ed. "Creed of Marcellus," 22–23.
3. Leith, ed. "Creed of Rufinus," 22–24.
4. The final version of The Apostles' Creed is designated *Textus Receptus*, a term meaning the received text. Leith, 22–25.

Appendix II. The Nicene-Constantinopolitan Creed

(325, 381)

WHAT APPEARS BELOW IS known as the Nicene Creed, although it might be called more accurately the Nicene-Constantinopolitan Creed or The Creed of the 150 Fathers of Constantinople. Its final version affirms what had been developed in Nicaea, but it goes further in asserting the full deity of the Holy Spirit. The phrase "proceeds from the Father" was later amended to "proceeds from the Father and the Son" to reflect the theology of the Western Church, especially as developed by Augustine. Although differences in temperaments, languages, and approaches to theology had been creating tensions between the Western (Latin) and Eastern Orthodox (Greek) branches of Christendom for centuries, it was disagreement over a single Greek word—*filioque*—that finally triggered the split in 1054 known as the East-West Schism. Members of the Eastern Orthodox branch believe that the Holy Spirit proceeds *only* from the Father, rather than from both Father and Son, and deny that the Eastern Church ever approved *dual procession*.

The road leading to ratification of the Nicene-Constantinopolitan Creed was fraught with conflict and controversy,[1] and between 325 and 381, various councils attempted to resolve them. Some claimed that the Son was unlike the Father, that he was fallible and could sin. Others claimed he resembled, but was not of the same substance or essence as,

---

1. See Latourette, *History of Christianity*, 153-164; Rusch, *The Trinitarian Controversy*.

APPENDIX II. THE NICENE-CONSTANTINOPOLITAN CREED

the Father. Setting aside the debate concerning procession, theologians in the Eastern Church, known as the three great Cappadocians,[2] were key to formulating the version in use today. We use this in the church I attend:

> We believe in one God,
>> the Father Almighty,
>> maker of heaven and earth,
>> of all things visible and invisible.
>
> And in one Lord Jesus Christ,
>> the only-begotten Son of God,
>> begotten from the Father before all ages;
>> God of God,
>> Light of Light,
>> true God from true God,
>> begotten, not made;
>> of the same essence as the Father.
>> Through Him all things were made.
>
> For us and for our salvation
>> he came down from heaven;
>> he became incarnate by the Holy Spirit of the virgin Mary,
>> and was made human.
>> He was crucified for us under Pontius Pilate;
>> he suffered and was buried.
>> The third day He rose again, according to the Scriptures.
>> He ascended into heaven
>> and is seated at the right hand of the Father.
>> He will come again with glory
>> to judge the living and the dead.
>> His kingdom will never end.

---

2. Gregory of Nazianzus, Basil of Caesarea, and Gregory of Nyssa. See LaTourette, 163.

APPENDIX II. THE NICENE-CONSTANTINOPOLITAN CREED

> And we believe in the Holy Spirit,
> the Lord and Giver of Life.
> He proceeds from the Father and the Son,
> and with the Father and the Son is worshipped and glorified.
> He spoke through the prophets.
> We believe in one holy catholic[3] and apostolic church.
> We affirm one baptism for the forgiveness of sins.
> We look forward to the resurrection of the dead,
> and to life in the world to come. AMEN.

What follows is a slightly different version,[4] which opens up some of the deeper meanings embedded in the creed:

> We believe in one God, the Father All Governing [Almighty], creator [Maker] of heaven and earth, of all things visible and invisible; And in one Lord Jesus Christ, the only-begotten Son of God, begotten from the Father before all time [all worlds], Light from Light, true [very] God from true [very] God, begotten not created [made], of the same essence (reality) [substance] as the Father, through [by] Whom all things came into being [were made], Who for us men and because of [for] our salvation came down from heaven, and was incarnate by the Holy Spirit [Ghost] and [of] the Virgin Mary and became human [was made man]. He was crucified for us under Pontius Pilate, and suffered and was buried, and rose on the third day, according to the Scriptures, and ascended to heaven, and sits on the right hand of the Father, and will come again with glory to judge the living [quick] and dead. His Kingdom shall have no end. And in the Holy Spirit, the Lord and life-giver, Who proceeds from the Father [and the Son], Who is worshipped and glorified together with the Father and Son, Who spoke through the prophets; and in one, holy, catholic, and apostolic Church. We confess [acknowledge] one baptism for the remission of sins. We look forward to the resurrection of the dead and the life of the world to come. Amen.

---

3. *Catholic*, as used here, means universal.
4. Leith, ed., *Creeds of the Churches*, 28–33. Bracketed alternate readings from MacGregor, *The Nicene Creed*, xi.

About the Author

CLINTON W. MCLEMORE TAUGHT six years full-time at Mount St. Mary's College, one summer at USC, nine years full-time in the doctoral clinical psychology program at Fuller Theological Seminary, and a part-time year at Fuller after that. He practiced as a psychotherapist for two decades and worked as an organizational psychologist for three. McLemore has consulted for many of the nation's largest and most respected corporations, and for over twenty years he served as the management psychologist for what many regard as the nation's premier think-tank. He has presented at many meetings of state and national associations, written several chapters in anthologies, and penned scores of entries in encyclopedias. He has also been interviewed many times on radio and television. For almost a decade, he led a research group investigating social dynamics. His many journal articles include a near-record-length contribution on interpersonal diagnosis to the flagship *American Psychologist,* which an anonymous reviewer described as a "seminal contribution" to the field. In 1983, he founded *Clinician's Research Digest*, now owned and operated by the American Psychological Association. In 2019, the APA gave McLemore its award for Outstanding Contributions to Continuing Professional Development in Psychology.

Bibliography

Ackroyd, P. R., and C. F. Evans, eds. *From the Beginnings to Jerome*. Cambridge History of the Bible 1. Cambridge: Cambridge University Press, 1970.
Ahlstrom, Sidney E. *A Religious History of the American People*. New Haven: Yale University Press, 1972.
Allen, Diogenes. *Three Outsides: Pascal, Kierkegaard, Simone Weil*. Cambridge, MA: Cowley, 1983.
Andersen, Kurt. "How America Lost Its Mind." *The Atlantic*, Sept. 2017.
Arendt, Hannah. *Eichmann in Jerusalem: A Report on the Banality of Evil*. New York: Viking, 1963.
Arsenault, Joseph, SSA. "Can Only Catholics Go to Heaven?" https://theleaven.org/can-only-catholics-go-to-heaven/.
Barrett, William. *The Illusion of Technique*. Garden City: Doubleday, 1978.
Bauckham, Richard J. *Jesus and the Eyewitnesses: The Gospels as Eyewitness Testimony*. Grand Rapids: Eerdmans, 2006.
Becker, Ernest. *The Denial of Death*. New York: Free, 1973.
Beckett, Wendy. *The Story of Painting*. London: Dorling Kindersley, 1994.
Behe, Michael J. *Darwin's Black Box: The Biochemical Challenge to Evolution*. 2nd ed. New York: Free Press, 2006.
Bellah, Robert N., et al. *Habits of the Heart: Individualism and Commitment in American Life*. Berkeley: University of California Press, 1985.
Benedict, Ruth. *Patterns of Culture*. Boston: Houghton Mifflin, 1934.
Benson, Bruce Ellis. *Pious Nietzsche: Decadence and Dionysian Faith*. Bloomington: Indiana University Press, 2008.
Berkouwer, G. C. *Sin*. Translated by Philip C. Holtrop. Grand Rapids: Eerdmans, 1971.
Billings, Malcolm. *The Crusades: Five Centuries of Holy Wars*. New York: Sterling, 1996.
Bloom, Harold. "Alfred, Lord Tennyson." In *The Best Poems of the English Language: From Chaucer through Frost*, 591–638. New York: HarperCollins, 2004.
Bodanis, David. *E=mc²*. New York: Walker, 2000.
Bonhoeffer, Dietrich. *The Cost of Discipleship*. New York: Scribner, 1963.
———. *Ethics*. New York: Simon & Schuster, 1995.
Book of Common Prayer. New York: Church Publishing Incorporated, 1979.

Boom, Corrie ten, with John Sherill and Elizabeth Sherill. *The Hiding Place*. Ada, MI: Revell, 1971.
Bosker, Bianca. "What Really Killed the Dinosaurs?" *The Atlantic*, Sept. 2018.
Branden, Barbara. *The Passion of Ayn Rand*. Garden City, NY: Anchor, 1986.
Bronowski, Jacob. "A Machine or a Self?" In *The Identify of Man*, 1–24. Garden City, New York: Natural History, 1965.
———. *The Ascent of Man*. 1973. BBC TV series.
Brooks, Arthur C. "The Satisfaction Trap." *The Atlantic*, Mar. 2022.
Brown, Colin. *Miracles and the Critical Mind*. Grand Rapids: Eerdmans, 1984.
Buber, Martin. *I and Thou*. New York: Charles Scribner, 1970.
Bunyan, John. *The Pilgrim's Progress from This World, to That Which Is to Come*. Edited by Cynthia Wall. New York: Norton, 2008.
Cahill, Thomas. *Desire of the Everlasting Hills: The World Before and After Jesus*. New York: Doubleday, 1999.
———. *The Gifts of the Jews: How a Tribe of Desert Nomads Changed the Way Everyone Thinks and Feels*. New York: Doubleday, 1998.
———. *How the Irish Saved Civilization: The Untold Story of Ireland's Heroic Role from the Fall of Rome to the Rise of Medieval Europe*. New York: Doubleday, 1995.
Calder, Todd. "The Concept of Evil." In *The Stanford Encyclopedia of Philosophy*, Winter 2022 ed., edited by Edward N. Zalta and Uri Nodelman. https://plato.stanford.edu/archives/win2022/entries/concept-evil/.
Cantini, Andrea, and Riccardo Bruni. "Paradoxes and Contemporary Logic." In *The Stanford Encyclopedia of Philosophy*, Summer 2024 ed., edited by Edward N. Zalta and Uri Nodelman. https://plato.stanford.edu/archives/sum2024/entries/paradoxes-contemporary-logic/.
Carson, D. A. *The Gospel According to John*. Pillar New Testament Commentary. Grand Rapids: Eerdmans, 1991.
Catechism of the Catholic Church, rev ed. New York: Doubleday, 1995.
Chambers Biographical Dictionary. 6th ed. Edinburgh: Chambers Harrap, 1997.
Chambers Dictionary of Etymology. Edinburgh: Chambers Harrap, 2001.
Chardin, Teilhard de. *The Phenomenon of Man*. New York: Harper, 2008.
Chesterton, G. K. *What's Wrong with the World?* New York: Dodd, Mead, 1910.
Clark, Kenneth. *Civilisation: A Personal View*. 1969. BBC.
———. *Civilisation: A Personal View*. Episode Six, "Protest and Communication." BBC.
———. *Civilisation: A Personal View*. New York: Harper & Row, 1969.
Collins, Francis. *Language of God: A Scientist Presents Evidence for Belief*. New York: Free Press, 2006.
Collins, Randall. *The Sociology of Philosophies: A Global Theory of Intellectual Change*. Cambridge, MA: Belknap, 1998.
Collodi, Carlo. *The Adventures of Pinocchio*. N.p., 1883.
Conant, James, and John Haugeland, eds. *The Road Since Structure: Philosophical Essays, 1970–1993, with an Autobiographical Interview*. Chicago: University of Chicago Press, 2000.
Copleston, Frederick. *A History of Philosophy*. Vol. 7. Westminster, Maryland: Newman, 1965.

Culp, John. "Panentheism." In *The Stanford Encyclopedia of Philosophy*, Fall 2023 ed., edited by Edward N. Zalta and Uri Nodelman. https://plato.stanford.edu/archives/fall2023/entries/panentheism/.

Daane, James. *The Anatomy of Anti-Semitism and Other Essays on Religion and Race.* Grand Rapids: Eerdmans, 1965.

Dalberg, John Emerich Edward (Lord Acton). *Bartlett's Familiar Quotations.* 17th ed. Boston: Little, Brown, 2002.

Darwin, Charles. *The Descent of Man, and Selection in Relation to Sex.* 1871.

———. *On the Origin of Species by means of Natural Selection, or the Preservation of Favoured Races in the Struggle for Life.* 1859.

Dawkins, Richard. *The God Delusion.* Boston: Houghton Mifflin Harcourt, 2006.

Dawson, Christopher. *Religion and the Rise of Western Culture.* New York: Sheed & Ward, 1950.

Diagnostic and Statistical Manual of Mental Disorders. 5th ed. Washington, DC: American Psychiatric Association, 2013.

Dominguez, Joe, and Vicki Robin. "Money Ain't What It Used to Be—and Never Was." In *Your Money or Your Life: Transforming Your Relationship with Money and Achieving Financial Independence*, 40–69. New York: Penguin, 1992.

Dostoevsky, Fyodor. *The Brothers Karamazov.* 1879.

———. *The Idiot.* 1868.

Douthat, Ross. *Bad Religion: How We Became a Nation of Heretics.* New York: Free Press, 2012.

Draper, John William. *History of the Conflict between Religion and Science.* 1874.

Duerrenmatt, Friedrich. *The Physicists.* Translated by Joel Agee. New York: Grove, 2010.

Durant, Will, and Ariel Durant. *The Lessons of History.* New York: Simon and Schuster, 1968.

Earhart, H. Byron, ed. *Religious Traditions of the World: A Journey through Africa, Mesoamerica, North America, Judaism, Christianity, Islam, Hinduism, Buddhism, China, and Japan.* New York: HarperSanFrancisco, 1993.

Edwards, David L. *Christianity: The First Two Thousand Years.* Maryknoll, NY: Orbis, 1997.

Egner, Robert B., and Lester E. Dennon, eds. *The Basic Writings of Bertrand Russell: 1903–1959.* New York: Simon & Schuster, 1961.

Ehrman, Bart. *Historical Jesus and Lost Christianities: Christian Scriptures and the Battle over Authentication.* Chantilly, VA: The Teaching Company, 2002.

———. *Misquoting Jesus: The Story Behind Who Changed the Bible and Why.* New York: HarperCollins, 2005.

Enns, Peter. *Inspiration and Incarnation: Evangelicals and the Problem of the Old Testament.* Grand Rapids: Baker, 2005.

———. *The Evolution of Adam: What the Bible Does and Doesn't Say about Human Origins.* Grand Rapids: Brazos, 2012.

Erickson, Millard J. "Salvation." In *The Concise Dictionary of Christian Theology*, 175. Rev ed. Wheaton, IL: Crossway, 2001.

———. "Sin." *The Concise Dictionary of Christian Theology*, 182. Rev ed. Wheaton, IL: Crossway, 2001.

Evans, C. Stephen. *Subjectivity and Religious Belief: An Historical Critical Study.* Grand Rapids: Christian University Press, 1978.

Farrer, Austin. "Images and Inspiration." In *The Truth Seeking Heart*, edited by Ann Loades and Robert MacSwain, 20–36. London: Canterbury Press Norwich, 2006.

———. *The Truth Seeking Heart: Austin Farrer and His Writings*, edited by Ann Loades and Robert MacSwain. London: Canterbury Press Norwich, 2006.

Fenichel, Otto. *Psychoanalytic Theory of Neurosis*. New York: Norton, 1945.

Ferguson, Niall. "Introduction: Rasselas's Question." *Civilization: The West and the Rest*, 1–18. New York: Penguin, 2011.

———. *Civilization: The West and the Rest*. New York: Penguin, 2011.

Ferry, Luc. *A Brief History of Thought: A Philosophical Guide to Living*. Translated by Theo Cuffe. New York: HarperCollins, 2011.

Flew, Antony. *David Hume: Writings on Religion*. Chicago: Open Court, 1992.

Frankfurt, Harry G. *On Bullshit*: Princeton: Princeton University Press, 2005.

Freud, Anna. *The Ego and the Mechanisms of Defense*. Rev. ed. New York: International Universities, 1966.

Freud, Sigmund. "Obsessive Acts and Religious Practices." In *Sigmund Freud: Collected Papers*, 2, 25–35. New York: Basic Books. Originally published 1907.

———. *Civilization and Its Discontents*. Translated by James Strachey. New York: Norton, 2010. Originally published 1930.

———. *The Future of an Illusion*. Translated by James Strachey. New York: Norton, 1989. Originally published 1927.

———. *Moses and Monotheism*. New York: Penguin, 1955. Originally published 1937.

———. *Totem and Taboo: Resemblances Between the Psychic Lives of Savages and Neurotics*. Translated by James Strachey. New York: Norton, 1990. Originally published 1913.

Fromm-Reichmann, Frieda. "Loneliness," *Psychiatry* 22.1 (1959) 1–15.

Fukuyama, Frank. *The End of History and the Last Man*. New York: Free Press, 1992.

Funk, Robert W., and the Jesus Seminar. *The Acts of Jesus: The Search for the Authentic Deeds of Jesus*. New York: HarperCollins, 1998.

Gabrieli, Francesco. *Arab Histories of the Crusades*. Translated by E. J. Costello. Berkeley: University of California Press, 1969.

Galbraith, John Kenneth. *Money: Where It Came From, Where It Went*. Boston: Houghton Mifflin, 1975.

Gibbon, Edward. *The History of the Decline and Fall of the Roman Empire*. New York: Everyman's Library, 2010. Originally published 1776–1789.

Gibbons, Ann. "Why 536 was 'the worst year to be alive.'" *Science Magazine*, Nov. 2018.

Gilbert, Douglas, and Clyde S. Kilby. *C. S. Lewis: Images of His World*. Grand Rapids: Eerdmans, 1973.

Gladwell, Malcolm. *Blink: The Power of Thinking Without Thinking*. New York: Little, Brown, 2005.

———. *Outliers: The Story of Success*. New York: Little, Brown, 2008.

Gombrich, E. H. *The Story of Art*. London: Phaidon, 1972.

Gopnik, Adam. "Blood and Soil: A Historian Returns to the Holocaust." Review of *Black Earth: The Holocaust as History and Warning*, by Timothy Synder. *The New Yorker*, Sept. 21, 2015.

Gould, Stephen Jay. *The Structure of Evolutionary Theory*. Cambridge, MA: Belknap, 2002.

Greene, Graham. *The End of the Affair*. New York: Viking, 1951.

Greene, Joshua. *Moral Tribes: Emotion, Reason, and the Gap Between Them and Us.* New York: Penguin, 2013.
Greenslade, S. L. *The West from the Reformation to the Present Day.* Cambridge History of the Bible 3. Cambridge: Cambridge University Press, 1963.
Haass, Richard. *World: A Brief Introduction.* New York: Penguin, 2020.
Habermas, Jürgen. *Between Facts and Norms: Contributions to a Discourse Theory of Law and Democracy.* Translated by William Rehg. Cambridge, MA: MIT Press, 1996.
Hagner, Donald A. "Paul, Judaism, and the Law." In *The New Testament: A Historical and Theological Introduction*, 366–79. Grand Rapids: Baker, 2012.
Haig, Matt. *The Midnight Library.* New York: Viking, 2020.
Hamel, Christopher de. *The Book: A History of the Bible.* London: Phaidon, 2001.
Harari, Yuval Noah. *Sapiens: A Brief History of Humankind.* New York: Harper, 2015.
Harvey, A. E. *The New English Bible Companion to the New Testament.* Oxford: Oxford University Press; Cambridge: Cambridge University Press, 1970.
Heine, Heinrich. *Religion and Philosophy in Germany.* 1835.
Herlihy, David. *The Black Death and the Transformation of the West.* Edited by Samuel K. Cohn Jr. Cambridge, MA: Harvard University Press, 1997.
Herodotus. *Histories.* 426 BC.
Hersey, John. *Hiroshima.* New York: Vintage Books, 1946, 1989.
Hildebrand, Dietrich von. *The Heart: An Analysis of Human and Divine Affectivity.* Edited by John Henry. South Bend, IN: St. Augustine's, 2007.
———. *Transformation in Christ.* Chicago: Franciscan Herald, 1948.
Hitler, Adolf. *Mein Kampf.* New York: Harper, 1998. Originally published 1925–1926.
Hobbes, Thomas. *Leviathan.* 1651.
Hoffer, Eric. *The True Believer: Thoughts on the Nature of Mass Movements.* New York: Harper & Row, 1951.
Holland, Tom. *Dominion: How the Christian Revolution Remade the World.* New York: Basic Books, 2019.
Hume, David. *Enquiry Concerning Human Understanding.* Oxford: Oxford University Press, 2008.
Hummel, Charles E. "The Faith Behind the Famous: Isaac Newton." *Christian History Magazine*, 1991.
Humphreys, W. Lee "Historical Contexts of the Biblical Communities." In *The Oxford Study Bible: Revised English Bible with the Apocrypha*, edited by M. Jack Suggs, et al., 33–47. New York: Oxford University Press, 1992.
Humphries, E. J. In *Letters of the Century*, edited by Lisa Grunwald and Stephen J. Adler, 223. New York: Random House, 1999.
Huntington, Samuel P. *Clash of Civilizations and the Remaking of the World Order.* New York: Simon & Schuster, 1996.
Infoplease. "Life Expectancy by Age, 1850–2011." 2023. https://www.infoplease.com/us/health-statistics/life-expectancy-age-1850-2011.
Inglehart, Ronald F. "Giving Up on God: The Global Decline of Religion." *Foreign Affairs* 99.5 (Sept./Oct. 2020) 110–18.
Jacobs, Alan. *The Book of Common Prayer: A Biography.* Princeton: Princeton University Press, 2013.
Jarvis, Brooke. "Buzz Off." Review of *The Mosquito: A Human History of Our Deadliest Predator*, by Timothy C. Winegard. *New Yorker*, Aug. 5 and 12, 2019.

BIBLIOGRAPHY

Jaspers, Karl. *Nietzsche and Christianity*. Washington: Henry Regnery, 1961.
Jewett, Paul K. *Man as Male and Female: A Study in Sexual Relationships from a Theological Point of View*. Grand Rapids: Eerdmans, 1975.
Johnson, Paul. *Jesus: A Biography from a Believer*. New York: Viking, 2010.
Jones, W. T. *Kant to Wittgenstein and Sartre*. In *A History of Western Philosophy*. 2nd ed., 4. New York: Harcourt, Brace & World, 1969.
Kahn, Herman. *On Thermonuclear War*. Princeton: Princeton University Press, 1960.
Kalish, Donald, et al. *Logic: Techniques of Formal Reasoning*. 2nd ed. Fort Worth: Harcourt Brace Jovanovich, 1980.
Kamen, Henry. *The Spanish Inquisition: A Historical Revision*. 4th ed. New Haven: Yale, 2014.
Kaufmann, Walter. *Critique of Religion and Philosophy*. Princeton: Princeton University Press, 1958.
Keller, Timothy. *Counterfeit Gods: The Empty Promise of Money, Sex, and Power, and the Only Hope that Matters*. New York: Dutton, 2009.
———. *The Reason for God: Belief in an Age of Skepticism*. New York: Dutton, 2008.
Kendall-Taylor, Andrea, Erica Frantz, and Joseph Wright. "The Digital Dictators." *Foreign Affairs* 99.2 (Mar./Apr. 2020) 103–15.
Kirsch, Jonathan. *The Grand Inquisitor's Manual: A History in the Name of God*. New York: HarperCollins Publishers, 2008.
Kreeft, Peter. *Between One Faith and Another: Engaging Conversations on the World's Great Religions*. Downers Grove, IL: InterVarsity, 2017.
———*Christianity for Modern Pagans: Pascal's Pensees*. San Francisco: Ignatius, 1993.
———. *Everything You Ever Wanted to Know About Heaven . . . But Never Dreamed of Asking?* San Francisco: Ignatius, 1990.
———. *Fundamentals of the Faith: Essays in Christian Apologetics*. San Francisco: Ignatius, 1988.
Kreeft, Peter, and Ronald K. Tacelli. "The Resurrection." In *Pocket Handbook of Christian Apologetics*, 69–78. Downers Grove, IL: InterVarsity, 2003.
———. *Handbook of Christian Apologetics: Hundreds of Answers to Crucial Questions*. Downers Grove, IL: InterVarsity, 1994.
———. *Pocket Handbook of Christian Apologetics*. Downers Grove, IL: InterVarsity, 2003.
Kuhn, Thomas S. *The Structure of Scientific Revolutions*. Chicago: University of Chicago Press, 1962.
Ladd, George Eldon. *A Theology of the New Testament*. Grand Rapids: Eerdmans, 1974.
Lampe, G. W. *The West from the Fathers to the Reformation*. Cambridge History of the Bible 2. Cambridge: Cambridge University Press, 1969.
Langworth, Richard M. *Churchill by Himself*. New York: Public Affairs, 2008.
Latourette, Kenneth Scott. *A History of Christianity*. New York: Harper & Row, 1953.
Laurentia, Digges. *Haunted by Hope*. New York: Macmillan, 1966.
Leith, John H., ed. *Creeds of the Churches: A Reader in Christian Doctrine from the Bible to the Present*. 3rd ed. Louisville: Westminster John Knox, 1982.
Lessing, Gotthold Ephraim. "On the Proof of the Spirit and of Power." In *Lessing's Theological Writings*, translated by Harry Chadwick, 51–56. Stanford, CA: Stanford University Press, 1956.
Lewis, C. S. *The Four Loves*. New York: Harcourt, Brace & World, 1960.
———. *The Great Divorce*. San Francisco: HarperOne, 1945.

———. *Mere Christianity.* New York: Macmillan, 1952.
———. *Miracles: A Preliminary Study.* New York: Macmillan, 1947.
———. "The Weight of Glory." In *The Weight of Glory and Other Addresses.* Grand Rapids: Eerdmans, 1963.
Lewis, Sinclair. *Elmer Gantry.* New York: Harcourt Brace, 1927.
———. *It Can't Happen Here.* Garden City: Doubleday, 1936.
Livingstone, David. *Darwin's Forgotten Defenders.* Vancouver: Regent College, 1984.
London, Perry. *The Modes and Morals of Psychotherapy.* New York: Holt, Rinehart and Winston, 1964.
Luscombe, David. *Medieval Thought.* Oxford: Oxford University Press, 1997.
MacFarquhar, Larissa. *Strangers Drowning: Impossible Idealism, Drastic Choices, and the Urge to Help.* New York: Penguin, 2015.
MacGregor, Geddes. *Dictionary of Religion and Philosophy.* New York: Paragon House, 1989.
———. *A Literary History of the Bible: From the Middle Ages to the Present Day.* Nashville: Abingdon, 1968.
———. "Logical Positivism." In *Dictionary of Religion and Philosophy,* 386. New York: Paragon House, 1989.
———. *The Nicene Creed: Illuminated by Modern Thought.* Grand Rapids: Eerdmans, 1980.
———. *Philosophical Issues in Religious Thought.* Boston: Houghton Mifflin, 1973.
———. *Reincarnation as a Christian Hope: A New Vision of the Role of Rebirth in Christian Thought.* Wheaton, IL: Theosophical Publishing, 1978.
———. "Textual Analysis." In *Dictionary of Religion and Philosophy,* 607. New York: Paragon House, 1989.
MacGregor, Geddes, ed. *Immortality and Human Destiny.* New York: Paragon House, 1985.
MacIntyre, Alasdair C. *The Unconscious: A Conceptual Analysis.* Bristol: Thoemmes, 1997.
———. "First Principles, Final Ends, and Contemporary Philosophical Issues." In *The Tasks of Philosophy: Selected Essays,* 1, 143–78. Cambridge: Cambridge University Press, 2006.
———. "Truth as a Good: Reflections on *Fides et Ratio*" In *The Tasks of Philosophy: Selected Essays,* 1, 197–215. Cambridge: Cambridge University, 2006.
Mander, William. "Pantheism." In *The Stanford Encyclopedia of Philosophy,* Fall 2023 ed., edited by Edward N. Zalta and Uri Nodelman.
Manuel, Frank E., and Fritzie P. Manual. "The Utopian Propensity." In *Utopian Thought in the Western World,* 1–29. Cambridge, MA: Belknap, 1979.
———. *Utopian Thought in the Western World.* Cambridge, MA: Belknap, 1979.
Markus, H., and P. Nurius. "Possible Selves." *American Psychologist* 41.9 (1986) 954–69. https://doi.org/10.1037/0003-066X.41.9.954.
Martinich, A. P. "Identity and Trinity." *Journal of Religion* 58.2 (Apr. 1978) 169–81. https://doi.org/10.1086/486611.
Marty, Martin E. *Protestantism: Its Churches and Cultures, Rituals and Doctrines, Yesterday and Today.* New York: Holt, Rinehart and Winston, 1972.
Mason, Richard. *The Drowning People.* New York: Warner Books, 1999.
Mavrodes, George I. *Belief in God: A Study in the Epistemology of Religion.* New York: Random House, 1970.

McCord, William. *Voyages to Utopia: From Monastery to Commune: The Search for the Perfect Society in Modern Times*. New York: Norton, 1989.

McGrath, Alister E. *Christian Theology: An Introduction*. 6th ed. Hoboken, NJ: Wiley-Blackwell, 2016.

———. *Christianity's Dangerous Idea: The Protestant Revolution—A History from the Sixteenth Century to the Twenty-First*. New York: HarperCollins, 2007.

———. *In the Beginning: The Story of the King James Bible and How It Changed a Nation, a Language, and a Culture*. New York: Doubleday, 2001.

McGrath, Alister E., and Joanna Collicutt McGrath. *Dawkin's Delusion? Atheist Fundamentalism and the Denial of the Divine*. Downers Grove, IL: InterVarsity, 2007.

McIntyre, Ben. *Forgotten Fatherland: The Search for Elizabeth Nietzsche*. New York: Farrar Straus Giroux, 1992.

McKenzie, John L. "Antioch." In *Dictionary of the Bible*, 36-37. New York: Touchstone. 1965.

McLaughlin, Rebecca. *Confronting Christianity: 12 Hard Questions for the World's Largest Religion*. Wheaton: Crossway, 2019.

McLemore, Clinton W. *Clergyman's Psychological Handbook: Clinical Information for Pastoral Counseling*. Grand Rapids: Eerdmans, 1974.

———. *Honest Christianity: Personal Strategies for Spiritual Growth*. Louisville: Westminster John Knox, 1984.

———. *The Scandal of Psychotherapy: A Guide to Resolving the Tensions between Faith and Counseling*. Wheaton, IL: Tyndale House, 1982.

———. *Street-Smart Ethics: Succeeding in Business without Selling Your Soul*. Louisville: Westminster John Knox, 2003.

———. *Toxic Relationships and How to Change Them: Health and Holiness in Everyday Life*. San Francisco: Jossey-Bass, 2003.

McLemore, Clinton W., and Anna M. McLemore. *Staying One: How to Avoid a Make-Believe Marriage*. Eugene, OR: Cascade, 2017.

McPherson, Conor. *The Seafarer*. New York: Dramatists Play Service, 2008.

Mead, Margaret. *Coming of Age in Samoa*. New York: Morrow, 1928.

Melamed, Yitzhak Y., and Martin Lin. "Principle of Sufficient Reason." In *The Stanford Encyclopedia of Philosophy, Summer 2020 ed.*, edited by Edward N. Zalta and Uri Nodelman. https://plato.stanford.edu/archives/sum2020/entries/sufficient-reason/.

Menninger, Karl A. *Theory of Psychoanalytic Technique*. New York: Basic Books, 1958.

Metaxas, Eric. *Bonhoeffer: Pastor, Prophet, Martyr, Spy*. Nashville: Thomas Nelson, 2010.

Metzger, Bruce, and Roland E. Murphy, eds. "Introduction to the New Testament." In *The New Oxford Annotated Bible, New Revised Standard Version*, iii–vi. Oxford: Oxford University Press, 1991.

———. "Modern Approaches to Biblical Study." In *The New Oxford Annotated Bible, New Revised Standard Version*, 388–92. Oxford: Oxford University Press, 1991.

Miller, J. Maxwell, and John H. Hayes. *A History of Ancient Israel and Judah*. 2nd ed. Louisville: Westminster John Knox, 2006.

Montaigne, Michel E. de. "Pedantry." Essays I, XXIV, 25. Translated by Charles Cotton. *Great Books of the Western World*. Chicago: University of Chicago, 1952.

More, Thomas. *Utopia*. Translated by Paul Turner. New York: Penguin, 2003.

BIBLIOGRAPHY

Muggeridge, Malcolm. *Chronicles of Wasted Time*. Vancouver, BC: Regent College, 2006.

———. *Jesus Rediscovered*. Garden City: Doubleday, 1969.

———. *Jesus: The Man Who Lives*. New York: Harper & Row, 1975.

———. *A Twentieth Century Testimony*. Nashville: Thomas Nelson, 1978.

Munger, Robert Boyd. *My Heart—Christ's Home*. Downers Grove, IL: InterVarsity, 1954.

Murray, John Courtney. *The Problem of Religious Freedom*. Westminster, MD: Newman, 1965.

Myers, David G. *The Pursuit of Happiness: Discovering the Pathway to Fulfillment, Well-Being, and Enduring Personal Joy*. New York: William Morrow, 1992.

Naphy, William G. *The Protestant Revolution*. London: BBC Books, 2007.

Nee, Watchman. *The Normal Christian Life*. Fort Washington, PA: Christian Literature Crusade, 1961.

Neiman, Susan. *Evil in Modern Thought: An Alternative History of Philosophy*. Princeton, NJ: Princeton University Press, 2002.

Nicholson, Adam. *God's Secretaries: The Making of the King James Bible*. New York: HarperCollins, 2003.

Nietzsche, Friedrich. *Beyond Good and Evil*. New York: Penguin, 2003. Originally published in 1886.

Nirenberg, David. *Anti-Judaism: The Western Tradition*. New York: Norton, 2013.

Nisbet, Robert. *History of the Idea of Progress*. New York: Basic Books, 1980.

O'Collins, Gerald, and Edward G. Farrugia. "Salvation." In *Concise Dictionary of Theology*, 233–34. Mahwah, NJ: Paulist, 2000.

———. "Sin." In *Concise Dictionary of Theology*, 243–44. Mahwah, NJ: Paulist, 2000.

O'Connor, David. *Hume on Religion*. London: Routledge, 2001.

O'Day, Gail R., and David L. Petersen, eds. *Theological Bible Commentary*. Louisville: Westminster John Knox, 2009.

O'Reilly, Bill, and Martin Dugand. *Killing Jesus: A History*. New York: Henry Holt and Company, 2013.

Oliver, Simon. "The Theodicy of Austin Farrer." *Heythrop Journal* 39.3 (July 1998) 280–97.

Orwell, George. *1984*. New York: Harcourt, Brace & World, 1949.

The Oxford Illustrated History of the Crusades, edited by Jonathan Riley-Smith. Oxford: Oxford University Press, 1997.

Parker, T. H. L. *Calvin: An Introduction to His Thought*. London: Geoffrey Chapman, 1995.

Pascal, Blaise. *Pensees*. Translated by A. J. Krailsheimer. New York: Penguin 1995.

Pasteur, Louis. *Literary Digest*, October 18, 1902. https://en.wikipedia.org/wiki/Louis_Pasteur.

Payton, James R. *Light from the Christian East*. Westmont, IL: InterVarsity, 2007.

Percy, Walker. *Lost in the Cosmos: The Last Self-Help Book*. New York: Farrar, Strauss & Giroux, 1983.

Pérez, Joseph. *The Spanish Inquisition: A History*. Translated by Janet Lloyd. New Haven: Yale, 2006.

Philbrick, Nathaniel. *In the Heart of the Sea: The Tragedy of the Whaleship Essex*. New York: Viking, 2000.

Plato. *Euthyphro, Apology, Crito, Phaedo.* Translated by Benjamin Jowett. Amherst, NY: Prometheus Books, 1988.
Polanyi, Michael. *Personal Knowledge: Toward a Post-Critical Philosophy.* Chicago: University of Chicago Press, 1958.
Polkinghorne, John. *Faith, Science and Understanding.* New Haven: Yale University Press, 2001.
Popkin, Richard H. "Pierre Bayle." In *The Encyclopedia of Philosophy*, edited by Paul Edwards, 157–262. New York: Macmillan, 1967.
Porter, Roy. *The Creation of the Modern World: The Untold Story of the British Enlightenment.* New York: Norton, 2000.
———. *The Greatest Benefit to Mankind: A Medical History of Humanity.* New York: Norton, 1997.
Principe, Lawrence M. *Course Guidebook, Science and Religion.* Chantilly, VA: The Teaching Company, 2006
———. *Science and Religion.* Chantilly, VA: The Teaching Company, DVDs, 2006.
Rachels, James. *The Elements of Moral Philosophy.* 4th ed. Boston: McGraw-Hill, 2003.
Rawls, John. *A Theory of Justice.* Cambridge, MA: Belknap, 1971.
———. *Justice as Fairness: A Restatement.* Cambridge, MA: Belknap, 2001.
Redding, Paul. "Georg Wilhelm Friedrich Hegel." In *The Stanford Encyclopedia of Philosophy*, Fall 2024 ed., edited by Edward N. Zalta and Uri Nodelman. https://plato.stanford.edu/archives/fall2024/entries/hegel/.
Reik, Theodore. *Listening with the Third Ear: The Inner Experience of a Psychoanalyst.* New York: Farrar, Strauss and Company, 1952.
Renault, Mary. *Last of the Wine.* New York: Pantheon, 1956.
Rokeach, Milton. *The Three Christs of Ypsilanti.* New York: Vintage, 1964.
Roszak, Theodore. *The Making of a Counter Culture: Reflections on the Technocratic Society and Its Youthful Opposition.* Berkeley: University of California Press, 1995.
Rousseau, Jean-Jacques. *Emile or On Education.* Translated by Allan Bloom. New York: Basic Books, 1979. Originally published in 1762.
Rusch, William G. *The Trinitarian Controversy.* Philadelphia: Fortress, 1980.
Russell, Bertrand. "The Value of Philosophy." In *The Problems of Philosophy*, 116-23. New York: Henry Holt, 1912.
Ryrie, Alec. *Unbelievers: An Emotional History of Doubt.* Cambridge, MA: Belknap, 2019.
Santayana, George. *Life of Reason: Reason in Common Sense.* Amherst, NY: Prometheus, 1998.
Sartre, Jean-Paul. *Being and Nothingness.* Translated by Sarah Richmond. New York: Washington Square, 2021.
Schilpp, Paul Arthur. *Albert Einstein: Philosopher-Scientist.* Evanston: Library of Living Philosophers, 1949.
Schmidt, Alvin J. *How Christianity Changed the World.* Grand Rapids: Zondervan, 2001.
Schofield, William. *Psychotherapy: The Purchase of Friendship.* Englewood, NJ: Prentice Hall, 1964.
Searle, John R. *Intentionality: An Essay in the Philosophy of Mind.* Cambridge: Cambridge University Press, 1983.
Sheehan, Jonathan. "Teaching Calvin in California." *International New York Times*, Sept. 12, 2016. http://nyti.ms/2cxt3sY.

Sherman, William Tecumseh. *Memoirs*. Edited by Charles Royster. New York: Library of America, 1990.
Shuster, Marguerite. *Power, Pathology, Paradox: The Dynamics of Evil and Good*. Grand Rapids: Zondervan, 1987.
Shute, Nevil. *On the Beach*. New York: William Morrow, 1957.
Singer, M. G. "The Concept of Evil." *Philosophy* 79 (2004) 185–214.
Skyrms, Brian. *Choice and Chance: An Introduction to Inductive Logic*. 4th ed. Belmont, California: Wadsworth, 2000.
Smedes, Lewis B. *All Things Made New: A Theology of Man's Union with Christ*. Grand Rapids: Eerdmans, 1970.
———. *Love Within Limits: A Realist's View of I Corinthians 13*. Grand Rapids: Eerdmans, 1978.
Smith, Christian, and Melina Lundquist Denton. *Soul Searching: The Religious and Spiritual Lives of American Teenagers*. Oxford: Oxford University Press, 2005.
Smith. Adam. *An Inquiry into the Nature and Causes of the Wealth of Nations*. 1776.
Solomon, Robert C., and Kathleen M. Higgins. *What Nietzsche Really Said*. New York: Random House, 2000.
Spangler, Ann, and Lois Tverberg, eds. *Sitting at the Feet of Rabbi Jesus: How the Jewishness of Jesus Can Transform Your Faith*. Grand Rapids: Zondervan, 2009.
Stark, Rodney. *God's Battalions: The Case for the Crusades*. New York: HarperOne, 2009.
———. *The Victory of Reason: How Christianity Led to Freedom, Capitalism, and Western Sciences*. New York: Random House, 2005.
Stefano, Joseph, and Lou Morheim. "The Bellero Shield." *Outer Limits*. Aired on February 10, 1964.
Styron, William. *Sophie's Choice*. New York: Random House, 1979.
Sullivan, Harry Stack. *The Psychiatric Interview*. New York: Norton, 1954.
Sykes, Christopher. "Lust." In *Seven Deadly Sins*, by Angus Wilson, et al. New York: Quill, 1962.
Szasz, Thomas. *The Myth of Mental Illness: Foundations of a Theory of Personal Conduct*. New York: Harper & Row, 1974.
Taylor, Shelley E. *Positive Illusions: Creative Self-Deception and the Healthy Mind*. New York: Basic Books, 1989.
Thackeray, William. *Vanity Fair*. Knoxville: Wordsworth, 1998. Originally published 1847–48.
Thiselton, Anthony C. *Life After Death: A New Approach to the Last Things*. Grand Rapids: Eerdmans, 2012.
Tillich, Paul. *Systematic Theology*. Vols. 1–3. Chicago: University of Chicago Press, 1951–63.
To Be a Christian: An Anglican Catechism. Wheaton, IL: Crossway, 2020.
Trevor-Roper, H. R. "Thomas Hobbes." In *The Oxford Book of Essays*, edited by John Gross, 566–71. Oxford: Oxford University Press, 1991.
Unamuno, Miguel de. *The Agony of Christianity*. Translated by Kurt F. Reinhardt. New York: Frederick Ungar, 1960. Originally published 1928.
———. *The Tragic Sense of Life*. Translated by J. E. Crawford Flitch. New York: Cosimo 2007. Originally published 1921.
Viereck, George Sylvester. "Freud." *Glimpses of the Great*. London: Duckworth, 1930. Reprinted in *The Norton Book of Interviews*, edited by Christopher Silvester, 263-72. New York: Norton, 1993.

BIBLIOGRAPHY

Vitz, Paul C. *Psychology as Religion: The Cult of Self Worship.* 2nd ed. Grand Rapids: Eerdmans, 1994.

Voltaire. *Candide.* 3rd critical ed. Edited by Nicholas Cronk. New York: Norton, 2016, 1759.

Walls, Andrew. "Christianity." In *The Penguin Handbook of the World's Living Religions,* edited by John R. Hinnells, 53-161. London: Penguin 2010.

Ware, Kallistos. *The Orthodox Way.* 2nd ed. Yonkers, NY: St. Vladimir's Seminary, 2019.

Watson, Peter. *Ideas: A History of Thought and Invention, from Fire to Freud.* New York: HarperCollins, 2005.

Waugh, Evelyn. *The Loved One: An Anglo-American Tragedy.* London: Little, Brown and Company, 1948.

Weil, Simone. "Some Thoughts on the Love of God." In *On Science, Necessity, and the Love of God.* Translated and edited by Richard Rees. London: Oxford University Press, 1968.

Weisberg, Joe. *The Americans.* TV series. Aired 2013–2018, on FX. https://en.wikipedia.org/wiki/The_Americans

Westminster Confession of Faith and Catechisms. Lawrenceville, GA: Orthodox Presbyterian Church, 2007.

White, Andrew Dickson. *Warfare of Science.* 1876. Later expanded into White, Andrew Dickson. *History of the Warfare of Science and Theology in Christendom.* Cambridge: Cambridge University Press, 1896.

Whitehead, Alfred North. *Process and Reality.* 2nd ed. New York: Free Press, 1979.

Wiker, Benjamin. *10 Books that Screwed Up the World.* Washington: Regnery, 2008.

Wills, Garry. "Renaissance and Reformation." In *Why I Am a Catholic,* 154–64. Boston: Houghton Mifflin, 2002.

———. *Papal Sins: Structure of Deceit.* New York: Doubleday, 2000.

———. *Why I Am a Catholic.* Boston: Houghton Mifflin, 2002.

Wilson, A. N. *God's Funeral.* New York: Norton, 1999.

Wood, James. *The Broken Estate: Essays on Literature and Belief.* New York: Random House, 1999.

Woods, Jr. Thomas E. *How the Catholic Church Built Western Civilization.* Washington: Regnery, 2005.

Wright, N. T. *The Last Word: Beyond the Bible Wars to a New Understanding of the Authority of Scripture.* New York: HarperOne, 2005.

———. *How God Became King: The Forgotten Story of the Gospels.* New York: HarperOne, 2012.

———. *Paul and the Faithfulness of God.* Minneapolis: Fortress, 2013.

———. *Paul in Fresh Perspective.* Minneapolis: Fortress, 2005.

———. *Paul: A Biography.* New York: Harper Collins, 2018.

———. *Surprised by Hope: Rethinking Heaven, the Resurrection, and the Mission of the Church.* New York: HarperCollins, 2008.

Wright, Robert. "Why We Fight—and Can We Stop?" *Atlantic,* Nov. 2013.

Yancey, Philip. *The Bible Jesus Read.* Grand Rapids: Zondervan, 1999.

Yerkes, Robert Mearns M. *Mental Life of Monkeys and Apes: A Study of Ideational Behavior.* New York: Henry Holt, 1916.

Yong, Ed. "The COVID-19 Manhattan Project." *Atlantic,* Jan./Feb. 2021.

Index

Abbey
    Kells, 316
    Melk, 315
Abelard, 216
Abrahamic religions, 160
Abstract Expressionism, 317
accommodation, 89, 182
Accuser, name for the devil, 389
acedia, meaning of, 7
adoption into God's family, 378, 389, 449
Adoptionism, form or Monarchianism, 215–16
Albigensian Crusade, 215. *See* Catharism
alignment, meta-category of prayer, 401
Alvarado, Pedro de, 333
agnostic suspends judgment, 119, 345
Apocrypha, 73, 179
Aquinas, Thomas, 72, 78, 251
Alberti, Leone Battista, 315
algebra, Islamic
altruism
    Holy Spirit nudges in direction of, 172
    human capacity to display, or its opposite, 178
    may not persist in, and revert to primal nature, 178
    people demonstrate heroic forms of, 147
    philosophers have failed to explain, 153
    psychologists unable significantly to increase, 153
American Bill of Rights, 62, 310, 320
altruism, remains an ideal in Western Culture, 301
Americans
    given up on God and quest for truth, 3
    less and more religious, 2–3
    many abandoned the search for God, 3
    opinions often taken as guide to truth, 3
    truth depends on point of view, 3
Amish, 333
Anabaptists, 43, 333
analog and digital knowledge, 49–50, 105
analytic reasoning
    analysis and intuitive involved in thinking, 102
    approaching a problem with, 102
    assumption we approach most problems with, 102–3
    intuitive reasoning and, 50
    left hemisphere, 50
    limitations of, 37
    may never of itself bring people to faith, 37

analytic reasoning *(continued)*
    sequential and, 50
    useful in matters of religion, 37
analysis
    intuition and, involved in thinking, 102
    intuition often trumps, 103
    of atheistic systems, 261
    of Nazi war crimes, 268
    spiritual transformation based on intuition and, 103
anesthetic of love before scalpel of truth, 437
angels or beasts, capacity to act like, 153, 241, 246, 339, 389
Anglican, 18, 60, 198, 214, 251, 333, 364, 369, 374, 380, 384
annihilationism, 349–50
anthropologists, some turned methodology into ideology, 60
anthropology, use of term in theology, 83
Antichrist, The, 284 (Nietzsche)
antisocial personality disorder, 137
apostle, meaning of, 4n7
Apostles' Creed, 20, 26, 51, 75, 110, 214, 365, Appendix I
apperceptive mass, 99
architecture, Christian contributions to, 314–15
Arendt, Hannah, treatment of evil, 268, 286–87
arguments
    in valid deductive, conclusions inexorably follow, 29
    circular, 31
    good theology guards against unsound, 111
    not all valid arguments sound, 29, 40, 69, 76, 206
    sound if consistent with rest of the Bible, 180
    sound only if premises true, 29, 40, 64, 69, 76, 206, 225
    unsound, 228–29
    valid versus sound, 29, 69, 76, 111, 206, 225, 229
Aristotle, 131, 226

Arius, 214–15
arrogance
    as distraction, 148–50
    hubris and, futility of, 149
    to presume always to know God's will, 405, 407
art
    Christian contributions to painting, 316–18
    first golden age of Byzantine, 316
    Gothic, influence of Byzantine art on, 316
    realistic, representational, figurative, 317
    second golden age of Byzantine, 316
Ascent of Man (Bronowski), 100
aseity, meaning of, 411n2m
assimilation, 89, 99, 182
assumptions
    altering fundamental, requires paradigm shift, 33–34
    can be sticky wickets, 30–31
    change in, fast or slow in science or religion, 32–33
    importance of examining, 4
    religion and rethinking basic, 34
    shift in basic, by companions of Jesus, 344
    useful to ask why a person accepts, 30
Assyrian Church, 108
astronomy, Islamic, 317
Athanasius, 190, 214–15
atheism
    agnosticism and, 345
    as non-rational as theism, 24
    by nature inferential not deductive, 28
    evil, strongest argument for, 160, 254
    functional, 135
    involves a leap of faith, 345
    like theism, an inference, 28
    of outspoken scientists, 234, 239
    reflects embedded sentiments, 24
    strident, 219
atheistic existentialism
    akin to nihilism, 150

INDEX

can resemble religion, 150
comforting as long as death remote, 151
Sartre and, 150
atonement, theological meaning of, 200, 376
attempts to prove or disprove religious truth-claims, 37
Augustine
    akin to Neo-Platonists, 262
    allusion to evolution, 235
    believe in order to understand, 367
    City of God, 78, 297, 308
    complete freedom only in heaven, 263
    Confessions, 78, 318
    denied evil as substance or property, 262
    desired to be holy but "not yet," 139
    difference, city of God and city of man, 297
    distinction between sacred and secular, 297
    evil, absence or corruption of good, 262
    evil no independent existence, 262
    fostered inward shift with *Confessions*, 318
    free will defense, 262
    greatest church father, 232
    influence on western theology, 454
    inherited disposition toward disobedience, 262
    interpretation of evil, 262–63
    Irenaeus and, 262
    just war theory introduced by, 327
    need clergy knowledgeable about science, 232
    original goodness lost, inclined toward evil, 262
    political realism made possible by, 297
    pride, the root of sin, 143–44
    seven propositions in support of the Trinity, 74
    two great books, nature and revelation, 237, 367
    understand in order to believe, 367
authentic religion not based on false beliefs, 44
autographs, use of term in biblical studies, 179
available moments, bank account of, 387
Avicenna, 368
avoidance of the big questions
    through distractions. *See* distractions
    through psychological defenses. *See* defense mechanisms
axiology, branch of ethics, 80n
Aztec Empire, 332

Baal, polytheistic god, 163–65
baby seal, use of term in translations, 6
Bach, Johann Sebastian, 152, 318
Bacon, Roger, 304
Ballantyne, Nathan, 219
Ballinger, Dan, xii
Baloche, Paul, 195
bank account of available moments, 387
Baptist, 19, 214, 380
Barth, Karl, 250–51, 273, 351
Basil the Great, 75
Bassi, Agostino, 363
Battle of Milvian Bridge and Constantine, 307
Bayle, Pierre, treatment of evil, 265–66
beasts or angels, capacity to act like, 153, 214, 246, 339, 389
Becker, Ernest, 138
Beethoven, Ludwig van, 318
begging the question
    arguments for God's existence from nature, 28
    confirmation bias related to, 238
    informal fallacy, 28
begotten
    Jesus uniquely, 73–74
    meaning of, in contrast to created, 74, 214
behavior of some Christians off-putting, 17

INDEX

being present (sitting with) powerful, 433
belief
   and unbelief intuitive, 24
   different from faith, 19, 25
   does not guarantee faith, 19
   erosion of in Western Culture, 362
   implies affirmation, 393
   necessary but not sufficient for faith, 24–24
beliefs
   and knowledge, relationship between, 4
   as all equally worthy, illogical, 57
   false, value of correcting, 90
   distinguishing between true and false, 4
   important to determine if likely true, 40
   may or may not mirror reality, 3, 36
   reached by induction, 76
   relationship to knowledge not straightforward, 4
   religious affiliation and, 4
   require justification, 3
   true and false religion, related to, 4
   two pivotal, in Christianity, 376–78
benefits
   do not prove religious truth-claims, 37
   not sound argument for Christianity, 87
   promised by primitive or psychopathic leaders, 154
Berkeley, George Bishop, 412
Bonhöffer, Dietrich, 337
Berger, Peter, 34
Beyond Good and Evil (Nietzsche), 125
bias(es)
   arbitrary, flawed information or faulty inferences, 64
   arbitrary, can be difficult to recognize or change, 64
   arbitrary, important to avoid, 5
   based on ethnicity, race, religion, unconscionable, 63
   based on reliable experience, beneficial and necessary, 63
   confirmation, 191, 237–38
   confusing two kinds of, 66,
   data-based, desirable and necessary, 64
   difference between accidental and dispositional, 64
   predisposition to perceive or act, 64
   prejudgments a type of, 64
   prejudgments necessary for survival, 64
   rejecting Christianity without examination arbitrary, 64
Bible
   composed over a thousand years, 42, 73
   God involved in development and preservation of, 73
   God continues to communicate through, 366
   discloses character of God, 5
   diverse collection of documents, 42, 178
   divine inspiration of, 179–80
   does not contain systematic theology, 42
   flawed criticism of, 237–38
   function of, 178
   higher criticism, 237–38
   individual interpretation discouraged, 75
   inspired, believed to be, 106
   lower criticism, 237
   nature of, 5
   not archaeology textbook, 367
   not proxy God, 78
   not scientific textbook, 77, 236–37
   not to be turned into idol, 78, 199
   own best commentary, 73, 189, 194
   problem of private interpretation, 75, 369
   record of divine revelation, 367
   Roman Catholic, 73
   source criticism, 237–38
   translations, attempts to convey essential meaning, 6
   trustworthy guide, 368
   written word of God, 367
biblical criticism, some flawed, 237–38

INDEX

biblical interpretation, ecumenical councils in Orthodoxy, 76
Big Bang
    compatible with creation from nothing (*ex nihilo*), 220, 373
    God's energy and, 412
    in relation to geologic time, 207
    occurred 13.8 billion years ago
Bill of Rights
    American, 62, 310, 320
    English, 307, 320
Bird respirator and ethics, 106
Birth of Tragedy, The (Nietzsche), 284
blessed not same as happy, 87
Bloody Mary, 333
Bohr, Niels, 225
Book of Common Prayer, 374, 384, 386, 408
Book of Kells, 316
Borgias, examples of corruption, 328
Bosch, Hieronymus, 316
Boyle, Robert, 312
Brahms, Johannes, 318
Braille, Louis, 314
brain
    causal relationship to consciousness unclear, 372
    consciousness, not identical with, 372, 413
    functions like gyroscope, 372
    left and right, 50
    necessary for consciousness, 372
    research, 50
Broad Street pump and cholera, 363
Bronowski, Jacob, 100–102
Brown, Warren S., xi
Brunelleschi, Fillipo, 315
Buber, Martin, 161, 356
Buddhism, 41, 275
Bultmann, Rudolf K., 377
Bunyan, John, 146
Butman, Richard, xi

Cahill, Thomas, 161, 179, 279
Caiaphas, 397
Calvin, John, 4, 6, 43, 101, 113, 173, 305, 333, 366, 370, 447
Calvinism, 43, 265, 346
Camus, Albert, held views on evil, 288
Candide (Voltaire), 267
canonical, meaning of in biblical studies, 179–80
Canterbury Tales (Chaucer), 319
capitalism
    alleged to turn people into factory cogs, 280
    better than systems previously tried, 81
    challenges to, 242
    evils attend, 281
    inequities arising from, 62
    view of as cause of class struggle, 280
captive to what we seek and serve, 7
Carver, George Washington, 312
Catharism
    belief in two Gods, 215
    related to Marcionism, 215
Cardenas, Paul, xii
caring and candor, importance of, 427, 437
Carolingian Empire, 298, 300
Caravaggio, Michelangelo Merisi da, 362
Catechism of the Catholic Church, 365
catechisms, definition of, 365
cathedral schools, 303
Catholicism. *See* Roman Catholicism
Celsus, 192
Cézanne, Paul, 317
Chalcedonian Creed
    addition of, to Apostles' and Nicene Creeds, 21
    embraced by many Christian traditions, 107, 214
    hypostatic union in, 107, 214
    rejected by some branches of Christianity, 107–08
charity
    derivation of word, 409
    modern Bibles translate as love, 409
Charter of Liberties, 329
Chaucer, Geoffrey, 319
Chesterton, G. K., 84

INDEX

chivalry
    blended together opposing ideals, 301
    established new code of morality, 301
    first version: affection, courtesy, refinement, 301
    enduring tensions in Western Culture, 301
    romantic love and, 301
    second version: hedonistic, 301
choice
    human, trivialization of, 136–38
    limitations of, 247
    spiritual implications of, 424
Chopin, Frédéric, 318
Christ. *See also* Jesus
    God entrusted universe to, 50, 174
    Greek for anointed or sent one, 21
    Greek translation of Hebrew *Messiah*, 21, 200
    legitimate to pray to, 108
    meaning of, 21, 88, 200
    one's ultimate authority as Lord, 21
    priestly, prophetic, and kingly functions, 396
    universe invisibly ruled by, 174
Christchurch, 241
Christian, becoming involves
    accepting reality of objective order, 395
    acknowledging Christ as supreme authority, 50
    believing we no longer stand accused, 398
    both objective and subjective, 38, 94
    change in basic assumptions, 2, 32
    change in worldview, 33
    choosing truth over duplicity, 64
    divine heart surgery, 38–39
    everyday experience new, 2, 22, 38, 449
    facing own flawed nature, 395
    forgiving, 64
    fundamental realignment, 2
    giving allegiance to God, 395
    intuition and imagination, 37
    Jesus indwelling one's heart, 103
    mysteries begin to make sense, 2, 40
    opening your mind and heart, 101
    penitent heart, 388
    paradigm shift, 33, 40
    potential crisis, 383
    preferring peace to war, 64
    propensity to love rather than hate, 64
    rebelling only with conflict, 378
    recognizing Jesus as unique, 395
    recognizing Jesus as embodying objective order, 395
    renewed life, 325
    reshaping personal biases, 64
    respecting others and their property, 64, 320
    risking time and attention, 387, 391
    shift in frame of reference, 35
    transformed heart, 325
Christian contributions to
    architecture, 314–15
    education, 313–14
    human life and dignity, 319–20
    literature, 319
    medicine and health care, 312–13
    music, 318–19
    painting, 316–18
    rule of law, 320
    science, 311–12
Christian faith
    historical data supportive of, 37
    involves objective analysis and subjective intuition, 94–95
    Jesus integral to one's life, 21
    love and trust as its center, 95
    loving God in response to God's love, 43
    may require a type of spiritual intelligence, 393
    more to it than following rules, 17
    must rest on knowledge, 393
    not arbitrary. 111
    objective, subjective, and personal, 95, 111
Christianity
    benefits, not sound argument for, 87
    could not remain Eurocentric, 60

center of gravity now in Southern Hemisphere, 59, 361
conceives of God as personal and involved, 55
continuation of faith begun in the Old Testament, 170
declared official state religion in fourth century, 307
end of gladiatorial games, 320
foundational beliefs and defining nature of, 50–51, 382
good reasons for accepting claims of, 40
mitigated violence, 339
no merit in watering down beyond recognition, 20
no other major religion claims founder resurrected, 210
not easy to define precisely, 20
pivotal role in development of Western Civilization, 119
rests on claims about God and Jesus, 40, 197
rooted in Judaism, 52
rule of law and, 320
tells of a different kind of God, 198
two pivotal beliefs, 377–88
Underground Railroad, involvement in, 320
understanding Christ's nature and significance, 50–51
Christianity and the Rise of Western Culture (Dawson), 291
Christian transformation. *See* transformation
Christianity's contribution to civilization
cathedral cities required to care for sick, 294
created disposition for exploration and discovery, 294
deep sense of individual worth, 295
development of two-track western mind, 295–96
first hospitals late in fourth century, 295
fostered embrace of language, valuation of words, 292, 294
educational tradition of understanding and improving, 290, 296
encouraged new modes of thought, 292
enhanced culture, 290
high value placed on human life, 294–95
modeled benevolence and charity, 294
monasteries, centers for health care, 295
monasteries, centers of learning, 303
new mediaeval economy, 293
open access to information and exchange of ideas, 294
promoted independence of thought, 290
promoted union of conceptual and practical, 292
rebuilt society after fall of Rome, 293
reinvigorated desire to think clearly and deeply, 291
relatively less thought-restricting, 292
religious orders formed to care for sick and dying, 295
returned Western Society to abstract thinking, 292
technological development, 296–97
translated words into charitable actions, 294
unrelenting pressure for intellectual freedom, 294
ultimately freed humanity from dependence on nature, 29
valuing both ideas and innovation, 293
Christina, Dowager Grand Duchess, 368
Christlike, cooperating with God to become more, 4
Christology
conclusions of church, 214–16
from above, 216
from below, 218
nature of, 83

INDEX

church
- Christians believe God continues to guide, 74, 379
- function of for Christians, 379–80
- set of values embedded in Western Culture, 305
- why attendance and involvement important, 451

church father, definition of, 68

Churchill, Winston, 281

church-state conflicts considerable by fourteenth century, 305

cities
- as social structures, 301–3
- based on voluntary economic associations, 302
- civic spirit worked against crude feudalism, 301
- communes based on compacts 302
- domains of comfort, security, and prosperity, 302
- economic well-being contingent on industriousness, 302
- efficient production of goods in, 302
- emergence of merchant class and trade associations, 302
- foundation for modern world, 302
- freedom to acquire property in, 302
- life no longer predominantly agrarian, 301
- life revolved around, 301
- medieval, centered on cathedrals. 303
- more important than chivalry to civilization, 301
- nobles ostracized or prohibited, 302
- powerful guilds in, 302
- revival of civic spirit, 301
- trade associations increasingly powerful, 302

City of God (Augustine), 78

civilization
- can be argued creation of the church, 290
- requirements for, 290, 293–94

claims by New Testament authors
- conspiracy unlikely, 202
- great art in their documents, 203
- maintained beliefs at personal risk and cost, 202–03
- paradox of the Gospels, 202
- reliability of, 202–04
- their ideas and conceptualizations, 203
- time-consuming tightly-written narratives, 202

clarity and precision, importance of, 106–8

Clark, Lord Kenneth, 290, 293

Clelland, Jackson, xii

Cleopas, 209

Collins, Francis, 311

colonialism
- and imperialism, 332–33
- byproduct, end of human sacrifice, 332
- priests opposed enslavement, 333

communication
- connecting with audience, 439
- involves heart as well as head, 440
- language in, 100, 111

communion, basic meaning of, 425

communism
- can foster corruption, emergence of racketeers, 283
- empowered workers sometimes become tyrants, 283
- minimizes important contributory elements, 282
- neglect of flexible economic policy, 282
- not monolithic entity, 281
- problems with, 282–83

Communist Manifesto (Marx and Engels), 281, 283

comparison level, 145

compassionate listening, value of, 421

compendium of evil, 257–60

conceptual
- clarity and spirituality, 17–18
- human experience essentially, 102, 104
- precision and religious experience, 17
- thinking, importance of, 99

confession, formal, commendable, 425

INDEX

Confessions (Augustine)
    fostered shift toward the subjective, 318
    superb example of attending to experience, 414
confessions of faith
    express distinctive beliefs, 365
    secondary to and less binding than creeds, 75, 365
confirmation bias, 191
confusion between subjective and objective reality, 3
conquistadors, 322
conscientiousness of Luke, 184–85
consciousness
    among God's great gifts, 372
    among ways we are like God, 50
    blend of objectivity and subjectivity, 98
    brain, necessary substrate for, 372
    continuity of, 355, 357, 381
    gift and mystery of, 372
    God must have something like, 70
    myth of objective, 98
    not reducible to firing of neurons, 37
    objective realities and subjective impressions, 96
    of our mortality, 127
    Paul's radical shift in, 52
    ultimately private, 96
consensual validation, 76
conservative arrangement in science, 33
conspiracy theory of resurrection, 212–13
Constable, John, 317
Constantine, Emperor, 20, 214–15, 294, 307, 329
consubstantiation, 43
contingent beings, humans as, 92
continued personal identity, 350–51, 355, 357, 381
conversion, term misleading, 54
cooperate with God
    death ends opportunity to, 129
    opportunity costs involved, 387
    possible while we are alive, 415
    to become more like Christ, 4

Copernicus, Nicolaus, 36, 99, 218, 232
Copleston, Frederick, 120
Coptic, language of some scriptures, 181, 190
Coptic Orthodox Church
    as denominational affiliation, 18
    Chalcedonian Council and, 108
Cornell, Ezra, 230
corporate codes of conduct, 241
correlation, spurious, 87
Cortés, Hernán, 332
Council of Chalcedon, 214
Council of Nicaea, 214, 294
Council of Trent
    position on justification, 366
    response to Protestantism, 331
    Vulgate Bible authorized by, 189
counterfeit gods and imitation heavens, 153–54
counterintuitive monotheism, 159, 176
counterphobic behavior, defense mechanism of, 139
Counter-Reformation, 331–32
covenant
    distinct from contract, 161
    Jewish, prelude to Christ, 162
    no sound reason to deny possibility of, 161
Creator-God, 6
creation
    by comparison, human history contemporary, 207
    earth 4.5 billion years ago, 207
    of true human beings 40,000 to 200,000 years ago, 207
    of universe 13.8 billion years ago
    science, 235
Creator-Provider-Sustainer. *See* God
credobaptism, meaning of, 333n
creed(s)
    Apostles,' 20, 26, 51, 75, 110, 214, 365, Appendix I
    basic Christian affirmations contained in, 20, 75
    Chalcedonian, 21, 107–8, 214
    centrally important defining documents, 20, 51, 75

INDEX

creed(s) *(continued)*
    continue to shape and reflect Christian beliefs, 21
    express in whom to place faith, 20
    formalize what is taken as essential, 365
    "I believe" versus "I know" in, 26
    Nicene, 20, 26, 51, 75, 110, 214, 326, 365, 378, 454–56, Appendix II
    not exhaustive, 20, 365
critical thinking
    fundamental method in philosophy and theology, 69
    necessary but not sufficient for sound theology, 69
    ultimate purpose of, 83
crucifixion
    asphyxiation, typical result of, 211
    common form of execution by Romans, 401
    evidence of asphyxiation in Gospel of John, 211
    horrors of, 377, 401
    Jesus absorbed human sins within himself through, 447
    Jesus submitted himself to horrors of, 204, 396
    jihad and, 327
    made it possible for God to see through Christ, 376
    no question Jesus died as a result of, 212
    purposes of, 327
    reincarnation misses significance of, and resurrection, 352
    Roman soldiers proficient at, 211
    scavenger birds feasted on victims, 203
    testimony to God's goodness toward us, 250
    victims sometimes survived for a day or more, 203
    way God attempted to get human attention, 205
crusade(s)
    aggression during Fourth, against Orthodox, 326
    Albigensian, 215
    Arab accounts of, 327
    conceived as just war, 327
    continued until end of seventeenth century, 300
    dates of, 327
    expressed goals of, 327, 329
    Fourth, sacked Constantinople, 326
    Great Schism, fifty years before first Mideast, 326
    may have contributed to fall of Byzantine Empire, 327
    response in part to aggression by Muslims, 300
    results of, 327
    unified and strengthened West, 300
    workaround of primogeniture for some, 327
cruise ship metaphor, 173
cultural
    bias, importance of guarding against, 59
    ignorance of other lands and cultures, 60
    literacy increasingly neglected by professors, 57
    narrowness and ethnocentrism, 59
    neutrality, operating principle for anthropologists, 56
    provincialism, documentation of, 59–60
    relativism, 61
    savvy 59–60
cynicism
    characteristic of our age, 21
    often understandable, 47
    skepticism peppered with, 151
cubism, 317

Dali, Salvador, 317
Dante, Alighieri, 319
Dark Ages, term inaccurate and misleading, 292–93
dark knight of the soul, 5
Darwin, Charles, 101, 233–35, 367
Darwinists and fundamentalists, 233–35
Darwinian and Lamarckian, theories of evolution 234–35

INDEX

data
    first-order (private), 96, 403
    second-order (potentially accessible to others), 97
Dawson, Christopher, 254, 291, 300
days of wine and roses, 130
death
    brings loss and separation, 129
    comes with a price, 141
    ends chance to love and worship God, 133
    ends relationships, love, conversation, 129, 133
    enemy and destroyer, 129
    facing mortality and, 141
    fear of, 129
    of Jesus attested, 211
    people avoid facing, with defense mechanisms, 141
Debussy, Claude, 318
decision, life-changing, 65
deductive reasoning
    can be powerful, 29–30
    conclusions reside within premises, 29
    conclusions sound if premises true, 29–30, 206
    example of potential power of, 29
    subtle example of, 30
defense mechanisms
    block out unwanted thoughts, 135
    can anesthetize us to God, 138–41
    compartmentalization, 141, 324
    counterphobic behavior, 139
    denial, 138
    intellectualization, 140
    isolation, 139–40
    often operate unconsciously, 136
    projection, 140
    rationalization, 139
    reaction formation, 138–39
    repression, 138
    ways we lie to ourselves, 141
Degas, Edgar, 317
deification
    in Eastern Orthodoxy and Eastern Catholicism, 374
    participating in God's energy and activities, 374
    theosis, 374n
    themes of, in Roman Catholicism, 374
deism, 45, 206, 223, 270, 362, 411
Delacroix, Eugène, 317
Dalberg, Emerich Edward (Lord Acton), 328
delusion
    argument that Christians accept, 47
    Christianity, if untrue, 387
    idea that Jesus suffered from a, 207
    indicative of major mental disorder, 209
    inconsistent with records in the New Testament, 180
    nature of, 209–10
    people do not sacrifice themselves for, 180
    rarely shared by more than two, 210
    unsound as explanation of the resurrection, 209–11
Democritus, 39
denial, defense mechanism of, 138
Denial of Death, The (Becker), 138
dependable
    false claims not, 90
    norm governing belief and judgment, 90
Descent of Man, The (Darwin), 234
determinism
    behavior according to, potentially explainable, 137
    definition of, 137
    foundation for and necessary assumption in science, 137
    freedom of choice an illusion, 70, 137
    related to metaphysical materialism, 226
    training in psychology and psychiatry, 137
Dewey, John, 36
digital and analogic knowledge, 49–50, 105
digital disappointments, 255
Diet of Worms, 306

INDEX

dilemma, morally ambiguous, 49
disciple(s)
    became outcasts, 212
    belief in Christ's divinity, 173, 210
    beloved, 193
    Cleopas, 209
    contemporary, share gospel with others, 415
    engaged with real post-resurrection person, 210
    initially disinclined to believe in resurrection, 343
    Jesus appeared to, 173, 197–98, 208, 210, 212, 343
    lost timidity after resurrection, 213
    meaning and etymology of, 52, 393
    remained loyal, 201
    reported to doubting Thomas, 344
    simple peasants, 213
    some tortured and executed, 212
    unlikely to have developed same delusion, 209
disputations
    common and amicable, 330
    long history of, 304
    salutary effect on reasoning, cognitive complexity, 304–5, 330
distraction(s)
    arrogance and hubris, 148–50
    can render us numb, 143
    intellectualism as, 150–51
    money, inordinate desire for, 144–46
    meaning of, 143
    pleasure, obsessive search for, 147–48
    power, quest for, 143–44
    pursuit of utopia on earth, 151–53
    status, excessive concern with, 146–47
    utopianism, 151–53
    ways of filling free mental space, 143
Divine Comedy, The (Dante), 319
divine right of kings
    conditional and revocable, 298
    viewed as ordained by God, 298
divinity
    ambiguous term, 51
    joined to humanity in Jesus, 54, 174, 207, 374–75, 395
    of Jesus denied, 216
divinization. *See* Eastern Orthodox, deification
docetism, meaning of, 107, 215
doctrinaire religionists, often wrong but never in doubt, 42
Dostoevsky, Fyodor, everything permitted, 124
doubt
    educational value of, 98
    history of, 24
Donner Party and cannibalism, 172
Dowson, Ernest, 130
Draper, John William
    author of influential book, 230
    faulty scholarship of, 231–32
    fomented warfare thesis, 218, 230–33, 239, 367
    ideas of, provoke laughter by contemporary students, 231
    suffused flawed ideas into popular culture, 231–32
dreams
    inability to turn off and psychiatric disorder, 100
Duerrenmatt, Friedrich, 367
Dun Scotus, 216
Dunant, Jean-Henri, 313
Durant, Will and Ariel, 291

Eastern Orthodox
    as denominational affiliation, 18, 380
    chrismation (sacrament of confirmation), 83
    civilizing influence of, 299
    deification, 374, 449
    denial of double procession, 326
    ecumenical councils and biblical interpretation, 76
    filioque, 326
    give special honor to church fathers, 76
    Great (East-West) Schism, 305, 326, 454

INDEX

humility toward history of Christian thought, 74
justification, 366
recognize seven sacraments, 83
relatively less inclined to overweight emotion, 17
relatively more inclined to appeal to church authority, 42
sin as destroying *koinonia* (community, fellowship), 388, 388n10
some branches of, reject Chalcedonian formulation, 107–08
take Bible to be authoritative, 73
two blended natures of Christ held by some, 107
Eastern Orthodoxy
Chalcedonian Creed not accepted by all, 107
controversy over authority of Pope, 75, 370
controversy over final version of Nicene Creed, 454
disagreement with Roman Catholicism over Holy Spirit, 369
deification, 374–75, 449
exercised civilizing influence, 299
less inclined to over-emphasize reason or emotion, 17–18
mistake to claim only Orthodox and Catholic have tradition, 369
most accept Chalcedonian Christology, 214
need for theological humility, 74
recognizes seven ecumenical councils, 76
scripture interpreted according to ecumenical councils, 76
special honor paid to three church fathers, 76
treat earlier theological work with respect, 74
East-West Schism, 305, 326, 454
ecclesiology, meaning of, 83
ecclesiastic suppression of science, a myth, 232

ecumenical councils
Eastern Orthodoxy recognizes seven, 76
Roman Catholicism recognizes twenty-one, 75
taken to be universal and worldwide, 76
Edgar, William, xi, 3
education, Christian contributions to, 313–14
egocentricity. *See* self-absorption
Eichmann, Otto Adolf, 286
Einstein, Albert, 33, 99, 101, 133, 255
elected representatives, origin in the church, 303
election
eliminative reductions, 36–37, 240, 285–86
Ellis, Courtney, xii
Ellis, Daryl, xii
Elmer Gantry (Lewis), 324
Emile (Rousseau), 269
English Bill of Rights, 307, 320
Emmaus, road to, 209, 343
emotional religion to neglect of intellectual, 18
empathy
as educated guess, 96
emotional food, 434
listening with the third ear, 434
not helped by platitudes or superficial advice, 435
psychopaths lack, 262, 324
requires tolerance for ambiguity, 435
scarce commodity, 434
taxing and costly, 435
Emperor Constantine, 20
empiricism
Hume, an empiricist, 347
sense perception ultimate criterion of truth in, 347
empiricists
may rule out or ignore human experience, 27
not always empirical, 27

encyclical, Papal
  Fides et ratio (Faith and Reason), 368
  meaning of, 75
End of the Affair, The (Greene), 110, 131
Engels, Friedrich, 280–81
Enlightenment increased religious skepticism, 218, 310, 362
Enlightenment thinkers
  encouraged tension between science and religion, 229
  favored deism, 270
environment, Christian duty to care for, 103
epigenetics, 235
epistemic
  distance of God, 263n
  trespassing, 219, 238
  value, 34
epistemology
  externalists, 27
  nature of, 27
epistles reflect thought-forms of Paul, 7
equity and fairness, human beings gravitate toward, 394
Erasmus, Desiderius, 189, 319, 330
eschatology, meaning of, 83
eternal (everlasting) life
  crucifixion and resurrection made possible, 184
  given to those who align with God, 350
  God's gift and promise to Christians, 65, 126, 131
  hope of, pointless if no resurrection of Jesus, 340
  implications of, 355
  Jesus' high priestly prayer, 395
  legacy, no substitute for, 92
  no longer genetically preprogrammed to die, 381
  omega point and, 173
  those not Roman Catholic may enjoy, 380
  transcendence of death and, 398
  umbrella line and, 51
eternities
  hints of God's existence, 40
  suspended between two, 39–40
ethical
  decisions today flow from those yesterday, 246
  decisions, moral and ethical, 70, 82
  dilemmas, complex, 61
  discourse, arena of, 248
  duties during and after war, 264
  duty to look out for one's neighbor, 307
  guidance not scientific in nature, 221
  implications of actions, people and God, 371
  little or no, or moral tension in some, 337
  makeover for Christians moral and, 389
  nihilism, 221
  relativism, 61, 66
  values, study of in philosophy, 81
ethics
  area of potential conflict with Christianity, 80
  difference between morality and, 241
  specialty in philosophy, 80
  universalism seems to trivialize, 351
ethics and morality
  difference between, 241
  sometimes in conflict, 241
Ethiopian Church, 108
Esser, Peter, xi
Euthyphro (Plato), 7n15
evangelism
  civilized large barbarian populations, 298
  civilizing influence via Byzantine Empire, 299
  Vikings became loving and peaceful because of, 299
Evans, C. Stephen, xii, 109, 120, 284, 351, 370
evil
  absence or corruption of good in Augustine, 262–63
  Arendt, treatment of, 268, 286–87
  Bayle, treatment of, 265–66

INDEX

benevolence, insufficient to prevent, 241–44
broad and narrow conceptions of, 243–44
compendium of, 257–60
concepts of, guiding force of modern thought, 261
continuum of, 243
created by lesser god, idea of, 215
deliverance from suffering and evil, 200
difficult precisely to define, 243–44
education insufficient to prevent, 241–42
egregious examples of, 257–60
enlightenment ambiguous and insufficient to prevent, 241–42
explaining away, 136–38, 241
family resemblances and, 244
Freud, views on, 285–86
God-given ability to do good or, 177
Hegel recognizes nature of, 274
hinders belief in goodness of God, 2
human sin, root of moral, 253–54
Hume, treatment of, 270–71
in contemporary thought, 287–88
intelligence insufficient to prevent, 241–42
Irenaeus, interpretation of, 263
Kant, treatment of, 271–73
Leibniz, treatment of, 266–68
love of money and, 144
Machiavelli, treatment of, 263–64
Marx, treatment of, 279–83
medicalization of psychological dysfunction and, 137–38
medicalizing, promotes illusion of understanding, 248
moral, 121, 240–41, 243–44, 250–51, 255, 262, 268, 271–72, 280
morally despicable, 244
metaphysical, 268
more than a social problem, 243
natural, 251, 255, 267–69, 278, 280
necessary condition for moral choice, 262–63
Nietzsche, treatment of, 283–84
not outdated or outmoded idea, 239
passivity to which denial of can lead, 268
philosophers increasingly interested in, 261, 288
problem of, 2, 160, 249–53, 255, 261–62, 265–66, 271–72, 368, 390, 414
psychopathology and, 248
reluctance to recognize, 241
remains inexplicable mystery, 243, 249
rescue and deliverance from, 195
rescue from imperfect or evil state, 200
Rousseau accurately recognizes, 268
Rousseau, Jean-Jacques, treatment of, 268–70
root of, pride and desire for power, 121
Sade, embrace of, 284–85
Schopenhauer, treatment of, 275–79
sense of objective moral order and, 246
smart people sometimes act in service of, 242
some define as opposite of good, 243
some define as intentionally harmful, 243
sometimes related to psychiatric disorder, 255
strongest argument of atheist, 160, 249
surd, 240
surrealistically unfathomable, horrendously malevolent, 243
triumph through Christ over, 205
two kinds, natural and moral, 240, 255, 268
Voltaire, treatment of, 266–67
evil, natural
attempt to harmonize with Christian beliefs, 267
distinguished from moral evil, 255
endemic to nature of human existence, 251
Marx and, 280
Rousseau and, 268–69

INDEX

evil, natural *(continued)*
    Schopenhauer and, 278
    Voltaire and, 267
evolution
    false dichotomy between, and God, 221
    theistic, 235
exegesis, definition of, 81
existence
    eventually transported to another dimension, 254
    hidden dimension of, 47, 254
    personal view of, changed, 1
existential dread
    from awareness of eventual death, 128–29
    many live with, 132–33
existentialism
    atheistic, meaning and significance of life, 85
    Nietzsche as example of atheistic, 124
    Sartre and, 150–51
    two kinds of, 150
experience
    assimilation of, 99
    helping someone else make sense of, 436
    making sense of new, 182
    making sense of what happens, 267
explanatory reductions, 36, 246, 286
Expressionism, 317

fairness, equality, and tolerance, 3
faith
    ambiguity needed to be meaningful, 24, 26, 49, 403
    analysis and subjective intuition involved in, 94–95
    as induction, 32, 34
    coerced belief would make impossible, 55
    different from belief, 19, 25–26
    content of versus act of, 25
    goes beyond but grounded in belief, 40
    implies trust in and reliance on God's goodness, 40, 49
    informed by objective knowledge, 95
    involves existential risk and intellectual choice, 19, 65
    leap of, 19
    presupposes belief, 19
    meaningless with complete knowledge, 26, 49, 110
    meaningless with no knowledge, 26, 49
    more than assenting to propositions, 26
    nothing true for faith but false for reason, 26
    reason not irrelevant to, 24
    relationship to knowledge, 5, 24, 26–27, 49
    relationship to reason, 24
    uncertainty creates occasion for, 49
    without passion, dry and lifeless, 22
fallacy
    collectivism, 232
    informal, 28
    nominal, 91, 248
false beliefs
    authentic religion cannot be based on, 44
    capable of causing harm, 90
    distinguishing between true and, 4
    knowledge blend of true and, 33–34
    misleading, 86–87
    sometimes useful even if incorrect, 83, 93
    value of correcting, 90
false religion
    important to distinguish from true, 4
    life off-kilter because of, 153
    many versions of, 154
    no foundation for authentic living, 153
    not a positive illusion, 132
    provides illusion of well-being, 153
family, devotion to, 7
fanaticism, 124, 242, 323
Faraday, Michael, 311
Farrer, Austin

God good and powerful, not contradictory
eschews philosophic treatments of evil, 251
evil when systems collide, 251
favors theological treatments of evil, 251
importance of writings by Paul, 198
mutual interference of systems, 251
views on evil, 250–52, 402
Fauvism, 317
fear
of the Lord, meaning of, 47
renders genuine love impossible, 40
feelings
not always trustworthy guides to action, 413
Ferguson, Niall, 308
fervent spirituality or intellectual precision, 17
feudalism
bond of loyalty between warrior and chief, 300
crusades began during feudal period, 300
French ideal of chivalry spread, 300
knights as indispensable agents of society, 300–1
knights increasingly chivalrous, 300
military values fostered gentility, 300
nobles became knights loyal to Christendom, 300
nobles, descendants of barbarian warriors, 300
nobles (knights) developed loyalty to church, 300
opened way for increased literacy, 300
primogeniture prevailed during, 300
rebellious nobles established warring states, 300
revival of religious, intellectual, artistic life, 300
Western Civilization increasingly militaristic, 300
fideism
definition of, 109, 367
skepticism as opposed to, 109
filioque, 326, 454
Firestone, Diana, xii
first-order data, 96
flesh, meaning of in New Testament, 171, 254
Fleskes, Diana, xii
Fleskes, Terry, xii
focus on self and focus on others, 103
Footprints, poem, 206
forgiveness
asking God for, 124, 448, Appendices I and II
central to Christianity, 428–29
Christians in the business of extending, 307
God's offer of, 381
may not sufficiently appreciate, 405
prayer as road to, 429
superficial, 428
Foucault, Michel, 3
frailties and failings
becoming more open about, 425
necessity of coming to terms with, 51
we all have, and their implications, 376, 385
freedom and self-determination
amendments to U.S. Constitution, 62, 310
Bill of Rights (American) 62
Bill of Rights (English), 307
Magna Carta, 62, 329
valued in the West, 58
freedom in Christ, abusing, 324
freedom of choice
can be diminished, 247
some always remains, 247
free will
attempts to address evil based on, 250
brain integrity and, 415
choice, an illusion without, 226, 372
defense, Augustine's, 262
developmental history imposes limits on, 414
genes impose limits on, 414
gift of, from God, 140, 372, 414–15

INDEX

free will *(continued)*
    God does not override human, 140, 172
    God has given us, 105
    if none, no accountability, 137
    may not depend entirely on brain, 415
    necessary for true moral choice, 262–63
    no accountability or responsibility without, 247–48, 372, 414
    no one has complete, 414
    people have at least limited, 372
    people retain some and can say no, 414
    possible, implications of, 246
    relationship to brain physiology unclear, 414
    result of obedience according to Augustine, 263
    trivialization of human choice, 136–38
Freud, Sigmund
    infantile needs for a father, explanation of religion, 132
    influenced by Nietzsche, 123
    not everything should be forgiven or tolerated, 285
    psychologically explains away Christianity, 36
    views on evil, 285–86
Fröbel, Friedrich, 314
fundamentalists and Darwinists, 233–35

Galbraith, John Kenneth, 144
Galileo affair, 218, 232–33
Galileo Galilei, 220, 368
Gallaudet, Thomas, 314
Garden of Earthly Delights (Bosch), 317
Gastil, Thomas, xii
Gatling gun, 245
Gauguin, Paul, 317
Geist, der, translated as spirit, mind, or intellect, 280
Gemara, 346
Genealogy of Morals (Nietzsche), 283
geologic science
    creation of human beings, 223
    creation of the earth, 223
    cataclysms, 222–23
    Pangaea, 222
Gifford Lectures, 98, 291
God
    access to through Jesus, 207
    alienation from self, others, and, 372
    ambiguity of the term, 227
    arguments for existence, begging the question, 28
    Bible discloses character of, 5
    cannot exist and not exist, 3
    challenge to determine nature of, 7
    chooses not to terrorize into belief, 47
    Christianity, claims about God and Jesus, 40
    communicates analytically and intuitively, 50
    connecting with, central business of life, 21
    conversation, ongoing through Christ, 19
    created universe out of love, 373
    Creator-Provider-Sustainer, 22, 50
    desire for truth and love of, 410
    desires relationships with human beings, 45
    divine nature revealed in Jesus, 44
    exists in three persons, 370. See Trinity
    has consciousness, 2, 70
    human consciousness reflective of God, 50
    human responsibility toward, 1
    humans, creations of, 1
    incomplete comprehension of, 49
    in three persons, took centuries to codify, 174
    invisible attributes self-evident, 178
    Jesus revealed nature and character of, 5
    keeps some things hidden, 40
    love of, entails pursuit of truth, 410
    love sacrificial, 205, 337
    loves us in spite of ourselves, 390

INDEX

loves us as individuals, 1, 48, 92, 195, 350
loving sustainer, 45
loving without reserve, 169
maintains necessary distance from humanity, 263
many people have abandoned search for, 3
many scientists believe in a transcendent, 227
married humanity in Jesus, 54, 374–75, 395
nature, reflected in Jesus, 2
not punitive judge or tyrant, 45
nothing you have done need alienate you from, 22
ongoing relationship with, and meaningful religion, 17
participating in divine existence and agenda, 54, 400
perceiving with spiritual ears, 397
perceiving with spiritual eyes, 37, 397, 403
proofs of, from nature unconvincing to many, 28, 233
proving existence of, inductive only, 26–29
purposes, desires, and intentions of, 2
refuses to intimidate into belief, 40
self-disclosure, 178–79, 370
sharing the mind of, 220, 400
suffers when we suffer, 390
truth and goodness, source of, 1
works through feelings as well as thoughts, 35
Gödel's incompleteness theorem, 30
God's gifts
consciousness, 50, 372, 412
cooperating with, and becoming like Christ, 4
death points us toward God, 132
discomfort leads us to God, 132
faith, 171
grace, by definition unmerited, 34
justification through Christ, 365–66
life beyond death, 65, 124, 173
life, God's greatest gift, 371, 429
mercifully we cannot read minds, 97
new and additional nature, 171–72
sacrificial love, 205
salvation, implies we require it, 372
spiritual insight, 34
time, necessary for choice and change, 371, 412
God's immutable attributes, 411
God's kingdom on earth, 21, 39, 184, 204, 307–8, 354–55, 375, 382, 449
God's love
rejecting and annihilationism, 350
some may continue to reject, 353
those who reject, may forever remain aware of, 415
trouble believing and accepting, 411
God's sustaining energy, 412
Gogh, Vincent van, 317
gospel
definition of, 22
news that God loves us anyway, 390
prosperity, 45, 87
Gospels
as memoirs, 185
as selective episodic biographies, 201
harmonies of, 185
Gould, Stephen Jay, 220
Gnosticism
adherents believed had secret knowledge, 215
body impediment to recognizing divine light within, 215
docetism, related to, 107, 215
grace
common, 408
giving to others, rather than law, 427, 435–36
meaning of, 53, 376, 390, 396, 405
sacraments as vehicles of, 379
Gratian, Emperor, 307
Great Divorce, The (Lewis), 386
Great Peasants' War, 330–31
Great Schism. *See* East-West Schism
Greene, Graham, 110, 131
Gregory of Nyssa, 75, 351
growing as a Christian, 448–50

INDEX

governments, forms of, not all of equal merit, 62
gyroscope, metaphor for brain and life, 129, 372
gyroscopic effect, 91

Hagia Sophia, 314
Hawthorne, Nathaniel, 361
hallucinations
    indicative of major mental disorder, 209
    nature of, 209–11
    unsound as explanation of resurrection, 209–11
Handel, Frideric, 318
harmonies of the Gospels, 185
Harvey, A. E., 49–50
hate crime, 241
Hayden, Joseph, 318
healing
    needed by everyone, 432
    takes other people to facilitate emotional, 432–33
heart
    capable of emulating beasts or angels, 153
    can never truly know another person's, 63, 97
    change of mind or, 384
    communication and the importance of, 440
    condemning God from, 251
    condition of, 385
    centrality of, 37
    crowd out worshipping from, 70
    culture reflects and shapes, 338
    deceitful, 337
    discerning, 233
    disease, 385
    disposition of, and acceptance of resurrection, 342
    God as heart surgeon, 38–39, 371, 385
    God prefers sincere, to pious recitations, 408
    God standing at the door of your, 173
    hardness of, 343, 353
    habits of, 246–47
    head and, matters of existential importance, 34
    head to the exclusion of, 150
    Holy Spirit and change of mind and, 170
    human, impression of morality on, 169
    Jesus indwelling your, 103
    living with a transformed, 376
    loving God with all your, 169
    mind reflects the, 416
    new eyes and a new, 378
    not always in the hearts of professed Christians, 257
    not loving God, 386
    only God fully knows a person's, 361
    open the eyes of my, 195
    reasons that reason knows not of, 37, 442–43
    reference to in the Bible, 103
    relative neglect by contemporary philosophers, 37
    renewed mind and, 22
    responsibility to nurture our own, 427
    transformed mind reflects transformed heart, 325
    worship of God begins in, 171
heaven(s)
    complete freedom only in, 263
    focusing excessively on, 184
    imitation, 154
    increasing joy and everlasting fulfillment, 133
    Jesus ascended to, 188, 216
    kingdom of, 92
    life on earth not a waiting room for, 355
    musings about, 355–57
    neither mindless nor boring, 133
    omnipresent as another dimension, 355
Hegel, Georg
    first to account for evil in secular terms, 274
    gap narrowing between is and ought. 275

INDEX

Geist, der, 274
   history a slaughterhouse, 274
   humanity on inexorable path of progress, 275
   redefines significance of evil, 275
   suffering and despair necessary, 275
   system builder, 82
   thesis, antithesis, synthesis, 275
   treatment of evil, 273–75
   working out of providence, 274
Heine, Heinrich, 69
heirs, Christians become joint, 449
hell, 279, 350, 352–54, 356–57, 386, 414–15, 453
helping others, seven ways of, 438
Henley, William Ernest, 148–49
Henry I, King, 329
Henry VIII, King, 58, 323
heresy, definition of, 53
hermeneutics, definition of, 367n3
Herodotus, 59–60
Hessenauer, Gary, xii
Hick, John, view on evil, 251
Hildebrand, Dietrich von, 37, 109, 325
Hinduism, 160, 275, 278, 351, 370
Historical and Critical Dictionary (Bayle), 256
History of the Conflict between Religion and Science (Draper), 230
History of the Warfare of Science and Theology (White), 219
Hobbes, Thomas
   life brutal without laws and enforcement, 58, 116
   people motivated by fear, 116
   restless desire for power in writings of, 116
Hoffer, Eric, 42
holiness as flawless moral beauty, 378
Holland, Tom, 337
Holocaust, Nazi, 152–53, 260–62, 286, 335, 339
holy intimacy
   enjoyed in heaven, 356
   possible on earth but has risks and costs, 423
Holy Spirit
   acted in incarnation of Jesus, 108
   Acts of the Holy Spirit, 170
   central to transformation in Christ, 448
   Christians as temples of, 390
   controversy between Catholicism and Orthodoxy over, 369
   creates awareness of lethal disease, 394
   creates new desires and capacities, 171
   creeds and the, 365, Appendices I and II
   eternal existence of, 74
   for Christians, struggle will always exist, 325
   gift of faith through, 171
   God operates on minds and hearts through, 371, 393, 404
   guided authors of biblical books, 368
   implanted by Jesus, 48
   incarnation, Appendix I
   influence us via Bible, 106
   leads to recognition of Christ, 34
   legitimate to pray to, 108
   motivates Christians to share God's love, 378
   moves people from skepticism to faith, 344
   not to be confused with Hegel's *Geist*
   nudges toward altruism and goodness, 172
   openness to, leads to desire for holiness, 416
   operates on mind and heart, 338
   personal presence of, 184
   prayers may be inspired by, 409
   prompts recognition of nature of Jesus, 37
   relationship to the Son, 326
   remaining open to guidance of, 449
   request for guidance from, 448
   same as Old Testament, 174
   single versus double procession, 326
   through the, change of heart and mind, 170
   uncreated, 214

INDEX

homo sapiens
  God breathed life into, 223
  groups of, displaced other groups, 334
  have existed at least 40,000 years, 220
  may have existed for 200,000 years, 207
  minuscule percentage of age of the earth, 223
  something turned, into true human beings, 223, 373

hope
  Christian, 91–93, 132–33, 381
  Christianity and, 35
  centerpiece of Jewish, 166
  confidence in loving creator, foundation for, 93
  confident expectation, good definition of, 341
  depression, loss, and vanishing, 93
  disciples had compelling, 202
  empty, 131–32
  false, based on unsound religion, 132
  false, offered by unscrupulous faith healers, 88
  finding sensible faith and, 5
  haunted by, 5
  in absence of underlying reality, 131–32
  long-term hope of individuals and species, 173
  loss of, 93
  of brighter side, only if there is one, 132
  of improving human nature, 153
  of living forever, not in vain, 66
  of eternal life, foundational to Christianity, 124, 341, 356
  of eternal life pointless if no resurrection, 340
  of human connectedness, 433
  of not being alone, 433
  of resurrected bodies, 349
  of showing Christ to others, 427
  oscillation between science as, and irrationalism, 221
  realistic, only if based on something true, 132
  utopian, false and unrealistic, 255–56
  without God, no realistic, 92

Hound of Heaven, The (Thompson), 140
how the heavens go, Galileo, 368
Hutterites, 333
Hubbard, David Allan, 206
human choice. *See also* free will
  trivialization of, 136–38
  rule of law, 320
  science, 311–12

human history
  emergence of true *Homo sapiens*, 223, 373
  infinitesimally small in relation to age of universe, 223
  stone age ended only recently, 223

human life and dignity, Christian contributions to, 319–20

human nature
  both animal (protoplasmic) and spiritual, 144, 177
  Christians realistic about, 283
  more than that of an animal, 223
  need a relationship with God to complete, 50
  primal may always emerge, 171–72, 178, 375
  require specific kind of spiritual nourishment, 50
  share divine attributes, 223

humanism did not imply atheism, 19–20

Hume
  begs the question in relation to miracles, 338
  benevolent and omnipotent God unlikely, 271
  causation just constant conjunction, 270
  denies existence and goodness of God based on experience, 270
  dismisses miracles on probabilistic grounds, 206
  distinguishes between moral and natural evil, 268

eschews metaphysical speculation, 348
fear and superstition basis of religion, 270
ferocious in his attack, 271
first thoroughly secular major thinker, 271
illegitimate to base religious belief on reason, 271
induction can never lead to certainty, 32
is and ought, not the same, 271
laws of nature probabilistic inferences, 224
no good argument for theism, 271
on evil, reason stumbles and skepticism prevails, 271
ruled out everything not observable or demonstratable, 340
skepticism toward inductive reasoning, 224
skepticism toward natural religion, 270
supreme skeptic, 347–49
treatment of evil, 270–71
with, skepticism comes into full bloom, 271
would fire God as architect, 270

humility
benevolence and, reflected in proper prayer, 408–9
epistemic, 110, 409
necessary in interpreting Bible, 42
necessary in trying to understand God, 50–51
need for, in approaching philosophic questions, 70
need for theological, 42–43
prayer to be undertaken with, 409
reflected in creeds, 110, 345
suggestion for, in approaching God, 447
toward history of Christian thought, 74

Hus, Jan, 305
Huygens, Christiaan, 345
hypostatic union, 107, 214

I and Thou (Buber), 356
"I believe in you," important, 443
Icelandic monasteries crucial in spawning scholars, 299
iconoclastic controversy, 316
Identity of Man, The (Bronowski), 100
ideology, methodology and, confusion between, 60–63
idiosyncrasy credits as invisible bank account, 58
illusion
inadequate as explanation for resurrection, 209
nature of, 208–09
of self-sufficiency, 92
of understanding created by medicalization, 248
imagination, Jesus came to expand human, 37, 105
Impressionism, 317–18
impact
can be unconscious, 441–42
seven thoughts on, 443–44
unpredictable, 440
Incarnation
carries implication for belief and practice, 108
definition of, 74
Hinduism and, 160
Jesus example of, 74
no specific word for in Bible, 108
may be difficult to accept for some, 216, 376
through the, Jesus emptied himself, 336
way God tried to get human attention, 205
Incas, 332–33
inductive reasoning
especially relevant in religion, 32
evaluation according to plausibility, 32
example of, 31–32
faith based in part on, 40
most knowledge based on, 32–33
nature of, 310
probabilistic by nature, 32

INDEX

inductive reasoning *(continued)*
    reach many if not most conclusions by, 32
    relationship to empiricism, 347
    weak inductive arguments, 68
indulgences
    definition and function of, 306, 330
    scathing criticism by Luther, 306
    sale of, 330
Industrial Revolution, effect on religious belief, 362
infinite qualitative difference, 273
infinities
    hints of God's existence, 40
    suspended between two, 39–40
Inglehart, 2–3, 236
inner testimony of the Spirit, 110
insight
    alone, not enough for emotional healing, 442
    Augustine provided considerable, 78
    becoming a Christian brings new, 383–94
    Bible assumed to provide unique, 71
    Christian, into human nature central, 299
    creative, in good theology, 76
    closing gap between belief and reality, 34
    Freud's, into working of the mind, 285
    important in matters of religion, 28
    into philosophies of major thinkers, 261
    into God's nature and relationship to humanity, 367
    into who and what we serve, 7
    narrowing gap between belief and reality, 28, 88, 93, 393
    of monotheism, fundamental in Christianity, 175
    overcoming false belief as, 89
    path to acquiring knowledge, 88
    relationship to belief, 88–90
    spiritual insight, 111, 393
    story of Joseph in Genesis, saturated with, 437
    survey results do not always provide, 44
    true philosopher more interested in, than cleverness, 410
    theological, into nature of Bible, 73
intellectual
    God not, abstraction, 70
    religion to neglect of emotion, 17
    pursuits may come to replace God, 70–71, 150
intellectualism
    as distraction, 150–51
    can crowd out faith, 70
    dry, in theology, 103
    vice of, 70
intellectualization, defense mechanism of, 140
intellectual precision and fervent spirituality, 17
intelligence
    abusing the gift of, 70
    implied in basic sanity, 97
    objectivity as expression of, 97
intelligent design, 235
interpersonal
    Christian faith as, 94, 96
    covenant, 161–62
    dynamics, research on, 428
    faith as, byproduct of monotheism, 161, 176
    nature of spiritual knowledge, 95–111
    relationships with God, 403
    relationships, ability to enjoy, similar to God's, 223
    relationships, heaven must allow, 355, 357
intimacy
    caring and candor necessary for, 427
    center of communion with Christ and others, 424
    characteristic of certain kind of friendship, 422
    costly, 426
    developing, a spiritual discipline, 427
    holy, may elude you, 425
    holy, requires authenticity, 427

INDEX

human beings created for, 424
implication of the Trinity, 424
Jesus came to restore, 424
not easy to create, 426
not optional, 424
provides glimpse ahead, 424
recommendations for fostering, 427–28
requires avoidance of superficial advice, 427
requires good judgment, 426
requires investment of time, 426
requires self-disclosure, 425, 427
taking risks and, 427
sacred or holy, 422
takes courage, 427
without, we remain wooden, 424
intuition
awareness of God, tacit knowledge based on, 111
by, know God exists, 132
can be misleading, 30
imagination and, central to faith, 37
often trumps analysis, 103
pattern recognition and, 50
personal decisions based heavily on, 103
right hemisphere and, 50
subjective, and objective analysis bear on faith, 94
thinking involves both, and analysis, 94, 102
intuitive
belief and unbelief, 24
hunches by scientists, 33
insight in grasping nature of Jesus, 103
leaps involved in understanding, 102
reasoning, nature and importance of, 99, 102
spiritual knowledge, 101
wisdom by mother, 436
Islamic architecture, 315
inquisitions
had been going on for centuries, 331
Counter-Reformation intensified violence of Spanish, 339
motives for, 332
Spanish, 322, 331
Inuit, 6
Invictus (Henley), 148–49
Irenaeus
evil necessary for moral development, 263
God maintains necessary distance from humanity, 263
human beings able to reach moral perfection, 263
human suffering necessary, 263
interpretation of evil, 263
suffering necessary for free will, 263
isolation, defense mechanism of, 139–40
ISSR (International Society for Science and Religion), 220

James, William, 36, 67, 86
Jaspers, Karl, 118–19. 122
Jefferson, Thomas
by deletions constructed own New Testament, 120, 320
law as codification of public opinion, 62
not recognizably Christian, 320
Jesus
access to God through, 207
appearances after resurrection, 173, 197–98, 208, 210, 212, 343
as rabbi (teacher), 22
before Abraham was, I am, 207
begotten, 108
both divine and human, 207
bridge to God, 53, 175, 376, 378, 381, 402
came from God, 395
came to expand human imagination, 37, 105
Christians died for their belief in, 204
church conclusions about, 214–16
claims about, many find compelling, 24
commissioned Christians to work through the church, 382

INDEX

Jesus *(continued)*
    continuation and fulfillment of Judaism, 52
    demonstrated God's nature, 2, 44
    deserved worship by disciples, 208
    divinity joined to humanity in, 54, 374–75, 395
    demonstrated divine justice and mercy, 374
    embodied or incarnate *Logos*, 172, 366
    enabled reconciliation with God, 366
    existence of, 201–2
    far more than unrealistic itinerant preacher, 22
    from another dimension of reality, 54
    fulfillment of a religion already existing, 175
    God in the flesh, 173
    God-Mortal, God-Man, 366
    God's unique self-disclosure, 74
    had been worshipping all along, 52
    identity, nature, and significance of, 37
    inaugurated new age, 382
    irreversible union of divine and human, 374
    joining of divinity to humanity, 54, 374–75, 395
    launched new humanity, 175 382
    love by, sacrificial, 205, 337
    made possible repair of broken relationship, 2, 48
    one toward whom Old Testament points, 52, 200
    only begotten Son of God, 378, 455–56
    overcame humanity's enemy death, 173
    parables, why taught in, 103
    perceiving with spiritual ears, 397
    perceiving with spiritual eyes, 37, 397, 403
    performed miracles, 204
    provided way to connect with God, 378
    recognition of, starting point for Christian faith, 37
    reconciled us to God, 382
    reconciler and rescuer, 36
    related to God in way we are not, 51
    replaced love of power with power of love, 175
    represented transcendent order of existence, 52
    resurrected and living Christ, 100
    revealed deep structure of existence, 48
    revealed God's nature as never before, 205, 373
    revealed nature of living in communion with God, 48
    same nature, essence, or substance as God, 214
    Seminar, 191
    showed humanity selfless love, 396, 398
    supreme commander for Christians, 173
    tempted but did not yield, 394
    undeserved gift to humankind, 2, 365, 381, 391, 447
    unique offspring of God, 108
    unique combination of God and humanity, 181, 205
    unparalleled divine self-disclosure, 22
    ushered in new emerging order, 175
    way, truth, and life, 207
    "Word made flesh," 366
Jesus Seminar, 191
Jesus' lament over Jerusalem, 416
jihad, waging of, 327
John Chrysostom, 75
Johnson, Paul, 6
Johnson, Samuel, 213
Jones, Jim, 324
Jonestown, 324
Josephus, dispassionate Jewish observer, 201
judgments
    affected by non-rational processes, 35
    cannot avoid making, 63

INDEX

conditioned by what we are drawn to, 35
shaped by what we think, 35
judging, injunctions again, can discourage thinking, 63
Judaism
   accountability, new sense of individual, 161
   both less and more than expected in Jesus, 175
   Christian heritage derived from, 175
   Christians indebted to, for monotheism, 159
   diaspora in, 168
   first part of two-part drama, 170
   God shaped thought-forms in, 162
   history of, foundational to Christianity, 162
   Israel, confusing use of in Bible, 163
   Jesus, culmination of new humanity, 175
   monarchy in, 162–63
   new sense of personal relationship with God, 161
   Northern Kingdom, history of, 163–64
   northern tribes secede, 163
   Second Temple, and redoubled focus on law, 169
   Shema, focal point of worship in, 170
   Southern Kingdom, history of, 164–67
   spiritual versus ceremonial, difference between in, 167–68
   twelve confederated tribes, 163
Juergensen, Mark, xii
justice, retributive, 286, 307
justification in God's sight
   because of Christ, 365–66
   Calvin, by faith alone, 366
   in Eastern Orthodoxy, 366
   in Roman Catholicism, 366
   Luther, by faith alone, 366
   parable of the religionist and the publican, 105
justified true belief, 27, 40, 108–9, 225
Justin Martyr, 185

Justinian, Emperor, 314
just war theory, 264

Kant, Immanuel
   coined term radical evil, 272
   insuperable sap between is and ought, 271
   noumenal and phenomenal, 273
   problem of evil impossible and immoral, 272
   treatment of evil, 271–73
Kaufman, Walter, 27
Keller, Tim, 447
Kelvin, Lord William, 311
kenotic theology, 336
Kepler, Johannes, 152, 220, 232, 311, 320
kerygma, meaning of, 47, 443
Kierkegaard, Søren, 19, 82, 120, 126, 150, 273–74
Killing Jesus (O'Reilly and Dugand), 375
Kingdom of God, already and not yet, 308
knights, medieval, 5
knowing versus proving, 27–29
knowledge
   about, different from knowledge of, 100
   amorphous blend of true and false beliefs, 34, 96
   accidental correctness not, 89–90
   accommodation and assimilation, relation to, 89
   beliefs, relationship between and, 4
   can be relied on, 93
   cannot be based on contradictions, 93
   central question, gap between conjecture and, 28
   claims to, often wrong, 4
   claims to, must be justified, 3
   coherence approaches to, 63, 76, 85–86
   coherence necessary but not sufficient, 86
   correspondence approaches to, 85–86

INDEX

knowledge *(continued)*
  externalists, only reliable source needed for, 27
  guessing correctly not, 89
  justified true belief, 27, 40, 108,
  materialism and only road to, 27
  mental templates, role in, 89
  not, if conclusion reached from false premises, 89–90
  not same as deductively proving, 27
  often flawed or incomplete, 33
  personal, 98–100
  pragmatic approaches to, 85–86, 224
  relationship to beliefs, not straightforward, 4
  relationship to faith, 5
  religious, possibility of, 110
  role of expert opinion in, 87
  role of tradition in, 87
  tacit, 38, 98–100, 104, 109, 111
  three basic approaches to, 85–87
  three categories of, 96
  when beliefs, thoughts, judgments align with reality, 84, 88–89, 93
Koch, Heinrich Hermann Robert, 363
koine Greek, commonly used, 181
koinonia, 388, 427
Kreeft, Peter, xii, 38n, 73, 173, 208n, 274, 344, 355
Kuhn, Thomas, 33

Lamb, Barbara, xii
Lamb, Warren, xii
language
  communication and, 100, 111
  inner and outer, both related to faith, 94
  of thought, 100
  thinking, 100–1, 111, 240
  thinking, may or may not include awareness of God, 101
  thinking, media in which creativity grows, 100
  thought and, 100–102
  two kinds, private and public, 94, 100
  when inner and outer converge, 100
Lavoisier, Antoine, 312

learning can become idolatry, 71
Leeuwenhoek, Antonie, 363
legacy, leaving, 92
Leibniz, Gottfried Wilhelm von
  best of all possible worlds, 250
  devout Lutheran, 311
  invented theodicy, 249
  natural and moral evil, 272
  symbolized one of two views on evil, 266–68
Lessing, Gotthold, difficult crossing ugly broad ditch, 206
Lessons of History (Durant and Durant), 291
Leo III, Emperor, outlawed human images, 316
Leonardo, da Vinci, 362
Lewis, Sinclair, 153n10, 324
Lewis, C. S.
  Christian conversion of, 38
  cooperated with God to promote faith, 38
  lay up our arms and surrender to God, 125
  letter to Arthur Greeves, 115
  people hold standard of justice, 278
  some prostitutes may be closer to heaven, 390
light
  Christians intended to shed, 378
  Gospels like shining, on a gem, 184
  Jews intended to be, of world, 168
  nature of, 225, 345
  interpreting scripture in, of rest of Bible
  love darkness rather than, 141
  of Christ, 39, 53
  of reason, 103
  opportunity to choose, over darkness, 416
  physical body impediment to recognizing divine, 215
  stopping at green, on way to rehearsal, 136
  switch, 279
life
  finite resource, 19

INDEX

fundamental unpredictability of, 154
energy, 7, 426
in Christ, meaning of, 103
like line of credit, 387
meaning and significance of, 85
purpose worthy of commitment, 85
linguistic philosophers
    more precision at cost of ignoring key problems, 27
    often define philosophic problems as ailments, 27
Lister, Joseph, 312, 364
listening, value of, 351, 403, 421, 426, 433–35, 437–38
Liszt, Franz, 318
literature, Christian contributions to, 319
liturgy, meaning of, 380
lizards, killing, 386–87
Locke, John, 320
logic
    good theology depends on, 255
    important things in life non-demonstrable, 26
    law of excluded middle, 63, 76
    of science, 206
    rules or principles of, 63
    subtlety of deductive, 29
logical positivism, 99, 102
logos
    Christ as pre-existing, 216
    entered space and time as man, 396
    etymology of, 181
    Jesus as incarnate, 366
    suggests order and rationality, 172
    with God from eternity, 396
Lord
    accepting Christ as, 393
    Christ as owner and, 78
    fear of, meaning of, 47
    Jesus as ultimate authority and, 21
    of the cosmos, 101
    Paul acknowledged Jesus as, 55
    question Paul asked on road to Damascus, 54
    Thomas owning Jesus as, 52
loss of unifying authority, 364

love
    accepting God's, 9, 43
    achievements and pleasures meaningless without, 92
    Aphrodite, goddess of, 159, 171
    chivalry and romantic, 301
    civilization's, of words and concepts, 294
    coercion precludes, 46–47
    commandments of Jesus and, 169
    confidence in God's, 93
    couples in, 97
    crucifixion demonstrated God's sacrificial, 48
    do not have to qualify for God's, 390
    death ends human, 129, 133
    divine, 123
    ensnared by, of the temporary, 397
    expressing, does not diminish us, 412
    from another human being, like God's, 351
    God's, for humanity, 2
    God's, for individuals, 1, 48, 92, 195, 350
    God's gift of Jesus, divine, 2
    God's, for us, 48, 83, 96, 110, 252, 350, 375, 379, 390
    God's, more enduring and substantial than ours, 110
    God's offer of, 103
    God's sacrificial, 19
    human standards of, more alike than different, 371
    implies caring about welfare of the beloved, 376
    impossible to, someone you fear, 40
    in Plato's *Euthyphro*
    inseparable from truth in good relationships, 426
    has several meanings, 43
    Jesus demonstrated God's, 48, 205, 377
    Lord your God, the, 169
    moved by, gave humanity Jesus, 395
    of novelty can overshadow, of God, 71
    of power versus power of, 175

INDEX

love *(continued)*
    of wisdom, philosophy as, 70
    one another, profound influence on culture, 307
    possible to, an idea 45
    rejecting divine goodness and, 388
    sacrificial, 205
    showing the world God's, 54
    truth and, inseparable, 426
    your neighbor as yourself, 169, 199
Loved One, The (Waugh), 138
Luther, Martin
    appalled by ignorance, 313
    church needs well-trained clergy, insistence that, 369
    consubstantiation versus transubstantiation, 43
    continued monastic idea of work as worship, 298
    contributed greatly to literacy, 313, 319
    controversy over nature of mass, 42
    critiqued selling of indulgences, 306
    kicked off Protestant Reformation, 189, 304–5, 328
    encouraged freedom of speech, 306
    endorsed idea of educating women, 313
    endorsed idea of state supported schools, 313
    Erasmus' acerbic quip to, 330
    excommunicated, 306, 313
    ninety-five thesis, scathing criticisms of pope, 306
    observed ecclesiastical opulence and clerical corruption, 306
    passionate belief in the power of scripture, 42
    position on mass, close to Roman Catholicism's, 42
    posting of ninety-five theses, 330
    presumed everyone competent to interpret Bible, 42
    priesthood of all believers, 333
    refused to subordinate himself to church or state, 306
    rejection of sacerdotalism, 333
    sola scriptura, doctrine of, 368
    standardized German language, 314
    supported compulsory school attendance, 313, 321
    theses, posting of ninety-five, 306
    translated Bible into colloquial German, 189
Lutheran, 18, 43, 118, 214, 311, 330, 337, 380,

Machiavelli
    descriptive or prescriptive, unclear, 263
    first to distinguish between virtue and practicality, 263
    no fan of Christianity or idealism, 264
    principal functions of government, 263
    redefined evil as expedience, 263–64
    treatment of evil, 263–64
    unethical actions sometimes necessary, 264
MacIntyre, Alasdair, 73, 90n, 136n
MacGregor, Geddes, 19, 456
Magna Carta, 62, 329
Manet, Édouard, 317
man, measure of all things, 20
Marcus Aurelius, 291
marriage, few secrets in a good, 46
Marshall, Cathy, xii
Marcionism, related to Catharism, 215
Marx, Karl
    alienation of workers from what they produce, 280
    capitalists versus proletariat, 280–81
    capitalists contribute little or nothing, 281
    challenge to Christianity, 36
    criticism of philosophers, 280
    determined to understand capitalism, 279
    dialectical materialism and, 280
    economic forces make progress inevitable, 280
    focused his attention on moral evil, 280
    history a record of class struggle, 280

keenly aware of nature of evil, 281
influenced by Hegel, French
    socialists, English economists,
    280
life, career, and impact, 279–83
little attention to innovation,
    capability, or risk-taking, 281
prodigious reader, 279
relentless fomenter of revolution,
    280
religion, opium of the masses
    (people), 36, 280
treatment of evil, 279–83
viewed Hegel's *Geist* as superfluous
    mystification, 280
Marxism, out of favor in philosophy
    departments, 151
Marxist governments often capitalist
    hybrids, 279
mass murder, 241
materialism, confusion between two
    kinds, 226–27
materialism, economic
    corruption in the church and, 299
    driving force in human events, 280
    not primary motive behind Spanish
        Inquisition, 332
materialism, methodological in science,
    226
materialism, philosophical
    (physicalism)
    definition of, 27
    difficulty making sense of all of life,
        350
    does not illumine nature of
        consciousness, 226, 350
    everything physically explainable,
        226
    for some, functions like religion,
        227
    fundamental thesis of, cannot be
        proved, 27
    not all scientists subscribe to, 226
    nothing logically to do with
        scientific method, 227
    not reached through empiricism, 27
    related to metaphysical naturalism,
        226
    reluctance to grasp spiritual nature
        of life, 226
    rules out divine creator, 226
    skepticism and, 27
mathematics, Islamic, 317
Matisse, Henri, 317
Maugham, Somerset, 128
Mavrodes, George, 249
Mayans, 332–33
McCarthy era, 334
McGrath, Alister E. 34, 77, 228, 369
McLemore, Kenneth S., xii, 422
McPherson, Conor, 353
meaningful life, 4
medicine and health care, Christian
    contributions to, 312–13
medicine, Islamic, 317
medieval Europe
    began to revolve around cities,
        301–3
    from 1150 began to resemble one
        society, 302
    work conceived as service to God
        and neighbor
Melk Abbey, 315
Melville, Herman, 172, 441
mental disorder(s)
    absurd explanation of New
        Testament events, 210
    evil and, 248
    human choice and, 255
    may or may not be implicated in
        evil, 255
    problem with medicalizing, 137
    Sade, Marquis de, 284
Mein Kampf, 125
Mendel, Gregor, 311
Mendelssohn, Felix, 318
Mennonites, 333
Merritt, Duncan, xii
Messiah (Jesus)
    allusion to as more than human, 175
    anointed or sent one, 21, 200
    belief in, 212
    followers believed Jesus to be, 201
    God coming to rescue, 205
    long-awaited, 343
    looked forward to as deliverer, 375

Messiah (Jesus) *(continued)*
    own realization he was, 402
    promised, 107, 180,
    reasoned arguments for, 205
    seen as blasphemous by Jews, 174
    Christ, Greek term for, 175
metanoia and *metalomai*, translated as repentance, 384
metaphysical evil, 268
metempsychosis, synonym for reincarnation, 351
Methodist, 18, 214, 380
Michael, Anna-Marie, xii
medieval church
    corruption and reform in, 299–300
    cross-national unifying force, 299
    growing movements for reform in, 299
    monastic system corrupted, 299
    reform began in eleventh century, 299
    reform became official policy, 299
    spawned representative government, checks, balances, 299
    tenth-century papal scandals, 299
medieval cities centered on cathedrals, 303
Michelangelo, di Lodovico Buonarroti Simoni, 362
Mill, James, 279
Milliron, Trevor, xii
mind
    ability to read another's, 356
    already made up, 206
    and body, each fundamental, 347
    and consciousness, not identical, 372, 413
    become a Christian when God acts on, 2
    by nature, subjective, 109
    cannot read anyone else's, 97
    central to being complete person, 413
    change of heart and, 105, 170
    closing one's, 43
    conforms to reality, not vice versa, 89
    contents of, shaped by reality, 95
    contingent on brain's integrity, 372, 415
    conventions, habits, and customs of, 122
    disease of the, 254
    dysfunctionally open, impaired ability to identify nonsense, 61
    eastern attitude of, 276
    freedom of, necessary for civilization, 290
    glimpsing into God's, 376
    God concerned with a person's, 416
    God gave us a, and we ought to use it, 191
    God must have something like a, 70
    God operates on the human, 371
    grasping Jesus' mind through the Gospels, 6
    Holy Spirit acting on, 338
    innate structures and templates of, 95
    insight into, 126
    Jesus indwelling your, 103
    knowing one another's, 46
    loving God with your heart and, 169
    makes us unique, 133
    meta- in good marriage, 97
    no such thing as a group, 96
    not reducible or equivalent to brain, 37
    of Christ, 83, 409, 424
    only mind that exists, 95, 109
    open, 194–95
    philosophy of, 81
    reality not invented by the, 20
    recognizing Jesus with heart and, 44
    reflects the heart, 416
    renewed heart and, 22
    repentance as change in one's, 384
    resentment, lethal state of, 428
    sin has corrosive effect on, 394
    speculative philosopher and the, 69
    states of, 154
    transformed by Christ, 325
    transformation of heart and, 50
    we are all shapers of others,' 439–40
    western, the, 295–96, 309, 317

will never fully understand the
workings of, 248
world exists outside our, 224
your, inaccessible to everyone but
God, 403
mind-body problem, 372, 413
minister without a professional veneer,
422
Mishnah, 346
miracles
cannot be categorically ruled out,
206, 217
one of a kind by definition, 204
perhaps more common than many
assume, 206
two great, on which Christianity
hinges, 206
Mitchell, Margaret, 130
Moby-Dick (Melville), 441
Monarchianism, 215
monasteries and monasticism
centers of European urban life, 298
centers of learning, 303
housed populations of dependent
workers, 298
Icelandic monasteries crucial in
spawning scholarship, 299
locus of quasi-theocratic
constitutionalism, 298
preservation of classical culture and
writings, 297
provided workshops, schools, care
for poor, 298
vehicle of Christian influence, 297
wellspring of new Christian culture,
297
Monet, Claude, 317
money
as a potential distraction, 144–46,
148, 154
can become false god, 374
desire for, among conquistadors,
332
disingenuous to claim not to care
about, 144, 146
half-life of pleasure and, 148
inordinate love of, 27

problem with inordinate desire for,
144–46
primarily important if you do not
have, 144
potential source of power, 143
pursuit of, 7
quest for, can choke off spiritual
growth, 449
monism, neutral, 347
monotheism, introduced problem of
evil, 160
Montaigne, 5
morally ambiguous dilemmas, 49
moral
advancements slower than scientific
and technical, 153
choices, tragic, 264
ever-widening gap between
goodness and capability, 153
evil, 121, 240–41, 243–44, 250–51,
255, 262, 268, 271–72, 280
More, Thomas, 152
moralistic therapeutic deism, 411
moral order, lack of a sense of objective,
246
morality
colored by subjective undertones,
241
Christian impact on, 319–20
morality and ethics
difference between, 241
sometimes in conflict, 241
Morris, Leon, 87
morphine addiction, 313
motif of realism within Christianity, 317
Mozart, Wolfgang Amadeus, 318
Muggeridge, Malcolm, 92n5, 151–52,
151n7, 246, 439, 439n
Munger, Bob, 435
Müntzer, Thomas, 333
Music
Christian contributions to, 318–19
Gregorian Chants, 318
monastic, 318
monophonic, 318
polyphonic, 318

INDEX

mutuality
  fragile, 97
  grows out of self-disclosure, 96
  sense of, we're in this together, 96
My Heart, Christ's Home, 435
myth of objective consciousness, 98

Native Americans, 332, 334–35, 339
natural evil, 251, 255, 267–69, 278, 280
natural theology, characteristics of, 233
navy chief, 1
Nazis, support of by some German clergy, 322
Nee, Watchman, 388
Neiman, Susan, 261, 271
Neo-Platonism, 262
Nero, Emperor, 203
New Testament
  authors unlikely to have colluded, 180
  differences add to historical credibility, 186
  differences among manuscripts, 190–91
  Gospels as memoirs, 185
  how best to read, 184–85
  important to let speak for itself, 198
  inadvertent and intentional alterations, 191–94
  inconsistencies and inaccuracies, 186–87
  less than one percent disputable, 194
  more source documents than other ancient books, 195
  other possible alterations, 193–94
  own best commentary, 194–95
  passages of uncertain authenticity, 187–89
  possible lost document "Q," 181
  provides insight into God's nature, 382
  read as set of historical documents, 24
  reading the Gospels, 184–85
  solidification of, 183
  textus receptus, 189
  themes running through, remarkably consistent, 195
  thousands of ancient manuscripts available, 190
  trustworthy guide to what God desires, 382
new Way, the 21, 173, 204
Neu, Dick, xii
new humanity, launched by Jesus, 175, 184, 382
new not always better than old, 39
Newton, John
  experienced Christian conversion, 325
  former slave ship captain, 325
  helped end slave trade in Great Britain, 325
  wrote words of hymn "Amazing Grace," 325
Newton, Isaac, 238–39, 311
Nicene Creed, 20, 26, 51, 75, 110, 214, 326, 365, 378, 454–56, Appendix II
Nietzsche, Friedrich
  alternative views of truth, 125
  ambiguities and inconsistencies in, 117
  attacks on Christianity, 119
  bypasses truth as discoverable, coherent, communicable, 123
  creative disruption together with incoherence, 117
  debt to Christianity, 119
  denies existence of all objective truth, 126
  egalitarianism, disparages, 117, 121, 126
  embraces Hobbesian idea of lust for power, 116
  eternal recurrence, doctrine of, 124
  iconoclastic, 118–21, 123
  influence on Freud, 123
  intellectual terrorist, 125
  intolerant toward the intolerant, 118
  Jesus for, a function of his fantasies, 120
  mental deterioration in, 123

moral codes in, mere conventions, habits, customs, 122
most powerful of atheistic philosophers, 125
nihilism and, 124, 221
no truth beyond what he proclaims, 118
not the first to announce death of God, 115
oblivious to own psychodynamics, 123
overman, concept of, 118–19, 122, 126
permission to be one's own god, 116–17
perhaps in search of meta-Christianity, 120
perspectivism, 122, 124
philologist, 19, 120
predilection for truth, from Christianity, 125
profound skepticism, 221
quest for truth ends in its repudiation, 117–18, 119
rejection of norms and conventions, 125–26
renounces all truth and objective reality, 125
theses and paradigms in, 117
treatment of evil, 283–84
ultimate truth cannot be found, 117
viewed Jesus as only honest decadent, 120
view of truth, 122–23
will, non-rational instinctive force, 123
will to power, 117–18, 121–22, 126
Nightingale, Florence, 313
nihilism, 124–25, 150, 221
nineteenth-century liberal Protestant theologians, 45, 120, 231
nominal fallacy, 91, 248
non-contradiction, law of, 3
non-propositional theology, *non sequitur*, 104
nuclear war and nuclear winter, 242
Notre Dame, 302, 314
numinous, 97

objective and subjective. *See* subjective and objective
objectivity
difficult to achieve in religion, 182–83
necessary for sanity, 97–98
rarely completely achieved, 98, 111
oceanic religious sentiments, 45
Ockham's Razor, 304
O'Hara, John, 128
Okholm, Dennis, xii, 7, 25, 351, 355
Old Testament
Creator-God, 6
culminates in God entering history as man, 374
omega point in history, 173
On the Beach (Shute), 142
ontological shock, 35
ontological status
Christians have no changed, 325
of fictional characters, 46
of Jesus, 108
open-mindedness, desirable if not unreflective, 56
opportunity costs, life with God requires paying, 388
order, whether universe has this and purpose, 4
Origen, 68, 190–92
Origin of Species, The (Darwin), 101, 234, 461
Orthodoxy. *See* Eastern Orthodoxy
Outer Limits, TV show, 423

paedobaptism, meaning of, 333n
painting, Christian contributions to, 316–18
paleolithic paintings, suggestive of, 13
panentheism, 346
pantheism, 45, 275, 346, 370
papal authority
disputes over, 369–70
ex cathedra, 370
formalized, 370
not acknowledged by, 75
papal failings, 328–29

INDEX

parable
  Book of Jonah, some regard as, 368
  Lazarus and the rich man, 415
  lost coin, 8
  one lost sheep, 8
  Pharisee and tax collector, 105
  prodigal or lost son, 8
  relentless widow, 400
  sower, 449
  wealthy landowner, 145
parables
  Jesus used to maximize spiritual impact, 94, 103–4
  nature of, 8, 49–50, 94, 204
  why Jesus spoke in, 104–6
paradigm shift
  often the nature of science, 33–34
  result of faith in God through Christ, 40
paradox of
  evil and divine goodness, 160, 249–52, 271
  free will and predestination, 415
  God's omnipotence and benevolence, 249–52
  Gospels, the 202
  informal traditions, 369
  losing life to gain it, 388
  power, 283, 328
  quest for satisfaction, a kind of, 145–46
  virtue, 328
parapraxes, 135
Paré, Ambroise, 312
partnering with God, 39, 406, 416
participating in God's ongoing existence, 389, 399–99, 424
Pascal, Blaise
  binomial equation, developer of, 28
  conic sections, work on, 28, 311, 321
  devout Christian, 311, 321
  heart has reasons of its own, 37, 442
  hydraulics, work on, 28, 311, 321
  nature most convincing to believers, 28
  people occupy themselves with distractions, 143
  people dread doing nothing, 143
  probability, work on, 28, 311, 321
  proofs of God from nature unconvincing to many, 233
  wager, 8
Pasteur, Louis, 312, 363
Patripassianism, 215
Paul (Apostle)
  colossal shift in consciousness, 52
  declared identity of unknown God, 132
  faith more than ritualistic animal sacrifice, 168
  good news (gospel), proclamation of, 392
  humanity's problem, reckoning with, 53
  initially persecutor of Christians, 205
  living according to the flesh, 426
  martyred for beliefs, 213
  mind of Christ, 409, 424
  Pharisee, lifelong, 52, 169, 205
  primary witness to historical Christ, 198
  proclaimed God all around us, 341
  promoted the Way, 205
  raised as orthodox Jew, 53
  reasoned arguments for faith in Christ, 205
  remained a Jew through life, 170
  shocked into realization of Jesus' true identity, 54
  spirit and flesh in, 171
  steeped in Hellenistic culture and Greek thought-forms, 53
  struggle between desires and behaviors, 325
  transformation on road to Damascus, 53, 169
  women in church, 193
peace, love of in converted Scandinavian tribes, 298
Pearl Harbor, 1
Peasants' Revolt, 330–31
pejorative terms, 39
Pensees (Pascal), 311
Pentecostal, 18, 380

INDEX

Pepe, Douglas, 428
Percy, Walker, 101
perspectivism
    close relative of subjectivism, 57
    denies existence of objective truth, 126
    Nietzsche's, 124, 126
    sham advocacy of absolute and universal values, 57
    truth relative and arbitrary, 122
    underpinning of several scholarly disciplines, 57
personal
    choice, 138. *See also* free will
    commitments implied by creeds, 110
    disciples' encounters with Jesus, 213
    disclosure, important in relationships, 427
    God no one's, agent, 407–9
    history, effects on individual, 286
    ideals of personal and social freedom, 292, 302
    identity beyond death, 350–51, 335, 357, 381
    knowledge, 98–100 *See also* tacit knowledge
    nature of Christian transformation, 338–39
    nature of faith, 95, 100
    nature of God, 45, 48, 55, 79, 233, 249, 371, 384
    probability, 34
    presence, God as, 184
    relationship with God, 171
    relationships with universal redeemer, 450
    religious knowledge always, 109
Personal Knowledge (Polanyi), 98
Peter (Apostle)
    act two of drama, 170
    almost certainly martyred, 202
    giving Christ, 427
    Paul certainly knew, 202
    ran to Jesus' tome, 193, 343
Pizarro, Francisco, 332
    plague 293, 329

Pharisee
    additional ritualistic requirements based on Torah, 53–54
    advocated meticulous observances of Jewish law, 52, 205
    invites Jesus to dine in his home, 405
    many sincere in efforts to honor God, 169
    not necessarily hypocrites, 52
    probably comfortable with abstractions, 106
    ritualistic observances sometimes burdensome, 169
philosophers and theologians, differences between, 71
philosophers
    Christians ought to resemble in best sense, 410
    Epicurean, 71, 291
    lovers of truth and wisdom 410
    representing themselves as theologians, 77
    some but not all not bound to defer to Bible, 74
    Stoic, 71, 148, 276, 291
    unlike theologians, not bound to religious beliefs,
philosophic
    naivete of scientists posing as philosophers, 221
    scientific question and, difference between, 219, 227–29
philosophic reasoning, 67
philosophy
    critical thinking in religion and, 69
    modes and branches of, 80–81
    speculative, 67–68
    some speculative philosophy Christian, 68
    two kinds, 67
Physicists, The (Duerrenmatt), 367
Piaget, Jean, 89
Picasso, Pablo, 317
Pilgrim's Progress (Bunyan), 146
Pierce, Charles Sanders, 36

Pilate, Pontius
　made sure Jesus was dead, 211–12
　mentioned in Apostles' Creed, 453
　mentioned in Nicene Creed, 455–56
　nervous about potential of Jewish insurrection, 211
　notice by, King of the Jews, 212
　ordered crucifixion of Jesus, 201
　political relationships with Jewish leaders, 375
Pinocchio, 356–57
Plantiga, Alvin, 73, 370–71
Plato
　allegory of the cave, 78
　Aristotle and, 131
　European philosophical tradition footnote to, 7
　Euthyphro, 141, 7n15
　questions raised by, remain relevant, 7–8
　reality behind appearances, 68
　souls indwelling bodies, 349
　uncertain authorship of some dialogues, 183
plausibility structure, 34
pleasure
　as a distraction, 147–48
　can become false god, 116
　capacity for often declines with age, 147
　chivalry and, 301
　empty and unenduring without companionship, 92
　half-life of, 148
　problems with obsessively seeking, 147–48
　pursuit of, 7
　quest for, can choke off spiritual growth, 449
　view by Christians of people existing at God's, 448
　we may serve, 7
Pocino, Mark, xii
Pocino, Sherilee, xii
point of departure, subjective, 72, 108
Polanyi, Michael, 98–101
Polkinghorne, John, both scientist and theologian, 77, 288

political correctness
　social pressure to demonstrate, 61
　sometimes poorly thought-out, 222
Pollack, Jackson, 317
polytheism
　can be attractive option, 160
　not necessarily primitive, 160
Pope (s)
　Alexander VI, 263
　Damascus, 189
　formal definition of, 75, 326
　Innocent III, 215
　John Paul II, 367
　Leo X, 330
　many, exemplary Christians, 328
　over 250 men have been, 328
　Pius IX, 370
　Pius XII, 336
　rival, 305
　Sylvester II, 297
Picture of Dorian Gray (Wilde), 66
Post-Impressionism, 317
postmodernism, key thesis of, 222
post-resurrection body
　Christian, 133
　of Jesus, same and different, 209, 213, 343
power
　as distraction, 143–44, 148
　as imitation god, 374
　Christianity not function of raw intellectual, 342
　deliverance from, of sin and death, 200, 361
　desire for, 116, 121, 133, 152, 389
　emotional, giving others, 427, 429
　God refrains from displays of, 47
　God's, obvious to receptive and discerning heart, 233
　ideas, sharing of, 442
　intellectual, of Paul, 292
　intoxicating elixir, 328
　Jewish, structure, 213
　limitations to royal, 329
　love of, replaced by power of love, 175
　lust for, 254, 389
　money, potential source of, 143

need for government with, to enforce in Hobbes, 58
of Reformation fueled by nobles, 332
of Christian faith rests on resurrection, 208
of Holy Spirit, 174
of reframing, 436
of scripture, belief in, 42
people have enormous, to help or harm, 431
political leaders and, 263–64
politically ambitious people often value, over truth, 48
problems with excessive concern with, 143–44
pursuit of, 7
redemptive, of God through Christ, 86
secular and ecclesiastical, 297, 306
serving, 7
use wisely, 429
we may serve quest for, 7
will to, in Nietzsche, 117–18, 121–22, 126
workers given, problem in communist regimes, 283
pragmatic maxim, 36
pragmatism
conception of truth, 85–87
development of, 36
Machiavelli, 264
necessary in science, 224
definition of truth, 36
prayer
acquiescence, trust, and holy, 402
as alignment with God's will, 400–2, 406
as assault on evil, 407
as gratitude, 404
as intimacy with God, 403
as participation, 406–7
as self-reckoning (confession), 405–6
as request (petition, supplication, intercession), 404
as worship, 404
can never know if outcome will change, 406
essential to remaining aligned with God, 402
fosters listening when authentic, 403
liturgical, 408
Luke's Gospel attests to importance of, 400
magic and, 407
modes of, 404–7
necessary for spiritual growth, 402
not type of magic, 399
participating in God's ongoing existence, 399
purpose of, to communicate and align with God, 400
resemble tribal shamans or witch doctors, 407
some treat God as an assistant, 407
spiritually toxic to pit God against medicine, 408
thy will be done, ultimate objective, 401, 405
two-way conversation, 403
praying
for enemies, corollary to loving and forgiving, 409
implies a measure of good will, 409
prehistoric cave drawings, possible metaphysical questions, 13, 349
Presbyterian, 18, 214, 365, 369, 380
premises
altered for those new to Christianity, 34
challenge to those, of speculative philosophers, 68
changed by fundamental inner transformation, 34–35
conclusions follow deductively and inexorably from, 29
condition conclusions based on, 394
deductive arguments sound only if based on true, 206
false, likely to lead to faulty conclusions, 69
fundamental change in perspective caused by changed, 40
fundamental, non-demonstrable, 30

premises *(continued)*
    God's existence, rock-bottom for theologians, 72
    implications of, an example from deductive logic, 30
    incorrect, can sometimes lead to correct conclusion, 89
    no reasoning sound if based on flawed, 76
    non-demonstrable, 30–31
    primary, as first principles, 31
    primary, cannot be shown to be true, 85
    primary, distorted by process of sin, 394
    religious, many cannot be objectively demonstrated, 40, 76
    true, basis of sound arguments, 29, 225
    wrong, correct conclusions by accident or coincidence, 69
primogeniture, 300, 327
Prince, The (Machiavelli), 263
Principe, Lawrence, 229, 231–32, 367
primal and cunning nature
    devout Christian can revert to, 172
    need way to transcend, 375
probability
    epistemic, 34
    personal, 34
    subjective, 34
problem of God, renewed interest in philosophy, 72
problem of evil, 2, 160, 249–53, 255, 261–66, 271–72, 368, 390, 414
procedural knowledge
    different from declarative, 442
    one of three basic kinds, 96
procession, single versus double (dual), 326, 454–55
professors
    increasingly neglect cultural literacy, 57
    sometimes discourage students from thinking, 56
projection, defense mechanism of, 140
prolegomena, definition, 71n
proofs of God, 72
properties, accidental and dispositional, 64
prophecy, change in meaning of, 166–67
propositions
    existential and universal, 29
    major and minor, 29
propositional, theology by nature, 104
prosperity evangelists, 45, 87
props
    identifying too closely with, 387
    we mistake for genuine life, 151
Protagoras, 20
provincialism, narrow-minded and religious, 59. 63
psychiatric afflictions, disorders, facilities, 28, 86, 336, 403
psychiatrists and psychologists as secular priests, 136
psychiatry and psychology
    achievement in humanizing treatments, 136
    advances in, 82
    delusions, nature of, 209
    hallucinations, nature of, 209–11
    have not made short work of evil, 248
    insufficiency of insight alone, 442
    loneliness, previous neglect of, 353
    Lucy Van Pelt, 437
    major insight into mental disorders, 432
    need for consultation from, 436
    nominal fallacy in, 248
    parapraxes, 135
    power motive in, 121
    practitioners, doing work of the church, 431
    sitting with the patient, value of, 433
    training in, fostering deterministic thinking, 137
    unconscious process, 136
psychopathology and evil, 248
public verifiability, 76
pulling weeds for health of relationships, 428
purgatory
    definition and function of, 306
    indulgence decreasing time in, 330

purpose
    might never know existed, 39
    renewed sense of, 38
    whether life and universe have, 4

Rachmaninoff, Sergei, 318
radical
    Christian transformation, 38
    etymology of, 1
    evil, 272, 286–87
    less, English Reformation, 305
    Reformation, European, 333
Raikes, Robert, 314
Ransey, Frank, 102
RAND Corporation, The, 148, 245
randomness of life, 40
rationalism
    reason ultimate criterion of truth in, 347
    Spinoza, a rationalist, 347
rationalization, defense mechanism of, 139
Rawls, John, 288, 393n4
reaction formation, defense mechanism of, 138–39
reason
    by itself insufficient, 39, 69
    can only take us so far, 39
    nothing true for reason incompatible with faith, 26
    relationship to faith, 24
reasoning, two basic modes, 23
rebellion
    built in disposition toward, 385
    great, the 92
    God cannot ignore our, 365, 373, 394
    human inclination toward, 115, 216, 385
    no longer participating in, 54, 92, 125
    our, with which we must reckon, 385
    reveling in, Nietzsche, 116, 122
reductions, eliminative versus explanatory, 36–37, 240, 285–86
reframing
    example from the Bible, 437

helpful only if appropriate, 436–37
maternal example of, 436–37
Reformation, Protestant
    debate over role of tradition, 42
    Calvin, John, leader in, 6
    Charles V convened Diet of Worms, 306
    Christianity's dangerous idea, 369
    controversies within highlight need for humility, 43
    controversies, major, about what Bible taught, 369
    end of unified Christendom in the West, 305
    Eck, Johann, interrogator of Luther, 306
    greatly increased literacy rate, 313
    growing concern for autonomy, 304
    had long been smoldering, 305
    history of, 305–8
    Hus, Jan, role in, 305
    impossible for Rome to ignore, 306
    in England, 305
    in Germany, Switzerland, Scotland, England, 42, 364
    Luther, Martin, kicked off, 189
    moved civilization forward, 310
    nobles and opportunistic prices contributed to, 332
    no overarching Protestant authority, a problem, 369
    Peasants' Revolt, 330
    pressure for separation of church and state, 305
    printing press contributed to, 306
    Protestants disagreed on what the Bible taught, 369
    triggered Thirty Years War, 42, 330
    unintended consequence of, 364
    Wycliff, John, role in, 305
    Zwingli, Huldrych, role in, 305
regeneration, definition, 52
reincarnation, 351–52
religion
    as what people most value, 41–42
    definition of, loose but worth pondering, 42
    possible origin of, 132

INDEX

religion *(continued)*
    relationship with science usually irenic, 220
religious provincialism, 59
relativism, absurdity of cultural and ethical, 61, 66
relationships, without feelings we could have no, 35
religion(s)
    authentic, cannot be based on false beliefs, 44
    and secular life, worth reflection on, 4
    based on flawed premises, 104
    family resemblances of, 19
    make incompatible truth-claims, 55, 65
    notoriously difficult to define, 19, 22
    nuanced and multifaceted, 19
    operate typically with explicit or implicit theology, 55
    recognize it when we see it, 19
    reflect assertions of belief, 19
    science and, relationship between, 219–20
    working characterization of, 19
religionists, misguided, sincere but potentially harmful, 77
religious
    affirmations remain beliefs, 4
    deductive proofs for truth-claims unconvincing, 29
    experience compatible with conceptual precision, 17
    ranking, United States, 2–3
    trends, 2–3
    truth-claims, competing, illogical to accept, 65
    truth-claims, incapable of logical demonstration, 76
    versus scientific truth, 367
    violence, psychodynamics of, 323–25
remaining focused as a Christian, 450
Renaissance, 19, 38, 243, 292, 300, 302, 309, 315, 317, 329–30, 362
Renoir, Pierre-Auguste, 317

repentance, meaning and necessity of, 384–86
repression, defense mechanism of, 138
resentment
    central to Nietzsche's thought, 283
    develop within communist countries, 282
    expressing, difficult but often important, 428–29
    forgiving difficult while carrying, 428
    importance of expressing and not harboring, 428
    lethal state of mind, 428
res ipsa loquitor, translation of, 183
resurrected bodies, Christian hope and expectation of, 341, 381
resurrection
    Apostles Creed and, 453
    after crucifixion, massively traumatized and infected, 212
    announcement God made through, 213
    as myth, 213–14
    assumption it could never have happened, 208
    belief in, after death, Christian hope and expectation, 341
    biblical accounts of, exceedingly detailed, 377
    can be no rigorous proof of, 204
    central to Christianity, 74, 204
    Christian hope pointless without, 340
    contemporaries not inclined to believe in, 211
    crucifixion and, made possible eternal life, 184
    disciples initially found incomprehensible, 342
    documentation of unshakable belief in, 210
    Gospels present remarkable parallel accounts of, 204
    evidence for, 208–11, 342
    if never happened, Christianity only an ethical system, 341

INDEX

inventing, would have required great creativity, 213
life and, I am, 207
implies God in person of Jesus crucified, 51
incarnation, crucifixion, and, only way to reach us, 205
life, death, and, culmination of Old Testament, 6
illusions, delusions, hallucinations, inadequate explanations, 208–11
implications of, New Testament resounds with, 204
major clue, 50
multiple encounters with Jesus after, 201, 208, 210–11, 213–14
new bodies similar to Christ's, 133
New Testament writers presuppose it occurred, 202, 208
Nicene Creed and, 456
no disagreement among Apostles about, 198
nothing in common with myth, 213–24
nothing to suggest Jesus needed medical attention, 212
of Jesus, prototype and one-time event, 341
of Lazarus, 342–43, 397
omitted, eviscerates Christianity, 208
physical, 206
power of Christian faith, 208
regarded by many as impossible, 339
reincarnation misses significance of crucifixion and, 352
steadfast belief in led to martyrdom, 202
sticky wicket for many, 201
swoon theory of, 211–12
unlikely so many trumped up belief in, 210
way God attempts to get our attention, 205
retributive justice, 286, 307
revelation, general and special, 371
Ricardo, David, 279
road to Emmaus, 209
rock climbing, 25–26
Roman Catholicism
accepts Chalcedonian Christology, 214
Bible in, 73
Catechism of the Catholic Church, 365
celibacy, formalization of requirement for priests, 328
conduct during WWII, 336
contents of Bible, 73
disagreement with Eastern Orthodoxy over Holy Spirit, 369
dispute with Luther over indulgences, 306
deification or divination alluded to in, 374, 449
Great Lisbon Earthquake and, 267
Great Schism, 305, 326, 454
inclined to appeal to authority of the church, 42
justification, view of, 366
less inclined to over-emphasize reason or emotion, 17–18
many of Luther's views aligned with, 42
mistaken views on, and tradition, 369
need for reform, 42, 330
need for theological humility, 74
Radical Reformation and, 333
real estate holdings confiscated by English church, 58
recognizes twenty-one ecumenical councils, 75
role of Pope, differences with Orthodox and Protestants, 370
role of tradition explicitly formalized in, 369
salvation, definition of, 100
salvation for those outside, 380
split with Eastern Orthodox Church, 326
strive to have affirmations align with Bible, 73
Thirty Years War, 42, 258, 330–31, 364

INDEX

Roman Catholicism *(continued)*
   transubstantiation, doctrine of, 42–43
Roman Catholic Missal, 408
Roman Catholics
   Greene, Graham
   Papal encyclicals, acknowledge authority of, 75
   Pope, acknowledge authority of, 75, 370
   submits to authority of Vatican, 75
   variation among, 75
Rousseau, Jean-Jacques, treatment of evil, 268–70
rule of law, Christian contributions to, 320
Russell, Bertrand,
   colleague of Alfred North Whitehead, 8
   critique of man as measure of all things, 20
   quip about Alfred North Whitehead, 57
Ryrie, Alec, 364

Sabellianism, non-trinitarian Modalism, 215
sacerdotalism
   definition of, 83, 379
   Eastern Orthodox, 83
   Protestant churches, 83
   Roman Catholic, 83
sacrament
   concept of, 83
   Protestant churches and, 83
sacred-secular tensions, 297
Sadducees, 106, 211
Sade, Marquis de (Donatien Alphonse François)
   embrace of evil, 284–85
   possible connection with unforgivable sin, 285
   psychotic, 284
   term sadism associated with, 284
St. Paul's Cathedral, 315, 321
St. Peter's Cathedral, 306, 315, 330

salvation
   alienation from God, self and others, 372
   available to those who desire it, 416
   empty quest for, 150
   from what, by whom, and why, 199
   idea of, 199–200
   issue must be addressed, 199
   implies we require it, 372
   history, overall arc of the Bible, 175
samsara, 352
sanctification, 378
sanity and objectivity, 97
Santayana, George, 36, 124
Sartre, Jean-Paul
   insisted we can always say no, 414
   involved in French resistance during WWII, 151
   held views on evil, 28
Sartrean existentialism
   all but dead as philosophic position, 151
   popular in salons, classrooms, English departments, 151
   quasi-religion, 151
   rarely popular in departments of philosophy, 151
savior
   gives potential to overcome self-centered existence, 381
   from consequences of previously rejecting God, 173
   grasping meaning of Jesus as, 88, 338
   idea of, rests on two pivotal beliefs, 376–77
   implication of the word Christ (*Messiah*), 21
   implies rescue of flawed and frail humanity, 173
   Lord and, for Christians, 217, 338
   need to affiliate with church proclaiming Jesus as, 380
   reconciled us to God, 382
   who has atoned for our rebellion and defiance, 381
Scarlet Letter, 361

INDEX

schism
- East-West, 305, 326, 454
- Western or Papal, 305

Schopenhauer, Arthur
- anticipated Nietzsche, 277
- antipathy toward Christianity, 275
- consummate pessimist, 276
- out of step with Enlightenment, 275
- renunciation in, 279
- treatment of evil, 275–79

Schubert, Franz, 318

science
- advances sometimes result from paradigm shifts, 33
- as quasi-religion, 221
- cannot demonstrate existence or nonexistence of miracles, 206
- cannot guide moral decisions, 221
- cannot reveal meaning or significance of life, 221
- Christian contributions to, 311–12
- Islamic, 317
- nature of, 32–33, 98–99, 223–25
- not philosophy, 238
- reason and faith in, 223–25
- relationship with religion usually irenic, 220
- religion and, compatible, 218–20
- religious truth and, 367
- rests on three core beliefs, 224
- unable to discover nonscientific conclusions, 206

science fiction, memorable, 423

science and religion, warfare thesis
- encouraged today by some celebrity scientists, 218
- popularized in nineteenth century, 218–19, 229–32
- reinforced by evolutionists and fundamentalists, 218

scientific and philosophic questions, difference, 219, 227–29

Scientific Revolution, effect on religious belief, 362

scientists
- attempt to disconfirm hypothesis as test, 33
- can be secular fundamentalists, 219
- conservative arrangement, 33
- ought not to pose as philosophers unless trained, 219, 227–29
- rarely try to prove a hypothesis, 33

Scopes trial, 235–36

Screwtape Letters (Lewis), 396

Scribes, 106

scripture, meaning of, 368

Seafarer, The, 353–54

second-order data, 97

Second Temple Judaism, 169

secrets, why God keeps, 48–50

secular humanism, 20

self-absorption
- antithesis of Christianity, 426
- Christians not immune from, 448
- countered and mitigated by Christian faith, 37
- cultural redefinition of, 301
- default modes of human beings, 37
- deliverance from, 398
- destructiveness of, 177
- eternal cut-off-ness, solitude, and 416
- God's offer to rescue and pull us out of, 177, 448
- most significant meaning of flesh in Bible, 254
- our natural built-in, 379
- our nature as skeptically inclined toward, 205
- our need for rescue from, 52
- poison of, 254
- potential to fall back into, 375
- precludes attention to others, 154
- pride and, 381
- prison of, 177
- profound, 375
- sometimes accompanies acquisition of power, 328
- transcendence of in heaven, 356
- virtue of, according to Ayn Rand, 389

self-insight
- brings awareness of personal shortcomings, 405
- pride can hinder or prevent, 406
- Rousseau's educational program and, 269

INDEX

self-centeredness. *See* self-absorption
selfishness. *See* self-absorption
selfism, 386, 416. *See also* self-absorption
self-sufficiency, illusion of, 92
Semmelweis, Ignaz Philipp, 363–64
sensus divinitis, 370
Sermon on the Mount, 49, 63, 376, 410
Schindler, Oskar, 336
Schweitzer, Albert, 191
Seurat, Georges-Pierre, 317
shapers of minds and hearts, 439
Sharkey, Paul, xii, 30
Shema, meaning of, 170
Sherman, William Tecumseh, 149–50
Simpson, James Young, 313
Singer, Marcus, 244
sin
    becoming more like Jesus and release from, 416
    blinded by, apart from Christian conversion, 251
    cause of human evil, 254
    central concept in Judaism, 53
    Christians perhaps unable to sin in heaven, 263, 355
    Christ's removal of consequences of, 366
    chronic human ailment, 389
    coming to grips with one's proclivity to, 52
    corrosive effect of, 394
    definitions of, 388
    distorting effects on thinking, 233, 370
    etymology of, 388
    God offers rescue from, 416
    hamartiology, study of, 388n7
    humanity's serious affliction, 361
    intentional versus unintentional, 411
    Jesus without, 393
    King David and, 447
    liberation from power of, 200
    like skin disease, 394
    missing the mark, and, 405
    new sense of personal accountability in Judaism, 161
    not prudent to euphemize or trivialize, 361, 405
    offenses against God and other people, 361
    of pride and self-centered living, 381
    operates as process within us, 388
    owning up to personal, necessary, 384–86
    pride as root of, according to Augustine, 144–45
    punishment of according to Gregory of Nyssa, 351
    rebels, captives to, 407
    reckoning with significance of, 406
    repentance, remorse, humility, and 105
    sin principle, 389
    soteriology, discipline concerning salvation from, 83
    spiritual or moral imperfection, 53
    substituting ourselves for God, 447
    will to gain power and, 121
    we all must reckon with, 388
sincerity
    gospel of, reflects confused thinking, 44
    important not to mistake for truth, 44
    naïve to endorse gospel of, 44
    no guarantee of truth, 40, 44, 55
    some turn into a religion, 44
    unreliable criterion for true beliefs, 44
skeptics, may have sincere and worthwhile questions, 216
skepticism
    atheistic existentialism and, 150–51
    cynicism and, of our age, 21
    Enlightenment increased, toward religion, 310
    from, to faith, 342–44
    has been increasing for centuries, 340
    healthy skepticism encouraged by education, disputations, 304
    Hume's, 224, 271, 347–49
    peppered with cynicism, 151
    philosophical materialism and, 27

INDEX

profound, 221
  toward possibility of truth and knowledge, 221
  toward rational inquiry and logical thought, 222
  truth unrelated or opposed to faith, 109
  understandable toward the resurrection, 341–42
Skinner, B. F., 147
Skinner Box, life in, 48
slavery
  abhorrent and incompatible with Christianity, 59
  abolition of, 320
  Emancipation Proclamation, 335
  indelible blot on record of Christians, 335
  Joseph sold into, 437
  moral horror of, 335
  perpetrated by self-identified Christians, 322, 335
  Slave Trade Act, 335
  Slavery Abolition Act, 335
  South had grown economically dependent on, 335
  Western Society took step backwards with, 59
sloth
  among seven deadly sins, 7
  busyness as well as laziness, 7
  from Latin *tristitia* (sadness) and *acedia* (apathy)
  meaning of in mediaeval theology, 7
  neglect of duty, 7
  originally called capital sin, 7
Smith, Adam, 279, 281
Snow, John, 363
social comparison, problem with, 146
Socialism, 216
Socrates, 29, 51, 141, 183, 200
sola scriptura, definition of, 368
soldier's disease, 313
solipsism, 95, 109
Sophie's Choice, (Styron), 61–62
Sophie Scholl (German film), 152
Sopranos, TV series, 237
soteriology, meaning of, 83, 199
sound judgment, 63, 84
Sozzini, Lelio, anti-trinitarian, 216
space and time
  created for our benefit, 40
  media in and through which we live, 412
  necessary for choice and change, 371, 412
space, question about where it ends, 8, 39
speculative philosophy. *See also* chapter 17
  alive and well, 69
  assumptions in, fundamental, 71
  ancient examples of, 68
  critical thinking important in, 69–70
  ideological biases easily influence, 228
  not always compatible with Christianity, 69
  not necessarily bound by religious assumptions, 78–79
  paths of, and Christian theology may separate, 69
  some forms distinctly Christian, 68
Spinoza
  a rationalist, 347
  first to challenge theistic religion, 206, 340
  history with Judaism, 346
  views on theism and miracles, 345–47
status
  as a distraction, 146–47
  can become false god, 374
  compulsive quest for, 148
  drive to be recognized as high, 146
  high, provides fund of idiosyncrasy credits, 58
  need to do and have more than others, 146
  perversely enhancing one's, 323
  problems from excessive concern with, 146–47
  pursuit of, 7
  striving for, 154
  what we may serve, 7

Stewart, Potter, 19
Stott, John, 447
Stravinsky, Igor, 318
Styron, William, 61–62
stochastic process. *See* randomness of life.
subjective
    displaced the objective for many, 3
    intuition, 94
    mind is by nature, 109
    people in the West increasingly favor, 413
    preferences, 3
    probability, 34
    shift toward the, 318, 414
    religion as only subjective, 413
    turn to the subject, 413
    well-being, 146
subjective and objective
    becoming a Christian involves both, 38
    continuous montage of both in consciousness, 96
    continual subtle interplay between, 99
    often in tension, 182
    two interacting worlds, 95
    we live in the tension between, 182
subjective point of departure, 108
subjectivism, close relative of perspectivism, 57
subjectivity
    and nature of one's mind, 109
    belief necessarily entails, 109
    may or may not be consistent with truth, 109
Sullivan, Harry Stack, 432
Summa Theologica (Thomas Aquinas), 78
Sunday School movement, enhanced literacy, 314
supernatural being
    no objective way to prove existence of, 397
    part of Christian statements of faith, 396
    with malevolent purposes, 396–97

survey questions sometimes meaningless, 44–45, 338
Swinburne, Richard, view on evil, 251
swoon theory of resurrection, 212–13
syncretism
    definition of, 164
    in ancient cults, 167–68
synoptic, meaning of for Gospels, 181
Syriac, language of some scriptures, 181, 190
Syrian Orthodox Church, 108
Szasz, Thomas, 248

tacit knowledge, 38, 98–100, 104, 109, 111
Tacitus, *Annals* of, 203
Taj Mahal, 315
Talmud, 346
Tchaikovsky, Pyotr Ilyich, 318
technological progress outpacing moral, 245–46
Teilhard de Chardin, 173
temporocentrism, 342
Ten Commandments
    educational function of, 169–70
    highlights dis-ease of our inner being, 170
    uniquely centered on monotheism, 169
Tennyson, Alfred Lord, 150
Tertullian, 174, 191, 215
Tetzel, Johann, 330
textual analysis and criticism, 186, 201
Thackeray, William, 146
theistic evolution, 235–36
theocracy, why never developed in Europe, 297
theologians
    amateur in domains of science, 77
    Christian, assume existence of personal God, 71, 79
theodicy
    attempt to harmonize theism and evil, 249
    difference between defense and theodicy, 250
    Leibniz introduced concept of, 266

INDEX

theology
- by itself may not bring anyone to faith, 37
- can crowd out faith, 103–4
- consensual validation in, 76
- continually evolving, 77, 106–8
- creativity, coherence, soundness as criteria, 76
- determines what religious leaders proclaim, 41
- different religions make incompatible claims, 43
- does it reflect reality, important question to ask, 43
- evaluating, 76–77
- few if any religions completely wrong, 43
- fosters tacit religious knowledge, 111
- guards against unsound beliefs, 111
- inescapable when higher power assumed, 43
- *kenotic*, 336
- modes or branches of, 81–83
- must accommodate conclusions from science, 225
- must be free of contradictions and make sense, 69
- natural, characteristics of, 233
- navigation charts and, 81
- necessary and unavoidable, 103–4
- no public verifiability, 76
- not all religions correct about Jesus, 43
- open-mindedness should not obscure differences, 43
- political and social action, not theology, 77
- reason and faith in, 223–25
- rests on scaffolding of careful reasoning, 225
- rigorous thinking foundational to, 69
- role of tradition in, 76
- scaffolding for faith, 104
- shade into politics, history, and social life, 4
- should not be confused with faith, 104
- study of God and God's ways with humankind, 41
- understanding God and divine expectations, 43
- wrong to consider outmoded, impractical or irrelevant, 41
- thinking language, 100–1, 111, 240
- akin to language of dreams, 100
- may include awareness of God, 101
- media in which creativity grows, 100
- when inner and outer languages converge, 100
- three ways of orienting toward God, 385
- through a glass darkly, 78
- thoughts, two modes of, 292
- *Thirty-Nine Articles of Religion*, 365, 369
- Thirty Years War, 42, 258, 330–31, 364
- Theodosius, Emperor, 307
- Tillich, Paul, 72
- time
  - geologic, 8
  - God offers us infinite, 93
  - mystery of when started or might end, 8, 39
  - spend on what we value, 35
- time and space
  - created for our benefit, 40
  - media in and through which we live, 411–12
  - necessary for choice and change, 371, 412
- tolerance
  - behavioral, no society has unlimited, 58
  - criminal codes specify limits of, 58
  - fashionable but dangerous without discernment, 56
  - in some areas of life noble but in others misguided, 56
  - norms not applied equally, 58–59
  - of belief or opinion, different from of bad behavior, 57
  - religious, desirable, 55
  - those promoting can prove intolerant, 56–57

INDEX

Tolstoy, Lev Nikolayevich, 288
Torquemada, Tomás de, 331
Toulouse-Lautrec, Henri de, 317
Toynbee, Arnold J, coined term postmodernism, 221
tradition
    all religious groups have formal or informal, 369
    explicitly formalized in Catholicism, 369
    medieval kingship and constitutional monarchy, 298
    misunderstandings about, 368–69
    need for theologians to work within a, 76
    Puritans generally followed Reformed, 333
    question of whether central or supplemental, 382
    role in acquisition of knowledge, 87
    warrior, culture and Christianity, 298
    wars of religion partly over, 42
tragic moral choice, 264
transformation
    accepting, offered by Christ, 52
    based on both analysis and intuition, 103
    Christian, 325, 384, 389
    death of opportunity for, 129
    God's Spirit central to, 448
    in Christ, 325, 388
    in how we perceive God and people, 384
    lack of Christian, noted by Nietzsche 121, 338
    likely to be radical, 38
    of medieval church into major political power, 328
    of earth, would require, 355
    of everyday experience, 2
    of society through Christianity, 291
    personal, by becoming a Christian, 338–39
    requires owning up, 384
    undergoing spiritual, 103
    when people are moved, captivated, shaken, 34

translations
    accord well with each other, 186
    all involve interpretations, 203
    attempts to convey essential meaning, 6
    dynamic equivalence, 6, 203
    English, copies of Greek texts, 182
    formal equivalence, 203
    good, get things right, 192
    influenced by personal biases, 203–4
    Jerome diligent in producing Vulgate, 189
    literal, 6
    often use belief and faith interchangeably, 24
    paraphrase, 6
    problems with dynamic equivalence, 203–4
    problems with formal equivalence, 203
    scholars labor hard to produce accurate, 186
    sincere attempts to convey meanings, 203
    some more literal, some more figurative, 203
    thought for thought, 6
    Vulgate ratified at Council of Trent, 189
    word for word, 6
transubstantiation, 43
treasury of merit, 330
Trinity
    God an eternal fellowship or communion, 108, 370, 424
    God's existence in three persons, 108, 370, 424
    Father, Son, Holy Spirit, 74, 382, 424
    monotheism and, 173–75
    most explicit statement of in Bible, 189
    Newton, Issac, and, 238
    no specific word for in Bible, 108
tristitia, meaning of, 7
truth
    absence of truth problematic, 90
    aim of in search for knowledge, 85
    all versions of, not tenable, 57

and love inseparable, 426
arrived at from false premises not knowledge, 90
arrived at by accident not knowledge, 90
assertion that all claims tenable itself untenable, 57
awkward truth in Christianity, 382
believed to be man-made, untrue, 20
can communicate only some through abstractions, 105
can rely on in life, 90
Christianity, pivotal role in valuing religious, 119
claim false that perceptions determine, 66
communicaiting through abstractions limited, 105
confused to insist we each have our own, 66
decreased concern with objective, 414
desirable, 90
determining depends on support by evidence, 108
does not depend on perceptions, 89
existence of overarching, 51
existence of versus absence of, 61
feelings not always trustworthy guides to, 413
God, the author of, 409
God's love grounded in eternal, 205
in Gospel of Luke, 185
Jesus, the way, truth, and life, 207
justice and, unbreakable connection for God, 373
love and, inseparable, 426
love of, in medieval Scandinavian tribes, 298
many have abandoned search for, 3
miracles not demonstrable, 206
more impact if people grasp, with their hearts, 105
none beyond what Nietzsche proclaims 118
not a matter of tastes and preferences, 57
opinions taken as guide to, 3, 57
passionate pursuit of, 410
pragmatic view and concept of, 85–87, 224
prayer and search for, 409
pursuit of and love for God, 410
quest for power over quest for, 48
reason, ultimate criterion in rationalism, 347
reflects what is the case, way things are, 57, 63, 76, 86, 93
relationship between, and reality, 88
religious and scientific, 367
scalpel of, first dip in anesthetic of love, 437
sense perception, ultimate criterion of in empiricism, 347
sincerity no guide to, 44, 55
some best communicated through stories, 105
some, requires left- and right-brain connection, 105
spiritual truth, recognition of, 216
stakes high regarding, 43
subjectivity can be compatible with, 109
taken as one's point of view, 3
understanding beneficial, 84
value of more than correcting false beliefs, 90
your truth versus my truth, 3, 221–23
truth-claims, Christianity makes unique, 65
truthful statements reflect way things are, 57, 76
Turner, William, 317
two eternities and two infinities hints of God's existence, 40
suspended between, 39–40
Tyndale, William, 319, 323

Ulfilas, Arian missionary, 215
Ulysses (Homer), 150
umbrella line and eternal life, 51

INDEX

Unamuno, Miguel de, 36, 385
unbelief
  help my, 390
  willful denial of evidence, 394
unconscious process
  conscious and, 35
  decision-making and, 102
  intuitive reasoning and, 102
  meaning of, 136
  nature of, 135–36
  personal and tacit knowledge, 98
  thinking language and, 100
understanding
  Christianity promotes, 91
  fosters good judgment, 84
  from grasping significance, 101
  genuine, not from dry facts or detached observation, 101
  grasping attributes and placing within matrix, 91
  information does not necessarily increase, 91
  involves creation of mind-map, 91
  involves intuitive leaps at times, 102
  locating within larger framework, 91, 93
  more than acquiring information, 93
  noting function or purpose, 91
  possible to hold true beliefs without, 90–91
  seeing principles relating to, 91, 93
  true judgments, contributes to, 90
unifying authority, loss of, 364
United States religious ranking, 2–3
universalism, 350–51
universe
  many no longer believe in objective order to, 117
  moral order, lack of sense of, 246
  moral order built into, 85
  natural order to, 240
  non-physical or trans-physical order to, 85
  ordered, 63
  physical laws in, 84
  purpose and order in, 4, 34
  randomness in, may turn out to be ordered, 40
  resistance to God jars alignment with order of, 373
  underlying pattern and order to, 34, 84, 221
universities
  Benedictine Age and, 303
  centers of learning, from cathedral schools to, 303
  emergence of, 303–05
  increased tension between sacred and secular, 303
  shift from Augustinian to Thomistic theology, 303
  tenure, crucial for protection of academic freedom, 304
  tenure, singular contribution to free speech, 304
utopianism
  avoidance through, 143
  definition and etymology of, 152
  evil and, 253–55
  frogs and scorpions, 253
  two alternatives, Christianity and, 151
  unrealistic quest for on earth, 151–54

value, epistemic, 34
values
  cultures condition and reflect, 62
  desirable to understand, 61
  flawed assumption that no set of preferable, 56
  in all cultures, not equally meritorious, 60
  some cultural, better than others, 59
  strong, those in the West hold, 62
values Christianity infused into Western Culture
  charity and ethical duty toward one's neighbor, 307
  emergence of focus on learning and universities, 309
  encouragement of forgiveness, 307
  high regard for human life and dignity, 308–09

ideological foundation for Bill of
    Rights, 307
individual freedom, 308
modern freedoms, 310
prohibition of cruel and unusual
    punishment, 307
promotion of literacy, 300, 309
right of self-determination, 308
separation of church and state, 308
transcendence of retributive justice,
    307
value theory, branch of ethics, 80n
Vanity Fair, (Thackeray), 146–47
Vatical Council I, 370
violence
    indigenous cultures damaged or
        destroyed by, 332
    no religion immune to, 324
    Protestant Reformation and, 330–31
    religious, psychodynamics of,
        323–35
    religious zealots can engage in,
        322–23
virtue signaling, 337
Volta, Alessandro, 312
Voltaire (François-Marie Arouet)
    Candide, 267
    limited impact on mass public
        opinion, 218
    Lisbon earthquake and, 266–67
    one of two views of God and the
        world, 266
    touch of God for him endured, 271
Vulgate Bible, 189–90

warfare thesis, origins of, 229–33
warriors and warrior cultures, 161, 244,
    297–301
Waugh, Evelyn, 138
Way, the New, 21, 173, 204
Wealth of Nations, The, 279
Weil, Simone
    disappointments associated with
        desires, 422
    God sometimes intervenes in
        nature, 253

God's act of renunciation, limiting
    divine power, 252
existence filled with uncertainty, 253
nature, context in which to exercise
    freedom, 253
nature indifferent, 252
no association between goodness
    and outcomes, 252
other realities and powers, 252
response to evil, test of faith, 253
universe operates by material
    causes, 253
universe has no inherent purpose,
    253
views on evil, 252
Western Canon and liberal education,
    57
Western Culture and Civilization
    disingenuous to argue nothing
        noble in, 61
    failure to understand and
        appreciate, 62
    insufficient appreciation of its
        religious heritage, 62
    people embarrassed to proclaim
        virtues of, 62
    secular motifs in, 3, 39
western domination due to six cultural
    trends, 308
Westminster Confession of Faith, 365,
    369
whaling ship *Essex* and cannibalism,
    172
Whitcomb, Susan, xii
White, Andrew Dickson
    co-founder and first president of
        Cornell University, 230
    faulty scholarship of, 231–32
    fomented warfare thesis, 219, 230–
        33, 239, 367
    suffused erroneous ideas into
        popular culture, 232
white supremacist, 241
Whitehead, Alfred North
    European philosophical tradition
        and Plato, 7
    quip about Bertrand Russell, 57

why God keeps secrets, 48–50
Wilberforce, William
    ended slave trade in Great Britain, 77, 320, 325
    Slavery Abolition Act, 335
    was not introducing a new theology, 77
Wilde, Oscar, 66
William of Ockham, 304
will, God's perfect and permissive, 400
Wills, Garry, 329
Witchcraft Act, 334
witches, burning of in New England, 322
witch-hunts, contemporary, 334
witch trial, mock, 334
Wittgenstein, Ludwig, 19
women
    as witnesses in ancient times, 214
    society took step backward in treatment of, 59

World as Will and Representation (Schopenhauer), 277
world religions, claims of often mutually exclusive, 44
World Trade Center, 153, 245, 253, 260–61
worldviews, constantly changing, 41
work as service to God, 298, 303
worship
    meaning of, 22, 404
    not groveling, 22
Wycliffe, John
    fourteenth century advocate for reform, 305
    translated modern word for love as charity, 408

Zwingli, Huldrych, 305

www.ingramcontent.com/pod-product-compliance
Lightning Source LLC
Chambersburg PA
CBHW052110010526
44111CB00036B/1620